THE GIANT BOOK OF
MYTHS AND LEGENDS

THE GIANT BOOK OF

MYTHS

AND

LEGENDS

EDITED BY
MIKE ASHLEY

SA PL MetroBooks

This edition published by MetroBooks, an imprint of
Friedman/Fairfax Publishers, by arrangement with Robinson Publishing.

2002 MetroBooks

ISBN 1-5866-3610-3

Printed and bound in the United States of America

02 03 04 05 06 07 MC 10 9 8 7 6 5 4 3

FG

For bulk purchases and special sales, please contact:
Friedman/Fairfax Publishers
Attention: Sales Department
230 Fifth Avenue, Suite 700-701
New York, NY 10001
212/685-6610 Fax 212/685-3916

Visit our website:
www.metrobooks.com

CONTENTS

PART IV: HEROES AND MONSTERS

PART V: BATTLES AND CONQUESTS

PART VI: LOVE, REVENGE AND SELF-SACRIFICE

INTRODUCTION

Mike Ashley

MYTHS HAVE FASCINATED me ever since I was about ten and was introduced to the tale of the Trojan War. I had heard of some of the characters before, particularly Achilles and Odysseus, but they hadn't been much more than names. But on that quiet autumn day, when my English teacher began to unravel the story of the Trojan War, reading, I think, from *The Greek Myths* by Robert Graves, I rapidly became hooked. In the years following I have explored and delighted in the world of myths and legends.

I suppose we all start with the Greek legends, the world of Classical mythology. Many of the heroes and their deeds have passed into our language. We talk of the strength of Hercules, an Oedipus complex, the music of Orpheus, the song of the Sirens, an Achilles heel. And we are almost as well acquainted with their Roman equivalents, when we refer to Mercury, as the messenger of the Gods, or the legend of Romulus and Remus, or even swear the oath 'By Jove!'

We may not be quite so aware that we are also fairly well acquainted with much non-Classical mythology. After all, the British Isles were, for some five centuries, dominated by the Saxons, and their own Nordic mythology passed into our language. Most of the days of the week are named after gods: Tuesday is named after Tiw or Tyr, the Teutonic god of war. (This was the Roman equivalent of Mars, so it is no coincidence that the French for Tuesday is *mardi*, after Mars.) Wednesday is named after Woden, the father of the Gods; Thursday after Thor, the god of thunder; and Friday after Freya, the wife of Woden. We are also well acquainted with such terms as Valhalla, the home of the Gods, and Ragnarok, the Nordic Armageddon. And probably because of the operas of Richard Wagner, we will be acquainted with the adventures of Siegfried which are fundamental to Norse mythology.

And then there are the many Turkish, Persian and Indian legends that found their way into the *Arabian Nights*. We remember them more today as fairy tales, or maybe just as material for Christmas pantomimes, and forget that these are every bit a part of distant myths and legends as any of the Greek and Nordic tales.

Britain, of course, has its own myths and legends. One has only to think of King Arthur or Robin Hood to consider two of the most popular characters in folklore. Folklore is only another term for legends although, for some reason, probably due to the influence of the Brothers Grimm, folklore has come to be more associated with fairy-tales, and thus with stories for children. But myths and folktales should not be reserved solely for children. In my own mind there is no difference between traditional fairy-tales, folklore, myths or legends. Indeed, the key word is 'tradition'. These are stories that captured the imagination and have been passed from generation to generation. Embellished and finely honed by the story teller's craft, such legends have, in fact, become some of our very best and most popular stories, and can and should be enjoyed by readers of all ages.

Legends don't have to be that old, and can frequently be replenished. We have only to think of our own legends of the Loch Ness monster or Jack the Ripper to know how events of fairly recent vintage can pass into the myth of the nation. Anything that captures the public imagination will do that. During the First World War Arthur Machen wrote a story called 'The Bowmen' which overnight created the legend of the Angel of Mons and this has been perpetuated ever since. A legend, quite clearly, is any story which strikes a chord with the public, regardless of whether it is based on fact.

And that is true of every nation. There is not a culture on earth that does not have its own traditional stories of far-off days and wonders. Stories which help explain the world about us and which bring with them keys which enable us to unlock the experience of others.

This volume gathers together a selection of those myths, legends and folk-tales. I have cast the net wide to include as many countries and cultures as I could, although far fewer than I would have liked. I have also sought to select a mixture of stories, some of which will be familiar and thus serve as home territory, so to speak, and many that you will probably not previously have encountered and yet will seem familiar – because that is the very magic of myth.

I have also tried to keep the selection varied in theme. It would be easy to have filled the anthology purely with stories of adventurous quests or heroic battles, but I wanted to show that myths cover the whole range of human experience.

For that reason I have set the stories in a sequence which parallels life. We start with birth or creation. Every culture has its own creation myths and some of the most colourful come from the tales of the native American Indians, a selection of which I have included here along with the Celtic legend of 'The Ever-Living Ones'.

We then enter our childhood, with our own struggles for self-discovery and identity. As we mature we set out on wider voyages of discovery and here I have included a range of stories of inner and outer quests from ancient Greece, Japan, Persia and India.

Our struggle for identity and our quests for discovery may make us into mighty heroes or heroines, and no book of myths would be complete without a few of their adventures. I have selected these from various nations of Europe, including some of the most famous Greek myths.

Warriors will naturally venture into battle, and I have included several stories of war and conquest from Europe and North America. But there is one thing that will conquer all heroes – love. And to show how universal that is I have included a wide range of stories about love, revenge and self-sacrifice from cultures the world over.

With maturity comes wisdom and with wisdom may come an exploration of more mystical or magical worlds. In this section I have included a variety of stories about magic, faith, monsters, and the mysteries of the world about us including the wonder of nature and the animal world.

The mysteries of life will lead us to consider the mysteries of death, and the anthology closes with a series of stories which seek to explore fate, death and the world beyond.

These divisions are there to provide some structure and cohesion to the volume and hopefully add to the enjoyment. They are, though, fairly arbitrary, as many myths include one or more of these themes and in the final analysis I have sorted stories into which I felt was the most satisfactory sequence.

Many of the stories are selected from the writings of Victorian explorers and antiquarians who were able to convey the thrill of their discoveries and were the first to begin the still unfinished task of identifying and cataloguing the world's myths and legends. Some of these stories I have edited to exclude any excesses of Victorian moralism, but most were compiled by master story-tellers and are left as written.

I have also been helped by Jessica Amanda Salmonson and Peter Tremayne. Jessica is an American writer and anthologist who has long been fascinated with legends, especially those from the Orient and from her native soil. Peter Tremayne, under his real persona of Peter Berresford Ellis, is an established authority on Celtic myth, history and culture, and he has provided several stories using a variety of Celtic backgrounds.

In total there are over fifty stories of ancient wonder. I hope this anthology serves as a key to open the door to the magic of the past, and to open the mind to the wonders of the world about us, and perhaps even to open the heart to the romance of legend. It stole my heart years ago, and it is a love that has never failed.

Mike Ashley,
Walderslade,
December 1994

PART I:
THE DAWN OF TIME

THE EVER-LIVING ONES

Peter Tremayne

I T WAS THE time of primal chaos; a time when the Earth
was new and undefined. Arid deserts and black bubbling
volcanoes, covered by swirling clouds of gases, scarred the
grim visage of the newborn world. It was, as yet, the time of
the great void.

Then into that oblivion, from the dull, dark heavens, there
came a trickle of water. First one drop, then another and
another, until finally there gushed a mighty torrent down upon
the earth. The divine waters from heaven flooded downwards
and soaked into the arid dirt, cooled the volcanoes which turned
into grey, granite mountains, and life began to spring forth
across the Earth. The dark, redden skies, grew light and blue.

From the darkened soil there grew a tree, tall and strong.
Danu, the divine waters from heaven, nurtured and cherished
this great tree which became the sacred oak named Bíle. Of the
conjugation of Danu and Bíle there dropped two giant acorns.
The first acorn was male. From it sprang The Dagda, 'The Good
God'. The second seed was female. From it there emerged
Brigantu, or Brigid, 'The Exalted One'. And The Dagda and
Brigid gazed upon one another in wonder for it was their task
to wrest order from the primal chaos and to people the Earth
with the Children of Danu, the Mother Goddess, whose divine
waters had given them life.

So there, by the divine waters of Danu, from where those
waters rose and flooded through the now fertile green valleys
of the Earth, eastwards towards a distant sea, The Dagda and
Brigid settled. And they called the great course of eastward
rushing water after the Mother Goddess, which is Danuvius,
whose children still know it as the mighty Danube. And four

great, bright cities they built there on its broad banks in which the Children of Danu would live and thrive.

The four cities were Falias, Gorias, Finias and Murias.

The Dagda became their father, thus humankind call him 'The Father of the Gods'. And Brigid became the wise-one, exalted in learning and much did she imbibe from the mighty Danu and from Bíle, the sacred oak. She was hailed as the mother of healing, of craftsmanship and of poetry; indeed, she excelled in all-knowledge. She showed her children that true wisdom was only to be garnered from the feet of Danu, the Mother Goddess, and so only to be found at the water's edge. Those who gathered such knowledge, also paid deference to Bíle, the sacred oak. Because they were not allowed to speak his holy name, they called the oak *draoi* and those learned in such knowledge were said to possess oak (*dru*) knowledge (*vid*) and thus were known as Druids.

The knowledge of the Children of Danu grew and each of their four great cities prospered. In Falias they held a sacred stone called the Lia Fáil or Stone of Destiny, which, when a righteous ruler set foot on it, would shout with joy; in Gorias, where Urias of the Noble Nature dwelt, they held a mighty sword called the 'Retaliator', fashioned before the time of the gods themselves, and which Urias presented to Lugh Lámhfada, who became the greatest warrior among the gods; in Finias, they held a magic spear, called 'The Red Javelin', which, once cast, would find its enemy no matter where he hid; and in Murias they held the 'Cauldron of Plenty' from which The Dagda could feed entire nations and it still would not be emptied.

For many aeons, the Children of Danu grew and prospered in their beautiful cities.

Then, one day, The Dagda, Father of the Gods, and Brigid, the Exalted One, called their children to them.

'You have tarried here long enough. The Earth needs to be peopled and needs your wisdom to advise and direct them so that they may live lives of virtue and merit. Our Mother, Danu, has directed you to move towards the place where the bright Sun vanishes each evening.'

'Why should we go there?' demanded Nuada, the favourite son of The Dagda.

'Because it is your destiny,' replied Brigid.

'And you, Nuada, shall lead your brothers and sisters, and their children, and the land that you shall come to will be called Inisfáil, the Island of Destiny. There shall you abide until your destiny is fulfilled.'

'If it is our destiny,' said another of The Dagda's sons, named Ogma, 'then we shall accept it.'

Ogma was the most handsome of the Children of Danu. From his long curly hair, the rays of the sun shone and he was called Ogma *grian-aineacg*, of the Sunny Countenance. To him fell the gift of honeyed words, of poetry and of languages, and he, it was, who devised how man could write in a form of calligraphy which was named after him as Ogham.

Brigid smiled at her eager children.

'I am allowed to give you one word of warning. When you reach Inisfáil you will find another people who will claim the Island of Destiny as their own. This people are the Children of Domnu, who is the sister of our mother Danu. But beware, for Domnu is not as Danu. For each sister is the inverse of the other, as winter is to summer.'

'Then,' Nuada said, 'should we not take something to defend ourselves with, less the Children of Domnu fight us for the possession of Inisfáil?'

The Dagda gazed at them kindly and replied: 'You may take the four great treasures of the cities of Falias, Gorias, Finias and Murias.'

And the Children of Danu took the treasures and they went to the mountains overlooking the headwaters of the Danuvius, the divine waters from heaven, and ascended in a great cloud which bore them westward to Inisfáil, the Island of Destiny. And among them were three beautiful young sisters who were the wives of the sons of Ogma. Their names were Banba, Fótla and Éire and each sister nurtured an ambition that this new land of Inisfáil would one day be named after her.

* * *

Night wrapped her darkened mantle over Magh Tuireadh, which is called the Plain of Towers, which lay in the west of the land of Inisfáil. On each side of the great plain, separated by the River Unius, myriads of small campfires glowed in the gloom. Two armies had gathered for combat.

Seven years had passed since the Children of Danu had landed in their cloud on the shores of the Island of Destiny. They had fought initially with a strange race of people called the Firbolg who challenged their right to rule in the Island of Destiny. These they had met at the Pass of Balgatan and the conflict went on for four days. And in that conflict there came forth a champion of the Firbolg named Sreng who challenged Nuada, the leader of the Children of Danu, to single combat. So strong and mighty was Sreng that, with one sweep of his great sword, he cut off Nuada's right hand.

But the Firbolg and their king, Eochaidh, were defeated and dispersed.

Dian Cécht, the god of all physicians, came to Nuada after the battle and fashioned him an artificial hand of silver, so strong and supple, that it was little different from the real hand. Thus did Nuada receive his full name Nuada Argetlámh, of the Silver Hand. Because he was maimed, the other Children of Danu had to choose another of their number to lead them, for they had been told by Brigid that no one with a blemish must rule them. In choosing a new leader, they made a disastrous choice. As an act of conciliation between themselves and the Children of Domnu, they chose Bres, son of Elatha, king of the Children of Domnu who were also known as the Fomorii, or those who dwelt beneath the sea. And to further consolidate the alliance, Dian Cécht married Ethne, the daughter of the foremost Fomorii warrior named Balor of the One Eye. And the condition was that if Bres did anything which displeased the Children of Danu then he would abdicate and depart in peace.

Those years marked a period of strife. Bres, being a Fomorii, refused to keep his word and began to lay heavy burdens on the Children of Danu. For a while Bres and the Children of Domnu, the children of darkness and evil, dominated the land, and the Children of Danu, the children of light and goodness, were helpless and as slaves.

Then finally, Miach, the son of Dian Cécht, aided by his sister, the beautiful Airmid, fashioned a new hand of flesh and bone for Nuada. His hand replaced Dian Cécht's silver one and now, without blemish, Nuada reclaimed the leadership of the Children of Danu. So jealous was Dian Cécht of his son's achievement that he slew Miach. But that is another story.

Nuada chased Bres back to the land of the Fomorii where Bres demanded that Elatha, his father, provide him with an army to punish the Children of Danu.

Thus, on the plain where ancient megaliths stood, thrusting their dark granite skywards, Magh Tuireadh, the Plain of Towers, on the evening of the Feast of Samhain (31 October), the Children of Danu faced the Children of Domnu in battle.

At dawn the battle commenced. Combats broke out all along the line as Nuada led his warriors, both male and female, against the warriors of Bres and his Fomorii. Across the battlefield, the Mórrígán, Great Queen of Battles, with her sisters, Badh the Crow, Nemain the Venomous and Fea the Hateful, rushed hither and thither with their wailing cries which drove mortals to despair and death.

As time passed, Indech, a Fomorii warrior, approached Bres, and pointed out that whenever the Children of Danu were slain, or their weapons broken and destroyed, they would be carried from the field and, shortly after, would appear alive and well again with their weapons intact. Bres summoned his son, Ruadan, to his side and ordered him to discover the cause of the endless supply of weapons. And he summoned the son of Indech, a warrior named Octriallach, to discover how the Children of Danu, once slain, could come alive again.

Disguising himself as one of the Children of Danu, Ruadan went behind the lines of warriors and came across Goibhniu, god of smiths, who had set up a forge to one side of the Plain of Towers. With Goibhniu were Luchtainé, god of carpenters, and Credné, god of bronze workers. As each broken weapon was handed to Goibhniu, the smith-god gave it three blows of his hammer, which forged the head. Luchtainé gave the wood three blows of his axe and the shaft was fashioned. Then Credné fixed the shaft and head together with his bronze nails so swiftly that they needed no hammering.

Ruadan went back to his father and told him what he had seen. In a rage, Bres ordered his son to kill Goibhniu.

In the meantime, Octriallach had found a mystic spring on the other side of the Plain of Towers at which stood Dian Cécht, the god of medicine, with his daughter Airmid at his side. Whenever one of the Children of Danu were slain, they were brought to the spring and Dian Cécht and his daughter plunged the body into the spring and they reemerged alive again. In a rage, Bres ordered Octriallach to destroy the healing spring.

Ruadan returned to the forge and asked for a javelin from Goibhniu who gave it without suspicion, thinking Ruadan was one of the Children of Danu. No sooner was the weapon in his hand, than Ruadan turned and cast it at Goibhniu. It went clean through the smith-god's body. Mortally wounded as he was, Goibhniu picked up the spear and threw it back, wounding Ruadan who crawled away back to his father and died at his feet. The Fomorii set up a great *caoine*, or keening, which was the first ever heard in the Island of Destiny.

Goibhniu also crawled away and came to the spring where Dian Cécht and Airmid plunged him in and he emerged healthy and healed.

That night, however, Octriallach, son of Indech, and several of his companions, came to the spring and each took a large stone from the bed of a nearby river and dropped them into the spring until they had filled it. So the healing waters were dispersed.

Bres, satisfied the Children of Danu were now mortal, and angered by the death of his son, determined that a pitched battle should be fought. The next morning, spears and lances and swords smote against buckler and shield. The whistle of darts and rattle of arrows and shouting of warriors made it seem as if a great thunder was rolling over the Plain of Towers. The River of Unius, which cut through the plain, was stopped up, so filled was it with dead bodies. The plain was red with blood, so cruel was the battle.

Indech of the Fomorii fell by the hand of Ogma. And Indech was not the first nor last of the leaders of the Fomorii to feel the steel of the Children of Danu.

Neither did the Children of Danu go away from the battle unscathed.

To the field of slaughter came Balor of the Evil Eye, son of Buarainench, the most formidable of the Fomorii champions. He had one great eye whose gaze was so malevolent that it destroyed whosoever looked upon it. So large and awesome was this eye that it took nine attendants, using hooks, to lift the mighty lid to open it for Balor. It happened on that fateful day of the battle that Balor came upon Nuada of the Silver Hand the leader of the Children of Danu, and hard and fierce was the contest. Yet in the end, after shield was shattered, after spear was bent and sword was broken into pieces, it was the blood of Nuada that gushed in a never-ending stream into the earth of the Island of Destiny. And not content in this slaughter, but Balor turned upon one of Nuada's beautiful wives, Macha the Personification of Battles, goddess of warriors, and slew her also. Nor did Dian Cécht have the means to restore life to them.

At the death of their leader, the Children of Danu wavered and became fearful.

It was then that Lugh Lámhfada, Lugh of the Long Arm, approached the battlefield. Now Lugh was the son of Cian, which means 'Enduring One', who was in turn son of Cainte, the god of speech. Now the council of the Children of Danu had forbidden him to come to the battle, for Lugh was all-wise and all-knowledgeable and it was thought that his life was too valuable to risk in battle for his was the wisdom needed to serve humankind. Indeed, so wise was Lugh, that Nuada had let him become ruler of the Children of Danu for thirteen days in order that they might receive his wisdom. Therefore the Children of Danu had him imprisoned for his own safety during the battle with nine warriors to guard him. But on hearing Nuada was slain, Lugh escaped his prison and his guards and, leaping into his chariot, he hurried to join his brothers and sisters on the Plain of Towers.

Bres was standing triumphantly with his Fomorii warriors when he saw a great light in the west.

'I wonder that the sun is rising in the west today,' he muttered, scratching his head.

One of the Fomorii shamans approached Bres trembling.

'It is not the sun, mighty Bres. The light stems from the countenance of Lugh Lámhfada! It is his radiance.'

Lugh, with his weapons sheathed, drove his chariot out from the lines of the Children of Danu; straight he drove up to the tightly packed lines of Fomorii champions.

'Where is Balor?' he cried. 'Let him who thinks himself a great warrior come forward and be taught the truth!'

The lines of Fomorii parted and the great figure of Balor was seen, seated on a gigantic chair. His one mighty eye was closed.

Lugh's challenge rang out again.

This time Balor heard it and said to his attendants: 'Lift up my eyelid that I may gaze upon this prattling little man.'

The attendants began to lift Balor's eye with a hook. They stood well out of range. For anyone on whom that eye fell upon would perish immediately.

Lugh was ready with a sling and in it set a *tathlum*, a slingshot made of blood mixed with the sand of the swift Armorian sea. As the lid was lifted, Lugh hurled his shot into the eye. It struck it, went through the brain and out the back of Balor's head. The great Fomorii champion's eye was knocked out and fell on the ground. In its dying glint, thrice nine companies of Fomorii warriors were destroyed for they saw its malignant gaze.

Balor fell screaming to the ground in blindness.

A great anxiety fell on the Fomorii.

Lugh now raised his sword, and the Mórrígán set up a paean of victory: 'Kings arise to the battle . . . .!' And so, the Children of Danu took heart, and echoing the song they began to move forward. Great was the slaughter now as they pressed back on the Children of Domnu. It is said that more Fomorii were killed on the Plain of Towers than there were stars in the sky or grains of sand on the seashore, or snowflakes in winter.

And Lugh came upon Bres, who was fleeing for his life from the battlefield.

'Spare my life, Lugh, great conqueror,' cried the son of Elatha, sinking to his knees, for he no longer had the strength nor spirit to fight. 'Spare it, and I will pay whatever ransom you require.'

'What ransom?' demanded Lugh, his sword held at the throat of the Fomorii leader.

'I will guarantee that there will be no shortage of milk from the cows of this land,' offered Bres.

Lugh then called the Children of Danu to him.

'What good is that if Bres cannot lengthen the lives of the cows?' they demanded.

Bres could not grant longer lives so he offered: 'If my life is spared, every wheat harvest in Inisfáil will be a good one.'

'We already have enough good harvests. We need no other guarantees.'

Finally, Bres agreed to instruct the Children of Danu as to the best times to plough, sow and reap and for this knowledge, which they had not, they spared his life.

And when the battle was over, when the Fomorii were pursued back into their undersea fortresses, and they accepted the right of the Children of Danu to live in peace on the Island of Destiny and rule over it as gods and goddesses of goodness and of light, the Mórrígán went to all the summits of the highest mountains of the island and on each summit she proclaimed the victory of the gods and goddesses of light and goodness. And she sang in triumphant voice a paean to the Mother Goddess, Danu.

> Peace mounts to the heavens
> The divine waters descend to earth
> And fructify our lives
> Earth lies under the heavens
> We are of the Earth now
> And everyone is strong . . .

And while Danu smiled on the victory of her children, her sister Domnu scowled from the depths of the earth and she chose the goddess Badh the Crow as her mouth to utter a prophecy to Danu and her children.

'All life is transitory. Even your Children are not immortal, my sister. The time will come when they will be defeated. The time will come when no one will want gods and goddesses to nurture them, when they will be driven into the darkness like my Children have been this day.

'The time approaches when the summers of Inisfáil will be flowerless, when the cows shall be without milk, and the men will be weak and the women shall be shameless; the seas will be without fish, the trees without fruit and old men will give false judgements; the judges will make unjust laws and honour will count for little and warriors will betray each other and resort to thievery. There will come a time when there will be no more virtue left in this world.'

* * *

Indeed, there came that time when the Children of Míl flooded into the Island of Destiny and when the Children of Danu were driven underground into the hills, which were called *sidhe*, which is pronounced *shee*, and in those mounds they dwelt, the once mighty gods and goddesses, deserted by the very people who they had sought to nourish. The descendants of Míl, who live in the Island of Destiny to this day, called the Children of Danu, the *aes sidhe*, the people of the hills, and when even the religion of Míl was forgotten, when the religion of the Cross replaced that of the Circle, the people simply called the *aes sidhe* by the name of fairies.

Of the greatest of the gods, the victor of the battle on the Plain of Towers, Lugh Lámhfada, god of all-knowledge, patron of all arts and crafts, his name is still known today. But as memory of the mighty warrior, the invincible god, has faded, he is known only as *Lugh-chromain*, little stooping Lugh of the *sidhe*, relegated to the role of a fairy craftsman. And, as even the language in which he was venerated has disappeared, all that is left of the supreme god of the Children of Danu is the distorted form of that name *Lugh-chromain* . . . leprechaun.

THE STAR MAIDS

Jessica Amanda Salmonson

THE STARMAIDS AND THE FLEA MAN

FIVE MAIDENS LIVED happily in the sky. They played together every night. Flea Man decided to marry all of them, so he hopped upward to catch them.

The star maids saw him coming and flew toward the East. They were swift, but Flea Man was persistent.

'That awful Flea Man is still coming,' said Moki-girl.

Moki was formerly a robin. She was the sister of that bad trickster Coyote. When she had to marry Salamander against her will, she fooled him into jumping into a hot spring so that he boiled to death.

'We should run faster!' said Kipi-girl.

Kipi was the famous girl who cut out Coyote's tongue to cook it, and it took him a very long time to grow another.

'If we make love to old scratchy,' said Tewe-girl, 'we'll go bald.'

Tewe's daughter was the well known Rabbit Huntress, who was strong like her mother.

'He's not strong enough to catch us,' said Pahalali.

Pahalali was the daughter of Frog-maid. Frog-maid was a warrior who battled the moon-devouring lizard. Every month, when the moon was nearly eaten by the lizard, Pahalali's mother ran forth with weapons to chase away the lizard and restore the moon.

'We'll go this way,' said Tukwishhemish. 'When Flea Man goes to sleep, we'll surely lose him.'

Tukwishhemish was the leader of the star maids. She was

a very clever girl and always decided their course across the night sky.

Flea Man went to sleep in the morning. When he woke up the next night, the star maids were way over by the horizon. 'Oh! My wives!' he shouted, and streaked eagerly across heaven.

'Here he comes again,' said Moki-girl.

'Let's get running,' said Kipi-girl.

'Is he close?' asked Tewe-girl.

'He's gaining,' said Pahalali.

'Let's go under the sea,' said Tukwishhemish, and led her companions downward.

The five star maids vanished under the sea. When they came back out, Flea Man still hopped after them, scratching and loping the whole way.

'Well, it's no use running,' said Moki.

'He'll never give up,' said Kipi.

'We'll have to try something desperate,' said Tewe.

'Let's kill him,' said Pahalali.

The star maids stopped running and turned around to face Flea Man.

'Come any closer,' Tukwishhemish warned, 'and we'll tear you to pieces.'

They stood their ground and Flea Man was afraid to come any closer. To this day, the five women are close together in the sky. Flea Man is that little speck of a star a little to one side.

THE STAR MAIDENS' LAUGHTER

MOKI, KIPI, TEWE and Pahalali were happy star maids and always laughing. But Tukwishhemish never laughed. Moki and Kipi slept side by side in the daytime, just as Tewe and Pahalali slept side by side. At night, they woke up to play and laugh.

But Tukwishhemish had no partner. She was the prettiest of the five and the others courted her, but she rebuffed their intimacy. In the daytime she slept alone.

One day, Tukwishhemish's companions leapt on her and held her down, tickling her all over her body. This made her open up her mouth and laugh. The others saw that she had two rows of teeth in her mouth! They laughed so hard that Tukwishhemish left them to live on the earth.

The star maids were sad without her. They came down from the sky to find her. They met Old-Mother-With-Dogs. She said, 'Tukwishhemish was adopted by Thunder Woman. The Thunder's daughter lures men and women to their deaths in the mountains. It is too late ever to reclaim her, so you girls had better fly back up to the sky.'

But the star maids would not stop looking. They sought Tukwishhemish despite the warning of Old-Mother-With-Dogs.

They spied Tukwishhemish high on a mountain carrying a basket of ice balls and arrows on her back. These she threw down at the star maids, but they dodged the ice balls and arrows. Then Tukwishhemish went down from the mountain through thorn bushes that opened in front of her and closed behind her. The star maids were scratched and bloodied, but would not give up the chase.

Tukwishhemish led them into the Valley of Rattlesnakes, while Thunder Mother shouted in the sky, waking up the serpents. So the star maids put on thick moccasins that went up to their knees and kept after Tukwishhemish.

But when they came to the Valley of Old Age, a thousand years went by in a second. The star maids became whitehaired and slow.

'We'll never catch her now,' said Moki-hag.

'I'm so tired,' said Kipi-hag.

'Let's stop here and rest,' said Tewe-hag.

'But if we delay,' said Pahalali, 'we'll continue to get older and then we'll die.'

They talked it over and all agreed they would rather die than live without Tukwishhemish. Therefore they sat down in the Valley of Old Age and waited. Tukwishhemish sent a magic bird which plucked out four of its feathers. These the star hags put in their hair and were made young and strong. They followed the magic bird through the air and came to the Sweat Lodge of Thunder Mother. Steam was pouring out of the mountain peak of the Sweat Lodge. The star maids went into the lodge and sat at the feet of Tukwishhemish and Thunder Mother.

'Come back with us to our home in the sky,' said Pahalali.

'We have missed you so much,' said the rest.

And Tukwishhemish opened her mouth wide and laughed for joy.

BEARSKIN WOMAN
AND GRIZZLY WOMAN

Jessica Amanda Salmonson

BEARSKIN WOMAN DREAMED of the spirit called Double Moon Woman, who only *kwame*[1] dream about. Thereby she knew where her future lay. She went into the forest and met a grizzly bear. They got along so well that Bearskin Woman went to live with Grizzly Woman in a cave.

When her father and brothers learned of it, they were furious. They gathered together some braves and surrounded the bear cave, intending to slay Grizzly Woman. But Bearskin Woman had also become a bear, due to an amulet that she had made. The two bears rushed out to confront Bearskin Woman's brothers, father, and the many braves that had accompanied them. The she-bears killed many who had set their faces against the bears. Only when Bearskin Woman's sister Sinopa stood before her did the two bears stop slaughtering.

The survivors had run off, so Bearskin Woman took her former shape and told her sister, 'Return to the tribe and tell them I have dreamed of Double Moon Woman and I am happy with Grizzly Woman in our cave together. We are holy women and cannot be destroyed. We will bring good luck to everyone, and cause the land to be green and fruitful, unless they trouble us again.'

The tribe was satisfied by this explanation, and were even glad to have holy women living in the forest with promises of good luck. But the six brothers felt insulted that their own sister and her bear-lover had defeated them and killed many of their

[1] lesbians

friends. They weren't about to let the women get away with it. So they gathered together a large number of prickly pear cacti. They slipped up to the cave in the deep of night and strew the prickly pears at the entrance. Then they made war-hollers and woke up Grizzly Woman and Bearskin Woman, who came running out, fierce and growling.

They got prickly pears in their paws, and roared with pain and anger. Even so, they came across the barrier so swiftly that the six brothers knew they would be defeated a second time.

Their younger sister Sinopa appeared from behind a bush. She had a bow and arrows. She didn't want any of her family killed, so she shot an arrow over the heads of her brothers, and it flew a great distance. As it was a magic arrow, her six brothers found themselves suddenly a surprising distance away, where the arrow had landed.

The two she-bears pursued. They were gaining on the brothers who were running across the prairie. Wherever the blood of the two bears' cactus-pierced feet touched the ground, trees sprang up. Wherever they angrily dug their claws into the earth, lakes appeared.

The six brothers were caught and scattered about the prairie like sticks. They got to their feet and ran to the biggest tree that had grown from the bloody footprints of the she-bears. Grizzly Woman and Bearskin Woman sat down underneath the tree and licked their paws. The six brothers knew that if they fell asleep, they would tumble out of the tree and be eaten.

Their little sister Sinopa appeared unexpectedly at the very top of the tree. She drew forth one of her arrows and fired it into heaven. One of her brothers vanished from the tree and became a star. She shot another arrow, and another, until all six brothers became stars. Then she rode upon the bow, which was the Moon, and joined her brothers, so that she was queen of six princes of heaven, and the seven stars are visible to this day.

Bearskin Woman and Grizzly Woman lived happily for many years. When they died, they became the Two Bears of Heaven, and still chase the six princes around and around the sky.

PART II:
YOUTH AND SELF-DISCOVERY

THE QUEST FOR DISCOVERY

Andrew Lang

IN OLDEN TIMES a young woman called Aethra bore a son. This was her only comfort, and she thought that she saw in him a likeness to his father, whose true name she did not know. Certainly he was a very beautiful baby, well formed and strong, and, as soon as he could walk he was apt to quarrel with other children of his own age, and fight with them in a harmless way. He never was an amiable child, though he was always gentle to his mother. From the first he was afraid of nothing, and when he was about four or five he used to frighten his mother by wandering from home, with his little bow and arrows, and staying by himself in the woods. However, he always found his own way back again, sometimes with a bird or a snake that he had shot, and once dragging the body of a fawn that was nearly as heavy as himself. Thus his mother, from his early boyhood, had many fears for him, that he might be killed by some fierce wild boar in the woods, for he would certainly shoot at whatever beast he met; or that he might kill some other boy in a quarrel, when he would be obliged to leave the country. The other boys, however, soon learned not to quarrel with Theseus (so Aethra had named her son), for he was quick of temper, and heavy of hand, and, as for the wild beasts, he was cool as well as eager, and seemed to have an untaught knowledge of how to deal with them.

Aethra was therefore very proud of her son, and began to hope that when he was older he would be able to roll away the great stone in the glen. She told him nothing about it when he was little, but, in her walks with him in the woods or on the sea shore, she would ask him to try his force in lifting large stones. When he succeeded she kissed and praised him, and told him stories of the famous strong man, Heracles, whose name was well known through all Greece. Theseus could not bear to be beaten at lifting any weight, and, if he failed, he would rise early and try again in the morning, for many men, as soon as they rise from bed, can lift weights which are too heavy for them later in the day.

When Theseus was seven years old, Aethra found for him a tutor, named Connidas, who taught him the arts of netting beasts and hunting, and how to manage the dogs, and how to drive a chariot, and wield sword and shield, and to throw the spear. Other things Connidas taught him which were known to few men in Greece, for Connidas came from the great rich island of Crete. He had killed a man there in a quarrel, and fled to Troezene to escape the revenge of the man's brothers and cousins. In Crete many people could read and write, which in Greece, perhaps none could do, and Connidas taught Theseus this learning.

When he was fifteen years old, Theseus went, as was the custom of young princes, to the temple of Delphi, not to ask questions, but to cut his long hair, and sacrifice it to the god, Apollo. He cut the forelock of his hair, so that no enemy, in battle, might take hold of it, for Theseus intended to fight at close quarters, hand to hand, in war, not to shoot arrows and throw spears from a distance. By this time he thought himself a man, and was always asking where his father was, while Aethra told him how her husband had left her soon after their marriage, and that she had never heard of him since, but that some day Theseus might find out all about him for himself, which no other person would ever be able to do.

Aethra did not wish to tell Theseus too soon the secret of the great stone, which hid she knew not what. She saw that he would leave her and go to seek his father, if he was able to raise the stone and find out the secret, and she could not bear to lose him, now that day by day he grew more like his father, her lost lover. Besides, she wanted him not to try to raise the stone till he came to his strength. But when he was in his nineteenth year, he told her that he would now go all over Greece and the whole world seeking for his father. She saw that he meant what he said, and one day she led him alone to the glen where the great stone lay, and sat down with him there, now talking, and now silent as if she were listening to the pleasant song of the burn that fell from a height into a clear deep pool. Really she was listening to make sure that no hunter and no lovers were near them in the wood, but she only heard the songs of the water and the birds, no voices, or cry of hounds, or fallen twig crackling under a footstep.

At last, when she was quite certain that nobody was near, she whispered, and told Theseus how her husband, before he disappeared, had taken her to this place, and shown her the great moss-grown boulder, and said that, when his son could lift that stone away, he would find certain tokens, and that he must then do what the gods put into his heart. Theseus listened eagerly, and said, 'If my father lifted that stone, and placed under it certain tokens, I also can lift it, perhaps not yet, but some day I shall be as strong a man as my father.' Then he set himself to move the stone, gradually putting out all his force, but it seemed rooted in the earth, though he tried it now on one side and now on another. At last he flung himself at his mother's feet, with his head in the grass, and lay without speaking. His breath came hard and quick, and his hands were bleeding. Aethra laid her hand on his long hair, and was silent. 'I shall not lose my boy this year,' she thought.

They were long in that lonely place, but at last Theseus rose, and kissed his mother, and stretched his arms. 'Not today!' he said, but his mother thought in her heart, 'Not for many a day, I hope!' Then they walked home to the house of Pittheus, saying little, and when they had taken supper, Theseus said that he would go to bed and dream of better fortune. So he arose, and went to his own chamber, which was built apart in the court of the palace, and soon Aethra too went to sleep, not unhappy, for her boy, she thought, would not leave her for a long time.

But in the night Theseus arose, and put on his shoes, and his smock, and a great double mantle. He girt on his sword of bronze, and went into the housekeeper's chamber, where he took a small skin of wine, and some food. These he placed in a wallet which he slung round his neck by a cord, and, lastly he stole out of the court, and walked to the lonely glen, and to the pool in the burn near which the great stone lay. Here he folded his purple mantle of fine wool round him, and lay down to sleep in the grass, with his sword lying near his hand.

When he awoke the clear blue morning light was round him, and all the birds were singing their song to the dawn. Theseus arose, threw off his mantle and smock, and plunged into the cold pool of the burn, and then he drank a little of the wine, and ate of the bread and cold meat, and set himself to move the stone. At the first effort, into which he put all his strength, the stone stirred. With the second he felt it rise a little way from the ground, and then he lifted with all the might in his heart and body, and rolled the stone clean over.

Beneath it there was nothing but the fresh turned soil, but in a hollow of the foot of the rock, which now lay uppermost, there was a wrapping of purple woollen cloth, that covered something. Theseus tore out the packet, unwrapped the cloth, and found within it a wrapping of white linen. This wrapping was in many folds, which he undid, and at last he found a pair of shoon, such as kings wear, adorned with gold, and also the most beautiful sword that he had ever seen. The handle was of clear rock crystal, and through the crystal you could see gold, inlaid with pictures of a lion hunt done in different shades of gold and silver. The sheath was of leather, with patterns in gold nails, and the blade was of bronze, a beautiful pattern ran down the centre to the point, the blade was straight, and double edged, supple, sharp, and strong. Never had Theseus seen so beautiful a sword, nor one so well balanced in his hand.

He saw that this was a king's sword; and he thought that it had not been wrought in Greece, for in Greece was no sword-smith that could do such work. Examining it very carefully he found characters engraved beneath the hilt, not letters such as the Greeks used in later times, but such Cretan signs as Connidas had taught him to read, for many a weary hour, when he would like to have been following the deer in the forest.

Theseus pored over these signs till he read: 'Icmalius me made. Of Aegeus of Athens am I.'

Now he knew the secret. His father was Aegeus, the king of Athens. Theseus had heard of him and knew that he yet lived, a sad life full of trouble. For Aegeus had no child by his Athenian wife, and the fifty sons of his brother, Pallas (who were called the Pallantidae) despised him, and feasted all day in his hall, recklessly and fiercely, robbing the people, and Aegeus had no power in his own kingdom.

'Methinks that my father has need of me!' said Theseus to himself. Then he wrapped up the sword and shoon in the linen and the cloth of wool, and walked home in the early morning to the palace of Pittheus.

When Theseus came to the palace, he went straight to the upper chamber of his mother, where she was spinning wool with a distaff of ivory. When he laid before her the sword and the shoon, the distaff fell from her hand, and she hid her head in a fold of her robe. Theseus kissed her hands and comforted her, and she dried her eyes, and praised him for his strength. 'These are the sword and the shoon of your father,' she said, 'but truly the gods have taken away his strength and courage. For all men say that Aegeus of Athens is not master in his own house; his brother's sons rule him, and with them Medea, the witch woman, that once was the wife of Jason.'

'The more he needs his son!' said Theseus. 'Mother, I must go to help him, and be the heir of his kingdom, where you shall be with me always, and rule the people of Cecrops that fasten the locks of their hair with grasshoppers of gold.'

'So may it be, my child,' said Aethra, 'if the gods go with you to protect you. But you will sail to Athens in a ship with fifty oarsmen, for the ways by land are long, and steep, and dangerous, beset by cruel giants and monstrous men.'

'Nay, mother,' said Theseus, 'by land must I go, for I would not be known in Athens, till I see how matters fall out: and I would destroy these giants and robbers, and give peace to the people, and win glory among men. This very night I shall set forth.'

He had a sore and sad parting from his mother, but under cloud of night he went on his way, girt with the sword of Aegeus, his father, and carrying in his wallet the shoon with ornaments of gold.

* * *

Theseus walked through the night, and slept for most of the next day at a shepherd's hut. The shepherd was kind to him, and bade him beware of one called the Maceman, who guarded a narrow path with a sheer cliff above, and a sheer precipice below. 'No man born may deal with the Maceman,' said the shepherd, 'for his great club is of iron, that cannot be broken, and his strength is as the strength of ten men, though his legs have no force to bear his body. Men say that he is the son of the lame god, Hephaestus, who forged his iron mace; there is not the like of it in the world.'

'Shall I fear a lame man?' said Theseus, 'and is it not easy, even if he be so terrible a fighter, for me to pass him in the darkness, for I walk by night?'

The shepherd shook his head. 'Few men have passed Periphetes the Maceman,' said he, 'and wiser are they who trust to swift ships than to the upland path.'

'You speak kindly, father,' said Theseus, 'but I am minded to make the upland paths safe for all men.'

So they parted, and Theseus walked through the sunset and the dusk, always on a rising path, and the further he went the harder it was to see the way, for the path was overgrown with grass, and the shadows were deepening. Night fell, and Theseus hardly dared to go further, for on his left hand was a wall of rock, and on his right hand a cliff sinking sheer and steep to the sea. But now he saw a light in front of him, a red light flickering, as from a great fire, and he could not be content till he knew why that fire was lighted. So he went on, slowly and warily, till he came in full view of the fire which covered the whole of a little platform of rock; on one side the blaze shone up the wall of cliff on his left hand, on the other was the steep fall to the sea. In front of this fire was a great black bulk; Theseus knew not what it might be. He walked forward till he saw that the black bulk was that of a monstrous man, who sat with his back to the fire. The man nodded his heavy head, thick with red unshorn hair, and Theseus went up close to him.

'Ho, sir,' he cried, 'this is my road, and on my road I must pass!'

The seated man opened his eyes sleepily.

'Not without my leave,' he said, 'for I keep this way, I and my club of iron.'

'Get up and begone!' said Theseus.

'That were hard for me to do,' said the monstrous man, 'for my legs will not bear the weight of my body, but my arms are strong enough.'

'That is to be seen!' said Theseus, and he drew his sword,

and leaped within the guard of the iron club that the monster, seated as he was, swung lightly to this side and that, covering the whole width of the path. The Maceman swung the club at Theseus, but Theseus sprang aside, and in a moment, before the monster could recover his stroke, drove through his throat the sword of Aegeus, and he fell back dead.

'He shall have his rights of fire, that his shadow may not wander outside the House of Hades,' said Theseus to himself, and he toppled the body of the Maceman into his own great fire. Then he went back some way, and wrapping himself in his mantle, he slept till the sun was high in heaven, while the fire had sunk into its embers, and Theseus lightly sprang over them, carrying with him the Maceman's iron club. The path now led downwards, and a burn that ran through a green forest kept him company on the way, and brought him to pleasant farms and houses of men.

They marvelled to see him, a young man, carrying the club of the Maceman. 'Did you find him asleep?' they asked, and Theseus smiled and said, 'No, I found him awake. But now he sleeps an iron sleep, from which he will never waken, and his body had due burning in his own watchfire.' Then the men and women praised Theseus, and wove for him a crown of leaves and flowers, and sacrificed sheep to the gods in heaven, and on the meat they dined, rejoicing that now they could go to Troezene by the hill path, for they did not love ships and the sea.

When they had eaten and drunk, and poured out the last cup of wine on the ground, in honour of Hermes, the God of Luck, the country people asked Theseus where he was going? He said that he was going to walk to Athens, and at this the people looked sad. 'No man may walk across the neck of land where Ephyre is built,' they said, 'because above it Sinis the Pine-Bender has his castle, and watches the way.'

'And who is Sinis, and why does he bend pine trees?' asked Theseus.

'He is the strongest of men, and when he catches a traveller, he binds him hand and foot, and sets him between two pine trees. Then he bends them down till they meet, and fastens the traveller to the boughs of each tree, and lets them spring apart, so that the man is riven asunder.'

'Two can play at that game,' said Theseus, smiling, and he

bade farewell to the kind country people, shouldered the iron club of Periphetes, and went singing on his way. The path led him over moors, and past farm-houses, and at last rose towards the crest of the hill whence he would see the place where two seas would have met, had they not been sundered by the neck of land which is now called the Isthmus of Corinth. Here the path was very narrow, with thick forests of pine trees on each hand, and 'here,' thought Theseus to himself, 'I am likely to meet the Pine-Bender.'

Soon he knew that he was right, for he saw the ghastly remains of dead men that the pine trees bore like horrible fruit, and presently the air was darkened overhead by the waving of vultures and ravens that prey upon the dead. 'I shall fight the better in the shade,' said Theseus, and he loosened the blade of the sword in its sheath, and raised the club of Periphetes aloft in his hand.

Well it was for him that he raised the iron club, for, just as he lifted it, there flew out from the thicket something long, and slim, and black, that fluttered above his head for a moment, and then a loop at the end of it fell round the head of Theseus, and was drawn tight with a sudden jerk. But the loop fell also above and round the club, which Theseus held firm, pushing away the loop, and so pushed it off that it did not grip his neck. Drawing with his left hand his bronze dagger, he cut through the leather lasso with one stroke, and bounded into the bushes from which it had flown. Here he found a huge man, clad in the skin of a lion, with its head fitting to his own like a mask. The man lifted a club made of the trunk of a young pine tree, with a sharp-edged stone fastened into the head of it like an axe-head. But, as the monster raised his long weapon it struck on a strong branch of a tree above him, and was entangled in the boughs, so that Theseus had time to thrust the head of the iron club full in his face, with all his force, and the savage fell with a crash like a falling oak among the bracken. He was one of the last of an ancient race of savage men, who dwelt in Greece before the Greeks, and he fought as they had fought, with weapons of wood and stone.

Theseus dropped with his knees on the breast of the Pine-Bender, and grasped his hairy throat with both his hands, not to strangle him, but to hold him sure and firm till he came to himself again. When at last the monster opened his eyes, Theseus gripped his throat the harder, and spoke, 'Pine-Bender, for thee shall pines be bent. But I am a man and not a monster, and thou shalt die a clean death before thy body is torn in twain to be the last feast of thy vultures.' Then, squeezing the throat of the wretch with his left hand, he drew the sword of Aegeus, and drove it into the heart of Sinis the Pine-Bender, and he gave a cry like a bull's, and his soul fled from him. Then Theseus bound the body of the savage with his own leather cord, and, bending down the tops of two pine trees, he did to the corpse as Sinis had been wont to do to living men.

Lastly he cleaned the sword-blade carefully, wiping it with grass and bracken, and thrusting it to the hilt through the soft fresh ground under the trees, and so went on his way till he came to a little stream that ran towards the sea from the crest of the hill above the town of Ephyre, which is now called Corinth. But as he cleansed himself in the clear water, he heard a rustle in the boughs of the wood, and running with sword drawn to the place whence the sound seemed to come, he heard the whisper of a woman. Then he saw a strange sight. A tall and very beautiful girl was kneeling in the thicket, in a patch of asparagus thorn, and was weeping, and praying, in a low voice, and in a childlike innocent manner, to the thorns, begging them to shelter and defend her.

Theseus wondered at her, and, sheathing his sword, came softly up to her, and bade her have no fear. Then she threw her arms about his knees, and raised her face, all wet with tears, and bade him take pity upon her, for she had done no harm.

'Who are you, maiden? You are safe with me,' said Theseus. 'Do you dread the Pine-Bender?'

'Alas, sir,' answered the girl, 'I am his daughter, Perigyne, and his blood is on your hands.'

'Yet I do not war with women,' said Theseus, 'though that has been done which was decreed by the gods. If you follow with me, you shall be kindly used, and marry, if you will, a man of a good house, being so beautiful as you are.'

When she heard this, the maiden rose to her feet, and would have put her hand in his. 'Not yet,' said Theseus, kindly, 'till water has clean washed away that which is between thee and me. But wherefore, maiden, being in fear as you were, did you not call to the gods in heaven to keep you, but to the asparagus thorns that cannot hear or help?'

'My father, sir,' she said, 'knew no gods, but he came of the race of the asparagus thorns, and to them I cried in my need.'

Theseus marvelled at these words, and said, 'From this day you shall pray to Zeus, the Lord of Thunder, and to the other gods.' Then he went forth from the wood, with the maiden following, and wholly cleansed himself in the brook that ran by the way.

So they passed down to the rich city of Ephyre, where the king received him gladly, when he heard of the slaying of the Maceman, Periphetes, and of Sinis the Pine-Bender. The Queen, too, had pity on Perigyne, so beautiful she was, and kept her in her own palace. Afterwards Perigyne married a prince, Deiones, son of Eurytus, King of Oechalia, whom the strong man Heracles slew for the sake of his bow, the very bow with which Ulysses, many years afterwards, destroyed the Wooers in his halls. The sons of Perigyne and Deiones later crossed the seas to Asia, and settled in a land called Caria, and they never burned or harmed the asparagus thorn to which Perigyne had prayed in the thicket.

Greece was so lawless in these days that all the road from Troezene northward to Athens was beset by violent and lawless men. They loved cruelty even more than robbery, and each of them had carefully thought out his particular style of being cruel. The cities were small, and at war with each other, or at war among themselves, one family fighting against another for the crown. Thus there was no chance of collecting an army to destroy the monstrous men of the roads, which it would have been easy enough for a small body of archers to have done. Later Theseus brought all into great order, but now, being but one man, he went seeking adventures.

On the border of a small country called Megara, whose people were much despised in Greece, he found a chance of advancing himself, and gaining glory. He was walking in the middle of the day along a narrow path at the crest of a cliff above the sea, when he saw the flickering of a great fire in the blue air, and steam going up from a bronze cauldron of water that was set on the fire. On one side of the fire was a foot-bath of glittering bronze. Hard by was built a bower of green branches, very cool on that hot day, and from the door of the bower stretched a great thick hairy pair of naked legs.

Theseus guessed, from what he had been told, that the owner of the legs was Sciron the Kicker. He was a fierce outlaw who was called the Kicker because he made all travellers wash his feet, and, as they were doing so, kicked them over the cliff. Some say that at the foot of the cliff dwelt an enormous tortoise, which ate the dead and dying when they fell near his lair, but as tortoises do not eat flesh, generally, this may be a mistake. Theseus was determined not to take any insolence from Sciron, so he shouted—

'Slave, take those dirty legs of yours out of the way of a Prince.'

'Prince!' answered Sciron, 'if my legs are dirty, the gods are kind who have sent you to wash them for me.'

Then he got up, lazily, laughing and showing his ugly teeth, and stood in front of his bath with his heavy wooden club in his hand. He whirled it round his head insultingly, but Theseus was quicker than he, and again, as when he slew the Pine-Bender, he did not strike, for striking is slow compared to thrusting, but like a flash he lunged forward and drove the thick end of his iron club into the breast of Sciron. He staggered, and, as he reeled, Theseus dealt him a blow across the thigh, and he fell. Theseus seized the club which dropped from the hand of Sciron, and threw it over the cliff; it seemed long before the sound came up from the rocks on which it struck. 'A deep drop into a stony way, Sciron,' said Theseus, 'now wash my feet! Stand up, and turn your back to me, and be ready when I tell you.' Sciron rose, slowly and sulkily, and stood as Theseus bade him do.

Now Theseus was not wearing light shoes or sandals, like the golden sandals of Aegeus, which he carried in his wallet. He was wearing thick boots, with bronze nails in the soles, and the upper leathers were laced high up his legs, for the Greeks wore such boots when they took long walks on mountain roads. As soon as Theseus had trained Sciron to stand in the proper position, he bade him stoop to undo the lacings of his boots. As Sciron stooped, Theseus gave him one tremendous kick, that lifted him over the edge of the cliff, and there was an end of Sciron.

Theseus left the marches of Megara, and walked singing on his way, above the sea, for his heart was light, and he was finding adventures to his heart's desire. Being so young and well trained, his foot and hand, in a combat, moved as swift as lightning, and his enemies were older than he, and, though very strong, were heavy with full feeding, and slow to move. Now it is speed that wins in a fight, whether between armies or single men, if strength and courage go with it.

At last the road led Theseus down from the heights to a great fertile plain, called the Thriasian plain, not far from Athens. There, near the sea, stands the famous old city of Eleusis. When Hades, the God of the Dead, carried away beautiful Persephone, the daughter of Demeter, the Goddess of corn and all manner of grain, to his dark palace beside the stream of Ocean, it was to Eleusis that Demeter wandered. She was clad in mourning robes, and she sat down on a stone by the way, like a weary old woman. Now the three daughters of the king who then reigned in Eleusis came by, on the way to the well, to fetch water, and when they saw the old woman they set down their vessels and came round her, asking what they could do for her, who was so tired and poor. They said that they had a baby brother at home, who was the favourite of them all, and that he needed a nurse. Demeter was pleased with their kindness, and they left their vessels for water beside her, and ran home to their mother. Their long golden hair danced on their shoulders as they ran, and they came, out of breath, to their mother the Queen, and asked her to take the old woman to be their brother's nurse. The Queen was kind, too, and the old woman lived in their house, till Zeus, the chief God, made the God of the Dead send back Persephone, to be with her mother through spring, and summer, and early autumn, but in winter she must live with her husband in the dark palace beside the river of Ocean.

Then Demeter was glad, and she caused the grain to grow abundantly for the people of Eleusis, and taught them ceremonies, and a kind of play in which all the story of her sorrows and joy was acted. It was also taught that the souls of men do not die with the death of their bodies, any more than the seed of corn dies when it is buried in the dark earth, but that they live again in a world more happy and beautiful than ours. These ceremonies were called the Mysteries of Eleusis, and were famous in all the world.

Theseus might have expected to find Eleusis a holy city, peaceful and quiet. But he had heard, as he travelled, that in Eleusis was a strong bully, named Cercyon; he was one of the rough Highlanders of Arcadia, who lived in the hills of the centre of Southern Greece, which is called Peloponnesus. He is said to have taken the kingship, and driven out the descendants of the king whose daughters were kind to Demeter. The strong man used to force all strangers to wrestle with him, and, when he threw them, for he had never been thrown, he broke their backs.

Knowing this, and being himself fond of wrestling, Theseus walked straight to the door of the king's house, though the men in the town warned him, and the women looked at him with sad eyes. He found the gate of the courtyard open, with the altar of Zeus the high God smoking in the middle of it, and at the threshold two servants welcomed him, and took him to the polished bath, and women washed him, and anointed him with oil, and clothed him in fresh raiment, as was the manner in kings' houses. Then they led him into the hall, and he walked straight up to the high seats between the four pillars beside the hearth, in the middle of the hall.

There Cercyon sat, eating and drinking, surrounded by a score of his clan, great, broad, red-haired men, but he himself was the broadest and the most brawny. He welcomed Theseus, and caused a table to be brought, with meat, and bread, and wine, and when Theseus had put away his hunger, began to ask him who he was and whence he came. Theseus told him that he had walked from Troezene, and was on his way to the court of King Peleus (the father of Achilles), in the north, for he did not want the news of his coming to go before him to Athens.

'You walked from Troezene?' said Cercyon. 'Did you meet or hear of the man who killed the Maceman and slew the Pine-Benders, and kicked Sciron into the sea?'

'I walk fast, but news flies faster,' said Theseus.

'The news came through my second-sighted man,' said Cercyon, 'there he is, in the corner,' and Cercyon threw the leg bone of an ox at his prophet, who just managed to leap out of the way. 'He seems to have foreseen that the bone was coming at him,' said Cercyon, and all his frends laughed loud. 'He told us this morning that a stranger was coming, he who had killed the three watchers of the way. From your legs and shoulders, and the iron club that you carry, methinks you are that stranger?'

Theseus smiled, and moulded upwards, which the Greeks did when they meant 'Yes!'

'Praise be to all the gods!' said Cercyon. 'It is long since a good man came my way. Do they practise wrestling at Troezene?'

'Now and then,' said Theseus.

'Then you will try a fall with me? There is a smooth space strewn with sand in the courtyard.'

Theseus answered that he had come hoping that the kind would graciously honour him by trying a fall. Then all the wild guests shouted, and out they all went and made a circle round the wrestling-place, while Theseus and Cercyon threw down their clothes and were anointed with oil over their bodies. To it they went, each straining forward and feeling for a grip, till they were locked, and then they swayed this way and that, their stamping the ground; and now one would yield a little, now the other, while the rough guests shouted, encouraging each of them. At last they rested and breathed, and now the men began to bet; seven oxen to three was laid on Cercyon, and taken in several places. Back to the wrestle they went, and Theseus found this by far the hardest of his adventures, for Cercyon was heavier than he, and as strong, but not so active. So Theseus for long did little but resist the awful strain of the arms of Cercyon, till, at last, for a moment Cercyon weakened. Then Theseus slipped his hip under the hip of Cercyon, and heaved him across and up, and threw him on the ground. He lighted in such a way that his neck broke, and there he lay dead.

'Was it fairly done?' said Theseus.

'It was fairly done!' cried the Highlanders of Arcadia; and then they raised such a wail for the dead that Theseus deemed it wise to put on his clothes and walk out of the court; and, leaping into a chariot that stod empty by the gate, for the servant in the chariot feared the club of iron, he drove away at full speed.

Though Cercyon was a cruel man and wild, Theseus was sorry for him in his heart.

The groom in the chariot tried to leap out, but Theseus gripped him tight. 'Do no hurry, my friend,' said Theseus, 'for I have need of you. I am not stealing the chariot and horses, and you shall drive them back after we reach Athens.'

'But, my lord,' said the groom, 'you will never reach Athens.'

'Why not?' asked Theseus.

'Because of the man Procrustes, who dwells in a strong castle among the hills on the way. He is the maimer of all mortals, and has at his command a company of archers and spearmen, pirates from the islands. He meets every traveller, and speaks to him courteously, praying him to be his guest, and if any refuses the archers leap out of ambush and seize and bind him. With them no man can contend. He has a bed which he says is a thing magical, for it is of the same length as the tallest or the shortest man who sleeps in it, so that all are fitted. Now the manner of it is this – there is an engine with ropes at the head of the bed, and a saw is fitted at the bed foot. If a man is too short, the ropes are fastened to his hands, and are strained till he is drawn to the full length of the bed. If he is too long the saw shortens him. Such a monster is Procrustes.

'Verily, my lord, King Cercyon was tomorrow to lead an army against him, and the King had a new device, as you may see, by which two great shields are slung along the side of this chariot, to ward off the arrows of the men of Procrustes.'

'Then you and I will wear the shields when we come near the place where Procrustes meets travellers by the way, and I think that tonight his own bed will be too long for him,' said Theseus.

To this the groom made no answer, but his body trembled.

Theseus drove swiftly on till the road began to climb the lowest spur of Mount Parnes, and then he drew rein, and put on one of the great shields that covered all his body and legs, and he bade the groom do the like. Then he drove slowly, watching the bushes and underwood beside the way. Soon he saw the smoke going up from the roof of a great castle high in the woods beside the road; and on the road there was a man waiting. Theseus, as he drove towards him, saw the glitter of armour in the underwood, and the setting sun shone red on a spear-point above the leaves. 'Here is our man,' he said to the groom, and pulled up his horses beside the stranger. He loosened his sword in the sheath, and leaped out of the chariot, holding the reins in his left hand, and bowed courteously to the man, who was tall, weak-looking, and old, with grey hair and a clean-shaven face, the colour of ivory. He was clad like a king, in garments of dark silk, with gold bracelets, and gold rings that clasped the leather gaiters on his legs, and he smiled and smiled, and rubbed his hands, while he looked to right and left, and not at Theseus.

'I am fortunate, fair sir,' said he to Theseus, 'for I love to entertain strangers, with whom goes the favour and protection of Zeus. Surely strangers are dear to all men, and holy! You, too, are not unlucky, for the night is falling, and the ways will be dark and dangerous. You will sup and sleep with me, and tonight I can give you a bed that is well spoken of, for its nature is such that it fits all men, the short and the tall, and you are of the tallest.'

'Tonight, fair sir,' quoth Theseus, 'your own bed will be full long for you.' And, drawing the sword of Aegeus, he cut sheer through the neck of Procrustes at one blow, and the head of the man flew one way, and his body fell another way.

Then with a swing of his hand Theseus turned his shield from his front to his back, and leaped into the chariot. He lashed the horses forward with a cry, while the groom also turned his own shield from front to back; and the arrows of the bowmen of Procrustes rattled on the bronze shields as the chariot flew along, or struck the sides and the seat of it. One arrow grazed the flank of a horse, and the pair broke into a wild gallop, while the yells of the bowmen grew faint in the distance. At last the horses slackened in their pace as they climbed a hill, and from the crest of it Theseus saw the lights in the city of Aphidnae.

'Now, my friend,' he said to the groom, 'the way is clear to Athens, and on your homeward road with the horses and the chariot you shall travel well guarded. By the splendour of Lady Athene's brow, I will burn that raven's nest of Procrustes!'

So they slept that night on safe beds at the house of the sons of Phytalus, who bore rule in Aphidnae. Here they were kindly welcomed, and the sons of Phytalus rejoiced when they heard how Theseus had made safe the ways, and slain the beasts that guarded them. 'We are your men,' they said, 'we and all our people, and our spears will encircle you when you make yourself King of Athens, and of all the cities in the Attic land.'

* * *

Next day Theseus said farewell to the sons of Phytalus, and drove slowly through the pleasant green woods that overhung the clear river Cephisus. He halted to rest his horses in a glen, and saw a very beautiful young man walking in a meadow on the other side of the river. In his hand he bore a white flower, and the root of it was black; in the other hand he carried a golden wand, and his upper lip was just beginning to darken, he was of the age when youth is most gracious. He came towards Theseus, and crossed the stream where it broke deep, and swift, and white, above a long pool, and it seemed to Theseus that his golden shoon did not touch the water.

'Come, speak with me apart,' the young man said; and Theseus threw the reins to the groom, and went aside with the youth, watching him narrowly, for he knew not what strange dangers might beset him on the way.

'Whither art thou going, unhappy one,' said the youth, 'thou that knowest not the land? Behold, the sons of Pallas rule in Athens, fiercely and disorderly. Thy father is of no force, and in the house with him is a fair witch woman from a far country. Her name is Medea, the daughter of Aeetes, the brother of Circe the Sorceress. She wedded the famous Jason, and won for him the Fleece of Gold, and slew her own brother Absyrtus. Other evils she wrought, and now she dwells with Aegeus, who fears and loves her greatly. Take thou this herb of grace, and if Medea offers you a cup of wine, drop this herb in the cup, and so you shall escape death. Behold, I am Hermes of the golden wand.'

Then he gave to Theseus the flower, and passed into the wood, and Theseus saw him no more; so then Theseus knelt down, and prayed, and thanked the gods. The flower he placed in the breast of his garment, and, returning to his chariot, he took the reins, and drove to Athens, and up the steep narrow way to the crest of the rock where the temple of Athene stood and the palace of King Aegeus.

Theseus drove through to the courtyard, and left his chariot at the gate. In the court young men were throwing spears at a mark, while others sat at the house door, playing draughts, and shouting and betting. They were heavy, lumpish, red-faced young men, all rather like each other. They looked up and stared, but said nothing. Theseus knew that they were his cousins, the sons of Pallas, but as they said nothing to him he walked through them, iron club on shoulder, as if he did not see them, and as one tall fellow stood in his way, the tall fellow spun round from a thrust of his shoulder. At the hall door Theseus stopped and shouted, and at his cry two or three servants came to him.

'Look to my horses and man,' said Theseus; 'I come to see your master.' And in he went, straight up to the high chairs beside the fire in the centre. The room was empty, but in a high seat sat, fallen forward and half-asleep, a man in whose grey hair was a circlet of gold and a golden grasshopper. Theseus knew that it was his father, grey and still, like the fallen fire on the hearth. As the king did not look up, Theseus touched his shoulder, and then knelt down, and put his arms round the knees of the king. The king aroused himself with a start. 'Who? What want you?' he said, and rubbed his red, bloodshot eyes.

'A suppliant from Troezene am I, who come to your knees, oh king, and bring you gifts.'

'From Troezene!' said the king sleepily, as if he were trying to remember something.

'From Aethra, your wife, your son brings your sword and your shoon,' said Theseus; and he laid the sword and the shoon at his father's feet.

The king rose to his feet with a great cry. 'You have come at last,' he cried, 'and the gods have forgiven me and heard my prayers. But gird on the sword, and hide the shoon, and speak not the name of "wife", for there is one that hears.'

'One that has heard,' said a silvery voice, and from behind a pillar came a woman, dark and pale, but very beautiful, clothed in a rich Eastern robe that shone and shifted from colour to colour. Lightly she threw her white arms round the neck of Theseus, lightly she kissed his cheeks, and a strange sweet fragrance hung about her. Then, holding him apart, with her hands on his shoulders, she laughed, and half-turning to Aegeus, who had fallen back into his chair, she said: 'My lord, did you think that you could hide anything from me?' Then she fixed her great eyes on the eyes of Theseus. 'We are friends?' she said, in her silvery voice.

'Lady, I love you even as you love my father, King Aegeus,' said Theseus.

'Even so much?' said the lady Medea. 'Then we must both drink to him in wine.' She glided to the great golden mixing-cup of wine that stood on a table behind Aegeus, and with her back to Theseus she ladled wine into a cup of strange coloured glass. 'Pledge me and the king,' she said, bringing the cup to Theseus. He took it, and from his breast he drew the flower of black root and white blossom that Hermes had given him, and laid it in the wine. Then the wine bubbled and hissed, and the cup burst and broke, and the wine fell on the floor, staining it as with blood.

Medea laughed lightly. 'Now we are friends indeed, for the gods befriend you,' she said, 'and I swear by the Water of Styx that your friends are my friends, and your foes are my foes, always, to the end. The gods are with you; and by the great oath of the gods I swear, which cannot be broken; for I come of the kin of the gods who live for ever.'

Now the father of the father of Medea was the Sun God.

Theseus took both her hands. 'I also swear,' he said, 'by the splendour of Zeus, that your friends shall be my friends, and that your foes shall be my foes, always, to the end.'

Then Medea sat by the feet of Aegeus, and drew down his head to her shoulder, while Theseus took hold of his hand, and the king wept for joy. For the son he loved, and the woman whom he loved and feared, were friends, and they two were stronger than the sons of Pallas.

While they sat thus, one of the sons of Pallas – the Pallantidae they were called – slouched into the hall to see if dinner was ready. He stared, and slouched out again, and said to his brothers: 'The old man is sitting in the embraces of the foreign woman, and of the big stranger with the iron club!' Then they all came together, and growled out their threats and fears, kicking at the stones in the courtyard, and quarrelling as to what it was best for them to do.

Meanwhile, in the hall, the servants began to spread the tables with meat and drink, and Theseus was taken to the bath, and clothed in new raiment.

While Theseus was at the bath Medea told Aegeus what he ought to do. So when Theseus came back into the hall, where the sons of Pallas were eating and drinking noisily, Aegeus stood up, and called to Theseus to sit down at his right hand. He added, in a loud voice, looking all round the hall: 'This is my son, Theseus, the slayer of monsters, and his is the power in the house!'

The sons of Pallas grew pale with fear and anger, but not one dared to make an insolent answer. They knew that they were hated by the people of Athens, except some young men of their own sort, and they did not dare to do anything against the man who had slain Periphetes and Sinis, and Cercyon, and Sciron, and, in the midst of his paid soldiers, had struck off the head of Procrustes. Silent all through dinner sat the sons of Pallas, and, when they had eaten, they walked out silently, and went to a lonely place, where they could make their plans without being overheard.

Theseus went with Medea into her fragrant chamber, and they spake a few words together. Then Medea took a silver bowl, filled it with water, and, drawing her dark silken mantle over her head, she sat gazing into the bowl. When she had gazed silently for a long time she said: 'Some of them are going towards Sphettus, where their father dwells, to summon his men at arms, and some are going to Gargettus on the other side of the city, to lie in ambush, and cut us off when they of Sphettus assail us. They will attack the palace just before the dawn. Now I will go through the town, and secretly call the trusty men to arm and come to defend the palace, telling them that the son of Aegeus, the man who cleared the ways, is with us. And do you take your chariot, and drive speedily to the sons of Phytalus, and bring all their spears, chariot men and foot men, and place them in ambush around the village of Gargettus, where one band of the Pallantidae will lie tonight till dawn. The rest you know.'

Theseus nodded and smiled. He drove at full speed to Aphidnae, where the sons of Phytalus armed their men, and by midnight they lay hidden in the woods round the village of Gargettus. When the stars had gone onward, and the second of the three watches of the night was nearly past, they set bands of men to guard every way from the little town, and Theseus with another band rushed in, and slew the men of the sons of Pallas around their fires, some of them awake, but most of them asleep. Those who escaped were taken by the bands who watched the ways, and when the sky was now clear at the earliest dawn, Theseus led his companions to the palace of Aegeus, where they fell furiously upon the rear of the men from Sphettus, who were besieging the palace of Aegeus.

The Sphettus company had broken in the gate of the court, and were trying to burn the house, while arrows flew thick from the bows of the trusty men of Athens on the palace roof. The Pallantids had set no sentinels, for they thought to take Theseus in the palace, and there to burn him, and win the kingdom for themselves. Then silently and suddenly the friends of Theseus stole into the courtyard, and, leaving some to guard the gate, they drew up in line, and charged the confused crowd of the Pallantids. Their spears flew thick among the enemy, and then they charged with the sword, while the crowd, in terror, ran this way and that way, being cut down at the gate, and dragged from the walls, when they tried to climb them. The daylight found the Pallantidae and their men lying dead in the courtyard.

Then Theseus with the sons of Phytalus and their company marched through the town, proclaiming that the rightful prince was come, and that the robbers and oppressors were fallen, and all honest men rejoiced. They burned the dead, and buried their ashes and bones, and for the rest of that day they feasted in the hall of Aegeus. Next day Theseus led his friends back to Aphidnae, and on the next day they attacked and stormed the castle of Procrustes, and slew the pirates, and Theseus divided all the rich plunder among the sons of Phytalus and their company, but the evil bed they burned to ashes.

THE STRANGE TALE
OF CARIBOU AND MOOSE

Cyrus Macmillan

T WO WIDOWS LIVED side by side in the forest. Their husbands had long been dead. Each widow had a little boy.
One boy was called Caribou; the other was called Moose. One
springtime the widows were gathering maple sap to make sugar.
The two boys played at home. They talked of the great forest,
and decided to travel, to see the big woods, and the mountains
far away. In the morning they set out on their journey. They
walked all day, and in the evening they came to a camp far
away in the woods. The camp was that of the Porcupines. The
Porcupines were kind to the boys, and gave them food. In the
morning they gave them new moccasins, and told them the road
to follow. The road, they said, had many giants.

The boys travelled all day without mishap. At last they came
to the edge of the wood where the giants lived. Here they met
a woman. She was half Indian, for her mother was an Indian
woman who had been carried off by a giant. Her mother had
long been dead. The woman they met knew that the boys
were of her mother's people, and she treated them kindly.
She told them that ahead of them were three great giants
they would have to overcome before they could pass on their
way. She gave them a box containing two dogs. The box was
very small; it could be hidden in one hand. The dogs were no
bigger than a fly, but when they were rubbed with the hand
they grew very large and very cross; and the more they were
rubbed, the larger and crosser they became. The dogs were to
be used, she said, to defeat the first giant. Then the woman
told them of the second giant. She said he was very terrible,

and that his head was covered with great toads, the poison of which would kill anyone who touched them. She told them that the giant would ask them to kill a toad because it hurt his head, hoping thereby to poison them. She warned them not to touch it, and she gave them some cranberries, and told them to crush the cranberries in their hands when the giant made his request and the noise would make the giant think they were crushing the poisonous toad. Then she told them of the third giant; and she gave them a knife with which to overcome him. It was a very wonderful knife that could not be turned aside from anything it attacked.

Then the boys went on their way. Soon they saw the first giant standing by the side of the path. He rushed at them as if to kill them; but they opened their magic box and took out the dogs. They rubbed them until they grew very large and cross, and when the giant came near they let them loose. The dogs soon killed the giant, and the boys went on their way, leaving the dogs to go back to the woman who gave them. Soon they came to the second giant. He was very ugly and terrible, and he had long hair covered with toads. He met the boys kindly, hoping to deceive them. Then, just as the woman had told them, he said, 'Something hurts my head. Do you see what it is?' And they said, 'Yes, it is a great toad.' 'Kill it,' said the giant. Then the boys put their hands close to his head and crushed the cranberries the woman had given them, and the giant thought the noise was that of the crushing of the toad. The boys then went on their way. The giant was well pleased, for he thought they would drop dead very soon because of the poison, and that next day he would find them and have a good meal. Soon the boys came to the third giant. He was very terrible, and he attacked them at once. But one of the boys drew the magic knife and plunged it into the giant's breast. The giant could not turn it aside; it pierced his heart, and he fell dead. Then the boys knew that they were safe.

The next morning the boys decided to separate, and to go each his own way. Moose went north, and Caribou went south. By and by Moose came to a tent where dwelt a woman with one daughter. The daughter wished to be married, but her mother was jealous of her daughter's charms, and she killed every suitor who wooed her daughter. Her mother had the power of a witch, which she had received from the Evil Spirit of the forest. The daughter loved Moose when she saw him. She warned him that her mother would try to kill him. Moose asked the mother if he might have the daughter as his wife, and the mother said, 'Yes; but first you must do whatever I bid you.' To this Moose agreed. When he went to bed, the daughter warned him to be on his guard. The mother put a thick skin over him for a blanket, covering him all up. Then she went to get another, saying that it was a cold night. Moose knew he would soon smother without air under the thick skins when she piled them over him, and while she was gone he cut a hole through the skin with his magic knife so that his nose would go through it. The woman came back with other skins, and covered him with a great many, but in each skin Moose cut a hole over his nose so that he might get air. The woman left him, believing that he would smother in the night, for she did not want her daughter to wed; but Moose breathed freely and slept soundly.

The next morning the woman uncovered him, thinking that he was dead; but Moose said he had slept well. The woman wondered greatly, and resolved upon another plan to kill him. A great tree grew near the tent. It was hemlock, and bigger than a haystack at the bottom. It had thick bark which was loose at the top. The woman gave Moose a long pole and told him to knock down the bark. Moose took the pole and knocked a piece off, but as it fell he jumped from under it, for he could jump far. The heavy bark fell with a great crash. Then he knocked off all the bark until the tree was stripped, but he was unharmed. The woman wondered greatly. She resolved upon another plan to kill him. The next day she took Moose to an island far off the coast. There were no trees on the island. They left their canoe on the beach and walked inland. The woman said, 'Wait here awhile; I will come back soon.' Then she went back to the beach. She took the canoe and paddled home, leaving Moose behind. 'Now,' she said, 'he will starve, for he cannot get off the island, and there is nothing there to eat.' When Moose came back to the beach, after waiting a long while, he saw the canoe a mere speck on the water far away. He was much troubled, for he thought that now he would surely die, and he cried loudly. But the seagulls flying above the beach heard his cries, and two large gulls came down to him. They told him not to cry, for they would save him. One went to each side of him and told him to take hold and hang on. So he put an arm around each gull's neck, and they rose into the air with him and flew over the sea. Moose was very frightened when he looked down at the water. But the gulls took him home safely. He sat a long time on the beach, and then the woman came paddling her canoe from the island. When she reached the land, Moose said, 'What kept you so long? I have been waiting for you a long time.' But he did not tell her how he had come home. The woman was so surprised she did not know what to say. But she resolved upon another plan to kill him.

The next day she invited Moose to a wrestling match on a high hill. The hill was full of stones. Moose decided that to save his own life he must kill the woman, because he had had enough of her treachery. They wrestled, and Moose let the woman throw him down, but because he was agile he saved himself from a great fall. He let her throw him a second time, but again he was unharmed, to her great surprise. The contest was three falls. The woman was sure she could kill him the third time. But the third time, Moose threw her down so hard that her back was broken on the stones. Then he tossed her high in the air, and she fell so hard that she was broken in pieces. Moose was then free from danger. He married the woman's daughter; but he was not very happy. The daughter was like her mother and caused him trouble, for she was often very wicked. She was a great fisher, and went often to the streams to fish. She could go under the water and stay a long time and bring up fish in her hands. One night in winter she went down through a hole in the ice to fish. It was very cold, and while she was down, the hole froze over and she could not get out. She called to Moose to break the ice, but Moose was glad to be rid of her and he would not let her out. So she was drowned in the stream.

Moose never married again and ever afterwards he lived a lonely life. He did not like company any more. That is why he is usually seen by himself, and why he usually travels alone in the forest. But Caribou, on the other hand, likes company, and that is why he is usually seen with five or six others of his kind, and why he seldom travels alone.

THE HERO MAKÓMA

Kingsley Fairbridge

A T THE TOWN of Senna on the banks of the Zambesi, was born a child. He was not like other children, for he was very tall and strong; over his shoulder he carried a big sack, and in his hand an iron hammer. He could also speak like a grown man, but usually he was very silent.

One day his mother said to him: 'My child, by what name shall we know you?'

And he answered: 'Call all the head men of Senna here to the river's bank.' And his mother called the head men of the town, and when they had come he led them down to a deep black pool in the river where all the fierce crocodiles lived.

'O great men!' he said, while they all listened, 'which of you will leap into the pool and overcome the crocodiles?' But no one would come forward. So he turned and sprang into the water and disappeared.

The people held their breath, for they thought: 'Surely the boy is bewitched and throws away his life, for the crocodiles will eat him!' Then suddenly the ground trembled, and the pool, heaving and swirling, became red with blood, and presently the boy rising to the surface swam on shore.

But he was no longer just a boy! He was stronger than any man and very tall and handsome, so that the people shouted with gladness when they saw him.

'Now, O my people!' he cried waving his hand, 'you know my name – I am Makóma, "the Greater"; for have I not slain the crocodiles in the pool where none would venture?'

Then he said to his mother: 'Rest gently, my mother, for I go to make a home for myself and become a hero.' Then, entering his hut he took Nu-éndo, his iron hammer, and throwing the sack over his shoulder, he went away.

Makóma crossed the Zambesi, and for many moons he wandered towards the north and west until he came to a very hilly country where, one day, he met a huge giant making mountains.

'Greeting,' shouted Makóma, 'who are you?'

'I am Chi-éswa-mapíri, who makes the mountains,' answered the giant; 'and who are you?'

'I am Makóma, which signifies "greater,"' answered he.

'Greater than who?' asked the giant.

'Greater than you!' answered Makóma.

The giant gave a roar and rushed upon him. Makóma said nothing, but swinging his great hammer, Nu-éndo, he struck the giant upon the head.

He struck him so hard a blow that the giant shrank into quite a little man, who fell upon his knees saying: 'You are indeed greater than I, O Makóma; take me with you to be your slave!' So Makóma picked him up and dropped him into the sack that he carried upon his back.

He was greater than ever now, for all the giant's strength had gone into him; and he resumed his journey, carrying his burden with as little difficulty as an eagle might carry a hare.

Before long he came to a country broken up with huge stones and immense clods of earth. Looking over one of the heaps he saw a giant wrapped in dust dragging out the very earth and hurling it in handfuls on either side of him.

'Who are you,' cried Makóma, 'that pulls up the earth in this way?'

'I am Chi-dúbula-táka,' said he, 'and I am making the river-beds.'

'Do you know who I am?' said Makóma. 'I am he that is called "greater"!'

'Greater than who?' thundered the giant.

'Greater than you!' answered Makóma.

With a shout, Chi-dúbula-táka seized a great clod of earth and launched it at Makóma. But the hero had his sack held over his left arm and the stones and earth fell harmlessly upon it, and, tightly gripping his iron hammer, he rushed in and struck the giant to the ground. Chi-dúbula-táka grovelled before him, all the while growing smaller and smaller; and when he had become a convenient size Makóma picked him up and put him into the sack beside Chi-éswa-mapíri.

He went on his way even greater than before, as all the river-maker's power had become his; and at last he came to a forest of bao-babs and thorn trees. He was astonished at their size, for every one was full grown and larger than any trees he had ever seen, and close by he saw Chi-gwísa-míti, the giant who was painting the forest.

Chi-gwísa-miti was taller than either of his brothers, but Makóma was not afraid, and called out to him: 'Who are you, O Big One?'

'I,' said the giant, 'am Chi-gwísa-míti, and I am planting these bao-babs and thorns as food for my children the elephants.'

'Leave off!' shouted the hero, 'for I am Makóma, and would like to exchange a blow with thee!'

The giant, plucking up a monster bao-bab by the roots, struck heavily at Makóma; but the hero sprang aside, and as the weapon sank deep into the soft earth, whirled Nu-éndo the hammer round his head and felled the giant with one blow.

So terrible was the stroke that Chi-gwísa-míti shrivelled up as the other giants had done; and when he had got back his breath he begged Makóma to take him as his servant. 'For,' said he, 'it is honourable to serve a man so great as thou.'

Makóma, after placing him in his sack, proceeded upon his journey, and travelling for many days he at last reached a country so barren and rocky that not a single living thing grew upon it – everywhere reigned grim desolation. And in the midst of this dead region he found a man eating fire.

'What are you doing? demanded Makóma.

'I am eating fire,' answered the man, laughing; 'and my name is Chi-ídea-móto, for I am the flame-spirit, and can waste and destroy what I like.'

'You are wrong,' said Makóma; 'for I am Makóma, who is "greater" than you – and you cannot destroy me!'

The fire-eater laughed again, and blew a flame at Makóma. But the hero sprang behind a rock – just in time, for the ground upon which he had been standing was turned to molten glass, like an overbaked pot, by the heat of the flame-spirit's breath.

Then the hero flung his iron hammer at Chi-ídea-móto, and, striking him, it knocked him helpless; so Makóma placed him in the sack, Woro-nówu, with the other great men that he had overcome.

And now, truly, Makóma was a very great hero; for he had the strength to make hills, the industry to lead rivers over dry wastes, foresight and wisdom in planting trees, and the power of producing fire when he wished.

Wandering on he arrived one day at a great plain, well watered and full of game; and in the very middle of it, close to a large river, was a grassy spot, very pleasant to make a home upon.

Makóma was so delighted with the little meadow that he sat down under a large tree, and removing the sack from his shoulder, took out all the giants and set them before him. 'My friends,' said he, 'I have travelled far and am weary. Is not this such a place as would suit a hero for his home? Let us then go, tomorrow, to bring in timber to make a kraal.'

So the next day Makóma and the giants set out to get poles to build the kraal, leaving only Chi-éswa-mapíri to look after the place and cook some venison which they had killed. In the evening, when they returned, they found the giant helpless and tied to a tree by one enormous hair!

'How is it,' said Makóma, astonished, 'that we find you thus bound and helpless?'

'O Chief,' answered Chi-éswa-mapíri, 'at mid-day a man came out of the river; he was of immense stature, and his grey moustaches were of such length that I could not see where they ended! He demanded of me "Who is thy master?" And I answered: "Makóma, the greatest of heroes." Then the man seized me, and pulling a hair from his moustache, tied me to this tree – even as you see me.'

Makóma was very wroth, but he said nothing, and drawing his finger-nail across the hair (which was as thick and strong as palm rope) cut it, and set free the mountain-maker.

The three following days exactly the same thing happened, only each time with a different one of the party; and on the fourth day Makóma stayed in camp when the others went to cut poles, saying that he would see for himself what sort of man this was that lived in the river and whose moustaches were so long that they extended beyond men's sight.

So when the giants had gone he swept and tidied the camp and put some venison on the fire to roast. At midday, when the sun was right overhead, he heard a rumbling noise from the river, and looking up he saw the head and shoulders of an enormous man emerging from it. And behold! right down the river-bed and up the river-bed, till they faded into the blue distance, stretched the giant's grey moustaches!

'Who are you?' bellowed the giant, as soon as he was out of the water.

'I am he that is called Makóma,' answered the hero; 'and, before I slay thee, tell me also what is thy name and what thou doest in the river?'

'My name is Chin-débou Máu-giri,' said the giant. 'My home is in the river, for my moustache is the grey fever-mist that hangs above the water, and with which I bind all those that come unto me so that they die.'

'You cannot bind me!' shouted Makóma, rushing upon him and striking with his hammer. But the river giant was so slimy that the blow slid harmlessly off his green chest, and as Makóma stumbled and tried to regain his balance, the giant swung one of his long hairs around him and tripped him up.

For a moment Makóma was helpless, but remembering the power of the flame-spirit which had entered into him, he breathed a fiery breath upon the giant's hair and cut himself free.

As Chin-débou Máu-giri leaned forward to seize him the hero flung his sack Woronówu over the giant's slippery head, and gripping his iron hammer, struck him again; this time the blow alighted upon the dry sack and Chin-débou Máu-giri fell dead.

When the four giants returned at sunset with the poles they rejoiced to find that Makóma had overcome the fever-spirit, and they feasted on the roast venison till far into the night; but in the morning, when they awoke, Makóma was already warming his hands at the fire, and his face was gloomy.

'In the darkness of the night, O my friends,' he said presently, 'the white spirits of my fathers came unto me and spoke, saying: "Get thee hence, Makóma, for thou shalt have no rest until thou hast found and fought with Sákatirína, who has five heads, and is very great and strong; so take leave of thy friends, for thou must go alone.'''

Then the giants were very sad, and bewailed the loss of their hero; but Makóma comforted them, and gave back to each the gifts he had taken from them. Then bidding them 'Farewell,' he went on his way.

Makóma travelled far towards the west; over rough mountains and waterlogged morasses, fording deep rivers, and tramping for days across dry deserts where most men would have died, until at length he arrived at a hut standing near some large peaks, and inside the hut were two beautiful women.

'Greeting!' said the hero. 'Is this the country of Sákatirína of five heads, whom I am seeking?'

'We greet you, O Great One!' answered the women. 'We are the wives of Sákatirína; your search is at an end, for there stands he whom you seek!' And they pointed to what Makóma had thought were two tall mountain peaks. 'Those are his legs,' they said; 'his body you cannot see, for it is hidden in the clouds.'

Makóma was astonished when he beheld how tall was the giant; but, nothing daunted, he went forward until he reached one of Sákatirína's legs, which he struck heavily with Nu-éndo. Nothing happened, so he hit again and then again until, presently, he heard a tired, far-away voice saying: 'Who is it that scratches my feet?'

And Makóma shouted as loud as he could, answering: 'It is I, Makóma, who is called "Greater"!' And he listened, but there was no answer.

Then Makóma collected all the dead brushwood and trees that he could find, and making an enormous pile round the giant's legs, set a light to it.

This time the giant spoke; his voice was very terrible, for it was the rumble of thunder in the clouds. 'Who is it,' he said, 'making that fire smoulder around my feet?'

'It is I, Makóma!' shouted the hero. 'And I have come from far away to see thee, O Sákatirína, for the spirits of my fathers bade me go seek and fight with thee, lest I should grow fat, and weary of myself.'

There was silence for a while, and then the giant spoke softly: 'It is good, O Makóma!' he said. 'For I too have grown weary.

There is no man so great as I, therefore I am all alone. Guard thyself!' And bending suddenly he seized the hero in his hands and dashed him upon the ground. And lo! instead of death, Makóma had found life, for he sprang to his feet mightier in strength and stature than before, and rushing in he gripped the giant by the waist and wrestled with him.

Hour by hour they fought, and mountains rolled beneath their feet like pebbles in a flood; now Makóma would break away, and summoning up his strength, strike the giant with Nu-éndo his iron hammer, and Sákatirína would pluck up the mountains and hurl them upon the hero, but neither one could slay the other. At last, upon the second day, they grappled so strongly that they could not break away; but their strength was failing, and, just as the sun was sinking, they fell together to the ground, insensible.

In the morning when they awoke, Mulimo the Great Spirit was standing by them; and he said: 'O Makóma and Sákatirína! Ye are heroes so great that no man may come against you. Therefore ye will leave the world and take up your home with me in the clouds.' And as he spake the heroes became invisible to the people of the Earth, and were no more seen among them.

PRINCE YAMATO TAKE

Theodora Ozaki

MANY, MANY YEARS ago, there was born a son to the Emperor Keiko, the twelfth in descent from the great Jimmu, the founder of the Japanese dynasty. This Prince was the second son of the Emperor Keiko, and he was named Yamato. From his childhood he proved himself to be of remarkable strength, wisdom and courage, and his father noticed with pride that he gave promise of great things, and he loved him even more than he did his elder son.

Now when Prince Yamato had grown to manhood (in the olden days of Japanese history, a boy was considered to have reached man's estate at the early age of sixteen) the realm was much troubled by a band of outlaws whose chiefs were two brothers, Kumaso and Takeru. These rebels seemed to delight in rebelling against the King, in breaking the laws and defying all authority.

At last King Keiko ordered his younger son Prince Yamato to subdue the brigands and, if possible, to rid the land of their evil lives. Prince Yamato was only sixteen years of age, he had but reached his manhood according to the law, yet though he was such a youth in years he possessed the dauntless spirit of a warrior of fuller age and knew not what fear was. Even then there was no man who could rival him for courage and bold deeds, and he received his father's command with great joy.

He at once made ready to start, and great was the stir in the precincts of the Palace as he and his trusty followers gathered together and prepared for the expedition, and polished up their armor and donned it. Before he left his father's Court he went to pray at the shrine of Ise and to take leave of his aunt the Princess Yamato, for his heart was somewhat heavy at the thought of the dangers he had to face, and he felt that he needed the protection of his ancestress, Amaterasu, the Sun Goddess. The Princess his aunt came out to give him glad welcome, and congratulated him on being trusted with so great a mission by his father the King. She then gave him one of her gorgeous robes as a keepsake to go with him and to bring him good luck, saying that it would surely be of service to him on this adventure. She then wished him all success in his undertaking and bade him good speed.

The young Prince bowed low before his aunt, and received her gracious gift with much pleasure and many respectful bows.

'I will now set out,' said the Prince, and returning to the Palace he put himself at the head of his troops. Thus cheered by his aunt's blessing, he felt ready for all that might befall, and marching through the land he went down to the Southern Island of Kiushiu, the home of the brigands.

Before many days had passed he reached the Southern Island, and then slowly but surely made his way to the headquarters of the chiefs Kumaso and Takeru. He now met with great difficulties, for he found the country exceedingly wild and rough. The mountains were high and steep, the valleys dark and deep, and huge trees and boulders of rock blocked up the road and stopped the progress of his army. It was all but impossible to go on.

Though the Prince was but a youth he had the wisdom of years, and, seeing that it was vain to try and lead his men further, he said to himself:

'To attempt to fight a battle in this impassable country unknown to my men only makes my task harder. We cannot clear the roads and fight as well. It is wiser for me to resort to stratagem and come upon my enemies unawares. In that way I may be able to kill them without much exertion.'

So he now bade his army halt by the way. His wife, the Princess Ototachibana, had accompanied him, and he bade her bring him the robe his aunt the priestess of Ise had given him, and to help him attire himself as a woman. With her help he put on the robe, and let his hair down till it flowed over his shoulders. Ototachibana then brought him her comb, which he put in his black tresses, and then adorned himself with strings of strange jewels just as you see in the picture. When he had finished his unusual toilet, Ototachibana brought him her mirror. He smiled as he gazed at himself – the disguise was so perfect.

He hardly knew himself, so changed was he. All traces of the warrior had disappeared, and in the shining surface only a beautiful lady looked back at him.

Thus completely disguised, he set out for the enemy's camp alone. In the folds of his silk gown, next his strong heart, was hidden a sharp dagger.

The two chiefs Kumaso and Takeru were sitting in their tent, resting in the cool of the evening, when the Prince approached. They were talking of the news which had recently been carried to them, that the King's son had entered their country with a large army determined to exterminate their band. They had both heard of the young warrior's renown, and for the first time in their wicked lives they felt afraid. In a pause in their talk they happened to look up, and saw through the door of the tent a beautiful woman robed in sumptuous garments coming towards them. Like an apparition of loveliness she appeared in the soft twilight. Little did they dream that it was their enemy whose coming they so dreaded who now stood before them in this disguise.

'What a beautiful woman! Where has she come from?' said the astonished Kumaso, forgetting war and council and everything as he looked at the gentle intruder.

He beckoned to the disguised Prince and bade him sit down and serve them with wine. Yamato Take felt his heart swell with a fierce glee for he now knew that his plan would succeed. However, he dissembled cleverly, and putting on a sweet air of shyness he approached the rebel chief with slow steps and eyes glancing like a frightened deer. Charmed to distraction by the girl's loveliness Kumaso drank cup after cup of wine for the pleasure of seeing her pour it out for him, till at last he was quite overcome with the quantity he had drunk.

This was the moment for which the brave Prince had been waiting. Flinging down the wine jar, he seized the tipsy and astonished Kumaso and quickly stabbed him to death with the dagger which he had secretly carried hidden in his breast.

Takeru, the brigand's brother, was terror-struck as soon as he saw what was happening and tried to escape, but Prince Yamato was too quick for him. Ere he could reach the tent door the Prince was at his heel, his garments were clutched by a hand of iron, and a dagger flashed before his eyes and he lay stabbed on the earth, dying but not yet dead.

'Wait one moment!' gasped the brigand painfully, and he seized the Prince's hand.

Yamato relaxed his hold somewhat and said:

'Why should I pause, thou villain?'

The brigand raised himself fearfully and said:

'Tell me from whence you come, and whom I have the honor of addressing? Hitherto I believed that my dead brother and I were the strongest men in the land, and that there was no one who could overcome us. Alone you have ventured into our stronghold, alone you have attacked and killed us! Surely you are more than mortal?'

Then the young Prince answered with a proud smile: 'I am the son of the King and my name is Yamato, and I have been sent by my father as the avenger of evil to bring death to all rebels! No longer shall robbery and murder hold my people in terror!' and he held the dagger dripping red above the rebel's head.

'Ah,' gasped the dying man with a great effort, 'I have often heard of you. You are indeed a strong man to have so easily overcome us. Allow me to give you a new name. From henceforth you shall be known as Yamato *Take*. Our title I bequeath to you as the bravest man in Yamato.'

And with these noble words, Takeru fell back and died.

The Prince having thus successfully put an end to his father's enemies in the West, now prepared to return to the capital. On the way back he passed through the province of Idzumo. Here he met with another outlaw named Idzumo Takeru who he knew had done much harm in the land. He again resorted to stratagem, and feigned friendship with the rebel under an assumed name. Having done this he made a sword of wood and jammed it tightly in the sheath of his own steel sword. This he purposely buckled to his side and wore on every occasion when he expected to meet the third robber Takeru.

He now invited Takeru to the bank of the River Hinokawa, and persuaded him to try a swim with him in the cool refreshing waters of the river.

As it was a hot summer's day, the rebel was nothing loath to take a plunge in the river. While his enemy was still swimming down the stream the Prince turned back and landed with all possible haste. Unperceived, he managed to change swords, putting his wooden one in place of the keen steel sword of Takeru.

Knowing nothing of this, the brigand came up to the bank shortly. As soon as he had landed and donned his clothes, the Prince came forward and asked him to cross swords with him to prove his skill, saying:

'Let us two prove which is the better swordsman of the two!'

The robber agreed with delight, feeling certain of victory, for he was famous as a fencer in his province and he did not know who his adversary was. He seized quickly what he thought was his sword and stood on guard to defend himself. Alas! for the rebel, the sword was the wooden one of the young Prince, and in vain Takeru tried to unsheathe it – it was jammed fast, not all his exerted strength could move it. Even if his efforts had been successful the sword would have been of no use to him for it was of wood. Yamato Take saw that his enemy was in his power, and swinging high the sword he had taken from Takeru he brought it down with great might and dexterity and cut off the robber's head.

In this way, sometimes by using his wisdom and sometimes by using his bodily strength, and at other times by resorting to craftiness, which was as much esteemed in those days as it is despised in these, he prevailed against all the King's foes one by one, and brought peace and rest to the land and the people.

When he returned to the capital the King praised him for his brave deeds, and held a feast in the Palace in honor of his safe coming home and presented him with many rare gifts. From this time forth the King loved him more than ever and would not let Yamato Take go from his side, for he said that his son was now as precious to him as one of his arms.

But the Prince was not allowed to live an idle life long. When he was about thirty years old, news was brought that the Ainu race, the aborigines of the islands of Japan, who had been conquered and pushed northwards by the Japanese, had rebelled in the Eastern provinces, and leaving the vicinity which had been allotted to them were causing great trouble in the land. The King decided that it was necessary to send an army to do

battle with them and bring them to reason. But who was to
lead the men?

Prince Yamato Take at once offered to go and bring the
newly-arisen rebels into subjection. Now as the King loved
the Prince dearly, and could not bear to have him go out of
his sight even for the length of one day, he was of course very
loath to send him on his dangerous expedition. But in the whole
army there was no warrior so strong or so brave as the Prince
his son, so that His Majesty, unable to do otherwise, reluctantly
complied with Yamato's wish.

When the time came for the Prince to start, the King gave
him a spear called the Eight-Arms-Length-Spear of the Holly
Tree (the handle was probably made from the wood of the
holly tree), and ordered him to set out to subjugate the Eastern
Barbarians as the Ainu were then called.

The Eight-Arms-Length-Spear of the Holly Tree of those old
days, was prized by warriors just as much as the Standard or
Banner is valued by a regiment in these modern days, when
given by the King to his soldiers on the occasion of setting out
for war.

The Prince respectfully and with great reverence received the
King's spear, and leaving the capital, marched with his army to
the East. On his way he visited first of all the temples of Ise for
worship, and his aunt the Princess of Yamato and High Priestess
came out to greet him. She it was who had given him her robe
which had proved such a boon to him before in helping him to
overcome and slay the brigands of the West.

He told her all that had happened to him, and of the great part
her keepsake had played in the success of his previous undertaking, and thanked her very heartily. When she heard that he was
starting out once again to do battle with his father's enemies,
she went into the temple, and reappeared bearing a sword and
a beautiful bag which she had made herself, and which was full
of flints, which in those times people used instead of matches
for making fire. These she presented to him as a parting gift.

The sword was the sword of Murakumo, one of the three
sacred treasures which comprise the insignia of the Imperial
House of Japan. No more auspicious talisman of luck and
success could she have given her nephew, and she bade him
use it in the hour of his greatest need.

Yamato Take now bade farewell to his aunt, and once more placing himself at the head of his men he marched to the farthest East through the province of Owari, and then he reached the province of Suruga. Here the governor welcomed the Prince right heartily and entertained him royally with many feasts. When these were over, the governor told his guest that his country was famous for its fine deer, and proposed a deer hunt for the Prince's amusement. The Prince was utterly deceived by the cordiality of his host, which was all feigned, and gladly consented to joint in the hunt.

The governor then led the Prince to a wild and extensive plain where the grass grew high and in great abundance. Quite ignorant that the governor had laid a trap for him with the desire to compass his death, the Prince began to ride hard and hunt down the deer, when all of a sudden to his amazement he saw flames and smoke bursting out from the bush in front of him. Realizing his danger he tried to retreat, but no sooner did he turn his horse in the opposite direction than he saw that even there the prairie was on fire. At the same time the grass on his left and right burst into flames, and these began to spread swiftly towards him on all sides. He looked round for a chance of escape. There was none. He was surrounded by fire.

'This deer hunt was then only a cunning trick of the enemy!' said the Prince, looking round on the flames and the smoke that crackled and rolled in towards him on every side. 'What a fool I was to be lured into this trap like a wild beast!' and he ground his teeth with rage as he thought of the governor's smiling treachery.

Dangerous as was his situation now, the Prince was not in the least confounded. In his dire extremity he remembered the gifts his aunt had given him when they parted, and it seemed to him as if she must, with prophetic foresight, have divined this hour of need. He coolly opened the flint-bag that his aunt had given him and set fire to the grass near him. Then drawing the sword of Murakumo from its sheath he set to work to cut down the grass on either side of him with all speed. He determined to die, if that were necessary, fighting for his life and not standing still waiting for death to come to him.

Strange to say the wind began to change and to blow from the opposite direction, and the fiercest portion of the burning bush which had hitherto threatened to come upon him was now blown right away from him, and the Prince, without even a scratch on his body or a single hair burned, lived to tell the tale of his wonderful escape, while the wind rising to a gale overtook the governor, and he was burned to death in the flames he had set alight to kill Yamato Take.

Now the Prince ascribed his escape entirely to the virtue of the sword of Murakumo, and to the protection of Amaterasu, the Sun Goddess of Ise, who controls the wind and all the elements and ensures the safety of all who pray to her in the hour of danger. Lifting the precious sword he raised it above his head many times in token of his great respect, and as he did this he renamed it *Kusanagi-no-Tsurugi* or the Grass-Cleaving Sword, and the place where he set fire to the grass round him and escaped from death in the burning prairie, he called *Yaidzu*. To this day there is a spot along the great Tokaido railway named Yaidzu, which is said to be the very place where this thrilling event took place.

Thus did the brave Prince Yamato Take escape out of the snare laid for him by his enemy. He was full of resource and courage, and finally outwitted and subdued all his foes. Leaving Yaidzu he marched eastward, and came to the shore at Idzu from whence he wished to cross to Kadzusa.

In these dangers and adventures he had been followed by his faithful loving wife the Princess Ototachibana. For his sake she counted the weariness of the long journeys and the dangers of war as nothing, and her love for her warrior husband was so great that she felt well repaid for all her wanderings if she could but hand him his sword when he sallied forth to battle, or minister to his wants when he returned weary to the camp.

But the heart of the Prince was full of war and conquest and he cared little for the faithful Ototachibana. From long exposure in travelling, and from care and grief at her lord's coldness to her, her beauty had faded, and her ivory skin was burnt brown by the sun, and the Prince told her one day that her place was in the Palace behind her screens at home and not with him upon the warpath. But in spite of rebuffs and indifference on her husband's part, Ototachibana could not find it in her heart to leave him. But perhaps it would have been better for her if she had done so, for on the way to Idzu, when they came to Owari, her heart was well-nigh broken.

Here dwelt in a Palace shaded by pine-trees and approached by imposing gates, the Princess Miyadzu, beautiful as the cherry blossom in the blushing dawn of a spring morning. Her garments were dainty and bright, and her skin was white as snow, for she had never known what it was to be weary along the path of duty or to walk in the heat of a summer's sun. And the Prince was ashamed of his sunburnt wife in her travel-stained garments, and bade her remain behind while he went to visit the Princess Miyadzu. Day after day he spent hours in the gardens and the Palace of his new friend, thinking only of his pleasure, and caring little for his poor wife who remained behind to weep in the tent at the misery which had come into her life. Yet she was so faithful a wife, and her character so patient, that she never allowed a reproach to escape her lips, or a frown to mar the sweet sadness of her face, and she was ever ready with a smile to welcome her husband back or usher him forth wherever he went.

At last the day came when the Prince Yamato Take must depart for Idzu and cross over the sea to Kadzusa, and he bade his wife follow in his retinue as an attendant while he went to take a ceremonious farewell of the Princess Miyadzu. She came out to greet him dressed in gorgeous robes, and she seemed more beautiful than ever, and when Yamato Take saw her he forgot his wife, his duty, and everything except the joy of the idle present, and swore that he would return to Owari and marry her when the war was over. And as he looked up when he had said these words he met the large almond eyes of Ototachibana fixed full upon him in unspeakable sadness and wonder, and he knew that he had done wrong, but he hardened his heart and rode on, caring little for the pain he had caused her.

When they reached the seashore at Idzu his men sought for boats in which to cross the straits to Kadzusa, but it was difficult to find boats enough to allow all the soldiers to embark. Then the Prince stood on the beach, and in the pride of his strength he scoffed and said:

'This is not the sea! This is only a brook! Why do you men want so many boats? I could jump this if I would.'

When at last they had all embarked and were fairly on their way across the straits, the sky suddenly clouded and a great storm arose. The waves rose mountains high, the wind howled, the lightning flashed and the thunder rolled, and the boat which held Ototachibana and the Prince and his men was tossed from crest to crest of the rolling waves, till it seemed that every moment must be their last and that they must all be swallowed up in the angry sea. For Rin Jin, the Dragon King of the Sea, had heard Yamato Take jeer, and had raised this terrible storm in anger, to show the scoffing Prince how awful the sea could be though it did but look like a brook.

The terrified crew lowered the sails and looked after the rudder, and worked for their dear lives' sake, but all in vain – the storm only seemed to increase in violence, and all gave themselves up for lost. Then the faithful Ototachibana rose, and forgetting all the grief that her husband had caused her, forgetting even that he had wearied of her, in the one great desire of her love to save him, she determined to sacrifice her life to rescue him from death if it were possible.

While the waves dashed over the ship and the wind whirled round them in fury she stood up and said:

'Surely all this has come because the Prince has angered Rin Jin, the God of the Sea, by his jesting. If so, I, Ototachibana, will appease the wrath of the Sea God who desires nothing less than my husband's life!'

Then addressing the sea she said:

'I will take the place of His Augustness, Yamato Take. I will now cast myself into your outraged depths, giving my life for his. Therefore hear me and bring him safely to the shore of Kadzusa.'

With these words she leaped quickly into the boisterous sea, and the waves soon whirled her away and she was lost to sight. Strange to say, the storm ceased at once, and the sea became as calm and smooth as the matting on which the astonished onlookers were sitting. The gods of the sea were now appeased, and the weather cleared and the sun shone as on a summer's day.

Yamato Take soon reached the opposite shore and landed safely, even as his wife Ototachibana had prayed. His prowess in war was marvelous, and he succeeded after some time in conquering the Eastern Barbarians, the Ainu.

He ascribed his safe landing wholly to the faithfulness of his wife, who had so willingly and lovingly sacrificed herself in the hour of his utmost peril. His heart was softened at the remembrance of her, and he never allowed her to pass from his thoughts even for a moment. Too late had he learned to esteem the goodness of her heart and the greatness of her love for him.

As he was returning on his homeward way he came to the high pass of the Usui Toge, and here he stood and gazed at the wonderful prospect beneath him. The country, from this great elevation, all lay open to his sight, a vast panorama of mountain and plain and forest, with rivers winding like silver ribbons through the land; then far off he saw the distant sea, which shimmered like a luminous mist in the great distance, where Ototachibana had given her life for him, and as he turned towards it he stretched out his arms, and thinking of her love which he had scorned and his faithlessness to her, his heart burst out into a sorrowful and bitter cry:

'Azuma, Azuma, Ya!' (Oh! my wife, my wife!) And to this day there is a district in Tokio called Azuma, which commemorates the words of Prince Yamato Take, and the place where his faithful wife leapt into the sea to save him is still pointed out. So, though in life the Princess Ototachibana was unhappy, history keeps her memory green, and the story of her unselfishness and heroic death will never pass away.

Yamato Take had now fulfilled all his father's orders, he had subdued all rebels, and rid the land of all robbers and enemies to the peace, and his renown was great, for in the whole land there was no one who could stand up against him, he was so strong in battle and wise in council.

He was about to return straight for home by the way he had come, when the thought struck him that he would find it more interesting to take another route, so he passed through the province of Owari and came to the province of Omi.

When the Prince reached Omi he found the people in a state of great excitement and fear. In many houses as he passed along he saw the signs of mourning and heard loud lamentations. On inquiring the cause of this he was told that a terrible monster had appeared in the mountains, who daily came down from thence and made raids on the villages, devouring whoever he could seize. Many homes had been made desolate and the men were afraid to go out to their daily work in the fields, or the women to go to the rivers to wash their rice.

When Yamato Take heard this his wrath was kindled, and he said fiercely:

'From the western end of Kiushiu to the eastern corner of Yezo I have subdued all the King's enemies – there is no one who dares to break the laws or to rebel against the King. It is indeed a matter for wonder that here in this place, so near the capital, a wicked monster has dared to take up his abode and be the terror of the King's subjects. Not long shall it find pleasure in devouring innocent folk. I will start out and kill it at once.'

With these words he set out for the Ibuki Mountain, where the monster was said to live. He climbed up a good distance, when all of a sudden, at a winding in the path, a monster serpent appeared before him and stopped the way.

'This must be the monster,' said the Prince; 'I do not need my sword for a serpent. I can kill him with my hands.'

He thereupon sprang upon the serpent and tried to strangle it to death with his bare arms. It was not long before his prodigious strength gained the mastery and the serpent lay dead at his feet. Now a sudden darkness came over the mountain and rain began to fall, so that for the gloom and the rain the Prince could hardly see which way to take. In a short time, however, while he was groping his way down the pass, the weather cleared, and our brave hero was able to make his way quickly down the mountain.

When he got back he began to feel ill and to have burning pains in his feet, so he knew that the serpent had poisoned him. So great was his suffering that he could hardly move, much less walk, so he had himself carried to a place in the mountains famous for its hot mineral springs, which rose bubbling out of the earth, and almost boiling from the volcanic fires beneath.

Yamato Take bathed daily in these waters, and gradually he felt his strength come again, and the pains left him, till at last one day he found with great joy that he was quite recovered. He now hastened to the temples of Ise, where you will remember that he prayed before undertaking this long expedition. His aunt, priestess of the shrine, who had blessed him on his setting out, now came to welcome him back. He told her of the many dangers he had encountered and of how marvelously his life had been preserved through all – and she praised his courage and his warrior's prowess, and then putting on her most magnificent robes she returned thanks to their ancestress the Sun Goddess Amaterasu, to whose protection they both ascribed the Prince's wonderful preservation.

PART III:
QUESTS OF FORTUNE

THE LAD WITH ONE SANDAL

Winifred Hutchinson

I

T HERE WAS A king in the olden time, whose name was Pelias, and he dwelt in the fair harbour-town of Iolcos, ruling a folk that were famous seafarers from the beginning. A bold man was he, and a crafty, but he went ever in fear of his life, for he had an ill deed on his conscience, and his sleep of nights was broken by dreams which boded a bitter reckoning for the same. Many and many a time he awoke with a shriek, as a dagger seemed to touch his throat, but the dream-shape that brandished it was dim and wavering, and he could never descry the countenance of that phantom foe. At last he sent a trusty messenger to the holy place of Delphi, where Apollo reveals hidden things to mortals by the mouth of his priestess, to ask the interpretation of the vision. For he thought, 'If I can but learn what man it is whose wraith appears to me, I shall make short work with him, and rid myself of this dread in which I live.' The messenger returned, and brought this answer from the god: 'Let Pelias know that the doom he dreams of will come from the hand of a near kinsman. I bid him beware, above all else, of the man who comes to him wearing one sandal, whether he be a stranger, or born and bred in Iolcos.'

When King Pelias heard this message, his blood froze with fear; it was indeed death, then, that the dreams foreboded. Yet it was some comfort that now at least he had a sign whereby to know when the danger drew near, and he still hoped that he might forestall it if he kept good watch. So he set guards day and night about his palace, and watchmen at all the city gates, and gave strict charge to them all to bring him instant warning, if ever they should see a man with one sandal. And as time went on, his heart grew somewhat lightened of its dread, for there was no such comer seen, and the evil dreams ceased to visit him.

But he that was foretold came in his destined hour to Iolcos, out of the mountains to the northward, and stood in the market-place, while it was yet morning, and the throng of folk was greatest. The watchmen at the gate had seen him pass, but they paid no heed to one who seemed a mere lad, and by his dress a hunter from the hill-country.

This youth carried two hunting-spears, and instead of a cloak a leopard skin hung from his shoulders, above a close-fitting tunic; his head was uncovered, and his long curls flamed golden-red in the sunlight. It was easy to guess, from the shy and wondering glances he cast about him, that he was new to the sights of a city, yet he bore himself with the noble grace of a king's son, and as he stood there silent, many eyes were drawn to the beauty of his face, and his stature, lofty as a god's. Men began to whisper to one another, asking who the stranger was, and when none could answer, a murmur went to and fro among the crowd that one of the Immortals was come among them.

'So might Apollo look,' they muttered, 'or the mailed warrior Ares, fair and terrible. Surely this is some god, or the son of a god.'

'Nay, friends,' said some of the old men, 'the gods come not thus in the sight of multitudes. Rather should we guess this mighty youth to be of that old race of the Earth-born Giants, but they all have perished long since, and only their huge graves are left for a witness to our days.'

Now, while the folks talked thus under their breaths, and durst not, for reverence, question the godlike stranger, a man of the King's household gazed with the rest, and marked on a sudden that he wore but the one sandal. For it chanced, as the youth crossed the ford of a mountain stream on his way to the city, that its fellow slipped from his foot and was carried away by the torrent. Quickly did that henchman bring word to the palace, and at his tidings, King Pelias came in hot haste to the market-place, urging the swift mules of his ivory car to their utmost speed. 'Way there for the King,' cried the slaves who ran beside him, and he drew rein in a cleared space, whence all the people had drawn back for his coming, save the stranger lad only. Pelias scanned him eagerly, and his soul sickened with affright as he saw the dreaded token of the single sandal on his right foot. But he cloaked the fear within him with haughty words, and said, eyeing the lad disdainfully, 'Stranger, what country do you call home? What grey-haired carline of low degree mothered such a dainty pet? Come, speak out your parentage, and disgrace it not with detested lying.'

Then the youth, undaunted, yet with gentlest courtesy, made reply –

'It is mine, rather, to render such answer as shall not disgrace the great Chiron, my teacher. For my home has been in his mountain-cave, and I had my rearing from the virtuous wife and mother of that wise Centaur. Twenty years have I numbered in the care of these foster-parents, and never yet done dishonour to their upbringing by deceitful act or word. But now I am come again to my own native land, to claim the ancient rights that were my father's, which Pelias, as I hear, holds in unlawful possession, even this kingdom of Iolcos.'

'Do you call yourself, then, the son of Aeson,' cried the King, 'who ruled this land until a better than he took it from him? Who knows not that his only child died at its birth?'

'Not so, for I am that child,' answered the stranger; 'but when Pelias, moved by reckless desires, had overthrown his kinsman King Aeson with force and fraud, then for fear of that violent oppressor, my parents feigned that their newborn son was dead, and made great mourning, with all their household. Then, at dead of night, they sent me privily out of the city, a babe wrapped in swaddling-bands of royal crimson, and at their bidding faithful friends conveyed me to Chiron's cave, where I might be reared in safety. And Jason was the name by which that twi-natured Being was wont to call me. Such in brief is my story, and now, good townsmen, since you know me for your countryman, come back to his own city, which of you will show me the ancient house of my fathers, that I know not, though I was born there?'

Before Jason made an end of speaking, King Pelias turned his mules and drove at a furious pace back to the palace; he knew that the folk held him in secret hate because he had dethroned Aeson, that gentle king, and he feared lest they should rise against him then and there, when they heard the lad with one sandal declare himself their rightful prince. But Jason also hurried from the market-place, eagerly following a band of willing guides. One thing he had not found courage to ask of a company of strangers, and would wait to learn within the doors of his home – was his father yet alive? Chiron had told him nothing of the old man's fate, only had bidden him go to Iolcos and claim his heritage from the usurper. Now when he was come to the house, and entered through its pillared porch, he crossed a wide courtyard, empty and silent, where grass was springing from the cracked pavement of marble, and in the hall beyond it he saw no one but an aged man, wrapped in a faded mantle, sitting in a low chair beside the embers of the hearth. The once lordly chamber was bare of furnishing; dust lay thick upon the floor, and cobwebs, where rich hangings should have been, drooped curtainwise from lintel and cornice. The home the youth had come to seemed a house of the dead, deserted save for that motionless figure cowering over the dying fire. But as he moved towards it, the snow-white head turned slowly, the dim eyes looked him in the face, and a trembling voice rang through the silence, 'My son, my son!' Jason sprang to the old king, for he indeed it was, and clasped him to his breast, while tears of joy fell fast from those withered eyelids. It was long before Aeson could find words, in the rapture of beholding his son, come back to him the fairest and goodliest of men, but he told at last how Pelias had stripped him little by little of all he possessed, on this pretext or that, till neither broad lands, nor flocks and herds, nor the rich treasures of his house were left, and he himself, with a few old slaves that tended him for love, lived on the secret doles of his well-wishers among the citizens.

'How comes it, my father,' asked Jason, 'that your two brethren have suffered you to be so evilly entreated of this tyrant, seeing that each of them is a king in his own country, if indeed they yet live?'

'They live and prosper,' answered his father, 'but it is far from hence to where they dwell, and they begrudge to waste blood and treasure in the cause of a feeble old man that cannot have long to live. But word will quickly reach them that you are

home again, and when they hear what manner of young man
their brother's son is become, I am much mistaken or they will
think his cause worth battling for. Be you patient till we have
news of them, for it comes in my mind that we shall shortly see
either themselves, or the princes, your cousins.'

The old king was a true prophet, and before many days, so
swiftly spread the rumour of Jason's return, those two brethren
and their sons came to greet him at Iolcos. The name of one was
Pheres, and his son was called Admetus; these two were men of
gracious and winning presence, speaking words of pleasantness,
but their souls within them were little and mean. Amythaon, the
other brother, was king in the far south-west; he had a name for
wisdom, but the son he brought with him had yet a greater in
the after time. For he was that Melampus of whom you may
read in the tale of 'The Prince who was a Seer.'

Jason and his father made these kinsmen right welcome,
although their hearts misgave them for the bareness of their
ancient dwelling and for the wherewithal to feast the princes
and their following. But at the first word that Aeson's kinsmen
were come to visit him, the townsfolk rejoiced openly because
at last strong helpers had appeared for the oppressed king, and
they feared not to make their gladness and goodwill manifest
by bringing him gifts in abundance of everything needful to
entertain his guests. Such store of sheep and oxen, of corn and
wine and oil, of tables, couches, vessels of every sort, and all
manner of household stuffs, as was gathered that day in Aeson's
courtyard, had not been seen within its gates for many a long
year. Moreover, the wealthier citizens sent their housethralls
both men and maids, by the score, to grind the corn, to bake,
and dress meat for the banquet, and to serve the king and his
kinsfolk in the hall. So that night there was feasting and good
cheer, torchlight and merry stir, in the house that had so long
been silent and deserted.

Now Jason had the charge of all, and gave command as
master, because of his father's great age and infirmity, and
carried himself as a princely host should do, overlooking no
point of courtesy, so that it was a marvel to his guests how
he had come by these manners in the cave of a Centaur. For
they knew not noble Chiron, who in the after time reared
Prince Peleus in the like gracious ways, and compassed for

him his marriage with the Sea-King's daughter, as I have told already.

Then, to do his kinsmen all honour, Jason feasted them with the best for five days and five nights, saying no word of the matter he had at heart, but tasting in their company the delicious joy of life at its sweetest.

But on the sixth day he began to speak of graver things, and when he had opened all his mind to them, they gave full consent to that which he declared it his purpose now to do, and rising all together from the banquet, they followed him forthwith to the house of Pelias. At the sound of their voices in his hall, King Pelias came hastily from the inner chambers to meet them, and then, with fair-flowing speech of gentle tone, Jason spoke thus: 'Son of a mighty sire, over quick are mortals to barter justice for the ways of iniquity, forgetting that the hour of reckoning must overtake them soon or late. But it well beseems both you and me to rule our hearts aright, and take thought what shall bring us good in days to come. Call to remembrance, I pray you, that your fathers and mine were of one blood, and that the divine Dispensers of weal and woe to men turn their faces from the sight of feuds between kindred. Let there be neither strife nor drawing of swords between us two, to make division of the great inheritance of our forefathers; for if you will follow my counsel, it shall not need. See now, I freely yield the rich lands, and all the goodly flocks and herds, of which you have despoiled the old man, my father; little care I for the wealth these bring into your house, only do you on your part restore me the sceptre that was Aeson's, and the kingly seat where he gave judgment to his people. These, I say, yield up and grudge me not, lest a worse thing come of it.'

Now Pelias was no ways minded to give up the kingship, even though he might keep all the fatness of the land for his own, and besides, he was utterly purposed to destroy the lad with the one sandal, because of the oracle he had heard concerning him. While Jason was yet speaking, his swift and cunning mind devised a plan for his undoing, and he answered with a show of mildness, in these words: 'Behold, I will deal according to your pleasure in all things, but I am now stricken in years, and you are in the flower of your youth, therefore it is for you to undertake a certain task that else were mine. Hear now what it is, since you seek to be head over all our kindred, for the matter touches him most nearly who is chief of our house. There was a prince of our blood, Athamas by name, whose wife died and left him with two young children, and in no long time he wedded another. Now this second bride proved a cruel stepdame, and when sons were born to her, she plotted death for Phrixus, the eldest born of the first wife, that her own children might inherit the kingdom. She caused all the seed sown in the land to be secretly poisoned, and when many that ate the corn sickened and died, she brought her husband to believe that the gods had sent a pestilence on the people, which must be stayed by some great sacrifice. Then did she bribe a wicked seer to declare that the wrath of the gods could be turned away by no other victim than the King's first-born son. But when the boy Phrixus was laid on the altarstone, and the knife upraised to slay him, the gods delivered him out of her hands in wondrous wise. For a ram with curly fleece of gold stood suddenly on the altar, and while all shrank back amazed, the boy threw himself upon its back, and it rose with him into the air. Over land and sea it flew till it brought him to the country of the Colchians in the unknown regions far northward, and there, by divine bidding, he sacrificed it to Ares, god of the land, and hung its golden fleece on a tree of his sacred grove. But that fleece of gold was the bane of the hapless youth not long after, for the king of the Colchians put him to death only to possess the marvellous thing. And now, O Jason, I would have you go to yonder land, and take the Golden Fleece from the keeping of that savage king, since I am given to know that our murdered kinsman's spirit cannot rest till this be done. Yes, such is the message his unquiet ghost has sent me in a dream, and when I sought counsel of the god at Delphi, answer came from the place of prophecy, that I should straightway launch a ship to sail on the hallowed quest. This quest, then, do you pledge yourself to follow in my stead, and I will swear a solemn oath, making Zeus my witness, to yield you the kingdom.'

Now all the tale Pelias told concerning Phrixus was true, but as for the dream and the message from Delphi, they were falsehoods cunningly devised to send Jason on a quest wherein he should surely perish. But the youth neither knew guile in his own heart, nor looked for it in another, so he made the covenant that Pelias asked, and took leave of him, filled with eagerness to achieve so strange an adventure. Then forthwith he sent out heralds to proclaim everywhere that he was bound on a perilous voyage, and would make all welcome to sail along with him who loved danger and renown better than to dwell at home in ignoble safety. At those tidings, high-hearted sons of kings gathered to Iolcos from far and near, for Queen Hera filled their hearts with keen desire to be Jason's shipmates, because she favoured him above all mortals from the day he came to the city to his life's end. And this was the reason: when he came to the ford where he lost his sandal, he saw an old beggar-woman sitting on the bank, crying and bewailing herself because she could not cross the rain-swollen stream. Jason spoke kindly to her, and, though she was both ragged and dirty, he took her up in his arms and carried her over. No sooner had he set her down again than her bent and shrunken form was changed into that of a fair woman in her prime, and her rags into shining raiment, and she said to him, 'For this good deed, count me your friend for ever.' Thereupon she vanished from his sight, and he went on his way with gladness, knowing that one of the Immortals had appeared to him in this shape. Now the beggar-woman was Hera, who was wandering that day on earth, to see what kindness mortals would show to one so feeble and wretched.

So the flower of all the heroes who then lived came to the house of Aeson, making offer to sail with Jason on the quest. The first who came were two noble youths in armour of gleaming silver; so like they were that none might know one from the other, and their silver chariot was drawn by horses white as snow. These were the twin brothers, Castor and Polydeuces, who for the great love they bore each other were never parted their lives long, nor did even death sunder them at the last. The next comer had neither chariot nor shining armour, but trudged on foot, bearing a great bow and quiver, with a tawny lion-skin girt about his sinewy, sun-browned limbs. He was a man in the prime of life, of gallant bearing, though without height or comeliness of person, and he passed unremarked through the crowd that were drawn to Jason's door to gaze on those glorious Twins.

But they, when they saw him stand within the hall, rose up in deepest reverence as at the coming of a god, and Jason also, for he knew by the lion-skin and bow that this was Heracles himself. Much had he heard from Chiron of that great helper of men, and he gazed with awe and wonder on him who had done such mighty deeds by land and sea. But now came into the hall a young minstrel clad in flowing robe of white, with a chaplet of ivy on his fair hair. 'I also, Jason,' he said, 'would fain be of your crew, though I have no weapon but this harp of mine. I am Orpheus of Thrace, come hither at Apollo's bidding, that your brave company may not lack for the minstrelsy warriors love so well.' Right gladly did the princes there assembled welcome that sweet singer, whose fame was gone out into all lands; of him it was told that beasts and birds, nay, the trees and rocks of the Thracian mountains, would follow the sound of his enchanting lyre.

It were long to tell what other heroes of ancient story mustered in Jason's hall that day, but none were so wondrous to behold as the last comers, Zetes and Calaïs, sons of the North Wind, who had bright feathered wings waving from their shoulders.

Meanwhile, the best-skilled craftsmen of Iolcos had wrought busily under Jason's watchful eye at the building of his ship; the tallest pines on Mount Pelion, whose woody top overhung the cave of Chiron, had been felled for her masts and timbers, and her fifty stout oars were hewn from giant ash-trees. When all was finished, and the good ship lay ready for launching, her young captain summoned his new comrades to the harbour, and said to them, 'Here, noble friends, is the bark that shall carry us to the far Colchian land, well found with all we need for the long voyage.' Then all the heroes clapped their hands at sight of the ship, and they called her Argo, that is to say, the Swift. And now Jason called upon Mopsos the seer, that dwelt in Iolcos, to offer sacrifice to Zeus, and entreat him for favourable signs at their setting forth, which the god granted both by the omens of the altar and by the lucky fall of lots that the seer cast to tell their fortunes. So that wise soothsayer bade them embark with all speed, for the hour was propitious to their sailing. But a greater sign followed, for when all were come aboard, and the anchors were raised on either side the prow, Jason stood up beside the helm, holding a golden cup in his hands, and poured wine therefrom into the sea, calling aloud on Zeus, lord of the lightning, on winds and waves, and nights of sea-faring, to be gracious to their outgoing and their homecoming. Immediately a peal of thunder gave answer from the clouds above, and lightning-flashes were seen to the right of the ship, cheering the hearts of all with happiest augury. At that, the seer bade the princely comrades betake them to their oars, and their mighty strokes bore the Argo swiftly out to sea. All that day, and many a day after, they rowed on untiringly, sped along by the strong south breeze that filled their sails. Fifty all told were those sailors, sons of gods and of kings, but none of Jason's kindred was among them, except only the brave Acastus, son of Pelias, who, for all his father could say, would not be turned from the quest of the Golden Fleece. So they fared ever northward, keeping in view the bays and promontories of the western mainland, till they had need of fresh water, and put in to a wooded cove, where a stream ran sparkling to the sea. And here misfortune befell them, for they lost Heracles, the best of their crew. There had followed him to Iolcos a fair lad called Hylas, who served him as cup-bearer. This boy, for his dauntless spirit, and the love Heracles had to him, was made one of Argo's crew, and he disembarked in this place with the rest. But while they drew water from the stream, he wandered along its banks into the woods, till he came to its source in a deep, clear pool. As he bent over its cool depths, the Water Fairies who abode therein fell in love with his beauty, and before he was aware they threw their white arms about him and drew him under. Hylas gave one cry for help as the water closed over him, and Heracles, who heard and knew the well-loved voice, rushed to find him, but in vain; nor, though the hero and his comrades searched the woods the livelong day, could they see or hear aught of the vanished lad. Then when morning dawned again, Heracles bade the others delay no longer from their journey. 'But I,' said he, 'must tarry, for I will never leave this place till I know what has become of Hylas.' Sadly Jason and the rest took farewell of their great companion; their hearts were sore for his grief, but they might not linger, and so once more they stood out to sea with oar and sail.

Now, after that, they came to a long strait of the sea, and on the shore of it there was an old blind man sitting at a table, who seemed to be weeping. 'Let us draw in to land,' said Jason, 'and

ask that old man what he does in this solitary place, and what
may be his sorrow.' So they brought Argo close in to the shelving
shore, and called to him, asking who he was. The old man turned
his sightless eyes upon them, and answered, 'I am Phineus, the
seer, of all men most miserable. Apollo, in my youth, bestowed
on me the power of prophecy, whereby I came to great honour,
and my house was filled with rich gifts from the folk who sought
to me for soothsay. But I offended the holy gods by greed of
gain, therefore in mine age they sent blindness upon me, and
a strange evil, the like of which came never on mortal man.
For whenever I sat at meat, two monstrous birds, with heads of
women, darted screeching upon my food, and snatched it away
before I could taste one morsel, leaving but fragments dropped
from their foul talons. They were in sight like vultures that prey
on carcases, and the deadly carrion smell of them polluted all
they touched, and all the air of the house, so that none could
endure to abide therein. And at last the men of my city thrust
me forth, because of those noisome guests, but that they might
still resort to me for prophecies, they builded me a hut on this
lonely shore, and daily bring me offerings of choice dainties,
such as I love. But woe's me! those fell winged creatures cease
not to haunt me, as you will shortly see.'

'Old man,' said Jason, 'our hearts are moved with pity for
your wretched lot. Tell us now, by your divine foresight, shall
none rid you of this strange pest?'

'Concerning that,' said Phineus, 'only this much is revealed to
me; my deliverers are even now aboard this your ship, O son of
Aeson, and bound for the far Colchian land. I know you, prince,
and your errand, and who your comrades are, but which of them
shall rescue me, and in what hour, is hidden from my ken.'

While they talked thus, certain men came thither from the
city, bearing baskets of rich viands which they spread on
the old man's table, and he put forth his hands to take of
them. Instantly, with hideous screams, two vulture-shapes,
woman-headed, swooped down from upper air, seized upon
the food and soared away swifter than an arrow's flight. And
the air was filled with a poisonous savour of decay, so that
Jason and his comrades were fain to push off their ship from
that tainted shore. But Phineus cried to them with tears not to
abandon him in his helpless plight, and they talked with him

from Argo's deck, and Jason asked him how the dire monsters were called. 'By mortals,' he answered, 'they are called the Harpies, that is the Snatchers, but the gods name them the Hounds of Zeus. You have seen their swiftness, how it is such that neither javelin nor arrow may overtake them; alas, what could Heracles himself avail me, were he yet with you!'

Then said Jason, 'I know a way,' and he filled a trencher with food, and bade the two Sons of the North Wind carry it ashore and set it before Phineus. They no sooner did so than the Harpies were seen darting upon the table; but swifter still, Zetes and Calaïs rushed between and drove them back with the flapping of their bright wings. The Harpies fled shrieking, pursued by those winged brethren over hill and dale, and the North Wind blew a fierce gale to speed his sons along, till on a desolate mountain they overtook the monsters, and drew their swords to slay them. But Zeus sent Iris, his messenger who rides upon the rainbow, to forbid them, because the Harpies were ministers of his vengeance upon sinners, and she commanded Zetes and Calaïs to put up their swords, and take an oath from them never more to come near Phineus. So the women-headed creatures swore it with human voice, by the great oath that binds the Immortal Gods, even by the Water of Styx, that icy stream which flows from Earth into the Nether World. And the sons of the North Wind flew back to the Argo.

Now when they had bidden Phineus farewell, the heroes sailed along the strait to its opening into another sea, stormy and cold, where never ship had sailed before. For at the mouth of the strait two steep cliffs made a gateway, and they were alive, and whatever passed between them they crushed to pieces, clashing suddenly together upon it. But the comrades were forewarned by Phineus of this dreadful place, and having cast anchor before it, they went ashore and built an altar of stones and sacrificed a bull to Poseidon, god of mariners, with prayers for aid. And Hera, in her love to Jason, prevailed with Poseidon to grant them safe passage through those gates that he had set up to keep mortals from the Northern Sea, and she came herself to the ship in the likeness of a damsel, carrying a white dove. 'Hail, Jason!' she said: 'A friend sends you this bird, even she whom you met by the ford of the stream, and bids you let it loose from Argo's prow. Then, when you see it pass between the Clashing Cliffs, let your comrades row forward at their utmost speed.' With that, she vanished, and Jason, glad at heart, bade his comrades bend to their oars, and let go the dove. Straight through the pass she flew, and the cliffs closed upon her with a roar like thunder, but by Hera's grace she sped between so swiftly that only her tail feathers were caught. Then, as the rocks rolled back with a grinding noise, Argo's crew rowed onward for their lives, and brought the good ship through by a hair's-breadth. The Clashing Cliffs met again that same instant, but too late, and that was the end of them, for their doom was, if ever they missed their prey, to dash each other to powder.

Poseidon, at Hera's entreaty, calmed the northern deep for those first voyagers, and with a fair wind ever behind them they came at last in sight of the low misty shores of an unknown land. It was towards evening when they drew near and saw at hand the mouth of a broad river that flowed between dark woods of beech and pine, and there in a creek of the spreading stream they moored their ship for the night.

II

WITH THE FIRST light of day Jason and two of his comrades set forth inland, that they might find some inhabited place, and learn if this was the country to which they were bound. Presently they spied smoke curling up through the trees of the forest, and they went towards it, and came to a great house of timber, standing in an open glade, with byres and barns around it. As they drew near, a lad met them, driving cows to pasture, and they asked him the name of the land, and who dwelt in that house. 'Strangers,' said he, 'this is the country of the Colchians, and yonder house is the palace of Aeetes, their king.' Then Jason, and the two comrades with him, who were Castor and Polydeuces, were glad, because they were at their journey's end; and they went into the palace and found the King sitting in the hall among his chieftains, dark-skinned men of fierce countenance, clad in golden armour of strange fashion. Aeetes looked grimly upon the strangers, but he bade them sit down and feast with him, and his slaves set food before them in plenty, and dark, sweet drink, brewed of herbs and honey. When they had eaten and drunk, the King asked them whence they came, and where they had left the ship that brought them, for he knew that they must have come by sea to his country, since by land it was walled about with trackless forests. And Jason answered discreetly, not making known his errand, but saying they were come from a land far south, and had moored their ship in the river not far away. 'It is well,' said the King. 'Let your two comrades now go and bring the rest of your crew hither, that I may feast them all. Today we will make merry, and you shall try your mettle in sword-play with my warriors, and tomorrow you shall tell me your errand.'

So the Twin Brethren went forth to fetch their comrades, but the King, under show of courtesy, kept Jason from returning to the ship lest the strangers should put to sea, and escape out of his hands. For this Aeetes was a cruel prince and a cunning, and he thought to make easy prey of these young men and their companions, and seize their fair-wrought arms, and any treasure they might have with them. But meantime he covered his evil purpose with friendly speech, bidding Jason refresh himself after his voyaging, and caused him to be led to a chamber where a bath was made ready. As the youth entered it he saw an ancient serving-woman pouring water into the bath out of a steaming cauldron, and she said to him, 'Prince Jason, when you leave this chamber the King's daughter will meet you, and offer you a posset in a silver cup. Beware you taste it not, for it is deadly, but pour it on the ground, and say, "For Those Below." Then give this to the King's daughter.' So saying, the old woman took a shining thing from her bosom, and gave it to Jason, and went quickly forth. But as she went out the fashion of her changed, and she shone with a beauty not earthly, so that he perceived some goddess had spoken to him. Now the shining thing was in the form of a four-spoked wheel, and it was golden, and the figure of a speckled bird, moulded in clay, was bound upon the spokes by the outspread wings and by the feet. Jason viewed it with wonder, and he bathed himself quickly, eager to see what should next betide. Then, when he was arrayed again, and come out of that chamber, there greeted him a dark maiden, robed in scarlet, and she offered him drink in a silver cup. But he took it from her hand, smiling, and poured the drink upon the ground, and said, 'For Those Below.' The King's daughter looked at the youth in silence, and her olive cheeks turned pale.

'Princess of the Colchians,' said he, 'let it not displease you that I deal thus with your gift, but take a gift in return.' And he laid the golden wheel in her hand, and left her standing mute. Now the daughter of Aeetes was a great enchantress, one that could draw the moon out of the sky by her incantations, and knew all spells that can be wrought with strange drugs and herbs of might. At her father's bidding she had mingled a potion for the stranger prince that would have destroyed him in three days, withering his veins with consuming fire. But, by his offering it to the Dead, she understood that he knew death was in the cup, and great fear of him took hold of her, for she deemed he had that knowledge by art magical, and that his gift was some potent charm. This in truth it was, as shall presently be told.

So soon as Argo's crew were come to the palace, King Aeetes made them cheer with a feast of good things, and after the banquet he had them forth into a meadow, and desired them to show him what skill they had with their weapons. And he set ten chosen warriors to sword-play with Jason and nine of his comrades, while he sat to watch on a grassy knoll, and his daughter beside him. Then, under colour of sport, the Colchian warriors aimed deadly strokes at the strangers, for so had the King given secret command, trusting to see his champions slay those youthful guests right speedily. But the ten comrades fought like young lions with their fierce adversaries, and when they saw the battle was for life or death, they spared not to smite them till all were slain upon the place. Sore wearied, but unwounded in that deadly fray, the heroes sheathed their resistless swords at last, and Jason cried to the King, 'We are guiltless, Aeetes, of the deaths of these men. In an evil hour have we come to such a host as this, who would make it his pastime to see guests slaughtered before his face.'

Aeetes rose up with a laugh, and answered, 'They that fare to strange lands must meet with strange customs. But since you like our Colchian manner of sport so little, I will henceforth deal with you in earnest.' With that he took them back to the palace, but because it was now late, he sent them to the guest-chambers, saying he would hear their errand in the morning.

That night the witch-princess could not sleep for thinking on the bright-haired stranger, and the meaning of the gift he had given her. She was afraid to keep it, and afraid to leave it, and she had it hidden in the folds above her girdle while she watched him fighting for his life with her father's best swordsman; nor for all her skill in enchantments did she know that the spell of it was at work upon her even then. At last she slept, and dreamed that a queen crowned with roses stood at her bedside, and asked her what thoughts those were that troubled her; but, when she essayed to answer, she could find no words, and fell to weeping.

Then said the rose-crowned queen, 'I am Aphrodite, known among gods and men for an enchantress of power, and to pleasure great Hera, I have put a charm upon you mightier than all your spells. For, as the bird is bound upon the wheel I bade Prince Jason give you, so your heart is bound with cords of desire to the giver, by the virtue of that charm. Rise now, and follow me to his chamber; the thoughts that you could not speak I know, and the struggle of your soul, but stronger than all is the thought that he must not die.'

The King's daughter awoke, and behold, she was no longer in her own chamber, but stood beside the sleeping stranger. Moonlight fell upon his face, and hair of ruddy gold, and the drawn sword by his side, and she looked at him long before she aroused him with a touch of her hand, calling him by name.

'Who calls me?' said Jason, springing to his feet and grasping his sword.

'It is I, Medea,' said the King's daughter; 'I am come to bid you fly from this house while it is yet night, for tomorrow Aeetes purposes to slay you and your comrades. Come, awaken the others, and I will unbar the gates meanwhile; the guards shall not hear us, for I have power to keep them slumbering soundly.'

'Noble Medea,' answered the prince, 'I have seen strange things on my way hither, but here is the strangest of all, that you, who would have destroyed me with your potion, are now fain to save my life. I thank whatever god has changed your heart towards me, and praise your kindly thought, but as for flight, neither I nor my true comrades will quit this place without the prize we are come in quest of.' And thereupon he took Medea by the hand, and seated her beside him on the couch, and told her all the tale from the beginning, of the task Pelias laid upon him, and the Argo's perilous voyage. Now, while he spoke of the dangers he had passed, and pleaded with her in sweet persuasive words for help to win the Golden Fleece, pity and love overflowed the heart of the witch-princess, and she forgot all the world but him only, and promised at last to aid him to the uttermost against her father. 'For your sake, prince'; she said, 'I will brave the wrath of Aeetes, though he kill me when he finds his treasure gone, and ask but this for reward, that you think sometimes of Medea when you dwell happily in that far southern home you tell me of.'

Then Jason vowed a solemn vow that he would not leave her to suffer her father's vengeance, but take her home to be his wife, and queen of fair Iolcos, and they plighted troth together in that same hour. Medea then fetched from her own chamber an ivory box of ointment, and bade him anoint himself therewith in the morning, and told him all else that he must do to outwit the crafty King. Thus did Queen Hera, with help of Aphrodite, accomplish victory for Jason over the enchantress, who else would have proved a foe too strong for him and all his crew.

No sooner had the King and his guests broken fast on the morrow, than he said to them, 'Let him that is captain among you now declare the cause of your coming hither'; and Jason made himself known to him, and in courteous words desired him to restore the Golden Fleece to the rightful heirs of Phrixus. Aeetes heard him in silence to the end; then he arose and beckoned Argo's crew to follow him, and they went after him, wondering, to a fallow field hard by the palace. There they saw a huge plough of bronze lying, and two dun oxen stood near it, wondrous to behold; they had horns and hoofs of bronze, and breathed forth smoke and flame from their nostrils. The King marked with his staff a furlong on the ground, took up the heavy brazen plough-yoke, and yoked those great beasts therewith, heedless of their scorching breath, that burnt black the grass around them, and the furious tossing of their terrible horns. Then, taking in hand a sharp-pointed goad of iron, he drove the oxen to the mark, and turned them, and so back again, cleaving the fallow soil with furrows deep and straight. And his guests watched with speechless amaze so great a marvel, till he unyoked his team beside them, and said, 'If your chief can do as you have seen me do, the Golden Fleece shall be his. But I am sworn to give it to no man who cannot yoke my oxen and plough with my plough.' Straightway Jason stripped off his saffron vesture and stepped boldly to the task, putting his trust in divine aid. Even as Aeetes had done, so did he; he took up the yoke as it were a feather's weight, laid it on the necks of the oxen, despite their plungings hither and thither, and goaded them forward with the one hand, while with the other he bore hard upon the plough-stilts, driving a true furrow alongside the King's. Aeetes looked to see him scorched to a cinder when he approached the fire-breathing bulls, but the flames had no power on his flesh by reason of Medea's enchanted ointment, and a wordless cry broke from the King, beholding him unscathed, and the god-like strength that was in him. But all Jason's comrades shouted with a great shout when the task was done, and crowded about him to clasp his hands with praises and glad greetings, and they crowned him with a garland of flowering grasses. In silent rage the King now led the way to the grove of Ares, where hung the Golden Fleece, yet he still had hopes that Jason, for all his prowess, would not be able to achieve the task that there awaited him. For the Fleece had a guardian stranger and more terrible than the oxen whose breath was flame. The grove of Ares was a gloomy wood of ancient oaks, that stooped their gnarled boughs low over dense undergrowths of brambles and juniper. A stone altar stood before it, stained with dark blood, and far within, the green gloom was broken by a spot of radiance like the clear shining of a lamp. No voice of bird sounded in that drear wood, for all winged creatures shunned it except the woodpeckers, whose tapping was heard ever and anon in the deathly stillness. 'Yonder light,' said Aeetes, 'is the glitter of the Golden Fleece, and you, bold prince, will need no other guide to lead you thereto.'

'King,' said Jason, who was forewarned by Medea's counselling, 'I fear to lay hands upon the sacred thing till I have offered sacrifice upon this altar, and besought mighty Ares not to be wroth at the taking away of the treasure which Phrixus dedicated here. Suffer us therefore to return to our ship for the night, and tomorrow we will bring offerings to the god of such things as we have.' Aeetes gave them leave willingly, for now he feared Jason exceedingly, and was well content that he should either depart at once from the land, if such were his secret purpose, or meet his doom on the morrow from the

guardian of the Fleece. And one of these things he trusted
would most surely befall, for that guardian was a dragon of
baleful glaring eye, whose dappled coils were in length and
thickness not less than Argo's hull that had fifty oars. So the
King returned to his house, and Jason and his comrades went
towards the river where their ship lay. But when they had gone
a little way, Jason told the others what had chanced in the night,
and how the King's daughter had wrought him deliverance from
the bulls, and shown him means to overcome a yet greater peril.
When they heard of the dragon in the grove, they were full eager
to fight the monster, and prayed their captain by no means to
encounter him alone, but Jason said, 'That task must be mine
only, and with Medea to aid, I shall not fail, if the gods so will.
Do you, my comrades, hasten to our ship, and make all ready
to sail whenever I shall come to you.'

With that, he turned back and went alone to the dark grove,
and at the setting of the sun, Medea came to him there.

But his comrades went on board the Argo, and looked well
to all her gear, and set her sails, and when they had taken their
supper, they sat each man at his oar, waiting in silence through
the first watch of the night, while the autumn moon rose golden
up the sky. And at midnight, they were aware of two stately
forms coming swiftly through the shadows of the wood, who
seemed to carry between them a huge, glittering shield. Then
the voice of Jason softly hailed them, and they saw that it was he
and the witch-princess who drew near, bearing a spear athwart
their shoulders, whereon hung the Fleece of Gold, shining like
a sun. Without word spoken, those two laid their burden on
Argo's deck, and Jason, with finger on lip, took his own place,
and made sign to his crew to give way. Silently they bent to their
oars, and the good ship stole out into the stream, and forth to
the open sea. The helmsman turned her prow southward, but at
that, Medea cried, 'Princes, steer not homeward on the course
by which you came, for that way will Aeetes send to pursue
you with a great host, and his ships sail fleeter than the wind
through his enchantments. Long must be your voyage, even half
the circuit of the world, but if you will trust to me for piloting,
I will guide you safe home at last.' The comrades hearkened
gladly to those wise words, and turned Argo northward again
at her command, and sailed for many days over a desolate sea

where no man had come since the making of the world. At last, where that sea narrowed into a gulf between hills of ice and snow, they came forth upon the boundless Ocean stream, that girdles the round world, and now, by Medea's guidance they steered eastward and southward, till the cold of the frozen north was left behind, and the sun's heat gladdened them again. Three moons had risen and set, while Argo bore them along the Ocean stream, before they saw on their right hand the red cliffs of a coast, and a wide channel of waters between.

'Through yonder strait lies our way,' said Medea, and they steered northward once again along that firth of ruddy shores. Now at the head of it, they found no passage for their ship, for dunes of yellow sand stretched before them, far as eye could see, and their hearts were discouraged. But Medea bade them draw Argo ashore, and said, 'Beyond this sandy waste lies the Midland sea, whose waters wash the shores of your own dear land. Be not downcast, brave comrades, for in twelve days Argo shall ride on that sea once more, if with stout hearts you endure the toil of bearing her thither.' So when they had rested there that night, she who had been their pilot over a thousand leagues of ocean, guided the crew across the pathless desert, and they, by main strength hoisting the ship to their shoulders, marched onward thus laden under a burning sun. Never in their long seafaring had they known a labour like this, but the spirit of the heroes and the might of their young limbs did not fail nor falter in all that toilsome journey. On the twelfth day, the glittering of water was seen among the sandhills, and they pressed onward joyfully, till they came to the margin of a vast and shallow mere. Now when they would have drunk of its water, they could not, for it was brackish, but Medea cast a certain herb therein, and forthwith it was sweetened. Then she said to them, 'This water is bitter with brine of the sea that neighbours it. Launch Argo now upon the mere, and let us seek a channel among the shallows that may bring us to the open main.'

So they pushed off from the reedy bank, and rowed slowly, steering warily through the shallows of that great lagoon, till the helmsman saw blue water sparkling ahead, and cried, 'The sea, the sea!' Then the glad heroes plied their oars with fresh vigour, and ere nightfall Argo was anchored in a bay of the Midland deep.

At early dawn, when they had hoisted sail and were drawing up the anchors, a voice hailed them from the shore, and they turned in wonder to see who might call them in that lonely place. There, at the waves' edge stood a man, stately and tall, and greeted them with kindly words, and desired them to tarry awhile, and be his guests that day. But Jason and the rest made courteous excuse, pleading their haste to be at home. 'Friends,' said the stranger, 'I will not seek to delay you, but at least take a guest-gift from my hands, for I would fain show you hospitality. I am the king of this desert land, and I know who you are, and the quest you sailed on. Be pleased to take this boon, the only one I have at hand.' So saying, he stooped down and took up a clod of earth of the shore, and held it forth to them. Now Argo's prow was nearest to the land, for thereby she had been moored, as the manner was, and it was not yet turned seaward, and he that stood nearest her curved beak was a young prince named Euphemos. He, springing to the bulwark, leapt lightly ashore, and clasped hands with the stranger, and took the clod, and knew not what gift that was, nor who gave it. But as he sprang on board again, and turned to speak thanks and farewell, the stranger vanished where he stood, and awe came on all the comrades, understanding that they had seen the god of that wilderness. Nevertheless, they set forth again rejoicing, because he had shown them favour and blessed them with a gift. Euphemos showed the clod to Medea and asked her what it might betoken, and she answered that the time was not yet come for him to know, but he must look well to the keeping of it, because there was a magic in it.

But when they had sailed three days, a gale blew from the south-west at twilight, and the waves rose high round the ship, and the enchanted clod was washed from the deck, where it was laid, by the driving spray. Then Euphemos called aloud to Medea, 'Alas, wise Lady, what shall I do? The precious thing is lost, carried overboard by a dashing wave, and it is sunk into the depths of the sea.'

'Nay,' said Medea, 'it has not sunk, for there is a magic in it, but is drifting even now to the shore of yonder island on our lee. Listen, heroes all, and I will tell you what power is in the clod, and what will come of it. It is fated that wherever it is laid upon the ground, the lord of that land shall be lord also of the soil whence it was taken. And if Euphemos had brought it to the fields of his own fair domain, and planted it there, then in the day when his children's children will seek new lordship over seas, they would have sailed to the land where we saw the solitary god, and made it their kingdom. But now, because the clod is flung by the salt waves on the strand of yonder isle, that is yet uninhabited, seventeen generations of men must pass away before the god's gift bears fruit. For the descendants of Euphemos will make their new home in that island, which then shall be called Thera, and long after, they will voyage thence to the land of the clod, and reign there as kings of many cities.' The comrades listened in silence to Medea's prophecy, and pondered it in their hearts, and Euphemos ever after kept it in memory, teaching it to his sons, and they to theirs. And in the seventeenth generation the words were fulfilled.

But now the gale freshened to a tempest, and Argo was driven before it out of her true course, and her crew were fain to run her for shelter under the white cliffs of another island, far to northward. There they found a fair haven where they anchored, and forthwith, an armed host came out to them from the city nigh at hand. Argo's men stared at these warriors with amaze, for they were women, and their leader, a tall, black-haired girl, clad in rich armour. She came to the harbour-side and greeted the strangers, asking who they were, and if they came peaceably.

'Peaceably, in truth, O Queen,' answered Jason. 'We are men of Iolcos, homeward bound from a long seafaring, and we do but seek shelter here till the storm is overpast. Tell me, I pray you, what land this is, and wherefore its warriors are women.' 'Stranger,' said the armed maiden 'This island is Lemnos, and my father was king of it. He and all our men-folk went forth to war against certain pirates of the mainland, and while they were abroad, Aphrodite took displeasure at us women, because we slighted her worship, and she caused us to become utterly hateful to our fathers and husbands when they returned. Therefore they thrust us away from bed and board, and would have taken them wives of the captives they brought home, but we, thus wronged, banded together for revenge, and slew them while they slept, with their own swords. Not one did we spare, except my father, but him, though I had sworn to show no mercy, I hid in a great chest, and had it thrown into the sea, that, if the gods so willed, he might drift to some other shore. Since then, I, Hypsipyle, am Queen, and none but women dwell in Lemnos. Arms we have, as you see, and have learnt the skill of them, to defend ourselves against all comers, but you, if you are what you say, we will welcome as guests.'

Jason had little will to enter that city of dark deeds, and consort with those women of fierce nature, but Medea said, 'Our ship was blown hither not without divine purpose. Let us go ashore, and lodge with the Queen, as she would have us.' So they sojourned seven days in Lemnos, for all that time the wind blew rough and contrary. Queen Hypsipyle entertained the comrades royally, and held games in their honour, setting forth prizes of golden goblets and broidered mantles for running and wrestling and throwing the spear. For these the warrior-women contended with the heroes, and overcame not a few of them, for they were cunning wrestlers, and marvellous fleet-footed. But in feats of strength they could not match Jason and his men, nor in the race for which the Queen gave the richest prize of all, a silver shield, embossed with wild bulls, and hunters driving them into the toils. That race was run by seven of the heroes in full armour, carrying their heavy shields, and there was laughter among the women when the seventh, whose name was Erginos, stepped to the starting-place, because he, though yet young, was grey-haired. Yet he outstripped the rest, and came foremost to the goal, and the mockers were ashamed when he took the silver shield, and the victor's garland from the Queen's hands. After this, the strangers found great favour with the island maidens, who would fain have had them for their wedded lords, and Hypsipyle made offer to Jason of her hand and kingdom, if he would abide in Lemnos. Now she was more beautiful than the Colchian enchantress, and Jason's heart was drawn to her, but false to his word he could not be, and that was given to Medea. But some of his comrades took them brides among the Lemnian damsels, and of these was Euphemos; and Medea, at his wedding, prophesied good fortune to the marriage, moreover, the gods, she said, had willed him to find a wife in that island, for which very cause they had driven Argo to its coast. And the truth of her saying was quickly made manifest, for that very day the wind blew fair again for Iolcos, so that the heroes longed to set sail for home without delay. They listened not to any pleading, but made Argo ready for sea, and put their island brides on board, and went their way. This was the last of their seafaring; the kindly breeze never failed till they dropped anchor once again in the haven where their good ship first floated.

Here ends the story of Jason's quest for the Golden Fleece, for it needs not to tell the joy of his father and of all Iolcos at his homecoming, nor how the brave comrades took farewell, when they had seen him receive the kingdom from Pelias, who durst not draw back from his oath to yield it. Jason and Medea were wedded with splendour and rejoicings, and thereafter they had such happiness as seemed good to the gods. But as for Pelias, although Jason did him no violence, he did not escape the death that was to be dealt him by his own kindred. For his daughters heard that Medea had made old Aeson young again by her spells, and entreated her to do the like for their father. Then the enchantress killed an old ram before them, and cut it in pieces, and threw the pieces with magic herbs into a boiling cauldron, and when she had said certain words over it, forthwith she drew out a lamb, alive and unhurt. And she gave a handful of herbs to the daughters of Pelias, saying, 'Do to your father as you have seen me do to this sheep, which has become a lamb again.' The princesses did so, but Medea had given them common herbs, and they had not bethought them to ask what those words were which she said over the cauldron, therefore they could not bring their slain father to life again. Thus perished Pelias, even as the oracle had forewarned him, by a doom that had its beginning in the coming to Iolcos of the lad with one sandal.

THE SONS OF TUIRENN

Peter Tremayne

N O ONE KNEW the reason of the feud between the sons of Cainte and the sons of Tuirenn. Perhaps it had its roots in a sharp word, some affront to honour, but the result was that the three sons of Cainte and the three sons of Tuirenn had sworn to shed each other's blood should they ever met with one another.

So it came about that the eldest son of Cainte, Cian, whose name means 'the enduring one', was crossing the great plain of Muirthemne, on his way to join the Children of Danu at Magh Tuireadh, for the news was that a great battle was being fought against the Fomorii. Cian was alone for his two brothers, Cú and Céthan, had gone on before him.

It was as he was on the open plain, some way from any shelter, that he saw three warriors heading towards him. Standing tall in his chariot, Cian narrowed his eyes to examine them. There was no mistaking the grim visage of Brían, whose name means 'exalted one', and his brothers Iuchar and Iucharba. Now Cian realised, because he was outnumbered, that discretion was the better part of valour. But there was no cover on the plain except for a herd of pigs feeding. Being one of the Children of Danu, Cian took a Druid wand and changed his shape into that of a pig, also causing his chariot and horses to be likewise transformed.

Brían, son of Tuirenn, chieftain of Ben Eadair, paused and stared across the plain.

'Brothers,' he said, turning to Iuchar and Iucharba, 'wasn't there a proud warrior crossing the plain a moment ago?'

They affirmed that their brother was right.

Brían saw the herd of pigs and he realised that the warrior

must have shape-changed. If this were so, then the warrior was no friend to the sons of Tuirenn. Now Brían realised that the herd of pigs belonged to Nuada himself and if he and his brothers harmed them, then Nuada would punish them. So he took his own Druidical wand and touched his brothers lightly. Iuchar and Iucharba were changed into two great hounds and straightaway, baying eagerly, they made for the herd, keen noses to the ground.

Cian realised that the hounds would sniff him out and so, still in the shape of a pig, he made a break from the herd. But Brían was standing ready and cast his spear through the pig shape. Cian screamed in agony.

'I am Cian, son of Cainte, and I plead for quarter,' cried the pig.

Brían, now joined by his brothers in their true shapes, stood before the bleeding pig.

'No quarter!' snapped Brían. 'We have all sworn an oath that none would survive our encounters should the sons of Cainte and the sons of Tuirenn meet.'

'Then grant me a last request,' cried Cian in resignation. 'Let me resume my human form before you kill me.'

This Brían granted.

Cian smiled triumphantly at him. 'You may kill me now but remember this, sons of Tuirenn; had you killed me as a pig, your punishment would have only been the *eric* fine paid on the unlawful slaughter of a pig. Since you now kill me as a man, then you will have to pay the *eric* fine of a man. Moreover, as I am Cian, the enduring, the son of Cainte, and the father of Lugh of the Long Hand, the punishment that shall be exacted will be great. Even the weapons which you kill me with shall cry out in horror at this deed.'

Brían thought for a while, for it was true that Cian was one of the Children of Danu. Then he smiled sneeringly at Cian.

'Then it shall not be with weapons you will be killed but with stones of the earth.'

So saying, he threw aside his weapons and picked up some stones and hurled them in hate at Cian. He was joined by his brothers and stone after stone flew until Cian was a disfigured and unrecognisable mess of a man. Then the brothers dug a grave and buried the battered body. But six times the earth refused to cover the corpse before, at the seventh time of burying, the earth accepted the body.

Yet as Brían and his brothers rode away they heard a voice calling from beneath the earth: 'The blood is on your hands, sons of Tuirenn, and there it will remain until we meet again.'

* * *

The sons of Tuirenn distinguished themselves in the great Battle of the Plain of Towers in which Bres and the Fomorii were defeated. But everyone remarked that Cian was absent from the battle which was strange as it was Cian's own son who had taken over the leadership of the Children of Danu when Nuada had been killed by the Fomorii Balor of the Evil Eye. So, after a fruitless search, Lugh Lámhfada finally came to the Plain of Muirthemne and as he was travelling across it the stones of the earth started to speak:

'Here lies the body of your father Cian! Killed by the sons of Tuirenn. Blood on their hands until they meet with Cian again!'

And Lugh had his father's body disinterred and he called his companions together that they might see how the deed was done. And Lugh swore vengeance. Lugh sang a lament over the body:

> Cian's death, death of a great champion,
> Has left me as a walking corpse
> Without a soul,
> Without strength, without power,
> Without a feeling for life.
> The Sons of Tuirenn have killed him
> Now my hatred will come against them
> And follow them to the ends of the world.

And Lugh buried his father's body with all pomp and ceremony and went back to the great hall of Tara where he summoned all the people. Even the sons of Tuirenn were among them but Lugh kept his counsel. Instead he asked those among the gods what they would do to take vengeance on those who had with malice slaughtered their fathers.

Each of the gods suggested ways, increasingly more horrible and more bloody, as a means of punishment. And when the last of them had spoken, the assembly roared its approval. Lugh saw that the sons of Tuirenn, not wishing to be conspicuous in the throng, were also applauding. Then Lugh, with a scowl on his usually sunny countenance, spoke up.

'The murderers of Cian have condemned themselves for they have joined in the agreement of you all as to their punishment. But I am merciful. I will not spill blood in Tara. I claim the right to put an *eric* fine on the murderers. If they refuse to accept it then they must meet me, one after the other, in bloody single combat at the door of Tara's Hall.'

All the while he spoke he was looking at the sons of Tuirenn.

Then Brían moved forward.

'It is known there was enmity between us and your father and his brothers Cú and Céthan. Your words seem addressed to us but Cian was not killed by any weapons of the sons of Tuirenn. Nevertheless, to show that we are honourable, each one of us will accept your *eric* fine.'

Lugh smiled grimly.

'You will not find it difficult. I wish for three apples, the skin of a pig, a spear, two horses and a chariot, seven swine, a hound-pup, a cooking spit and three shouts to be delivered on a hill.'

Not only the sons of Tuirenn stood amazed but the entire assembly could not believe their ears at the little Lugh demanded in compensation for his father's death. The sons of Tuirenn were visibly relieved and clamoured to accept the fine.

'If you think it is too heavy,' Lugh added, 'I will not press the fine.'

'We do not consider it heavy,' replied Brían. 'In fact it seems so light that I suspect some trickery. Are you intending to increase the sum . . .?'

'I swear by our mother, Danu, the divine waters, that the fine will not be increased. And in return for this oath, do you swear you will faithfully complete the *eric* fine?'

They did so with mighty acclaim.

'Very well,' Lugh chuckled grimly, after they had sworn. 'The three apples must come from the Garden of Hesperides in the east. They are of gold in colour and have immense power and virtue. They are as big as the head of a month-old child and never grow less no matter how much is eaten from them. They have the taste of honey and a bite will cure a sick or wounded man. A warrior can perform any feat with one and should he for once cast it from his hand it will return to him.'

The sons of Tuirenn looked thunderstruck.

'The skin of the pig is that owned by Tuis, king of Greece. In whatever stream that pig walked, the water turned to wine, and the wounded and sick became well when they drank of it. These magical properties are enshrouded in that skin.'

The sons of Tuirenn began to look grim.

'The spear is that which belongs to Pisear of Persia and it is called "slaughterer". It has to be kept in a cauldron of blood to prevent it killing for only blood cools its angry blade.'

Lugh paused but the sons of Tuirenn now stood expressionless as they realised the trap that he had set for them.

'The steeds and chariot which I require are those belonging to Dobhar of Siogair. If one of the horses is killed it will come to life again if its bones are brought together in the same place.

'The seven swine are those of Easal, king of the Golden Pillars, which, though killed each day for the feast, are found alive the following morning. The hound pup is Failinis, owned by the king of Ioruiadh. The wild beasts are helpless before her. The cooking spit I want is that from the island of Fianchuibhne which is protected by mighty women warriors. And the hill on which you must give three shouts is that of Miodchaoin in Lochlainn which is constantly guarded by Miodchaoin and his three fierce sons, Aedh, Corca and Conn. Their task is solely to prevent any person from raising their voices on the hill.

'This, sons of Tuirenn, is the *eric* fine I ask of you.'

* * *

When Tuirenn heard of what had befallen his sons, he was upset but he went to them and gave them advice.

'No one can set out on this voyage without the magical ship of the god of the oceans Manánnan Mac Lir. But Lugh owns this ship, the Wave-sweeper, which can navigate itself across the seas. But listen to me, Lugh is under a *geis*, a sacred proscription never to refuse a second request. So go to him and ask for a loan of Manánnan's fabulous horse, Aonbharr, which can gallop over land and water. He will refuse. Then ask for the Wave-sweeper and that he cannot refuse.'

And this they did and it happened as Tuirenn had said. Lugh was forced to give them the loan of Manánnan's boat. And Tuirenn and his daughter Eithne went to see them off from the harbour at Ben Eadair. Their sister Eithne sung a lament of farewell for as much as she loved them, she knew that they had done an evil thing and therefore only evil would come of it.

The three warriors climbed into the Wave-sweeper and Brían commanded it to cross to the Garden of Hesperides. The boat leapt forward at his command and ploughed through the white crested waves more swiftly than if the winds of Spring were blowing into its sail. So fast did it travel that within the wink of an eye it came safely to the harbour of Hesperides on the extreme western edge of the ocean.

The three brothers climbed out. They learnt that the apple orchards of Hesperides were so well guarded that they had no chance of entering without discovery. Then Brían drew up his Druid's wand and changed his brothers and himself into hawks. On his instructions they rose into the air and circled high above the orchard and then they swooped down, travelling so fast that the arrows and spears of the guards could not hit them. Each in turn, they seized one of the golden apples and rose again into the air and raced back to the harbour where they had left their boat.

Now the king of Hesperides had three daughters who were sorceresses and when they heard the news they transformed themselves into three griffins and pursued the hawks, breathing great tongues of fire after them. So fierce were the flames that the hawks were burnt and blinded and could bear the heat no longer. Then Brían used his Druid's lore and changed them into swans who were able to glide down to the sea. The griffins confused flew off still looking for the hawks and the sons of Tuirenn made their way back to the Wave-sweeper.

Next they commanded the boat to take them to Greece and entered the harbour close to the palace of Tuis.

Brían's brothers wanted him to disguise them as animals but

he told them that poets from Inisfáil were well respected in Greece and they would go up to the king's palace and present themselves as such. Indeed, this was truly thought out for the guards allowed the three 'poets' into the king's palace. Tuis himself greeted them and invited them to a great feast. At the end of the feast, the king's poets rose and recited their poems. Then the sons of Tuirenn were invited to recite.

Brían stood up and intoned these verses.

> I conceal not your fame, O Tuis
> Great as an oak among kings,
> A pigskin is a reward without meanness,
> And this I claim in return for this poem.
>
> A war may come when warriors clash
> A war may be averted by a gift
> And he who gives without fear,
> Shall lose nothing.
>
> A stormy army and tempestuous sea
> Are weapons that no one would oppose,
> But a pigskin, a reward freely given
> Is that which we claim.

'It sounds an excellent poem,' mused Tuis, 'yet I do not understand it.'

'I will interpret it,' smiled Brían. 'It means that as an oak excels above other trees, so do you in kingship. We claim the pigskin you have as a reward for our poem, but if it is refused it means that there will be a war between us.'

Tuis stared in surprise.

'I would like your poem if you had not mentioned my magical pigskin. You seem a foolish man, poet, to ask for it. I would even refuse the kings and warriors of your land had they demanded it. So now I refuse you. Yet your poem is good and I will reward you with gold. And three times in gold what that pigskin will hold will be your fee.'

'Generous as you are, king,' Brían laughed, 'let us watch while the gold is measured in the skin.'

The king agreed and the sons of Tuirenn were brought to the treasure house and the skin was brought from its special place.

And when the skinfuls of gold were weighed, Brían suddenly grabbed the skin, drawing his sword and cutting the arm of the man who held the skin clean off. He wrapped the skin about himself and the three brothers fought their way from the palace. In rage and fury Tuis and his court attacked them but not one noble, nor champion of Greece, was able to halt them. Tuis himself fell before the slashing sword of Brían.

They fought their way back to the Wave-sweeper and straightaway they called on it to take them to Persia. It was agreed that the disguise of poets worked well for them and so they presented themselves to the court of Pisear in the same manner. Once more they were asked to recite a poem and Brían did so.

> Small esteem of any spear with Pisear
> His enemies are already broken
> Pisear has little cause for worry
> Since it is others who receive wounds.
>
> The yew is the finest tree in the forest
> The yew is king without opposition
> May the great spear shafts drive on
> Through the wounds of those they slay.

When Pisear asked Brían to spell out the meaning of the poem, Brían told him that he wanted his magic spear in payment for the poem.

When Pisear threatened to kill him and his brothers for audacity, Brían remembered that he had one of the apples of Hesperides with him. He took it from his bag and threw it at Pisear, so hard, it knocked the king's head off and returned safely to his hand. Then Brían and his brothers drew their swords and fought their way to the room where the blazing spear was kept in its great cauldron of blood, hissing and bubbling. They took it and went back to the Wave-sweeper.

On they went to Dobhar's kingdom of Siogair. Here they appeared before his court as three champions of Inisfáil seeking hospitality. When asked what they wanted they told Dobhar the king that they would serve him for payment. They spent a long time in Siogair because they were unable to find the steeds and the chariot which were faster than the winds of Spring. Finally, Brían tricked the king into ordering that the chariot be brought to the court, harnessed and ready.

And when the sons of Tuirenn turned and demanded the prancing horses and the beautiful chariot as the price for their service, Dobhar flew into a rage and ordered his guards to kill them.

Brían sprang into the chariot, hurling the charioteer to the ground. He took the reins in his hands and unloosed the spear of Pisear so that the guards of Dobhar were slain and those who were not simply fled. And with Iuchar and Iucharba behind him, Brían drove the chariot back to the waiting Wave-sweeper.

Next the magic boat of Manánnan Mac Lir brought them to the land of the Golden Pillars, the entrance of the Middle Sea, where Easal ruled. And when they came to the shore they saw great armies gathered for now the fame of the deeds of the sons of Tuirenn had travelled before them and news of their banishment from Inisfáil and the nature of their tasks had proceeded them.

Easal the king came down to the harbour to meet them and he demanded to know if it was true that they had come for his swine. They told him it was. Now Easal was a peaceful man and he went and sat in council with his chieftains. Eventually they decided that they would hand the swine to the sons of Tuirenn to avoid the slaughter of the innocent. That night Easal invited the brothers to a feasting where the seven pigs were handed to them. Brían sang a paean in praise of Easal's wisdom and generosity.

When Easal learnt that the sons of Tuirenn were going next to the country of Ioruiadh, the king asked that he be allowed to accompany them for his daughter was the wife of the king of Ioruiadh. Easal promised, in return, to do his best to secure the hound-pup from the king, his son-in-law, without bloodshed.

The king of Ioruiadh would have none of Easal's advice. 'You may be weak, old man, but the gods have not given strength or luck enough to any warrior to take my hound-pup by force.'

Easal was saddened for he knew what bloodshed and mayhem would follow.

A great and bloody battle began. And Brían cleaved through the warriors of Ioruiadh, throwing them back by the nine times one hundred until he reached the spot where the king of Ioruaidh stood. And he bodily picked up the king and fought his way back until he threw the craven man at Easal's feet.

'There is your daughter's husband, o king. It would have been easier to kill him than to return with him alive.'

The warriors of Ioruiadh, seeing their king defeated, threw down their arms. And the king of Ioruiadh now heeded the peaceful tones of Easal and handed over the hound-pup and the sons of Tuirenn took their leave in friendship.

Now only two tasks remained to be filled.

They were to find the cooking spit of Fianchuibhne and give three shouts on the Hill of Miodchaoin.

But so excited were they at their successes that they forgot about the last two tasks. Some have it that Lugh Lámhfada had prevailed upon his Druid to send a cloud of forgetfulness to seep into the brothers' minds after they had left Ioruaidh.

Whatever the cause, the Wave-sweeper returned to Inisfáil. Lugh heard of their coming and was suddenly troubled for he had followed the successes of the sons of Tuirenn with mixed feelings. He was happy that these gifts that they had secured were for him but apprehensive that they might be turned against him. He was also bitter because the brothers were fulfilling the conditions of the *eric* fine which he had devised to cause their deaths.

So when the Wave-sweeper entered the mouth of the Boyne river, Lugh went to the fort of Cathair Crofinn and armed himself with the magical armour of the Ocean god, Manánnan, who was his foster father. He also put on the cloak of invisibility of Fea the Hateful, one of the goddesses of war. For Lugh also feared their coming, thinking the three brothers might mean him harm now that they possessed such wonderful weapons. And when they sent word to Lugh, asking him to come and take his *eric* fine, Lugh sent back asking that they hand over the spoils to the Bodb Dearg, son of The Dagda, who had now succeeded Lugh as ruler of the Children of Danu. Only when the Bodb Dearg reported that he had control of the wondrous gifts did Lugh emerge and come to examine them.

'But where is the cooking spit?' demanded Lugh, 'And I did not hear the three shouts on the Hill of Miodchaoin.'

The sons of Tuirenn then remembered and they were sorely

grieved. So they left and spent a night with their father, Tuirenn, and sister Eithne, at their fortress at Ben Eadair. Now they did not have the benefit of the magical ship the Wave-sweeper for they had foolishly surrendered it to Lugh. So they set sail in an ordinary ship in search of Fianchuibhne. However, the task was a long one. For three months they searched, visiting many islands and asking many travellers if they knew of such a place. No one knew.

Finally, they met an old man; toothless and without eyes for there were so many wrinkles and folds of flesh on his walnut coloured face, that they were hidden. He told them that the island of Fianchuibhne did not lie on the surface of the sea but deep down in its depths.

Brían, telling Iuchar and Iucharba to wait for him, leapt over the side of their ship and sank down into the waves. For two periods of nine days he walked the ocean bed in his search and found many houses, and great palaces. Then he entered a house with its doors open where one hundred and fifty beautiful women were engaged in needlework and embroidery. In the middle of them lay a cooking spit.

Brían saw that the women neither moved nor spoke as he entered. So, without more ado, he walked to the spit, seized it, turned and walked out. At that point the women all burst out laughing. They rose and surrounded Brían who saw they had a formidable assortment of weapons.

'Brave man are you Brían son of Tuirenn. There are one hundred and fifty of us here, every one a warrior, and each one of us able to slay you. But you are brave and courageous to make this attempt knowing the dangers. You shall be rewarded. Take the spit for this is one of many which we have.'

And Brían thanked them and swam upwards to the ship in which his brothers were anxiously waiting. They were overjoyed.

They turned the ship northward now to the great fjords of Lochlainn, for that is what the name means, the place of lochs and fjords. They saw the great hill of Miodchaoin rising upwards and, leaving their ship, they walked to the bottom of it. But there, on the massive slopes, stood Miodchaoin, who was a mighty warrior.

Miodchaoin saw Brían and unsheathed his great sword.

'Killer of my friend and foster-brother Cian! Now you have come to shout upon this hill. You will do that deed only when I am dead.'

Brían flew at Miodchaoin and the two great warriors set about one another. So fierce was their onslaught that the ringing of the swords upon their shields could be heard in every corner of the world. No quarter was asked nor given until Miodchaoin fell dead with Brían's sword thrust through his giant heart.

Then the three sons of Miodchaoin, Aedh, Corca and Conn, having heard the noise of battle, came racing up and fell on the three sons of Tuirenn. The sky reddened and blackened, blood flowed from that mountain slope like the gushing waters of a mountain spring, and the earth trembled from the stamping of their feet even as far to the east as Hesperides.

For three days and three nights the great combat shook the mountains of Lochlainn. Then the sons of Miodchaoin managed to find the flesh of the sons of Tuirenn with their spear points. Each one of the sons of Tuirenn, Brían, Iuchar and Iuchara, were pierced and wounded. Yet the sons of Tuirenn would not give in for they thrust their spears into the bodies of Aedh, Corca and Conn and the three sons of Miodchaoin fell dead.

The sons of Tuirenn fell on the blood-stained grass and it seemed that a heavy veil of darkness was being drawn before their eyes. It was Brían, coughing blood, who called faintly: 'Brothers, how is it with you?' 'Dead are we,' they gasped, 'or as near it as makes no difference.'

'We must climb the hill and give three shouts before death claims us,' replied Brían. 'Only then may we rest in peace.'

With Brían supporting his two brothers on his mighty arms, the three went forward up the steep slopes, stumbling and moving as in a dream until they reached the summit. Then they paused and gave three shouts, weak as they were, they were shouts nevertheless.

Brían, still supporting his brothers, then guided them to the ship and they turned her prow for Inisfáil.

In a delirium they drifted and drifted towards the distant island. Suddenly Brían raised his head:

'I see Ben Eadair and the fort of our father, Tuirenn.'

His brothers raised their heads so that they might see the green hills of their home before they died. The ship gently nudged ashore and Tuirenn came down with Eithne to greet his sons.

'Father, take the spit to Lugh,' instructed Brían, 'and tell him that the three shouts on the Hill of Miodchaoin have been given.'

And Tuirenn mounted his chariot and rode to Tara with the news. And he pleaded with Lugh to loan him the magic pigskin of Tuis which would heal the sick and wounded or one of the apples of Hesperides but Lugh refused him coldly. And Tuirenn returned to his dying sons and lamented:

> If all the jewels of the world
> Were given to Lugh to ease his anger
> It would not be enough to save you
> From a gloomy grave.

MY LORD BAG OF RICE

Theodora Ozaki

L ONG AGO THERE lived in Japan a brave warrior known to all as Tawara Toda, or 'My Lord Bag of Rice.' His true name was Fujiwara Hidesato, and this is the story of how he came to change his name.

One day he sallied forth in search of adventures, for he had the nature of a warrior and could not bear to be idle. So he buckled on his two swords, took his huge bow, much taller than himself, in his hand, and slinging his quiver on his back started out. He had not gone far when he came to the bridge of Seta-no-Karashi spanning one end of the beautiful Lake Biwa. No sooner had he set foot on the bridge than he saw lying right across his patch a huge serpent-dragon. Its body was so big that it looked like the trunk of a large pine tree and it took up the whole width of the bridge. One of its huge claws rested on the parapet of one side of the bridge, while its tail lay right against the other. The monster seemed to be asleep, and as it breathed, fire and smoke came out of its nostrils.

At first Hidesato could not help feeling alarmed at the sight of this horrible reptile lying in his path, for he must either turn back or walk right over its body. He was a brave man, however, and putting aside all fear went forward dauntlessly. Crunch, crunch! he stepped now on the dragon's body, now between its coils, and without even one glance backward he went on his way.

He had only gone a few steps when he heard someone calling him from behind. On turning back he was much surprised to see that the monster dragon had entirely disappeared and in its place was a strange-looking man, who was bowing most ceremoniously to the ground. His red hair streamed over his shoulders and was surmounted by a crown in the shape of a dragon's head, and his sea-green dress was patterned with shells. Hidesato knew at once that this was no ordinary mortal and he wondered much at the strange occurrence. Where had the dragon gone in such a short space of time? Or had it transformed itself into this man, and what did the whole thing mean? While these thoughts passed through his mind he had come up to the man on the bridge and now addressed him:

'Was it you that called me just now?'

'Yes, it was I,' answered the man: 'I have an earnest request to make to you. Do you think you can grant it to me?'

'If it is in my power to do so I will,' answered Hidesato, 'but first tell me who you are?'

'I am the Dragon King of the Lake, and my home is in these waters just under this bridge.'

'And what is it you have to ask of me!' said Hidesato.

'I want you to kill my mortal enemy the centipede, who lives on the mountain beyond,' and the Dragon King pointed to a high peak on the opposite shore of the lake.

'I have lived now for many years in this lake and I have a large family of children and grandchildren. For some time past we have lived in terror, for a monster centipede has discovered our home, and night after night it comes and carries off one of my family. I am powerless to save them. If it goes on much longer like this, not only shall I lose all my children, but I myself must fall a victim to the monster. I am, therefore, very unhappy, and in my extremity I determined to ask the help of a human being. For many days with this intention I have waited on the bridge in the shape of the horrible serpent-dragon that you saw, in the hope that some strong brave man would come along. But all who came this way, as soon as they saw me were terrified and ran away as fast as they could. You are the first man I have found able to look at me without fear, so I knew at once that you were a man of great courage. I beg you to have pity upon me. Will you not help me and kill my enemy the centipede?'

Hidesato felt very sorry for the Dragon King on hearing his story, and readily promised to do what he could to help him. The warrior asked where the centipede lived, so that he might attack the creature at once. The Dragon King replied that its home was on the mountain Mikami, but that as it came every night at a certain hour to the palace of the lake, it would be better to wait till then. So Hidesato was conducted to the palace of the Dragon King, under the bridge. Strange to say, as he followed his host downwards the waters parted to let them pass, and his clothes did not even feel damp as he passed through the flood. Never had Hidesato seen anything so beautiful as this palace built of white marble beneath the lake. He had often heard of the Sea King's palace at the bottom of the sea, where all the servants and retainers were salt-water fishes, but here was a magnificent building in the heart of Lake Biwa. The dainty goldfishes, red carp, and silvery trout, waited upon the Dragon King and his guest.

Hidesato was astonished at the feast that was spread for him. The dishes were crystallized lotus leaves and flowers, and the chopsticks were of the rarest ebony. As soon as they sat down, the sliding doors opened and ten lovely goldfish dancers came out, and behind them followed ten red-carp musicians with the koto and the samisen. Thus the hours flew by till midnight, and the beautiful music and dancing had banished all thoughts of the centipede. The Dragon King was about to pledge the warrior in a fresh cup of wine when the palace was suddenly shaken by a tramp, tramp! as if a mighty army had begun to march not far away.

Hidesato and his host both rose to their feet and rushed to the balcony, and the warrior saw on the opposite mountain two great balls of glowing fire coming nearer and nearer. The Dragon King stood by the warrior's side trembling with fear.

'The centipede! The centipede! Those two balls of fire are its eyes. It is coming for its prey! Now is the time to kill it.'

Hidesato looked where his host pointed, and, in the dim light of the starlit evening, behind the two balls of fire he saw the long body of an enormous centipede winding round the mountains, and the light in its hundred feet glowed like so many distant lanterns moving slowly towards the shore.

Hidesato showed not the least sign of fear. He tried to calm the Dragon King.

'Don't be afraid. I shall surely kill the centipede. Just bring me my bow and arrows.'

The Dragon King did as he was bid, and the warrior noticed that he had only three arrows left in his quiver. He took the bow, and fitting an arrow to the notch, took careful aim and let fly.

The arrow hit the centipede right in the middle of its head, but instead of penetrating, it glanced off harmless and fell to the ground.

Nothing daunted, Hidesato took another arrow, fitted it to the notch of the bow and let fly. Again the arrow hit the mark, it struck the centipede right in the middle of its head, only to glance off and fall to the ground. The centipede was invulnerable to weapons! When the Dragon King saw that even this brave warrior's arrows were powerless to kill the centipede, he lost heart and began to tremble with fear.

The warrior saw that he had now only one arrow left in his quiver, and if this one failed he could not kill the centipede. He looked across the waters. The huge reptile had wound its horrid body seven times round the mountain and would soon come down to the lake. Nearer and nearer gleamed fireballs of eyes, and the light of its hundred feet began to throw reflections in the still waters of the lake.

Then suddenly the warrior remembered that he had heard that human saliva was deadly to centipedes. But this was no ordinary centipede. This was so monstrous that even to think of such a creature made one creep with horror. Hidesato determined to try his last chance. So taking his last arrow and first putting the end of it in his mouth, he fitted the notch to his bow, took careful aim once more and let fly.

This time the arrow again hit the centipede right in the middle of its head, but instead of glancing off harmlessly as before, it struck home to the creature's brain. Then with a convulsive shudder the serpentine body stopped moving, and the fiery light of its great eyes and hundred feet darkened to a dull glare like the sunset of a stormy day, and then went out in blackness. A great darkness now overspread the heavens, the thunder rolled and the lightning flashed, and the wind roared in fury, and it seemed as if the world were coming to an end. The Dragon King and his children and retainers all crouched in different parts of the palace, frightened to death, for the building was shaken to its foundation. At last the dreadful night was over. Day dawned beautiful and clear. The centipede was gone from the mountain.

Then Hidesato called to the Dragon King to come out with him on the balcony, for the centipede was dead and he had nothing more to fear.

Then all the inhabitants of the palace came out with joy, and Hidesato pointed to the lake. There lay the body of the dead centipede floating on the water, which was dyed red with its blood.

The gratitude of the Dragon King knew no bounds. The whole family came and bowed down before the warrior, calling him their preserver and the bravest warrior in all Japan.

Another feast was prepared, more sumptuous than the first. All kinds of fish, prepared in every imaginable way, raw, stewed, boiled and roasted, served on coral trays and crystal dishes, were put before him, and the wine was the best that Hidesato had ever tasted in his life. To add to the beauty of everything the sun shone brightly, the lake glittered like a liquid diamond, and the palace was a thousand times more beautiful by day than by night.

His host tried to persuade the warrior to stay a few days, but Hidesato insisted on going home, saying that he had now finished what he had come to do, and must return. The Dragon King and his family were all very sorry to have him leave so soon, but since he would go they begged him to accept a few small presents (so they said) in token of their gratitude to him for delivering them forever from their horrible enemy the centipede.

As the warrior stood in the porch taking leave, a train of fish was suddenly transformed into a retinue of men, all wearing ceremonial robes and dragon's crowns on their heads to show that they were servants of the great Dragon King. The presents that they carried were as follows:

> First, a large bronze bell.
> Second, a bag of rice.
> Third, a roll of silk.
> Fourth, a cooking pot.

Hidesato did not want to accept all these presents, but as the Dragon King insisted, he could not well refuse.

The Dragon King himself accompanied the warrior as far as

the bridge, and then took leave of him with many bows and good wishes, leaving the procession of servants to accompany Hidesato to his house with the presents.

The warrior's household and servants had been very much concerned when they found that he did not return the night before, but they finally concluded that he had been kept by the violent storm and had taken shelter somewhere. When the servants on the watch for his return caught sight of him they called to everyone that he was approaching, and the whole household turned out to meet him, wondering much what the retinue of men, bearing presents and banners, that followed him, could mean.

As soon as the Dragon King's retainers had put down the presents they vanished, and Hidesato told all that had happened to him.

The presents which he had received from the grateful Dragon King were found to be of magic power. The bell only was ordinary, and as Hidesato had no use for it he presented it to the temple near by, where it was hung up, to boom out the hour of day over the surrounding neighbourhood.

The single bag of rice, however much was taken from it day after day for the meals of the knight and his whole family, never grew less – the supply in the bag was inexhaustible.

The roll of silk, too, never grew shorter, though time after time long pieces were cut off to make the warrior a new suit of clothes to go to Court in at the New Year.

The cooking pot was wonderful, too. No matter what was put into it, it cooked deliciously whatever was wanted without any firing – truly a very economical saucepan.

The fame of Hidesato's fortune spread far and wide, and as there was no need for him to spend money on rice or silk or firing, he became very rich and prosperous, and was henceforth known as *My Lord Bag of Rice*.

PRINCE SEYF EL MULOUK

François Pétis de la Croix

I HAVE ALREADY had the honour of telling your majesty that I am the son of the late Sultan of Egypt, Asem Ben Sefouan, and brother of the prince who succeeded him. One day, being in my sixteenth year I found the door of my father's treasury open. I entered, and I began to scrutinise with much attention the things which seemed rarest to me. I lingered particularly over a little box of red sandalwood, strewn with pearls, diamonds, emeralds, and topazes. It opened with a little gold key, which was in the lock. I opened it, and perceived within a ring of marvellous beauty, with a gold box which contained the portrait of a woman.

The features were so regular, the eyes so fine, her appearance so charming, that I thought at first it was a fancy portrait. 'The works of nature are not so perfect,' I said. What honour to the brush which produced it does this do!' I admired the imagination of the painter who had been capable of forming so beautiful an idea to himself.

My eyes could not detach themselves from this painting, and, what is most surprising, it inspired me with love. I thought it was perhaps the portrait of some living princess, and the more amorous I became the more I persuaded myself of it. I closed the box and put it in my pocket with the ring; then I left the treasury.

I had a confidant named Saed. He was the son of a great lord of Cairo. I loved him, and he was a few years older than me. I related my adventure to him; he asked me for the portrait and I gave it him. He took it out of the box to see whether there were not some writing at the back which could tell us what I longed passionately to know – that is to say, the name of the person portrayed.

We perceived round the box inside these words in Arabic characters: 'Bedy-Aljemal, daughter of the King Achahbal.'

This discovery charmed me; I was enchanted to learn that I was not in love with an imaginary person. I bade my confidant discover where King Achahbal reigned.

Saed asked it of the best informed people of Cairo, but no one could tell him, so that I resolved to travel, to scour the world if necessary, and not to return to Egypt until I had seen Bedy-Aljemal. I begged the sultan, my father, to permit me to go to Baghdad to see the court of the caliph and the marvels of that town of which I had heard so much. He granted me this permission. As I wished to travel incognito, I did not make a pompous exit from Cairo; my suite consisted only of Saed and some slaves whose zeal was known to me. I soon put on my finger the beautiful ring which I had taken from my father's treasury, and the whole way I talked with my confidant only of the Princess Bedy-Aljemal, whose portrait I had always in my hands. When I arrived at Baghdad and had seen all that was curious there, I asked of some wise men if they could not tell me in what part of the world were situated the States of the King Achahbal. They replied in the negative; but if I wished very much to know I had only to take the trouble to go to Bassora and find an old man aged a hundred and seventy, named Padmanaba. This person knew everything, and would doubtless satisfy my curiosity.

I left Baghdad immediately, flew to Bassora, and inquired for the old man. His dwelling was pointed out to me. I went to him. I saw a venerable man still full of vigour, although nearly two centuries had passed over him.

'My son,' he said to me, with a laughing air, 'what can I do for you?'

'My father,' I said to him, 'I would like to know where the King Achahbal reigns. It is of the utmost importance for me to know. Some wise men of Baghdad whom I have consulted, and who have not been able to throw any light upon it, have assured me that you would tell me the name of and the road to the Kingdom of Achahbal.'

'My son,' replied the old man, 'the wise men who have sent you to me think me less ignorant than I am. I do not know exactly where the States of Achahbal are, I only remember to have heard some traveller speak of them. This king reigns, I believe, in a neighbouring island to that of Serendib, but it is only a conjecture, and I am perhaps in error.'

I thanked Padmanaba for having at least indicated a spot where I might hope to be informed of what I wished to know. I formed the resolution to go to the island of Serendib. I embarked with Saed and my slaves on the Gulf of Bassora in a merchant vessel which was going to Surat. From Surat we went to Goa, where we learnt on arrival that a vessel was going to sail in a few days and take the direction of the island of Serendib. We profited by the occasion.

We left Goa with a favourable wind, which took us far on our way the first day; but the second day the wind changed, and towards evening so violent a tempest arose that the sailors, seeing our destruction to be inevitable, abandoned the vessel to the mercy of the wind and sea. Sometimes the waves, opening as if to engulf us, presented frightful abysses to our frightened eyes, and sometimes rising they lifted us to the clouds. The vessel soon filling, we took to the boats. I threw myself into one with Saed. Hardly had we left the vessel than it foundered with a terrible sound, and we lost sight of our companions.

Having drifted all night, we saw at daybreak a little island. We landed on it. Trees, laden with very fine fruit hanging to the ground, first met our view, which rejoiced us all the more that we began to feel very hungry. We picked and ate of them, and found them excellent. When we had taken a little refreshment, we fastened our boat and advanced further into the island. I have never seen a more delightful spot: sandal and aloe woods grew there; there were springs of fresh water, and all sorts of fruits, as well as the most beautiful flowers.

What surprised us most was that this island, although so pleasant to look upon, seemed to be deserted.

'Whence comes it,' I said to Saed, 'that this island is not inhabited? We are not the first to visit it; others before us have doubtless discovered it. Why is it abandoned?'

'My prince,' replied my confidant, 'since no one lives here, it is a sure proof that no one can live here; there is something about it which renders it uninhabitable.' Alas! when the unfortunate Saed spoke thus, he little knew with what truth he was speaking.

We spent the day in rejoicing, and when night fell we stretched ourselves on the grass, which was sprinkled with a thousand sweet-smelling flowers. We slept deliciously; but on awaking I was very astonished to find myself alone. I called Saed repeatedly. As he did not reply I rose to seek him, and, after having searched a part of the island, I returned to the same place where I had spent the night, thinking he might perhaps be there. I awaited him in vain the whole day and even the following night; then, despairing of seeing him again, I made the air resound with cries and groans. 'Ah! my dear Saed,' I cried every minute, 'what has become of you? Whilst you were with me you helped me to bear the burden of my misfortune; you relieved my troubles in sharing them; by what misfortune or by what enchantment have you been carried off from me? What barbarous power has separated us? It would have been sweeter to die with you than to live quite alone.'

I could not console myself for the loss of my confidant; and what troubled me was that I could not think what could have happened to him. I was in despair and resolved to perish also on that island. I said to myself, 'I will scour it thoroughly; I will find either Saed or death.' I walked towards a wood that I saw, and when I had arrived there, I discovered in the middle a very well-built castle, surrounded by a large moat full of water, the drawbridge of which was let down. I entered a large courtyard paved with white marble, and advanced towards the door of a fine block of buildings. It was made of aloe-wood; several figures of birds were represented in relief upon it, and a great padlock of steel, made in the form of a lion, kept it closed. The key was in the padlock; I took hold of it to turn it; the padlock broke like a piece of glass, and the door opened more of itself than from the effort I made to open it, which caused me extreme surprise. I found a staircase of black marble. I ascended, and first entered a great hall ornamented with a gold and silken tapestry with sofas of brocade. From there I entered a room richly furnished, but what I looked at with most attention was a perfectly beautiful young lady. She was reclining on a large sofa, her head resting on a cushion, richly dressed, and beside her was a little jasper table. As her eyes were closed, and I had reason to doubt her being alive, I approached her gently and perceived that she breathed.

I remained for some moments in contemplation of her. She seemed charming to me, and I should have become enamoured of her had I not been so absorbed in Bedy-Aljemal. I was extremely desirous of knowing why I found in a deserted island a young lady alone in a castle where I saw no one. I sincerely hoped she would wake, but she slept so soundly I did not dare disturb her rest. I left the castle, resolved to return some hours later. I walked about the island, and saw with alarm a great number of animals as large as tigers, and formed something like ants. I should have taken them for cruel and ferocious beasts had they not fled at sight of me. I saw other wild animals who seemed to fear me, although they had an alarmingly ferocious appearance. After having eaten several fruits whose beauty charmed me, and having walked for some time, I returned to the castle, where the lady was still asleep. I could no longer resist the desire I had to speak to her. I made a noise in the room and coughed to awake her. As she did not awake, I approached her and touched her arm, but without effect. 'There is some enchantment here,' I then said to myself; 'some talisman keeps this lady asleep, and if this is the case it is not possible to awake her from this slumber.' I despaired of succeeding, when I perceived on the jasper table of which I have spoken several graven characters; I thought this graving might hold the secret. I was about to study the table, but I had hardly touched it when the lady gave a deep sigh and awoke.

If I had been surprised to find so beautiful a person in this castle, she was not less astonished to see me. 'Ah! young man,' she said to me, 'how did you get in here? What have you done to surmount all the obstacles which should have prevented your entering this castle, and which are beyond the reach of human power? I cannot believe you to be a man. You are doubtless the prophet Elias?'

'No, madam,' I said to her, 'I am only a simple man, and I can assure you I have come here without any difficulty. The door of this castle opened as soon as I had touched the key. I mounted to this apartment without any power resisting me. I have not awakened you with ease; that is what I found most difficult.'

'I cannot believe what you tell me,' replied the lady. 'I am so persuaded that it is impossible to men to do what you have done, that I do not believe, whatever you may say, that you are merely a man.'

'Madam,' I said, 'I am perhaps something more than an ordinary man. A sovereign is the author of my being, but I am only a man for all that. I have much more reason to think that you are a superior being to myself.'

'No,' she replied, 'I am, like you, of the race of Adam. But tell me why you have left your father's court, and how you came to this island.'

I then satisfied her curiosity. I ingenuously admitted that I had become enamoured of Bedy-Aljemal, daughter of the king Achahbal, on seeing her portrait, which I showed her. The lady took the portrait, looked at it very attentively, and said; 'I have heard speak of the King Achahbal. He reigns in a neighbouring island to Serendib. If his daughter is as beautiful as her portrait, she indeed deserves that you should love her ardently, but one must not trust in the portraits which are taken of princesses; they are usually painted beautiful. Finish telling me your history,' she added; 'after that I will relate mine to you.'

I gave her a long and detailed account of all my adventures, and then I begged her to relate hers to me. She began thus:

'I am the only daughter of the King of Serendib. One day as I was with my women in a castle of my father's near the town of Serendib, the fancy took me to bathe in a white marble basin which was in the garden. I was undressed, and entered the basin with my favourite slave. We had hardly entered the water than a wind arose. A whirlwind of dust formed in the air above us, and from the midst of this whirlwind there suddenly flew a great bird who pounced on me, took me in his claws, carried me off and brought me to this castle, where, immediately changing its shape, it appeared before me in the form of a young genie. "Princess," he said to me, "I am one of the most considerable genii in the world. As I was passing the island of Serendib today, I saw you in your bath. You charmed me. 'There is a beautiful princess,' I said to myself, 'it would be a pity she should make the happiness of a son of Adam; she deserves the attachment of a genie. I must carry her off and transport her to a desert island.' So, princess, forget the king, your father, and think only of responding to my love. You shall want for nothing in this castle. I will take care to provide you with everything you need."

'Whilst the genie was speaking thus to me, I only wept and lamented. "Unfortunate Malika," I said to myself, "is this the fate which was reserved for you? Has the king, my father, brought me up with so much care only to have the sorrow to lose me so miserably? Alas! he does not know what has become of me, and I fear my loss will be fatal to him." "No, no," said the genie to me, "your father will not succumb to his grief; and as for you, my princess, I trust you will yield to the evidences of affection which I propose to give you." "Do not flatter yourself," I said, "with this false hope. I shall have all my life a mortal aversion to the man who has carried me off." "You will change your sentiment," he replied; "you will accustom yourself to me; time will produce this effect." "It will not work this miracle," I interrupted with bitterness, "it will rather increase the hatred that I feel for you." The genie, instead of appearing offended, smiled, and, persuaded that I should accustom myself by degrees to listen to him, he spared nothing to please me. He went, I know not where, to get magnificent clothes which he brought me. He did his best to inspire in me an inclination for him; but, perceiving that far from making any progress in my heart, he became daily more odious to me, he finally lost patience, and resolved to revenge himself for my contempt. He threw me into a magic sleep; he stretched me on the sofa in the attitude in which you have found me, and put beside me this marble table on which he had traced talismanic characters to keep me in a deep sleep through the centuries. He also made two other talismans; one to make this castle invisible, the other to prevent the door being opened. Then he left me in this apartment and quitted the castle. He returns hither from time to time. He wakes me up and asks me whether I wish at last to become sensible to his passion, and as I persist in refusing him, he plunges me anew in the unconsciousness which he has invented for my punishment.

'Nevertheless, my lord,' continued the daughter of the King of Serendib, 'you have awakened me, you have opened the door of this castle which has not remained invisible to you. Have I not reason to doubt your being a man? I will even tell you that it is surprising that you still live; for I have heard the genie say that the wild beasts devour all those who wish to stop in this island, and that it is on that account deserted.'

Whilst the princess Malika was speaking thus, we heard a great noise in the castle. She ceased speaking in order to hear better, and soon terrible cries met our ears.

'Great Heaven!' then said the princess, 'we are lost. It is the genie; I recognise him by his voice. You will perish; nothing can save you from his fury. Ah! unhappy prince; what fatality has brought you to this castle?'

I thought my death inevitable. The genie entered looking furious. He had a steel club in his hand; his body was enormous. He shuddered at the sight of me; but instead of giving me a blow on the head, or adopting a threatening tone, he approached me trembling, threw himself at my feet, and spoke thus:

'Oh! prince, son of a king, you have only to command me as you please; I am prepared to obey you.'

This speech surprised me. I could not understand why this genie was so grovelling to me, and spoke as a slave. But my surprise vanished when, continuing to speak to me, he said:

'The ring which you have on your finger is the seal of Solomon; whoever possesses it cannot perish from accident. He can cross the most stormy seas in a simple skiff without fearing that the waves will swallow him up. The most ferocious beasts cannot hurt him, and he has a sovereign power over genii. Talismans and all charms yield to his marvellous seal.'

'It is then by virtue of this ring that I still live,' I said to the genie.

'Yes, my lord,' he replied, 'it is that ring which has saved you from the beasts which are on this island.'

'Tell me,' I said to him, 'if you know what has become of the companion I had on arriving?'

'I know the present and the past,' replied the genie, 'and I will tell you that your comrade has been eaten by the ants, who devoured him at night at your side. Those sort of ants are in great numbers and make this island uninhabitable. They do not prevent, however, the neighbouring peoples, and above all the inhabitants of the Maldives, coming here every year to cut sandalwood; but they do not carry it away without difficulty; they come here during the summer; they have on board their vessels very swift horses, which they disembark, and on which they mount; they gallop in whatever direction they see sandalwood, and as soon as they see the ants approaching they throw them great pieces of meat with which they are provided for the purpose. Whilst the ants are occupied in eating these pieces of meat, the men mark the trees they wish to cut, after which they return. They come back in the winter and cut the trees without fear of the ants, who do not show themselves at this season.'

I could not hear the strange fate of Saed without feeling grieved. Then I asked the genie where the dominion of the king Achahbal was and if the princess Bedy-Aljemal his daughter still lived.

'My lord,' he replied, 'there is in these seas an island where there reigns a king named Achahbal, but he has no daughter. The princess Bedy-Aljemal of whom you speak, was indeed the daughter of a king called Achahbal, who lived in the time of Solomon.'

'What!' I replied, 'Bedy-Aljemal lives no longer?'

'No,' he replied, 'she was a wife of the great Prophet.'

I was very mortified to hear that I loved someone whose life was long over. 'Oh! madman that I am!' I cried, 'why did I not ask the sultan, my father, whose portrait it was I found in his treasury? He would have told me what I have just heard. What trouble and anxiety I should have spared myself! I should have nipped my love in the bud. It would perhaps not have gained such control over me. I should not have left Cairo; Saed would be still living. Must his death be then the sole outcome of my chimerical sentiments? All that consoles me, beautiful princess,' I continued, turning to Malika, 'is having been able to be useful to you: thanks to my ring, I am in the position to give you back to the king your father.' At the same time I addressed the genie: 'Since I am happy enough,' I said, 'to be the possessor of the seal of Solomon, since I have the right to command genii, obey me. I order you to transport me immediately with the princess Malika, to the kingdom of Serendib, to the gates of the capital.'

'I am going to obey you, my lord,' replied the genie, 'however unhappy the loss of the princess may make me.'

'It is very fortunate for you,' I replied, 'that I content myself with only exacting from you that you should bear us both to the island of Serendib; you deserve, for having carried off Malika, that I should punish you to the full extent of the power which the seal of the Prophet gives me over rebel genii.'

The genie replied nothing; he prepared immediately to do what I had ordered him: he took us in his arms, the princess and myself, and bore us to the gates of Serendib. 'Is that all,' then said the genie to me, 'that you wish me to do? Have you nothing further to command me?' I replied in the negative, and he immediately disappeared.

We went to lodge at the first caravanserai on entering the town, and there we deliberated whether we would write to the court or whether I should go myself to inform the king of the arrival of the princess. We decided on the latter course. I betook myself to the palace, which seemed to me a singular structure. It was built on a thousand columns of marble, and the ascent to it was by a staircase of three hundred steps of beautiful stone. I passed a guard in the first hall; an officer approached me, asked me whether I had any business at the court, or whether curiosity alone brought me thither. I replied that I wished to speak to the king on an important matter. The officer led me to the grand vizir, who presented me to the king, his master.

'Young man,' said the monarch to me, 'of what country are you, and what do you come to Serendib for?'

'Sire,' I replied, 'Egypt was my birth-place. I have been long absent from my father, and I have experienced all sorts of misfortunes.' Hardly had I said these words than the king, who was a kind old man, began to weep.

'Alas!' he said to me, 'I am no happier than you. I have lost my only daughter, in a manner which increases my grief at not seeing her again.'

'My lord,' I replied, 'I have come to this palace only to give you news of this princess.'

'Ah! what news,' he cried, 'can you give me of her? You have come to announce her death to me? You have doubtless been the witness of her sad end?'

'No, no,' I replied, 'she still lives, and you will see her today.'

'Ah! where have you found her?' said the king; 'where was she hidden?'

Then I related all my adventures to him. I dilated particularly on that of the castle and the genie, which he listened to with all the more attention that he was himself interested in it. As soon as I had finished he embraced me.

'Prince,' he said to me, for I had discovered my birth to him in relating my history, 'what do I not owe to you? I love my daughter dearly: I did not hope to see her again. You have been the cause of my finding her. How can I acquit myself towards you? Let us go together,' he continued; 'let us go to the caravanserai where you have left her, I am burning with impatience to embrace my dear Malika.'

Saying these words, he gave the order to his vizir to have a litter prepared, which was promptly executed.

The king then made me enter the litter with him, and followed by several officers on horseback we went to the caravanserai where Malika awaited me impatiently. No words can express the mutual joy which the King of Serendib and the princess his daughter felt on seeing each other again. After their first transport the monarch wished Malika herself to give a detailed account of her being carried off and her rescue, which she did in a way that gave him much satisfaction. He thought how happily she had preserved her life from the power of the genie, and declared that he could not carry his gratitude to her liberator too far. He seemed charmed with my bearing and my courage.

We all returned to the palace, where the king gave me a magnificent apartment. He ordered public prayers to return thanks to Heaven for the return of the princess. The inhabitants celebrated it with endless rejoicing. There was a magnificent feast at the court; all the nobility of the island were invited.

The King of Serendib showed me every attention; he took me hunting with him: I joined in all his pleasure parties. He evinced such friendship for me that he said to me one day: 'O my son, it is time to reveal to you a plan I have formed. You have brought me back my daughter. You have consoled an afflicted father. I wish to acquit myself towards you. Be my son-in-law and the inheritor of my crown.'

I thanked the king for his kindness, and begged him not to take it ill if I refused the honour he wished to do me. I told him the reasons which had compelled me to leave Cairo. I confessed to him that I could not detach myself from the image of Bedy-Aljemal, nor cease to nourish a futile passion. 'Would you,' I added, 'give your daughter to a man whose heart she cannot possess? Ah! my lord, the Princess Malika deserves a happier fate.'

'How can I,' replied the king, 'recognise the service you have done me?'

'Sire,' I replied, 'I am sufficiently rewarded for it. The reception your majesty has given me – the pleasure alone of having delivered the Princess of Serendib from the hands of the genie who had carried her off, is a sufficient reward for me. All that I ask of your gratitude is a vessel to take me to Bassora.'

The king did as I wished; he ordered a vessel to be filled with provisions and to be held ready to depart when I thought convenient. He kept me, however, some time at his court, and he told me every day that he was sorry that I did not wish to remain at Serendib. Finally the day of my departure arrived. I took leave of the king and the princess, who overwhelmed me with civilities, and I embarked.

We experienced several storms on the way, severe enough to have caused our shipwreck, but the virtue of my ring prevented our being submerged. So, after a long voyage, I arrived happily at Bassora, whence I went to grand Cairo with a caravan of Egyptian merchants.

I found many changes had taken place at the court: my father lived no more, and my brother was on the throne. The new sultan received me at first as a man sensible to the bonds which united us; he assured me he was glad to see me again; he told me that a few days after my departure, my father, being in his treasury, had opened by chance the little coffer which contained the seal of Solomon and the portrait of Bedy-Aljemal; that not seeing them he had suspected me of having taken them. I confessed everything to my brother, and placed the ring in his hands.

He seemed touched at my misfortune, and marvelled at the strangeness of my adventures; he pitied me, and I felt that his sympathy relieved my trouble. All the sensibility that he evinced was, however, only perfidy. The very day of my arrival he had me enclosed in a tower, where he sent at night an officer who had orders to take my life; but this officer had pity on me, and said: 'Prince, the sultan, your brother, has ordered me to assassinate you; he fears lest a desire to reign may possess you and incite you to make trouble in the state; he thinks your death necessary to his safety. Happily for you he has addressed himself to me, he imagines that I shall execute his barbarous order and he expects to see me return covered with your blood. Ah! rather may my hand shed my own! Escape, prince; the door of your prison is open to you, profit by the darkness of the night; leave Cairo, fly, and do not stop till you are in safety.'

After having thanked this generous officer as he deserved, I took flight, and abandoning myself to Providence, I hastened to leave my brother's states. I had the good fortune to arrive in yours, my lord, and to find a safe refuge at your court.

THE JOURNEY
TO CONSTANTINOPLE

Hans Shück

T HE EMPEROR KARL the Great was sitting under an olive tree. The queen sat by his side, and round about him stood his twelve paladins. These were the bravest and wisest men to be found in the length and breadth of the land, and they always accompanied the emperor on all his journeys and campaigns. These paladins were Archbishop Turpin, the old Duke Nemes, the emperor's nephew Roland, who was looked upon as the finest knight in France, the valiant Ogier the Dane, about whom our folk-songs still have so much to tell, his companion-in-arms the courtly Oliver, and, besides these, Bernard, Villifer, Bering, Ernald, Eimer, Bertram, and Gerin.

The emperor was blithe of heart, and said jestingly to his spouse:

'Do you know any king in the wide world who wears his crown as well as I, or one whom armour equally becomes?'

Without further thought on the matter she answered heedlessly:

'No man should so vaunt himself; for I know a king who wears a higher crown than you and who cuts a more stalwart figure in his armour.'

She had hardly uttered these words before the emperor's good humour vanished, and wrath mounted to his brow.

'Have a care,' said he, 'what you are saying, or it may cost you your life.'

'There is no cause for you to be angry. The king I mean is certainly mightier than you, and richer in lands and gold, but he is not so good a knight, nor yet so brave, as you.'

But seeing that the emperor's wrath was not yet appeased, despite her excuse, she fell upon her knees before him and besought him thus:

'Forgive me, for God's pity's sake, for you know indeed that I am your wife, and would do everything to gratify you.'

'Only tell me the name of him you meant.'

'Ah, my emperor and lord, there is no such king in the whole world. It was but my foolish tongue that wagged and ran away from my wits.'

'Do not attempt evasion. Tell me his name at once, or you will repent it.'

'Well, then, as you refuse to give me peace on any other condition, the king I mean is King Hugo of Constantinople, and no one is so rich and strong and majestic as he, save you alone.'

'Good,' answered the king. 'That we must put to the test, and if you have uttered an untruth it will cost you dear.'

Then he turned to his paladins and addressed them thus:

'You know I have long desired to fare to Jerusalem to behold the places where our Saviour lived and taught. This journey we must now undertake, and, on our way back, we shall visit King Hugo of Constantinople to see if the queen has spoken the truth. Prepare yourselves, therefore, for the journey, which I trow will be long indeed, and, as we are to appear before so illustrious a king, it behoves us to be well equipped, that we may not appear before him like beggars. Let us, therefore, take with us seven hundred camels loaded with gold and silver, but until we have left Jerusalem we must be clad as becomes humble pilgrims, bearing staves and wearing weeds.'

They repaired to the church dedicated to St Dionysius, the patron saint of all the land of France, and, in front of the high altar, solemnly assumed the Cross, whereupon Archbishop Turpin said Mass for them. When all the preparations for the journey were accomplished they mounted their steeds, and rode forth accompanied by their attendants. They took ship at Marseilles, and at length reached Jerusalem, where they found quarters.

On the morrow after their arrival they all went to the church that is called Pater Noster, wherein the Saviour Himself and His apostles had celebrated the holy rites. The church, however, was reckoned so holy that none had a right to enter it without special permission from the Patriarch of Jerusalem. Now the latter, when he heard that some had dared to disregard his orders, hastened at once to the church. The emperor, on seeing him, arose and greeted him reverently. Then the patriarch asked him who he was, adding: 'You are the first who has dared to enter this holy room without my leave.'

'I am Karl the Great, emperor of that land which is called France, and these are my paladins. We have come hither to visit the Holy Sepulchre; we knew nothing about your prohibition, and it was not our intention to show you any discourtesy.'

'Nor do I believe it either, now that I know who you are. I have long heard talk about the mighty emperor Karl the Great, for the fame of his valour and that of his paladins is spread throughout the whole world. Welcome to Jerusalem and the Holy Sepulchre, which has no nobler protector than yourself, before whose sword the Infidels have so long trembled.'

The patriarch then brought out the most precious relics that were to be found, and presented them as a gift to the emperor, who accepted them with thanks and had them preserved in a magnificent gold shrine which he handed over to the care of Archbishop Turpin, and, directly they had performed their devotions once more in the church of Pater Noster, they started for Constantinople, accompanied by the patriarch's good wishes.

When they got within three miles of the town their path led through a splendid garden full of all sorts of wonderful trees and flowers, the like of which they had never beheld before. They saw in the garden thousands of knights clad in purple and ermine, and also as many damsels, each fairer than the other, disporting together, some playing chess and draughts, others amusing themselves with round dances, holding one another all the time by the hand. Now when Karl saw all this magnificence and all that crowd of courtiers, surpassing everything to which he had been accustomed, he had at once a feeling that his queen had not perhaps been altogether wrong when she described this court as the finest in the world; but if he could not rival the mighty King Hugo in riches, still he thought he might, nevertheless, do so in other respects. He, therefore,

turned to a knight and asked him where the latter's king was
to be found.

'Our king,' answered he, 'you will find down there where
they are carrying the purple canopy that you see.'

Karl the Great immediately went there, and saw beneath
the costly canopy a man sitting in a golden chariot, holding
in his hand a rod likewise of gold, wherewith he goaded the
oxen that drew his chariot, and to this chariot was attached a
golden plough wherewith he ploughed. The emperor saluted
him courteously, but at first he only got a careless nod in return.
When the king, however, saw that the stranger was a man of
birth he stopped and asked him who he was.

'I am Karl the Great, king of France and emperor of Rome.
I have just been to Jerusalem and visited the Holy Sepulchre,
and I have now come hither to meet you.'

'Welcome. For many years past I have heard talk of you and
praise of your valour; so it is, therefore, a great honour to me
that you desired to pay me a visit, and I hope you will be in no
haste to leave me. I will unyoke my oxen, and, that done, follow
you to the castle, where I trust you will take up your quarters
and treat it as if it were your own.'

'But is not someone going to take charge of that costly
plough?' asked Karl. 'I am afraid it will be stolen if you leave
it behind in that way.'

'It appears,' said King Hugo, with a smile, 'that customs
are different in our country. Thank God, justice is so well
administered in my land that were I to leave this golden plough
lying on the highway for seven years not a soul would dream
of venturing to steal it; and even if that did happen, I should,
fortunately, be able to bear the loss.'

Karl, whose pride had, for the second time, received a
certain humiliation, accompanied King Hugo to the castle, which the latter pointed out to him as his abode in
Constantinople. Immediately on their arrival twelve hundred
knights approached, took their horses, and followed the guests
into the huge banqueting-hall, which occupied the middle of
the building. This hall, which was the most spacious Karl had
ever seen, was perfectly round; and a lofty dome, adorned with
paintings of exceeding splendour, was thrown across it. This
dome was supported by a massive pillar, which shot up from the

centre of the hall, and around it rose a forest of smaller pillars, which did not serve the purpose of props, but merely supported magnificent statues of gold, silver, bronze and marble. These statues, which represented children at play, stretching out their hands to one another, were so well executed that they looked like living creatures, and all of them had horns at their mouths, whereon they were blowing. The emperor marvelled exceedingly at all this, and began to realise more vividly that the queen was right in what she had said. Soon he had further reason to be still more astounded.

The pillars were hollow, and the wind from outside played into them and came out of the horns borne by the statues, and these gave forth musical notes which sounded like the loveliest minstrelsy. The wind, however, rose and increased to a storm, and then it began to make such a din in the hall that the noise was as the noise of a mill, and with the increasing violence of the wind, the floor likewise began to whirl round like the wheel of a mill, and the gusts grew so violent at last that the Franks had some difficulty in keeping on their feet. They thought that their last hour had come, and tried in vain to open the door in order to rush out of this perilous abode; but at that moment King Hugo entered and smilingly requested them not to be alarmed at such a thing, which was really a matter of no importance to men so brave as they.

'The storm,' said he, 'will most likely subside towards evening,' and he had hardly uttered these words before it grew calm and still once more. The Franks were therefore ashamed of their terror, and no longer looked as if they wished to leave the quarters the king had assigned them.

On a signal from the king a table was now brought in groaning beneath the weight of the most toothsome dishes – venison, wild boars, geese, peacocks, and all sorts of game; and between the baked meats there stood drinking-horns filled with mead, bastard, red wine, and other good drinks. Minstrels entered and played at the same time, and bassoons, fiddles, harps, and other stringed instruments made music while the guests took their seats at table. King Hugo sat in the seat of honour, on his right hand the emperor Karl the Great, and on his left his queen and her daughter, the fairest damsel you could see, with a complexion of roses and lilies.

Many were the glances which the knights in the emperor's retinue cast across the table at the young princess; but she seemed used to such homage on the part of men, and paid no heed to the admiration she excited.

At last the emperor Karl the Great turned to the king and exclaimed: 'How comes it that your daughter, who has already reached the age for marriage, has not chosen herself a husband? With us young maids tarry not so long, and your daughter's beauty makes me believe that she has not lacked suitors.'

'I have never sought to constrain her, but have left her free choice. I have perhaps done wrong, for she has now made up her mind only to accept the prince whose wisdom is on a par with his valour. To every suitor who has come to woo, she has, with this purpose, proposed three riddles which he must resolve if he would win her hand. Besides this, as he must set his head for wager, you can understand that not many have had the courage to make the attempt, and those who were brave enough to do so have paid with their lives the penalty of their rashness. I am sorry, for her sake and for theirs, that it should be so, but as I have given my word, the thing cannot be altered.'

'If such be the state of affairs, then I do not think my paladins can cherish any hopes, for Archbishop Turpin, as a priest, may not marry, Duke Nemes is too old to think of love, and the rest of them have during their lives devoted themselves rather to wielding their swords than to guessing riddles. They would assuredly be worsted at the outset in a task like that, and so we must not indulge in the hope of ever seeing the princess in our fair France. The night, however, is far spent, and we have abused your hospitality too long.'

On a sign from the king the tables were removed, and then he took the emperor by the hand, and led him and his paladins into another hall that was to serve as their bedchamber. This hall was also vaulted, and on the top of the dome there gleamed a carbuncle which blazed as brightly by night as by day. Twelve costly beds of bronze stood in the hall, but the thirteenth, which was in the middle, was wrought of gold. When King Hugo had bidden them take their rest after the fatigues of their journey, he wished them good-night and then withdrew.

Now, in the centre of this hall there was a cunning pillar of stone that supported the dome. This pillar was likewise hollow, and in it King Hugo had concealed a spy who was afterwards to relate to him the conversation of the strangers when they were by themselves. The emperor and his friends, however, went to bed, but as the mirth engendered of the banquet had not yet departed, they found it hard to go to sleep at once, but began instead to talk to each other. They talked about all the marvellous things they had seen, and how far these had surpassed what they had dreamt of in France. When they had got more and more awake through talking, the emperor proposed that they should begin a game which was a great favourite with Frankish knights – to wit, every one was to mention by way of jest some remarkable feat he meant to perform, the object being to hit upon the most improbable and astonishing deed there could be. The emperor himself began.

'Let King Hugo,' said he, 'pit against me the doughtiest knight he has, and clothe him with two coats of steel. Let him, moreover, place four helmets on his head, and give him his strongest horse, which may, if he choose, have a triple covering of mail; yet I will give this knight such a blow that both he and his horse shall be cloven into two equal parts, and my sword shall penetrate a spear's length into the ground.'

Then Roland said: 'Let the king give me his horn Oliphant, and I will go some way off from the castle, and blow so deep a blast on the horn that all the doors of the castle shall fly off their hinges, and if the king himself shall venture to look out, I will blow his hair and beard and clothes off him.'

Then it came to Villifer's turn.

'You have seen,' said he, 'a ball lying out in the courtyard, which is wrought of gold and silver. It is so heavy and big that thirty men are not strong enough to move it from its place. Tomorrow I shall take this ball, lift it with one hand, and hurl it against the castle so that 500 feet of wall at the very least shall crack and tumble down.'

'Well,' said Ogier the Dane, 'I shall do far more injury to King Hugo's castle. You remember the great pillar that stood in the middle of the banqueting-hall. Early tomorrow I shall seize it with my arms and shake it till the whole house comes rattling down.'

'That is mere child's play to what I think of doing,' said the old Duke Nemes. 'Let King Hugo give me four coats of ring-armour, the heaviest to be found in his kingdom. I will put these on and then jump 500 feet higher than the highest towers of the castle, and, when I come down to the ground again, I shall shake myself and all the rings in the armour shall jump out one after the other, and fall to the ground like burnt straw.'

'That should be a very pleasant sight to see,' rejoined Bering, 'but the feat I intend performing is harder still. I shall ask King Hugo to collect all the swords there are here, and stick them in the courtyard with their points upwards and their hilts buried in the ground. When the whole courtyard has been covered in this manner with sword points, I shall walk up to the highest tower and throw myself down, so that the sword-points shall be broken and the blades snap asunder, yet I myself shall be unscathed.'

After this came the turn of Archbishop Turpin, who spoke thus:

'Tomorrow I shall go to the river that flows some way out of the town, divert it from its course, and make it pour all over Constantinople till every house is filled with water. The king himself shall be so frightened that he will flee to his highest tower, and will not venture to come down until I let him.'

'Now, listen,' said Ernald, 'to what I mean to do. I think of asking King Hugo for four loads of lead. When this has been boiled till it melts I shall pour it into a cauldron, and I myself shall go down and sit in it till the lead gets hard again. I shall next shake myself till the lead falls off me and not a single drop remains on my body. Now, beat this who can.'

'I consider myself capable of a more difficult feat even than that,' said Eimer. 'I have a hat, and when I put it on my head I am invisible to everyone. I shall put that on tomorrow when King Hugo has sat down to table. I shall go up to him, eat up his meat and drink up his wine without his perceiving who it is that is playing him that trick. Finally, I shall go behind him and give him a push that will send him falling head foremost on the table. As he will not see who has given him the blow, I shall act in such a manner that he and his knights shall come to blows with one another, and tear and rend each other's beards.'

'As for me,' said Bertram, 'I shall go into the forest to-morrow, and shriek so loud that it shall be heard a hundred miles off. Yes, I shall roar in such a way that the beasts in the forest shall be terrified and flee away, and the fishes in the river jump out of the water in their fright.'

'Now,' said Gerin, 'it is my turn to tell what I intend to do. If the king will give me a spear that weighs a man's weight and the point of which is an ell long, and will then place a couple of small coins, one on the top of the other, on the summit of the tower, I will go three miles hence, hurl the spear and hit one of the coins so that it falls pierced to the ground without the other being displaced in the least. And I shall run back so fast that I shall catch the spear before it has come through the air to the ground.'

'That is something like fleetness,' said Bernard, 'but I fancy I am as quick and nimble as yourself. Tomorrow, if the king will take three of the fastest horses he owns and will drive them in the wildest way, I will run up to them, jump over the first two, and stand on the third; and, in quicker time than it takes to make a single step, I shall take up four apples from the ground, and if I miss a single one of them may the king take my head.'

Now Oliver was the only one who had said nothing as yet of the marvellous things he meant to accomplish, and, when at length he was asked how he thought of rivalling the rest, he answered:

'You have all promised to perform marvels of bodily strength and agility, but we have trained ourselves to such exercises and are to some extent accustomed to them. I shall, on the other hand, attempt something new, and therefore mean to try tomorrow to solve the princess's three riddles. She will either be mine or King Hugo may take my head.'

After he had said this, they began to talk and dispute as to which of them had composed the most extraordinary story; but sleep at last claimed its rights, and they went to sleep. As soon as the hall was hushed to silence, the terrified spy crept back to King Hugo and told him what appalling promises the strangers had made.

'I have never heard the like in impudence,' said he, 'and they have spent the whole night in scoffing and mocking at you.'

King Hugo was exceedingly wroth when he had heard the spy's account of their conversation, and said to him:

'I acted like a madman when I received the emperor with so

many marks of respect, and sneers and ridicule have been my sole reward; but I shall punish these braggarts as they deserve, and if they cannot perform all the labours they have said they would do it shall cost them their lives.'

Then the king had ten thousand knights summoned in haste, and these presented themselves at the castle on the following day to succour their lord in case of need. Meanwhile the emperor Karl the Great and his paladins awoke, got out of their beds, and went to Mass without any presentiment of evil, or further thought of the jesting of the previous night. As they came out of church King Hugo met them, and addressed them in severe language.

'I am aware,' said he, 'that you have spent your night in mocking me, and have repaid with insults the hospitality I showed you; but now it is my turn to speak and tell you of the wonderful things I intend doing. If there is one of you who cannot perform what he asserted he could last night, I mean to have his head, and however intrepid you may say you are, you will hardly, I fancy, be strong enough to withstand the ten thousand knights I have gathered around me.'

When the emperor heard these words he became utterly shamefaced, and for a long time did not know what reply to make. At last he exclaimed:

'When we went to bed last night we were joyous and mirthful, thanks to the wine you gave us in such abundance, and, perhaps in consequence of that, we chattered nonsense; but we did not think of insulting you. You must know that it is customary with us Frankish knights, before going to sleep after a banquet, to vie with one another in such extravagances; and we never thought of engaging in such impossible undertakings as those we were talking about, or of intending by such talk to offend you. But you did not act aright in spying on us when we were alone. I do not say this as a reproach: the one rebuke may outweigh the other, and, on these grounds, I beseech you to let these trifles be forgotten.'

'You cannot smooth over your sneers at me so easily,' replied King Hugo, 'and it shall be as I have said – either you perform the exploits you promised or else I shall cut off your heads. In the course of an hour we shall meet again, and then you are to begin your experiments.'

With these words he left Karl and his paladins. For a long time they stood silent without daring to raise their eyes from the ground, so ashamed were they of their boasting. As brave men I do not suppose they feared death, but they blushed at being compelled to forfeit their lives for such a paltry reason. At last the emperor said:

'We have been foolish, and we must now pay the penalty of our foolishness. I have vaunted myself over others and did not deem that any one could be my peer, and it is, therefore, no more than just that the Lord should now humiliate me and punish my pride. Let us, then, bear our fate without cowardly shrinking, and show that we can at least die like men, even if we have lived like fools. An hour yet remains to us before our heads must fall by the sword. Let us use this time to pray in church for forgiveness of our sins.'

With these words he went back to the church he had just left, and his paladins followed him solemnly and silently. After Archbishop Turpin had celebrated Mass, and each of them had confessed his sins and prayed for forgiveness of them, they arose from their knees, fully resolved on meeting their approaching fate with courage. But at that very instant an angel appeared to them and said:

'The Lord has heard your prayer and will succour you. You have been mad and rash in having trusted to your own strength, and forgotten that you have merely been instruments of the Lord's will. Let the humiliation which has now befallen you serve as a lesson, and do not vaunt yourselves hereafter over your peers. If you will do this, then the Lord will be satisfied, and will not exact the uttermost penalty. So meet King Hugo without apprehension, and I will stand at your side and perform for you all the exploits you have promised to do. Go, therefore, and henceforward sin no more.'

When they heard these comforting words their sorrow vanished straightway. With joyous mien they walked up to King Hugo again and said:

'Once more we beseech you to be assured that we were only jesting and did not in the least degree intend to flout you, for whose hospitality we are deeply indebted; but, since you insist on claiming the fulfilment of the promises we made in jest, we are now prepared, with God's help, to perform the exploits we spoke of; but you yourself must name the person who is to begin.'

'Good,' replied the king; 'we shall begin with the least dangerous, so let Oliver come forward and resolve the riddles my daughter shall propose to him.'

Oliver drew near the throne on which the princess had taken her seat. All the court was assembled around the throne, and the princess began:

'Tell me what the name of that tree is under which race after race sprouts up and withers away. It dies perpetually, but perpetually grows anew. One side turns itself towards the light, but the other is as black as night, and is not touched by the sun's rays. As it grows it plants new rings, and by these rings one can mark the flight of time.'

'The riddle, noble princess,' replied Oliver, 'is easy to guess. The tree is *the year*.'

'Correctly guessed,' said the princess, slightly changing colour. 'My next riddle will therefore be harder. Tell me, now, what kind of picture it is which continually grows and gives fresh images. Its frame is the smallest, yet this picture embraces more than any other. It is more precious than any stone of price; it gives light of itself, yet does not burn. All the great and beautiful world is depicted in it, but the image is often more lovely than the reality.'

'I can solve even that riddle. The picture you mean is *the human eye*, and when I gaze into your eyes methinks the image of the object therein reflected is fairer than the thing itself.'

'Well, solve me the last riddle, then. Name me the implement that is most often despised, but which, nevertheless, becomes even an emperor. It is made to wound, and though it inflicts wounds by thousands, blood does not flow from them. It impoverishes no one, but enriches many a man; it has laid the foundation of the highest sovereignty on earth, and yet has never been employed in war.'

'That implement I should certainly have found difficulty in naming if it had not been the first thing I beheld when I came hither to your father's kingdom, and I saw him with my own eyes ploughing with a golden plough; the implement you mean is *the plough*, is it not so, princess?'

'It is so, and you have saved your head. But do not rejoice

prematurely, for there remain twelve other feats for you to accomplish, and those ought to be harder than this.'

'We have once expressed our willingness to do what we promised,' said the emperor. 'Oliver has kept his promise, and not only saved his own life, but even won the hand of the princess. We will not, however, base any claim on that reward for him, so name only one of us whose strength you wish to test.'

'Well, then,' replied King Hugo, 'let Villifer take the golden ball which lies in this courtyard, and if he is not able to lift it and throw it as he boasted last night, his life and the lives of his companions will be forfeited.'

But Villifer only smiled, being certain that the angel would help him as it had already helped his friend Oliver, whereupon he went up to the huge globe and lifted it with one hand as if it had been a glove, and hurled it against the castle wall, so that the whole edifice tottered, and a rent ten times larger than that which he had promised appeared.

When King Hugo saw this exhibition of strength he was not, as you can well understand, happy in his mind. His beautiful castle was ruined, and he began to fear that these strangers could do more than he had imagined they could. He would not, however, yield yet, but summoned Archbishop Turpin, and called on him to carry out what he had promised.

'As you please,' answered the archbishop. 'With God's help I think the river will rise.'

Then he went down to the shore, fell upon his knees, and besought help from heaven; then he arose, stretched forth his hand, and blessed the water. Then a great miracle took place, for the river began to bubble, and gradually rose out of its channel, making its way over fields and meadows, and rushed at a mighty speed towards the chief city, and there it soon filled all the streets and houses, to the intense alarm of all the inhabitants. King Hugo himself quite lost his presence of mind, and fled for safety to the loftiest tower in his castle. On looking down he saw Karl and his paladins standing under an olive tree which the water had not yet reached, and he called on them piteously to help him.

'Is it your intention,' he cried to Karl the Great, 'to drown me utterly in this flood? If you will save me I promise henceforward to be your vassal and pay you tribute, and you may demand what treasures you will if you will but remove this plague from me.'

'Yes,' answered the emperor, 'I like to show mercy to all who ask it, and I will willingly do what I can for you.'

At the prayer of Karl and Turpin the water withdrew from the town and subsided, after a time, into its old channel. When the ground became dry King Hugo came down from his tower and went up to the tree under which Karl the Great was standing, and said:

'I have now discovered that you are dear to God, and that He is with you in all things. I do not blush, therefore, to do you homage, as my emperor and overlord, in the presence of your knights and mine. I am your vassal, and my kingdom is yours.'

'But,' said Karl with a smile, 'there still remain no less than ten feats for us to accomplish.'

'For God's sake,' exclaimed King Hugo, 'say no more about them. I have had quite enough, and have no wish to make further proof of your strength. If you were to keep on in the same way as you have begun, before night-time I should have lost both my crown and my life.'

'Just so,' answered Karl; 'neither should I like our promises that were made in jest to have grave consequences. Let all be forgotten, and suffer us to go to church instead, to thank God, who has taken compassion on our foolishness, and directed all for the best. In one respect only do I wish to take advantage of the victory we have won, and that is on behalf of my poor Oliver. He has honourably obtained your daughter's hand, and it seems to me that it would not be fair to withhold it any longer. You will have no cause to regret this choice, for a braver and more honourable knight does not live.'

'Let it be done according to your wish.'

Then they all assembled and went to church in a solemn procession, at the head of which walked Karl the Great, and after him, among his other vassals, followed King Hugo. Karl was quite a head taller than King Hugo, and, moreover, wore his crown more majestically. The Franks in the church whispered among themselves: 'Our queen was wrong when she thought there was any king in the whole world to be compared with our emperor, and we never shall come to a country where we shall see his like.'

When they reached church Archbishop Turpin said Mass, thanked God for His goodness, and ended by placing the hand of the princess in Oliver's, after which he pronounced a blessing over them both, and made them man and wife.

A lordly marriage feast awaited them as they came out of church. The cakes offered were of the very rarest, and wine flowed in torrents. During the banquet King Hugo arose and said:

'Let every Frank take of my treasures what he wishes, and carry it to his own land.'

But Karl replied:

'Not a farthing will we take of you, who have shown us right royal hospitality, which we are loth to abuse. We thank you for all the kindness you have shown us, and will withdraw to our own land once more.'

On saying this, Karl and his paladins arose from table, took their leave, and prepared for their journey. And when Karl was about to mount his horse, the king of Constantinople bowed, and held the stirrups for the Frankish emperor.

Whereupon they made their way back to France.

HUON'S QUEST

A. R. Hope-Moncrieff

I

A CHRISTIAN KNIGHT had lost his way in the glades of a Syrian forest. For three days he wandered at a venture without meeting any man, and finding no food but berries and wild honey. On the third day the blows of an axe guided him to a clearing, where he saw a tall figure, half-naked, but almost covered with grizzled hair. So uncouth seemed he, and so sturdily he swung his axe, that the knight's first thought was to rein in his steed and lay hand to his sword. For a time they looked hard upon each other; then suddenly the wild man flung down his axe, and rushed forward to throw himself on his knees, exclaiming:

'Sir Huon of Bordeaux, my good lord!'

'Who art thou?' cried the knight, amazed to hear himself called by name, and his native tongue in this paynim land.

'Who but Geraume, brother of the Mayor of Bordeaux!'

'The most faithful vassal of my father's house! But how comes a Christian here?'

'Years ago, fighting by your good father's side, I was made slave to the Saracens, who in vain sought to turn me from the true faith, till after many sufferings at their hands I broke my chains and escaped to the wilderness. Here I have since lived as a hermit, little hoping ever again to see a kindly face. But say, my lord, what brings a knight of France so far from home?'

'That were a long tale for a hungry mouth,' said Huon; whereon Geraume led him to his hut hard by, and set before him such poor fare as he had to offer.

When refreshed, the knight told at length how he had fallen

under the displeasure of Charlemagne, his sovereign lord. In defence of his own brother he had slain Charlot, the king's spiteful son. In vain he knelt at the father's knees, imploring pardon for a chance blow in a quarrel forced upon him. When Charlot's body was brought in, Charlemagne grew so furious that he would have slain Huon forthwith, had not the twelve peers joined to denounce his injustice. In the end the angry king was moved to spare his life, but only on condition of his undertaking a desperate enterprise. He must go alone to the city of Babylon, where reigned the Emir Gaudisse, from whom Charlemagne had already demanded homage by fifteen messengers, one after another, but not one of them had come back. There, sword in hand, he must haughtily call on the emir to pay tribute, and, as proof of obedience, take from him certain tokens, without which Huon durst not return to France.

'You are sending him to his death!' the peers had cried with one voice; and Charlot's wrathful father did not say them nay.

Learning thus on what a perilous errand the knight was bound, Geraume asked no better than to accompany him as guide and squire; and Huon gladly consented, since the country was as strange to him as its speech. Two ways led to Babylon, the old man told him: the one, safe and easy, making a year's journey; the other much shorter, but full of perils. The bold knight did not hesitate to choose the latter, though Geraume warned him that it led at once through an enchanted forest, haunt of Oberon, the fairy king, who had power to turn them both into monstrous beasts.

'His enchantments have no power over me,' quoth Huon, 'for I come newly from Rome, armed with the blessing of the Holy Father.'

They set out, then, and at nightfall found the forest growing thicker and darker about them, where strange shapes of beasts and birds flitted across their way. A storm of wind and thunder broke out, roaring through the fearsome shades, lit up by flashes of lightning. All at once Huon's horse started aside, rearing in terror, as there glided forth an unearthly figure, a young child in stature, but wrinkled and grey with age, magnificently attired in a jewelled robe that shone like daylight, and round his neck was hung an ivory horn.

'The saints defend us! 'Tis Oberon!' whispered Geraume, and seized his master's bridle to drag him back; but Huon, making the sign of the cross, looked steadfastly on the fairy prince.

'Nay, Sir Huon of Bordeaux, fear me not,' spoke the dwarf in mild and benevolent tones, as if reading his thoughts.

'Thou knowest me, then?'

'And wish thee well! In me see one that, unknown to thee, has watched over thy welfare from the cradle. Now am I here to aid thee in the perilous enterprise on which thou art bound. Trust me; dismount; and my goodwill shall be proved.'

For a moment the knight hesitated; then he leaped from his steed. Oberon waved his wand. Instantly the darkness became dazzling light, and with the sound of entrancing music there sprang up around them, like vapour, such a magnificent palace as no king in Christendom could boast. One moment Sir Huon stood on the ground damp with rain, where the storm wind roared above his head among dripping branches, the next he found himself in a lofty hall, where the walls were of glittering crystal and the pillars of gold, and the roof was starred with gems of every hue. On a carpet of blooming flowers stood a table loaded with sumptuous dishes, at the head of which Oberon sat on a golden throne. The knight's horse was led away, as if by spirits of the air; unseen hands held before him a jewelled basin of perfumed water; the same invisible attendants relieved him of his armour, throwing around him a robe of embroidered silk. Then, before he had fully recovered from his amazement, the enchanter motioned him to a seat by his side, and the invisible hands served them with meat and drink. The guest at that banquet had only to form a wish, then it seemed that a spirit stood beside him who knew and obeyed his slightest thought. Oberon did not eat, but while Huon satisfied his appetite, he pledged him in a cup of wine, and spoke thus:

'I have vowed friendship and protection to thy house; nothing that concerns them is hid from me. I know the purpose of this journey and the charge laid upon thee. For slaying the king's son in a chance fray, a good knight is doomed to do penance after strange fashion. He must ride alone to the palace of Gaudisse, the Emir of Babylon, and present himself in the hall while that miscreant shall be sitting at meat among his vassals and friends. Before speaking a word, he must cut off the head of whomever he finds sitting at the emir's right hand, must then kiss his fair daughter Esclarmonde thrice, and must take from Gaudisse a handful of his beard and four of his great teeth. Having further made the emir swear to be tributary to the crown of France, he is to return with these trophies, or expect no welcome but a shameful death. Say I not truly, and art not thou this luckless knight?'

'Marvellous sage, it is even as thou hast said!' replied Huon. 'All this am I bound to do, who would liefer die by Saracen swords than on the gallows!'

'Fear not, Huon, thou shalt not die, if thou art a worthy son of my friend thy father, and wilt but accept my aid and obey my directions.'

'Noble Oberon, I will obey thee in all things,' vowed Huon, as with a benignant smile the enchanter placed in his hands a crystal goblet and an ivory horn.

'Take these gifts, and learn their value. The goblet will, at the wish of any good man, fill with meat or drink; while in the hands of the treacherous and base it remains for ever empty. When assailed by numbers, let this horn be thy defence. Sound it softly if the danger be slight, and watch what befalls; but in utmost need blow loudly, and I myself will appear with all the host of fairyland. Yet, remember, these charms serve only him whose heart is true and his honour pure; no summons from the coward or the liar will reach my ear.'

'May I never prove unworthy of thy protection!'

'Beware, also, of rashness. I foresee too surely that the hot blood of youth will carry thee into perils where my aid may be of no avail. Above all, take heed to shun the tower of Angoulafre, the ruthless giant of whom all these countries are in dread. His enchantments are even stronger than mine, and he can be slain only by him who wears a coat of magic mail stolen from me years ago.'

'Show me the way to that tower!' was Huon's eager reply.

'Said I not well? Thy imprudence is too strong for good counsel.'

'Nay, friendly enchanter, the imprudence is thine, to let me know this danger that may be sought and overcome. If I am destined to leave my bones in the tower of Angoulafre, so be it; but it shall never be said that Huon heard of a perilous achievement and passed it by.'

'Thy task is already a full hard one,' said Oberon, and sighed to think of the misfortunes that might yet lie before this gallant knight.

But now the morning began to break, when at the first beam of the rising sun the enchanted palace vanished away like a dream, and Huon found himself again in the heart of the forest. The fairy prince conducted him to the verge of it, and gave directions as to the way he must now follow. Then, earnestly repeating his injunctions, he took leave of him with all good wishes.

II

FOR SEVERAL DAYS the bold knight and his squire travelled over a barren desert, where they might have starved but for the magic goblet that never failed to fill in Huon's hands, furnishing them with whatever meat or drink they desired; while they met no enemy on whom to test the virtue of Oberon's horn.

At last they came upon a richer country, where the road led them to a Saracen city named Tormont. At the gate, Geraume begged his master not to enter it; and when the knight laughed his fear to scorn, he added:

'Know that the lord of this paynim stronghold is no other than thine own uncle.'

'My uncle – lord among the unbelievers!' exclaimed Huon in astonishment.

'Even so, to the shame and sorrow of all his kin. Carried away captive by pirates, Sir Eudes, thy father's brother, was sold to the Emir of Babylon; then to save his life, he denied the Cross and turned infidel. Thus he gained that master's favour, who married him to his own niece and made him ruler of this city. Now he hates the Christians, so that he hangs or imprisons all who fall into his hands.'

'It is my duty to visit so heartless a renegade!' declared Huon. 'Before one of his own blood he cannot but blush for the cowardice that made him deny his father's faith.'

'Alas! you know him not. Hardened by debauchery and power, he is past repentance, and will answer such reproaches by a cruel death.'

But Huon was not to be moved from his purpose. He entered the city and took lodging at an inn, where he called together all the poor to entertain them by meat and drink out of his magic cup. The news of such liberality soon came to the ears of Eudes, and he sent to summon the knight to his palace.

That renegade's surprise was not less than his displeasure to find in this stranger his own nephew. Yet he feigned to meet him with joy, while secretly plotting to rid himself of so unwelcome a visitor. Huon, for his part, burned with indignation to see Eudes wearing a green turban crowned by a crescent of gems. It was all he could do to bridle his tongue, awaiting a favourable moment for denouncing the uncle's apostasy. But he, as if divining the nephew's mind, cunningly avoided being alone with him. The whole morning they spent among the train of courtiers and attendants in examining the palace and its gardens, till the hour of dinner sounded and the sultan gave Huon his hand to lead to the hall. Now the young man could no longer restrain his impatience.

'Oh, my uncle!' he whispered in his ear; 'oh, prince, brother of my father, in what a hateful disguise have I the grief and shame to find thee!'

Eudes secretly gnashed his teeth; but he pretended to be moved by this reproach; he gently pressed his kinsman's hand, and replied in the same tone:

'Silence for the present, dear nephew! Tomorrow morning I will explain all.'

Huon, deceived by his uncle's air, calmed himself and sat down by his side with a lighter heart. The muftis, the cadis, and the other officers of the court took their places; there were also some dervishes present, upon whom, like a good Catholic, our knight looked with the greatest contempt and abhorrence. As for Geraume, he remained without, and kept a watchful eye on what was doing in the palace. He began to suspect treachery, and his suspicions were increased when he saw armed men mustering about the hall. But before he could warn his master, what he dreaded had already come about.

At first Huon addressed himself to do honour to the feast, eating with the appetite of youth and a good conscience. All kinds of rich meats were served to him, but, according to the law of the Prophet, no wine appeared on the table. So, after a time, he drew from his bosom the magic goblet, which, at his wish, was at once filled with red and sparkling wine. At this sight the Saracens frowned and stroked their beards, but, feigning not to observe these signs of displeasure, he courteously handed the cup to Eudes, saying:

'Dear uncle, pledge me in this goblet. It is excellent wine of your own native province, and will remind you of your mother's milk.'

Eudes often drank the juice of the grape in secret, though before others he made pretence of abhorring it. Not for long had he tasted the good wine for which his birthplace was famed; the very name of it made his mouth water; surely for once he might transgress the law: so, forgetting what watchful eyes were upon him, he stretched out his hand towards the crystal goblet in which the liquor glowed like a heap of rubies. He felt a thrill of delight as he already thought to taste the delicious flavour, when lo! the cup was empty at his lips, the contents disappearing as if by enchantment. Huon could not restrain a laugh at his confusion and disappointment, yet he drew back from the uncle whose falsity was thus revealed.

'Insolent!' cried Eudes, as soon as surprise allowed him to speak. 'Do you dare to mock me in the midst of my court? Ho! without there!'

And he hurled the goblet at Huon, who, catching it in his hand, replied by tearing the sultan's jewelled turban from his head, and trampling it on the floor. The cadis, agas, dervishes, and muftis rose from the table, uttering cries of horror at this insult. At the same moment the doors of the hall were flung open on every side, and a crowd of soldiers and eunuchs, armed to the teeth, rushed in, running upon the young knight in such haste that the foremost of them tripped and fell in a struggling heap before him.

This gave Huon a moment's respite. He stepped back while his assailants were picking themselves up, and did not even take the trouble to draw his sword, but brought out the ivory horn of Oberon, on which he began to blow gently. Immediately the effects were seen. At the first soft and melodious notes every Saracen stood upright, then fell a-trembling in all his limbs, and, as the sound continued, had, willy-nilly, to break into a dance. The music of the horn was heard over all the palace, and each note thrilled through every limb. The dervishes whirled themselves into the middle of the hall; the eunuchs gambolled like kids; their weapons dropped from the hands of the soldiers, staggering as if they were drunk; the grave muftis and cadis flung their turbans on the floor, and spun round among the crowd; even their lord himself, after stamping and wriggling in a vain effort to keep his dignity, was forced to caper with the rest; and soon all the assembly was one wild reel.

Standing at the head of the hall, Huon blew faster and faster, and the dancers were hurried round and round with more and more vehemence. Howling, leaping, tumbling, tottering, skipping, tripping over their long garments, panting, perspiring, frantically clinging to chairs and tables, and even to each other's beards, dashing their heads against the walls, kicking their slippers up to the ceiling, raging, crying, entreating, struggling, they whirled on, and kept up the dance till they could neither stand nor speak, but still their limbs must jerk, like a child's toy, of which the enchanter did not cease to pull the string. At last Huon had pity on this wretched rout. He suddenly took the horn from his lips, then in one moment every Saracen fell flat on the ground, breathless and exhausted.

Seeing that they were no longer able to do him harm, the knight made his way through the piles of helpless bodies, and sought out the inn, where his prudent squire was already saddling their horses for immediate departure.

III

BEFORE ONE OF the Saracens had recovered strength to move hand or foot, Huon and Geraume left the city and took the road to Babylon. Again they journeyed on without meeting any hindrance, till they arrived upon a plain in the midst of which a huge tower reared itself, losing its battlements in the clouds.

'It is the tower of Angoulafre!' cried Huon.

'Do not approach it!' begged Geraume, not so eager for adventures as his master. 'Call to mind the warnings of Oberon. Back, if you love your life!'

But the knight feigned not to hear his squire's advice. He was determined at any cost to visit this appallingly mysterious tower.

As they drew nearer, they perceived that the wall was pierced here and there with deep windows that resembled human eyes, but through which no human being could be seen. All without and within was dark, silent, and threatening. Round the whole pile ran a wide, deep ditch, crossed by a drawbridge but three feet wide, leading to a gate even narrower. The gate was defended by two tall brazen statues, that whirled round long flails of the same metal, like the arms of a windmill; so broad were these flails and so rapid was their motion, that not even a bird could pass between them without being crushed to pieces.

The more he saw of this fearsome place, the more Geraume urged his master to hold back from it. But Huon was only tempted on by these desperate obstacles. At a little distance from the tower he dismounted, bade his companion remain with the horses, and advanced alone and on foot towards the entrance, where hung a great basin of brass, as large as a shield. He struck it with the hilt of his sword, and the brass gave forth a deep, dreadful clang, echoed throughout the tower.

'Now we shall see who lives here,' said Huon to himself; and a sorrowful cry made him turn his eyes upwards to the loophole above the gate, through which he caught a glimpse of the face of a young and beautiful lady. Before a minute had passed, the whirling arms of the statues suddenly ceased their motion, and the lady appeared at the wicket.

'Rash man, what do you here?' she cried, all pale and shuddering, as Huon ran lightly across the drawbridge. 'You are but hastening upon your death.'

'Nay; what harm can await me in the abode of such a fair one?' said Huon gallantly.

'Alas,' replied she, casting looks of compassion upon him, 'it is not me ye have to fear, but the cruel tyrant that holds me as his prisoner!'

'The giant Angoulafre?'

'No other. At this moment, happily for you, he sleeps. Had he awakened, you were surely lost! When I heard the noise you made, I gave you up for lost; then, perceiving the cross which adorns your shield, I judged that you must be a Christian knight, and would save your life if I could. Now you are warned; oh, fly while there is yet time!'

'Noble and beautiful damsel, I have not come here to fly. And now that I have seen you, and know you to be the captive of this monster, I am more than ever eager to combat him for your deliverance. But tell me, lady, before I seek the giant, who are you, and how came you into his power?'

'Ah! the tale of my misfortunes is soon told. My name is Sibille. I came with my noble father, Guerin of Guienne, on a pilgrimage to the Holy Land; then, returning, would have sailed to France, where a good knight, nephew of Ogier the Dane, waited to make me his wife. But a furious tempest threw us upon this hateful coast; Angoulafre discovered and attacked us; my father and all his knights were slain, and I became his prisoner. For three years have I pined in this house of horror, and now for the first time I hear my native tongue and see the face of a countryman.'

'Nay, fair Sibille, of a kinsman! Know that I am Huon of Bordeaux, the eldest son of your father's brother, and therefore your cousin, and doubly bound to deliver you from this wicked giant. Lead me to him forthwith, and let me deal with the robber of ladies!'

'But ah! he is strong and fierce and — '

'Say no more. Am I not one of the peers of France?'

Sibille, scarcely able to suppress her exclamations of joy, no longer delayed to admit this welcome kinsman; and, walking on tiptoe, led the way to the chamber from which the monster's snoring could be heard all over the tower.

There he lay on his back, a hideous form, seventeen feet long, with such a fierce countenance as even in sleep would have made most men shudder. Huon stood over him and raised his sword; his first impulse was to bury it to the hilt in the giant's throat. But he bethought him that he was a knight, and must in no case attack an enemy who could not defend himself. Moreover, he fortunately remembered that this monster could not be slain except by the man wearing that enchanted coat of mail of which Oberon had spoken; and, while Angoulafre still slept heavily, the knight and his cousin searched for it throughout the tower. It was soon discovered in a cedar coffer that stood in one of the next apartments. Huon seized it, put it on, and was rejoiced to find that it fitted him marvellously well.

'Now, fair cousin,' he said gaily, 'excuse me if I leave you

here for a little. I am going to awake Angoulafre, and put him
to the death he deserves.'

But it was no easy task to rouse the giant from his nap. Not
till Huon had shaken him, and struck him, and shouted in his
ear, and pulled his beard, and tweaked his nose, did he begin
to move, and slowly raised his head, gaping and rubbing his
bloodshot eyes. Then, as he caught sight of this unexpected
visitor, he stared wildly, with a bellow that shook all the walls,
and sent Sibille, anxiously watching without, to her knees.

'Puny creature, what madness has brought you here to your
death? Miserable wretch, tell me your name before I crush you
with one blow, and you be never more heard of on earth!'

'Odious monster, my name is Huon of Bordeaux, and I am
come to punish you for all your evil deeds. Arm, and prepare
for the combat.'

Angoulafre might well be astonished at this bold language. He
regarded the knight with attention, and was still more astonished
to see him encased in the magic coat of mail.

'By Mahomet,' he said, 'it was generous of you not to have
slain me in my sleep, as you might well have done. Come, I
pardon you; it would cost me too much trouble to take your
life. Only give up that armour, and on this condition I will let
you go free and unharmed.'

'Nay, give you up this tower, and the princess whom you hold
captive in it; and, moreover, consent to renounce Mahomet,
and to follow me to the court of the Emir of Babylon, where
I have a certain errand to do; on these conditions will I spare
your life.'

The giant laughed loudly, making a gesture of scorn.

'Fool, if I let you go, you could not come at the Emir of
Babylon without my aid. He is my vassal, and this golden ring
betokens the respect due to me by him and all his. Four gates
guard his palace, each of which will fly open at the sight of my
ring. Without it you cannot hope to pass. At the first gate they
would cut off your right hand, at the second your left, at the
third one of your feet, at the fourth another, and when thus
you reached the hall it would be but a moment before your
head were shorn from your shoulders. Be wise, then; take this
ring, and return my armour.'

'Ring, and armour, and all that you have is already mine,'

quoth the bold Huon. 'We but waste our time; arm, and let me slay thee without more to-do.'

Seeing that he could by no persuasion win back from Huon the enchanted mail, Angoulafre withdrew to prepare for the combat. In a short time he returned, covered from head to foot with massive armour, and wielding a huge scythe in both his brawny hands.

'I am ready to fight if you are ready to die!' he roared, brandishing this terrific weapon over Huon's head.

'Look to thyself, pagan,' replied Huon, deftly escaping the blow.

The scythe, swung with all the giant's strength, struck against a pillar, and sank into it to the depth of three feet. Angoulafre made desperate efforts to draw it out; but before he could succeed, Huon rushed forward and cut off both his hands at the wrists. The giant, uttering a hideous howl of pain, turned to fly. He hurled himself into the chamber where the pale Sibille was trembling for the result of this combat, but, missing his footing, fell headlong, and his huge bulk rolled at her feet. She screamed out; but Huon was close at his heels; one good blow of the keen sword ended the cruel monster's life, and the cousins threw themselves into each other's arms.

When Huon had drawn the giant's ring from his finger, they hastened to leave this gloomy abode, and Geraume rejoiced to see his master come back safe. To him the knight confided the care of Sibille, directing him to take her to the nearest seaport and put her on board a ship bound for France, while he himself was achieving his enterprise. So they parted with all good wishes, and Huon pursued his journey alone with the ring of Angoulafre, the enchanted coat of mail, the wonderful goblet and horn, and his own good sword to be his guide.

IV

A FEW DAYS more brought Huon in sight of the rich and beautiful city of Babylon, where upon a high hill rose the marble palace of Gaudisse, the emir, or admiral of that country. Glad to arrive at the end of this long journey, Huon left his horse at the foot of the hill, to climb impatiently up its steep side, wondering whether Gaudisse would easily comply with the requests he had to make, and if his daughter Esclarmonde were indeed of such surpassing beauty as fame reported her.

As a loud flourish of trumpets announced that the emir and his guests were sitting down to dinner, Huon presented himself at the outermost gate of the palace, and demanded admission. That same hour Oberon was dining in fairyland, when suddenly he rose and uttered a cry of pain.

'Alas!' cried the enchanter; 'the brave knight whom I loved so well is at this moment perjuring himself basely, and thus deprives me of both the power and the will to succour him.'

It was too true. Huon had just been asked by the guard whether he belonged to their religion, this day being a high festival among the Saracens, in which none might take part who were not faithful followers of the Prophet. The knight had thoughtlessly answered 'Yea', and was at once allowed to enter without further question. But he no sooner found himself within the precincts of the palace, than his conscience began to smite him for having thus spoken a falsehood and denied his faith. He would have given much to be able to recall the words, but it was now too late. He could only determine not again to be guilty of the like weakness. And when he had advanced as far as the second gate, which was closed and guarded like the first, he drew his sword and called out at the height of his voice:

'Infidel dogs! I command ye to open to a Christian knight!'

The guards sprang to their arms. The barrier bristled with spears and sword-points, and in another moment a cloud of darts would have been hurled upon this rash intruder. But the captain of the guard caught sight of the giant's ring upon the stranger's hand, and called out:

'Forbear! Know ye not the ring of Angoulafre, to whom our lord owes tribute and homage?'

Instantly the weapons were lowered, the gate was flung open, and as the knight passed through, looking sternly around him, the guards fell upon their knees, and the captain, bowing low, conducted him across a courtyard to the third barrier that must be passed.

Here Huon bethought him of again trying the effect of the giant's ring.

'Behold,' he cried, 'the sign before which you must tremble and fall at my feet!'

Again the effect was magical. At this gate, as also at the fourth, he was received with every mark of profound respect. Then, crossing the last court, Huon made his way into the great hall where the banquet was being served, and found himself face to face with the personages upon whom he was to perform his strange mission.

At the head of the board sat the turbaned emir in all his pomp. On his right was the King of Hircania, a cruel tyrant, of whom all the neighbouring lands stood in dread. On the left of Gaudisse was his daughter Esclarmonde, the most beautiful princess of the East, her fair face pale and her bright eyes red with weeping. Sore against her will she had just been betrothed to this hateful king, and in honour of the betrothal was gathered a brilliant assembly of warriors and chiefs, both of Babylon and Hircania, who filled the hall, placed according to their rank. The King of Hircania was rising to kiss his destined bride at the moment when Huon entered; but now every eye turned upon the knight, as, with open visor and naked sword, he marched up the hall amid such a silence of amazement that no sound could be heard but the trampling of his mailed feet and the clattering of his scabbard.

The attendants shrank right and left out of his way, and, thus unopposed, Huon reached the emir's seat. Then, before a word was spoken, he swung his sword, with one mighty blow to hew off the head of the King of Hircania, and it rolled at the emir's feet. Esclarmonde uttered a cry. The feasters sprang up in confusion. Gaudisse, all bespattered by the blood of his guest, and speechless from surprise, gazed openmouthed upon the audacious stranger. What was his amazement to see him calmly walk up to the princess, who, half-terrified, half-rejoiced at the fate of her unwelcome suitor, stood as if spellbound and did not shrink while the handsome knight stooped and saluted her coral lips once, twice, thrice, before all the bewildered beholders! With the last kiss her father found words to express his feelings.

'Madman! Who are you, and in the name of the Prophet, what would you here?'

Huon did not concern himself to reply till he had courteously bowed to the blushing lady. Then he turned to the emir, and said in a clear voice that could be heard in the farthest corner of the hall:

'My name is Huon of Bordeaux, and I am sent hither by Charles, the great king, to do as I have done; and, furthermore, to have from thee a handful of that grizzled beard and four of thy strongest teeth, as tokens of the tribute owed him. Be pleased to do me this favour without delay.'

'This to my face!' bellowed Gaudisse, stamping, and choking, and glowing like a live coal. 'My friend! My beard! My daughter! My teeth! Am I alive to hear such things! Impossible! Outrageous! Irreverence! Audacity! Madness! Never! Ho, my guards, my slaves, my vassals — '

Suddenly the emir checked himself as Huon raised his hand, and displayed the ring of Angoulafre.

'The ring of my sovereign lord, to whom I owe homage and tribute! Stranger, I am bound to hear the man that bears this token. But, speak the truth, how came you by it, and where last saw you the mighty Angoulafre?'

The knight had too well repented of one falsehood to tell another.

'Pagan, thy sovereign lord is no longer to be feared even by such as thou! This arm has ended his wicked life. Think no more of him, but prepare to obey the commands of my king.'

'Angoulafre dead!' exclaimed the emir, and now cared not to restrain his wrath. 'Then, robber and murderer and insolent fool, prepare to meet thy death. My beard and teeth, forsooth! What next? Cowards, how long will ye suffer him to insult your prince. Seize him! Bind him! Off with his head! Tear him in pieces!'

At the first word out leaped the scimitars of the Saracens, and a score of warriors rushed furiously upon the dauntless knight. He stepped back quickly and loudly blew his horn, looking round in confident expectation. But, alas! the charm was broken. The offended enchanter did not regard the summons, and the knight must defend himself alone. The hall rang with the clash of weapons, and above all rose the furious voice of Gaudisse, bidding his men take the intruder dead or alive. The fair Esclarmonde clasped her hands and wept to see the fray. The indignation she should have felt against her father's enemy was lost in regard for this daring youth; and despite of filial duty she could not but wish for his escape.

But wishes were in vain, when one stood against so many. Huon's shield was covered with darts; his sword was forced from his hand; the Saracens rushed in and threw themselves upon him. He was seized, dragged away, loaded with chains, and hurled into the emir's darkest and deepest dungeon, with the assurance that he might expect no better fate than to be flayed alive.

Exhausted from loss of blood, he lay insensible on the cold stones; and when at last he came to himself his condition was most pitiable. He could scarcely move for pain; the emir's dreadful threats rang in his ears; in all that country he had no friend to speak a word or shed a tear for him; and, worst of all, it was by his own fault that he had come into such misfortune. Bitterly he reproached himself for the falsehood by which he had forfeited the favour of Oberon, but for which he might now have been reigning a victor where he pined in fetters, and might have sought the hand of that beautiful princess whose charms had at first sight made such an impression on his heart.

All night long he was tormented by these sad reflections, and the day brought no ray of light to his gloomy prison. He began to feel the want of food; his magic goblet as well as his horn had been torn from him in the struggle, and no one had come near him since he entered the dungeon. Was it the intention of his enemies to reduce his strength by starvation before bringing him to the torture, that they might have the satisfaction of seeing a Christian knight die with unmanly weakness? A burning thirst also distressed him. Thus he passed that day in anguish of mind and body, thinking sorrowfully of fair France and the gallant comrades in arms he should never see more. The death of Charlot was indeed avenged, and his unjust king might well be satisfied.

At last, towards evening, he heard footsteps without. The bolts were drawn back; the key grated in the door of the dungeon. The knight summoned all his fortitude, and prepared to meet his executioners. The door opened softly to let pass a veiled figure bearing in one hand a lamp and in the other a basket. Huon strove to rise, but could not for the weight of his fetters. The figure advanced slowly towards him; the veil was drawn back, the lamp raised, and he saw the pitiful face of Esclarmonde.

V

WHEN SOME weeks had gone by, a stranger arrived at the court of Babylon, who spoke the language of the country well, and made believe to be heir of one of the great sultans of the East. Such a guest the emir received with open arms, hoping to find in him a husband for his daughter to take the place of the King of Hircania. A great feast was held in his honour, and, as they sat at dinner, the stranger spoke of the death of Angoulafre, with which all the country rang, and asked for news of the Christian knight who had slain him.

'That knight will do no more murders,' said Gaudisse grimly. 'Long ere this he has starved in my dungeons.'

'Dead!' exclaimed the stranger in such tones that Esclarmonde eagerly fixed her eyes upon him and caught a meaning in his words that her father perceived not.

'Aye, dead, and too soon to get all his deserts,' said the emir. 'Know you not how that madman came here, and how he fared?'

The stranger was not unaware of Esclarmonde's glances, and as her father told his tale at full length, he, as if thoughtlessly, drew aside his robe and let her see a rosary that hung beneath this disguise. At the sight of it she started and blushed, and he knew he had not been deceived.

When the emir had ended his story and gone to sleep, the stranger sought private speech of the princess, then, as soon as they were alone, he fell on his knees, crying: 'Lady, tell me the truth, for you can and will. I am come to seek out my dear master, Sir Huon of Bordeaux.'

'You are his faithful squire, Geraume, of whom he has so often spoken to me?'

'I am no other, But say, does he live? Is he in health? Where may I see him?'

'Follow me,' replied the princess, and led the way to a dungeon below the palace. She drew back the bolts, and in another moment the knight and his squire were embracing each other with mutual joy.

Soon now Huon's tale was told, while Esclarmonde stood by, the darkness hiding how her cheeks glowed as she heard him speak of her part in his deliverance. His courage, as well as his misfortunes, had so moved her heart that she could not rest for thinking of his unhappy lot. Overcoming all scruples, she persuaded his jailer to let her visit the prisoner and supply him with food. The more she saw of this knight, the more she was grateful to have been delivered from the hateful King of Hircania. Deserted by the enchanter, Huon now found himself succoured by the powerful magic of love. She secretly restored to him his goblet and ivory horn; and when her father ordered the captive to be led forth to the most cruel death that could be devised, she bribed the jailer to say that he was already dead of hunger, and in proof to exhibit the emaciated body of a prisoner who had really died that very day.

The emir, wrathful to see his vengeance thus escape him, had the jailer executed forthwith, and tried to gratify his hatred by inflicting all imaginable tortures on the senseless corpse believed to be that of his enemy. Esclarmonde shuddered at the horrors from which she had preserved Huon, who became dearer to her day by day. She was easily persuaded of the errors of her faith; she consented to be baptized as soon as possible, and asked nothing better than to be allowed to fly with her lover to his native land, abandoning gladly for his sake her friends, her rank, and her religion.

With the aid of Geraume, they now began to concert measures for escape. It soon seemed that there was need of haste, for the approach was announced of the giant Agrapard, King of Nubia and brother of Angoulafre, who, the emir understood, was coming to seek his daughter's hand. Esclarmonde grew pale at the thought, but Gaudisse exulted in the prospect of such a match, and forthwith began to look coldly on Geraume. He, without exciting suspicion, took his leave and hurried to the seacoast, where it was agreed that he should have a vessel in readiness, while Huon and Esclarmonde watched for the first favourable moment of escape.

But as Agrapard drew nearer the city it appeared that he had come intent on far other thoughts than those of love. He sent a herald before him to reproach Gaudisse with having lost a single day in avenging his brother's death, and to defy him to mortal combat, or to demand a tribute which would exhaust his revenues.

The emir was in despair; vainly through all his host he sought a warrior bold enough to accept the challenge of this terrible giant; and, when there seemed to be no hope for him but in submission, he cursed his gods and shed tears of rage before his daughter, who seized the moment to make him regret the loss of the vanquisher of Angoulafre.

'Ah,' cried the emir, 'I let him starve to death, and now it repents me to have lost such a champion! He alone could save me from this monster. Willingly would I give half my state to bring him to life.'

'Learn,' said Esclarmonde joyfully, 'that he of whom you speak is not dead.'

'Not dead? But no – I saw his corpse! Do you mock me, child?'

'It was the corpse of another. The brave knight, Huon, is still alive, and, if you are willing, will maintain your cause against the giant.'

Gaudisse was astonished, but this was not a time to ask questions. He desired that Huon should be sent for, and was surprised to find him as stout and vigorous as the day on which he was thrown into chains. This must be explained when the present danger was overpast; in the meantime he welcomed the knight and declared what was required of him.

'The brother of the giant whom you slew so doughtily is under our walls, full of threats and fury. As you conquered Angoulafre, so must you conquer Agrapard. Go forth, brave youth, and if you rid me of this foe I promise to give you my daughter and to obey the wishes of your king.'

Huon replied by demanding his armour. It was brought forth to him all rusty and battered, and his sword notched with many a blow. Right glad was he to find himself again harnessed like a warrior. They brought him the best horse in the emir's stables, and after taking a tender leave of Esclarmonde, and assuring her father that there need now be no fear of the giant, he mounted and rode forth to defy Agrapard without the walls.

The combat was long and desperate. For hours Esclarmonde's heart was torn with anxiety, and the emir remained trembling in the middle of his army, till a great shouting announced the victory of their champion, and soon Huon appeared leading the humbled giant bound to his saddle and covered with blood. He brought him thus to the feet of the emir, sitting on the terrace of the palace, and after he had lovingly embraced his lady he turned to her father and said, while Agrapard was being dragged to the dungeon he himself had lately quitted:

'Behold, I have kept my promise. Now it is for thee to perform thine.'

'My promise?' answered the wily Saracen. 'What promise? Thou art still alive: what ask ye more?'

'Emir, the commands of my king are still unfulfilled. Make haste to give me your teeth and beard; and, moreover, you must renounce the law of your false prophet that has taught you thus to lie.'

'Dog of a Christian, I would perish a thousand times rather than consent to such insolent demands. Now will I load thee with ten times heavier chains, from which this time none shall set thee free.'

Esclarmonde screamed and clung to her father's knees, begging for mercy, till she swooned away from terror. Huon ran to support her with the cry:

'Ungrateful miscreant, as well threaten the winds! I grant you one moment to obey me, or else fear my wrath.'

'Seize him! Slay him! Away with them both to the dungeon!' replied Gaudisse, waving his scimitar and shouting to his men; but he held back, not caring to measure himself with the knight that came from proving his strength upon Agrapard.

The guards rushed forward. Huon smiled and drew forth his horn. Rightly he judged that now the enchanter must be appeased by his repentance and his sufferings. He gave one blast so loud that all the walls of the palace quivered, and lo! in a moment Oberon was by his side, and the ground shook with the trampling of invisible horses and the tread of marching men.

The emir's soldiers could not stand against such a foe. As they paused and looked round, to ask each other whence came these martial sounds with which the air was filled, the host of fairyland fell upon them. The dwarf waved his enchanting wand and their arms were struck from their hands; their leaders were seized and dragged away before their eyes; horses and men rolled in the dust; the blood flowed from the wounds of phantom steel; whole troops were laid low, as trees by a hurricane; destruction swept through the ranks like a thunderbolt, and the terror-stricken Saracens turned to fly in wild confusion, without being able to see a single one of their assailants.

Gaudisse beheld this rout of his army with dismay; but what were his feelings when he found himself in the grasp of invisible hands, and loaded with the very chains he had ordered for Huon! Before he could beg for mercy, the irresistible hands had plucked the beard from his chin; he opened his mouth to roar in agony, and four of his largest teeth were torn from his jaws.

'Be this the fate of all cruel and unbelieving princes!' said Oberon, and gave the beard and the teeth to Huon. 'Take now these tokens; return to the King of France; salute him from me, and say that, through my aid and thine own stout heart, thou hast performed the task, and mayst well be forgiven. Take, too, this fair lady to be thy bride, and, so long as ye are loving and true, Oberon the Enchanter will be your friend.'

Thus made master of Babylon, Huon bestowed it as a reward upon his faithful squire. Gaudisse and Agrapard he sent to be kept in prison in the tower of Angoulafre. He loaded the emir's treasures upon camels, and set forth homewards, not forgetting to take with him the most precious treasure of all, the fair Esclarmonde. Arriving at the seacoast, they embarked in the ship which Geraume had provided, and, after many more perilous adventures, reached the city of Rome. There Esclarmonde was christened by the Pope and married to Huon; after which they repaired to France, and the knight, presenting the tokens of his success, was in due time restored to the king's favour.

PART IV:
HEROES AND MONSTERS

PERSEUS AND THE GORGON

Charles Kingsley

W HEN HE WAS FIFTEEN years old Perseus had grown to be a tall lad and a sailor, and went many voyages after merchandise to the islands around. All the people in Seriphos said that he was not the son of mortal man, and called him the son of Zeus, the king of the Immortals. For though he was but fifteen, he was taller by a head than any man in the island; and he was the most skilful of all in running and wrestling and boxing, and in throwing the quoit and the javelin, and in rowing with the oar, and in playing on the harp, and in all which befits a man. And he was brave and truthful, gentle and courteous; for good old Dictys had trained him well – and well it was for Perseus that he had done so. For now Danaë and her son fell into great danger, and Perseus had need of all his wit to defend his mother and himself.

Dictys' brother was Polydectes, king of the island. He was not a righteous man, like Dictys, but greedy and cunning and cruel. And when he saw fair Danaë, he wanted to marry her. But she would not; for she did not love him, and cared for no one but her boy and her boy's father, whom she never hoped to see again. At last Polydectes became furious, and while Perseus was away at sea he took poor Danaë away from Dictys, saying: 'If you will not be my wife, you shall be my slave.' So Danaë was made a slave, and had to fetch water from the well, and grind in the mill, and perhaps was beaten, and made to wear a heavy chain, because she would not marry that cruel king. But Perseus was far away over the seas in the isle of Samos, little thinking how his mother was languishing in grief.

Now one day at Samos while the ship was loading, Perseus wandered into a pleasant wood to get out of the sun, and sat down on the turf and fell asleep. And as he slept a strange dream came to him – the strangest dream which he had ever had in his life.

There came a lady to him through the wood, taller than he or any mortal man, but beautiful exceedingly, with great grey eyes, clear and piercing, but strangely soft and mild. On her head was a helmet and in her hand a spear. And over her shoulder above her long blue robes hung a goatskin, which bore up a mighty shield of brass, polished like a mirror. She stood and looked at him with her clear grey eyes; and Perseus saw that her eyelids never moved, nor her eyeballs, but looked straight through and through him, and into his very heart, as if she could see all the secrets of his soul, and knew all that he had ever thought or longed for since the day that he was born. And Perseus dropped his eyes, trembling and blushing, as the wonderful lady spoke.

'Perseus, you must do an errand for me.'

'Who are you, lady? And how do you know my name?'

'I am Pallas Athené; and I know the thoughts of all men's hearts, and discern their manhood or their baseness. And from the souls of clay I turn away, and they are blest, but not by me. They fatten at ease, like sheep in the pasture, and eat what they did not sow, like oxen in the stall. They grow and spread, like the gourd along the ground; but like the gourd they give no shade to the traveller, and when they are ripe, death gathers them, and they go down unloved into hell, and their name vanishes out of the land.

'But to the souls of fire I give more fire, and to those who are manly I give a might more than man's. These are the heroes, the sons of the Immortals, who are blest, but not like the souls of clay. For I drive them forth by strange paths, Perseus, that they may fight the Titans and the monsters, the enemies of gods and men. Through doubt and need, danger and battle, I drive them; and some of them are slain in the flower of youth, no man knows when or where; and some of them win noble names, and a fair and green old age. But what will be their latter end I know not, and none, save Zeus, the father of gods and men. Tell me now, Perseus which of these two sorts of men seem to you more blest?'

Then Perseus answered boldly: 'Better to die in the flower

of youth on the chance of winning a noble name, than to live at ease like the sheep, and die unloved and unrenowned.'

Then that strange lady laughed, and held up her brazen shield, and cried: 'See here, Perseus; dare you face such a monster as this and slay it, that I may place its head upon this shield?'

And in the mirror of the shield there appeared a face, and as Perseus looked on it his blood ran cold. It was the face of a beautiful woman, but her cheeks were pale as death and her brows were knit with everlasting pain and her lips were thin and bitter like a snake's; and instead of hair, vipers wreathed about her temples and shot out their forked tongues, while round her head were folded wings like an eagle's, and upon her bosom claws of brass.

And Perseus looked awhile, and then said: 'If there is anything so fierce and foul on earth, it were a noble deed to kill it. Where can I find the monster?'

Then the strange lady smiled again, and said: 'Not yet; you are too young and too unskilled; for this is Medusa the Gorgon, the mother of a monstrous brood. Return to your home and do the work which waits there for you. You must play the man in that before I can think you worthy to go in search of the Gorgon.'

Then Perseus would have spoken, but the strange lady vanished and he awoke; and behold, it was a dream. But day and night Perseus saw before him the face of that dreadful woman, with the vipers writhing round her head.

So he returned home; and when he came to Seriphos, the first thing which he heard was that his mother was a slave in the house of Polydectes.

Grinding his teeth with rage, he went out and away to the king's palace and through the men's rooms and the women's rooms, and so through all the house (for no one dared stop him, so terrible and fair was he) till he found his mother sitting on the floor, turning the stone hand-mill, and weeping as she turned it. And he lifted her up and kissed her and bade her follow him forth. But before they could pass out of the room Polydectes came in, raging. And when Perseus saw him, he flew upon him as the mastiff flies on the boar. 'Villain and tyrant!' he cried. 'Is this your respect for the gods, and your mercy to strangers and widows? You shall die!' And because he had no sword he caught up the stone hand-mill and lifted it to dash out Polydectes' brains.

But his mother clung to him, shrieking: 'Oh, my son, we are strangers and helpless in the land; and if you kill the king, all the people will fall on us, and we shall both die.'

Good Dictys too who had come in, entreated him: 'Remember that he is my brother. Remember how I have brought you up and trained you as my own son, and spare him for my sake.'

Then Perseus lowered his hand; and Polydectes, who had been trembling all this while like a coward because he knew that he was in the wrong, let Perseus and his mother pass.

Perseus took his mother to the temple of Athené, and there the priestess made her one of the temple-sweepers; for there they knew she would be safe, and not even Polydectes would dare to drag her away from the altar. And there Perseus and the good Dictys and his wife came to visit her every day, while Polydectes, not being able to get what he wanted by force, cast about in his wicked heart how he might get it by cunning.

Now he was sure that he could never get back Danaë as long as Perseus was in the island; so he made a plot to rid himself of him. And first he pretended to have forgiven Perseus and to have forgotten Danaë, so that for a while all went as smoothly as ever.

Next he proclaimed a great feast, and invited to it all the chiefs and landowners and the young men of the island, and among them Perseus, that they might all do him homage as their king and eat of his banquet in his hall.

On the appointed day they all came; and as the custom was then, each guest brought his present with him to the king: one a horse, another a shawl or a ring or a sword; and those who had nothing better brought a basket of grapes or of game. But Perseus brought nothing, for he had nothing to bring, being but a poor sailor-lad.

He was ashamed, however, to go into the king's presence without his gift, and he was too proud to ask Dictys to lend him one. So he stood at the door sorrowfully, watching the rich men go in; and his face grew very red as they pointed at him and smiled and whispered: 'What has that foundling to give?'

Now this was what Polydectes wanted; and as soon as he heard that Perseus stood without, he bade them bring him in, and asked him scornfully before them all: 'Am I not your king, Perseus, and have I not invited you to my feast? Where is your present then?'

Perseus blushed and stammered, while all the proud men round laughed, and some of them began jeering him openly. 'This fellow was thrown ashore here like a piece of weed or driftwood, and yet he is too proud to bring a gift to the king.'

'And though he does not know who his father is, he is vain enough to let the old women call him the son of Zeus.'

And so forth, till poor Perseus grew mad with shame, and hardly knowing what he said, cried out: 'A present! Who are you who talk of presents? See if I do not bring a nobler one than all of yours together!'

So he said boasting; and yet he felt in his heart that he was braver than all those scoffers, and more able to do some glorious deed.

'Hear him! Hear the boaster! What is it to be?' cried they all, laughing louder than ever.

Then his dream at Samos came into his mind, and he cried aloud: 'The head of the Gorgon.'

He was half afraid after he had said the words; for all laughed louder than ever, and Polydectes loudest of all.

'You have promised to bring me the Gorgon's head? Then never appear again in this island without it. Go!'

Perseus ground his teeth with rage, for he saw that he had fallen into a trap; but his promise lay upon him, and he went out without a word.

Down to the cliffs he went, and looked across the broad blue sea; and he wondered if his dream were true, and prayed in the bitterness of his soul:

'Pallas Athené, was my dream true? And shall I slay the Gorgon? If thou didst really show me her face, let me not come to shame as a liar and boastful. Rashly and angrily I promised; but cunningly and patiently will I perform.'

But there was no answer, nor sign; neither thunder nor any appearance; not even a cloud in the sky.

And three times Perseus called weeping, 'Rashly and angrily I promised; but cunningly and patiently will I perform.'

Then he saw afar off above the sea a small white cloud, as

bright as silver. And it came on, nearer and nearer, till its brightness dazzled his eyes.

Perseus wondered at that strange cloud, for there was no other cloud all round the sky; and he trembled as it touched the cliff below. And as it touched it broke and parted, and within it appeared Pallas Athené, as he had seen her at Samos in his dream, and beside her a young man more light-limbed than the stag, whose eyes were like sparks of fire. By his side was a sword of diamond, all of one clear precious stone, and on his feet were golden sandals, from the heels of which grew living wings.

They looked upon Perseus keenly, and yet they never moved their eyes; and they came up the cliffs towards him more swiftly than the seagull, and yet they never moved their feet, nor did the breeze stir the robes about their limbs; only the wings of the youth's sandals quivered, like a hawk's when he hangs above the cliff. And Perseus fell down and worshipped, for he knew that they were more than man.

But Athené stood before him and spoke grimly, and bid him have no fear. Then:

'Perseus,' she said, 'he who overcomes in one trial merits thereby a sharper trial still. You have braved Polydectes, and done manfully. Dare you brave Medusa the Gorgon?'

And Perseus said: 'Try me; for since you spoke to me in Samos a new soul has come into my breast, and I should be ashamed not to dare anything which I can do. Show me then how I can do this!'

'Perseus,' said Athené, 'think well before you attempt; for this deed requires a seven years' journey in which you cannot repent or turn back nor escape; but if your heart fails you, you must die in the Unshapen Land, where no man will ever find your bones.'

'Better so than live here useless and despised,' said Perseus. 'Tell me then, oh tell me, fair and wise goddess, of your great kindness and condescension, how I can do but this one thing, and then, if need be, die!'

Then Athené smiled and said:

'Be patient and listen; for if you forget my words, you will indeed die. You must go northward to the country of the Hyperboreans, who live beyond the pole, at the sources of the cold north wind, till you find the three Grey Sisters, who have but one eye and one tooth between them. You must ask them the way to the nymphs, the daughters of the Evening Star, who dance about the golden tree in the Atlantic island of the west. They will tell you the way to the Gorgon, that you may slay her, my enemy, the mother of monstrous beasts. Once she was a maiden as beautiful as morn, till in her pride she sinned a sin at which the sun hid his face. And from that day her hair was turned to vipers, and her hands to eagle's claws, and her heart was filled with shame and rage, and her lips with bitter venom; and her eyes became so terrible that whosoever looks on them is turned to stone; and her children are the winged horse and the giant of the golden sword; and her grandchildren are Echidna the witch-adder and Geryon the three-headed tyrant, who feeds his herds beside the herds of hell. So she became the sister of the Gorgons, Stheino and Euryte the abhorred, the daughters of the Queen of the Sea. Touch them not, for they are immortal; but bring me only Medusa's head.'

'And I will bring it!' said Perseus. 'But how am I to escape her eyes? Will she not freeze me too into stone?'

'You shall take this polished shield,' said Athené, 'and when you come near her look not at her herself, but at her image in the brass; so you may strike her safely. And when you have struck off her head, wrap it, with your face turned away, in the folds of the goatskin on which the shield hangs, the hide of Amaltheié, the nurse of the Aegisholder. So you will bring it safely back to me and win to yourself renown and a place among the heroes who feast with the Immortals upon the peak where no winds blow.'

Then Perseus said: 'I will go, though I die in going. But how shall I cross the seas without a ship? And who will show me my way? And when I find her, how shall I slay her, if her scales be iron and brass?'

Then the young man spoke: 'These sandals of mine will bear you across the seas, and over hill and dale like a bird, as they bear me all day long; for I am Hermes, the far-famed Argus-slayer, the messenger of the Immortals who dwell on Olympus.'

Then Perseus fell down and worshipped, while the young man spoke again:

'The sandals themselves will guide you on the road, for they are divine and cannot stray; and this sword itself, the Argus-slayer, will kill her, for it is divine and needs no second stroke. Arise and gird them on and go forth.'

So Perseus arose, and girded on the sandals and the sword.

And Athené cried: 'Now leap from the cliff and be gone.'

But Perseus lingered.

'May I not bid farewell to my mother and to Dictys? And may I not offer burnt-offerings to you, and to Hermes the far-famed Argus-slayer, and to Father Zeus above?'

'You shall not bid farewell to your mother, lest your heart relent at her weeping. I will comfort her and Dictys until you return in peace. Nor shall you offer burnt-offerings to the Olympians; for your offering shall be Medusa's head. Leap, and trust in the armour of the Immortals.'

Then Perseus looked down the cliff and shuddered; but he was ashamed to show his dread. Then he thought of Medusa and the renown before him, and he leapt into the empty air.

And behold, instead of falling he floated and stood and ran along the sky. He looked back, but Athené had vanished, and Hermes; and the sandals led him on northward ever, like a crane who follows the spring toward the Ister fens. So Perseus started on his journey, going dry-shod over land and sea; and his heart was high and joyful, for the winged sandals bore him each day a seven days' journey.

And he went by Cythnus and by Ceos and the pleasant Cyclades to Attica, and past Athens and Thebes and the Copaic lake and up the vale of Cephissus and past the peaks of Oeta and Pindus and over the rich Thessalian plains, till the sunny hills of Greece were behind him and before him were the wilds of the north. Then he passed the Thracian mountains and many a barbarous tribe, Paeons and Dardans and Triballi, till he came to the Ister stream, and the dreary Scythian plains. And he walked across the Ister dry-shod, and away through the moors and fens day and night, toward the bleak north-west, turning neither to the right hand nor the left, till he came to the Unshapen Land, and the place which has no name.

And seven days he walked through it, on a path which few can tell; for those who have trodden it like least to speak of it, and those who go there again in dreams are glad enough when they awake; till he came to the edge of the everlasting night, where the air was full of feathers and the soil was hard with ice, and there at last he found the three Grey Sisters, by the shore of the freezing sea, nodding upon a white log of driftwood, beneath the cold white winter moon; and they chanted a low song together: 'Why the old times were better than the new.'

There was no living thing around them, not a fly, not a moss upon the rocks. Neither seal nor seagull dare come near, lest the ice should clutch them in its claws. The surge broke up in foam, but it fell again in flakes of snow, and it frosted the hair of the three Grey Sisters and the bones in the ice-cliff above their heads. They passed the eye from one to the other, but for all that they could not see; and they passed the tooth from one to the other, but for all that they could not eat; and they sat in the full glare of the moon, but they were none the warmer for her beams. And Perseus pitied the three Grey Sisters, but they did not pity themselves.

So he said: 'Oh, venerable mothers, wisdom is the daughter of old age. You therefore should know many things. Tell me, if you can, the path to the Gorgon.'

Then one cried: 'Who is this who reproaches us with old age?' And another: 'This is the voice of one of the children of men.'

And he: 'I do not reproach, but honour your old age, and I am one of the sons of men and of the heroes. The rulers of Olympus have sent me to you to ask the way to the Gorgon.'

Then one: 'There are new rulers in Olympus, and all new things are bad.' And another: 'We hate your rulers and the heroes and all the children of men. We are the kindred of the Titans and the Giants and the Gorgons and the ancient monsters of the deep.' And another: 'Who is this rash and insolent man who pushes unbidden into our world?' And the first: 'There never was such a world as ours, nor will be: if we let him see it, he will spoil it all.'

Then one cried: 'Give me the eye, that I may see him'; and another: 'Give me the tooth, that I may bite him.' But Perseus, when he saw that they were foolish and proud, and did not love the children of men, left off pitying them and said to himself: 'Hungry men must needs be hasty; if I stay making many words here, I shall be starved.' Then he stepped close to them and watched till they passed the eye from hand to hand. And as they groped about between themselves, he held out his own hand gently, till one of them put the eye into it, fancying that it was the hand of her sister. Then he sprang back, and laughed, and cried:

'Cruel and proud old women, I have your eye; and I will throw it into the sea, unless you tell me the path to the Gorgon, and swear to me that you tell me right.'

Then they wept and chattered and scolded; but in vain. They were forced to tell the truth, though when they told it Perseus could hardly make out the road.

'You must go,' they said, 'foolish boy, to the southward into the ugly glare of the sun, till you come to Atlas the giant who holds the heavens and the earth apart. And you must ask his daughters, the Hesperides, who are young and foolish like yourself. And now give us back our eye, for we have forgotten all the rest.'

So Perseus gave them back their eye; but instead of using it, they nodded and fell fast asleep and were turned into blocks of ice, till the tide came up and washed them all away. And now they float up and down like icebergs for ever, weeping whenever they meet the sunshine and the fruitful summer and the warm south wind which fill young hearts with joy.

But Perseus leapt away to the southward, leaving the snow and ice behind, past the isle of the Hyperboreans and the tin isles and the long Iberian shore, while the sun rose higher day by day upon a bright blue summer sea. And the terns and the seagulls swept laughing round his head and called to him to stop and play, and the dolphins gambolled up as he passed and offered to carry him on their backs. And all night long the sea-nymphs sang sweetly, and the Tritons blew upon their conchs as they played round Galataea their queen in her car of pearled shells. Day by day the sun rose higher and leapt more swiftly into the sea at night and more swiftly out of the sea at dawn, while Perseus skimmed over the billows like a seagull, and his feet were never wetted; and leapt on from wave to wave, and his limbs were never weary, till he saw far away a mighty mountain, all rose-red in the setting sun. Its feet were wrapped in forests, and its head in wreaths of cloud; and Perseus knew that it was Atlas, who holds the heavens and the earth apart.

He came to the mountain and leapt on shore and wandered upward among pleasant valleys and waterfalls and tall trees and strange ferns and flowers; but there was no smoke rising from any glen, nor house, nor sign of man.

At last he heard sweet voices singing; and he guessed that he was come to the garden of the nymphs, the daughters of the Evening Star.

They sang like nightingales among the thickets, and Perseus stopped to hear their song; but the words which they spoke he could not understand – no, nor no man after him for many a hundred years. So he stepped forward and saw them dancing, hand in hand, around the charmed tree which bent under its golden fruit; and round the tree-foot was coiled the dragon, old Ladon the sleepless snake, who lies there for ever, listening to the song of the maidens, blinking and watching with dry bright eyes.

Then Perseus stopped, not because he feared the dragon, but because he was bashful before those fair maids; but when they saw him, they too stopped, and called to him with trembling voices:

'Who are you? Are you Heracles the mighty, who will come to rob our garden, and carry off our golden fruit?' And he answered:

'I am not Heracles the mighty, and I want none of your golden fruit. Tell me, fair nymphs, the way which leads to the Gorgon, that I may go on my way and slay her.'

'Not yet, not yet, fair boy; come dance with us around the tree in the garden which knows no winter, the home of the south wind and the sun. Come hither and play with us awhile; we have danced alone here for a thousand years, and our hearts are weary with longing for a playfellow. So come, come, come!'

'I cannot dance with you, fair maidens; for I must do the errand of the Immortals. So tell me the way to the Gorgon lest I wander and perish in the waves.'

Then they sighed and wept, and answered:

'The Gorgon! She will freeze you into stone.'

'It is better to die like a hero than to live like an ox in a stall. The Immortals have lent me weapons, and they will give me wit to use them.'

Then they sighed again and answered: 'Fair boy, if you are

bent on your own ruin, be it so. We know not the way to the Gorgon; but we will ask the giant Atlas, above upon the mountain peak, the brother of our father, the silver Evening Star. He sits aloft and sees across the ocean, and far away into the Unshapen Land.'

So they went up the mountain to Atlas their uncle, and Perseus went up with them. And they found the giant kneeling, as he held the heavens and the earth apart.

They asked him, and he answered mildly, pointing to the seaboard with his mighty hand: 'I can see the Gorgons lying on an island far away, but this youth can never come near them, unless he has the hat of darkness, which whosoever wears cannot be seen.'

Then cried Perseus: 'Where is that hat, that I may find it?'

But the giant smiled. 'No living mortal can find that hat, for it lies in the depths of Hades in the regions of the dead. But my nieces are immortal, and they shall fetch it for you if you will promise me one thing and keep your faith.'

Then Perseus promised; and the giant said: 'When you come back with the head of Medusa, you shall show me the beautiful horror, that I may lose my feeling and my breathing, and become a stone for ever; for it is weary labour for me to hold the heavens and the earth apart.'

Then Perseus promised; and the eldest of the nymphs went down and into a dark cavern among the cliffs out of which came smoke and thunder, for it was one of the mouths of Hell.

And Perseus and the nymphs sat down seven days and waited trembling, till the nymph came up again; and her face was pale and her eyes dazzled with the light, for she had been long in the dreary darkness, but in her hand was the magic hat.

Then all the nymphs kissed Perseus, and wept over him a long while, but he was only impatient to be gone. And at last they put the hat upon his head, and he vanished out of their sight.

But Perseus went on boldly, past many an ugly sight, far away into the heart of the Unshapen Land, beyond the streams of Ocean, to the isles where no ship cruises, where is neither night nor day, where nothing is in its right place and nothing has a name, till he heard the rustle of the Gorgons' wings and saw the glitter of their brazen talons; and then he knew that it was time to halt, lest Medusa should freeze him into stone.

He thought awhile with himself, and remembered Athené's words. He rose aloft into the air and held the mirror of the shield above his head and looked up into it that he might see all that was below him.

And he saw the three Gorgons sleeping, as huge as elephants. He knew that they could not see him because the hat of darkness hid him; and yet he trembled as he sank down near them, so terrible were those brazen claws.

Two of the Gorgons were foul as swine, and lay sleeping heavily as swine sleep, with their mighty wings outspread; but Medusa tossed to and fro restlessly, and as she tossed Perseus pitied her, she looked so fair and said. Her plumage was like the rainbow, and her face was like the face of a nymph; only her eyebrows were knit and her lips clenched, with everlasting care and pain, and her long neck gleamed so white in the mirror that Perseus had not the heart to strike, and said: 'Ah, that it had been either of her sisters!'

But as he looked, from among her tresses the vipers' heads awoke and peeped up with their bright dry eyes and showed their fangs and hissed. And Medusa, as she tossed, threw back her wings and showed her brazen claws; and Perseus saw that, for all her beauty, she was as foul and venomous as the rest.

Then he came down and stepped to her boldly, and looked steadfastly on his mirror, and struck with Herpé stoutly once. And he did not need to strike again.

Then he wrapped the head in the goatskin, turning away his eyes, and sprang into the air aloft, faster than he ever sprang before.

For Medusa's wings and talons rattled as she sank dead upon the rocks, and her two foul sisters woke and saw her lying dead.

Into the air they sprang yelling and looked for him who had done the deed. Thrice they swung round and round, like hawks who beat for a partridge; and thrice they snuffed round and round, like hounds who draw upon a deer. At last they struck upon the scent of the blood, and they checked for a moment to make sure; and then on they rushed with a fearful howl, while the wind rattled hoarse in their wings.

On they rushed, sweeping and flapping like eagles after a hare; and Perseus' blood ran cold, for all his courage, as he saw them come howling on his track; and he cried: 'Bear me well now, brave sandals, for the hounds of Death are at my heels!'

And well the brave sandals bore him, aloft through cloud and sunshine, across the shoreless sea; and fast followed the hounds of Death, as the roar of their wings came down the wind. But the roar came down fainter and fainter, and the howl of their voices died away; for the sandals were too swift, even for Gorgons, and by nightfall they were far behind, two black specks in the southern sky, till the sun sank and he saw them no more.

Then he came again to Atlas and the garden of the nymphs; and when the giant heard him coming, he groaned and said: 'Fulfil thy promise to me.' Then Perseus held up to him the Gorgon's head, and he had rest from all his toil, for he became a crag of stone, which sleeps for ever far above the clouds.

Then he thanked the nymphs, and asked them. 'By what road shall I go homeward again, for I wandered far round in coming hither?'

And they wept and cried: 'Go home no more, but stay and play with us, the lonely maidens, who dwell for ever far away from gods and men.'

But he refused, and they told him his road, and said: 'Take with you this magic fruit, which, if you eat once, you will not hunger for seven days. For you must go eastward and eastward ever, over the doleful Libyan shore, which Poseidon gave to Father Zeus, when he burst open the Bosphorus and the Hellespont, and drowned the fair Lectonian land. And Zeus took that land in exchange – a fair bargain, much bad ground for a little good – and to this day it lies waste and desert, with shingle and rock and sand.'

Then they kissed Perseus and wept over him, and he leapt down the mountain and went on, lessening and lessening like a seagull, away and out to sea.

So Perseus flitted onward to the north-east, over many a league of sea, till he came to the rolling sand-hills and the dreary Libyan shore.

And he flitted on across the desert: over rock ledges and banks of shingle and level wastes of sand, and shell-drifts bleaching in the sunshine and the skeletons of great seamonsters and dead bones of ancient giants, strewn up and down upon the old sea-floor. And as he went the blood drops fell to the earth from the Gorgon's head, and became poisonous asps and adders, which breed in the desert to this day.

Over the sands he went – he never knew how far or how long – feeding on the fruit which the nymphs had given him, till he saw the hills of the Psylli, and the dwarfs who fought with cranes. Their spears were of reeds and rushes, and their houses of the egg-shells of the cranes; and Perseus laughed, and went his way to the north-east, hoping all day long to see the blue Mediterranean sparkling, that he might fly across it to his home.

But now came down a mighty wind, and swept him back southward toward the desert. All day long he strove against it; but even the winged sandals could not prevail. So he was forced to float down the wind all night; and when the morning dawned there was nothing to be seen, save the same old hateful waste of sand.

And out of the north the sandstorms rushed upon him, blood-red pillars and wreaths, blotting out the noonday sun; and Perseus fled before them, lest he should be choked by the burning dust. At last the gale fell calm, and he tried to go northward again; but again came down the sandstorms, and swept him back into the waste, and then all was calm and cloudless as before. Seven days he strove against the storms, and seven days he was driven back, till he was spent with thirst and hunger, and his tongue clove to the roof of his mouth. Here and there he fancied that he saw a fair lake, and the sunbeams shining on the water; but when he came to it it vanished at his feet, and there was nought but burning sand. And if he had not been of the race of the Immortals, he would have perished in the waste; but his life was strong within him, because it was more than man's.

Then he cried to Athené, and said:

'Oh, fair and pure, if thou hearest me, wilt thou leave me here to die of drought? I have brought thee the Gorgon's head at thy bidding, and hitherto thou hast prospered my journey; dost thou desert me at the last? Else why will not these immortal sandals prevail, even against the desert storms? Shall I never see my mother more, and the blue ripple round Seriphos, and the sunny hills of Hellas?'

So he prayed; and after he had prayed there was a great silence.

The heaven was still above his head and the sand was still beneath his feet, and Perseus looked up, but there was nothing but the blinding sun in the blinding blue, and round him nothing but the blinding sand.

And Perseus stood still awhile, and waited, and said: 'Surely I am not here without the will of the Immortals, for Athené will not lie. Were not these sandals to lead me in the right road? Then the road in which I have tried to go must be a wrong road.'

Then suddenly his ears were opened, and he heard the sound of running water.

And at that his heart was lifted up, though he scarcely dare believe his ears; and weary as he was he hurried forward, though he could scarcely stand upright; and within a bowshot of him was a glen in the sand and marble rocks and date trees and a lawn of gay green grass. And through the lawn a streamlet sparkled and wandered out beyond the trees, and vanished in the sand.

The water trickled among the rocks, and a pleasant breeze rustled in the dry date branches; and Perseus laughed for joy and leapt down the cliff and drank of the cool water and ate of the dates and slept upon the turf and leapt up and went forward again, but not toward the north this time. For he said: 'Surely Athené hath sent me hither, and will not have me go homeward yet. What if there be another noble deed to be done before I see the sunny hills of Hellas?'

So he went east, and east for ever, by fresh oases and fountains, date palms and lawns of grass, till he saw before him a mighty mountain wall, all rose-red in the setting sun.

Then he towered in the air like an eagle, for his limbs were strong again; and he flew all night across the mountain till the day began to dawn and rosy-fingered Eos came blushing up the sky. And then, behold, beneath him was the long green garden of Egypt and the shining stream of Nile.

And he saw cities walled up to heaven, and temples and obelisks and pyramids and giant gods of stone. And he came down amid fields of barley and flax and millet and clambering gourds, and saw the people coming out of the gates of a great city and setting to work, each in his place, among the watercourses, parting the streams among the plants cunningly with their feet, according to the wisdom of the Egyptians. But when they saw him they all stopped their work and gathered round him and cried:

'Who art thou, fair youth? And what bearest thou beneath thy goatskin there? Surely thou art one of the Immortals, for thy skin is white like ivory and ours is red like clay. Thy hair is like threads of gold and ours is black and curled. Surely thou art one of the Immortals!' And they would have worshipped him then and there, but Perseus said:

'I am not one of the Immortals, but I am a hero of the Hellenes. And I have slain the Gorgon in the wilderness, and bear her head with me. Give me food therefore that I may go forward and finish my work.'

Then they gave him food and fruit and wine, but they would not let him go. And when the news came into the city that the Gorgon was slain, the priests came out to meet him, and the maidens, with songs and dances and timbrels and harps; and they would have brought him to their temple and to their king, but Perseus put on the hat of darkness, and vanished away out of their sight.

Therefore the Egyptians looked long for his return, but in vain, and worshipped him as a hero, and made a statue of him in Chemmis, which stood for many a hundred years. And they said that he appeared to them at times, with sandals a cubit long, and that whenever he appeared the season was fruitful and the Nile rose high that year.

Then Perseus went to the eastward, along the Red Sea shore; and then, because he was afraid to go into the Arabian deserts, he turned northward once more, and this time no storm hindered him.

He went past the Isthmus and Mount Casius and the vast Serbonian bog and up the shore of Palestine, where the dark-faced Aethiops dwelt.

He flew on past pleasant hills and valleys, like Argos itself, or Lacedaemon, or the fair vale of Tempe. But the lowlands were all drowned by floods, and the highlands blasted by fire, and the hills heaved like a bubbling cauldron before the wrath of King Poseidon, the shaker of the earth.

And Perseus feared to go inland, but flew along the shore above the sea. And he went on all the day, and the sky was black with smoke; and he went on all the night, and the sky was red with flame.

And at the dawn of day he looked toward the cliffs, and at the water's edge, under a black rock, he saw a white image stand.

'This', thought he, 'must surely be the statue of some seagod; I will go near and see what kind of gods these barbarians worship.'

So he came near; but when he came it was no statue, but a maiden of flesh and blood, for he could see her tresses streaming in the breeze. And as he came closer still he could see how she shrank and shivered when the waves sprinkled her with cold salt spray. Her arms were spread above her head, and fastened to the rock with chains of brass; and her head drooped on her bosom, either with sleep or weariness or grief. But now and then she looked up and wailed and called her mother; yet she did not see Perseus, for the cap of darkness was on his head.

Full of pity and indignation, Perseus drew near and looked upon the maid. Her cheeks were darker than his were, and her hair was blue-black like a hyacinth; but Perseus thought: 'I have never seen so beautiful a maiden, no, not in all our isles. Surely she is a king's daughter. Do barbarians treat their king's daughters thus? She is too fair at least to have done any wrong. I will speak to her.'

And lifting the hat from his head he flashed into her sight.

She shrieked with terror and tried to hide her face with her hair, for she could not with her hands; but Perseus cried:

'Do not fear me, fair one; I am a Hellene, and no barbarian. What cruel men have bound you? But first I will set you free.'

And he tore at the fetters, but they were too strong for him, while the maiden cried:

'Touch me not; I am accursed, devoted as a victim to the sea-gods. They will slay you if you dare to set me free.'

'Let them try,' said Perseus, and drawing Herpé from his thigh, he cut through the brass as if it had been flax.

'Now', he said, 'you belong to me and not to these sea-gods, whosoever they may be!' But she only called the more on her mother.

'Why call on your mother? She can be no mother to have left you here. If a bird is dropped out of the nest, it belongs to the man who picks it up. If a jewel is cast by the wayside, it is his who dare win it and wear it as I will win you and will wear you. I know now why Pallas Athené sent me hither. She sent me to gain a prize worth all my toil and more.'

And he clasped her in his arms and cried: 'Where are these sea-gods, cruel and unjust, who doom fair maids to death? I carry the weapons of Immortals. Let them measure their strength against mine! But tell me, maiden, who you are and what dark fate brought you here.'

And she answered, weeping:

'I am the daughter of Cepheus, King of Iopa, and my mother is Cassiopoeia of the beautiful tresses, and they called me Andromeda, as long as life was mine. And I stand bound here, hapless that I am, for the sea-monster's food, to atone for my mother's sin. For she boasted of me once that I was fairer than Atergatis, Queen of the Fishes; so she in her wrath sent the sea-floods. And her brother the Fire King sent the earthquakes, and wasted all the land, and after the floods a monster bred of the slime, who devours all living things. And now he must devour me, guiltless though I am – me, who never harmed a living thing, nor saw a fish upon the shore but I gave it life and threw it back into the sea, for in our land we eat no fish for fear of Atergatis their queen. Yet the priests say that nothing but my blood can atone for a sin which I never committed.'

But Perseus laughed, and said: 'A sea-monster? I have fought with worse than him: I would have faced Immortals for your sake; how much more a beast of the sea?'

Then Andromeda looked up at him, and new hope was kindled in her breast, so proud and fair did he stand, with one hand round her, and in the other the glittering sword. But she only sighed and wept the more and cried:

'Why will you die, young as you are? Is there not death and sorrow enough in the world already? It is noble for me to die, that I may save the lives of a whole people; but you, better than them all, why should I slay you too? Go you your way; I must go mine.'

But Perseus cried: 'Not so; for the lords of Olympus, whom I serve, are the friends of the heroes and help them on to noble deeds. Led by them I slew the Gorgon, the beautiful horror, and not without them do I come hither, to slay this monster with that same Gorgon's head. Yet hide your eyes when I leave you, lest the sight of it freeze you too to stone.'

But the maiden answered nothing, for she could not believe his words. And then, suddenly looking up, she pointed to the sea, and shrieked:

'There he comes, with the sunrise, as they promised. I must die now. How shall I endure it? Oh, go! Is it not dreadful enough to be torn piecemeal, without having you to look on?' And she tried to thrust him away.

But he said: 'I go; yet promise me one thing ere I go: that if I slay this beast you will be my wife, and come back with me to my kingdom in fruitful Argos, for I am a king's heir. Promise me, and seal it with a kiss.'

Then she lifted up her face and kissed him, and Perseus laughed for joy and flew upward, while Andromeda crouched trembling on the rock, waiting for what might befall.

On came the great sea-monster, coasting along like a huge black galley, lazily breasting the ripple and stopping at times by creek or headland to watch for the laughter of girls at their bleaching, or cattle pawing on the sandhills, or boys bathing on the beach. His great sides were fringed with clustering shells and seaweeds, and the water gurgled in and out of his wide jaws as he rolled along, dripping and glistening in the beams of the morning sun.

At last he saw Andromeda, and shot forward to take his prey, while the waves foamed white behind him, and before him the fish fled leaping.

Then down from the height of the air fell Perseus like a shooting star – down to the crests of the waves, while Andromeda hid her face as he shouted. And then there was silence for a while.

At last she looked up trembling and saw Perseus springing toward her, and instead of the monster a long black rock, with the sea rippling quietly round it.

Who then so proud as Perseus, as he leapt back to the rock, lifted his fair Andromeda in his arms and flew with her to the cliff-top, as a falcon carries a dove?

Who so proud as Perseus, and who so joyful as all the Aethiop people? For they had stood watching the monster from the cliffs, wailing for the maiden's fate. And already a messenger had gone to Cepheus and Cassiopoeia, where they sat in sackcloth and ashes on the ground in the innermost palace chambers, awaiting their daughter's end. And they came, and all the city with them, to see the wonder, with songs and with dances, with cymbals and harps, and received their daughter back again, as one alive from the dead.

Then Cepheus said: 'Hero of the Hellenes, stay here with me and be my son-in-law, and I will give you the half of my kingdom.'

'I will be your son-in-law,' said Perseus, 'but of your kingdom I will have none, for I long after the pleasant land of Greece, and my mother who waits for me at home.'

Then Cepheus said: 'You must not take my daughter away at once, for she is to us like one alive from the dead. Stay with us here a year, and after that you shall return with honour.' And Perseus consented; but before he went to the palace he bade the people bring stones and wood, and built three altars – one to Athené, one to Hermes and one to Father Zeus – and offered bullocks and rams.

And some said: 'This is a pious man.' Yet the priests said: 'The Sea Queen will be yet more fierce against us, because her monster is slain.' But they were afraid to speak aloud, for they feared the Gorgon's head. So they went up to the palace; and when they came in there stood in the hall Phineus, the brother of Cepheus, chafing like a bear robbed of her whelps, and with him his sons and his servants and many an armed man; and he cried to Cepheus:

'You shall not marry your daughter to this stranger, of whom no one knows even the name. Was not Andromeda betrothed to my son? And now she is safe again, has he not a right to claim her?'

But Perseus laughed and answered: 'If your son is in want of a bride, let him save a maiden for himself. As yet he seems but a helpless bridegroom. He left this one to die, and dead she is to him. I saved her alive, and alive she is to me, but to no one else. Ungrateful man! Have I not saved your land and the lives of your sons and daughters, and will you requite me thus? Go, or it will be worse for you!' But all the men-at-arms drew their swords and rushed on him like wild beasts.

Then he unveiled the Gorgon's head, and said: 'This has

delivered my bride from one wild beast: it shall deliver her from many.' And as he spoke Phineus and all his men-at-arms stopped short, and each man stiffened as he stood; and before Perseus had drawn the goatskin over the face again, they were all turned into stone.

Then Perseus bade the people bring levers and roll them out. And what was done with them after that I cannot tell.

So they made a great wedding-feast, which lasted seven whole days, and who so happy as Perseus and Andromeda?

But on the eighth night Perseus dreamed a dream, and he saw standing beside him Pallas Athené, as he had seen her in Seriphos, seven long years before. And she stood and called him by name, and said:

'Perseus, you have played the man, and see, you have your reward. Know now that the gods are just, and help him who helps himself. Now give me here Herpé the sword and the sandals and the hat of darkness, that I may give them back to their owners, but the Gorgon's head you shall keep awhile, for you will need it in your land of Greece. Then you shall lay it up in my temple at Seriphos, that I may wear it on my shield for ever, a terror to the Titans and the monsters and the foes of gods and men. And as for this land, I have appeased the sea and the fire, and there shall be no more floods nor earthquakes. But let the people build altars to Father Zeus and to me, and worship the Immortals, the lords of heaven and earth.'

And Perseus rose to give her the sword and the cap and the sandals, but he woke, and his dream vanished away. And yet it was not altogether a dream, for the goatskin with the head was in its place, but the sword and the cap and the sandals were gone, and Perseus never saw them more.

Then a great awe fell on Perseus. And he went out in the morning to the people and told his dream and bade them build altars to Zeus, the father of gods and men, and to Athené, who gives wisdom to heroes, and fear no more the earthquakes and the floods, but sow and build in peace. And they did so for a while, and prospered. But after Perseus was gone they forgot Zeus and Athené, and worshipped again Atergatis the queen, and the undying fish of the sacred lake, where Deucalion's deluge was swallowed up; and they burnt their children before the Fire King, till Zeus was angry with that foolish people and brought a strange nation against them out of Egypt, who fought against them and wasted them utterly, and dwelt in their cities for many a hundred years.

And when a year was ended Perseus hired Phoenicians from Tyre and cut down cedars, and built himself a noble galley, and painted its cheeks with vermilion and pitched its sides with pitch. And in it he put Andromeda and all her dowry of jewels and rich shawls and spices from the East, and great was the weeping when they rowed away. But the remembrance of his brave deed was left behind; and Andromeda's rock was shown at Iopa in Palestine till more than a thousand years were past.

So Perseus and the Phoenicians rowed to the westward across the sea of Crete, till they came to the blue Aegean and the pleasant Isles of Hellas and Seriphos, his ancient home.

Then he left his galley on the beach, and went up as of old, and he embraced his mother and Dictys his good foster-father, and they wept over each other a long while, for it was seven years and more since they had met.

Then Perseus went out, and up to the hall of Polydectes; and underneath the goatskin he bore the Gorgon's head.

And when he came into the hall, Polydectes sat at the table-head, and all his nobles and landowners on either side, each according to his rank, feasting on the fish and the goat's flesh, and drinking the blood-red wine. The harpers harped and the revellers shouted, and the wine-cups rang merrily as they passed from hand to hand, and great was the noise in the hall of Polydectes.

Then Perseus stood upon the threshold and called to the king by name. But none of the guests knew Perseus, for he was changed by his long journey. He had gone out a boy, and he was come home a hero; his eye shone like an eagle's and his beard was like a lion's beard, and he stood up like a wild bull in his pride.

But Polydectes the wicked knew him, and hardened his heart still more; and scornfully he called:

'Ah, foundling! Have you found it more easy to promise than to fulfil?'

'Those whom the gods help fulfil their promises; and those who despise them, reap as they have sown. Behold the Gorgon's head!'

Then Perseus drew back the goatskin, and held aloft the Gorgon's head.

Pale grew Polydectes and his guests as they looked upon that dreadful face. They tried to rise up from their seats: but from their seats they never rose, but stiffened, each man where he sat, into a ring of cold grey stones.

Then Perseus turned and left them, and went down to his galley in the bay. And he gave the kingdom to good Dictys, and sailed away with his mother and his bride.

THE CHIMAERA

Nathaniel Hawthorne

T HERE WAS ONCE a fountain which gushed out of a hill-side in the marvellous land of Greece. And for aught I know, after so many thousand years, it is still gushing out of the very selfsame spot. At any rate, there was the pleasant fountain, welling freshly forth and sparkling down the hill-side in the golden sunset, when a handsome young man named Bellerophon drew near its margin. In his hand he held a bridle, studded with brilliant gems, and adorned with a golden bit. Seeing an old man, and another of middle age, and a little boy, near the fountain, and likewise a maiden, who was dipping up some of the water in a pitcher, he paused, and begged that he might refresh himself with a draught.

'This is very delicious water,' he said to the maiden, as he rinsed and filled her pitcher, after drinking out of it. 'Will you be kind enough to tell me whether the fountain has any name?'

'Yes; it is called the Fountain of Pirene,' answered the maiden; and then she added, 'My grandmother has told me that this clear fountain was once a beautiful woman; and when her son was killed by the arrows of the huntress Diana, she melted all away into tears. And so the water, which you find so cool and sweet, is the sorrow of that poor mother's heart!'

'I should not have dreamed,' observed the young stranger, 'that so clear a well-spring, with its gush and gurgle, and its cheery dance out of the shade into the sunlight, had so much as one tear-drop in its bosom! And this, then, is Pirene? I thank you, pretty maiden, for telling me its name. I have come from a far-away country to find this very spot.'

A middle-aged country fellow (he had driven his cow to drink out of the spring) stared hard at young Bellerophon, and at the handsome bridle which he carried in his hand.

'The water-courses must be getting low, friend, in your part of the world,' remarked he, 'if you come so far only to find the Fountain of Pirene. But, pray, have you lost a horse? I see you carry the bridle in your hand; and a very pretty one it is, with that double row of bright stones upon it. If the horse was as fine as the bridle, you are much to be pitied for losing him.'

'I have lost no horse,' said Bellerophon, with a smile. 'But I happen to be seeking a very famous one, which, as wise people have informed me, must be found hereabouts, if anywhere. Do you know whether the winged horse Pegasus still haunts the Fountain of Pirene, as he used to do in your forefathers' days?'

But then the country fellow laughed.

Pegasus was a snow-white steed, with beautiful silvery wings, who spent most of his time on the summit of Mount Helicon. He was as wild, and as swift, and as buoyant in his flight through the air, as any eagle that ever soared into the clouds. There was nothing else like him in the world. He had no mate; he had never been backed or bridled by a master; and for many a long year he led a solitary and a happy life.

Oh, how fine a thing it is to be a winged horse! Sleeping at night, as he did, on a lofty mountain-top, and passing the greater part of the day in the air, Pegasus seemed hardly to be a creature of the earth. Whenever he was seen up very high above people's heads, with the sunshine on his silvery wings, you would have thought that he belonged to the sky, and that, skimming a little too low, he had got astray among our mists and vapours, and was seeking his way back again. It was very pretty to behold him plunge into the fleecy bosom of a bright cloud, and be lost in it for a moment or two, and then break forth from the other side. Or, in a sullen rain-storm, when there was a grey pavement of clouds over the whole sky, it would sometimes happen that the winged horse descended right through it, and the glad light of the upper region would gleam after him. In another instant, it is true, both Pegasus and the pleasant light would be gone away together. But anyone that was fortunate enough to see this wondrous spectacle felt cheerful the whole day afterwards, and as much longer as the storm lasted.

In the summer time, and in the beautifullest of weather, Pegasus often alighted on the solid earth, and, closing his silvery wings, would gallop over hill and dale for pastime, as fleetly as the wind. Oftener than in any other place, he had been seen near the Fountain of Pirene, drinking the delicious water, or rolling himself upon the soft grass of the margin. Sometimes, too (but Pegasus was very dainty in his food), he would crop a few of the clover-blossoms that happened to be sweetest.

To the Fountain of Pirene, therefore, people's great-grand-fathers had been in the habit of going (as long as they were youthful, and retained their faith in winged horses), in hopes of getting a glimpse at the beautiful Pegasus. But of late years he had been very seldom seen. Indeed, there were many of the country folk, dwelling within half an hour's walk of the fountain, who had never beheld Pegasus, and did not believe that there was any such creature in existence. The country fellow to whom Bellerophon was speaking chanced to be one of those incredulous persons.

And that was the reason why he laughed.

'Pegasus, indeed!' cried he, turning up his nose as high as such a flat nose could be turned up. 'Pegasus, indeed! A winged horse, truly! Why, friend, are you in your senses? Of what use would wings be to a horse? Could he drag the plough so well, think you? To be sure, there might be a little saving in the expense of shoes; but then, how would a man like to see his horse flying out of the stable window? – yes; or whisking him up above the clouds, when he only wanted to ride to mill? No, no! I don't believe in Pegasus. There never was such a ridiculous kind of a horse-fowl made!'

'I have some reason to think otherwise,' said Bellerophon quietly.

And then he turned to an old, grey man, who was leaning on a staff, and listening very attentively, with his head stretched forward, and one hand at his ear, because, for the last twenty years, he had been getting rather deaf.

'And what say you, venerable sir?' inquired he. 'In your younger days, I should imagine, you must frequently have seen the winged steed!'

'Ah, young stranger, my memory is very poor!' said the aged man. 'When I was a lad, if I remember rightly, I used to believe there was such a horse, and so did everybody else. But, nowadays, I hardly know what to think, and very seldom think about the winged horse at all. If I ever saw the creature, it was a long, long while ago; and, to tell you the truth, I doubt whether I ever did see him. One day, to be sure, when I was quite a youth, I remember seeing some hoof-tramps round about the brink of the fountain. Pegasus might have made those hoof-marks; and so might some other horse.'

'And have you never seen him, my fair maiden?' asked Bellerophon of the girl, who stood with the pitcher on her head, while this talk went on. 'You certainly could see Pegasus, if anybody can, for your eyes are very bright.'

'Once I thought I saw him,' replied the maiden, with a smile and a blush. 'It was either Pegasus or a large white bird, a very great way up in the air. And one other time, as I was coming to the fountain with my pitcher, I heard a neigh. Oh, such a brisk and melodious neigh as that was! My very heart leaped with delight at the sound. But it startled me, nevertheless; so that I ran home without filling my pitcher.'

'That was truly a pity!' said Bellerophon.

And he turned to the child who was gazing at him, as children are apt to gaze at strangers, with his rosy mouth wide open.

'Well, my little fellow,' cried Bellerophon, playfully pulling one of his curls, 'I suppose you have often seen the winged horse.'

'That I have,' answered the child, very readily. 'I saw him yesterday, and many times before.'

'You are a fine little man!' said Bellerophon, drawing the child closer to him. 'Come, tell me all about it.'

'Why,' replied the child, 'I often come here to sail little boats in the fountain, and to gather pretty pebbles out of its basin. And sometimes, when I look down into the water, I see the image of the winged horse in the picture of the sky that is there. I wish he would come down and take me on his back, and let me ride him up to the moon! But, if I so much as stir to look at him, he flies far away out of sight.'

And Bellerophon put his faith in the child, who had seen the image of Pegasus in the water, and in the maiden, who had heard him neigh so melodiously, rather than in the middle-aged clown, who believed only in cart-horses, or in the old man, who had forgotten the beautiful things of his youth.

Therefore, he hunted about the Fountain of Pirene for a great many days afterwards. He kept continually on the watch, looking upward at the sky, or else down into the water, hoping for ever that he should see either the reflected image of the winged horse, or the marvellous reality. He held the bridle, with its bright gems and golden bit, always ready in his hand. The rustic people, who dwelt in the neighbourhood, and drove their cattle to the fountain to drink, would often laugh at poor Bellerophon; and sometimes take him pretty severely to task. They told him that an able-bodied young man like himself ought to have better business than to be wasting his time in such an idle pursuit. They offered to sell him a horse, if he wanted one; and when Bellerophon declined the purchase, they tried to drive a bargain with him for his fine bridle.

Even the country boys thought him so very foolish that they used to have a great deal of sport about him, and were rude enough not to care a fig although Bellerophon saw and heard it. One little urchin, for example, would play Pegasus, and cut the oddest imaginable capers by way of flying, while one of his schoolfellows would scamper after him, holding forth a twist of bulrushes, which was intended to represent Bellerophon's ornamental bridle. But the gentle child, who had seen the picture of Pegasus in the water, comforted the young stranger more than all the naughty boys could torment him. The dear little fellow often sat down beside him, and, without speaking a word, would look down into the fountain and up towards the sky, with so innocent a faith that Bellerophon could not help feeling encouraged.

Now you will, perhaps, wish to be told why it was that Bellerophon had undertaken to catch the winged horse. And we shall find no better opportunity to speak about this matter than while he is waiting for Pegasus to appear.

If I were to relate the whole of Bellerophon's previous adventures, they might easily grow into a very long story. It will be quite enough to say that, in a certain country of Asia, a terrible monster, called a Chimaera, had made its appearance, and was doing more mischief than could be talked about between now and sunset. According to the best accounts which I have been able to obtain, this Chimaera was nearly, if not quite, the ugliest and most poisonous creature, and the strangest and unaccountablest, and the hardest to fight with, and the most difficult to run away from, that ever came out of the earth's inside. It had a tail like a boa-constrictor; its body was like I do not care what; and it had three separate heads, one of which was a lion's, the second a goat's, and the third an abominably great snake's. And a hot blast of fire came flaming out of each of its three mouths! Being an earthly monster, I doubt whether it had any wings; but, wings or no, it ran like a goat and a lion, and wriggled along like a serpent, and thus contrived to make about as much speed as all the three together.

Oh, the mischief, and mischief, and mischief, that this naughty creature did! With its flaming breath, it could set a forest on fire, or burn up a field of grain, or, for that matter, a village, with all its fences and houses. It laid waste the whole country round about, and used to eat up people and animals alive, and cook them afterwards in the burning oven of its stomach. Mercy on us, little children, I hope neither you nor I will ever happen to meet a Chimaera!

While the hateful beast (if a beast we can anywise call it) was doing all these horrible things, it so chanced that Bellerophon came to that part of the world on a visit to the king. The king's name was Iobates, and Lycia was the country which he ruled over. Bellerophon was one of the bravest youths in the world, and desired nothing so much as to do some valiant and beneficent deed, such as would make all mankind admire and love him. In those days, the only way for a young man to distinguish himself was by fighting battles, either with the enemies of his country or with wicked giants, or with troublesome dragons, or with wild beasts, when he could find nothing more dangerous to encounter. King Iobates, perceiving the courage of his youthful visitor, proposed to him to go and fight the Chimaera, which everybody else was afraid of, and which, unless it should be soon killed, was likely to convert Lycia into a desert. Bellerophon hesitated not a moment, but assured the king that he would either slay this dreaded Chimaera or perish in the attempt.

But in the first place, as the monster was so prodigiously swift, he bethought himself that he should never win the victory by fighting on foot. The wisest thing he could do, therefore, was to get the very best and fleetest horse that could anywhere be found. And what other horse in all the world was half so fleet as the marvellous horse Pegasus, who had wings as well as legs, and was even more active in the air than on the earth? To be sure, a great many people denied that there was any such horse with wings, and said that the stories about him were all poetry and nonsense. But, wonderful as it appeared, Bellerophon believed that Pegasus was a real steed, and hoped that he himself might be fortunate enough to find him; and, once fairly mounted on his back, he would be able to fight the Chimaera at better advantage.

And this was the purpose with which he had travelled from Lycia to Greece, and had brought the beautifully ornamented bridle in his hand. It was an enchanted bridle. If he could only succeed in putting the golden bit into the mouth of Pegasus, the winged horse would be submissive and own Bellerophon for his master, and fly whithersoever he might choose to turn the rein.

But, indeed, it was a weary and anxious time while Bellerophon waited and waited for Pegasus, in hopes that he would come and drink at the Fountain of Pirene. He was afraid lest King Iobates should imagine that he had fled from the Chimaera. It pained him, too, to think how much mischief the monster was doing, while he himself, instead of fighting with it, was compelled to sit idly poring over the bright waters of Pirene, as they gushed out of the sparkling sand. And as Pegasus came thither so seldom in these latter years, and scarcely alighted there more than once in a lifetime, Bellerophon feared that he might grow an old man, and have no strength left in his arms nor courage in his heart, before the winged horse would appear. O, how heavily passes the time while an adventurous youth is yearning to do his part in life, and to gather in the harvest of his renown! How hard a lesson it is to wait! Our life is brief, and how much of it is spent in teaching us only this!

Well was it for Bellerophon that the child had grown so fond of him, and was never weary of keeping him company. Every morning the child gave him a new hope to put in his bosom, instead of yesterday's withered one.

'Dear Bellerophon,' he would cry, looking up hopefully into his face, 'I think we shall see Pegasus today!'

And at length, if it had not been for the little boy's unwavering faith, Bellerophon would have given up all hope, and would have gone back to Lycia, and have done his best to slay the Chimaera without the help of the winged horse. And in that case poor Bellerophon would at least have been terribly scorched by the creature's breath, and would most probably have been killed and devoured. Nobody should ever try to fight an earth-born Chimaera, unless he can first get upon the back of an aerial steed.

One morning the child spoke to Bellerophon even more hopefully than usual.

'Dear, dear Bellerophon,' cried he, 'I know not why it is, but I feel as if we should certainly see Pegasus to-day!'

And all that day he would not stir a step from Bellerophon's side; so they ate a crust of bread together, and drank some of the water of the fountain. In the afternoon there they sat, and Bellerophon had thrown his arm around the child, who likewise had put one of his little hands into Bellerophon's. The latter was lost in his own thoughts, and was fixing his eyes vacantly on the trunks of the trees that overshadowed the fountain, and on the grape-vines that clambered up among their branches. But the gentle child was gazing down into the water; he was grieved, for Bellerophon's sake, that the hope of another day should be deceived, like so many before it; and two or three quiet tear-drops fell from his eyes, and mingled with what were said to be the many tears of Pirene, when she wept for her slain children.

But, when he least thought of it, Bellerophon felt the pressure of the child's little hand, and heard a soft, almost breathless whisper.

'See there, dear Bellerophon! There is an image in the water!'

The young man looked down into the dimpling mirror of the fountain, and saw what he took to be the reflection of a bird which seemed to be flying at a great height in the air, with a gleam of sunshine on its snowy or silvery wings.

'What a splendid bird it must be!' said he. 'And how very large it looks, though it must really be flying higher than the clouds!'

'It makes me tremble!' whispered the child. 'I am afraid to look up into the air! It is very beautiful, and yet I dare only look at its image in the water. Dear Bellerophon, do you not see that it is no bird? It is the winged horse Pegasus!'

Bellerophon's heart began to throb! He gazed keenly upward, but could not see the winged creature, whether bird or horse; because, just then, it had plunged into the fleecy depths of a summer cloud. It was but a moment, however, before the object reappeared, sinking lightly down out of the cloud, although still at a vast distance from the earth. Bellerophon caught the child in his arms, and shrank back with him, so that they were both hidden among the thick shrubbery which grew all around the fountain. Not that he was afraid of any harm, but he dreaded lest, if Pegasus caught a glimpse of them, he would fly far away, and alight in some inaccessible mountain-top. For it was really the winged horse. After they had expected him so long, he was coming to quench his thirst with the water of Pirene.

Nearer and nearer came the aerial wonder, flying in great circles, as you may have seen a dove when about to alight. Downward came Pegasus, in those wide, sweeping circles, which grew narrower and narrower still as he gradually approached the earth. The nigher the view of him, the more beautiful he was, and the more marvellous the sweep of his silvery wings. At last, with so slight a pressure as hardly to bend the grass about the fountain, or imprint a hoof-tramp in the sand of its margin, he alighted, and, stooping his wild head, began to drink. He drew in the water with long and pleasant sighs, and tranquil pauses of enjoyment; and then another draught, and another and another. For, nowhere in the world or up among the clouds, did Pegasus love any water as he loved this of Pirene. And when his thirst was slaked, he cropped a few of the honey-blossoms of the clover, delicately tasting them, but not caring to make a hearty meal, because the herbage just beneath the clouds on the lofty sides of Mount Helicon, suited his palate better than this ordinary grass.

After thus drinking to his heart's content, and, in his dainty fashion, condescending to take a little food, the winged horse began to caper to and fro and dance, as it were out of mere idleness and sport. There never was a more playful creature made than this very Pegasus. So there he frisked, in a way that it delights me to think about, fluttering his great wings as lightly as ever did a linnet, and running little races, half on earth and half in air, and which I know not whether to call a flight or a gallop. When a creature is perfectly able to fly, he sometimes chooses to run just for the pastime of the thing; and so did Pegasus, although it cost him some little trouble to keep his hoofs so near the ground. Bellerophon, meanwhile, holding the child's hand, peeped forth from the shrubbery, and thought that never was any sight so beautiful as this, nor ever a horse's eyes so wild and spirited as those of Pegasus. It seemed a sin to think of bridling him and riding on his back.

Once or twice Pegasus stopped and snuffed the air, pricking up his ears, tossing his head, and turning it on all sides, as if he partly suspected some mischief or other. Seeing nothing, however, and hearing no sound, he soon began his antics again.

At length – not that he was weary, but only idle and luxurious – Pegasus folded his wings, and lay down on the soft green turf. But, being too full of aerial life to remain quiet for many moments together, he soon rolled over on his back, with his four slender legs in the air. It was beautiful to see him, this one solitary creature, whose mate had never been created, but who needed no companion, and, living a great many hundred years, was as happy as the centuries were long. The more he did such things as mortal horses are accustomed to do, the less earthly and more wonderful he seemed. Bellerophon and the child almost held their breath, partly from a delightful awe, but still more because they dreaded lest the slightest stir or murmur should send him up, with the speed of an arrow-flight, into the farthest blue of the sky.

Finally, when he had had enough of rolling over and over, Pegasus turned himself about, and, indolently, like any other horse, put out his fore legs, in order to rise from the ground; and Bellerophon, who had guessed that he would do so, darted suddenly from the thicket, and leaped astride of his back.

Yes, there he sat, on the back of the winged horse!

But what a bound did Pegasus make, when, for the first time, he felt the weight of a mortal man upon his loins! A bound, indeed! Before he had time to draw a breath, Bellerophon found himself five hundred feet aloft, and still shooting upward, while the winged horse snorted and trembled with terror and anger. Upward he went, up, up, up, until he plunged into the cold misty bosom of a cloud, at which, only a little while before, Bellerophon had been gazing, and fancying it a very pleasant spot. Then again, out of the heart of the cloud, Pegasus shot down like a thunderbolt, as if he meant to dash both himself and his rider headlong against a rock. Then he went through about a thousand of the wildest caprioles that had ever been performed either by a bird or a horse.

I cannot tell you half that he did. He skimmed straightforward, and sideways, and backward. He reared himself erect, with his fore legs on a wreath of mist, and his hind legs on nothing at all. He flung out his heels behind, and put down his head between his legs, with his wings pointing right upward. At about two miles' height above the earth, he turned a somersault, so that Bellerophon's heels were where his head should have been, and he seemed to look down into the sky, instead of up. He twisted his head about, and looking Bellerophon in the face, with fire flashing from his eyes, made a terrible attempt to bite him. He fluttered his pinions so wildly that one of the silver feathers was shaken out, and floating earthward, was picked up by the child, who kept it as long as he lived, in memory of Pegasus and Bellerophon.

But the latter (who, as you may judge, was as good a horseman as ever galloped) had been watching his opportunity, and at last clapped the golden bit of the enchanted bridle between the winged steed's jaws. No sooner was this done, than Pegasus became as manageable as if he had taken food all his life out of Bellerophon's hand. To speak what I really feel, it was almost a sadness to see so wild a creature grow suddenly so tame. And Pegasus seemed to feel it so likewise. He looked round to Bellerophon, with the tears in his beautiful eyes, instead of the fire that so recently flashed from them. But when Bellerophon patted his head, and spoke a few authoritative, yet kind and soothing words, another look came into the eyes of Pegasus; for he was glad at heart, after so many lonely centuries, to have found a companion and a master.

Thus it always is with winged horses, and with all such wild and solitary creatures. If you can catch and overcome them, it is the surest way to win their love.

While Pegasus had been doing his utmost to shake Bellerophon off his back, he had flown a very long distance; and they had come within sight of a lofty mountain by the time the bit was in his mouth. Bellerophon had seen this mountain before, and knew it to be Helicon, on the summit of which was the winged horse's abode. Thither (after looking gently into his rider's face, as if to ask leave) Pegasus now flew, and, alighting, waited patiently until Bellerophon should please to dismount. The young man, accordingly, leaped from his steed's back, but still held him fast by the bridle. Meeting his eyes, however, he was so affected by the gentleness of his aspect, and by his beauty, and by the thought of the free life which Pegasus had heretofore lived, that he could not bear to keep him a prisoner if he really desired his liberty.

Obeying this generous impulse, he slipped the enchanted bridle off the head of Pegasus, and took the bit from his mouth.

'Leave me, Pegasus!' said he. 'Either leave me, or love me.'

In an instant, the winged horse shot almost out of sight, soaring straight upward from the summit of Mount Helicon. Being long after sunset, it was now twilight on the mountain-top, and dusky evening over all the country round about. But Pegasus flew so high that he overtook the departed day, and was bathed in the upper radiance of the sun. Ascending higher and higher, he looked like a bright speck, and at last could no longer be seen in the hollow waste of the sky. And Bellerophon was afraid that he should never behold him more. But, while he was lamenting his own folly, the bright speck reappeared, and drew nearer and nearer, until it descended lower than the sunshine; and behold, Pegasus had come back! After this trial, there was no more fear of the winged horse making his escape. He and Bellerophon were friends, and put loving faith in one another.

That night they lay down and slept together, with Bellerophon's arm about the neck of Pegasus, not as a caution, but for kindness. And they awoke at peep of day, and bade one another good-morning, each in his own language.

In this manner, Bellerophon and the wondrous steed spent several days, and grew better acquainted and fonder of each other all the time. They went on long aerial journeys, and sometimes ascended so high that the earth looked hardly bigger than the moon. They visited distant countries, and amazed the inhabitants, who thought that the beautiful young man, on the back of the winged horse, must have come down out of the sky. A thousand miles a day was no more than an easy space for the fleet Pegasus to pass over. Bellerophon was delighted with this kind of life, and would have liked nothing better than to live always in the same way, aloft in the clear atmosphere; for it was always sunny weather up there, however cheerless and rainy it might be in the lower region. But he could not forget the horrible Chimaera, which he had promised King Iobates to slay. So, at last, when he had become well accustomed to feats of horsemanship in the air, and could manage Pegasus with the least motion of his hand, and had taught him to obey his voice, he determined to attempt the performance of this perilous adventure.

At daybreak, therefore, as soon as he unclosed his eyes, he gently pinched the winged horse's ear, in order to arouse him. Pegasus immediately started from the ground and pranced about a quarter of a mile aloft, and made a grand sweep around the mountain-top, by way of showing that he was wide awake, and ready for any kind of an excursion. During the whole of this little flight, he uttered a loud, brisk and melodious neigh, and finally came down at Bellerophon's side, as lightly as ever you saw a sparrow hop upon a twig.

'Well done, dear Pegasus! well done, my sky-skimmer!' cried Bellerophon, fondly stroking the horse's neck. 'And now, my fleet and beautiful friend, we must break our fast. Today we are to fight the terrible Chimaera.'

As soon as they had eaten their morning meal, and drank some sparkling water from a spring called Hippocrene, Pegasus held out his head, of his own accord, so that his master might put on the bridle. Then, with a great many playful leaps and airy caperings, he showed his impatience to be gone; while Bellerophon was girding on his sword, and hanging his shield about his neck, and preparing himself for battle. When everything was ready, the rider mounted, and (as was his custom, when going a long distance) ascended five miles perpendicularly, so as the better to see whither he was directing his course. He then turned the head of Pegasus towards the east, and set out for Lycia. In their flight they overtook an eagle, and came so nigh him, before he could get out of their way, that Bellerophon might easily have caught him by the leg. Hastening onward at this rate, it was still early in the forenoon when they beheld the lofty mountains of Lycia, with their deep and shaggy valleys. If Bellerophon had been told truly, it was in one of those dismal valleys that the hideous Chimaera had taken up its abode.

Being now so near their journey's end, the winged horse gradually descended with his rider; and they took advantage of some clouds that were floating over the mountain tops, in order to conceal themselves. Hovering on the upper surface of a cloud, and peeping over its edge, Bellerophon had a pretty distinct view of the mountainous part of Lycia, and could look into all its shadowy vales at once. At first there appeared to be nothing remarkable. It was a wild, savage, and rocky tract of high and precipitous hills. In the more level part of the country there were ruins of houses that had been burnt, and here and there the carcasses of dead cattle strewn about the pastures where they had been feeding.

'The Chimaera must have done this mischief,' thought Bellerophon. 'But where can the monster be?'

As I have already said, there was nothing remarkable to be detected, at first sight, in any of the valleys and dells that lay among the precipitous heights of the mountains. Nothing at all; unless, indeed, it were three spires of black smoke, which issued from what seemed to be the mouth of a cavern, and clambered sullenly into the atmosphere. Before reaching the mountain-top, these three black smoke-wreaths mingled themselves into one. The cavern was almost directly beneath the winged horse and his rider, at the distance of about a thousand feet. The smoke, as it crept heavily upward, had an ugly, sulphurous, stifling scent, which caused Pegasus to snort and Bellerophon to sneeze. So disagreeable was it to the marvellous steed (who was accustomed to breathe only the purest air) that he waved his wings, and shot half a mile out of the range of this offensive vapour.

But, on looking behind him, Bellerophon saw something that induced him first to draw the bridle, and then to turn Pegasus about. He made a sign, which the winged horse understood, and sunk slowly through the air, until his hoofs were scarcely more than a man's height above the rocky bottom of the valley. In front, as far off as you could throw a stone, was the cavern's mouth, with the three smoke-wreaths oozing out of it. And what else did Bellerophon behold then?

There seemed to be a heap of strange and terrible creatures curled up within the cavern. Their bodies lay so close together that Bellerophon could not distinguish them apart; but, judging by their heads, one of these creatures was a huge snake, the second a fierce lion, and the third an ugly goat. The lion and the goat were asleep; the snake was broad awake, and kept staring about him with a great pair of fiery eyes. But – and this was the most wonderful part of the matter – the three spires of smoke evidently issued from the nostrils of these three heads! So strange was the spectacle, that, though Bellerophon had been all along expecting it, the truth did not immediately occur to him that here was the terrible three-headed Chimaera. He had found out the Chimaera's cavern. The snake, the lion, and the goat, as he supposed them to be, were not three separate creatures, but one monster.

The wicked, hateful thing! Slumbering, as two thirds of it was, it still held, in its abominable claws, the remnant of an unfortunate lamb – or possibly (but I hate to think so) it was a dear little boy – which its three mouths had been gnawing before two of them fell asleep!

All at once Bellerophon started as from a dream, and knew it to be the Chimaera. Pegasus seemed to know it at the same instant, and sent forth a neigh that sounded like the call of a trumpet to battle. At this sound the three heads reared themselves erect, and belched out great flashes of flame. Before Bellerophon had time to consider what to do next, the monster flung itself out of the cavern and sprung straight towards him, with its immense claws extended, and its snaky tail twisting itself venomously behind. If Pegasus had not been as nimble as a bird, both he and his rider would have been overthrown by the Chimaera's headlong rush, and thus the battle have been ended before it was well begun. But the winged horse was not to be caught so. In the twinkling of an eye he was up aloft, half-way to the clouds, snorting with anger. He shuddered, too, not with affright, but with utter disgust at the loathsomeness of this poisonous thing with three heads.

The Chimaera, on the other hand, raised itself up so as to stand absolutely on the tip-end of its tail, with its talons pawing fiercely in the air, and its three heads spluttering fire at Pegasus and his rider. My stars, how it roared, and hissed, and bellowed! Bellerophon, meanwhile, was fitting his shield on his arm, and drawing his sword.

'Now, my beloved Pegasus,' he whispered in the winged horse's ear, 'thou must help me to slay this insufferable monster; or else thou shalt fly back to thy solitary mountain-peak without thy friend Bellerophon. For either the Chimaera dies, or its three mouths shall gnaw this head of mine, which has slumbered upon thy neck!'

Pegasus whinnied, and, turning back his head, rubbed his nose tenderly against his rider's cheek. It was his way of telling him that, though he had wings and was an immortal horse, yet he would perish, if it was possible for immortality to perish, rather than leave Bellerophon behind.

'I thank you, Pegasus,' answered Bellerophon. 'Now, then, let us make a dash at the monster!'

Uttering these words, he shook the bridle; and Pegasus darted down aslant, as swift as the flight of an arrow, right towards the Chimaera's three-fold head, which all this time was poking itself as high as it could into the air. As he came within arm's-length, Bellerophon made a cut at the monster, but was carried onward by his steed before he could see whether the blow had been successful. Pegasus continued his course, but soon wheeled round, at about the same distance from the Chimaera as before. Bellerophon then perceived that he had cut the goat's head of the monster almost off, so that it dangled downward by the skin, and seemed quite dead.

But, to make amends the snake's head and the lion's head had taken all the fierceness of the dead one into themselves, and spit flame, and hissed, and roared, with a vast deal more fury than before.

'Never mind, my brave Pegasus!' cried Bellerophon. 'With another stroke like that, we will stop either its hissing or its roaring.'

And again he shook the bridle. Dashing aslantwise as before, the winged horse made another arrow-flight towards the Chimaera, and Bellerophon aimed another downright stroke at one of the two remaining heads as he shot by. But this time neither he nor Pegasus escaped so well as at first. With one of its claws the Chimaera had given the young man a deep scratch on his shoulder, and had slightly damaged the left wing of the flying steed with the other. On his part Bellerophon had mortally wounded the lion's head of the monster, insomuch that it now hung downward, with its fire almost extinguished, and sending out gasps of thick black smoke. The snake's head, however (which was the only one now left), was twice as fierce and venomous as ever before. It belched forth shoots of fire five hundred yards long, and emitted hisses so loud, so harsh, and so ear-piercing, that King Iobates heard them fifty miles off, and trembled till the throne shook under him.

'Well-a-day!' thought the poor king; 'the Chimaera is certainly coming to devour me!'

Meanwhile Pegasus had again paused in the air, and neighed angrily, while sparkles of a pure crystal flame darted out of his eyes. How unlike the lurid fire of the Chimaera! The aerial steed's spirit was all aroused, and so was that of Bellerophon.

'Dost thou bleed, my immortal horse?' cried the young man, caring less for his own hurt than for the anguish of this glorious creature, that ought never to have tasted pain. 'The execrable Chimaera shall pay for this mischief with his last head!'

Then he shook the bridle, shouted loudly, and guided Pegasus, not aslantwise as before, but straight at the monster's hideous front. So rapid was the onset, that it seemed but a dazzle and a flash before Bellerophon was at close grips with his enemy.

The Chimaera, by this time, after losing its second head, had got into a red-hot passion of pain and rampant rage. It so flounced about, half on earth and partly in the air, that it was impossible to say which element it rested upon. It opened its snake-jaws to such an abominable width that Pegasus might almost, I was going to say, have flown right down its throat, wings outspread, rider and all! At their approach it shot out a tremendous blast of its fiery breath, and enveloped Bellerophon and his steed in a perfect atmosphere of flame, singeing the wings of Pegasus, scorching off one whole side of the young man's golden ringlets, and making them both far hotter than was comfortable from head to foot.

But this was nothing to what followed.

When the airy rush of the winged horse had brought him within the distance of a hundred yards, the Chimaera gave a spring, and flung its huge, awkward, venomous, and utterly detestable carcass right upon poor Pegasus, clung round him with might and main, and tied up its snaky tail into a knot! Up flew the aerial steed, higher, higher, higher, above the mountain peaks, above the clouds, and almost out of sight of the solid earth. But still the earth-born monster kept its hold, and was borne upward, along with the creature of light and air. Bellerophon, meanwhile, turning about, found himself face to face with the ugly grimness of the Chimaera's visage, and could only avoid being scorched to death, or bitten right in twain, by holding up his shield. Over the upper edge of the shield he looked sternly into the savage eyes of the monster.

But the Chimaera was so mad and wild with pain, that it did not guard itself so well as might else have been the case. Perhaps, after all, the best way to fight a Chimaera is by getting as close to it as you can. In its efforts to stick its horrible iron claws into its enemy, the creature left its own breast quite exposed; and perceiving this, Bellerophon thrust his sword up to the hilt into its cruel heart. Immediately the snaky tail untied its knot. The monster let go its hold of Pegasus, and fell from that vast height, downward: while the fire within its bosom, instead of being put out, burned fiercer than ever, and quickly began to consume the dead carcass. Thus it fell out of the sky, all aflame, and (it being nightfall before it reached the earth) was mistaken for a shooting star or a comet. But, at early sunrise, some cottagers were going to their day's labour, and saw, to their astonishment, that several acres of ground were strewn with black ashes. In the middle of a field there was a heap of whitened bones a great deal higher than a haystack. Nothing else was ever seen of the dreadful Chimaera!

And when Bellerophon had won the victory, he bent forward and kissed Pegasus, while the tears stood in his eyes.

'Back now, my beloved steed!' said he. 'Back to the Fountain of Pirene!'

Pegasus skimmed through the air, quicker than ever he did

before, and reached the fountain in a very short time. And there he found the old man leaning on his staff, and the country fellow watering his cow, and the pretty maiden filling her pitcher.

'I remember now,' quoth the old man, 'I saw this winged horse once before, when I was quite a lad. But he was ten times handsomer in those days.'

'I own a cart-horse worth three of him!' said the country fellow. 'If this pony were mine, the first thing I should do would be to clip his wings!'

But the poor maiden said nothing, for she had always the luck to be afraid at the wrong time. So she ran away, and let her pitcher tumble down and broke it.

'Where is the gentle child,' asked Bellerophon, 'who used to keep me company, and never lost his faith, and never was weary of gazing into the fountain?'

'Here am I, dear Bellerophon!' said the child, softly.

For the little boy had spent day after day, on the margin of Pirene, waiting for his friend to come back; but when he perceived Bellerophon descending through the clouds, mounted on the winged horse, he had shrunk back into the shrubbery. He was a delicate and tender child, and dreaded lest the old man and the country fellow should see the tears gushing from his eyes.

'Thou hast won the victory,' said he, joyfully, running to the knee of Bellerophon, who still sat on the back of Pegasus. 'I knew thou wouldst.'

'Yes, dear child!' replied Bellerophon, alighting from the winged horse. 'But if thy faith had not helped me, I should never have waited for Pegasus, and never have gone up above the clouds, and never have conquered the terrible Chimaera. Thou, my beloved little friend, hast done it all. And now let us give Pegasus his liberty.'

So he slipped off the enchanted bridle from the head of the marvellous steed.

'Be free for evermore, my Pegasus!' cried he, with a shade of sadness in his tone. 'Be as free as thou art fleet!'

But Pegasus rested his head on Bellerophon's shoulder and would not be persuaded to take flight.

'Well, then,' said Bellerophon, caressing the airy horse, 'thou shalt be with me as long as thou wilt; and we will go together, forthwith, and tell King Iobates that the Chimaera is destroyed.'

Then Bellerophon embraced the gentle child, and promised to come to him again, and departed. But, in after years, that child took higher flights upon the aerial steed than ever did Bellerophon, and achieved more honourable deeds than his friend's victory over the Chimaera. For, gentle and tender as he was, he grew to be a mighty poet!

HERCULES IN HELL

Mike Ashley

E URYSTHEUS, KING of Tiryns, sighed as he looked upon the undaunted countenance of Hercules. There stood the man-mountain, proud and defiant.

'Twelve tasks I have agreed to complete,' Hercules was saying. 'Eleven are accomplished. What is your final test?'

Eurystheus winced. How he hated Hercules. The man might be a blood relative, but his supporters were legion, and his claim to the throne of the sons of Perseus which Eurystheus held had only been thwarted by his delayed birth. There had to be some way to be rid of him, yet although he had set him eleven impossible tasks, every time he had triumphed. Was there no way Eurystheus would see this man in Hell?

And with that thought the idea of the final task came to mind and for the first time in many years, Eurystheus smiled.

'Cousin, as you say, one task remains. I want you to fetch Cerberus from the Underworld.'

Eurystheus expected to see even Hercules hesitate. This task surely was impossible. Even if Hercules could survive the journey into the realms of darkness, Cerberus itself would be unconquerable and the Dark Lord Pluto would not agree to Cerberus being taken.

Yet Hercules bowed, and walked from Eurystheus' chamber seemingly without concern. 'Clearly he's mad,' Eurystheus spoke to the air, 'just as we all knew.' Eurystheus was referring to the reason Hercules was under his control in the first place. Some years before Hercules had been seized with a fit of madness and had murdered his own sons and nephews. For atonement the oracle at Delphi had ordered Hercules to serve Eurystheus and to undertake twelve tasks. Although Hercules' madness had passed, Eurystheus was convinced the man could never be totally sane. He was mad with his own strength, the power that he drew from Zeus, his father, which no mortal could contain. But perhaps set against the Lord of the Underworld, Hercules might at last meet his match.

Hercules, armed as ever with his poisoned arrows and his massive club, left Tiryns and headed for the city of Eleusis, on the coast beyond Athens. To venture into the depths of Hell, Hercules knew he must be purified of all sin, and only the Lords of the Mysteries at Eleusis could cleanse him of his past. But for the first time in his labours, Hercules met the opposition of his fellow man. The initiation ceremonies at Eleusis were reserved for Athenians alone and Hercules was no Athenian. Regardless of his power, Hercules could not be admitted.

A younger Hercules would have torn the temple apart, but now more mature and trying to control his power Hercules sought to reason. He had learned on previous adventures that sometimes the mind was more powerful than muscle. On his quest to obtain the Golden Apples of the Hesperides, Hercules had asked Atlas to help him. Atlas was only too welcome and, for a while, Hercules took the burden of the Heavens upon his shoulders while Atlas sought out the Apples. But when he returned Atlas decided he did not want to take back the Heavens and prepared to take the Apples to Eurystheus himself. Hercules outwitted Atlas, though, by asking him to place a pad upon Hercules' neck to help spread the load. As Atlas did so, Hercules slipped out leaving Atlas bearing the full weight of the Heavens again.

Perhaps reason could work again here. Supposing Hercules became an Athenian? Would they accept an adopted son of Athens? Hercules appealed to the king of Athens, his friend Theseus, and Theseus agreed, suggesting that one of the senior citizens be an adoptive father. This threw the Eleusinians into a quandary, but not wishing to argue with Theseus or Hercules, they consented.

The studies and rites were extensive and arduous, testing Hercules' mind in ways far harder than ever his muscles. But he applied himself and after almost a year the Eleusinians agreed that Hercules was ready for his initiation. This led to further debate because the ceremony at Eleusis was only for

Athenians. As a result they agreed to hold a special ceremony outside Eleusis. Thus in the earliest days of spring, Hercules bathed and cleansed himself in the river Ilissus and was purified by the priest.

Now Hercules, his mind and body both spiritually strong, was ready to enter the darkest depths of Hell.

It was a new Hercules who set out. Gone was the lion skin that he had worn since, as a youth, he had killed the lion that ravaged the cattle at Cithaeron, the first of his mighty deeds. Instead he wore a simple linen tunic, white and pure.

Hercules prayed to Zeus for guidance. To help him Zeus sent Hermes who led Hercules south across the Peloponnese to the southernmost point of the Greek mainland to the rich marble quarries of Taenarum. There Hermes bade Hercules to search for the entrance.

Hercules first went to pay homage to Poseidon, whose Temple was at Taenarum. Poseidon had always admired Hercules' strength, though he had never supported him because Hercules was always fighting and killing Poseidon's own offspring. But he saw no reason why he should not help Hercules on his way, particularly as the trip into Hell might be the best way to be rid of him.

As Hercules prayed at the Temple, Poseidon caused a spring to burst forth from the ground. Hercules, hearing the trickling water, followed the sound and found where the water bubbled from the rocks. The trickle formed a small stream which Hercules followed, and the stream led to a dark cave. There at the mouth stood Hermes.

'Beware Hercules,' Hermes warned. 'The waters of Acheron are poisonous. Do not drink therefrom or bathe in it.'

Hercules now followed Hermes into the dark mouth of the cave. His descent into the Underworld had begun.

The moment they were out of the sun a chillness settled about them. Hercules, dressed only in his linen tunic, found the cold more numbing than anything he had previously experienced. This would test his strength past endurance.

Led by light from Hermes' staff, the two followed the stream down through the dark caverns. Gradually, as Hercules' eyes became accustomed to the darkness, he became aware of other shapes moving along the walls. Shapes that vanished when he turned to look at them fully, but which returned when he looked ahead. A few at first they began to increase in number, some coming close to whisper his name, but vanishing as soon as he turned his head.

'What visions are these?' Hercules grunted, as he unleashed his club from around his waist. But Hermes stayed his hand.

'What do you expect to find in the Underworld, son of Zeus, but wraiths of the dead? You cannot harm them, and they can harm you no more.'

But though the shades could not injure Hercules physically, they could taunt his mind and threaten his madness. He needed to draw upon all that he had learned at Eleusis to control his fear.

The dark waters of Acheron led them further into gloom and at length the passageway opened onto a vast cavern whose ceiling was lost in the heights. The cavern glowed with a dim twilight, lit by the fires of the river Phlegethon. Here the Acheron flowed into another river, the Styx.

Through the twilight of the cavern Hercules perceived a short way off a boat, and in the boat waited Charon, the ancient boatman who ferried the souls of the dead across to Hades. Charon was a strong old man with a hideous countenance and a long white beard. His garment was ragged and dirty and his forehead covered with wrinkles. He looked on Hercules with piercing eyes.

'You are living,' said he. 'Get thee hence. My boat is for the dead.'

'You shall ferry me across,' Hercules affirmed. 'By the will of Zeus I go to bring Cerberus to the light of day.'

'Where is thy money to pay me?' asked Charon. 'Without it you cannot pass, but must wander by these shores a hundred years.'

'I have no money, but that will not stop me.'

So saying Hercules leaped into the boat. Despite his fearsomeness, Charon was terrified of the might and will of Hercules. He gave way and ferried him over, all the while grumbling, 'Pluto will have me in prison for this; no one can pass without payment.'

All the while they crossed Hercules was aware of the wailing of souls about him as spirits awaited their fate. The waters of the Styx were oily black and silent as death. As Hercules peered into them he was aware he could see no reflection. Instead the water seemed to draw him toward it. He felt as if it were sucking his very soul from his body. Again he had to draw upon the strength of his initiation to fight back. Only a pure mind could combat the agonies of Hell.

Eventually Charon reached the far shore where all the new spirits were gathered. At the sight of Hercules most fled, but two stood their ground. Hercules found it hard at first to see either as they seemed to fade as he looked directly and were always at the side of his vision. But gradually one face came to him which did not fade. This face had hair that seethed and writhed, and an expression of total hatred. It was a face that no one could look upon and live, the face of the gorgon, Medusa.

'Hercules,' it whispered, 'do you know me?'

Hercules put up his arm to shield his face.

'I know you, daughter of Phorcys, but you do not trouble me.'

Hercules reached for his club, but Hermes stayed his hand.

'Pass her by, Hercules. The dead cannot harm you.'

But still the monster taunted. 'Once I had life, Hercules, until your forebear, Perseus, struck me dead. I shall have revenge upon his seed.'

As she spoke the hissing of the snakes about her head increased, their sibillance luring Hercules to sleep. Slowly he lowered his arm. Deep down his soul cried for help.

There was a flash of brilliance within the cave which caused Hercules to again shield his eyes. In that moment the goddess Athene appeared and held her shield in front of Medusa's head. The serpents were forced to obey their goddess and the writhing and hissing ceased.

Athene spoke through the blinding light.

'Pass on, Hercules. Your mission awaits you.'

But now the other spirit called to Hercules. Again as his vision cleared Hercules recognised his old friend Meleager, the mighty hero whom Hercules had accompanied on the hunt for the Calydonian Boar, and who had been one of the Argonauts in Jason's quest for the Golden Fleece. Fate had struck Meleager a savage blow. His life had been safe so long as a certain log had remained unburnt. But Meleager, like

Hercules, suffered bouts of madness and in one such fit had killed his brothers. In anger his mother, who had kept the log safe, threw it on the fire, and as it burned so Meleager died.

'Hercules, my old friend,' Meleager whispered. 'My sister Deianeira believes you dead and weeps for you.'

Hercules remembered Deianeira with much love and tenderness. He vowed to Meleager that once he had finished this final labour he would seek out Deianeira and look after her. Little did Hercules know at that moment that he was sealing his fate, though it would be many years and many adventures before that day came.

Hercules now passed Meleager by, following the river Styx toward the Gates of Hell itself. At this point Hermes stopped Hercules and spoke to him.

'You are now on the Plains of Hell, Hercules, and ahead lie the Gates of Hades. This is where I agreed to take you, and is where I leave you. Fare well, son of Zeus, until we meet again.' And so saying Hermes rose on his winged feet and vanished into the darkness above.

Alone on the Plains of Hell, Hercules detected a sound of chains ahead of him. Were these the tormented souls of Hell?

As Hercules drew near he saw two men chained to a rock as black as pitch. Suddenly Hercules recognised them. They were his past comrades in adventures, Theseus, king of Athens, and Pirithous, king of the Lapithae. Hercules could not help but laugh at seeing these two heroes in their plight.

Theseus explained what had transpired in the year while Hercules studied at Eleusis. Hercules learned of the battle between the Lapithae and their half-brothers the Centaurs. This had happened after the centaur Eurution, far the worse for drink, had abducted Pirithous' bride Hippodameia. In the subsequent battle Hippodameia had died. Theseus, who had helped in the fight, agreed that each would aid the other find a new bride. Theseus had abducted the young Helen of Troy, which had led to further adventures, though not the famous Trojan War. But Pirithous would settle for no one less than Persephone, the wife of Pluto.

Now Persephone was under an agreement to spend part of her life in the upper world, but rather than wait for her to appear, Pirithous insisted on seeking her in the Underworld.

Against his better judgement Theseus agreed to help. But even before they had reached the gates of Hades, Pluto thwarted their presumption and had them chained to a rock to live forever amongst the dead.

Now Pirithous pleaded with Hercules to set them free. Hercules agreed provided they return to the upper world and forget their quest. Theseus agreed. With one tug from his mighty wrists, Hercules broke the chain that bound Theseus and set him free.

But Pirithous argued and was determined to claim Persephone. This angered Pluto who began to shake the rocks around Pirithous until he sank into a crack.

'You deserve your fate, Pirithous,' Hercules shouted into the chasm. 'There you shall remain until you mend your ways. But do you, dear Theseus, return to the world of light. I must continue on my quest.'

Hercules was now nearing the Gates of Hell. Around him gathered the souls of the dead, and the magnitude of these ghosts daunted even the spirit of Hercules. He decided to appease them with a gift of blood.

Nearby on the Plain of Hell were the cattle of Pluto. Hercules slaughtered one of them, pouring the blood over the Earth on which the ghosts feasted as their one last taste of life.

But the herdsman Monoetius challenged Hercules. 'You have no right to slaughter Pluto's cattle,' he cried, shaking his fist.

'I have no argument with you, Monoetius. Let me pass.'

But Monoetius would not and challenged Hercules to a wrestling match. Hercules first prayed to Zeus for his blessing, and then rose to meet Monoetius. The herdsman was a mighty man, but pale of skin and with long white hair. The two grappled and Hercules soon gripped Monoetius by the waist crushing his ribs. Had Hercules continued he would have broken the herdsman's back and killed him. But a voice from the darkness cried stop.

Hercules dropped Monoetius and looked ahead into the gloom. From out of the darkness came Persephone, the wife of Pluto. She was beautiful and fair, but her countenance was sad and pale. She always longed for the flowery valleys of earth, the light of the sun and the laughter of the living.

'Welcome, Hercules my brother, but stay your hand.

Monoetius is proud and loyal, but does not deserve to die. Spare him and I will grant you audience with Pluto.'

Hercules bowed his head to Persephone, the Queen of the Night, and agreed to follow her.

Persephone led Hercules along the banks of the Styx. Shortly, on either side of the river rose monstrous silver columns that stretched and vanished into the twilight, and there at the Gates of Hell waited Cerberus.

Though dog-shaped, Cerberus had three heads, a neck of hissing serpents and the tail of a scorpion. As Hercules approached the dog rose, baring its poisonous teeth and growled deeply in each of its three throats, but as Persephone raised her hand the dog ceased its growling and allowed them to pass.

Hercules now entered the Palace of Hell. There sat Pluto, high on a throne of sulphur set over the point where all the rivers of Hell met. He was a hard-hearted and inexorable god of a grim and dismal countenance.

'Hail, Pluto,' said Hercules. 'I am commanded by Eurystheus to bring Cerberus from your kingdom and into the eye of day.'

'Thou may be Hercules,' said Pluto, his voice darker than dread, 'but neither you nor Eurystheus have authority over me. Thou art a madman to make such a request. Who then would guard the gates of my kingdom?'

Hercules tensed at the reference to being mad, and called upon the Mysteries to contain his ire.

'Pluto, you have many servants to do thy work. But as for me, I am alone to do the work which Zeus has laid upon me. Eleven labours have I performed. I have been to the ends of the earth, and felt the weight of the heavens on my back; and now this last labour will I perform, if I have to pull down the walls of Hades and perish in the undertaking.'

'I believe you would, Hercules. Very well. If you think you are so powerful, then take Cerberus, but you must capture him first. And if you succeed, you must return him to me within the month. But do not believe that you have conquered Hades. That thou never will. A place awaits you here after your adventures and wanderings. And the next time you shall never leave.'

Hercules thanked Pluto and bowed deeply to the Dark Lord

and his wife. He then returned to the Gates of Hell where Cerberus waited as he had for eternity stopping any souls from leaving.

The monster's eyes glowed red and its three jaws opened revealing huge teeth dripping with venom. It moved out toward the centre of the Gates and crouched low, ready to spring.

But Hercules sprang first taking the beast by surprise. With one hand Hercules gripped the hellhound by the throat and with the other he grasped its poisonous tail and held the monster over his head. No matter how it writhed and struggled it could not escape Hercules' mighty grip. Hercules now tightened his grip around the creature's throat where all three necks joined. Although huge and as strong as iron the throat began to yield to Hercules' almighty strength and the beast found itself choking. Knowing it could not beat Hercules it ceased its struggling and relaxed. Gradually Hercules placed the beast on the ground where it lay in submission. Hercules gathered the chains that had previously bound Theseus to the rock and bound Cerberus.

Persephone had followed Hercules and watched the battle.

'You have achieved your quest, Hercules. Go, take Cerberus back to the land of life, but return him hence or my Lord Pluto will take his revenge.'

Hercules agreed and bowing to Persephone hefted Cerberus onto his mighty shoulders.

As he left he took one final glance back at Persephone. 'Remember me to the world,' she said, and then she turned and went back to Darkness.

Hercules seized Cerberus and carried him aloft out of the Halls of Hell. Charon readily ferried him back across the Styx. He had already received his punishment from Pluto for allowing Hercules in and was commanded to take Cerberus' place until Hercules returned.

As Hercules began to approach the upper world Cerberus began to struggle. The monster had never seen the sun and daylight and was afraid. With a blow of his fist Hercules knocked him unconscious, but as they emerged into the daylight, the dog's venomous spittle spattered the ground, and thereabout the plant aconite grew thereafter.

At last, after an absence of almost two years, Hercules returned to Tiryns. He cast the fearful monster at the feet of

Eurystheus. Cerberus held him in his baleful glare, his teeth dripping venom.

Eurystheus quailed and implored Hercules to keep hold of the monster. 'Very well, Hercules. You have performed the tasks I placed upon you. You are free to go. But first you must join me in a sacrifice of thanks to the gods.'

Hercules had no trust in Eurystheus but could not taunt the gods. At the celebrations Eurystheus handed Hercules a small portion of meat, whilst granting much larger portions to his sons. Hercules' temper could hold no longer.

'Eurystheus, I am no longer bound to you and you have no hold over me. From this day forth live in fear for the day shall come when not I, but my children, shall avenge me.'

As Hercules stormed from the Palace, three of Eurystheus' sons jumped upon him with their swords, but with one swing of his club he dashed out their brains. Eurystheus looked on in horror and wept. He watched his doom go forth.

Hercules now had to complete his promise to Pluto. Shouldering again the burden of Cerberus, which continued to whimper against the sunlight, Hercules returned to the Halls of Hell. The beast was much pleased to behold the fearful gates and the thousand thousand gliding shadows of the dead and the dim uncertain light of his own land.

But Hercules did not pass through the Gates of Hell this time. He turned back to light and life. He was now free from the yoke of Eurystheus and the world was his. There was still much for Hercules to achieve, but first he had his promise to Meleager to fulfil and the next step along the road to fate was about to begin.

SIEGFRIED AND
THE DRAGON FAFNIR

James Baldwin

R EGIN THE BARD took up his harp, and his fingers smote the strings; and the music which came forth sounded like the wail of the winter's wind through the dead tree tops of the forest. And the song which he sang was full of grief and wild hopeless yearning for the things which were not to be. When he had ceased, Siegfried said, 'That was indeed a sorrowful song for one to sing who sees his hopes so nearly realized. Why are you so sad? Is it because you fear the curse which you have taken upon yourself? or is it because you know not what you will do with so vast a treasure, and its possession begins already to trouble you?'

'Oh, many are the things I will do with that treasure!' answered Regin; and his eyes flashed wildly, and his face grew red and pale. 'I will turn winter into summer; I will make the desert-places glad; I will bring back the golden age; I will make myself a god: for mine shall be the wisdom and the gathered wealth of the world. And yet I fear –'

'What do you fear?'

'The ring, the ring – it is accursed! The Norns, too, have spoken, and my doom is known. I cannot escape it.'

'The Norns have woven the woof of every man's life,' answered Siegfried. 'Tomorrow we fare to the Glittering Heath, and the end shall be as the Norns have spoken.'

And so, early the next morning, Siegfried mounted Greyfell, and rode out towards the desert-land that lay beyond the forest and the barren mountain-range; and Regin, his eyes flashing with desire, and his feet never tiring, trudged by his side. For seven days they wended their way through the thick greenwood, sleeping at night on the bare ground beneath the trees, while the wolves and other wild beasts of the forest filled the air with their hideous howlings. But no evil creature dared come near them, for fear of the shining beams of light which fell from Greyfell's gleaming mane. On the eighth day they came to the open country and to the hills, where the land was covered with black boulders and broken by yawning chasms. And no living thing was seen there, not even an insect, nor a blade of grass; and the silence of the grave was over all. And the earth was dry and parched, and the sun hung above them like a painted shield in a blue-black sky, and there was neither shade nor water anywhere. But Siegfried rode onwards in the way which Regin pointed out, and faltered not, although he grew faint with thirst and with the overpowering heat. Towards the evening of the next day they came to a dark mountain-wall which stretched far out on either hand, and rose high above them, so steep that it seemed to close up the way, and to forbid them going farther.

'This is the wall!' cried Regin. 'Beyond this mountain is the Glittering Heath, and the goal of all my hopes.'

And the little old man ran forwards, and scaled the rough side of the mountain, and reached its summit, while Siegfried and Greyfell were yet toiling among the rocks at its foot. Slowly and painfully they climbed the steep ascent, sometimes following a narrow path which wound along the edge of a precipice, sometimes leaping from rock to rock, or over some deep gorge, and sometimes picking their way among the crags and cliffs. The sun at last went down, and one by one the stars came out; and the moon was rising, round and red, when Siegfried stood by Regin's side, and gazed from the mountain-top down upon the Glittering Heath which lay beyond. And a strange, weird scene it was that met his sight. At the foot of the mountain was a river, white and cold and still; and beyond it was a smooth and barren plain, lying silent and lonely in the pale moonlight. But in the distance was seen a circle of flickering flames, ever changing – now growing brighter, now fading away, and now shining with a dull, cold light, like the glimmer of the glow-worm or the fox-fire. And as Siegfried gazed upon the scene, he saw the dim outline of some hideous monster moving hither and thither, and seeming all the more terrible in the uncertain light.

'It is he!' whispered Regin, and his lips were ashy pale, and his knees trembled beneath him. 'It is Fafnir, and he wears the Helmet of Terror! Shall we not go back to the smithy by the great forest, and to the life of ease and safety that may be ours there? Or will you rather dare to go forwards, and meet the Terror in its abode?'

'None but cowards give up an undertaking once begun,' answered Siegfried. 'Go back to Rhineland yourself, if you are afraid; but you must go alone. You have brought me thus far to meet the dragon of the heath, to win the hoard of the swarthy elves, and to rid the world of a terrible evil. Before the setting of another sun, the deed which you have urged me to do will be done.'

Then he dashed down the eastern slope of the mountain, leaving Greyfell and the trembling Regin behind him. Soon he stood on the banks of the white river, which lay between the mountain and the heath; but the stream was deep and sluggish, and the channel was very wide. He paused a moment, wondering how he should cross; and the air seemed heavy with deadly vapors, and the water was thick and cold. While he thus stood in thought, a boat came silently out of the mists, and drew near; and the boatman stood up and called to him, and said, 'What man are you who dares come into this land of loneliness and fear?'

'I am Siegfried,' answered the lad; 'and I have come to slay Fafnir, the Terror.'

'Sit in my boat,' said the boatman, 'and I will carry you across the river.'

And Siegfried sat by the boatman's side; and without the use of an oar, and without a breath of air to drive it forwards, the little vessel turned, and moved silently towards the farther shore.

'In what way will you fight the dragon?' asked the boatman.

'With my trusty sword Balmung I shall slay him,' answered Siegfried.

'But he wears the Helmet of Terror, and he breathes deathly poisons, and his eyes dart forth lightning, and no man can withstand his strength,' said the boatman.

'I will find some way by which to overcome him.'

'Then be wise, and listen to me,' said the boatman. 'As you go up from the river you will find a road, worn deep and smooth, starting from the water's edge, and winding over the moor. It is the trail of Fafnir, adown which he comes at dawn of every day to slake his thirst at the river. Do you dig a pit in this roadway – a pit narrow and deep – and hide yourself within it. In the morning, when Fafnir passes over it, let him feel the edge of Balmung.'

As the man ceased speaking, the boat touched the shore, and Siegfried leaped out. He looked back to thank his unknown friend, but neither boat nor boatman was to be seen. Only a thin white mist rose slowly from the cold surface of the stream, and floated upwards and away towards the mountain-tops. Then the lad remembered that the strange boatman had worn a blue hood bespangled with golden stars, and that a gray kirtle was thrown over his shoulders, and that his one eye glistened and sparkled with a light that was more than human. And he knew that he had again talked with Odin. Then, with a braver heart than before, he went forwards, along the river-bank, until he came to Fafnir's trail – a deep, wide furrow in the earth, beginning at the river's bank, and winding far away over the heath, until it was lost to sight in the darkness. The bottom of the trail was soft and slimy, and its sides had been worn smooth by Fafnir's frequent travel through it.

In this road, at a point not far from the river, Siegfried, with his trusty sword Balmung, scooped out a deep and narrow pit, as Odin had directed. And when the gray dawn began to appear in the east he hid himself within this trench, and waited for the coming of the monster. He had not long to wait; for no sooner had the sky begun to redden in the light of the coming sun than the dragon was heard bestirring himself. Siegfried peeped warily from his hiding-place, and saw him coming far down the road, hurrying with all speed, that he might quench his thirst at the sluggish river, and hasten back to his gold; and the sound which he made was like the trampling of many feet and the jingling of many chains. With bloodshot eyes, and gaping mouth, and flaming nostrils, the hideous creature came rushing onwards. His sharp, curved claws dug deep into the soft earth; and his bat-like wings, half trailing on the ground, half flapping in the air, made a sound like that which is heard when Thor rides in his goat-drawn chariot over the dark thunder-clouds. It was a terrible moment for Siegfried, but still he was not afraid. He crouched low down in his hiding-place, and the bare blade of the trusty Balmung glittered in the morning light. On came the hastening feet and the flapping wings: the red gleam from the monster's flaming nostrils lighted up the trench where Siegfried lay. He heard a roaring and a rushing like the sound of a whirlwind in the forest; then a black, inky mass rolled above him, and all was dark. Now was Siegfried's opportunity. The bright edge of Balmung gleamed in the darkness one moment, and then it smote the heart of Fafnir as he passed. Some men say that Odin sat in the pit with Siegfried, and strengthened his arm and directed his sword, or else he could not thus have slain the Terror. But, be this as it may, the victory was soon won. The monster stopped short, while but half of his long body had glided over the pit; for sudden death had overtaken him. His horrid head fell lifeless upon the ground; his cold wings flapped once, and then lay, quivering and helpless, spread out on either side; and streams of thick black blood flowed from his heart, through the wound beneath, and filled the trench in which Siegfried was hidden, and ran like a mountain-torrent down the road towards the river. Siegfried was covered from head to foot with the slimy liquid, and, had he not quickly leaped from his hiding-place, he would have been drowned in the swift-rushing stream.

The bright sun rose in the east, and gilded the mountain-tops, and fell upon the still waters of the river, and lighted up the treeless plains around. The south wind played gently against Siegfried's cheeks and in his long hair, as he stood gazing on his fallen foe. And the sound of singing birds, and rippling waters, and gay insects – such as had not broken the silence of the Glittering Heath for ages – came to his ears. The Terror was dead, and Nature had awakened from her sleep of dread. And as the lad leaned upon his sword, and thought of the deed he had done, behold! the shining Greyfell, with the beaming, hopeful mane, having crossed the now bright river, stood by his side. And Regin, his face grown wondrous cold, came trudging over the meadows; and his heart was full of guile. Then the mountain vultures came wheeling downwards to look upon the dead dragon; and with them were two ravens, black as midnight.

And when Siegfried saw these ravens he knew them to be Odin's birds – Hugin, thought, and Munin, memory. And they alighted on the ground near by; and the lad listened to hear what they would say. Then Hugin flapped his wings, and said, 'The deed is done. Why tarries the hero?'

And Munin said, 'The world is wide. Fame waits for the hero.'

And Hugin answered, 'What if he win the Hoard of the Elves? That is not honor. Let him seek fame by nobler deeds.'

Then Munin flew past his ear, and whispered, 'Beware of Regin, the master! His heart is poisoned. He would be thy bane.'

And the two birds flew away to carry the news to Odin in the happy halls of Gladsheim.

When Regin drew near to look upon the dragon, Siegfried kindly accosted him: but he seemed not to hear; and a snaky glitter lurked in his eyes, and his mouth was set and dry, and he seemed as one walking in a dream.

'It is mine now,' he murmured: 'it is all mine, now – the Hoard of the swarthy elf-folk, the garnered wisdom of ages. The strength of the world is mine. I will keep, I will save, I will heap up; and none shall have part or parcel of the treasure which is mine alone.'

Then his eyes fell upon Siegfried; and his cheeks grew dark with wrath, and he cried out, 'Why are you here in my way? I am the lord of the Glittering Heath: I am the master of the Hoard. I am the master, and you are my thrall.'

Siegfried wondered at the change which had taken place in his old master; but he only smiled at his strange words, and made no answer.

'You have slain my brother!' Regin cried; and his face grew fearfully black, and his mouth foamed with rage.

'It was my deed and yours,' calmly answered Siegfried. 'I have rid the world of a Terror: I have righted a grievous wrong.'

'You have slain my brother,' said Regin; 'and a murderer's ransom you shall pay!'

'Take the Hoard for your ransom, and let us each wend his way,' said the lad.

'The Hoard is mine by rights,' answered Regin still more

wrathfully. 'I am the master, and you are my thrall. Why stand you in my way?'

Then, blinded with madness, he rushed at Siegfried as if to strike him down; but his foot slipped in a puddle of gore, and he pitched headlong against the sharp edge of Balmung. So sudden was this movement, and so unlooked for, that the sword was twitched out of Siegfried's hand, and fell with a dull splash into the blood-filled pit before him; while Regin, slain by his own rashness, sank dead upon the ground. Full of horror, Siegfried turned away, and mounted Greyfell.

'This is a place of blood,' said he, 'and the way to glory leads not through it. Let the Hoard still lie on the Glittering Heath; I will go my way from hence; and the world shall know me for better deeds than this.'

And he turned his back on the fearful scene, and rode away; and so swiftly did Greyfell carry him over the desert land and the mountain waste, that, when night came, they stood on the shore of the great North Sea, and the white waves broke at their feet. And the lad sat for a long time silent upon the warm white sand of the beach, and Greyfell waited at his side. And he watched the stars as they came out one by one, and the moon, as it rose round and pale, and moved like a queen across the sky. And the night wore away, and the stars grew pale, and the moon sank to rest in the wilderness of waters. And at day-dawn Siegfried looked towards the west, and midway between sky and sea he thought he saw dark mountain tops hanging above a land of mists that seemed to float upon the edge of the sea.

While he looked, a white ship, with sails all set, came speeding over the waters towards him. It came nearer and nearer, and the sailors rested upon their oars as it glided into the quiet harbor. A minstrel, with long white beard floating in the wind, sat at the prow; and the sweet music from his harp was wafted like incense to the shore. The vessel touched the sands: its white sails were reefed as if by magic, and the crew leaped out upon the beach.

'Hail, Siegfried the Golden!' cried the harper. 'Whither do you fare this summer day?'

'I have come from a land of horror and dread,' answered the lad; 'and I would fain fare to a brighter.'

'Then go with me to awaken the earth from its slumber, and

to robe the fields in their garbs of beauty,' said the harper. And he touched the strings of his harp, and strains of the softest music arose in the still morning air. And Siegfried stood entranced, for never before had he heard such music.

'Tell me who you are!' he cried, when the sounds died away. 'Tell me who you are, and I will go to the ends of the earth with you.'

'I am Bragi,' answered the harper, smiling. And Siegfried noticed then that the ship was laden with flowers of every hue, and that thousands of singing birds circled around and above it, filling the air with the sound of their glad twitterings.

Now, Bragi was the sweetest musician in all the world. It was said by some that his home was with the song-birds, and that he had learned his skill from them. But this was only part of the truth: for wherever there was loveliness or beauty, or things noble and pure, there was Bragi; and his wondrous power in music and song was but the outward sign of a blameless soul. When he touched the strings of his golden harp, all Nature was charmed with the sweet harmony: the savage beasts of the wood crept near to listen; the birds paused in their flight; the waves of the sea were becalmed, and the winds were hushed; the leaping waterfall was still, and the rushing torrent tarried in its bed; the elves forgot their hidden treasures, and joined in silent dance around him; and the ström-karls and the musicians of the wood vainly tried to imitate him. And he was as fair of speech as he was skilful in song. His words were so persuasive that he had been known to call the fishes from the sea, to move great lifeless rocks, and, what is harder, the hearts of kings. He understood the voice of the birds, and the whispering of the breeze, the murmur of the waves, and the roar of the waterfalls. He knew the length and breadth of the earth, and the secrets of the sea, and the language of the stars. And every day he talked with Odin the All-Father, and with the wise and good in the sunlit halls of Gladsheim. And once every year he went to the North-lands, and woke the earth from its long winter's sleep, and scattered music and smiles and beauty everywhere.

Right gladly did Siegfried agree to sail with Bragi over the sea; for he wot that the bright Asa-god would be a very different guide from the cunning, evil-eyed Regin. So he went on board with Bragi, and the gleaming Greyfell followed them, and the sailors sat at their oars. And Bragi stood in the prow, and touched the strings of his harp. And, as the music arose, the white sails leaped up the masts, and a warm south breeze began to blow; and the little vessel, wafted by sweet sounds and the incense of spring, sped gladly away over the sea.

THE SLAYING OF GRENDEL

Alfred J. Church

IN THE DAYS of old the House of the Scyldings ruled in Denmark. The first of the line was Scyld, whom men called 'Son of the Sheaf' because he came no man knew whence, being a little child in a boat with a sheaf of corn. He grew to be a mighty man of valour, subduing the robber tribes that sailed over the seas seeking for plunder, and compelling the nations round about to pay him tribute. A good and great King was he and God gave him a son for the comfort of his people, for He knew in what evil case that nation stands that lacks a king to rule over it.

Now the time came that King Scyld must die, for he had grown old and feeble. So he said to his warriors, 'Carry me, comrades, to the shore, for as I came by the sea, so by the sea must I go.' So they carried him to the shore; there stood his ship, newly adorned, and with sails set as for a voyage. There in the middle of the ship, hard by the mast, did the comrades of Scyld the King lay down their dead lord. And they laid with him many precious things, ornaments gathered from many far countries. Never have I heard of ship that was adorned in more comely fashion with warriors' gear and weapons of war, battle-axes and coats of mail. Rich in truth was the store that they put in his keeping that he might carry them with him far away into the land of waters. Not less, then, was the wealth that he took than that which he brought. With empty hands he came, but he departed with a king's treasure. And over his head they set up a banner wrought in gold. And the helm they left free that the sea might take him whithersoever it would. But who received that burden not the wisest man that is under heaven knows to this day.

King Scyld having thus gone to his place, Beowulf his son
reigned in his stead for many years even unto old age; and
after Beowulf, Healfdene, a hero famous in war; and after
Healfdene, Hrothgar, who excelled all that had gone before
him in valiant deeds.

It came into the mind of this Hrothgar that he would build a
banqueting-hall, greater than man had ever before heard tell
of. And as he purposed so he did. Quickly was the hall set up,
and when it was finished it was the stateliest hall in all the earth,
a home of peace, towering high into the air. Nor did any that
beheld it dream that there should ever be strife within it, or
that its splendour should be devoured by flames.

And when the great hall was built, the King's warriors
resorted to it with much joy and gladness, till there came
within its doors an evil guest that worked desolation and
woe. Grendel was his name, and he dwelt among the moors
and fens. He was of an accursed race, the race of Cain the
murderer, whom the Lord separated from the children of men.
For, indeed, of this first father come all strange broods, giants,
and elves, and ogres.

On a certain night, when the darkness had fallen, this Grendel
set forth to search out this lofty hall, and to see how the Danes
had bestowed themselves in it. A princely troop he found
sleeping after the feast. Thirty of them did the monster seize,
and hied him back to his den, rejoicing with loud cries over his
prey. But when the day broke all men might see what desolation
he had wrought, and great was the grief of the King. Again,
on the very next night, the monster came, and seized a fresh
prey. And so it happened for the space of twelve winters. No
man dared abide in the hall for fear of Grendel; nor did they
escape him in the chambers of the castle. Whether a man was
a tried warrior, or a youth, it mattered not; all were his prey.
And over the moors he wandered, seizing such as found access
there. Only to the throne itself he could not approach, for God
would not suffer him so to do. Oft did the nobles take counsel
together how they might abate this plague; often did they offer
sacrifices to their gods if haply they might win help from them;
but neither sacrifice nor counsel availed.

Now in the land of the Goths there was a certain King,
Hygelac by name, and this King had a nephew, whose name

was Beowulf, a youth that had in him the strength of thirty men. To him came the report of King Hrothgar's trouble, and he conceived in his mind the purpose to help him. So he set sail to the land of the Danes, having fourteen comrades with him, the bravest that he could find in all the land of the Goths. All that day and all that night they sailed, and on the morrow, at the very hour of their setting out, they saw land, a land of great cliffs and of headlands jutting far out into the sea. So they drove the ship to the beach, and sprang ashore in their warriors' gear, and made fast their craft.

When the warden of the coast espied them, he rode down to the shore, with a great spear in his hand. 'Who are ye,' he said, 'who come so boldly to this land? Many years have I been warden in this place, having been set to watch the sea-robbers, lest they should work mischief to the land of the Danes, but never have I seen men land in more open guise. Nor do ye know, I take it, any password or token such as kinsmen have between them. Say then who ye are, for, indeed, I see among you one whose peer may not easily be found, so stalwart and strong is he to look upon. No common man is he that has decked himself out with splendid armour. But say, strangers, who ye are before ye go further into the land of the Danes.'

Then Beowulf made answer: 'We are of the race of the Goths, and we are come with friendly purpose to thy lord, King Hrothgar; nor is there any need to hide it. We have heard – and whether it be true or no thou knowest – that some monster comes by night to devour the King's warriors in his hall. For this evil we bring a remedy.'

The warden said: 'Yea, I know it well; a faithful squire must needs know the troubles of his lord. But ye, for ye seem to be a friendly company, pass on with your weapons of war, and I will bid my comrades keep watch and ward over your ship till ye return, that it may carry you safely back to the land of your birth.'

So Beowulf and his company marched on, with the warden for guide of their way; and as they went, the sun shone on the golden boars' heads that they carried on their helmets. Eager for battle they went on till they could see before them the hall of the King where it stood in its splendour. Then the warden pointed with his hand and said: 'Now I must depart; for I must needs return to the shore to keep it against the approach of the enemy. And may the Almighty Father keep you in your way!'

So they marched along the path of stone till they came to the hall; there they set up their shields against the wall, and stacked their spears together, and sat down upon a bench, for they were weary with their journey.

To them came forth an officer of the King, and questioned them of their kindred and country: 'Whence do ye bring,' he said, 'your warriors' gear, your shields and spears? Know that I am squire and herald to King Hrothgar. Never yet have I seen so fair a company of strangers. 'Tis, I trow, on some bold errand that ye are come.'

The chief made reply: 'We sit at the table of Hygelac, King of the Goths. As for me, I am Beowulf; my errand I will set forth to the King, if he will grant us of his good grace that we may see him.'

Then said Wulfgar the herald: 'I will ask the King his pleasure, and bring thee back his answer without delay.'

So the herald went to where King Hrothgar sat, an old man among his warriors, and spake: 'Certain men are newly come, my lord, to this place far across the sea from the land of the Goths, and the name of their chief is Beowulf. They make petition that they may see thee, and I would counsel that thou refuse not their request, for their gear is that of worthy men, and their chief is a noble prince.'

The King made answer: 'I knew him well when he was yet a boy. His father was Egthean, to whom Hethel the Goth gave his only daughter in marriage. And now he has grown to man's estate, and is come to visit us. And indeed it is well, for they who carried our gifts over the seas to the Goths say that he has in his grip the strength of thirty men. Haply God has sent him of His grace to help us against the monster Grendel. Go, therefore, and say to him and his company that they are welcome to the land of the Danes.'

So Wulfgar the herald returned and said: 'The King bids you welcome to the land of the Danes, for he knows of what race ye are. Leave, therefore, your shields and spears till ye have spoken with him.'

So Beowulf and some of his company went in to speak to

the King, and the others tarried behind to keep watch over the war gear.

And when they stood before the King, Beowulf stood forth and said: 'Hail to thee, King Hrothgar! I am Beowulf, kinsman to King Hygelac. Many deeds of note have I done in my youth, and now the report of the doings of Grendel the monster has brought me to this land. For strangers from over the sea have told us how that this fair hall stands empty of guests so soon as the evening falls. 'Twas my comrades that put the thought in my heart, for they had seen my valorous deeds, how I had conquered the foes of my country, and brought the race of the giants low, and slain monsters both on sea and on land. So now I am come, my lord King, to fight single-handed against this Grendel. Now, therefore, I make my petition to thee, O Prince, first that I may undertake this enterprise alone, and next, seeing that this monster despises weapons, that I may also forego all use of the same, and carry neither sword, nor shield, nor coat of mail to this battle. With the grip of my hands only will I deal with this enemy, struggling with him, life for life. But who shall live and who shall die, let it be as God shall will. I doubt not, O King, that if he have his way he will devour the champions of the Goths, even as he has devoured the champions of the Danes. And as for me, thou wilt not need to lay my body in the earth and raise a mound over it, for he will carry it off to the moors where he dwells and devour it there. Only I would pray thee to send back to King Hygelac the armour that I wear; for it came to me by inheritance, and Weland, the smith of the gods, wrought in the old time. But that which Fate has ordered shall come to pass.'

To him King Hrothgar made answer: ''Tis well, O Beowulf, that thou art come to help me in this my need, for I knew thy father in the old time; he was a mighty man of valour, and there was a bond of friendship between him and me. But as for this Grendel, it is a shame to tell what desolation he has wrought in my hall. He has swept away the whole company of my warriors. Who can stay him in his ill-deeds? God doubtless can do so, but I know of none besides. Often have my warriors boasted, when they were merry with their drink, that they would stand up, sword in hand, against the monster. But when morning came, lo! the hall was bespattered with gore, and the benches reeked with blood, and I was the poorer by many brave warriors. But now, I pray thee, sit down to the feast, thou and thy brave comrades with thee.'

So a table was cleared, and the warriors of the Goths sat down together in the pride of their strength. And one of the King's thanes waited on them, bearing the ale-can in his hands, and, once and again, a minstrel sang with clear voice of the deeds of the men of old, and there was mirth in the hall.

But while they feasted envy stirred in the heart of Unferth, son of Ecglaf. He was the King's orator, and he took it ill that Beowulf should have come to the land of the Danes on this great enterprise, for he was one who could not endure that any man under heaven should do greater deeds than himself. Therefore he stood up in the hall and spake: 'Art thou that Beowulf who contended with Breca in swimming on the open sea? 'Twas, indeed, a foolhardy thing so to put your lives in jeopardy, yet no man could turn you from your adventure. Seven days and nights ye toiled, one against the other, but he in the end prevailed, for he had the greater strength. And on the eighth morning the waves cast him ashore on the land of the Heathoram, whence he journeyed back to the city of the Bronding, of which he was lord. So did Breca, son of Beanstan, make good his boast against thee. And thou, I trow, wilt have worse luck than this, though doubtless thou art a sturdy warrior in the shock of battle, if thou shalt dare to abide for the space of a night the strength of the monster Grendel.'

Then said Beowulf: 'Surely the ale-can has wrought with thee, friend Unferth, that thou hast said such things about Breca, the son of Beanstan, and how he strove with me in swimming. But I say to thee that in buffeting the waves of the sea I have more strength than any other man under heaven. Now hear the truth. This Breca and I, in our boyhood, when we were pages at the King's court, were wont to talk of this, how we would put our lives in jeopardy on the sea, and we made agreement to contend the one against the other. So we swam, each of us holding in one hand a sword wherewith to defend ourselves against the whale-fishes of the sea. Not one whit further than I could he swim, nor I one whit further than he. So for the space of five days and five nights we twain swam together; but on the sixth day the floods parted us, for the wind blew mightily against us from the north, and the waves were rough. So was I left alone, and then the rage of the sea-monsters was roused against me; but my coat of mail stood me in good stead against their attacks. Yet did one great beast – spotted he was with spots – seize me in his grip and drag me to the bottom of the sea. Yet strength was given me to pierce the monster with my sword, and then I slew him. Nor yet in truth was I quit of my enemies; for they pressed against me in my rage, and I dealt them blows with my sword and stinted not. They counted to devour me, foul robbers of the sea that they were, to devour me for their supper. But they fared far otherwise. Verily they lay the next morning high and dry upon the shore, having met their fate by the sword. And truly it was a good deed to slay them, for never more would they hinder in their course such as fare across the sea. And when I had finished my task, lo! it was morning, and I saw the headlands. So does fortune rescue the warrior if he be not doomed of Fate, and if he be bold of heart. Verily it came of my good luck that I was able to slay with my sword nine monsters of the deep and to escape with my life. Never was a man more hardly pressed by the waves of the sea or come into greater peril of death. After this the sea cast me up on the land of the Finns. I have heard of no such deeds as done by thee, Unferth, son of Ecglaf; no, nor hath Breca achieved the like. And this I say to thee, that Grendel had never wrought such woe and desolation for thy King hadst thou in truth possessed the courage of which thou makest boast. But he, methinks, takes but small heed of the spearmen of the Danes, nor fears lest they requite him, slaughter for slaughter. Rather he takes toll from them at his will; he slaughters and he feasts, but he has no thought of fight. But now there has come one who shall show him what a Goth can do in battle, and shall make King Hrothgar's hall a fit abiding-place again for men.'

So Beowulf spake, and the old King heard him with great joy, seeing that he was steadily purposed in his heart to contend and to prevail. So there was mirth in the hall, and much laughter of heroes, and music, and songs of rejoicing.

Then came Elfrida, Queen of King Hrothgar, into the hall, clad in cloth of gold, and she bore a great beaker in her hand, for she was careful to observe all ancient customs. To the King of the East Danes first she handed the great cup, wishing him joy and the love of his lords. And after him she went the round to all the warriors where they sat in their places, the old by themselves and the young by themselves; last of all she brought the cup to Beowulf, and greeted him right courteously, and gave thanks to God that He had given them such an answer to their prayers. 'For now,' she said, 'I believe that we have a warrior who will rid us of our troubles.' Beowulf made answer to the Queen: 'Lady, when I embarked on this voyage with my fellows, I promised that I would either do this deed, or perish by the hands of this monster. And to this I am bound; either I will fulfil this promise, or I will meet my death in this hall.' Well pleased was the Queen with this saying, and she went in her gold attire to sit by the side of her lord, King Hrothgar.

So all the company of Danes and Goths sat in the hall, and made good cheer, till the King rose from his place to go to his chamber. Well he knew that the time was come when the monster issued forth to his cruel deeds, for Grendel was of the creatures of darkness that come forth when the sun has set. And when he rose, all the company stood up. Then said the King to Beowulf, the while he wished him all good fortune, 'Never since I first laid my right hand to the sword and bare the shield on my left have I given this hall of the Danes to any man to keep. And now I give it in trust to thee. Do thou keep it as befits its grace. Be of good hope; be valiant; watch. And verily, if thou comest with thy life out of this conflict, there is no wish in thy heart which thou shalt not see fulfilled.' So King Hrothgar went to his chamber, and his chiefs followed him. But Beowulf abode still in the hall, resolved in his heart to do the service which he had promised. And first he took from off his body his stout coat of mail and doffed his helmet, and then he gave to his squire his good sword. 'Keep thou,' he said, 'all my warrior's gear.' But before he climbed up on his bed he spake aloud saying, 'Now indeed I reckon myself to be not one whit behind this Grendel in deeds of war. Therefore I am resolved not to make an end of him with the sword, as well I might, for he knows nought, I trow, of the noble art of arms, how to strike with the sword and parry, though he be expert in deeds of darkness. So it shall be that when we come to trial of our strength this night we will have no weapon in our hands. And may He who knows all things give the victory as it shall please Him.'

So saying, the warrior laid him down on a bed and round

him lay many valiant lovers of the sea, his comrades in this enterprise. Without fear they lay, though there was not one who thought that he should ever see again land, and kindred, and the home of his youth, for they knew what havoc the monster Grendel had wrought in that same hall among the Danish folk. But they fared better than they had thought, for God gave them deliverance by the hand of a single champion. It pleased Him so to do, and verily He is the ruler of the world.

Meanwhile the destroyer came on his way, bent on his errand of mischief. And they who should have guarded the hall slept all of them: Beowulf only kept watch and ward, awaiting the trial of battle. In haste the monster approached, hoping to catch some man for his prey. Many a time before had he visited King Hrothgar's hall, and never had he gone away empty. But, of a truth, he had not found it before in the keeping of so stout a warrior.

And now he was come to the hall, and straightway, at the first touch of his hands, the door, fastened though it was with bars of iron wrought by a cunning smith, flew open. Thereafter he looked about him, with ravening eyes, whose light was like to burning fire. And as he looked he saw, fast bound in sleep, a troop of warriors, kinsmen all of them. And as he saw he laughed, thinking to himself that ere the day should dawn he would slay them all, for he deemed that fortune had favoured him again. But it was not so decreed of fate, but rather that he should not after that night make his meal again of the flesh of man.

Great was the rage in the heart of Beowulf when he saw the monster, but he held it back, waiting to see what the creature would do. Nor indeed did Grendel long delay. Speedily he seized a sleeping warrior and tore him in twain, crunching the bones with his teeth, and drinking the blood from his veins. In a trice he had devoured the body to the very feet and hands. This done, he came near to the bed of Beowulf, and stretched out to lay hold on him. But the champion seized the monster's arm with such a grip as he had never felt before. Nowhere had he found such strength in mortal man. Great was his fear and eager his desire to depart. Such grim entertainment he had not met before in King Hrothgar's hall. But Beowulf remembered what boast he had made that night, how he would carry this work to its full accomplishment. Therefore he stood up in his place, and grappled with the monster, holding him fast, though it seemed as if his fingers would burst. And when Grendel turned to flee, then the Earl followed him. Fain would the ogre have fled to his dwelling in the moors, for he knew that the grip of a deadly foe was on him. That was in truth a rash journey that he had made to King Hrothgar's hall.

Loud were the cries of the two as they fought together, and great the terror of all that were in the hall, Danes and Goths alike. The very bravest could not hear it with an untroubled heart. Verily it was a wonder that the house itself endured such conflict; nor had it stood but that it was cunningly set up within and without with stanchions of iron. And still Beowulf held the monster fast, with all his strength – nor, indeed, was there in any man such strength as his – for he was not minded to let so evil a thing escape. And then, for all their fear, the Earl's comrades unsheathed their swords, thinking to help their lord, and rescue him, if it might be, from his great peril. So they thought, but they knew not that not the keenest sword on earth, no, nor the stoutest battle-axe, could avail to touch that evil thing, for he had guarded himself by enchantments against all edge of steel. Nevertheless there was now come upon him a woeful end, fit recompense for one that had wrought such woe to men. He could not by any means free himself from the strong hand-grip of the Earl. And as he strove, there came in his shoulder a great crack, and the sinews sprang apart and the joints of the bones burst asunder. Then at last he fled to his hiding-place in the moors; but he had suffered a deadly loss, for his arm he left behind him in the champion's grip.

So did Beowulf accomplish that which he had promised, delivering the hall of the Danes from the terror which had made it desolate. In token thereof he hung up high on the gable of the roof hand and arm and shoulder.

The tidings of what had befallen were soon noised abroad, and the chiefs of the Danes came from far and near to see the place and the signs of the battle. Glad of heart were they as they tracked the monster's course, seeing it red with blood, till they came to the place where he had hidden himself in his terror, knowing that his end was come, even the lake of the pixies. And when they looked on the face of the lake, they saw that it was dark with blood, the blood of Grendel. Then they rode back again in great glee, and many sang of Beowulf's mighty deed. 'There is not on earth,' so said they all, 'among warriors that bear the shield, a champion mightier or more worthy to bear rule than he!' So they sang, yet did not fail in due honour to King Hrothgar. Verily he was a worthy king! Then the bard, the maker of lays, after telling of the dreadful deeds of Grendel and of how Beowulf had vanquished him, sang thus:

> How shall we praise him? to whom compare?
> To Sigemund, Waelson, the dragon-slayer.
> Never, I trow, did braver lord
> In the battle-press bear shield and sword;
> And ever, where fiercest ran the tide
> Of the great war-torrent, by his side
> Stout Fitela stood, his sister's son,
> A stalwart comrade and true; but one,
> And the dourest deed of all, alone
> King Sigemund wrought, by the Dragon-stone,
> Where the dreadful Worm from days of yore
> Kept watch and ward o'er the treasure-store,
> A fearsome beast, but the Waelsing Lord,
> Nothing afraid, with his noble sword
> Shore him through with so stout a blow
> That the good steel sank in the earth below,
> And the treasure-store of gems and gold
> He stored away in his swift ship's hold.

So the company returned with great gladness to the town, and King Hrothgar himself came forth from his chamber, and the Queen with him, and a bevy of fair ladies in gay apparel. And when the King saw the gable of the hall, and the hand and arm of Grendel fixed upon it, he brake forth in speech, saying:

'Now let us thank Almighty God for giving us to see this sight with our eyes! Many things have I suffered from this Grendel, and now the Lord hath wrought a wonderful deliverance. I never thought to see a remedy, for this hall evermore ran with blood, and my warriors and counsellors availed nothing to abate this woe. Yet now hath this warrior achieved our deliverance, God helping him. Happy the mother, and favoured of the Almighty, who bare such a son! And now hearken, Beowulf. I love thee as though thou wert my son; and indeed from this day forth thou shalt be as a son to me. Nothing that thou shalt desire shalt thou lack, so far as I have power to give it. And indeed I have given noble gifts and great honours to many a one who was not thy match in courage or great deeds.'

Beowulf made answer to the King: 'We did our work with a good heart. Only I would that thou hadst the creature himself. I thought, indeed, to have held him down in the place where I grappled him till he died. But I could not; I did not hold him fast enough. Nevertheless he left his hand, aye and his arm and shoulder also, behind him. Nor will he live one hour the longer for that he has escaped. From the deadly wound that he has suffered there is no flight.'

So spake Beowulf, and there was mirth in the hall. But one man sat and spake nothing, and he was Unferth, the son of Ecglaf. For had he not spoken scornfully of the hero? – and lo! there before his eyes and the eyes of all the nobles of the land, high up on the gable of the roof, was the hand of the monster! Like to spurs of steel were all the fingers, spurs or spikes, so keen were they and so hard. Not the most famous sword that the great smiths of old had wrought by their craft had availed to sever such a hand as the hand of Grendel.

Then King Hrothgar commanded that they should adorn the hall anew. So they adorned it with willing hands, both men and women. Grievously desolated had it been by the monster Grendel; not a part of it had escaped save the roof only, but now it was decked out with tapestries woven with threaded gold and with pictures. And when the work of adorning was finished, King Hrothgar came into the hall and sat down to the feast, and a fair company of guests, kinsmen, and nobles sat down with him. From end to end it was filled with friends, friends true at heart, for in those days no man of the Danish race cherished a thought of treachery in his heart.

Then King Hrothgar gave to Beowulf an ensign of gold on a staff richly dight, and a helmet, and a coat of mail, and a great sword from the royal treasury. Eight horses also, each with cheek-plates of gold, did the King give him, and one of these was saddled with a saddle adorned with silver. 'Twas the

King's own warhorse, on which he was wont to ride in the days
when he entered into the battle. These were the gifts that King
Hrothgar in true kingly wise gave to the champion Beowulf.
Also he gave gifts, precious things that had come down to him
as an inheritance from the kings of old, to each one of the
comrades of Beowulf. And he gave also a blood-price, many
pieces of gold, for him whom Grendel slew cruelly in the hall.
So they sat in the hall and feasted, the King with his nobles and
his guests about him, and a minstrel sang to the harp the lay of
the Sons of Finn:

> To the Frisian land,
> With a chosen band,
> Brave sons of the Dane,
> O'er the ocean plain
> Did Hnaef of the race of the Scyldings go:
> In the stress of battle Fate laid him low.

And when the lay of the Sons of Finn was ended, the drawers
filled up the cups and the revellers drank again. And as they
drank came Elfrida the Queen, with the crown of gold upon
her head. To the King she came, and said to him: 'Take this
beaker, my lord King, and drink, and speak comfortable words
to our guests from Gothland. Dear they are to thee, and their
chief Beowulf thou wouldst gladly count for a son of thine own.
And indeed thou doest well to love them, for thy hall is purged
of its troubles by their means, and the years that are coming
shall be years of peace. And when the time shall be for thee
to depart hence, thou wilt leave thy people and thy realm to
thy children after thee. And if thy sons be over young for
government, then shall Hrothulf thy neighbour counsel them
dutifully, remembering how we two gave him nurture in time
past when he was yet but an infant.' So saying, she turned
to the bench where sat the two lords her sons, Hrethin and
Hrothmund, and the sons of the nobles sat by them, all the
youths together.

And the Queen bade Beowulf drink of the cup, and she
gave into his hand chains of twisted gold, and armlets, and
a mantle and rings. Never were seen jewels so precious since
Hama carried away the necklace of the Brisings, which Freia

the goddess wore. And when the Queen gave him these gifts, she said: 'Wear this collar, dear youth, with good fortune, and put this mantle about thy shoulders, and prosper. Make thyself fame by thy valour, and be happy as long as thou shalt live. And, I pray thee, help these my sons with counsel wise and kind. Verily thou shalt have thy reward.'

So spake the Queen, and went back to her chair. And with great joy did the company revel in the hall. And when they had enough of feasting, then they cleared away the tables and spread out the beds. So the warriors lay down to their rest, each man setting up his shield at his head, and over it his helmet, and his coat of mail, and his spear. But for one of them that lay down it was decreed of fate that he should not rise up again. But no man knows his doom, whether it shall come soon or late.

*   *   *

In peace and confidence the warriors laid them down to sleep, but there was one among them that was doomed to pay dearly for his rest. And this was the way in which the matter came to pass. Grendel, indeed, was dead, but an avenger lived, even his mother, a troll-wife that dwelt in the moorland streams. Of savage temper was she, neither did ruth dwell in her heart, and now she was wrought to fury by the death of her son. Therefore she came to King Hrothgar's hall, and burst in upon the warriors as they slept. Great was the fear among them – not so great, of a truth, as it was when Grendel himself had come among them, for the might of a woman is not as the might of a man, but the thing troubled them much.

Now the troll-wife was in great haste, for though she was bent on avenging her son, yet she desired to escape with her life. Therefore she was content to seize but one of the sleepers in the hall. Him she grappled with her hands, crushing him to death as he slept, and then she returned with all speed to her dwelling among the trees; but she did not forget to take away with her the hand and arm of her son. From the gable she took it down and carried it off with her.

Great was King Hrothgar's trouble when he heard of this cruel deed; for the man that had perished in this way was dearer to him than all his thanes. So he sent a messenger to Beowulf, bidding him come with all speed, for Beowulf had not slept in the hall, but a chamber had been prepared for him elsewhere, in which he might take his rest and also bestow the precious gifts which had been given him. And when he had heard from the messenger the King's desire he went, and his comrades with him. And first he said: 'Hast thou slept well, O King?'

King Hrothgar made answer: 'Talk not of welfare to me. Aescher is dead, Aescher who was my scribe and counsellor, aye, and the squire of my body in the old time when we stood together in the battle. And now he is dead. The destroyer has slain him in my hall, and whither the creature is gone, carrying with her the prey, I know not. Grendel thou didst slay yesterday, grappling him right manfully in thy hands, and now this creature has avenged his death, and the bravest and best of my lords lies dead, slain by her hands.

'Now hear how I come to know that it is she that has done this deed. Often have the dwellers in the moorland seen these two. One was in the semblance of a man, only more huge than any man has been seen: this was Grendel, the same that was slain by thee; and the other was in woman's shape. These two were wont to dwell in secret places in the wilderness. If thou wouldst know more closely the place, hearken to my words. There is a certain lake, not many miles from this hall. All about it are woods, whose great roots go down to the water. Night by night on its waters may be seen a flame, and as for its depth, no man knows what it is. A fearful place is this lake; the stag, however sorely the hounds may have pressed him in the hunt, would sooner die than plunge his head in the water. And now it is to thee, O Beowulf, that we look for help and counsel. The place thou hast not seen, but yet, if thou darest to track this monster to her lair, go and prosper. Verily, if thou returnest again victorious, I will recompense thee with great store of treasure.'

Then said Beowulf: 'Be of good comfort my lord King. 'Tis better for a man to avenge his friend than that he should sit down and spend his time in useless lamenting. Verily for every one of us there is ordained a certain end of life; let us therefore take such occasion as God may give us of winning renown while life still remains to us, for there is nothing better for a man than renown. Come, then, my lord King, let us go and track the path of this foul creature that is of Grendel's kindred. And this I vow. She shall not escape, nor hide herself from me; no, neither in the bowels of the earth, nor in the secret places of the wood, nor in the depths of the sea. Have patience, then, in thy troubles, for I am assured that all will go well with thee.'

Then King Hrothgar gave thanks to God for Beowulf's comfortable words, and commanded that his horse should be saddled. In stately guise he rode, and his warriors round about him. Nor was it a hard matter to follow the track of the monster. That was indeed easy to see across the moor, the evil path by which it had carried off King Hrothgar's best beloved comrade. So Beowulf and a few of his warriors with him, the stoutest and bravest of all his company, followed the track with light steps, over rocky heights, and through narrow glades, where the pixies dwelt. And of a sudden they came upon a wood. Gloomy of aspect it was, and dark the rocks on which it grew, and dreary the water that lay beneath in its shade. A gloomy place it was, and terrible the sight, for there on the rock by the water's edge was the head of the brave man Aescher, King Hrothgar's chosen counsellor, and the lake itself seethed and bubbled with blood. Then he that bore the horn sounded, once and again, a cheering blast, and Beowulf and his company sat down and looked. Strange was the sight; great serpents and monstrous snakes of the sea at their gambols, and dragons, and many another monstrous thing. But when they heard the bugle-blast they were fain, one and all, to depart. Only Beowulf set an arrow to the string, and drew the bow and let fly the shaft. It pierced one of the monsters in a mortal part, and stayed him from his swimming for ever. Then Beowulf's comrades, with boat-poles, armed with harpoons, dragged the monster to the shore, marvelling much, so huge was he and so terrible to behold.

Then Beowulf donned his war-gear. Light of heart he was, though great was the danger. And first he put upon him his coat of mail. Well it knew how to protect the champion's body from the grip of the enemy, but now for the first time it was to make trial of the water. And so was it with the helmet that guarded his head. It also must be plunged into the deep, with its ornaments of silver, and the boar-figures, wrought of old by the hand of some cunning smith, that were set about it, keeping it safe from all the sword-strokes of the enemy.

But of all the things that helped his valour the best was the good sword which the orator of King Hrothgar sent to him. A precious heirloom it was, and its edge was tempered with the blood of men. Never in the stress of battle had it failed the man who wielded it with undoubted hands. Nor was it now the first time that it was called to do a hero's work. Unferth, son of Ecglaf, it was who lent it to Beowulf, for he remembered no longer how he had scoffed at the champion, and indeed he knew that he lacked courage in his heart to plunge into the sea on such errand as that to which Beowulf now addressed himself.

And when the champion was now altogether ready for the fight, he said: 'Remember now, my lord King, what we two have talked together. Thou hast promised that if the doom of death should overtake me in thy service, thou wouldst be in the place of a father to me. Protect, therefore, I pray thee, my kinsmen and comrades, and cause the gifts which thou hast given me to be sent to King Hygelac. So will he understand, when he sees so great a store of gold and jewels, that I had good luck while fortune favoured me. And let Unferth the orator have the sword Hardedge, with its damasked blade, that has come down to me from my fathers, and I with the sword Hrunting will either achieve high renown, or perish.'

So spake the lord of the Goths, nor did he await reply, but plunged headlong into the lake. It was morning when he leapt, but the day was far spent when he reached the land that lay at the bottom of the mere. Not long was the monster in perceiving that one of the sons of men was visiting her dwelling-place for the first time in a hundred years. Swiftly she flew at him, and caught him in her talons; but for all their strength and sharpness she could not break through the coat of mail with which his body was girt about. But though she could not reach his flesh to tear it with her claws, she carried him away to the hall in which she dwelt at the bottom of the mere, nor could he, for all his strength, resist her, or wield his weapons against her. In her grip she carried him, and as he went the great water-beasts butted at him with their tusks.

The dwelling of the monster was indeed a marvellous place.

Under the water it was, but the water troubled not them that
were in it, for it was kept from them by the roof. Also there was
a strange light in it, a light as of fire. And by this light Beowulf
saw of what shape was the creature that had assailed, that it was
the monster which men had sometime seen upon the moor in
the form of a woman. Straightway he dealt a great blow at her
with his sword, even the mighty sword Hrunting that Unferth,
the King's orator, had lent him. Mighty was the blow, but the
edge of the sword could not bite. For the first time since its
forging it failed its master. Oft had it dealt death in the press
of battle, cleaving buckler and corslet and helmet, but now it
availed nothing. In great wrath Beowulf threw away the blade.
He would trust to the grip of his hands only. Thus had he
vanquished Grendel, thus would he vanquish Grendel's dam.

So should a man bear himself, to work his work as best he
may and have no thought of life.

Then, heedless of peril, Beowulf sprang upon Grendel's dam,
and seized her by the shoulder. Full of rage he was, and he
grappled the dreadful creature so mightily that she sank down
upon the ground. But she was not yet overcome. No, indeed,
for in her turn she grappled with him, closing in upon him, and
flinging him, strongest among men though he was, upon the
pavement of the floor; for his breath failed him, and his strength
was spent. Then the hag sat upon him and drew her knife, broad
of blade it was and brown; willingly would she have slain him,
for she was minded to take vengeance for the death of her son.
Then of a truth had Beowulf perished, but for the coat of mail
that was about his body. This the hag could not pierce; neither
with blade nor with point could she drive her knife through it.
So did the Almighty Father help the champion in his need.

Then again Beowulf, with a great struggle, threw the hag from
off him, and stood upright on his feet. And as he looked about
the hall, he saw among the armour that was hanging about it
a great sword, a weapon of giants, keen of edge, a very king
among swords; only it was so huge that no other man upon earth
could wield it in the press of battle save only Beowulf the Goth.
He seized it with his hands, thinking to himself, 'If this avails
me not, I die,' and smote the beldam so fiercely on the neck
that the steel shore her body right through, and she fell dead
upon the pavement of the hall. And even as she fell, the light

that he had seen at the first, blazed up again and showed him all the place. By the wall side he went, still holding the sword of the giants in his hand. And as he went he saw Grendel lying dead upon the floor. With his sword he cut the monster's head from his body and so turned him to depart.

Meanwhile King Hrothgar and the Danish lords sat by the side of the mere and watched the water. And when they saw how it grew troubled, and how the surf was red with blood, they said among themselves, 'The champion will not come back, bringing victory with him. Without doubt we shall not see him any more. The she-wolf has torn him in pieces.' So thinking, the King and his nobles departed. But the Goths sat still by the mere side and waited, though they were sick at heart. Greatly did they long to look upon their captain again, but there was no hope in their hearts.

But now, beyond all expectation, he came back. Nought did he take from the hall under the mere, though there were many precious things in it, and he saw them with his eyes. Only the head of Grendel he brought with him in one hand, and in the other the hilt of the giant's sword. There was nothing left of it save the hilt only, for in the blood of Grendel and of Grendel's dam there was so deadly a fire that it devoured all the blade. Glad of heart were the Goths when they saw the chief returning, and they thanked the merciful God who had delivered them from the hand of the enemy.

After this they set out to return to King Hrothgar's hall by the same way by which they had come. And in the midst of the company four stout warriors bare upon a pole the head of Grendel. And when they came to the hall, Beowulf took the head from the pole and carried it within, holding it by the hair. Truly a marvellous thing it was for the King and his nobles and Queen Veleda to behold. Never had any man looked on so terrible a face.

Then said Beowulf to King Hrothgar: 'Hail, O King. Gladly do we bring to thee from the mere the spoils that thou seest before thee, in token that the work is done. Hardly, indeed, did I win through it with life; in the battle beneath the water I had failed, but that the Almighty shielded me. As for the sword Hrunting I could do nothing with it, though it be a good weapon; but by the grace of God I saw hanging upon the wall an old sword exceeding large and heavy, and He who helps men when of other help there is none, put it in my heart that I should lay hold of that weapon. And this I did, and dealt therewith to the monster a mighty and effectual blow. See now the hilt of this sword, for the blade has melted away into nothing with the blood of the monster. Now, therefore, O King, I bid thee sleep in peace, nor fear, as heretofore, any danger in the night.'

So saying, he gave the hilt into the hands of the King. And when the King looked upon it he saw that there was written upon it the story of how the Flood swept away the herd of the Giants who had hardened themselves against the Ruler of the world. This was written upon it, and also for whom the Smiths of old had wrought this marvellous work.

And when King Hrothgar had perused the hilt, he said to Beowulf: 'Friend, thy fame is spread abroad throughout the world, but thou bearest it modestly and discreetly. Behave thyself so, and thou shalt be a comfort to thy people and their lords. Not so did Herenod that was King of Denmark before the days of Scyld. For did he not slay the chiefs, his comrades, at the feast? and did he not wander away alone from all companionship of man? God had given him strength and power beyond all other men, but he used them so ill that there was not one that loved him. Take thou, therefore, warning by him, O Beowulf. Sometimes God gives a man a wide dominion and great power and much prosperity. Sickness comes not near him, nor does old age bow him down, nor care trouble his heart. All his neighbours are at peace with him, and everything falls out to his mind. Then there grow up within his heart pride and arrogancy; and conscience, that should keep watch in his soul against evil, falls into a deep sleep, and wicked thoughts take possession of his heart. Then he thinks to himself that his abundance is not sufficient for him; he grows covetous for himself, and grudges others their due. The end of that man is that he is overthrown and that another takes the wealth which he has gathered. Take thou, therefore, good heed, O Beowulf, against pride and arrogancy. Now, indeed, thou art in the pride of thy strength and the power of thy age, but there will come of a surety, sooner or later, either sickness or the sword; the fire shall consume thee, or the floods swallow thee up. Be it in one fashion or another, death will subdue thee who hast so mightily subdued others. So I myself reigned for fifty years over the Danes, and had the mastery over all my enemies, so that I feared no rival from the one end of heaven to the other. Then there befell me great trouble, and I had heaviness in the place of mirth, for this Grendel came an evil guest to my hall. From this thou hast delivered me and my people, for do I not see with mine eyes the head of the enemy? And now let us come to the feast; tomorrow I have other gifts to give thee.'

So they sat down to the feast, King Hrothgar and his lords, and Beowulf and his comrades. And in a while they went to their beds; right glad was Beowulf, after all his toils, to lay him down to sleep.

And now the time was come for the champion to depart. First he gave back the good sword Hrunting to Unferth the orator. ''Tis a right good sword,' he said, 'and will serve thee well in war, though it availed not against the evil hag, the mother of Grendel.'

To the King he said: 'We now must needs return to our own land and to Hygelac our King. Thou hast used great hospitality to us and hast given us many and great gifts. If, then, there is aught else in which I can do thee service, willingly will I do it. If thy neighbours press thee hard, then will I come again, and a thousand warriors with me. And if Prince Hrethin, thy son, is minded to come as a guest to our court, verily he will find there many friends.'

King Hrothgar made answer to him: 'God puts into thy mouth words of wisdom, O Beowulf. Never have I heard from man so young speech so weighty. Good service hast thou done to me; and this also thou hast achieved that there shall be henceforth mutual friendship between thy heart and mine.'

Then the King gave him twelve jewels from his store; and after this he threw his arms about the young man's neck, weeping the while, for he knew in his heart that he should see his face no more, and indeed he loved him no less than a father loves his son.

So Beowulf and his comrades rode down to the shore. And when the warden of the shore saw them from the peak whereon he kept his watch, he made haste to meet them, not as heretofore with suspicion, but with greeting of welcome. 'Glad am I to see you safe returning;' and he led them down to their ship where it lay on the beach. Then Beowulf gave to the warden of the boat a sword bound with gold; high place did the man hold thenceforth among his fellows by reason of this gift.

Then the Goths embarked upon their ship, and set sail; and the wind blew fair behind, stretching the canvas to the full, and the prow divided the sea-waves, throwing the foam on either side, till the men beheld the cliffs of Gothland, headlands well known to their eyes. High up on the beach was the ship driven, and the shore-warden was ready to receive it, glad to welcome his countrymen. He bade some fasten the ship with anchor-cables on either side, lest haply it should be broken by the violence of the waves; and others he commanded to bear the precious gifts, gold and jewels, to the hall of King Hygelac, for the hall was night at hand, where the King dwelt with Hygda his Queen, a gracious dame, young and fair. And one ran and told the King, saying: 'Beowulf is come again, safe and sound from the battle.'

So the King said, 'Bring him hither to me.' And they brought him, and he sat down by the King's side, and Hygda, the gracious lady, went about the hall carrying in her hands the meadbowl to the men of war.

Said King Hygelac: 'How hast thou fared, my kinsman? Hast thou rid King Hrothgar of his troubles? I entreated thee, as thou knowest, to let the Danes settle their own quarrel with Grendel. But now I give thanks to God that I see thee again safe and sound.'

Thereupon Beowulf told the tale of how he had grappled with Grendel in the hall, and how the monster had wrenched himself away, but with an hand and arm the less, wounded to the death; and how he had sought for Grendel's dam in the mere among the hills and found her, and done fierce battle with her, and vanquished her, but hardly and after long struggle, and with grievous peril of his life.

And when he had ended the tale of his doings he said: 'Now for these things King Hrothgar gave me many gifts and precious. To me he gave them, but I give them to thee, O King; for indeed it was for thee I won them, and if thou art satisfied, then am I well pleased.'

Then he bade his comrades bring into the hall a helmet with a crest that towered in the press of battle, and a coat of mail, and a mighty sword. 'This,' he said, 'King Hrothgar gave me, having had it from his fathers before him.' Also he gave to the King four noble steeds, so like that none could tell the one from the other. And to Hygda he gave a jewel marvellously wrought that Queen Veleda had bestowed upon him, and three palfreys, gaily caparisoned.

After this King Hygelac bade them bring the great sword, mounted in gold, that had belonged to King Hrethet, his father. In all Gothland there was not a treasure of greater account than the sword of King Hrethet. And he gave him also a great revenue in money, and a stately dwelling, and a high place among his lords.

Now it came to pass as time went on that King Hygelac made war against the men of Friesland, and he took with him a great host and many famous chiefs, of whom Beowulf was the greatest. But the men of Friesland had made alliance with the Chatti and with others of the nations round about; and the battle went against King Hygelac and the Goths, and the King was slain and all his nobles with him, save Beowulf only. He, indeed, when the enemy pressed him hard, leapt into the sea. Thirty sets of war-harness had he on his arm when he leapt. Small cause had the Chatti to rejoice that day, seeing that few only of their host escaped from the sword of Beowulf to go back to their home. So the champion escaped by swimming, and came back to Gothland lonely and sad of heart. Then Queen Hygda would have had him take the throne to himself, for her son was but of tender years and she feared that he would not have strength to guard the realm against the assaults of the enemy. But she did not prevail with Beowulf, no, nor did the nobles of the land, when they joined with her in her prayers. 'Nay,' said Beowulf, 'but I will keep the kingdom for the boy till he become of years to keep it for himself.' So he kept it faithfully and with a prudent soul. But after a while there came to the court of King Heardred – he was Hygelac's son – two outlawed men, sons of Ohthere the Swede, who had rebelled against their lord the King of Sweden. Heardred showed them hospitality, but they for recompense slew him with the sword. Lo, and when he was dead, the nobles took counsel together, and came to Beowulf saying, 'There is now none who can be King over the Goths save thou only.' So Beowulf consented to their desire, and took the kingdom upon himself, ruling the people prudently for fifty years. Well did he avenge the death of Hygelac and his son. But the tale of how he also came to his end yet remains to be told.

THE LAMBTON WORM

Jessie Adelaide Middleton

> For nine generations direct in their line,
>   No one in his bed shall die;
> In red war and in surgy sea,
>   And some by their own hand lie.
>
> (OLD BALLAD)

L ONG AGO, in the days when the Lambtons were so brave and powerful that they feared neither God nor man, the young heir of Lambton went a-fishing in the river Wear on a Sunday, according to his profane custom, and, meeting with no success, he vented his ill-luck in curses loud and deep, to the horror of the pious folk who passed him on their way to Mass.

At last he felt a sharp tug at his line, and joyfully began to draw the expected fish to land; but, to his surprise and disappointment, he found he had hooked a worm of disgusting appearance, which he hastily tore off his hook, and threw into a neighbouring well.

He continued to fish, and presently a stranger of venerable appearance drew near.

'What sport?' quoth he.

'Why, I think I've catched the devil,' was young Lambton's reply; 'go and look in yonder well.'

The stranger looked at the Worm long and silently. 'I never saw the like of it before,' he said gravely. 'It betokens no good. Why, it has nine holes on each side of its mouth.'

Lambton laughed and went on with his fishing, and presently the stranger passed on his way.

Left in the well, the Worm throve apace. It grew and grew until the well became too small to hold it, and then it crawled forth to seek a new resting place. As the old chap-book version of the story says:

> It betook itself to Wear's cool stream,
>   Nurs'd by the flood, so fast
> It grew till, within nine circling folds,
>   A neighbouring hill it grasp'd.

It soon found a stone crag in the river Wear, round which it lay coiled during the daytime, and in the evening it wrapped itself nine times round the foot of a neighbouring hillock, which is called to this day the Worm Hill. It now became the terror of the whole countryside, laying waste the land, injuring the cattle, frightening the villagers, devouring lambs, and sucking the milk from the cows.

Meanwhile young Lambton had repented him of his evil life, and, having bathed himself in holy water and made the sign of the Cross, he joined the Crusaders and went off to distant lands. He was, therefore, quite in ignorance of the fact that the worm he had caught was devastating the country round his home, and laying waste the lands of his forefathers. His father, the old lord, bowed down by grief and sorrow, lived still at Lambton Hall, and on its hill the Worm held sway.

The household met in council, and an old retainer, far advanced in years, suggested that the large trough belonging to the courtyard should be filled with milk to propitiate the Worm. This was accordingly done. The Worm approached, drank the milk, and retired to the hill with its appetite appeased, and from that day forth it demanded a daily supply of milk of 'nine kye', and if refused it would plunder and slay without mercy, and tear up the trees in the park with violent lashing of its tail.

Of course, such a state of things could not be borne, and many a gallant knight set out to slay the Worm, but each one as he came was vanquished, with loss of life or limb, for no sooner was the Worm cut asunder than it immediately joined itself together again and renewed the attack.

So, after a time, it was left in undisputed possession of its hill.

Years passed by, and Lambton returned from the holy wars. He had fought the Saracen foe, trodden on Calvary's Hill, and imprinted a kiss on his Saviour's grave. Full of horror, he listened to the story of the Worm's depredations, and with eyes full of tears beheld the broad lands of his ancestors now made barren as a wilderness. After tenderly greeting his father (who had long thought him dead and was overjoyed at his return), he crossed the river to see for himself the monster who had wrought such devastation, and which the boldest knight had failed to kill:

> By the struggling light of early morn
> It lies in its resting-place,
> Its argus head on the waters clear,
> The rock in its embrace.

Next morning he consulted a sibyl, or wise woman, who consented to help him to overcome the Worm, but before giving him advice, the knight, she added, must take a solemn vow that, if successful, he would offer as a sacrifice the first living thing he met after the combat. Should he fail to do this, his race would be accursed, and *the lords of Lambton for nine generations would never die in their beds.*

Lambton agreed to the conditions, and the sibyl then bade him put on his coat of mail, well studded with spear-blades, take his trustiest sword in his hand, and boldly attack the Worm on the water before it hied from the Wear to the Hall to partake of its morning meal.

Lambton instructed his aged father that if he vanquished the Worm he was to blow three blasts on his horn. This would be the signal to let loose his favourite greyhound, which would immediately fly to the sound of the horn, and would thus be the first thing to meet him and be slain, according to the sibyl's condition. The father promised to carry out these instructions, and the knight, having made the solemn vow in Brigford Chapel, armed himself cap-à-pie, and started out to the fray.

He took his stand on the rock with his sword in his hand, and when the Worm saw him it left the hill round which it was coiled, and went down to the river to attack him.

Then began a fearful combat between the Knight and the Worm. The Knight struck at it again and again with all his might as it closed on him with its deadly embrace, coiling round him and trying to strangle him in its folds. But now the spear blades upon his coat did their work, for the closer the Worm pressed the more frightfully was it cut through and through by their sharp edges. Even so, the several pieces quickly united again, and the fierce combat went on till the Wear ran red with blood. Then Lambton, calling upon the Saints to help him, stepped to the river, raised his sword, and with a mighty stroke cut the Worm in two. This time the pieces were carried away by the stream, and the vanquished monster was unable to reunite himself:

> Thrice does he kiss the cross round his neck,
>   Thrice to the saints he prays,
> Then draws his sword so sharp and long,
>   Nor to the combat he delays.
>
> For anon unto Wear's strong stream he goes,
>   His sword direct he wields,
> The monster's gore thick crimsons the Wear,
>   And nor wound nor cut now heals.
>
> For the Wear's strong stream fast floods away
>   The parts that are cut in twain
> By the razored coat that the Worm enfolds,
>   Or the sword strokes made amain.

The victorious knight blew three loud blasts on his horn as a signal for the greyhound to be released, but his aged father was so filled with rapture at hearing the tidings of his son's victory, that, in his impatience to embrace him, he forgot everything else, and in the excitement of the moment ran forward to meet him.

Now was Lambton face to face with a dreadful alternative. Either he must become a parricide, or bring the curse upon his descendants. He again blew his horn, and the greyhound bounded forward, and was sacrificed with the still reeking sword; but it was killed in vain, for the vow had stipulated that the *first* creature he met should die, and so the curse fell upon the Lambtons, and the sybil's prediction was fulfilled.

But no Christian might his father slay,
No penance the deed atone;
And no Lambton for nine ages past
To die in his bed was known.

Afterword

Popular tradition traces the curse back to Robert Lambton, who died in 1442, leaving by his will 100 marks to his brother, John Lambton, Knight of Rhodes. A curious old manuscript, lately owned by the Middletons of Offerton, has the following entry: 'John Lambton that slew ye worm was Knight of Rhodes and Lord of Lambeton and Wod Spilton after the dethe of four brother, sans esshew malle.' Nine succeeding generations brought the curse down to Henry Lambton, whose death in 1761 broke the spell. During his lifetime there was great curiosity to know whether the curse would hold good to the end; but to the relief of the superstitious he died in his coach while crossing a bridge within a mile of Lambton Hall. His brother, General Lambton, it is said, was so afraid that his servants would forcibly fulfil the ancient prophecy in him as well, that, during his last illness, he kept a horsewhip by his bedside.

The Lambtons, on whom the curse fell, died various deaths, both valorous and untimely. Sir William Lambton was slain at Marston Moor, while serving under Charles I and his son William received his death-wound at the battle of Wakefield. Robert, the son of John Lambton, who slew the Worm, was drowned in Newbig, and others died 'in red war and in surgy sea.'

The ruins of the Chapel of Brigford, where Lambton vowed his rash vow, were still to be seen in 1820, and so is the Worm Hill today, near Fatfield, about a mile and a half from old Lambton Hall. The Worm Well lies between the hill and the river Wear; it once had a reputation as a wishing well, and midsummer eve revels were carried on round it.

At Lambton Hall, the seat of the present Earl of Durham, two stone figures are preserved, the exact date of which is not known. One represents a knight, armed cap-à-pie, his visor raised, and part of his coat of mail inlaid with spear blades. Coiled round his legs is the Worm, which is not represented as a reptile, but as a creature bearing a strong family likeness to the dragon – 'full of fyre and also of venyme,' so dear to the hearts of the ballad-monger of the fourteenth century. The other is a female figure supposed to represent the sibyl.

PART V:
BATTLES AND CONQUESTS

THE SHADOWY ONE

Peter Tremayne

'A YOUNG BOY is approaching the gate, Scáthach,' announced Cochar Croibhe, the gatekeeper of Dún Scaith, whose great fortifications rose on the Island of Shadows in Alba, an island which today is still called the Island of Scáthach or Skye.

'A boy?' Scáthach was a tall woman, of pleasing figure and long fiery red hair. A closer look at her form would show the well-toned muscles. The easiness of her gait belied a body so well trained that in a moment the great sword, which hung from her slender waist, would be in her hand and that sword was not for ornament. Indeed, Scáthach was acclaimed one of the greatest warriors in all the world. No one had ever bested her in combat which was why all the warriors, who had ambition to be champions, were sent to her academy where she taught them the martial arts. Her school was famous in every land.

Cochar Croibhe, the gatekeeper, was himself a warrior of no mean abilities, for such he had to be in order to guard the gates of Dún Scaith. He shrugged.

'A boy,' he confirmed, 'but accoutred as a warrior.'

'Does he come alone?'

'He is quite alone, Scáthach.'

'A talented boy, then,' mused Scáthach, 'for such he would have to be to reach this place by himself.'

Cochar Croibhe conceded the fact after some thought. After all, Scáthach's military academy lay on the Island of Shadows and to reach it one had to pass through black forests and desert plains. There was the Plain of Ill-Luck, for example, which could not be crossed without sinking into bottomless bogs for it was one great quagmire. There was the Perilous Glen which was filled with countless ravening beasts.

It was with curiosity that Scáthach mounted the battlements of her fortress to view the approach of the boy. She decided that Cochar Croibhe did not lie but the youth was more than a mere boy. He was short, muscular and handsome, and he carried his weapons as a veteran used to arms.

'He may have crossed the Plain of Ill-Luck and the Perilous Glen,' sneered Cochar Croibhe, at her side, 'but he still has to cross the Bridge of Leaps.'

Now Scáthach's island, the Island of Shadows, was separated from the mainland by a deep gorge through which tempestuous, boiling seas, flooded. And the sea was filled with ravening creatures of the sea. The only way across was by a high bridge which led to the gate of her fortress. The point of this bridge was that it had been constructed by a god in a time before time. When one man stepped upon one end of this bridge, the middle would rise up and throw him off, and if he leapt into the centre then it would do likewise so that he might be flung into the gorge to the waiting creatures of the deep. Only Scáthach knew the secret of the safe crossing and only when her pupils had graduated from her academy and sworn a sacred oath of friendship, did she reveal to them the secret.

As Scáthach watched, the youth trotted up to the end of the bridge. She smiled and turned to Cochar Croibhe.

'We will wait to see if he can overcome this obstacle to assess his worthiness.'

They waited. The youth came and examined the bridge and then, to their surprise, he sat down on the far shore and built a fire where he rested.

'He cannot cross,' chuckled Cochar Croibhe. 'He waits for us to go out and show him the way.'

Scáthach shook her head.

'Not so. I think he does but rest from his long journey here and when his strength is recovered he will attempt the crossing.'

Sure enough, when the grey mists of evening were approaching, the youth suddenly stood up. He walked back a distance and made a run at the bridge. As soon as his foot touched the end of it, it rose up and flung him backwards. He landed without dignity on his back on the ground. Cochar Croibhe laughed sourly.

'He is not finished yet,' smiled Scáthach. 'Look.'

The youth tried once more, and again he was flung off the bridge but thankfully not into the foaming waters below. A third time he tried and with the same result. Then the youth stood for a while in thought. They saw him walk back a distance and run for the bridge.

'My best sword as a wager that he will be thrown into the sea this time,' cried Cochar Croibhe eagerly.

'Done! My best shield will answer your wager,' cried Scáthach in reply.

With the fourth leap, the youth landed on the centre of the bridge. In a fraction of a second, it started to rise but the youth had made a further leap and was safely across and at the gates of Dún Scaith, demanding entrance.

'Let us go down and admit this young man for his courage and vigour has won him a place in this academy whatever his name and station.'

Grumbling at the loss of his best sword, Cochar Croibhe went and brought the youth in and escorted him into the presence of Scáthach.

'What is your name?' she asked.

'I am named Setanta and I am from the kingdom of Ulaidh.'

Scáthach's eyes widened as she gazed on the handsome, muscular youth.

'I have heard that a youth named Setanta, coming late to a feast at the fortress of Cullan, was confronted by a ferocious hound, which Cullan, thinking his guests were all in the fortress, had loosed to guard the place. This hound was so strong that Cullan had no fear of attack save only if an entire army marched on his fortress. The story I heard was that this youth was named Setanta. When attacked by the hound, he killed it. And while the warriors of Ulaidh were amazed by the feat, Cullan was sorrowful that his faithful hound had died for the safety of his house. The youth Setanta then offered to guard Cullan's house until such time as a hound whelp had been trained to take its sire's place. So Setanta became Cullan's hound – Cúchullain.'

'I am that Setanta, the hound of Cullan,' replied the youth solemnly.

'Then you are thrice welcome, Cúchullain.'

Cochar Croibhe glowered in the background for jealousy was in his soul.

It happened that Scáthach had a beautiful daughter and her name was Uathach, which means 'spectre'. It was Uathach's duty to serve at the table when the students of her mother's academy were having their evening meal. One evening, therefore, when Uathach was serving meat, she came to the young man Setanta. She held out the dish of meat to him and he took it.

Their eyes met and through their eyes their souls found attraction.

In this moment, Setanta forgot his strength and, in taking the dish of meat from the girl's hands, his hand closed upon hers and her finger broke in his grasp.

Uathach let out a scream of anguish.

Setanta dropped to his knees before her and asked for her forgiveness. This the girl, in spite of her pain, willingly gave.

But Cochar Croibhe, the jealous doorkeeper, who already had cause to dislike the young man, came running into the feasting hall in answer to the girl's cry. Now it was known that Cochar Croibhe coveted Uathach and his amorous suit had twice been rejected by her in spite of the fact that he was acclaimed the bravest champion at Dún Scaith . . . with the exception of Scáthach, of course.

Straightaway he challenged Setanta to single combat as reparation for the injury.

Uathach protested that she had already forgiven the young man but Cochar Croibhe grew insulting and spoke of a boy hiding behind the apron of a girl.

Setanta stood quietly, for he was not one to lose his temper without just cause.

Osmiach, the physician, having heard Uathach's scream, came into the feasting hall and set the girl's finger and applied pain-killing poultices.

All the while Cochar Croibhe, in spite of Uathach's protests, taunted young Setanta. Finally, he pointed out that everyone knew that Setanta had no father for was it not common knowledge that his mother, Dectera, had vanished one day from the court of Conchobhar Mac Nessa and then reappeared with the boy child which she named Setanta?

Now this was true, for Dectera had been beloved of none

other than the great god Lugh Lámhfada, and the child was Lugh's gift to Ulaidh. But Setanta could not bear to hear his mother so insulted.

'Choose your weapons,' he finally snapped at Cochar Croibhe, who was a master of all weapons, but was incomparable with the spear or javelin.

'Javelin and buckler!'

And with that the two went out into the courtyard of Dún Scaith.

Scáthach had the power to stop the fight but she did not.

'We shall see,' mused Scáthach to herself, watching from a window. 'If Setanta bests Cochar Croibhe in combat than it will mean that I am right to have accepted him for he will become the greatest champion of Ulaidh.'

And the combat commenced.

Cochar Croibhe came running forward, buckler before him, javelin held high.

Setanta merely stood there, watching his advance with a frown. He did not even raise his buckler to defend himself. Yet his muscles tightened on his javelin and moved it back into position. Then Cochar Croibhe halted in his run, halted a split second, dropped his buckler and held back his arm for the throw. At that point, Setanta loosed his own javelin. So fast and so swiftly did it cleave the air that it transfixed Cochar Croibhe before he had time to cast his own spear. Spear and buckler dropped from his grasp and he sank on his knees, staring in horrified surprise. Then he collapsed on his side.

'Dead,' exclaimed Osmiach the physician dispassionately.

Setanta's gaze met that of Uathach but she was not distressed. Admiration shone from her eyes.

Scáthach appeared, standing frowning at the young man.

'You have slain my gatekeeper,' she said without emotion.

'Then as I fulfilled the duties of Cullan's hound, and guarded Cullan's fortress, let me now be your gatekeeper for as long as I stay here.'

So it was, that for a year and a day, Setanta stayed at the martial arts academy of Scáthach and each night Uathach warmed his bed. And Scáthach herself taught Setanta all he needed to know to become the greatest warrior in all Éireann and the fame of Cúchullain, or Cullan's hound, for as such he was better known than as Setanta, spread far and wide.

At the end of a year and a day, Scáthach drew Setanta to her and led the way down to a large underground cavern where none but they were allowed to enter. Inside, lit by brand torches, was a great pool of bubbling sulphur, warm and liquid grey.

'Here we will make the final test,' Scáthach announced. 'We will wrestle and it shall be the winner of three throws shall be the greater.'

'I cannot wrestle you!' protested Setanta, for as much as he realised that she was the greatest female champion of Alba, it was against his sense of honour to wrestle a woman.

'You will wrestle as I direct or it shall be known that you feared a challenge from me,' she said simply.

So the two of them stripped off, there and then, and took their places on either side of the sulphur pool. At the first clash, Scáthach threw Setanta. The next time they touched, Setanta, no longer fearful to harm her, threw her. And then the third time they came together in the centre of the sulphur pool. They held each other so tightly in an embrace that neither could throw the other. And after an hour Scáthach released her hold and said:

'The pupil has become the master.'

Setanta then made love with her for it is written that the apprentice must show his willingness to marry his vocation.

In return, Scáthach gave Setanta a special spear which was called the Gae-Bolg, or belly spear. This spear was thrown by the foot. It made one small wound when it entered a man's body but then thirty terrible barbs opened so that it filled every limb and crevice with mortal wounds. Scáthach gave this to Setanta and taught him how to cast it.

And both Scáthach and Uathach knew that the time was now approaching when Setanta would leave Dún Scaith.

It happened about this time that Scáthach received a challenge to combat from her own sister Aoife, whose name means 'radiantly beautiful'. Now she was Scáthach's twin sister and they had both been born of the goddess of war, the Mórrígán. Each was as proficient as the other in arms but each claimed to be the superior of the other. Sibling rivalry warped their relationship.

Aoife had sent Scáthach a message saying: 'I hear that you have a new champion at Dún Scaith. Let us test his mettle. My champions and your champions will contest together.'

When she read this, Scáthach was fearful for the safety of Setanta for she knew, deep in her heart, that her sister was the greater of the two; that she was the fiercest and strongest champion in the world. But the challenge could not be rejected and so Scáthach prepared her warriors to go out and meet her sister Aoife.

The night before they were to set forth, Scáthach called Osmiach, the physician, to her and told him to prepare a potion which would send a man to sleep for four and twenty hours. And Osmiach prepared the sleeping draught and it was administered in secret to Setanta.

The warriors of Scáthach set out to meet the warriors of Aoife.

What Scáthach overlooked was that the potion which might have served to cause an ordinary man to sleep for four and twenty hours, only held Setanta in sleep for one hour.

As the armies gathered, great was Scáthach's astonishment when Setanta's chariot came careering up and he joined her lines, for he had followed Scáthach's army by the tracks of the chariots.

The champions met in combat and great deeds were wrought that day. Setanta and two sons of Scáthach fought with six of Aoife's mightiest warriors and slew them. Several of Scáthach's pupils were cut down but they did not fall alone. As the day grew dark, both armies were still evenly matched.

Then Aoife challenged Scáthach directly to combat to resolve matters.

Setanta intervened and claimed the champion's right to meet Aoife in place of Scáthach and such was the ethics of the situation that Scáthach could not refuse him.

'Before I go,' Setanta said, 'tell me what your sister Aoife loves and values most in the world.'

Scáthach frowned.

'Why, she loves her two horses, her chariot and her charioteer, in that order.'

So Setanta drove out into the battlefield to meet Aoife.

At first he was amazed that Aoife was so like Scáthach, but her

beauty seemed more radiant than Scáthach's and she handled
her weapons with greater dexterity. It was truly said that she
was the greater warrior of the two. They clashed together,
Setanta and Aoife. They fought in single combat and tried
every champion's feat they knew. Blow to blow, shield to
shield, eye to eye. Then skill was with Aoife. She aimed such
a blow that the sword of Setanta shattered at the hilt. She raised
her sword for the final strike.

Setanta cried out: 'Look! Your horses and chariot have fallen
from the cliff into the gorge!'

Aoife hesitated and glanced round fearfully.

At once Setanta rushed forward, seized her around the waist
and flung her to the ground. Before she could recover, there was
a knife at her throat and Setanta was demanding her surrender.
Angrily, she realised that she had no option but to plead for her
life and Setanta granted it on condition that she made a lasting
peace with her sister Scáthach and gave Scáthach hostages for
the fulfilment of the pledge.

'You are the first person who has bested me in combat,' Aoife
ruefully admitted, staring at the handsome youth. 'Albeit, it was
by a trick.'

'Victory is victory however it was achieved,' replied Setanta
calmly.

'There is wisdom on your tongue,' agreed Aoife. 'Come and
join me at my fortress that we may get better acquainted.'

To this invitation, Setanta agreed.

Scáthach and her daughter Uathach watched his departure
with Aoife in sadness but in resignation of his Destiny. He would
become Aoife's lover and she would bear his son, Connla, whom
the gods would force him to kill. In sadness, he would stride
forth to become the defender of Ulaidh, his name praised in
the mouths of all men; charioteers and warriors, kings and sages
would recount his deeds and he would win the love of many. He
would be – Cúchullain. And whenever the name of Cúchullain
was spoken, the name of his famous tutor would also drop from
the tongue – Scáthach, the Shadowy One, ruler of Dún Scaith
on the Isle of Skye.

BRAN AND BRANWEN

Peter Tremayne

T HERE WAS GREAT rejoicing throughout the Isle of the Mighty when Bran, son of Llyr, announced that his beautiful sister Branwen, 'the Fair Blossom', would be married to Matholwch, king of Éireann. It was a union that everyone rejoiced in, for it meant peace between the two kingdoms. Others rejoiced that Branwen should find a husband in the handsome warrior-king and a king so rich that he had sent no less than thirteen great ships to Aber Alaw, which is now called Aberffraw, filled with rich gifts. It was at Aber Alaw that the wedding feast was to be held.

Great pavilion tents were pitched around the sea port and for nine days and nine nights there was feasting and entertainment.

Branwen and Matholwch gazed upon one another and neither could find fault in the choice.

Bran, the king of the Isle of the Mighty, was much pleased with the match for, above all things, he desired peace for his people. But there were some in the kingdom, and within his own family, who did not. Some were ready for mischief and war. Penardun, the daughter of Dôn, who, by Llyr was the mother of Bran and Branwen, had married again to a champion called Eurosswyd. To him she bore twins. One was called Nisien and the other was Efnisien. The first grew to be a youth of gentle nature and a lover of peace, while the second was one who loved nothing better than strife and conflict.

Because this was known, Bran the king decided that Efnisien should not be invited to Branwen's wedding feast. So enraged did Efnisien become that he came to the celebrations anyway, although he did not make his presence known. He slunk into the camp of Matholwch in disguise and proceeded to cut off the tails, ears, eyebrows and lips of all the king of Ireland's horses.

Matholwch stormed into Bran's tent the next morning and demanded an explanation for the great insult that had been paid him. Bran explained that the deed had been done without his knowledge and, as token of his good faith, Bran would replace every horse that had been mutilated. In addition he gave Matholwch a plate of purest gold as big as his face and a staff of silver as tall as Matholwch himself. To this Bran also added a special gift. It was a magical cauldron that had been brought from Éireann.

Matholwch was mollified by these gifts. In fact, he was more than delighted with the cauldron. Matholwch knew of this magical cauldron and knew where it had once been kept, at a spot called the Lake of the Cauldron in the heart of his kingdom. Walking by that lake many years before, Matholwch had met a tall, ugly man, with a wife larger and uglier than himself. The man, who was called Llassar Llaesgyfnewis, had the cauldron strapped to his back. Every six weeks his wife, called Cymideu Cymeinfoll, gave birth to a fully armed warrior. And if any one warrior was killed, Llassar would put the corpse in the cauldron and the warrior would emerge as alive as ever but lacking the power of speech.

At first they had taken service with Matholwch but the continual growth of the warrior family, who could never be killed, and their incessant bickering caused the king of Éireann many a heartache. Finally he could stand no more and knew that the only thing to do was to destroy Llassar and Cymideu and all their children together.

He had enticed them all into a house made of iron and had coals heaped on it hoping that it would roast the whole family to death. As soon as the iron walls grew white hot, Cymideu and Llassar had burst through them, but their bickering children had remained behind and were roasted to death. Cymideu and Llassar, together with their magic cauldron, had crossed to the Isle of the Mighty where Bran had allowed them to settle and, in return for this kindness, they had given Bran the magic cauldron.

So Matholwch was well pleased at receiving the cauldron but

without the fierce pair who had previously owned it and all the warriors to which they gave birth.

So the wedding feast continued and, at the end of the nine days and nights, Matholwch and his beautiful bride, Branwen, set sail for his court at Tara in Éireann. And before the year was out Branwen bore Matholwch a son who was called Gwern and because he was the heir to the five kingdoms of Éireann he was sent to be fostered among the greatest families of the land.

In the second year of their marriage, tales of the insult Matholwch had suffered at his wedding feast were made known to the people of Éireann. Stories were spread that Matholwch was weak, having accepted a token compensation from Bran. The people of Éireann, prompted by these stories, grew indignant. They demanded that Matholwch should seek vengeance. Now Matholwch was rather worried at this for he knew that behind the stories were his foster brothers who were envious of his throne. They were stirring up this trouble in order to oust him as king and claim the throne for themselves.

So Matholwch decided to appease his people by publicly degrading Branwen. He had her removed to the kitchens of the palace and forced her to cook and clean and ordered the chief cook to give her a blow on the ears every day so that she would know her place. All traffic of ships between Éireann and the Isle of the Mighty was forbidden so that no news of how Branwen was being punished should reach her brother.

For three years Branwen bore the punishment, working from sunrise to sunset in the kitchens and being sent to sleep in a draughty attic at night. It was in the attic, in the brief period before dawn, that she found a young starling with a broken wing. She mended the wing and taught the starling how to fly. Then she wrote a letter to her brother Bran, telling him what was taking place. The starling took the message under its wing and flew up into the sky.

Away eastward from Éireann it flew until it alighted at Caer Seiont in Arfon. Indeed, not only did it alight in Caer Seiont but it set down on the very shoulder of Bran, the king himself.

Bran's rage grew as he read the letter from his sister and he called his son Caradawc to him and told him to send out to all the chieftains of the Isle of the Mighty to prepare a great army to invade Éireann. No less than one hundred and forty-four kings came to his aid. Leaving Caradawc to rule the Isle of the Mighty in his absençe, Bran set sail with his great armada.

Messengers soon came to Matholwch telling him that a great forest was growing on the sea and this vast wood was moving towards the shores of Éireann.

Branwen heard the news and cried in joy. 'It is the masts and yards of the fleet of Britain.'

The chief cook reported this outburst to Matholwch who immediately sought the advice of his council. They decided that the army of Bran was so vast that it could not be met in battle where advantage was with it. Matholwch, however, ordered a great palace to be constructed for Bran to placate him. A great feasting would be held and all homage done to the king of the Isle of the Mighty. Branwen would be released and her son Gwern brought to the court.

However, this was an outward subterfuge. The plan was that Bran and all his sub-kings and chieftains would be invited into the new palace feasting hall. Of course, according to ancient law, no one could enter a feasting hall with arms. So the Britons would be defenceless. Matholwch secretly arranged that at each of the pillars behind the seats at the feasting tables were to be hung two leather bags. And in each bag would be an armed warrior of Éireann. A signal would be given and the warriors would then fall on the guests and slaughter them.

Now it chanced that Efnisien had come with Bran's army and while Matholwch was greeting Bran and inviting him to the banquet, Efnisien entered the feasting hall. Efnisien saw the bags and asked one of Matholwch's attendants: 'What is in this bag?' 'Meal, good soul,' replied the servant. So Efnisien put his hand in the bag and felt the head of the warrior inside. He squeezed the head until his fingers met together in the brain as the bone cracked. He went to the next bag and asked the same question. The attendant tried to brazen it out. But Efnisien went through the entire hall and crushed all two hundred warriors' heads while they were hiding in the bags, even the head of one warrior who was wearing an iron helmet.

When the feasting began, Matholwch made a great play of preaching peace and concord. Branwen, suitably clothed once more as a princess, was told to enter the feast and pretend to her brother Bran that her letter of despair was all a mistake.

Matholwch had brought her son – the boy Gwern – to the feasting hall and threatened to kill him if Branwen disobeyed. And when the boy was led in Bran and his followers embraced their young nephew in whom the kingship of Éireann rested. But when the boy came to Efnisien, the boy's half-uncle, Efnisien seized him and flung him into the blazing fire in the hearth saying: 'No son of Matholwch can be trusted, for treachery runs deep in his blood!' Branwen with a cry of despair would have leapt after him but Bran seized her and held her back.

Matholwch called his warriors to strike but they lay dead in their sacks.

Realising now that he had been betrayed by Matholwch, Bran ordered his men to arms while Matholwch and his nobles beat a hurried retreat from the feasting hall. Thereafter, the men of the Isle of the Mighty and the men of Éireann closed in battle and the combat continued far into that first night.

During the night the men of Éireann told Matholwch that they were losing too many warriors. And so Matholwch ordered that the magic cauldron be readied and the bodies of the dead were thrown inside. Come the next morning, the dead warriors emerged alive but without the power of speech. The fresh army of Matholwch renewed the attack on the exhausted army of Bran and there was great slaughter.

Now Efnisien, who had inherited a little of the purity of spirit of his mother Penardun, for he was still half-brother to Bran and Branwen, was filled with remorse for what he had done. He realised that he was responsible for everything that had come to pass since the wedding of Branwen. 'It is up to me to find a way of delivering my people safely from this catastrophe,' he said. And so he hid himself that evening among the dead warriors of Éireann. He was taken up with their corpses and transferred to the hidden place of the cauldron during the night. Then he was flung inside with the others and once inside he rent the cauldron into four pieces so that it could not be used again. Such was the effort of his deed that his own heart burst asunder.

The men of Éireann and the men of the Isle of the Mighty continued to wage war but, finally, all the men of Éireann were slain and only five pregnant women of Éireann were left to repopulate that ravaged land. And among the warriors from the Isle of the Mighty only seven remained. Bran himself was

wounded in the foot by an arrow bearing poison and he knew
that the poison was spreading through his body. So he called
the remaining warriors of Britain to him.

They were Bran's brother Manawyddan ap Llyr; Pryderi, son
of Pwyll and Rhiannon; the great bard Taliesin; Gluneu son
of Taran; Ynnawc; Grudye son of Muryel; and Heilyn son of
Gwynn Hen.

Bran gazed at them sadly.

'I am dying. Before the poison reaches my head and destroys
my soul, cut off my head. Take it with you to the fortress of Llyr
and bury it on the White Hill. There shall my head be placed so
that it faces east and then no foreigner will invade Britain while
it is there. Once you have cut off my head, I shall remain and
talk to you through my head, and be pleasant company on your
sad journey back to the Isle of the Mighty. I shall remain with
you until you have completed your task.'

Then the seven cut off Bran's head and, together with a
sorrowing Branwen, those survivors left the ravaged shores of
Éireann where so many had perished. And although the Head
of Bran talked and was as joyful as it had been in life, the more
Branwen grew mournful and depressed. And when the party
reached the shores of the Isle of the Mighty and came to Aber
Alaw, where she had once been so happy at her marriage feast,
Branwen sat down in grief.

'Grief is on me that I was ever born. Two island kingdoms
have been destroyed because of me. Though yesterday my grief
was unbearable, today it is twice so.'

Without another word, the beautiful Branwen groaned and
her heart broke.

> Softened were the voices in the brakes
> Of the wondering birds
> On seeing the fair body of Branwen.
> Will there not be a relating again
> Of that sadness that befell the Fair Blossom
> At the stream of Alaw?

The seven survivors gathered round and they built her a
four-sided grave on the banks of the Alaw which spot they
called Ynys Branwen.

As they journeyed eastward, the seven found that Caswallon son of Beli had overthrown Caradawc, Bran's son, and destruction had settled upon the Isle of the Mighty. Caradawc had died of grief and only Pryderi's foster father, Pendaran had escaped the destruction. And while Manawyddan should have been king of the Isle of the Mighty, Caswallon ruled instead for the destiny had been laid on the seven that they should first accompany the head of their beloved leader to its final resting place.

They journeyed onward, eating, drinking and feasting with the noble head of Bran.

Finally, they came to the fortress of Llyr, Llyr's dun, which is now called London, and they took the head to a hill overlooking the place, called the White Hill, where in later years the Tower of London was raised. Here they buried the head with its face to the east. And it came to pass for many centuries no conquerors truly conquered the Isle of the Mighty and Britain remained under the rule of the descendants of the Children of Dôn.

It is said that ages afterwards, Arthur, in his Christian pride, thought it beneath his dignity to rely on the prophecy wrought by Bran, and he had the fabulous head dug up and thrown into the sea. Within a short time, Arthur was slain at Camlann and the godless hosts of Angles and Saxons were swarming into Britain across the Northern Sea.

KING LAURIN'S ROSE-GARDEN

Wilhelm Wägner

I

K ING DIETRICH WAS one day about to mount his horse, and set out to visit his brother monarch, the Emperor Ermenrich, when a warrior rode into the court. The king at once knew him to be Heime. He was not much pleased to see him back at Bern, but when Heime told him that he had been victorious in many battles against giants and robbers, he consented to receive him once more into the ranks of his comrades, and desired him to accompany him and certain of his followers to Romaburg.

At Fritilaburg, where they rested, Dietrich accepted the offered service of a man who called himself Ilmenrik, son of a Danish yeoman Soti; and enrolled him amongst his servants.

When they came to Romaburg, they were received with all honour by the emperor, who gave them both board and lodging. But the emperor forgot one thing in his plans, and that was, to provide food for the servants. Ilmenrik fed them the first night. On the second, his private resources being exhausted, he pawned Heime's armour and horse for ten gold pieces; on the third, he pawned Wittich's goods for twenty; and on the fourth, he got thirty for the weapons and horse of the king. On the fifth day, when the king gave orders for their return home, Ilmenrik asked for money to free the articles he had pawned. Dietrich was astonished and angry when he heard how extravagant his servant's ideas had been. He took him before

Ermenrich, who at once said he would pay the sum required, and asked how much it was. The emperor and all his court made merry at Ilmenrik's expense, especially Walter of Wasgenstein (Vosges), who asked him if he was a were-wolf, and well up in strange knowledge of all kinds. Ilmenrik modestly answered that he had learnt to perform many feats of strength and skill from his father, such as putting the stone and throwing the hammer; and that he would wager his head against the lord of Wasgenstein's that he could beat him in this. Walter accepted his challenge, and the trial began.

Such skill as Ilmenrik displayed had never been seen before. The heroes all feared for the life of the brave warrior of Wasgenstein. The emperor then called the young victor to him.

'Hearken to me, young sir,' he said; 'I will buy the head of my vassal from you at whatever price you list. Gold for blood is the old law.'

'Fear not, sire,' answered Ilmenrik, 'the head of the brave hero is in no danger from me. I do not want it. But if you wish to do me a kindness, lend me so much money as I have expended for the keep of the servants, that I may redeem the weapons, garments, and horses that I pawned.'

'Treasurer,' said the emperor, turning to one of his ministers, 'weigh out sixty marks of red gold, that the fellow may redeem his pledges, and another sixty marks to fill his purse.'

'Thank you, my lord,' returned the young man, 'I do not need your gift, for I am a servant of the rich king of Bern, who will see that I lack nothing; but if you will keep us another day here, I will, with this sixty marks, treat the servants to a better feast than before, and also my master, all his warriors, and you yourself, should you desire to join the party, even if I have to pawn horses and coats of mail again.'

The warriors all laughed at the merry youth, but Heime frowned, and said that if ever he pawned his horse again it should cost him his life.

The feast which the servant prepared them was of royal magnificence. All were pleased except Heime, who secretly feared that his property was again in pawn. The young fellow seated himself at his side, and asked him in a low voice if he knew who had given him that scar on his forehead. Heime answered that it was Dietleib, son of Yarl Biterolf, adding that he would know him again in a moment, and that the scar should be avenged in blood.

Ilmenrik replied:

'Methinks, bold warrior, your memory has gone a-woolgathering. If you look me in the face, you will see that I am that Dietleib whom you and your robbers attacked as he was riding through a forest with his father. We slew the robber Ingram and his companions, but you escaped with that wound, thanks to the speed of your good horse. If you don't believe me, I have a witness here that will prove my words in the open field. But if you will trust me, the matter may remain a secret between us.'

Towards the end of the feast, Dietrich told the youth that he should no longer be a servant, but should be received into the ranks of his comrades; and he, thanking him, answered that he was really Dietleib, son of Yarl Biterolf, whose glorious deeds were known far and wide.

All the king's followers, except Heime, received the young hero into their ranks with pleasure. He returned to Bern with the king, and proved himself his trusty comrade in many an adventure. But he was of a restless mind, and wished to see more of the world; so after a time he took service under Etzel, king of the Huns, at whose court he found his father settled. Father and son together were the doers of many a daring deed. King Etzel, wishing to keep them in his service, offered them the land of Steiermark (Styria) as a fief. Biterolf gave up his share to his son, who was therefore surnamed the Styrian.

II

DIETLEIB ONCE CAME unexpectedly on a visit to Master Hildebrand at his castle of Garden. He looked sadder than of old, and returned the master's greeting without an answering smile. Hildebrand inquired the cause of his sadness, and he replied that he had a sweet and wise sister named Künhild, who had kept house for him in Styria. One day, when she was dancing with other maidens in a green meadow, and he looking on, she suddenly vanished from the circle, and no one knew what had become of her.

'Since then,' he continued, 'I have learnt from a magician that it was the dwarf king Laurin that hid her under a cap of darkness, and carried her off to his hollow mountain. This mountain is in Tyrol, where the dwarf has also a wonderful Rose-garden. Now, good master, I have come to you for advice. How can I free my sister from the power of the goblin?'

'It is a ticklish matter,' said Hildebrand, 'and may cost many a good life. I will go with you to Bern, to see Dietrich and our other comrades, and then we can agree in council what is the best plan to pursue. For the dwarf is powerful, not only because of the extent of his empire, but from his knowledge of magic.'

When the heroes heard what had brought Hildebrand and Dietleib to Bern, Wolfhart spoke first, and said that he would adventure himself alone upon the quest, fetch home the maiden safe and sound, and bring the royal mannikin to Bern bound to his saddle-bow. Dietleib then asked Hildebrand if he knew the way to the Rose-garden. He replied that he did, but that Laurin watched over the garden himself, and exacted the left foot and right hand of any one who was bold enough to venture within its bounds, and spoil the roses.

'He cannot exact this tribute,' said Wittich, 'unless he gets the better of the warrior in fair fight.'

'Well then,' added the king, 'we will not touch the lovely flowers. All we want is to save our friend's sister from the hands of the dwarf, and that is a labour beseeming a warrior.'

The heroes all swore to do no hurt to the garden, and then Hildebrand consented to be their guide. The adventurers were Hildebrand, Dietrich, Dietleib, Wittich, and Wolfhart.

Their road led them northward among the wild mountains, and over crevasses, ice, and snow. It was a perilous way they trod, but they recked nothing of fatigue or danger, for their hearts beat high with hope. At length they reached the garden: a lovely place, where spring reigned eternally, making it a flowery oasis in a wintry desert. The heroes feasted their eyes on the beautiful sight, and felt as though they had reached the gates of paradise.

Wolfhart was the first to break the spell: setting spurs to his horse, he called to his comrades to follow, and galloped towards the garden. His mad career was soon checked by an iron door with golden letters inscribed on it. He tried to break open the door, but in vain; his comrades came to his aid, and the door was at last beaten in by the four strong men. The garden was still defended by a golden thread, such as used to surround the palaces of the Ases in the olden time. The warriors trod down the thread, and then, in spite of Hildebrand's warnings, began to pluck the roses and trample the garden. Dietrich did not join in the work of destruction, but stood apart under a linden tree.

Suddenly Hildebrand called out, 'Draw your swords! Here comes the master of the garden.'

They all looked up, and saw something bright advancing rapidly towards them. Soon they were able to distinguish the form of a horseman riding a steed that was swift as the wind. He was small of stature, and habited in a complete suit of armour. His helmet was of specially beautiful workmanship, and was further adorned with a diadem of jewels, in the midst of which a carbuncle blazed like a sun. On beholding the damage that had just been done, he drew rein, and exclaimed angrily:

'What harm have I ever done you, robbers as you are, that you should thus destroy my roses? If you had aught against me, why did you not send me a challenge like honourable men? You must now expiate your crime by each giving me his right hand and left foot.'

'If you are King Laurin,' answered Dietrich, 'we do indeed owe you reparation, and will pay you a fine in gold; but we cannot afford to lose our right hands, for we require them to wield our swords; and as to our left feet, we could not well ride were we deprived of them.'

'He would be a coward who talked of paying any fine except in blows,' cried Wolfhart; 'and I am determined to dash that hop-o'-my-thumb, together with the cat he is riding, against the cliffs over yonder, and then his bones will break into such tiny pieces that even his grasshopper subjects can never collect them.'

Upon this Laurin answered in words of defiance, and the combat with Wolfhart began, only to end in the latter's overthrow the moment he felt the touch of the dwarf's spear. Wittich was not more fortunate than his friend, for he also was thrown from his saddle at the first encounter.

Laurin sprang from his horse, drew out a large knife, and

approached the hero, who lay senseless on the ground. Dietrich sprang forward to rescue his comrade.

'Do not venture the spear thrust, but close with him,' said Hildebrand in a low voice. 'Laurin has three magic charms of which you must deprive him; and these are, a ring with the stone of victory on his finger, a belt that gives him the strength of twelve men round his waist, and in his pocket a cap of darkness, which makes him invisible when he puts it on.'

After a long and fierce wrestle, Dietrich managed to get possession of the ring, which he at once gave into the master's charge. Again the combat raged, neither side gaining any advantage. At last Dietrich begged for a short truce, which Laurin granted.

The truce over, the two kings renewed the fight. Dietrich caught Laurin by the belt, and at the same moment the latter clasped him round the knees so tight that he fell backwards. The violence of his fall broke the belt he was holding, and it slipped from his hand. Hildebrand then rushed forward and caught it before the dwarf could pick it up. No sooner was this done than Laurin went out of sight. Dietrich still felt the blows he gave, but could not see him. Filled with a berserkir rage at his own powerlessness, he forgot the pain of his wounds; he flung away both sword and spear, sprang like a tiger in the direction in which he heard the whistling of the invisible sword, and seized his adversary for the third time. He tore away the cap of darkness, and Laurin stood before him praying for peace.

'I shall first cut off your right hand and left foot, and then your head, and after that you may have peace,' cried the angered hero, setting off in pursuit of the dwarf, who now took to his heels.

'Save me, Dietleib, my dear brother-in-law,' cried Laurin, running up to that warrior; 'your sister is my queen.'

Dietleib swung the little creature on horseback before him, and galloped away into the wood. There he set him down, and told him to hide himself until the king's anger was abated.

Coming back to the place of combat, the warrior found Dietrich on horseback, and as furious as before.

'I must have either the dwarf's head or yours,' cried Dietrich.

In another moment their swords were flashing; a second fight would have begun had not Hildebrand held back the king by main force, while Wittich did the same to Dietleib. After a little they succeeded in making peace between the angry men, and also in gaining grace for the dwarf. Later still the warriors might have been seen in friendly converse with each other and with Laurin, who was then and there admitted as one of Dietrich's comrades.

This point settled, the dwarf proposed to show them the wonders of his hollow mountain, saying that Dietleib should then give his sister to him as wife, with the usual ceremonies.

'It is the old law,' answered the hero of Steierland, 'that when a maiden has been carried away from her home and is recovered by her friends, she should have free choice given her either to remain with her husband, or return to her people. Are you willing that it should be so in this case?'

'By all means,' said the dwarf. 'Now let us go. Do you see that snow-capped mountain? My palace is there – so to horse, that my eyes may no longer be pained by seeing the wreck you have wrought in my garden. The roses will bloom again in May.'

The journey to the snow-capped mountain was much longer than the warriors had imagined. It lasted till noon of the following day. Below the snow, they came to a meadow that was as beautiful as the rose-garden. The air was filled with the perfume of flowers. Birds were singing in the branches, and little dwarfs were to be seen hurrying to and fro. They followed Laurin into the dark entrance of his underground kingdom. The only one of their number who felt the least distrust was Wittich, who had not forgotten the thrust of the dwarf king's spear.

III

A SOFT TWILIGHT reigned in the vast hall of the palace to which they now came. The walls were of polished marble, inlaid with gold and silver. The floor was formed of a single agate, the ceiling of a sapphire, and from it there hung shining carbuncles like stars in the blue sky of night. All at once it became light as day. The queen came in surrounded by her maidens. Her girdle and necklace were jewelled, and in her coronet was a diamond that shone like the sun, bringing the brightness of day wherever it came. But the lady herself was more beautiful than aught else. None could take their eyes off her face. She seated herself beside Laurin, and signed to her brother Dietleib to sit down at the other side of her. She embraced him and asked him many questions about her old home and friends. By this time supper was ready. Laurin was a perfect host, and his guests were soon quite at their ease. Even Wittich forgot to be suspicious. When the meal was over, the dwarf king left the hall, and Dietleib seized the opportunity to ask his sister whether she was willing to remain in that underground paradise as its queen. She answered with tears that she could not forget her home and friends; that she would rather be a peasant girl in the upper world than a queen among the dwarfs, and that though she must admit that Laurin was very good and kind, yet he was not as other men. Dietleib then promised to save her, or lose his life in the attempt.

Laurin now returned, and asked the hero if he would like to retire to his bedchamber. He took him there, and remained talking with him for some time. At last he told him that his comrades were all condemned to death, and that he had only spared him because he was his brother-in-law.

'Traitor, false dwarf!' cried Dietleib. 'I live and die with my comrades, but you are in my power!'

He started forward, but the dwarf was gone, and the door was shut and locked on the outside.

Laurin then returned to the hall, filled the goblets of the warriors from a particular jar, and entreated them to drink the wine, which would insure them a good night's rest. They did so, and immediately their heads sank upon their breasts, and a heavy drugged sleep fell upon them. Then turning to the queen, Laurin desired her to go to her room, for these men must die in punishment for the wreck they had made of his rose-garden; adding that her brother was safely locked up in a distant room, that he might escape the fate of his comrades. Künhild wept aloud, and said that she would die if he carried out his cruel purpose. He gave her no distinct answer, but reiterated his command.

As soon as the queen had retired, he sounded his horn, and immediately five giants and a number of dwarfs hurried into the room. He commanded them to bind the warriors so tight with cords that they could not move when they awoke. After that he had them dragged to a dungeon, where they might remain until he should decide their fate next morning. Having seen his orders carried out, he went to bed, and began to think whether it would be better to let the men off to please the queen, or to punish them for their evil deed. The last seemed to him the wiser plan, and he fell asleep, gloating over the intended slaughter of his helpless victims.

Dietrich awoke soon after midnight; he felt that he was bound hand and foot, and called to his comrades for aid; but they were as powerless as he. Then Dietrich's wrath was roused to such a pitch, that his fiery breath burnt the cords that bound one hand, and left it free. After that, it was a matter of little difficulty to untie the knots at his wrist and feet, and then to set his comrades at liberty. What was to be done now? They could not break open their dungeon door. They had neither weapon nor coat of mail. They were helpless victims. At this very moment, while they were looking at each other in despair, they were startled by hearing a woman's voice asking in a low whisper if they were yet alive.

'We thank you, noble queen,' answered Hildebrand, 'we are alive and well, but totally unarmed.'

So Künhild opened the door, and appeared on the threshold with her brother. She placed her finger on her lips to enforce silence, and led the way to where the heroes' armour was piled. As soon as they were ready, the queen gave each of them a ring, by means of which he could see the dwarfs, even when they wore their caps of darkness.

'Hurrah!' cried Wolfhart. 'We can make as much noise as we like, now that we have our armour on, and our weapons in our hands.'

Laurin, wakened by Wolfhart's loud tones, knew that the prisoners were free, and at once summoned his dwarfish army to his assistance. The battle began, and raged for a long time without any advantage being gained by either side. Laurin was pleased in his heart of hearts that matters had turned out as they had, for he was a bold little fellow, and liked open war better than trickery. At length the underground forces were routed with great loss, and Laurin himself was taken prisoner.

Dietrich spared the life of the dwarf king at fair Künhild's request, but deposed him from royal power, and gave the mountain to Sintram, another dwarf of high rank, for a yearly tribute. When everything was ordered to their liking, the heroes returned to Bern, taking Laurin with them as a prisoner.

There was great joy in Bern at the return of the heroes, who were much praised for their valiant deeds, while the unfortunate Laurin was laughed at by all. There was only one person who showed him any sympathy, and that was Künhild. One day she met him when he was wandering about alone and melancholy, She spoke to him kindly, tried to comfort him, and told him he would soon gain the king's friendship if he proved himself to be faithful and true.

'Ah,' he laughed bitterly; 'they think that they have kicked a dog who will lick their hands; but a trodden snake bites! You may know what I intend to do. I have sent to inform Walberan, my uncle, who rules over the dwarfs and giants from the Caucasus to Sinai, of what has happened, and he is coming at the head of his forces to be my avenger. He cannot fail to win the day, slay strong Dietrich and his comrades, and lay the whole land waste. When that is done, I will take you back to my kingdom, and replant my Rose Garden, that it may be lovelier in May than it ever was before.'

'Laurin,' she answered, 'you carried me away from home by trickery and magic spells; but I have not been blind to your love, and feel myself honoured by its greatness. I cannot live in your underground kingdom, but I will love you and be your queen in the Rose Garden, if you will think of love and faithfulness, and not of revenge.'

She left him, and he sat pondering the matter for a long time.

A few days afterwards, Dietrich came to the Dwarf King, and, taking him by the hand, said, that he had been his prisoner long enough, that he must now sit with his comrades, or return to his own home, whichever he liked best.

'And then,' continued the king, 'I will go with you to your Rose Garden next spring, and see it in its beauty.'

The dwarf silently followed the king into the hall. He sat at Dietrich's side at the feast, and thought over the vengeance he would take when his uncle came.

But lovely Künhild appeared and filled his goblet, saying a few kind words the while, and immediately love conquered hatred, and he cried, emptying the goblet to the last drop –

'Henceforward I am your faithful comrade in life and death.'

Whilst the warriors were still at the feast, a messenger from King Walberan came in, and declared war on Dietrich in the name of his master, unless Laurin were at once restored to his kingdom, and unless the hero of Bern sent Walberan all the money and all the weapons in the country, as well as the right hand and left foot of every warrior who had taken part in the destruction of the Rose Garden.

Dietrich answered proudly, that he intended to keep his money, arms, hands, and feet, and those of his subjects also.

'And tell him,' added Laurin, 'that I send him my thanks and greeting for coming to my assistance, but that I am now free, and have entered into a bond of love and friendship with the King of Bern.'

Both sides prepared for battle, but before a blow was struck, Laurin rode into his uncle's camp, and tried to make peace between Walberan and Dietrich. His uncle told him he was no better than a broken-spirited serf, and refused to listen to his words. So the fight began, and raged furiously for many hours. At length, late in the afternoon, Dietrich and Walberan met, and challenged each other to single combat. It was a terrible struggle – both kings were severely wounded, and it seemed to the onlookers as if both must die. Suddenly Laurin threw himself unarmed between their swords, flung his arms round King Walberan, and entreated him to make peace. Almost at the same moment Hildebrand did the same by the angry Dietrich, and after much expenditure of words, the peacemakers had their way.

So the fighting was changed to feasting, and the kings entered into a friendly alliance at the banquet that evening. The hero of Bern made a long speech in praise of Laurin, who had endangered his life in endeavouring to make peace, and to whom he therefore restored the free and independent rule over his kingdom and Rose Garden. When he had finished, Queen Virginal came forward, leading fair Künhild, and laid the hand of the maiden in that of Laurin, saying that she knew he would regard her reward of his faithfulness as the greatest he had that day received; for Künhild had promised to be his wife if her brother did not object. As no dissentient voice was heard, the marriage was celebrated there and then.

In the May-month of the following year, when the roses were again in bloom, the dwarfs put the finishing touches to a beautiful palace, which they had built in the Rose Garden. Many a herdsman and Alpine hunter has seen it; but to those who go in search of it from mere curiosity, it remains ever invisible.

To this day, Laurin and Künhild show themselves at odd times in the valleys of Tyrol, and there are people yet alive who are reported to have had a distant glimpse of the wonderful Rose Garden.

IV

DIETRICH WAS NOW a man in the prime of life – a perfect hero, and man of valour. The number of his comrades had much increased, and many doughty deeds had been done.

Once when the king was feasting with many of his comrades, he looked round the table with pride, and said he believed that no ruler on earth had such heroes about him, that no other had prospered so well as he with the help of his chosen comrades, and that none might be compared with them. The warriors shouted their approbation. One alone was silent. The king turned to him, and asked whether in all his journeys he had seen bolder warriors.

'That I have,' cried Herbrand. 'I have seen some that have not their match upon earth. It was at the good town of Worms, near the River Rhine, in the land of Burgundy. It is there that the great Rose Garden lies – five miles long by two-and-a-half broad. The queen and her ladies tend it themselves, and twelve great warriors keep watch and ward lest any one enter the garden without the queen's permission. Whoever does so must fight with the guard, and no one yet, whether giant or warrior, has been able to withstand them.'

'Let us go and pluck the roses that have been watered with the blood of heroes,' cried Dietrich. 'I think that my comrades and I will get the better of the guard.'

'If you mean to try your luck,' said Herbrand, 'you must

know that the victor will receive a kiss and a wreath of roses from lovely women.'

'Ah, well,' said the old master, 'for the sake of a rose and a woman's kiss I would not risk a single hair of my head or beard. He who wishes to pluck roses or kiss women will find enough at Bern; he need not go to the Rhine to find them.'

Trusty Eckehart and a few more of the comrades agreed with him, for well they knew what the Burgundian warriors were like. But Dietrich loudly declared that he was not going to fight for the sake of roses and kisses, but for honour and fame; and that if his comrades did not wish to go with him, he could go alone. Of course, they would not hear of that, and all who were present agreed to go. The names of those who thus adventured their lives were: Dietrich himself, Master Hildebrand, strong Wittich, Henne called the Grim, Wolfhart, the young heroes Siegestab and Amelung (or Omlung), Trusty Eckehart, and Hertnit, Prince of the Reussen; but they only numbered nine in all, and twelve were needed to meet the twelve watchmen of the garden. Hildebrand knew what was to be done. He said –

'Good Rüdiger of Bechelaren will not refuse to be the tenth; the eleventh must be brave Dietleib of Styria, and the twelfth my pious brother, the monk Ilsan.'

They started forth at once to induce the chosen three to join them. They went first to Bechelaren, in the land of the Danube. Rüdiger received them hospitably, and at once consented to go with them, but said that he must first get leave of absence from Etzel, whose margrave he was. The heroes then went on to Styria to visit Dietleib. They did not find him at home, but his father Biterolf, who was there, earnestly entreated them to give up the journey to the Rhine, because, he said, only a fool would undertake a conflict for life or death with the world's bravest warriors, for the sake of a rose and a kiss. But when they met the young hero a short time after, they found him ready to go with them. This settled, they went on to Münchenzell, the monastery to which Hildebrand's brother belonged. As soon as Ilsan heard the object of their journey, he went straight to the abbot, and asked leave to accompany the hero of Bern to the Rose Garden. The abbot told him that such was scarcely a monkish quest, but Ilsan grew so angry, and so loudly affirmed that valiant deeds were in his eyes as seemly for a monk as for any other man, that the abbot quailed before him, and gave him leave to go. So Ilsan donned his armour under his monkish dress, and started with his friends. His heart beat high with joy that he was again bound on one of Dietrich's adventures, while his brother monks stood by and shook their heads, saying they feared it would not end well, seeing it was no saintly quest, but a worldly.

The heroes went first to Bern, which was to be the general meeting-place. Margrave Rüdiger was the last to arrive, for he had been detained by his visit to Etzel. Rüdiger was now sent on before the others as ambassador to King Gibich at Worms, to inform him of their intended invasion of the Rose Garden. The Margrave was well known in the Rhineland, and was received as an old friend by the king, who rejoiced to hear of his leader's enterprise.

The garden was entered on the appointed day, and the warriors stood opposite each other ready for battle; twelve against twelve, and yet always one against one. It was a terrible sight, for many a hero fell dying amongst the roses, and watered them with his heart's blood. When proud Wolfhart had slain his adversary, he contemptuously refused the kiss offered him by a lovely maiden, and contented himself with the garland of roses. The monk, Ilsan, walked into the lists on foot, clad in his grey robes. He jumped about among the roses with such strange agility that his opponent thought he had a madman to deal with. But he soon found that his reverend foe was made of sterner metal than he supposed, for he lay vanquished, a wiser man, though wounded almost to the death. The victor received the wreath of roses on his tonsured head, but when he kissed the lovely maid who gave it him, she shrieked aloud, for his bristly beard had stung her rosy lips. Seeing this, he said with comical disgust –

> 'The maidens of Rhineland are fair to see,
> But far too tender to pleasure me.'

Many other heroes received the prize of victory, while others were severely wounded. Peace was not concluded until sunset. The brave hero of Bern soon afterwards returned home, pleased with the result of his quest.

THE CHILDREN OF LOKI

Annie & Eliza Keary

I

Now, IN THE city of Asgard dwelt one called Loki, who, though amongst the Aesir, was not of the Aesir, but utterly unlike to them; for to do the wrong, and leave the right undone, was, night and day, this wicked Loki's one unwearied aim. How he came amongst the Aesir no one knew, nor even whence he came. Once, when Odin questioned him on the subject, Loki stoutly declared that there had been a time when he was innocent and noble-purposed like the Aesir themselves; but that, after many wanderings up and down the earth, it had been his misfortune, Loki said, to discover the half-burnt heart of a woman; 'since when,' continued he, 'I became what you now see me, Odin.' As this was too fearful a story for anyone to wish to hear twice over Odin never questioned him again.

Whilst the Aesir were building their city, Loki, instead of helping them, had been continually running over to Jötunheim to make friends amongst the giants and wicked witches of the place. Now, amongst the witches there was one so fearful to behold in her sin and her cruelty, that one would have thought it impossible even for such a one as Loki to find any pleasure in her companionship: nevertheless, so it was that he married her, and they lived together a long time, making each other worse and worse out of the abundance of their own wicked hearts, and bringing up their three children to be the plague, dread, and misery of mankind. These three children were just what they might have been expected to be from their parentage and education. The eldest was Jörmungand, a monstrous serpent; the second Fenrir, most ferocious of wolves; the third was Hela, half corpse, half queen. When Loki and his witch-wife looked at their fearful progeny they thought within themselves, 'What would the Aesir say if they could see?' 'But they cannot see,' said Loki; 'and, lest they should suspect Witch-wife, I will go back to Asgard for a little while, and salute old Father Odin bravely, as if I had no secret here.' So saying, Loki wished his wife good-morning, bade her hide the children securely indoors, and set forth on the road to Asgard.

But all the time he was travelling Loki's children went on growing, and long before he had reached the lofty city Jörmungand had become so large, that his mother was obliged to open the door to let his tail out. At first it hung only a little way across the road; but he grew, Oh, how fearfully Jörmungand grew! Whether it was from sudden exposure to the air, I do not know; but, in a single day he grew from one end of Jötunheim to the other, and early next morning began to shoot out in the direction of Asgard. Luckily, however, just at that moment Odin caught sight of him, when, from the top of Air Throne, the eyes of this vigilant ruler were taking their morning walk. 'Now,' said Odin, 'it is quite clear, Frigga, that I must remain in idleness no longer at Asgard, for monsters are bred up in Jötunheim, and the earth has need of me.' So saying, descending instantly from Air Throne, Odin went forth of Asgard's golden gates to tread the earth of common men, fighting to pierce through Jötunheim, and slay its monstrous sins.

In his journeyings Odin mixed freely with the people of the countries through which he passed; shared with them toil and pleasure, war and grief; taught them out of his own large experience, inspired them with his noble thoughts, and exalted them by his example. Even to the oldest he could teach much; and in the evening, when the labours of the day were ended, and the sun cast slanting rays upon the village green, it was pleasant to see the sturdy village youths grouped round that noble chief, hanging open-mouthed upon his words, as he told them of his great fight with the giant of long ago, and then pointing towards Jötunheim, explained to them how that fight was not yet over, for that giants and monsters grew round them on every side, and they, too, might do battle bravely, and be heroes and Aesir of the earth.

One evening, after thus drinking in his burning words they all trooped together to the village smithy, and Odin forged for them all night arms and armour, instructing them, at the same time, in their use. In the morning he said, 'Farewell, children; I have further to go than you can come; but do not forget me when I am gone, nor how to fight as I have taught you. Never cease to be true and brave; never turn your arms against one another; and never turn them away from the giant and the oppressor.'

Then the villagers returned to their homes and their field-labour, and Odin pressed on, through trackless uninhabited woods, up silent mountains, over the lonely ocean, until he reached that strange, mysterious meeting-place of sea and sky. There, brooding over the waters like a grey sea fog, sat Mimer, guardian of the well where wit and wisdom lie hidden.

'Mimer,' said Odin, going up to him boldly, 'let me drink of the waters of wisdom.'

'Truly, Odin,' answered Mimer, 'it is a great treasure that you seek, and one which many have sought before, but who, when they knew the price of it, turned back.'

Then replied Odin, 'I would give my right hand for wisdom willingly.'

'Nay,' rejoined the remorseless Mimer, 'it is not your right hand, but your right eye you must give.'

Odin was very sorry when he heard the words of Mimer, and yet he did not deem the price too great; for plucking out his right eye, and casting it from him, he received in return a draught of the fathomless deep. As Odin gave back the horn into Mimer's hand he felt as if there were a fountain of wisdom springing up within him – an inward light; for which you may be sure he never grudged having given his perishable eye. Now, also, he knew what it was necessary for him to do in order to become a really noble Asa,* and that was to push on to the extreme edge of the earth itself, and peep over into Niflheim. Odin knew it was precisely that he must do; and precisely that he did. Onward and northward he went over ice-bound seas, through twilight, fog, and snow, right onward in the face of winds that were like

* Asa – the singular of Aesir.

swords until he came into the unknown land, where sobs, and sighs, and sad, unfinished shapes were drifting up and down. 'Then,' said Odin, thoughtfully, 'I have come to the end of all creation, and a little further on Niflheim must lie.'

Accordingly he pushed on further and further until he reached the earth's extremest edge, where, lying down and leaning over from its last cold peak, he looked into the gulf below. It was Niflheim. At first Odin imagined that it was only empty darkness; but, after hanging there three nights and days, his eye fell on one of Yggdrasil's mighty stems. Yggdrasil was the old earth-tree, whose roots sprang far and wide, from Jötunheim, from above, and this, the oldest of the three, out of Niflheim. Odin looked long upon its time-worn, knotted fibres, and watched how they were for ever gnawed by Nidhögg the envious serpent, and his brood of poisonous diseases. Then he wondered what he should see next; and one by one spectres arose from Naströnd, the Shore of Corpses – arose and wandered pale, naked, nameless, and without a home. Then Odin looked down deeper into the abyss of abysses, and saw all its shapeless, nameless ills; whilst far below him, deeper than Naströnd, Yggdrasil, and Nidhögg, roared Hvergelmir, the boiling cauldron of evil. Nine nights and days this brave wise Asa hung over Niflheim pondering. More brave and more wise he turned away from it than when he came. It is true that he sighed often on his road thence to Jötunheim; but is it not always thus that wisdom and strength come to us weeping.

II

WHEN, AT LENGTH, Odin found himself in the land of giants – frost giants, mountain giants, three-headed and wolf-headed giants, monsters and iron witches of every kind – he walked straight on, without stopping to fight with any one of them, until he came to the middle of Jörmungand's body. Then he seized the monster, growing fearfully as he was all the time, and threw him headlong into the deep ocean. There Jörmungand still grew, until, encircling the whole earth, he found that his tail was growing down his throat, after which he lay quite still, binding himself together; and neither Odin nor anyone else has been able to move him thence. When Odin had thus disposed of

Jörmungand, henceforth called the Midgard Serpent, he went on to the house of Loki's wife. The door was thrown open, and the wicked Witch-mother sat in the entrance, whilst on one side crouched Fenrir, her ferocious wolf-son, and on the other stood Hela, most terrible of monsters and women. A crowd of giants strode after Odin, curious to obtain a glance of Loki's strange children before they should be sent away. At Fenrir and the Witch-mother they stared with great eyes, joyfully and savagely glittering; but when he looked at Hela each giant became as pale as new snow, and cold with terror as a mountain of ice. Pale, cold, frozen, they never moved again; but a rugged chain of rocks stood behind Odin, and he looked on fearless and unchilled.

'Strange daughter of Loki,' he said, speaking to Hela, 'you have the head of a queen, proud forehead, and large, imperial eyes; but your heart is pulseless, and your cruel arms kill what they embrace. Without doubt you have somewhere a kingdom; not where the sun shines, and men breathe the free air, but down below in infinite depths, where bodiless spirits wander, and the cast-off corpses are cold.'

Then Odin pointed downwards towards Niflheim, and Hela sank right through the earth, downward, downward, to that abyss of abysses, where she ruled over spectres, and made for herself a home called Helheim, nine lengthy kingdoms wide and deep.

After this, Odin desired Fenrir to follow him, promising that if he became tractable and obedient, and exchanged his ferocity for courage, he should not be banished as his brother and sister had been. So Fenrir followed, and Odin led the way out of Jötunheim, across the ocean, over the earth, until he came to the heavenly hills, which held up the southern sky tenderly in their glittering arms. There, half on the mountain-top and half in air, sat Heimdall, guardian of the tremulous bridge Bifröst, that arches from earth to heaven.

Heimdall was a tall, white Van, with golden teeth, and a wonderful horn, called the Giallar Horn, which he generally kept hidden under the tree Yggdrasil; but when he blew it the sound went out into all worlds.

Now, Odin had never been introduced to Heimdall – had never even seen him before; but he did not pass him by without speaking on that account. On the contrary, being altogether much struck by his appearance, he could not refrain from asking him a few questions. First, he requested to know whom he had the pleasure of addressing; secondly, who his parents were, and what his education had been; and thirdly, how he explained his present circumstances and occupation.

'My name is Heimdall,' answered the guardian of Bifröst, 'and the son of nine sisters am I. Born in the beginning of time, at the boundaries of the earth, I was fed on the strength of the earth and the cold sea. My training, moreover, was so perfect, that I now need no more sleep than a bird. I can see for a hundred miles around me as well by night as by day; I can hear the grass growing and the wool on the backs of sheep. I can blow mightily my horn Giallar, and I for ever guard the tremulous bridge-head against monsters, giants, iron witches, and dwarfs.'

Then asked Odin, gravely, 'Is it also forbidden to the Aesir to pass this way, Heimdall? Must you guard Bifröst, also, against them?'

'Assuredly not,' answered Heimdall. 'All Aesir and heroes are free to tread its trembling, many-coloured pavement, and they will do well to tread it, for above the arch's summit I know that the Urda fountain springs; rises, and falls, in a perpetual glitter, and by its sacred waters the Nornir dwell – those three mysterious, mighty maidens, through whose cold fingers run the golden threads of Time.'

'Enough, Heimdall,' answered Odin. 'Tomorrow we will come.'

III

ODIN DEPARTED FROM Heimdall, and went on his way, Fenrir obediently following, though not now much noticed by his captor, who pondered over the new wonders of which he had heard. 'Bifröst, Urda, and the Norns – what can they mean?'

Thus pondering and wondering he went, ascended Asgard's Hill, walked through the golden gates of the City into the palace of Gladsheim, and into the hall Valhalla, where, just then, the Aesir and Asyniur were assembled at their evening meal. Odin sat down to the table without speaking, and, still absent and meditative, proceeded to carve the great boar, Saehrimnir, which every evening eaten, was every morning whole again. No one thought of disturbing him by asking any questions, for they saw that something was on his mind, and the Aesir were well-bred. It is probable, therefore, that the supper would have been concluded in perfect silence if Fenrir had not poked his nose in at the doorway, just opposite to the seat of the lovely Freyja. She, genius of beauty as she was, and who had never in her whole life seen even the shadow of a wolf, covered her face with her hands, and screamed a little, which caused all the Aesir to start and turn round, in order to see what was the matter. But Odin directed a reproving glance at the ill-mannered Fenrir, and then gave orders that the wolf should be fed; 'after which,' concluded he, 'I will relate my adventures to the assembled Aesir.'

'That is all very well, Asa Odin,' answered Frey; 'but who, let me ask, is to undertake the office of feeding yon hideous and unmannerly animal?'

'That will I, joyfully,' cried Tyr, who liked nothing better than an adventure; and then, seizing a plate of meat from the table, he ran out of the hall, followed by Fenrir, who howled, and sniffed, and jumped up at him in a most impatient, un-Aesir-like manner.

After the wolf was gone Freyja looked up again, and when Tyr was seated once more, Odin began. He told them of everything that he had seen, and done, and suffered; and, at last, of Heimdall, that strange white Van, who sat upon the heavenly hills, and spoke of Bifröst, and Urda, and the Norns. The Aesir were very silent whilst Odin spoke to them, and were deeply and strangely moved by this conclusion to his discourse.

'The Norns,' repeated Frigga, 'the Fountain of Urd, the golden threads of time! Let us go, my children,' she said, rising from the table, 'let us go and look at these things.'

But Odin advised that they should wait until the next day, as the journey to Bifröst and back again could easily be accomplished in a single morning.

Accordingly, the next day the Aesir and Asyniur all rose with the sun, and prepared to set forth. Niörd came from Noatun, the mild sea-coast, which he had made his home, and with continual gentle puffings out of his wide, breezy mouth, he made their journey to Bifröst so easy and pleasant, that they all felt a little sorry when they caught the first glitter of Heimdall's golden teeth. But Heimdall was glad to see them; glad, at least, for their sakes. He thought it would be so good for them to go and see the Norns. As far as he himself was concerned he never felt dull alone. On the top of those bright hills how many meditations he had! Looking far and wide over the earth how much he saw and heard!

'Come already!' said Heimdall to the Aesir, stretching out his long, white hands to welcome them; 'come already! Ah! this is Niörd's doing. How do you do, cousin,' said he; for Niörd and Heimdall were related.

'How sweet and fresh it is up here!' remarked Frigga, looking all round, and feeling that it would be polite to say something. 'You are very happy, Sir,' continued she, 'in having always such fine scenery about you, and in being the guardian of such a bridge.'

And in truth Frigga might well say 'such a bridge,' for the like of it was never seen on the ground. Trembling and glittering it swung across the sky, up from the top of the mountain to the clouds, and down again into the distant sea.

'Bifröst! Bifröst!' exclaimed the Aesir, wonderingly; and Heimdall was pleased at their surprise.

'At the arch's highest point,' said he, pointing upward, 'rises that fountain of which I spoke. Do you wish to see it today?'

'That do we, indeed,' cried all the Aesir in a breath. 'Quick, Heimdall, and unlock the bridge's golden gate.'

Then Heimdall took all his keys out, and fitted them into the diamond lock till he found the right one, and the gate flew open with a sound at the same time sad and cheerful, like the dripping of leaves after a thunder-shower.

The Aesir pressed in; but, as they passed him, Heimdall laid his hand upon Thor's shoulder, and said 'I am very sorry, Thor; but it cannot be helped. You must go to the fountain alone by another way; for you are so strong and heavy, that if you were to put your foot on Bifröst, either it would tremble in pieces beneath your weight, or take fire from the friction of your iron heels. Yonder, however, are two river-clouds, called Körmt and Ermt, through which you can wade to the Sacred Urd, and you will assuredly reach it in time, though the waters of the clouds are strong and deep.'

At the words of Heimdall Thor fell back from the bridge's head, vexed and sorrowful. 'Am I to be sent away, then, and have to do disagreeable things,' said he, 'just because I am so strong? After all, what are Urda and the Norns to me, and Körmt and Ermt? I will go back to Asgard again.'

'Nay, Thor,' said Odin, 'I pray you, do not anything so foolish. Think again, I beseech you, what it is that we are going to see and hear. Körmt and Ermt lie before you, as Bifröst before us. It is yonder, above both, that we go. Neither can it much matter, Thor, whether we reach the Fountain of Urd over Bifröst or through the cloud.'

Then Thor blushed with shame at his own weakness, which had made him regret his strength; and, without any more grumbling or hanging back, he plunged into the dreadful river-clouds, whose dark vapours closed around him and covered him. He was hidden from sight, and the Aesir went on their way over the glittering bridge.

Daintily and airily they trod over it; they swung themselves up the swinging arch; they reached its summit on a pale, bright cloud. Thor was there already waiting for them, drenched and weary, but cheerful and bold. Then, all together, they knocked at the door of the pale, bright cloud; it blew open, and they passed in. Oh! then what did they see! Looking up to an infinite height through the purple air, they saw towering above them Yggdrasil's fairest branches, leafy and of a tender green, which also stretched far and wide; but, though they looked long, the Aesir could distinguish no topmost bough, and it almost seemed to them that, from somewhere up above, this mighty earth-tree must draw another root, so firmly and so tall it grew. On one side stood the Palace of the Norns, which was so bright that it almost blinded them to look at it, and on the other the Urda fountain plashed its cool waters – rising, falling, glittering, as nothing ever glitters on this side the clouds. Two ancient swans swam under the fount, and around it sat Three. Ah! how shall I describe them – Urd, Verdandi, Skuld. They were mighty, they were wilful, and one was veiled. Sitting upon the Doomstead, they watched the water as it rose and fell, and passed golden threads from one to another. Verdandi plucked them with busy fingers from Skuld's reluctant hand, and wove them in and out quickly, almost carelessly; for some she tore and blemished, and some she cruelly spoiled. Then Urd took the woof away from her, smoothed its rough places, and covered up some of the torn, gaping holes; but she hid away many of the bright parts, too, and then rolled it all round her great roller, Oblivion, which grew thicker and heavier every moment. And so they went on, Verdandi drawing from Skuld, and Urd from Verdandi; but whence Skuld drew her separate bright threads no one could see. She never seemed to reach the end of them, and neither of the sisters ever stopped or grew weary of her work.

The Aesir stood apart watching, and it was a great sight. They looked in the face of Urd, and fed on wisdom; they studied the countenance of Verdandi, and drank bitter strength; they glanced through the veil of Skuld, and tasted hope. At length, with full hearts, they stole away silently, one by one, out by the pale, open door, re-crossed the bridge, and stood once more by the side of Heimdall on the heavenly hills; then they went home again. Nobody spoke as they went; but ever afterwards it was an understood thing that the Aesir should fare to the Doomstead of the Nornir once in every day.

IV

YEARS PASSED AFTER Odin had brought Fenrir home with him to Asgard. All this time Odin entertained some hope that the wholesome, bright air of Gladsheim, the sight of the fair faces of the Asyniur and the hearing of the brave words which day by day fell from the lips of heroes, would, perhaps, have power to change the cruel nature Fenrir had inherited from his father, and make him worthy of his place as a dweller in the City of Lords.

To Tyr, the brave and strong-handed, Odin assigned the task of feeding Fenrir, and watching him, lest, in his cruel strength, he should injure any who were unable to defend themselves. And truly it was a grand sight, and one that Asa Odin loved, to see the two together, when, in the evening after the feast was over in Valhalla, Fenrir came prowling to Tyr's feet to receive his food from the one hand strong enough to quell him.

Tyr stood up in his calm strength like a tall, sheltering rock in which the timid sea-birds find a home; and Fenrir roared and howled round him like the bitter, destroying wave that slowly undermines its base.

Time passed on. Tyr had reached the prime of his strength; but Fenrir went on growing, not so rapidly as to awaken fear, as his brother Jörmungand had done, but slowly, surely, continually – a little stronger and a little fiercer every day.

The Aesir and the Asyniur had become accustomed to his presence; the gentlest lady in Asgard no longer turned away from the sight of his fierce mouth and fiery eye; they talked to each other about the smallest things, and every daily event was commented on and wondered about; but no one said anything of Fenrir, or noticed how gradually he grew, or how the glad air and the strong food, which gave valour and strength to an Asa, could only develop with greater rapidity fierceness and cruelty in a wolf. And they would have gone on living securely together while the monster grew and grew, if it had not been that Asa Odin's one eye, enlightened as it was by the upspringing well of wisdom within, saw more clearly than the eyes of his brothers and children.

One evening, as he stood in the court of Valhalla watching Tyr as he gave Fenrir his evening meal, a sudden cloud of care fell on the placid face of All-Father, and when the wolf, having satisfied his hunger, crouched back to his lair, he called together a council of the heads of the Aesir – Thor, Tyr, Bragi, Hoenir, Frey, and Niörd; and, after pointing out to them the evil which they had allowed to grow up among them unnoticed, he asked their counsel as to the best way of overcoming it before it became too strong to withstand.

Thor, always ready, was the first to answer. 'One would think,' he said, 'to hear the grave way in which you speak, Father Odin, that there was no such thing as a smithy near Asgard, or that I, Asa Thor, had no power to forge mighty weapons, and had never made my name known in Jötunheim as the conqueror and binder of monsters. Set your mind at rest. Before tomorrow evening at this time I will have forged a chain with which you shall bind Fenrir; and, once bound in a chain of my workmanship, there will be nothing further to fear from him.'

The assembled Aesir applauded Thor's speech; but the cloud did not pass away from Odin's brow.

'You have done many mighty deeds, Son Thor,' he said; 'but, if I mistake not, this binding of Fenrir will prove a task too difficult even for you.'

Thor made no answer; but he seized Miölnir, and, with sounding steps, strode to the smithy. All night long the mighty blows of Miölnir rang on the anvil, and the roaring bellows breathed a hot blast over all the hill of Asgard. None of the Aesir slept that night; but every now and then one or other of them came to cheer Thor at his work. Sometimes Frey brought his bright face into the dusky smithy; sometimes Tyr entreated permission to strike a stout blow; sometimes Bragi seated himself among the workers, and, with his eyes fixed on the glowing iron, poured forth a hero song, to which the ringing blows kept time.

There was also another guest, who, at intervals, made his presence known. By the light of the fire the evil form of Fenrir was seen prowling round in the darkness, and every now and then a fiendish, mocking laugh filled the pauses of the song, and the wind, and the ringing hammer.

All that night and the next day Thor laboured and Fenrir watched, and, at the time of the evening meal, Thor strode triumphantly into Father Odin's presence, and laid before him Laeding, the strongest chain that had ever yet been forged on earth. The Aesir passed it from one to another, and wondered at its immense length, and at the ponderous moulding of its twisted links.

'It is impossible for Fenrir to break through this,' they said; and they were loud in their thanks to Thor and praises of his prowess; only Father Odin kept a grave, sad silence.

When Fenrir came into the court to receive his food from Tyr, it was agreed that Thor and Tyr were to seize and bind him. They held their weapons in readiness, for they expected a fierce struggle; but, to their surprise, Fenrir quietly allowed the chain to be wound round him, and lay down at his ease, while Thor, with two strokes of Miölnir, riveted the last link into one of the strongest stones on which the court rested. Then, when the Aesir were about to congratulate each other on their victory, he slowly raised his ponderous form, which seemed to dilate in the rising, with one bound forward snapped the chain like a silken thread, and walked leisurely to his lair, as if no unusual thing had befallen him.

The Aesir, with downcast faces, stood looking at each other. Once more Thor was the first to speak. 'He who breaks through Laeding,' he said, 'only brings upon himself the still harder bondage of Dromi.' And having uttered these words, he again lifted Miölnir from the ground, and, weary as he was, returned to the smithy and resumed his place at the anvil.

For three days and nights Thor worked, and, when he once more appeared before Father Odin, he carried in his hand Dromi – the 'Strong Binding'. This chain exceeded Laeding in strength by one half, and was so heavy that Asa Thor himself staggered under its weight; and yet Fenrir showed no fear of allowing himself to be bound by it, and it cost him very little more effort than on the first evening to free himself from its fetters.

After this second failure Odin again called a council of Aesir in Gladsheim, and Thor stood among the others, silent and shamefaced.

It was now Frey who ventured first to offer an opinion. 'Thor, Tyr, and other brave sons of the Aesir,' he said, 'have passed their lives valiantly in fighting against giants and monsters, and, doubtless, much wise lore has come to them through these adventures. I, for the most part, have spent my time peacefully in woods and fields, watching how the seasons follow each other, and how the silent, dewy night ever leads up the brightly-smiling day; and, in this watching, many things have been made plain to me which have not, perhaps, been thought worthy of regard by my brother Lords. One thing that I have learned is, the wondrous strength that lies in little things, and that the labour carried on in darkness and silence ever brings forth the grandest birth. Thor and Miölnir have failed to forge a chain strong enough to bind Fenrir; but, since we cannot be helped by the mighty and renowned, let us turn to the unknown and weak.

'In the caverns and dim places of the earth live a tiny race of people, who are always working with unwearied, noiseless fingers. With Asa Odin's permission, I will send my messenger, Skirnir, and entreat aid of them; and we shall, perhaps, find that what passes the might of Asgard may be accomplished in the secret places of Svartheim.'

The face of Asa Odin brightened as Frey spoke, and, rising

immediately from his seat, he broke up the council, and entreated Frey to lose no time in returning to Alfheim and despatching Skirnir on his mission. In spite of the cloud that hung over Asgard all was fair and peaceful in Alfheim. Gerda, the radiant Alf Queen, made there perpetual sunshine with her bright face. The little elves loved her, and fluttered round her, keeping up a continual merry chatter, which sounded through the land like the sharp ripple of a brook over stony places; and Gerda answered them in low, sweet tones, as the answering wind sounds among the trees.

These must have been pleasant sounds to hear after the ringing of Miölnir and the howling of Fenrir; but Frey hardly gave himself time to greet Gerd and his elves before he summoned Skirnir into his presence, and acquainted him with the danger that hung over Asgard, and the important mission which the Aesir had determined to trust to his sagacity. Skirnir listened, playing with the knot of his wondrous sword, as he was wont to do, in order to make known to everyone that he possessed it; for, to confess the truth, it was somewhat too heavy for him to wield.

'This is a far different mission,' he said, 'from that on which you once sent me – to woo fairest Gerd; but, as the welfare of Asgard requires it, I will depart at once, though I have little liking for the dark caves and cunning people.'

Frey thanked him, and, putting a small key into his hand, which was, indeed, the key to the gate of Svartheim, he bade him farewell, and Skirnir set out on his journey.

The road from Alfheim to Svartheim is not as long as you would be apt to imagine. Indeed, it is possible for a careless person to wander from one region to another without being at once aware of it. Skirnir, having the key in his hand, took the direct way. The entrance-gate stands at the opening of a dim mountain-cave. Skirnir left his horse without, and entered; the air was heavy, moist, and warm, and it required the keenest glances of Skirnir's keen eyes to see his way. Innumerable narrow, winding paths, all leading downwards, opened themselves before him. As he followed the widest, a faint clinking sound of hammers met his ear, and, looking round, he saw groups of little men at work on every side. Some were wheeling small wheelbarrows full of lumps of shining metal along the ledges of the rock: some, with elfin pickaxes and spades, were digging ore from the mountain-side; some, herded together in little caves, were busy kindling fires, or working with tiny hammers on small anvils. As he continued his downward path the last remnant of daylight faded away; but he was not in total darkness, for now he perceived that each worker carried on his head a lantern, in which burned a pale, dancing light. Skirnir knew that each light was a Will-o'-the-wisp, which the dwarf who carried it had caught and imprisoned to light him in his work during the day, and which he must restore to the earth at night.

For many miles Skirnir wandered on lower and lower. On every side of him lay countless heaps of treasure – gold, silver, diamonds, rubies, emeralds – which the cunning workers stowed away silently in their dark hiding-places. At length he came to the very middle of the mountain, where the rocky roof rose to an immense height, and where he found himself in a brilliantly-lighted palace. Here, in truth, were hung all the lights in the world, which, on dark, moonless nights, are carried out by dwarfs to deceive the eyes of men. Corpse-lights, Will-o'-the-wisps, the sparks from glow-worms' tails, the light in fire-flies' wings – these, carefully hung up in tiers round and round the hall, illuminated the palace with a cold blue light, and revealed to Skirnir's eyes the grotesque and hideous shapes of the tiny beings around him. Hump-backed, cunning-eyed, open-mouthed, they stood round, laughing, and whispering, and pointing with shrivelled fingers. One among them, a little taller than the rest, who sat on a golden seat thickly set with diamonds, appeared to be a kind of chief among them, and to him Skirnir addressed his message.

Cunning and wicked as these dwarfs were, they entertained a wholesome fear of Odin, having never forgotten their one interview with him in Gladsheim; and, therefore, when they heard from whom Skirnir came, with many uncouth gesticulations they bowed low before him, and declared themselves willing to obey All-Father's commands. They asked for two days and two nights in which to complete their task, and during that time Skirnir remained their guest in Svartheim.

He wandered about, and saw strange sights. He saw the great earth central fire, and the swarthy, withered race, whose task it is ceaselessly to feed it with fuel; he saw the diamond-makers, who change the ashes of the great fire into brilliants; and the dwarfs, whose business it is to fill the cracks in the mountain-sides with pure veins of silver and gold, and lead them up to places where they will one day meet the eyes of men. Nearer the surface he visited the workers in iron and the makers of salt-mines; he drank of their strange-tasting mineral waters, and admired the splendour of their silver-roofed temples and dwellings of solid gold.

At the end of two days Skirnir re-entered the audience-hall, and then the chief of the dwarfs put into his hand a slender chain. You can imagine what size it was when I tell you that the dwarf chief held it lightly balanced on his forefinger; and when it rested on Skirnir's hand it felt to him no heavier than a piece of thistledown.

The Svart King laughed loud when he saw the disappointment on Skirnir's face. 'It seems to you a little thing,' he said; 'and yet I assure you that in making it we have used up all the materials in the whole world fit for the purpose. No such chain can ever be made again, neither will the least atom of the substances of which it is made be found more. It is fashioned out of six things. The noise made by the footfall of cats; the beards of women; the roots of stones; the sinews of bears; the breath of fish; and the spittle of birds. Fear not with this to bind Fenrir; for no stronger chain will ever be made till the end of the world.'

Skirnir now looked with wonder at his chain, and, after having thanked the dwarfs, and promised to bring them a reward from Odin, he set forth on his road home, and, by the time of the evening meal, reached Valhalla, and gladdened the hearts of the Aesir by the tidings of his success.

V

FAR AWAY TO the north of Asgard, surrounded by frowning mountains, the dark lake, Amsvartnir, lies, and, above the level of its troubled waters, burns Lyngvi, the island of sweet broom, flaming like a jewel on the dark brow of Hela. In this lonely isle, to which no ship but Skidbladnir could sail, the Aesir, with Fenrir in the midst, assembled to try the strength of the dwarfs' chain.

Fenrir prowled round his old master, Tyr, with a look of

savage triumph in his cruel eyes, now licking the hand that had so long fed him, and now shaking his great head, and howling defiantly. The Aesir stood at the foot of Giöll, the sounding rock, and passed Gleipnir, the chain, from one to another, talking about it, while Fenrir listened. 'It was much stronger than it looked,' they said; and Thor and Tyr vied with each other in their efforts to break it; while Bragi declared his belief that there was no one among Aesir or giants capable of performing so great a feat, 'unless,' he added, 'it should be you, Fenrir.'

This speech roused the pride of Fenrir; and, after looking long at the slender chain and the faces of the Aesir, he answered, 'Loath am I to be bound by this chain; but, lest you should doubt my courage, I will consent that you should bind me, provided one of you put his hand into my mouth as a pledge that no deceit is intended.'

There was a moment's silence among the Aesir when they heard this, and they looked at one another. Odin looked at Thor, and Thor looked at Bragi, and Frey fell behind, and put his hand to his side, where the all-conquering sword, which he alone could wield, no longer rested.

At length Tyr stepped forward valiantly, and put his strong right hand, with which he had so often fed him, into the wolf's cruel jaws.

At this signal the other Aesir threw the chain round the monster's neck, bound him securely with one end, and fastened the other to the great rock Giöll. When he was bound Fenrir rose, and shook himself, as he had done before; but in vain he raised himself up, and bounded forward – the more he struggled the more firmly the slender chain bound him.

At this sight the Aesir set up a loud shout of joy; for they saw their enemy conquered, and the danger that threatened Asgard averted. Only Tyr was silent, for in the struggle he had lost his hand.

Then Thor thrust his sword into the mouth of Fenrir, and a foaming dark flood burst forth, roared down the rock and under the lake, and began its course through the country a turbid river. So it will roll on till Ragnarök be come.

The sails of Skidbladnir now spread themselves out to the wind; and the Aesir, seated in the magic ship, floated over the lake silently in the silent moonlight; while, from the top of Bifröst, over the Urda fount and the dwelling of the Norns, a song floated down. 'Who,' asked one voice, 'of all the Aesir has won the highest honour?' and, singing, another voice made answer, 'Tyr has won the highest honour; for, of all the Aesir, he has the most worthily employed his gift.'

'Frey gave his sword for fairest Gerd.'

'Odin bought for himself wisdom at the price of his right eye.'

'Tyr, not for himself, but for others, has sacrificed his strong right hand.'

WHEN THE WOMAN CHIEF
WAS YOUNG

· ——————————— ·

Jessica Amanda Salmonson

T HE CHIEF OF the Klamath nation was wise and valiant. As
he grew older, he became a man of considerable wealth.
One day he looked about and saw that he had achieved all his
life's goals but one. He had no son to be his heir. With heavy
heart he asked, 'To whom will I teach the ways of justice?' In
his distress, he sought the counsel of three prophets who knew
the ways of divine beings as intimately as the chief knew the ways
of mortals. These wise men put their heads together and spoke
with great spirits of sun, earth, wind, and water. They perceived
that come autumn, at the time of the wapato root harvest, the
chief's wife would bear a child worthy to be his heir.

The following autumn, a child was born. To the chief's
chagrin, his wife bore a baby girl.

As she grew, her father the chief, remembering the prophesies
of his wise men, saw to the instruction of his daughter. She
learned to hunt; she rode in battle; she learned the ways of
wisdom in mediating disputes and rendering fair judgments.
Her name was Chao, the Antelope, though many years later
she was called Wolkotska the Cougar.

She was as lovely as the dawn, and the Klamaths loved her for
her courage and kindness. That she went clad in the garments
of a hunter only heightened the effect of her beauty. One day
she was hunting in the mountains and was seen by Llao, ruler
of the demons of Crater Lake and of the world below. From
his lofty throne at the lake's western edge, he observed the
boyish maiden for a long while, admiring her tracking skills.
Everything about her appealed to him, her quill-worked shirt

of fawn skin, her mantle of cougar fur, her high beaded moccasins, the colorfully fletched arrows in her quiver. The demon king came down from his rocky throne and said to Chao, 'Live with me at the center of the world. You will be wealthy beyond dreams as queen of powerful armies.' Chao laughed and refused him. He dared not take her by force, as she gleamed with a personal magic, and she was armed with a bow, sharp arrows, and a knife.

The following day the demon-king was seen coming across a meadow toward the Klamath village. The people saw his big grey face, his horned ears, his tough sinewy arms and taloned claws, and the people were greatly alarmed. When he smiled, his teeth were not reassuring, and when he hailed the chief with friendly words, the harshness of his voice was disheartening.

Llao entered into a bargaining with Chao's father and mother. Because he was a god, he was able to offer good hunting and fishing, fair weather, and large harvests in exchange for Chao as his wife. In addition he would provide personal wealth in the form of dentalia shells, obsidian for making spear and arrow heads, copper beads from under the earth, and a great many furs of black otters and white foxes.

The chief said, 'As you can see, my daughter is not like other maidens; she is also my son and will rule the Klamaths when I have gone to the land of the spirits. I do not wish to anger you, yet must ask that you turn your heart to another.'

Llao glowered silently for some while before he replied, 'You will regret this' and strode away across the meadow.

* * *

The following autumn there was a poor wapato harvest, and other roots were just as hard to find. Then came a terrifyingly cold winter. The game fled to warmer climes and the salmon could not be expected until late in spring, by which time many Klamaths would starve to death. The chief called together the three prophets. They said, 'What mortal can oppose the dark god Llao, ruler of the underworld? We must seek a champion, and who better than Skell, king of the skyworld?'

Skell's lodge was beyond the Yamsay River. As it happened, he had one day seen Chao running in pursuit of a deer. She had hunted far and wide to assist her hungry people, and so wandered into Skell's country seeking meat. He fell in love with the huntress at once and followed her secretly to her village.

The deer which Chao carried to her people was insufficient to feed everyone. Skell saw his chance to win his way into her heart. He commanded his eagles to fetch a large number of hares and bring them to the hungry village at once. When golden eagles appeared from every part of the forest with their offerings, the Klamaths were astonished and delighted. Then Skell came forth and said to the chief, 'My heart aches for your daughter. You did wisely to refuse her hand to Llao, for as his queen she would have lived miserably in the darkness of the world-cavern, worshipped by slavering monsters. At my side, she will become queen of sun and sky. Flowers will arise in the places of her footsteps. She will rule the children of the fox, the deer, and all that dwells in the forest; it shall be as though she were their only mother, before whom all life bows.'

The chief felt despair welling inside him. He had hoped to seek out Skell as a champion for his people against the malignant Llao, but now he must risk angering even the good god, saying, 'Great Skell, once I was without an heir, and I made sacrifices and supplications to the spirits of sky and earth, wind and water, and you were yourself among the divinities whose intercession I requested. Through my wise men I was promised an heir, and Chao was sent to me. I asked, "Is it possible the gods have made an error?" and I answered, "Indeed not; this girl will be my heir." This being so, how can I send her to live in the sky? I am old and will soon rest forever. Chao must remain with her people, who have already accepted her as my son. As chief of the Klamaths, she will choose her spouse, and not be chosen.'

Skell said, 'Well do I remember your prayers and sacrifices, but even gods may err, for each of us has his own design. Little did I know what giving you Chao would mean for me, or for my rival Llao. Know this, Chief of the Klamaths, that for the sake of your daughter, the huntress Chao, there will be war between the upper world and the lower world. When gods do battle, mortals invariably feel the tragic repercussions of divine severity.'

* * *

Thereafter Skell took it upon himself to protect the Klamaths from Llao's hostilities. When Llao called forth clouds of icy storms, Skell called forth warm sunlight to soften the stormy blows. When Llao's forces tried to frighten away all the game of the region, Skell sent troops of game from his own country to sacrifice themselves before the arrows of Klamath hunters. When Llao's underground fiends blighted essential roots and berries, Skell secretly arranged sunlit meadows with plenitude, revealing these sites to Chao.

The Klamaths moved their village to Klamath Lake near which Skell's meadows were discovered. Here Llao's evil influences were weakest, due to Skell's handiwork. Llao discovered that the fish in this lake were beyond his command. He became increasingly annoyed with Skell for negating his efforts to starve and punish the Klamaths.

One night when Llao's frustrations had reached a peak, the demon king called forth a large number of his shadowy, monstrous soldiers. They gathered with the demon-king upon Llao's rock, and he said to them, 'For so long as Skell lives as the protector of the Klamaths, I will not be able to slay the old chief and steal away Chao for my under-world bride.'

For five days they chanted dirge-like war songs and beat huge base drums made from the skins of tattooed men. Demons arrived in increasing numbers from the bottom of the lake and from the black depths of caves, bearing clubs and knives and savage faces, waving their knotted fists, eager for a fight. All this while Llao breathed forth a fetid smokiness that spread across the land.

At the end of the five days, the world was as dark by day as by night, as choking as a cedar lodge with its smoke-holes closed tight. Then Llao sent his legions into Skell's country to wreak havoc.

As Skell was a divinity of sunlight, the smoky darkness bewildered him. He called upon his legions of foxes, eagles, mountain goats, elk, bear, antelope and cougars, but all these were made sleepy and befuddled by the incessant night. They feared the smoke as a harbinger of fire, and knew not which way to run. Meanwhile the shades which Llao brought from the underworld roved about the land unchecked. When they came to the lodge of Skell they dragged him out into the blinding smoke. They bludgeoned him with their clubs, laughing hideously as they rent him piece from piece with their dreadful knives. Finally they carved out Skell's immortal beating heart and ran howling and hooting back to Crater Lake in Llao's land.

The conjured smoke dispersed from the countryside. A natural night descended, filled with stars and a fat bright moon reflecting on the cold waters of Llao's perfectly round lake. He and his legions gathered on the throne-rock, screeching their victory chants. Then Llao threw the beating heart of Skell into the lake, where numerous giant, brilliantly red crawfishes caught it and threw it from one clawed monster to another. They played with the heart of Skell as though it were a ball at a festival game. Llao and his army sat along the cliffs cheering and encouraging the moonlit sport of the giant crawfishes.

The game went on all night long. At dawn, the huntress Chao appeared unexpectedly at the eastern edge of the lake, the opposite side from Llao's Rock. She called across the waters in a chiding manner, 'How weak you are! Can't you throw Skell's heart any higher than that? The smallest child in my village could throw it higher!'

The crawfishes were insulted. Llao's legion chanted to the players, 'Throw it higher! Throw it higher!' Skell's heart was given a mighty toss from a crawfish's claw. When another crawfish caught it, Chao laughed mockingly, and said, 'Is that so high? Oh, such weaklings!' Each time Chao chided them, the crawfishes threw the heart still higher. Then an eagle streaked across the sky, caught Skell's heart in its talons, sped over the lake's surface pursued by crawfishes, and dropped the heart into Chao's upstretched hands.

The huntress immediately fled with the prize. Llao shouted, 'After her! After her!' and all the legions chased her through the wilderness toward the land of the River Yamsay.

The huntress was as swift as the antelope for which she was named. The rising sun burned the eyes of her pursuers. Wolves and bears leapt at the demons with claws and teeth, while foxes and deer led them astray. With this assistance, Chao left her pursuers far behind, and came alone to the lodge of Skell. Outside the lodge, Skell's pale lifeless limbs lay strewn about in pieces. His head was upside-down by a stump. His torso lay before the door of the lodge. Chao carefully put his body back together, then inserted the heart in his chest, so that the god sprang back to life.

*   *   *

For the span of half a moon, Chao nursed the sky-god, during which time Llao continued to terrorize the band of Klamaths. The tribe moved from Klamath Lake to Little Klamath Lake in their efforts to avoid the demon-king's minions. Throughout this time the Klamaths had no news of their princess and grieved that both she and Skell had been slain in the war against Llao.

One night the demons of Llao surrounded the harried village at Little Klamath Lake and began to take the people prisoner. They bound everyone with hazel rope and marched them away. The old chief and his wife they whipped with a cord. All through the night they tramped toward Crater Lake; men and women, old and young, all were so dispirited by events and weakened by weeks of poor nourishment that they could do nothing in their own behalf.

When the lake was reached, the people saw against the moonlight the terrible shadow of Llao atop his great rock. In a bellowing, thunderous voice he demanded, 'Where have you hidden Chao the Beautiful One, my chosen bride? Reveal her at once, or you shall all be fed to my crawfishes!'

Hearing their name called, the crawfish-monsters raised their beady-eyed faces above the water and created a froth in the starlit waters about them, stirring with their clacking claws. Yet the terror of this vision was not as effective as it might otherwise have been, for the Klamaths realized for the first time, by Llao's own demand, that he had failed to capture or slay their princess! The old chief stepped forth, his back bleeding from the whipping the devils had given him. He said, 'We have not seen Chao for half a moon. Perhaps she is licking her wounds in some secret place, we don't know. When she is able, she will return, and wage an avenging battle against you, like a good son.'

The Klamaths laughed and hollered in agreement and began to sing the name of Chao. The devils backed away, disliking the sound of human laughter. It was then that the spirit-canoe appeared in the east of the lake, and in it stood the huntress Chao and the sky-god Skell. Skell flew out of the canoe and over the lake, landing alongside Llao on the throne-rock. They were shadows against the moon, locked arm in arm in mortal combat. They fell to their sides still embracing, and no one could tell whose knife it was that glinted on the left, and whose knife glinted on the right.

Chao stepped out of the spirit-canoe and confronted five devils. She unleashed two arrows before the devils ran away, two of them severely wounded. She hurried to her mother and father and untied their hands, and soon everyone was untying someone else. Just as everyone's spirits were highest, they were stunned to hear the thunderous voice of Llao cry out, 'Feast, my crawfishes, upon the arms of Skell!'

The shadowy king threw two severed body parts into the lake, which the crawfish rent into small pieces as the waters grew black with the god's blood.

The dark figure atop the rock bent down to again hack at the corpse. Then he stood and cried out, 'Feast, my crawfishes, upon the legs of Skell!'

The monsters caught the falling limbs and began to devour them with rapacious delight.

A third time the Klamaths heard the horrible bellowing, 'Feast, my beauties, upon the heart and torso of Skell!' as he threw the greater part of his foe into the roiling waters.

The hearts of the Klamath people were dashed low. The devils, no longer cowed, came forth from the places where Chao had sent them hiding. However, in the next moment, the Klamaths were cheering excitedly, for it was Skell upon the rock! Skell laughed in his own handsome voice, crying out, 'Last of all I give to you the head of your master Llao!'

As Llao's head struck the surface of the water, it was transformed into Wizard Island. His gaping mouth became the island's burning crater. The crawfishes in a horror of having eaten their king sank away into the unnatural depths of the lake, never to be seen again. The devilish warriors along the lakeshore ran forth planning to avenge their ruler by battling the Klamaths, who were all unarmed save Chao. But as they ran forward, they began to dissipate in the rising dawn. Their shadowy forms faded into morning's mist which clung a while to the surface of the lake, then was gone.

*   *   *

It was not long after these events that the father of Chao died peacefully in the fulfillment of his life. His wife's spirit followed after him in due course. For many years thereafter, in the long past age that is today but an echo of a dream, the Maklak clan of Klamaths dwelt among their lakes and the vales, ruled by a noble and wise woman chief whose footfalls in the forest were as light as Wolkotska the Cougar, who was as gracefully fleet-footed as Chao the Antelope, and who was beloved of all her people.

TEWDRIG,
TYRANT OF TREHEYL

Peter Tremayne

'TEWDRIG! A STRANGE ship has appeared in the estuary,' cried Wron the Druid, bursting into the great feasting hall of Tewdrig, king of Treheyl and emperor of all Kernow, that south-western peninsula of the Isle of the Mighty that is today called Cornwall.

Tewdrig glanced up in agitated surprise.

'What guards do I have that I am not warned of the sight of a strange sail until a ship sails into the estuary?' he demanded vehemently. 'I should be informed as soon as a sail appears on the distant horizon.'

Wron made a dismissive gesture.

'Better to learn late than learn never, my king.'

'Does it come in war or does it come in peace?' demanded Tewdrig, buckling on his great sword, and taking up his rounded buckler.

Tewdrig was a strong man, as tall as a spear and as straight, with long black hair and a face that was saturnine and cruel. Skill with his weapons had brought Tewdrig power and his domains spread through the land of Kernow as far east as the great River Tamar, the quietly flowing river that marked the border with the kingdom of Dumnonia.

It was not strength alone, however, by which Tewdrig had kept his kingdom secure. He believed in the gods and the old ways in a world that was rapidly changing. In the east, whole kingdoms were falling before the hordes of Saxons with their mighty gods of war. Countless tribes had fled north, west and south to escape massacre by the children of Woden.

So far, the kingdom of Kernow had been kept safe. But Tewdrig was ever vigilant. Only a battle hardened king could keep harm from his people.

Now he hurried to the battlements of his fortress at the place of the estuary, Treheyl, and looked out across its waters. The estuary of the river, which was also called Heyl, formed a wide sac stretching two miles which, at low tide, was a stretch of mud banks on which numerous seabirds nested. The ramparts of Tewdrig's fortress rose dominantly above them.

Wron had obviously alerted the guards for they were gathered ready, their weapons in their hands.

Tewdrig came to the battlements and halted.

Indeed, there was a ship sailing into the estuary, its sails filled before the wind. It was heading towards the quay below Treheyl.

The king's eyes narrowed.

'It bears a strange emblem on the sail, Wron. Can you identify it?'

The Druid peered forward and shook his head.

'I cannot identify it, my king. It is not a symbol that is familiar in this land. Though from the cut of the vessel I would say that it is from the western island of Ywerdhon.'

Ywerdhon was the name by which the people of Kernow called the land of the goddess Éire.

Tewdrig bit in irritation at his lip, a habit he had often tried to control since childhood.

'Well, if they are foreign and mean us harm, they can harm us little. There is not room enough on that little craft for many warriors and their approach is open enough.'

Wron nodded: 'Nevertheless, my king, it would be best to have the men stand ready.'

Tewdrig turned to Dinan, chieftain of Pendinas, who was the captain of his guard, and told him to take a company of warriors to the quay to greet the strangers. Dinan was, in fact, Tewdrig's own brother and as fair as Tewdrig was dark yet they were both born at the same hour of the same mother and father. Dinan was Tewdrig's right hand and his shield at every battle. Firm in battle and as shrewd in war was Dinan. Some said that without Dinan, Tewdrig could not have maintained his kingdom. Though this was never said before either Tewdrig or Dinan. Further, many said that Tewdrig was as evilly tempered to those nearest to him as Dinan was amiable and obliging. Indeed, at Tewdrig's sharp commands, Dinan smiled but a gentle acknowledgement of his brother's order and went down in obedience to it.

Tewdrig turned back to examine the sail and its strange emblem again. It consisted of two curving lines which crossed each other so that the emblem appeared as if it was meant to be the outline of a fish.

Tewdrig was seated in the great hall of his palace when Dinan escorted the visitors to him. Wron the Druid stood at his right elbow for Wron was his chief counsellor.

There were five people who came before him; three men and two women. And while they were all clad in simple attire they stood tall and had the look of nobility on their faces. Around the neck of each one of them there hung a silver cross on a leather thong. Tewdrig's eyes narrowed for the cross seemed to be a badge of their fellowship.

'These, my brother, are travellers from Ywerdhon,' Dinan announced.

Their leader stepped forward. He was a tall, elderly man with a regal countenance.

'The Blessing of the Living God on you, Tewdrig of Treheyl,' he greeted.

Tewdrig frowned before he replied.

'The prosperity of each of the gods of my ancestors on you, stranger. Who are you and what do you seek in this land?'

'I was a king in my own country but have given up earthly pomp to follow a more glorious life. My name is Germoe.'

'Welcome then, Germoe. And what is more glorious in your eyes than temporal splendour?' smiled Tewdrig indulgently, wondering if the man was mad.

'To follow the ways of the Son of God and teach His truth and peace to your people.'

Wron drew his brows together.

'The Son of God? The Father of the Gods had many sons, each of them gods in their own right. Of which do you speak?'

'The one and indivisible God,' replied Germoe. 'Him we shall speak of anon if you allow me and my band to stay in your kingdom.'

'And who are these others?'

'I am Coan,' said one of the two young men.

'I am Elwyn,' announced the other.

'My name is Breage,' one of the young women added.

'I am Crowan,' said the last.

'We are all servants of the Living God,' Germoe said. 'We seek your permission to settle in peace and preach the new faith of our God.'

Wron glanced at the king.

'To settle in peace?' he sneered. 'Yet you would preach against our faith, destroy our beliefs and our laws. Do you call this peace?'

'Once you have opened your ears to the word of our Lord in heaven, it will be peace,' replied Germoe confidently. 'Our God is not a God of war, strife or dissension.'

'I would hear them, brother,' Dinan suddenly said. 'Let them go where they will in our land. For what can five people do to shake the faith of a nation?'

Wron flashed an angry glance at Dinan.

'I like it not. If they must stay let them go south away from this place so that they may not contaminate our good government.'

Tewdrig chuckled suddenly in humour.

'We will give in to our brother's urgings,' he said. 'For I agree – what harm can five strangers do in our midst? But Wron is my counsellor. Go southward, strangers, and preach as you wish.'

They all left Treheyl and journeyed south. But Crowan was the first to break away and took an eastern road until she came to a spot where she built a round enclosure and she prospered. They call this place Crowan to this day.

The others continued southwards. Then Coan also turned east and found a river called the Fal. On its eastern bank he started to preach the word of the Son of the Living God. But it is said that this land owed allegiance to Wron the Druid who stirred up the people against Coan and in their anger they stoned him to death. So the place where this happened was afterwards called Merther, which stands between Tresillian and St Michael Penkevil. The word *merther*, in the Cornish tongue, means 'martyr'.

The others continued southwards. And first Germoe halted

at the southern coast of Kernow and established a house where he taught and the spot became named after him. The others continued to the south-east following the coast. Then Breage stopped and under the shadow of a fortress called Pencaire, between the hills of Tregonning and Godolphin, she built her house and began to teach and so the place was called Breage after her. Finally, the young man named Elwyn came to the sea's edge and to a small port where he established himself and taught. The place was thereafter called Porth Elwyn, or Elwyn's port which is now Porthleven.

Now Tewdrig watched the progress of the strangers, with their strange stories of the Son of God, with anxiety on his brow. His people, who had followed the wise Druids of old, had begun to fall away from the rituals at the stone circles and the worship of the old gods. In spite of the martyrdom of Coan, the other members of Germoe's party were gaining converts throughout the southern lands of Kernow.

What Tewdrig did not realise was that his own brother had listened to the word and accepted the truth of the new faith.

It happened that a year and a day after the coming of Germoe and his followers, Wron came running to Tewdrig who was seated in his feasting hall.

'Tewdrig! A strange ship has appeared in the estuary,' cried Wron.

Tewdrig glanced up from his wine in agitated surprise.

'What guards do I have that I am not warned of the sight of a sail until a ship sails into the estuary?' he demanded vehemently. 'I should be informed as soon as a sail appears on the distant horizon.'

Wron made a dismissive gesture.

'Better to learn late than learn never, my king.'

'Does it come in war or does it come in peace?' demanded Tewdrig, buckling on his great sword, and taking up his rounded buckler.

'Perhaps it does not matter,' said Wron slyly, 'for the last strange ship that came here was supposed to come in peace and its honey-tongued crew have sewn dissension through the land.'

They climbed to the battlements and Tewdrig's eyes narrowed. Indeed, there was a ship sailing in the broad estuary before Treheyl, a ship with its sails filled before the wind.

Tewdrig gasped and pointed.

'See, Wron, look at its sail. It carries the same design as the ship of Germoe.' And, indeed, he was right for the sail carried two curving lines which crossed each other forming the outline of a great fish.

Wron drew in a deep breath.

'Then this ship is of the same nation as Germoe and his tribe. We would do well to slaughter them before they come ashore.'

Even so, Tewdrig hesitated and by the time he had made up his mind, his brother Dinan had gone down to the quay to welcome the strangers to Treheyl.

So Tewdrig hurried to the hall of his palace and slumped upon his throne while Wron stood moodily at his side.

Five strangers entered with Dinan.

'These, my brother, are travellers from Ywerdhon,' he said.

Tewdrig was filled with apprehension for though this time there were three men and two women, like the five that had come before them, they each carried a silver cross hung around their necks, and while the clothes they wore were simple, they all carried themselves with noble bearing.

'The Blessing of the Living God on you, Tewdrig of Treheyl,' greeted their leader.

He was a tall, handsome man.

'The prosperity of the gods of my ancestors greet you,' replied Tewdrig, frowning.

'I am called Gwinear, I was a prince in my own land but I have given up all temporal pomp to serve the true God.'

'All the gods are true,' snapped Wron, irritably.

'There is but one God,' replied the woman at Gwinear's side.

Tewdrig's eyes bulged a little as he beheld her, for never had he seen a maiden so comely as this.

Gwinear smiled, not noticing the look in the king's eyes: 'This is my sister, Piala.'

'My name is Ia,' the second maiden said. She was as fair as Piala was dark but just as beautiful, or so Dinan thought for he had not taken his eyes from the girl since she had set foot on the quay of Treheyl.

'I am called Erth, and I am brother to Ia,' announced one of the young men.

'While I am Uny,' added the third man, 'brother of Ia and Erth.'

'And I suppose you want to stay in my kingdom and live in peace?' queried Tewdrig, a hint of sarcasm in his voice. But the derision was taken from his voice when his eyes dwelt on the beauty of Piala.

'That is our earnest request,' Gwinear responded.

'But in doing so you would want freedom to preach your religion?' Wron prompted.

'That is what we desire,' Piala smiled sweetly in innocence at Tewdrig.

The heart of the king gave a lurch and a passion began to throb within him.

'My king, we cannot grant this,' Wron leant forward and whispered into the ear of the king of Treheyl.

Tewdrig glanced up startled.

'Why so?'

Wron closed his eyes in anguish.

'Have you forgotten so soon how Germoe and his followers are disrupting the kingdom in the south?'

Tewdrig bit his lip and then stared across at Piala.

'Then we will allow these good people to stay with us, provided they stay within sight of Treheyl that we may know what they are doing.'

Now this idea had occurred to Tewdrig not because of the reason he implied to his Druid but because he wanted to be near the beautiful Piala. Further, he rose and went down to Piala, smiling, and said: 'And in good faith, and to keep you safe, I will grant you land at the gate of my fortress and there you may preach to those of Treheyl who would hear you.'

Thus did the spot where Piala set up her dwelling become known as Phillack, in her honour, yet it was under the shadow of the king's gloomy fortress at Treheyl.

Piala's brother, Gwinear, wandered a mile or so further to the east and established himself at a spot which is still named after him. And Erth also stayed within a short distance from Treheyl and the spot where he taught also took the name of St Erth. And Uny crossed the estuary opposite to Tewdrig's fortress and the place he taught was called the enclosure of the church – Lelant.

Now Ia tarried a while with Dinan, for in those days the sons and daughters of the church could marry and did so. Love and marriage between men and women, even though they be of the church was not then forbidden as it was in later centuries. Ia was as attracted to Dinan as he was to her. Dinan promised her that he would hand over to her a tiny island at the end of a small bay to the west on which he had a fortress. That fortress was called Pendinas. Ia established her church on this island and there lived with Dinan.

Wron the Druid was angered by these happenings and began to wonder whether the land of Kernow was in need of a new king to govern. The preachers of the new religion were gaining converts from the old and in teaching love and forgiveness were allowing their enemies to rage and pillage unchecked along the eastern border of the kingdom where ran the mighty River Tamar. Within the kingdom, there was also rumblings and dissent, and many came to call Tewdrig a tyrant and godless king.

To the south-east, Geraint, chieftain of Gerrans, was openly preaching insurrection for he had been converted to the new religions. In spite of Wron's pleas, Tewdrig would not stir against him.

'Plenty of time to teach him a lesson,' Tewdrig assured Wron. 'Let him have his say. The howling of a dog at the moon will not change its course.'

Tewdrig was too infatuated with Piala to notice the danger. In fact, desire still burned deep within him. Piala was polite and greeted him in friendship, not being of the world to read the depth of the craving in his eyes. Indeed, there was a fearful emotion which smouldered restlessly there. Like a dog, Tewdrig followed her about, pretending interest in her teachings in order to sit in her company for hours on end.

Wron realised that the veil of desire must be lifted from his king's eyes or else Kernow would be doomed. It would be wracked by internal dissension and then it would be attacked from without. So Wron sat and pondered the problem and a crafty plan began to form in his mind. He would create blood-shed between Tewdrig and the Ywerdhon; if the Ywerdhon died then well and good, if Tewdrig died, then he would be able to rouse all Kernow against all the Ywerdhon preachers there. Then Wron arose with a great smile on his thin features and, saddling his horse, he rode for the church of Gwinear.

'Greetings, Ywerdhon,' he said.

'Blessings of God on you, Wron of Treheyl.'

'I will come straight to the point,' Wron said, as he dismounted and sat before Gwinear's fire.

'A good place to start,' acknowledged Gwinear.

'My king is besotted with your sister Piala.'

Gwinear at once looked troubled for he had seen the carnal fire in the eyes of the tyrant of Treheyl.

'My sister has sworn to celibacy, for she will serve no other than the Son of God.'

Wron hid his contempt and simply nodded.

'Very laudable,' he exclaimed. 'But Tewdrig has sworn to have no other woman seated by his throne.'

'This is grave news. Perhaps I should speak to the king and explain our ways?'

'An excellent idea. I know that this evening, Tewdrig goes to plight his troth to Piala. Be there at the ninth hour. Tewdrig is a reasonable man and will listen to argument.'

So saying, Wron mounted his horse and rode back to Treheyl. There he sought out the sulking Tewdrig.

'What ails you, my king?' Wron asked.

'I am as restive and fretful as a young man in the first vapours of love. I send Piala tokens and she dispenses them as charity to the poor. What am I to do?'

Wron's thin lips twitched but he controlled his cunning smile.

'If that is all that ails you, fret no more.'

'What do you mean?' demanded Tewdrig.

'I have just come from the lady. She does return your love. This she has told me. But she says she must act with decorum before her brother, for these Ywerdhon have strange beliefs and ways. Though under that faint cloak they are as passionate as we. However, it is clearly fear of her brother's anger which bids her hold you at arm's length. He is the problem here.'

'Speak further,' Tewdrig invited, much intrigued.

'She tells me that she shares your passions. Her cloak of indifference shall be discarded if you come to her just before the ninth hour and, because of her customs, you must not heed her protest but take her like the great man and mighty king she knows you to be.'

A smile of lascivious joy spread over Tewdrig's face.

Wron went off to his meal well pleased with his day's work.

So it happened, as dusk was falling before the ninth hour, Tewdrig went to the place where Piala had set up her church, which is called Phillack. Those the beautiful maiden was instructing in the ways of the new religion had departed to their houses and Piala was kneeling praying before the image of a young man hanging on a cross. Two candles were lit before it.

Tewdrig entered the church, his body tingling with desire as his lustful eyes fell on the maiden.

Piala started at the noise of his entry and turned round, her eyes widening as she beheld the tyrant of Treheyl.

'Why, King Tewdrig,' she said, scrambling from her knees, 'what brings you here at this hour of the night?'

'That you know well,' smiled Tewdrig, confidently.

Piala bit her lip in agitation for she now recognised the meaning of the many presents Tewdrig had bestowed on her during the last months.

'I must tell you the ways of those who follow the Son of God, Tewdrig!'

Tewdrig let forth an oath.

'You may tell me later, for my body aches for our union.'

Piala went pale as she discerned his purpose.

'This must not be!' she gasped. 'I am sworn to celibacy in the service of . . .'

But Tewdrig moved forward and seized her, delighting in her struggles because he believed it to be, as Wron had told him, her way of greeting his love-making.

An angry exclamation halted Tewdrig. He turned in annoyance as a figure burst into the church.

It was Gwinear, his face working in anger.

'Lecherous dog! You dare the sacrilege of this place by attacking a daughter of the church?'

Tewdrig pushed Piala to one side and drew for his sword.

'Begone, little man! Preach not to me for I am not of your faith.'

Now it has been said that Gwinear was a king in his own land before he followed the path of the Son of God. The blood of champions still flowed in his veins and a battle rage came upon him. He moved forward with only his wooden staff for courage. Tewdrig, whatever else he was, was a great warrior but he lacked the warrior's will to self-control. He saw Gwinear's approach and made only three strokes of his sword. The first stroke cut the staff into two useless pieces; the second stroke pierced Gwinear's heart while the third stroke decapitated his head.

Piala let forth a tremendous shriek. She rushed to her brother's side and picked up his head and kissed it fervently. The eyes of Gwinear flicked open, for the ancients rightly believed that the soul resided in the head, and his voice spoke: 'I have sinned. Do not you do likewise, my sister. Unto him that smiteth thee on the one cheek offer also the other. Remember.'

With that Gwinear's soul departed.

Piala, too, was born of the blood of champions and it burnt with a fierce fire. It is one thing to hear a philosophy with the mind but blood is strong.

In blind vengeance she seized the dagger which Gwinear wore in his belt, for each man must carry a means to cut his meat. She seized it and lunged forward.

It can be said for Tewdrig that he acted only out of instinct. The point of his sword met Piala's onward rush at breast level and entered it. The blood spurted from her heart and she fell to the ground.

Tewdrig stood in a daze at the swiftness of what had happened.

Then Wron entered, for the sly Druid had been watching all the time, and while he was pleased at what had befallen he pretended horror at the scene.

'Now the remaining Ywerdhon will preach rebellion against you, Tewdrig, and join with Geraint of Gerrans. You must act to stop this rebellion before it has time to flower and bear fruit.'

Tewdrig moved in a stupor and Wron had to shout to snap him out of it.

'Take the head of Gwinear and wash it in the well, then place it on a spike and have it carried before you so all Kernow may know your serious intent to rid the land of the Ywerdhon.'

Now the reason for this was not so much to put fear in people but because of the religious symbolism of the head wherein the

Druids believed the soul dwelt. To carry the head of your enemy endowed you with the strength and valour and intellect of that enemy.

Soon, Tewdrig came to his old self and realised that Wron was right. Before the next dawn, Tewdrig and his men had ridden to the churches of Erth and Uny and the brothers were slain before they had time to raise an alarm.

'Where is Ia, the last of this breed?' Tewdrig commanded as he stood by the bloody remains of Uny.

His warriors looked uncomfortably at each other.

'Why she is with your brother Dinan at Pendinas,' they said.

Anger was on Tewdrig's face now.

'Then we will go to Pendinas and finish this job. And woe to any, brother or no, who tries to defend this Ywerdhon from my wrath!'

His army arrived at Pendinas the next day and were surprised when they found Geraint of Gerrans with an army there before them. Geraint had gathered the rebellious men of Kernow from the four corners of the kingdom. Before this great hosting stood Breage, Crowan and Elwyn as well as Ia. By Ia's side, on his warhorse, sat Tewdrig's own brother Dinan. And before all of them was Geraint, a handsome young man of princely countenance. At his side was the venerable Germoe and Germoe carried a great cross of silver to act as their standard.

Tewdrig rode forward and by his side rode Wron, who carried the pole on which the head of Gwinear was set. And Geraint came forward with Germoe riding by his side bearing the silver cross.

'You are in rebellion against your just king,' cried Tewdrig in anger.

Geraint smiled gently.

'Is it not written in our ancient law – what makes a king weaker than a servant on the poorest farm? It is because the people ordain the king, the king does not ordain the people. While you sat in justice, promoting our commonweal, Tewdrig, we followed you. But a bad deed you have done and we will now have done with you.'

'Then, by the gods, I challenge you to the right of single combat!' cried Tewdrig.

Both men drew their swords.

Now as Tewdrig was about to spur forward, the head of Gwinear, set atop the great pole held by Wron, suddenly fell. It fell straight and true and struck Tewdrig on the head with such impact that his iron helm was shattered and he was knocked to the ground.

Wron dismounted and examined his king and when he looked up there was fear in his eyes.

'His skull has been crushed by the head of Gwinear,' he whispered.

'The true God has spoken,' cried Germoe. 'Vengeance is mine, says the Lord. Geraint is king.'

And they departed, each to his own place. The head of Gwinear was buried at the town named after him. Ia continued to preach at Pendinas with support of the prince Dinan, rejecting all worldly treasures, and eventually the spot was named after her and is known today as St Ives. Geraint became a good and just king whose name is still spoken of today and Gerrans, named after him, still exists. He, it was, who encouraged many saints to come to Kernow and soon all the land was following the faith of the Son of God.

As for Wron, he departed the field unseen and was never punished. They say he went to hide in a cold, dark granite cave, within the sound of the blustery billows of the sea, and is there waiting for his time for he was sure that that time, which was, must be and will come again.

RED WOLF'S DAUGHTER
AND BLOODY CHIEF'S SON

Jessica Amanda Salmonson

A FIERCE BATTLE was engaged in the snowy forest of pine and tamaracks above Wallowa Lake. Red Wolf's Chute-pa-lu band whirled ravenously in the midst of the ambushed Blackfoot scouting party.

For long moons, Blackfeet had been striving to displace Red Wolf's Chute-pa-lu Nez Perce from their ancient fishing and hunting grounds. With a thousand streams, and rivers, and lakes, it was good country, worth a fight. When the interlopers first began troubling the established tribe, it seemed they could not hope to succeed and would soon return to their lands defeated.

All the early battles fell to the valor of Red Wolf and his courageous followers, familiar as they were with the region. But by degrees, Blackfeet had increasingly mastered the forest, it became more and more difficult to surprise the foe. A great leader had arisen among them. That man was Bloody Chief, a clever tactician who drew more Blackfeet from beyond Shining Mountain to join him. Increasingly it was Red Wolf's men who were surprised by ambushes.

Today, however, the Nez Perce met with good luck. A band of enemy scouts came running up the forest slope away from the lake, shouting among themselves about something hideous they had seen. They made so much ridiculous noise they gave themselves away while still at some distance. Then they stopped short, shocked to discover they had fled straight into the arms of Red Wolf and his warriors.

The cluster of eight Blackfoot scouts spun about as though

intending to run back the way they came. Yet they were seemingly even more afraid of retreating in that direction than they were of facing impossible odds against the Nez Perce. In that moment of indecision, the Nez Perce were upon them. Red Wolf swung his long warclub of polished hardwood beveled along an edge and inlaid with the teeth of wolves. His opponent tried ineffectually to deflect a blow. In the next moment, blood and brain spattered freshly tramped snow. He fell backward and lay with tongue and one eye hanging out.

After a few hard breaths, it was done. All the birds had flown away. The forest was silent save for the harsh breathing of the victors. The Blackfeet lay dead at the feet of their enemies, whereas Red Wolf had but one man down. Red Wolf stalked amidst the Blackfoot corpses, saw one man not yet fully dead, and bashed his skull. Then he knelt beside the injured Nez Perce. He looked at the gaping wound, took the warrior's arm and said, 'Press your hand here, so.' Then he motioned four men to carry the one, and they started down the hill. When they reached the snowline, they knew their village was near.

One of Red Wolf's warriors said, 'I wonder what those scouts were running from?'

'Strong spirits guard this place,' said Red Wolf. 'They are Chute-pa-lu spirits, angered by the presence of Blackfeet.'

His men did not contradict this, for they hoped Red Wolf's opinion was inspired by the spirit-power that was in him. They would not like to see him proven wrong.

*   *   *

At a bonfire in the center of the village, the people gathered for a communal feast. They ate trout, crawfish and fernbrake. It was a good meal, but nothing compared to what in better times was expected from the rich forest. With the present war, there had been little opportunity to hunt elk or bear.

As the warriors told expansive versions of that day's successful battle, the tribe became cheerful. Each man in turn was encouraged to tell of the battle from his point of view. With every retelling, the story was embellished and improved. The part about the Blackfeet petrified in their tracks, too frightened either to attack or run away, won screeches of laughter.

But underlying the momentary cheerfulness of women, old men and children there was a continuous thrum of fear. Reflected on the waters of icy Wallowa Lake was the greater bonfire of Blackfeet on the further shore. They were dancing and hollering and pounding drums. Perhaps as yet they did not know eight of their men were killed. When they learned of it, they would seek swift vengeance. The sound of the Blackfoot celebration reached the Chute-pa-lu, muted but clear, and Chute-pa-lu laughter was insufficient to shut out the noise of the big gathering of their foe.

The sorry fact was, the Nez Perce village had lost the majority of its young warriors during a year of raids back and forth, whereas the Blackfeet seemed to spring in ever increasing numbers, as though descending from out of the sky.

Red Wolf declined to tell his version of the victory. He was not able to eat. He accepted a carved juniper trough with a fat portion of trout, but could only look at it as though it were something he disliked. He stood from the circle of his men and walked away without a word, carrying the trough with him. All knew by his moodiness and demeanor that they must not call after him. He faded into the darkness outside the circle of firelight.

* * *

In a tipi near an old spruce, the injured man lay upon a bearskin robe, his lower body covered with a blanket of marmot skins. He was not young, though he was famous for the many adventures of his youth. He was proud to be called Old Strength. Often Red Wolf had tried to convince him to remain in the village as its guard. Always he replied, 'What! Like an old man? Let's go kill Blackfeet!' Now, if he recovered, the muscle of his arm was so deeply cut he would never again be strong enough to fight.

His bare chest glistened with sweat, though the early autumn evening was chill. A small fire burned in the center of the floor. A trail of smoke rose in a thin line and escaped where the tipi's braces joined. He was attended by Red Wolf's daughter Wahluna, a shamanic healer. She was singing a magic song that went, 'Healing spirits, healing spirits, see this man, see him.' It was like a lullaby.

From a medicine bag she drew forth herbs which she pounded in a mortar, adding pure lakewater until she had a green paste. This she smeared on Old Strength's broad, ragged wounds. There were two wounds, made with a single thrust of a spear that bared a rib at his side and parted the flesh of the inner muscle of his right arm. Wahluna pressed boiled moss into the paste upon the wounds. Over the curative concoction she bound muskrat hides. Through all her endeavors, Old Strength scarcely winced, though his jaw quivered with the pain.

When Red Wolf entered the tipi, his daughter Wahluna ceased her soft chant. The wounded man tried to sit up, as it was improper to lay in the presence of Red Wolf. Wahluna put her hand on his chest to hold him down. She said, 'If you move, you will not live long.' Red Wolf sat on the ground near the sad-looking warrior. He broke a piece of the tender trout and held it to Old Strength's mouth. At first Old Strength turned his head away, but he turned back with moist eyes and let himself be fed. Wahluna took up her healing lullaby while Old Strength was fed like a baby.

'You are Red Wolf, and should not serve me so,' said Old Strength.

Red Wolf said, 'You served my father, and you have served me. You were like an uncle when I was small. Haven't the Blackfeet killed all your sons? Didn't your wife die of grief? Who are your relatives now? A chief must be every man's father. Wahluna must be every man's mother.'

At this, Old Strength smiled in earnest. Not only was he deeply touched, but he was amused to think of the young princess as an aging warrior's mother. She helped prop him against a rolled fur so he could sit up. She pulled the marmot blanket to his shoulders. Old Strength grew extremely serious. He asked, 'How long, Red Wolf, can we go on? We are slowly being picked off, while more Blackfeet come from their nation into ours. Today we were fortunate. But what will happen tomorrow?'

'Tomorrow?' Red Wolf echoed, and his gaze rose along the little column of smoke until he spotted one star through the opening where the poles joined. 'Today, the warriors are filled with boasts and hold their hands above their heads. Tomorrow, it may be their shoulders will sag with weight of sorrows. You were my father's counselor. Should I pretend in your presence that things are well? Tomorrow? There is only today, Old Strength. And today we are victorious.'

Having said so much, Red Wolf left the tipi of Old Strength. He stood alone by Wallowa Lake, listening dejectedly to chants and drums of Blackfeet on the far shore.

*   *   *

Wahluna covered Old Strength with the blanket, then looked about until she found a well-worn buffalo robe and laid that on him too. Then she asked the warrior, 'Old Strength, why do the Blackfeet fight us? Why do we fight the Blackfeet?'

Old Strength replied, 'You are too young to understand.'

'I am old enough to be your mother,' she teased.

'Ha! Well then, little mother, you are not a child after all. So I will tell you that not one of us can know the reason why men kill men. Your grandfather, who died when you were little, of the same sickness that carried away your mother, was called Red Wolf like your father. He was a great buffalo hunter. Today we lake people do not go to the place of the buffalo, but when I was young, we went every summer. There were many Blackfeet that came from their place beyond the buffalo grounds. We watched each other killing buffalo, and when they made a mistake, we laughed. When we failed, they made light of us and hooted. Then they stole some of our horses, thinking themselves clever. We stole them back, and some of theirs as well.

'Somehow it came about that every year when we went to hunt buffalo, we went to kill Blackfeet as well. They had the best horses, so we had to be smarter. We found out what route they took to reach the buffalo grounds. One year we went early. From a high point, overlooking a narrow canyon, we were able to kill very many Blackfeet. Among the Chute-pa-lu, however, not one man fell! It is my thought, little mother, that if some of us had died on that day, the Blackfeet would not hate us so much. They have avenged themselves many times since, but they remember that first humiliation, when your grandfather led us home to the mountain country, bringing Blackfoot horses! We built great fires and danced for days and nights. Oh! Those were good days, little mother. I miss those days so much.'

Then Wahluna let Old Strength sleep. She went out to see if she could find her father. But Red Wolf had vanished into the forest to commune with his own heart. Under the starry sky, Wahluna felt alone on the earth. She could hear her people laughing and telling stories. So too she could hear the whooping Blackfeet across the lake. They did not seem entirely real to her. They were ghosts from a bad, bad dream.

She went among the thickly draping willows at the lake's edge. From the willow roots a stream leapt forth into the lake, the rippling music erasing all the other sounds of night. Hidden as she was amidst draping leaves, Wahluna's sad loneliness became a boon of solitude while she watched the moon reflected on the water.

Against the moon she saw a nighthawk dipping and flitting. She thought to herself, 'My soul is with the nighthawk. I am up there dipping and flitting. What is my soul seeking? It seeks happiness and peace. Can you hear me, spirit of Wallowa? Does not the bloodshed hurt you, as it hurts me? I call to you, spirit of the lake! I call to the mother-spirit and the father-spirit. I call to the tree-spirits and the wind-spirits. I pray to all of you, give me strength, give me wisdom. Show me by what means I may stop the killing. No price is too great for me to pay! I would be a slave to the Blackfeet if that would bring peace. I will give my life!'

As she spoke, she saw the waters stirring in the light of moon and stars. Then she spotted an empty skin-canoe at the lake's edge. As she had not seen it a moment before, it seemed to her a thing materialized from a vision. She took the appearance of the canoe to be an invitation to go upon the lake.

Wahluna paddled silently through the darkness. She crossed the lake to the enemy village. She left with such stillness the Nez Perce did not hear her go, nor did the Blackfeet detect her arrival until she was within the circle of a bonfire. At the sight of this beautiful maiden appearing as though from nowhere, celebrant drummers ceased beating their tomtoms. Singers stilled their voices. The only sound was the crackling of the fire as Wahluna approached Bloody Chief who sat crosslegged on a blanket alongside Tlesca, his son, each wearing beautifully woven robes of feathers, quills and fibers, the insignias of their rank.

'I am Wahluna, princess of my tribe, come to speak to a great chief,' she began. 'Many of the young men of my tribe have been slain. I despair for the survival of my people. Today the remnant of our fighters met Blackfoot scouts lurking in our forest. All those scouts were slain. It has made my people joyous, but such joy cannot be sustained, for our women have long sung songs of mourning.

'I hear your followers gasp with anger to learn of our luck in today's battle, though I speak of these things not to boast. Tomorrow, you may seek revenge for eight lives. Perhaps my family and all my people, with all that I have known in this life, will be exterminated once and for all. Yet I have come to you to say, 'Have pity!' for there can be no greatness in slaying old men, women and small children, for this is nearly all that is left of us now. If you will allow me to take to my father your offer of peace, it may be that we can learn to share the bounty of the forest and the lake without so great an enmity.'

Bloody Chief barely considered her words before he answered, 'What cowardly people send a girl to beg? Such a tribe merits death!'

But Tlesca was impressed with the maiden. Though a great warrior of necessity, his spirit was inclined to gentleness. He said, 'Father, open your heart to her words. This maiden bravely loves her people. As for me, I am moved beyond my capacity for speech. Never again will I kill one of her people.'

Having made such a bold statement, he stood from the blanket on which he had been sitting. He removed his cloak of authority as he stepped to Wahluna's side.

Bloody Chief made a growling sound in his throat, for he had often wished for a harsher son. Even so, he greatly loved Tlesca, and could not dismiss his son's words. He said, 'My son, one day you must become a great chief. You cannot rely on kindheartedness to rule. Her people are mere dogs. Come! Put on your robe, for this girl must die.'

Tlesca was insistent. 'We have battled Red Wolf's bravest warriors. Remember how Red Wolf fought, days on end, to save his people? I recall how impressed you were! For many weeks we gave him no opportunity to capture game; we harried him until he was weak from hunger. We even saw him stagger! Even then, when he was at his weakest, who was brave enough to fight him face to face? I alone answered his challenge. He fought like a cougar. With his warclub, he broke my shoulder, which was long in healing.

'How often I think of that day! Many of our warriors fell before Red Wolf as they rushed forth to draw me away when you, my father, commanded me not to try to fight one-handed. Do you say we were routed by a dog, my father? Did my shoulder hurt because I was weaker than a dog?

'No, my father, Red Wolf is a noble warrior, and this maiden who has come before us is noble too. Look! I have taken off my robe of authority to place it about the shoulders of this maiden! See? It suits her well. She looks as powerful as a warrior!'

Bloody Chief closed his eyes and thought. The people gathered near were motionless. Then Bloody Chief raised his eyes and addressed the crowd. 'My son speaks well. I have heard his words. Therefore will I rise and place my robe upon his.'

Wahluna stood straight and tall as Bloody Chief wrapped his robe about her. The two robes were tokens of a promise of peace, to be worn before her father Red Wolf so that he would know for whom she spoke of truce.

As she turned to leave the circle of firelight, no one followed. Prince Tlesca strode away into woods above the lake. Yet when Wahluna arrived at her canoe by the lakeside, there stood Tlesca, who had hurried to skirt the edge of the village, to reach the lake in secret. He wished to see Wahluna off without detection. He said, 'Wahluna, truly my heart is made lighter in your presence.'

She replied, 'I, too, was moved by your manly beauty and the fairness of your speech. But you must not hope the two of us will become as one. If my father suspected my love for a Blackfoot prince, he would rise up and fight to the death. If your father thought you loved a Chute-pa-lu princess, he would exterminate my people rather than give his blessing to such a union. You must turn your heart toward a Blackfoot maiden. As for me, I have sworn my life to the spirit of Wallowa Lake in exchange for a prosperous peace for our peoples.'

'Blackfoot girls are beautiful and many have expressed their love for Tlesca,' he admitted. 'Even so, my heart seeks none but Wahluna.'

She said, 'What you desire cannot be.'

'It may be that we must keep our feelings to ourselves,' he said, taking her by the arm for fear that she would leave too soon. 'But Wahluna, listen. We can meet secretly in our canoes on dark nights in the middle of the lake. No one will suspect. When I wish to see you, you will hear me make the sound of a coyote. When you wish to see me, call to me in the voice of the owl. By these signals we will come together and speak.'

'I cannot promise such a thing,' she said, though already she knew she would lay awake nights listening for the coyote call. Then, warm in the cloaks of chief and prince, she knelt into her canoe and paddled to her village.

* * *

The successful peace-talks which ensued were greatly facilitated by Wahluna's previously unsuspected skill as a mediator. Many meetings were required. Many bad feelings were mollified. For six moons, as the truce held, Red Wolf and Bloody Chief met in neutral places in the mountains, bringing with them none but Wahluna and Tlesca, whose natures were more giving than their hardened fathers.

Many times she despaired, fearing these two men would never acknowledge how each saw greatness in the other. Many nights she lay awake thinking she was failing at mediation, and the soothing speeches of Tlesca were failing also. So too it was painful to see the youth she secretly loved, under conditions which demanded that neither give evidence of the affection which intensified daily.

One evening as she lay worrying in her tipi, she heard a coyote singing. At first she did not heed the call, for it sounded like a true coyote. When it called again, she thought it sounded as though it were in the middle of the lake. Only then did she rise swiftly to slip to the lakeside where she called out like an owl. She knelt in her canoe which lay hidden in shallows amidst overhanging willows.

She paddled toward the center of the lake and stopped alongside Tlesca. They reached their hands to one another to pull the canoes closer, and Tlesca said, 'I am in an agony of lonely sorrow. I see you only in the presence of our fathers. When can we tell our peoples of our love?'

Wahluna, too, was steeped in melancholy. She said, 'I have sworn myself to the spirit of the lake. I offered everything to this spirit, even my life, in exchange for peace between our tribes. For six moons there has been no arrow exchanged by Blackfeet and Nez Perce. By this I know the spirit has heeded my prayer. Were I to accept all that is in your heart, the lake would only take it from me, for all that I receive belongs to the spirit of the Wallowa.'

'If it is so,' said Tlesca, 'then what good is my life? My heart is yours even now. I will fight this spirit!'

'You must not say so!' exclaimed Wahluna.

The water had become agitated. As they gazed at the dark surface, a slowly funneling maelstrom encircled them and caused their canoes to turn around and around. Tlesca gaped in amazement. Wahluna said, not to Tlesca but to the spirit of the lake, 'Do not grow angry, O Spirit of Wallowa!'

At her plea, the water grew still, and Tlesca said softly, 'If the power of this lake possesses all that is yours, then this power possesses me. I will not fight it, but will share in your destiny.'

* * *

When the most difficult matters of the truce were settled, joy at last arose among the Nez Perce. One morning a great many children, women and men old and young arrived from the Blackfoot village singing songs of friendship. The men brought fresh-killed dear and bear hunted in the mountains. The women bore fish trapped in streams.

Throughout the festivities, Wahluna and Tlesca exchanged meaningful glances whenever they thought no one could see them flirting. Wahluna and other Nez Perce women assisted the Blackfoot wives and daughters in preparing the great feast. It seemed to her that a real affection had developed between the tribes. She began to allow herself to hope her fondness for the Blackfoot prince might after all be revealed without reawakening anger.

As the afternoon progressed into evening, Wahluna became bolder when casting glances at Tlesca, thus several Nez Perce girls noticed. They began to whisper, 'There is something going on between Wahluna and that beautiful young Blackfoot.'

The gossip spread throughout the village. Soon all the Nez Perce women were considering the possibilities. Some were joyful at the thought; a few were jealous, for they had been trying to catch a glance from the prince without success. Not everyone agreed such a match would be a good idea, for the friendship between the two peoples was as yet very new and untested. There remained many suspicions and ill-healed wounds of grief because of sons lost in battles.

Divided opinions fueled the rumors, which soon spread to the Blackfoot women as well.

In evening's dusk, when half the people were done feasting, several women began gambling with engraved beaver teeth, tossing like dice. A Blackfoot woman, tall and handsome, won a Nez Perce woman's woven conical hat. Sorry to have wagered the hat, the stout Nez Perce woman said, 'Take these moccasins instead, for I love that hat.'

The tall woman answered, 'Your moccasins are worn thin; I'll keep this.'

They argued back and forth until the Nez Perce woman leapt at the Blackfoot and knocked her to the ground. They rolled in the dust while the other gambling women broke into opposing camps to cheer and encourage their champion. Blackfeet cheered the tall woman; Nez Perce cheered the woman who was stout.

Into this fracas Tlesca strode in order to separate the women. The hat was damaged during their wrestling match. The woman who had won the hat spat on the ground and said, 'You think your princess is worthy of our prince? They will never marry!'

The Nez Perce woman shot back, 'Who says she wants to marry him? As our young men have become bones for wolves to gnaw, so should this haughty chief's son be killed and left to rot in the forest!'

They tried to get at each other again, but Tlesca held them apart, alarmed though he was by what they were saying.

Bloody Chief and Red Wolf had all this while been smoking the pipe together. The women's quarrel was on everyone's tongue except for these two chiefs, who knew not what to say.

After a long silence between them, Bloody Chief finally spoke. 'My son's heart reaches for your daughter. He is a great warrior and will rule after me. Your Wahluna has proven herself a great mediator. Who else is their equal? Perhaps we should not stand in their way.'

Red Wolf and his people had suffered so long at the hands of the Blackfoot warriors, it was painful to accept such a marriage. Yet Red Wolf was a wise man and came to a sensible conclusion. He said, 'Yes, I too have heard of their secret meetings. I confess I turned my face and hoped it was not so. Yet now, if in truth Wahluna's heart reaches out to Tlesca, she may go with him to his lodge.'

* * *

In days that followed, Red Wolf sent runners to announce the wedding to friends among the Cayuse, Wenatchees and Yakamas. A three-day wedding feast was planned. People came into the Nez Perce village from far and near, for the joining of two famous families who were formerly rivals was a great thing and deserved to be attended by many.

The Blackfoot village was empty of all but a few dogs and ponies, for all had left to participate in the extravagant affair with the Nez Perce. At sunset on the first day of the feast, the newly joined couple set out in a canoe to head for Tlesca's lodge across the lake, where they could be alone. People stood on the shore and the hillside watching the beautiful couple paddling across Wallowa Lake, with the high mountains forming a dark backdrop against a fading sky of red dusk.

Halfway across the lake, the lake's calm was disrupted. At first there were only mild ripples upon the water, which caused their boat to wobble. But the ripples rose into a roil so that the canoe was greatly endangered. Tlesca dropped the paddle and clung to Wahluna. They spoke to one another earnestly and did not look frightened. The tumultuous waters rose in waves, spinning the little skin canoe around and around.

Old Strength, the aged warrior, shoved one of the largest canoes into the lake, intending to assist the couple who were caught in the inexplicable maelstrom. Red Wolf leapt into the big canoe with Old Strength. Others followed close behind, Nez Perce and Blackfeet, including Bloody Chief. All were eager to save Wahluna and Tlesca before their vessel was swamped and carried under.

As the would-be helpers neared, Wahluna cried out, 'Old Strength! Father! Come no nearer!'

Tlesca called, 'Father, hold back!'

The tiny fleet of canoes halted. The little skin canoe continued to turn around and around as Wahluna called out in calm resignation, 'This is what I promised the spirit of the lake in exchange for peace between our tribes!'

Tlesca added, 'With open eyes, I have sworn to share Wahluna's fate! Live in peace, my father and my father-in-law! Do not fight again! Do not grieve too long for us!'

The waters abruptly parted, revealing a monstrous creature. Its furred neck rose higher and higher. Its head was like the head of a gigantic pony, with the down-turned horns of a buffalo. It swept its gaze from side to side, watching the fleet of canoes as hollering Nez Perce and Blackfeet paddled madly for their respective shores. Then the creature raised its long, heavy tail from out of the water and thrashed it downwards, hard upon the tiny canoe, cutting it in half.

Wahluna and Tlesca continued to cling tightly to one another as they were thrown into the water. Even now they conveyed no fear of dying; they offered no useless struggle. They closed their eyes, placed their faces each upon the shoulder of the other, and the quickening maelstrom sucked them down and down forever.

The dragon dove after them into the funnel of water. Afterward, all grew still beneath night's canopy of stars. Only a few small bubbles broke the surface of the lake, to mark the passing of beast and lovers.

* * *

At dawn, when it was certain the lovers were truly lost, there arose among Nez Perce women a continuous lamentation lasting many days. Their grief inspired many new songs of sorrow. Some sang that Wahluna had been taken from them because she had wrongly loved the enemy, while others sang in guilty sadness how all were punished for feeling critical of the marriage as their small hearts continued to despise Blackfeet.

Bloody Chief believed he had lost his son because his people tried to conquer the Nez Perce in order to take possession of their lake and forest. The monster had come to punish the Blackfeet for their greed. Feeling nothing beyond self-blame and sorrow, Bloody Chief led his people away from the accursed lake which had stolen his son.

The Blackfeet left Wallowa afoot and on horseback. Their heads hung low; they moaned with grievous sorrow. Along the way, they stopped but once, at a crossroad where Red Wolf and Old Strength stood waiting to bid last farewells.

Although neither chief could find words, they spoke deeply through the tragedy reflected in their eyes. Red Wolf stepped forth to the side of Bloody Chief's pony and tried to return to him the pair of robes that had been given to Wahluna by Tlesca and Bloody Chief. But the Blackfoot chief would not take them. Red Wolf had thought this might occur and so handed the robes to Old Strength. Then he removed from the strap at his side the famous warclub inlaid with wolf teeth. This he gave to Bloody Chief as a parting gift. Only then did the long line of Blackfeet continue on their way to their country beyond the Shining Mountain, returning nevermore to the Land of Many Waters.

PART VI:
LOVE, REVENGE AND SELF-SACRIFICE

EAST OF THE SUN
AND WEST OF THE MOON

William Morris

E AST OF THE sun, west of the moon!
All day long Gregory's fishing boat had been flitting hither and thither upon the broad Norwegian firth, so belike it was the memory of that long day's cruise that led him at night-time to dream of a country whose direction was so quaint and puzzling. And as the dream lingered in his mind next morning, and pleased him, idle though it was, he took pains to turn it into verses, which many a generation has listened to within the halls and cottages of Norway.

Here is the story which came to him in his dreams.

A well-to-do husbandman in a certain part of Norway farmed his own land with the help of his two elder sons. He had a third son, but this John, although a tall, strong lad, was of little use upon the farm. Many an hour he trifled away at the fireside in winter, and still more in the woods and orchard when summer came round. Whatever he might make of his handsome face, his dreamy wits, the store of old rhymes and such other scraps of learning as were his, he would never prove a good farmer, said his father. 'Let John go his own ways,' the goodman would exclaim; 'he is not worth training on my fields!'

One summer morning the farmer went to look at a meadow where he expected his rich crop of hay would soon be ready for the scythe, but, alas! a melancholy sight met his eyes when he looked across the wattled fence – a great patch of the meadow grass was trampled down, so that no mower could possibly pass his scythe through the tangle.

The farmer came home with a frown on his brow. 'Thorolf,'

he cried to his eldest son, 'tonight you must take your crossbow, and lie in watch amongst the hawthorns that skirt the south meadow. Someone has come by night and beaten down the ripening grass; whether it be an enemy of ours – who would have thought we had any! – or a mischievous vagrant, he shall be well punished if he plant foot within the meadow a second time!'

So Thorolf went out after supper to keep watch over the meadow, but what with his hard day's work, and a very comfortable meal at the close of it, he was not long in falling into a doze, and from that he passed into a deep sleep that lasted well into the morning. When he arose from his bed of wood-sorrel he found that the long grass was trodden down in fresh places, and he was obliged to go home and own, to his father's chagrin, that matters were now worse than ever.

The next evening Thord, the second son, was sent in place of Thorolf, but when he returned to confess with downcast face that he had done no better than his elder brother, and that by this time there was only one corner of the meadow left untrodden, the farmer altogether lost his temper, and rated them both soundly, calling them good-for-nothing, slothful young fellows.

Hearing his brothers called names that were generally bestowed upon him alone, John, who was strolling past the group, stopped, and stretching himself lazily: 'I am truly sorry you have not done your work better, my brothers,' he said, with a pretence at reproach in his voice, 'for now our good father will insist upon sending me out to take a turn at night watching. Well, well, father, you need vex no more; by this time tomorrow I shall have found out where the mischief comes from.'

'You!' cried his father indignantly. 'Do you think you can succeed where Thorolf and Thord have both failed? If you find out the offender it will be the first time in your life, my boy, that you have shown yourself worth your keep. Go and try the post tonight, by all means, but I cannot say that I expect to learn more from you than from my other brave watchers.'

Quite unmoved by his father's scoff, John went calmly on his way. He spent the day in sleep – a wise enough preparation for night work – and when the time came for him to go on watch, he went down to the meadow without bow or knife in his hand. 'If I have to deal with a rough set of men, they would soon make an end of me should I draw bow upon them,' thought he, 'and still less use have I for weapons, if the trespassers prove, as methinks they will, to be gentle fairy-folk.'

Amongst the hawthorn bushes he found a hiding-place close to the untrodden part of the hayfield. Hour after hour passed, and yet no visitant, either of earth or fairy-land, set foot upon the meadow. The dawn broke, a light breeze stirred the long grass, and one by one the birds in the wood began to twitter shyly. Up to this time John had kept wide awake, but now drowsiness would have overpowered him had he not heard a strange, rushing sound of wings overhead, and, parting the boughs that screened his face, he watched breathlessly to see what manner of bird might alight. Slowly seven white swans came circling towards the meadow, and dropped on the dewy grass only a stone's cast from where he lay crouching beneath the hawthorn. He was ready to raise a shout, and frighten them from the place, if need be; but so long as they did no harm to his father's crops, he took pleasure in watching them close beside him, bridling, and preening their snow-white feathers.

Satisfied that they were moving about on the edge of the field where there was nothing to spoil, he closed his eyes for a few moments. A sudden hush made him start, and he glanced round to see if the stately birds were still before him. No, they were not; but on the grass stood seven maidens, as fresh and lovely as the white feathers that they had cast down at their feet! One of them was standing with her face turned away from the hawthorn brake, so that John saw but the ripples of her golden hair, over which the morning breeze was playing lightly; yet as he hearkened to the sweet notes of her voice, his heart beat wildly, and he cried to himself that she was the fairest of the fays, and the queen of his heart now and for ever! And when at length she turned, and he eagerly scanned her features, one glance told him that he had judged aright by her voice, for indeed the sweetness of her face passed all imagining.

A while the seven sisters stood murmuring softly to one another, glad, it seemed, to indulge in talk when they regained their voices along with their human form; then, as if to enjoy all that they might, before they again put on their feathery dress, they danced lightly and merrily over the long, dewy grass, and laughed for joy as they frolicked carelessly in the farmer's dearly prized meadow. Not for worlds would the watcher amongst the hawthorns have disturbed them. Every smile, every word, and every movement of the swan-maiden whom he had singled out for his love, made his heart thrill with happiness. But ah! what would he do when she flew away with her sisters, and he was left to mourn, perchance never to see her again? The swan-skin which she had cast aside, lay within his reach. If he hid it from her, at least she would have to speak a word to him before she could recover it and soar away, thought he, and, yielding to the impulse, he stretched out his hand stealthily, and drew the skin into his nest beneath the thorn-trees.

The sun, that had shot its first level beams across the meadow when the maidens started upon their dance, now rising high in the heavens, warned them that it was no longer safe to linger where men might soon be passing to their day's work. In a long line they tripped back, one after another, and slipped on their snow-white swan-skins; but when she upon whom John's eyes were bent, came to look for hers, a sharp cry of distress rang from her lips – the downy wrap was not to be found! In vain she searched for it, in vain her sisters flitted through the tangled grass, looking for what lay hidden securely in John's keeping beneath the hawthorn boughs. Every minute the sun beat more strongly upon wood and field, a stern reminder to the swan-maidens that fate forbade them to remain longer upon earth. The six fair white birds clustered around their poor sister, striving without avail to comfort her, and she, softly stroking their plumes with one hand in silent farewell, hid her tearful eyes with the other as they unwillingly prepared to take their flight. So long as they were with her, she tried to conceal her anguish, but when she heard them rise on the wing and soar away far above the meadow, her grief broke out wildly; her whole body was shaken with sobs, and the tears splashed down on the grass through the slim fingers that hid her face.

A sound of footsteps amongst rustling twigs startled her even in the midst of her distress, and in fear of being seen by mortal eyes, she fled across the trampled ground, and cowered low down in the beaten grass, like a wounded bird that lies in terror of its destroyer. The eyes that met hers, however, were not such as could inspire fear; they were almost as startled and timid as her own. Moved by her grief, John had come to own, in shame, that he had stolen the swan-skin; and though at first the maiden had trembled at his coming, she saw now that he was looking tenderly upon her, and she divined that it was love for her, and a longing to keep her beside him, that had prompted his theft. 'Ah! do you think,' she cried passionately, 'that because you have been cruel enough to hide my swan-skin, and keep me bound to earth, I can love you and live happily amongst mortal men?' Wisely she worked upon his feelings, begging him, since he did not wish to do her harm, to win her grateful thanks by letting her fly away safely. 'You make it too hard for me to set you free, maiden,' he answered; 'every word from your lips, every glance from your bright eyes so enthralls me that I cannot bear to let you go.'

'Alas!' she sobbed, 'what can I do? I would fain listen to your love, but I must not dwell with mortals upon earth; it would be death alike to you and to me if you kept me beside you any longer. Will you not come with me, and share our life in our far-distant country? Nay, nay; it would be too much to ask you to leave your home and your kinsfolk for my sake. Let me bid you farewell, then; be wise, and yield to fate; let me soar away in my swan-skin, and do you turn back and dwell contentedly in your own land, knowing that you have won my heart by your gentleness, your pity, and your love.'

'Nay,' said he eagerly; 'I will not let you go alone. Take me with you, I pray, and let me live for ever in your far country, for worthless would I count my life on earth if I should never look again on your dear face.'

So the swan-maiden, though she doubted the wisdom of his choice, suffered him to lead her to the shade of a neighbouring beech-wood, where, taking from him her white swan-skin, she made ready for their strange journey. First, she set a gold ring with a dark green stone upon his finger as a seal to their love; then, bidding him lie down on the withered leaves beneath a beech-tree, she laid a spell upon him, and immediately his eyes grew dim, and sleep stole over his senses.

A long, long time passed until at length his eyes opened upon a new world. His love stood beside him in a beautiful land, whose sunshine and flowers were as unmatched by what he had hitherto known, as was the girlish beauty of her upon whom the pink blossoms were now falling from the trees. 'My land and yours!' she cried, following his bewildered gaze with a smile.

'You look too grave, sweetheart; does it not please you well?' But the only reason why the earth-born stranger looked so grave was that he was striving to recall something of the gloom and trouble that overshadowed mortal life, so that he might the better gauge the joy of his new home, where all was unclouded peacefulness and bliss.

Three harvests had been gathered in his father's fields when John began to think wistfully of the life that had once been his in Norway. It was not that he was dissatisfied with the fairyland in which he dwelt, or that his love was growing cold towards the lady of his heart, but more and more he yearned to share again his brothers' lot and to see how things sped with them. He fancied that he showed no sign of uneasiness, however, so the swan-maiden's question surprised him when one morning she asked: 'What burden lies heavy upon your spirit? Do you fear that I have hid from you the knowledge of coming trouble, and that our careless, happy years are soon to have an end? Yes; you are right. I have said nothing of what I foresaw, because so long as we could close our eyes to it, there was no call to disturb our peaceful days, but now, alas! our parting is at hand.'

John turned to her anxiously. 'Parting?' said he. 'Why should we part?'

Then the swan-maiden told him that fate willed he should return to his own country for a time, and that their future happiness depended solely upon whether he could keep the commands that must be laid upon him whilst he revisited his old home. 'Let not a sigh for me escape your lips,' she warned him solemnly, 'for were you to call on me, I would have to appear beside you upon earth, and ill would it be for both of us if I were seen of mortals. Yet though you must not ask me to join you, I have power to call you back, should I need you sorely. Every evening you shall go to the meadow where you first saw me, wait there an hour, and if I would recall you, I will send a sign. Rest contented, nor strive to return until you are bidden of me, and above all, sweetheart, let no one know the story of our love.' Then, telling him that he must not delay his departure, she led him to the spot where he had first awakened in her fairyland, and, bending over him with sad and tender farewell, she soon sang him to sleep beneath a mystic spell. He knew that he was being wafted farther and farther away from her, for her sweet voice, half choked with sobs, grew fainter each moment, and before his eyes there flitted a countless number of forms, unlike what he had ever seen either on earth or in fairyland – birds of gorgeous plumage, giant trees that seemed like overgrown ferns, dim-eyed beasts, and unthought-of creatures that aped mankind. By and by he became unconscious, as on his former journey, and when he awakened he was lying in a thick wood, where he had spent many an hour bird-nesting in his boyhood. He was again in Norway!

How well he remembered every step that he took towards his father's house! When he reached open ground he saw the farm-roofs, studded with bright house-leeks, rising above a distant clump of trees, and at the same time he heard the horn summoning the field workers to dinner – a summons which they were not slow to answer, for every one was at table when John, a few minutes later, came up to the porch, his footsteps unnoticed amid the general clatter of tongues and dishes. He listened anxiously until he caught the sound of his father's voice, for he had feared that by this time the old man might be dead; but now, reassured by the cheerfulness that reigned in the homestead, he stepped forward briskly, took the horn from its peg beside the door, and wound it, as a stranger might, to announce his arrival.

The honest farm-folk stared in amazement when they saw upon the threshold a stranger whose dress was a mass of gold from head to foot. No one recognised John; even his father thought he was a nobleman, and, rising up, he courteously invited him to rest in the hall and share their simple meal, if he were so inclined.

John thanked him, and, feeling that it was not a fit time at which to declare himself, he answered that he would be glad to rest with them a while, for he was a stranger in those parts, and, having had the mishap to lose his horse that morning, he had been forced to walk till he was footsore. Satisfied with the explanation, the goodman gave him a place at the head of the table, and treated him with the utmost honour; but his mother, on the other hand, was less convinced by his story, and watched him narrowly, wondering why he should so strongly remind her of her youngest boy, whom, in spite of his waywardness, she had loved most tenderly, and whose sudden disappearance had caused her untold suffering.

Meanwhile John had been taking note of all who were at table. Father and mother, his two brothers Thorolf and Thord, and most of the old servants were still there. A few new faces there were, one of which he looked at with interest – by his younger brother's side sat a handsome woman, whom he rightly guessed to be Thord's bride. For one glance that John gave this Thorgerd, she shyly returned two, for she was much charmed by the good looks and the pleasant manners of the stranger.

When dinner was over the men returned to their work in the fields; but before they left, the master of the house begged his guest to rest in the farmhouse as long as he pleased, and John answered that he would be glad to stay a while. The women were sent to their tasks by their mistress, who gave her orders to her young daughter-in-law, Thorgerd, amongst the others. Unwillingly Thorgerd rose from the table, and, throwing a last glance towards John, left him and his mother alone in the hall. But not yet did the goodwife dare to ask this handsomely dressed stranger the question that was trembling on her lips. If he really were her son he would soon show it, she believed; and instead of leading him to talk, she slipped out of the hall, and prepared to test him by a simple little device. She sent a maid to throw down an armful of clothes on the settle close to which the stranger was resting, and the maid having done so, John was again left alone in the hall. His eyes fell upon the bundle of clothes beside him, and he immediately recognised them to be a masquerader's quaint cloak and hood which he had worn four years ago at a Yule-tide gathering.

The whole scene came back to him: the snowy ground, the figures around him, and the song that they sang that evening:

> News of a fair and a marvellous thing,
> *The snow in the street and the wind on the door.*
> Nowell, nowell, nowell we sing!
> *Minstrels and maids, stand forth on the floor.*

He rose dreamily, threw off his gold-embroidered coat, and, wrapping himself in the spangled finery, he paced the floor singing verse after verse of the old carol. His mother stole back to the hall, and saw what she had expected – her own boy, recalled by the memories of a past night, breaking into songs of the countryside, and hugging the quaint cloak about him as he wandered up and down the room in his dreamy fashion as of old.

He ran towards her as he caught sight of her loving eyes fixed upon him. 'Mother,' he cried, looking into the wistful face, and kissing her fondly, as he had done when he was but a boy, 'mother, your ne'er-do-well has come back, and glad am I that I may yet be a joy to you. I have come to see you but for a time, for my new home is far distant, and ere long I must return to it. But if I give you news of how I have fared these three years, tell me in return all that has come to pass amongst you in that time.'

So mother and son sat and talked hand-in-hand until the others came in at nightfall, when John rose, and told them that he was indeed the lad who had disappeared three summers ago. Mindful of the warning given him by the swan-maiden, he told no one, not even his old mother, the true story of his fairy love, but spoke of how he had met people from a far country the morning that he had been on watch beside the south meadow, and how they had taken him with them, and, settling in their midst, he had fared surpassingly well, and was now wedded to a lovely princess.

There was great rejoicing amongst the simple folk when they learned that the handsome stranger was the idle young dreamer whose chances of fortune had seemed so slender in the past. His elder brothers welcomed him without the least touch of jealousy; while the goodman, for the first time in his life, felt proud of his youngest son, and his only regret was that John would have to quit Norway again, when the seamen who had brought him on this visit should return to take him back to his new home.

And now John had got his desire. He was free to enjoy life on his father's farm as of old; but just as he had wearied for the pleasure of that rough life when he was shut off from it in the swan-maiden's country, so now that he was again upon earth, what would he not have given to see his love at his side? He began to grieve sadly, and the people in the homestead noticed that he came home more unhappy each evening from his solitary walk to the south meadow. They would fain have discovered why he took his nightly walk alone; but he did not encourage them to talk about his affairs, and, saving Thorgerd, no one ventured to question him. His sister-in-law, however, had fallen hopelessly in love with him, and she did everything in her power to win his heart and learn the secrets that lay buried there. She would slip out to join him on his way back from the meadow at nights, when he, love-lorn and despairing, sometimes wondered if he might not tell the story of his woe to this soft-eyed friend who was so anxious to listen to his talk and try to comfort him.

It was only by remembering how earnestly the swan-maiden had entreated him to keep the secret of her love from mortal ears, that he withstood his longing to unburden himself to Thorgerd. And yet, although he never willingly revealed the reason of his sadness, there came at length a night when rash words escaped him, and brought grievous trouble upon him and his beloved.

On Christmas Eve the snow lay thick upon the ground, and heavy grey clouds were resting on the hillsides, to be ever and again swept along by a bitingly cold wind that howled around the old farmhouse as John set out on his customary evening walk to the meadow. The chill and dreary look of the country was in keeping with his sense of misery, and in a sudden fit of despair he cried aloud when he reached the spot where he had first seen the swan-maiden: 'Come to me, sweetheart! I cannot live without you. Come to me now!'

Would a fair white swan float down towards him from that cold, wind-swept mass of clouds? No; no answer came either by sight or sound. A long time he waited breathlessly, trembling at his rashness in having called his beloved; but the sky grew darker and darker, night closed in, and at last he realised that it was useless to wait longer. Bitterly reproaching his love for having deceived him in saying that she would come at a sigh from him, he turned, and strode homeward. A slender woman wrapped in a grey cloak stood waiting him as he entered the courtyard; here, surely, was his swan-maiden! Not a word could he cry, for joy and surprise overmastered him. He saw her glide up to him, and felt her soft, warm hand slipped into his. Then he stammered,

'Oh, sweetheart, I have done no wrong, have I? I called on you because I could no longer endure life without you.'

A gentle voice answered that in her eyes he could do no wrong, and that to know he loved her was the one desire of her heart. But when he recognised the speaker, John dropped her hand quickly, for it was not his swan-maiden, but Thorgerd, who had come to meet him. Forgetting that there was a listener beside him, he cried recklessly 'O my beloved, do you care for me no longer? Have I been indeed deceived? Yet think not that my love can fail like yours; while life lasts, never shall I cease to mourn for you!'

Thorgerd did not interrupt him. Silently she walked beside him across the snowy courtyard to the hall-door, then, stopping abruptly, she asked him in a smothered voice who it was that he had hoped to see that night – was it not she herself? She had loosened her grey cloak, and the light from the open door sparkled upon her golden hair and on the rich, embroidered robe which she wore in honour of the Christmas feast. A more beautiful woman could hardly have been found in all Norway; but John had not a thought to give her, and cared not though his words pained her deeply. He answered that the lady-love whom he longed to see was afar off. 'Ah, if she would but cross this threshold tonight!' he sighed despairingly; and as Thorgerd heard him, she turned away sullenly, knowing that there would never be a place for her in his heart, and wild with shame and anger that she had vainly betrayed to him the secret of her love.

The great Yule-tide feast was being celebrated in the hall, and everyone belonging to the homestead was there, John and Thorgerd among the rest; she, trying to bury her chagrin in forced merriment, he, weary at heart, still thinking of his lost love. It was late in the evening before he could rouse himself to join in the revelry around the table; but at length he made the effort to bear his part, and, rising to his feet, he was about to call some well-known toast, when a horn rang out clear, though far away across the fields, and at the sound of the blast the words died upon his lips. Again the horn was wound, this time louder than before, and John grew pale and trembled at the thought of what it might betoken. When for the third time the blast was heard, now close at hand, he could neither speak nor move, and the other men snatched up their weapons, not knowing what enemy might be upon them at that late hour; another minute, and the arms were dropped, for the door opened, and upon the threshold stood a gentle lady in robes white as the snow that lay about her feet – John's true love had come to him!

'Joy and peace to the house,' she said in her pretty, birdlike voice, looking round the smoky hall with a bright inquiring glance. 'I have come to join my loved one. Will you give me your welcome, John?'

How timidly, and yet with what rapture, did John come forward to whisper his joy at seeing her; how proudly he led her before his father and the others, telling them that for his sake his bride had come a far journey to his home! If anyone had been inclined to doubt the story of John's fortunes, there was none now but believed it every whit, when they saw his mate, whom no princess in their country could equal in sweetness and beauty. The evening that had begun so gloomily for John, had now become a season of bewildering joy, and he watched with delight how his beloved won the hearts of all at table. She spoke gently and lovingly to the goodman and his wife, wishing them many long years of happiness together; she joined in the mirth around her, and when a shade of doubt and anxiety crossed John's face, she smiled upon him gaily, as if to assure him that he must not regret the rash words which brought her to his world.

'Let us be glad together for at least one night,' she whispered; and so, in spite of secret misgivings, he smiled back to her, and gave himself up to the enjoyment of her sweet presence.

Hours after, when the banquet was over and the house wrapped in slumber, a poor, heart-broken little swan-maiden arose, and bent tearfully over John, who was lying fast asleep. 'Farewell, dearest,' she sobbed as she drew the gold ring off his finger. 'Alas that we should have to part! Yet so it must be, because in your impatience you called me to appear amongst mortals. How mournful henceforth will your life be, and oh! how desolate mine, when I go to dwell in that land far beyond the world's end, *east of the sun and west of the moon*! Ah! love, would that these words might reach you in your sleep, and sink deep into your memory, so that you might afterwards arise and seek me in that home of hapless lovers, whither no one has yet journeyed of his own will!'

Then she turned, and stole softly downstairs to the deserted hall, and out into the white world of snow on which the moon was pouring its silver light. But where her path led, no one might ever know, for when John discovered his loss in the morning, and ran out, wild with grief, to try and trace her steps, he found that the snow had fallen afresh, and not a print remained to tell of her passing.

In speechless anguish, he fled from his old home before any of the household was astir, and all day he wandered aimlessly through the countryside until at nightfall he reached a small seaport. He had but one thought, and that was to roam the wide world, so long as life lasted, in search of his beloved. But where was he to turn his steps? He was haunted by the memory of a phrase – part of a forgotten dream, he fancied – which told of a dreary land where the love-lorn dwell, far removed from earth's joys; but, try as he might, he could not recall the exact words which might help him upon his well-nigh hopeless quest.

Having determined to seek his lost one overseas, he had to wait many weeks at the little seaport until the wintry weather gave place to a mild springtide, when the sailing boats could safely leave the harbour. At length, one fair March evening, he went on board the first ship that was southward bound that season, and although he had nothing to guide him in his wanderings, he felt it a comfort at least to be moving onward to a new country. His dreams that night were of travels, untried and perilous, yet full of promise, and when he awakened in time to see the sun rise while the moon was still shining faintly, the words that had haunted his memory since that sad Christmas night suddenly flashed upon him, and he cried; '*East of the sun and west of the moon!* That is the land where I shall find my swan-maiden. But oh! my sweetheart, how am I to reach you there?'

He looked up gratefully at sun and moon, which together had reached the phrase that henceforth was go guide his steps, and little else he thought of, for the rest of his voyage; but how he could journey to that unknown abode of the love-lorn. When his ship reached the shores of England he disembarked at the easterly port of Dunwich, and since he could expect no news of foreign lands in the quiet country villages around, he turned his steps towards London, where he might hear talk amongst the seamen on the wharfs about strange journeys – perchance of what lay beyond the world's end.

Sometimes when he stopped for the night at a hostle or abbey, he would relate this own sad love-story (always pretending, however, that it was the tale of another man), in the hope that some listener might rise to tell something more about that land of exiled lovers. But though his audience heard him with deep interest, and told him that no minstrel could have given them a merrier tale, yet never a man had a word to add about the country of which the poor wanderer was fain to hear. In time he reached London, and went down to the riverside, where he mixed with all sorts of travellers and heard indeed of many a curious voyage; but to that land east of the sun and west of the moon no one seemed ever to have journeyed, or at least no one had ever returned from its shores. Then he resolved that he would begin travelling himself, and form that time onward he sailed from one quarter of the globe to another, till many years had been spent in fruitless search that brought him no nearer to his heart's desire.

Once he returned to his father's house in Norway, but when he learned that his mother was dead, the ties which bound him to his kinsmen were severed; and after he had seen his father and brothers, strong and hearty as ever, and Thorgerd no less beautiful, he bade them farewell hastily, for the place reminded him too sadly of his swan-maiden, and scarcely could he restrain himself from falling down in a passion of tears to kiss the threshold on which her slender white feet had rested that fateful Christmas night.

Reckless of dangers, he continued to roam through many countries until he found himself in an Eastern land in the company of certain traders who were preparing for a cruise to far-distant shores, where they expected to find great abundance of gold and precious stones. At his request they took him aboard, and presently they set out upon their voyage with every prospect of success.

Time passed, however, and the land which the sailors expected to have sighted was nowhere visible; day after day they sailed on, and still nothing but sea and sky met their gaze; then seamen and merchants grew alike disquieted, while, strange to say, John felt calmer and more hopeful than his wont.

Standing one evening by the prow, he gazed at the setting sun with hopes so bright that he was almost afraid to harbour them in his heart. While the sun dropped upon the western horizon he saw the sickle of the new moon shining aloft; and at the sight of sun and moon he pondered on the course he wished to keep – east of the sun, west of the moon, and something seemed to whisper to him that this evening he was approaching his long journey's end. He cared not that the sailors were anxiously watching a heavy bank of grey clouds that lay upon the water's edge in the east; the threatening storm had no terrors for him, and at night-time he lay down and slept, while the others, open-eyed, and shuddering at the great waves that rose like mountains above the ship's side, crouched together in fear of instant death. The night grew darker and darker, and the sea tossed the frail timber-built vessel, as though it were made of paper, now to the crest of a huge billow and again down into a trough at the very roots of the waves. And still John slept, until a great wave swept over the deck and hurled him against the mast, around which he had the presence of mind to fling both arms, so that he escaped being washed overboard. Whether others, like himself, were still clinging to the wreck, he could not see, but it was soon plain that all were alike doomed, for the ship was rapidly filling with water. On and on he was swept through the billows, while through his mind rushed crowded memories of his loved swan-maiden; and horror of the shipwreck and the raging black sea was lost in strangely peaceful dreams of her for whose sake he was even then drifting to an untimely end. Then the wrecked vessel reeled beneath a last, violent shock, the waves met with a roar above his head, and John sank down quietly into depths where he felt and knew no more.

But all was not over. The swan-maiden's lover awoke to find himself on a sunny stretch of sand where the green sea rippled gently at his feet, without a trace of the storm that had raged the night before. A strange contentment filled his heart as he thought of all the toils and perils he had safely passed through;

surely, said he, his life would not have been preserved, had he not been destined to see his beloved once again. For a little while he lay at ease, basking in the warm sunshine, and wondering vaguely what country this might be, which had all the charm of earth's fairest places and was yet unlike any land that he had ever visited.

At length he rose, and with a last gaze upon the ocean, which he was dimly conscious he would not cross again, he passed inland over daisied slopes, where never a building of any kind nor a human being was to be seen.

From the sea-level the ground rose first to grassy hills and then to an unbroken line of lofty, rugged mountains, which, having no passes, would have to be scaled by the stranger who wished to make his way to the valley beyond. John stopped to take his first refreshment in this lonely outland, from an apple-tree on whose boughs blossoms and delicious ripe fruit hung side by side, and then he pressed uphill until the sun set, and he was forced to wait till dawn before he gained the heights from which he hoped to look down into the heart of the country. So early indeed was he afoot next day that the sun had but risen when he reached the summit. Looking eagerly inland, he saw beneath him a wonderfully beautiful vale, in which the hand of man had been at work, cultivating fruits and raising pleasant homesteads by the side of the stream that flowed between the low meadows. On the slopes immediately beneath the bare rocky brow of the hill, lay terraced vineyards and rich wheat fields; lower down, there were patches of orchards which skirted the fertile meadows on the level ground. Cottages and trim farmhouses were there in plenty, and as John gazed down upon the valley, which the sun was now flooding with a golden haze, he fancied that the happy folk who dwelt there must be sheltered from all the woes that afflict mortals whose lot is cast in less pleasant places.

From this restful scene his eyes turned to the wan ghost of the moon, which hung low above the hills facing him, and then, feeling the sun waxing warm upon his shoulders, he gave a sudden shout of joy. '*East of the sun and west of the moon*! At last, at last I have reached the land where my loved one is to be found!'

He looked to find a path from the rocky ridge down to the hollow, and, seeing that it was impossible to descend the steep cliffs at the point where he stood, he made his way along the crest of the hill for some little distance, until the valley beneath him, which had at first been but narrow, widened out to a great expanse of sheltered lowland, through which the river swept in a wide bend. Far away upon the curve of the river, gleamed the golden roofs of a castle, and at the sight of it John's heart beat fast, for there, surely, was the abode of the love-lorn! Presently the hillside became less precipitous, and, climbing down the rocks, he reached the grassy slopes, where men were afoot, making ready for their day's work in field and orchard. They were a well-thriven race, comely for the most part, and of honest appearance, but never had John seen such grave faces as they wore. They showed no interest in the stranger; if their sad eyes happened to meet his, they gave him no second glance, and none answered his greeting. On his way to the palace he hailed in turn a woodman, an elderly dame, riding upon a mule, and a young boy, who was walking by her side, but for all the notice that they took of his questions, they might have been dead folk. Indeed, so much did he doubt whether they were living men and women, that when he passed a group of girls filling their jars with water at the palace fountain, he laid his fingers lightly upon the soft hand of a maid to feel if there were any warmth in it. Yes; the blood coursed freely in her veins, but his touch could not rouse her from the indifference in which she, like the others in this enchanted land, seemed to be irretrievably lost.

Through groups of servants, men-at-arms, and gentlefolk, he passed from the court to the hall, where all were streaming in to their early meal without a summons from either bell or horn. He stood aside and watched the dumb figures take their places until only one seat remained empty, and that was the throne in the centre of the dais. Then in his sea-stained, tattered clothes, he strode barefooted, past the handsomely dressed knights and ladies, and seated himself in the chair of honour. Just as no one had questioned his right to enter the palace, so no one showed either displeasure or surprise at his taking his seat upon the throne. The meal was taken in unbroken silence; unasked, the servants brought John all that he could wish; and then, smiling at the absurdity of a poor wanderer like himself having been entertained so royally, he wandered out of the hall before the others, and turned his steps along a cool cloister.

A maid brushed closely past him, walked to the end of the paved way, and disappeared through a door in the wall. The disappointment which John had felt when he saw that his swan-maiden was not amongst the people in the hall, gave place suddenly to overwhelming excitement. The door in front of him led, without doubt, to the women's courts, and there, if anywhere in this enchanted castle, he would find his lost one With bated breath he hastened to raise the latch, and stepped into a court which was shaded by pink-blossomed trees and cooled by the playing of a fountain in the midst. There in the centre of a busy group of girls, bending silent-tongued over their spinning, sat his dearly loved swan-maiden!

Her face was as joyless as those around her; she had no smile upon her lips, and her eyes were heavy and downcast, but except for her sadly changed expression, her beauty was as exquisite as ever. John's joy unnerved him, and, too faint to move, he stood for a time and feasted his eyes upon that sweet form which for many a long year he had seen only in dreams. When would she raise her face, he wondered; and would her eyes brighten when they fell upon him? With trembling limbs he crossed to where she sat listlessly working at a piece of embroidery. Like all others banished to this land of hopeless love, she was deaf to any sound, and even when his glad, faltering words of greeting were uttered, she did not notice the man who stood before her; only, as if she were troubled by a dream, she gave a little start and clenched her white hands.

'Sweetheart,' he sobbed, 'surely your love has not grown cold? Ah! look into my eyes, I pray you, and behold your true lover, who all these years has found no rest nor happiness without you.' Then he poured into her unheeding ears the story of his love, from the morning when she won his heart in the meadow by his old Norwegian home, on to the late sad years when he had roamed the whole world in his distress. 'Have not we both been sorely punished for my folly and impatience in calling you to join me amongst mortal men?' he pleaded. 'Through all those bitter years I have never ceased to believe that our punishment would one day come to an end, and that I would find you in that country of which you must have whispered when you left me in my sleep that Christmas night. Did you not tell me, sweetheart, that

I must seek you in this strange land, *east of the sun and west of the moon?'*

The potent words had no sooner crossed his lips than his loved one awakened from her languor. She rose to her feet, raised her eyes, and, seeing her devoted lover, with the sweetest of glad cries she sprang forward to welcome him fondly. Words came again to her lips, joy took possession of her soul, and she became, as of old, a light-hearted swan-maiden, radiant with love and happiness.

But it was not to his beloved alone that John brought deliverance. The spell that bound all the dwellers in that country of lost loves was broken, once for all, when the name of the land, *east of the sun and west of the moon,* was uttered by one whose devotion had led him, through countless toils and perils, to win back his sweetheart from that silent, gloomy life. One and all awoke now to enjoy renewed speech and laughter, and to praise the constancy of the Norwegian, who had rested not until he had accomplished the journey, which no other mortal ever undertook of his own free will.

THE BARNACLE MAID

Jessica Amanda Salmonson

O UT IN DECEPTION PASS, with the ebb and flow of the tide, the hair of a sea maiden can be seen drifting back and forth, back and forth, like a bed of kelp. Many people claim to see her even to this day. In her mortal life, this maiden had been the tribal princess Ko-Kwalawut, famed far and wide for her beauty and wisdom.

She lived before the coming of white settlers. In those days, the Samish people were famous fishermen. The coastline was dense with ancient forests and the many streams and rivers were pure and clear. It was a paradise given to the Indians to oversee and defend. The men were commonly out in their canoes, either upon the rivers or on Puget Sound. The women were more apt to be gatherers of clams, oysters, and crabs along the shoreline.

One day Princess Ko was filling her basket with shellfish. She had struggled to dig up an especially large clam, but when she grasped it in her hand, it seemed to come to life and sprang into the shallows. She waded out to get the shellfish, but when she picked it up, it leapt into a deeper part of the water, as though upon invisible feet! She waded farther, and the same thing happened once more, so that she was standing waist deep in the cold, swift water.

When she started back toward the beach, a long nubbly arm covered with sand and seaweed reached upward from the sand at her feet. It caught hold of her wrist and held her fast. She struggled to get free, but could not shake the chill and powerful grip. Then a voice from the water said to her, 'Do not fear me. I, a prince of the sea, have greatly admired your beauty. I have fallen in love with you, and now that I have gotten hold of you, I will never let go.'

'But you must let me go,' said Princess Ko, a brave calmness in her voice. 'Do you not know that I will drown if you drag me into your world.'

'How can I let you leave me after I have planned so long to capture you?' the prince asked.

She moved her foot back and forth to see if she could uncover his face in the sandy sea bottom, but all she detected was the upraised arm. Still, when he spoke, she heard him clearly. He said, 'If you will promise to visit me in this cove from time to time, I will let you go.'

She agreed, and during each of their meetings, the sea spirit held her hand for longer and longer periods of time. He spoke loving words to her, and finally asked her to marry him. Princess Ko said, 'Only the chief, my father, can give me into marriage. You must ask his permission, and I must abide by his decision.'

The spirit rose out of the sea and followed the princess to the village. Princess Ko was unafraid, but the people were frightened of his appearance, for he was encrusted with barnacles. Seaweed hung all about him. He had eyes like a fish, perfectly round and with no eyelids.

Everyone dreaded the prospect of their beautiful princess marrying such a monster. His presence caused a coldness throughout the village. When he asked the chief for Princess Ko's hand, her father was incensed. He said, 'No! If my daughter entered the sea, she would die!'

'She shall not die,' said the sea's prince. 'She shall become one among my people, and live forever. I have such love for her, believe me, she would not be harmed.'

'No! She is the pride of our people, and I will not permit her to go into the sea. Go away at once!'

An icy wind exuded from the sea spirit. His chest swelled and he seemed to inhale all the luck of the tribe. His eyes narrowed with anger and his massive, encrusted fingers coiled into a fist. In a low, threatening voice he said, 'If you refuse me, the water in all the streams will be undrinkable. The fish will depart. Your people will die of thirst and famine.'

'Go! Go!' shouted the chief, angered by such threats.

* * *

So it was that the streams turned dark with foul scum and mud, or were made salty by the invasion of the sea, or dried up altogether. There were no fish to be caught, no clams or oysters or crabs to be found. Night and day, a coldness filled the longhouses, and bonfires burned without heat. The people grew thin and ill. The children cried out constantly for food and water.

Princess Ko went to the cove where she had often met with the spirit, and chastised him for his cruelty to her people. 'How can I return your affection when you perform evil deeds?' she scolded. She demanded he restrain himself from his heartless acts. If he would take away the curse, she would beg her father to permit her marriage. Having heard her words, the sea spirit relented a little, and there was almost enough to eat, although it was still a hard time for the Samish.

Princess Ko went every day to talk to her father, and at last he was convinced of her desire to marry the sea-spirit. He said he would give his blessing to the marriage under one condition. Once each year, his daughter must be allowed to return to the Samish village, so that everyone could judge her happiness for themselves, and because otherwise they would miss her too much. The spirit arose from the sea until he stood atop the waters of Deception Pass. At the spirit's feet, water roiled furiously. The chief shivered at the coldness.

Then Princess Ko in her beautifully beaded and feathered wedding garments walked out on the surface of the water. She took her husband's hand, and slowly they sank downward together, until all that was visible was the beautiful dark hair of Princess Ko waving to and fro with the tide.

* * *

From that day on, the rivers ran crystal clear. Salmon hurried up the streams, coming from the sea, and the nets of the Samish people were filled. The beaches were dense with shellfish and all the women's baskets were filled with razor clams and butter clams and oysters. There was greater prosperity than ever before, because the sea had married a Samish princess.

A year later, the princess came to visit. The salmon catch had been excellent the day before her arrival, which had been a sign of her coming, and everyone greeted her with reverence and awe. In spite of her friendliness, her relatives were uncomfortable around her, because Princess Ko exuded the terrible coldness of creatures of the sea, and this affected the atmosphere wherever she passed.

There was a great feast, and everyone danced and sang. Yet for all the joy of the reunion, a degree of superstitious dreadfulness underlay the festivities, for Ko's people felt strange about her new life. Her coloring had become ever so slightly mottled and greenish, and the chilliness her body generated made people want to sit or stand apart from her.

The following year there was another extraordinarily fine catch, followed by the arrival of the princess. But during the feast, everyone thought Princess Ko looked uncomfortable and agitated, as though she hated to be so long out of the sea. They feared her a little more than they had on her first visit, since strange things so often frightened people. Their fear made the princess melancholy in their presence.

The year after that, it was even more difficult for the people to get into a festive mood, despite so much food and singing. For by now, their beloved princess had undergone dramatic changes. Her beautiful eyes had become like the eyes of a fish, flat and round and unblinking. Upon her arms and on her neck, barnacles had taken hold. As she stood among her people, a cold wind whipped about her, and even her loving father could not stand close to her without shaking with a chill.

On the fourth year, she came again. The people were horrified. That face that had once been so beautiful was now entirely sheathed in barnacles. Her arms were like barnacle-encrusted driftwood. Seaweed clung to her everywhere. Only her raven hair was still the same, assuring the people that she was indeed their beloved princess.

* * *

Sad though it made her father the chief, he released his daughter from her vow to return once each year, for she was not happy out of the sea, and the people had become afraid of her coldness and appearance.

The Samish chanted this tale to the beat of drums. The old

songs and the old ways are rarer now than they once were. But the people remember Princess Ko, and to this day her hair can be seen flowing to and fro with the tides. They say she is still protecting the Samish people.

BATTLE ON
THE BRIDGE OF THE GODS

Jessica Amanda Salmonson

T HE GIANTESS LOOWIT had lived to great old age. She could
hardly believe it, but after thousands of years, she had
become a terrible looking crone. Her cheeks sagged; her
chin sagged too. Her hair that once was a splendid midnight
waterfall had become white and wild like a tormented frothing
river. Underneath her tired old eyes were large red cups full
of melancholy which at times spilled forth to wet the earth
in sundry sorrows. Her hands, that once were so delicate
and slender, were like the claws of eagles, with long sharp
dark nails.

Even so, in her heart, she had never aged. When she went
to the river with a bucket, she betimes chanced to see her own
reflection. She was startled by her appearance, her crinkled
complexion, her eagle's nest of wild white hair.

Where, she wondered, was the beautiful maiden she once had
been? That maiden was still present, inside an old woman.

* * *

Loowit was a very great shaman in the days when humanity
was newly made. All people were giants then and often
mingled with gods. Loowit was the inventor of a firemaking
device. For a long time she kept this device a secret, hidden as it was in her cavernous home in the heart of a
certain mountain today called Mount St. Helens. This mountain's hollow was well-lit on account of her ingenious invention. The mountain was like a tipi to Loowit, with the

smoke of her miraculous fire rising through the smoke-hole at the top.

Then as now, the means and methods of certain arts were protected as secrets among artisans. Those who did not know the secrets of an art imagined such things were done solely by magic. Having told no one of her invention, various valley peoples and peoples near the sea believed Loowit manufactured fire by a supernatural method. Such peoples came to the door of Loowit's cavern and paid homage to her. She would then deposit a single coal inside a clamshell which each visitor brought along for the purpose. By this means, these individuals were able to deliver fire to their various villages.

But if in a village the fire went out, they knew not how to make another. In the winter, travel was difficult, and they might not be able to reach Loowit's mountain. They must therefore live in misery until the journey could be made. Then again, since Loowit was an ascetic, she was not always available with a new coal, for she was deep in the labyrinth of her cavern, lost in meditations. Thereby many made the terrible journey only to find their efforts fruitless, since Loowit did not invariably come forth proffering the burning coals. No one expected Loowit to be at the instant beck and call of people foolish enough to let their fires die. Therefore none complained to her about how often they went without fire.

Yet when Loowit went into the world in the guise of an elderly beggar, she saw that people suffered cold misery during many a winter. Rain, wind, flood, or some error of neglect, was apt to douse a fire, after which there befell terrible woe. People lived in blind fear of the night, wherein ghosts cried out with the voices of owls. So, too, having no fire to cook their venison and salmon, they ate raw flesh, their white teeth gnawing.

Loowit became heartsick to see the peoples wet and cold. She said to herself, 'If I show them my ingenious device, each will be able to make a fire without need of my services. Their lot will be improved. But once I have revealed my secret, what will I be but an old woman of no importance to anyone?'

Even so, her heart could not deny the world. Children had frozen to death, and Loowit could not allow such tragedies to continue. She went to her cavern and prayed to Tyhee Saghalie, Chief of the Gods. He heard her in his heavenly place and came striding down the Milky Way from the north and trod along the Cascade peaks. As he was visible from a long way off, two of his earthly sons saw him, and they arose from their places to join their father. These sons were called Pahtoe and Wyeast, who dwelt in the mountains later known as Adams and Hood. The Great Chief together with his powerful sons sat in counsel with Loowit, who was indeed a great Shaman to speak with such gods as these.

She showed Tyhee Saghalie her invention, which was a drill that made fire when it was whirled with correct dexterity. For his own needs, Tyhee Saghalie always made fire with great explosions of lightning. This was not entirely practical for just anyone. So he was very impressed by Loowit's cleverness.

Loowit said, 'Tyhee Saghalie, I am too old to travel about the nations of all the peoples of the valleys and the shores in order to teach this great secret. So I am giving my drill to you. As you can see, it is easily duplicated. Will you and your sons deliver my gift to the peoples, so that they may easily achieve their needs whenever fire is required?'

'I and my sons will do as you have asked,' said Tyhee Saghalie. He held the drill in his hand, and parted it by a miraculous means, so that there were two drills. He gave one to his right-hand son, and the other to his left-hand son, instructing them, 'Tell the peoples this is the gift of the mountain witch Loowit.' And the two princes sat in awe of the soul of Loowit, which was a very great and giving soul.

Then to the old Shaman woman, Tyhee Saghalie said, 'But what of your own future? Do you think I did not see you had horded your invention? Do you think I knew not why you kept the secret for so long? Now that you have given away the only thing you possessed, you will have nothing.'

'Will I not have the affection of the people?'

'You will have the affection of the people,' said Tyhee Saghalie, 'and in honor of your selflessness, potlatches will be held each year, and the richest of every tribe will give their wealth to others. Never will such selflessness go unrewarded by Tyhee Saghalie. To you, Loowit, I will grant whatever is the one thing you have most in your life desired. What is there you would have from me?'

'I am forlorn of my youth,' said Loowit, 'and would live in

happiness to be once more that which in my heart I have always remained.'

Therefore the Chief of the Gods restored Loowit to her former maidenliness. And because she was a priestess, but no longer sole guardian of fire, he made her, instead, the guardian of the Bridge of the Gods. This was the bridge which in former times joined the Washington Cascades to the Oregon Cascades, spanning the Columbia River, a river known to Chinookan peoples as Wauna.

The bridge over the Wauna was made in days before there were people, when Coyote was digging in the ground as coyotes do even now. Coyote dug through under the mountain range so that the Wauna flowed to the sea, and salmon swam to villages on the upper Wauna. Beneath the bridge there arose a lonesome island, invisible in the darkness, upon which dead fish, broken canoes, rotting bits of lodges and human corpses were strewn as flotsam. There was good magic above the bridge so that mystagogues were able to pass from it onto the Milky Way, and visit the country of Tyhee Saghalie.

'By this bridge,' said the Chief of Gods, 'I am visited by the giants of the earth. You, Loowit, will be the guide who opens and shuts the spirit-bridge that exists in tandem with the physical bridge. Those who are giants of body but not of soul must never have the spirit bridge opened to them, but you will advise them on the Road of Mountains. Those who are giants in spirit, whatever their physical proportions, for these you may reveal the spirit-bridge, that I may see them.'

Having been greatly honored with a signal duty, Loowit left the cavern of her mountain. She went to live in a small stone house in the middle of the bridge high above the Columbia.

Loowit was thereafter very beautiful. Many people came to the Bridge of the Gods to worship her as a Goddess. The sons of all the chiefs in every tribe desired her in marriage, but she rebuffed them in a kindly way. She remained an ascetic and a guide to many, belonging to no one man.

The princes Pahtoe and Wyeast had been impressed by the greatness of her soul even when she had the appearance of a crone. Now, whenever they gazed upon her, they each knew there was no other wife for them. They boasted each in turn that he and he alone would marry her. When they were rebuffed as swiftly as were her common beaus, the two mountainous princes declared to one another their intent to induce her by any means to choose between them.

After they had given to the peoples the gift of fire, in accordance with the directions of their father and Loowit, each returned to the Bridge of the Gods in order to woo the maiden. She said, 'I am flattered by your sincere attentions, but must ask that you desist, as I am an ascetic and devoted to the well-being of the whole of the world. I cannot be restricted to the needs of a single man or a single house. Simply put, I do not wish to marry, and will remain pure in my duties as a priestess.'

The princes said to one another, 'If she will not decide between us, we will do battle with one another. Who wins will take Loowit by main force, whether or not she agrees.' Having said this, they threw off their white robes, and rushed at one another.

They had many of the powers of their father the Great Chief. For this reason, their battle was terrible to see. Their feet gouged new rivers in the land, and heaped up new mountains, changing the direction of the Wauna River and causing whole forests to become submerged. Where the princes fell down wrestling, a vast wilderness was wasted. They rolled about clinging body to body so that prairies were ironed out. They dashed at one another, Wyeast with hurricanes, Pahtoe with fiery bolts of lightning. They were not yet worn out when they began to shove one another back and forth along the Bridge of the Gods until that mighty span collapsed into the Wauna River.

Now they sat in the rushing river of the gorge, alarmed by the destruction they had wrought. At the sound of the bridge crashing down, Tyhee Saghalie came striding down the Milky Way and stood atop the Cascades with his arms folded, his eyes flashing with anger. He snatched Wyeast and fixed him in the heart of Mount Hood, from whence he never could escape to cause mischief. He grabbed Pahtoe from the river as well, and fixed him in the heart of Mount Adams.

Loowit sat on the edge of the river, looking at the ruins of the bridge. She said, 'Now I am guardian neither of fire nor of the wonderful bridge. Was it my vanity that brought about this ruin? O Tyhee Saghalie, I will retire anew to the furnaces of my cavern, and never go forth among people, lest the beauty you have bestowed upon me inspire further harm.'

Taking pity on her, Tyhee Saghalie said, 'The Spirit of the Bridge of Gods exists within you, Loowit. Only the material bridge is ruined. I have reduced the size of humanity, so that no two may commit such harm as my sons have committed; but the hearts of people I have not changed. Some have great hearts, some have little. At my command, Loowit, you will unfold the spirit-bridge for those of the earth who are giant of heart. But if my will, and my laws, and my creation are hampered and harmed in future generations, then know that I have bestowed upon you a very grave power of destruction, so that even my spirit-bridge may fall, if ever I command thee.'

STORY OF
THE THREE STRONG MEN

Charles G. Leland

T HERE WAS A chieftain in the days of yore. He had a great desire for a poor girl who was a servant, and who worked for him. To win this girl he first must lose his wife. He took his wife afar into the woods to gather spruce-gum, and then left her there.

She soon found out that she had lost her way, and, wandering, she lost it more and more for many days, until she came at last to a bear's den, where, going in, she found the Chief of all the bears, who welcomed her, provided for her wants, and furnished her with pleasant food; but as the meat was raw he went into a neighboring town for fire. And as she lived with him she was to him in all things as he wished, and as a wife.

So that it came to pass, as time went on, that a new-comer was expected, and she bade the Bear provide the baby's clothes. And when the long-expected infant came it was a boy, large, beautiful, and strong; he was in everything beyond all other boys.

And as the child was born in a strange way, he very soon displayed a magic power. No baby ever grew so rapidly: when four months old he wrestled with the Bear and threw him easily upon the floor. And so the mother saw that he would be a warrior, and the chief of other men.

She loathed the life she led, and wished to leave, and live as she had done in days of old. To this the Bear would in no wise consent, and as her son was human, like herself, he loved his mother best, and thought with her.

One day he said, 'Now I can wrestle well and throw the Bear

as often as I choose. When I next time cast him upon the ground, catch up a club; the rest remains for you!'

They waited yet a while till he had grown so strong that the Bear was nothing in his grasp. One day they wrestled as they ever did, and then the woman, with a vigorous blow, strengthened by hate and famishing desire of freedom and a better human life, laid him in death upon the mossy floor.

They went their way back to the chieftain's town, and found him married to the servant-girl. The mother only spoke, and the wild boy tore down the wigwam of the Indian chief just with a blow, and then he called aloud unto the Lightning in the sky above, 'Come down to me and help me in my need! Build a grand wigwam such as man ne'er saw! Build it, I say, and for my mother here!'

The Lightning came, and with a single flash built such a home as man had never seen.

And then he said, 'Mother, I mean to go and travel everywhere, until I find another man who is as strong as I. When he is found I will return to thee.'

So on he went afar until he saw a man who lifted up a vast canoe with many people in it. This he did, raising it in the water; but the boy bore it ashore, and lifted it on land.

And so the two agreed that they would go on together until they found a third equal to them in strength, if such a man were living anywhere in all the world.

So traveling by hill and lake, they went, until one day, far in a lonely land, they saw a man rolling a mighty rock, large as the largest wigwam, up a hill. But the Bear's son, lifting the stone with ease, threw it afar over the mountain-top – threw it afar beyond the rocky range; they heard it thunder down the depths below.

Then the three strong men went to hunt the moose. He who had tossed the ship remained in camp to do the cooking, while the others went with bow and spear afar to find their game.

Now when the sun was at the edge of noon, just balancing to fall, there came a boy, a little wretched, elfish-looking child, as sad and sickly as a boy could be, who asked the man for food. He answered him, 'Poor little fellow! there, the pot is full of venison, so go and eat your fill.'

He ate, indeed, the dinner for the three. When he had done he did not leave a scrap; then walked into the stony mountain-side, as any man might walk into the fog, and in a second he was seen no more.

Now when the two returned and heard the tale they were right angry, being hungry men. The man who rolled the stone stayed next in turn, but when the little fellow came to him he seemed so famished and he shed such tears that this one also gave him leave to eat. Then, in a single swallow, as it seemed, he bolted all the food, and yelled aloud with an insulting laugh. The man, enraged, grappled him by the throat, but the strange boy flung him away as one would throw a nut, and vanished in the mountain as before.

On the third day the mighty man himself remained at home, and soon the starveling child came and began to beg, with tears, for food. 'Eat,' said the chief, 'as other people eat, and no more tricks, or I will deal with you.' But as it was with him the day before, so it went now; he swallowed all the meat with the same jeering yell. Then the strong man closed with the boy. It was an awful strife; they fought together from the early morn until the sun went down, and then the elf – for elf he was – cried out, 'I now give in!' So both his arms were tightly bound behind, and with a long, tough cord of plaited hide the strong man kept his prey, the lariat fast noosed about his neck. The child went on, the strong man ever following behind, holding the cord well twisted round his hand.

And so they went into the mountain-side, and ever on, a long and winding way, down a deep cavern, on for many a mile, – the light of sorcery shining from the elf made it all clear – until at last the guide stopped in his course, and said:

'Now list to me. I am the servant of a frightful fiend, a seven-headed devil, whom I deemed no man could ever conquer, he and I being of equal strength; but I believe that thou mayst conquer him, since I have found, by bitter proof, that thou canst conquer me. Here is a staff, the only thing on earth that man may smite him with and give him pain. Now, do your best; it is all one to me which of you gains, so one of you be slain, for well I wot 't will be a roaring fight.'

In came the evil being with a scream, and clutched the Indian with teeth and claws. There, in the magic cavern, many a mile from the sun's rays, they fought for seven days, the stubborn devil and the stubborn man, whose savage temper gave him fresher strength with every fresh wound; the more his blood ran from his body all the more his heart grew harder with the love of fight, until he beat away the monster's seven heads. And so he slew him, and the watching elf burst into laughter at the victory.

'Now,' said the elf, 'I have a gift for thee. I have three sisters: all are beautiful, and all shall be thine own if thou wilt but unbind my hands.' The strong man set him free. And so he led the man to another cave, and there he saw three girls so strangely fair they seemed to be a dream. The first, indeed, was very beautiful, and yet as plump as she was lovely; then the second maid was tall, superb, and most magnificent, in rarest furs, with richest wampum bands, the very picture of a perfect bride; but fairer than them both, as much more fair as swans outrival ducks, the youngest smiled. And the young chieftain chose her for his own.

With the three girls he went into the day. Far on the rocks above him he could see his two companions, and a sudden thought came to his mind, for he was quick to think; and so he called, 'I say, let down a rope; I have three girls here, and they cannot climb.' And so the two strong men let down a cord: then the first fairy-maid went up by it, and then the second. Now the chief cried out, 'It is my turn; now you must pull on me!' And saying this, he tied a heavy stone, just his own weight, unto the long rope's end, then bid them haul. It rose, but as it came just to the top the traitors let it fall, as he supposed they would, to murder him.

And then the chieftain said unto the elf, 'You know the mountain and its winding ways: bear me upon thy back, and that in haste, to where those fellows are!' The goblin flew, and in an instant he was by their side.

He found the villains in a deadly fight, quarreling for the maids; but seeing him they ceased to wrestle, upon which he said, 'I risked my life to bring away these girls; I would have given each of you a wife: for doing this you would have murdered me. Now I could kill you, and you both deserve death at the stake, vile serpents that you are; but take your lives – you are too low for me, – and with them take these women, if they wish to wed with such incarnate brutes as you!'

They went their way; the women followed them along the forest paths, and ever on. Into this story they return no more.

And then the strong man said to his young bride, 'I must return unto my village; then I'll come again to you; await me here.' But she, as one to elfin magic born, replied, 'I warn you of a single thing. When you again are at your wigwam door a small black dog will leap to lick your hand. Beware, I say; if he succeed in it, you surely will forget me utterly.' As she predicted so it came to pass.

And so she waited in the lonely wood beside the mountain till a month was gone, and then arose and went to seek her love. All in the early dawn she reached the town, and found the wigwam of the sagamore. She sought a neighboring hiding-place, where she might watch unseen, and found a tree, a broad old ash, which spread its stooping boughs over the surface of a silent pool.

An old black Indian had a hut hard by. His daughter, coming, looked into the spring, and saw a lovely face. The simple girl thought it was hers, her own grown beautiful by sorcery which hung about the place. She flung away her pail, and said, 'Aha! I'll work no more; some chief shall marry me!' and so she went to smile among the men.

Then came the mother, who beheld the same sweet, smiling, also girlish face. She said, 'Now I am young and beautiful again; I'll seek another husband, and at once.' She threw her pail afar and went away, losing no time to smile among the men.

And then in turn the old black Indian came, and looking in the spring beheld the face. He knew right well that it was not his own, for in his youth he never had been fair. So looking up above he saw the bride, and bade her come to him; and then he said, 'My wife has gone away; my daughter, too. You were the cause of it; it is but right that you should take the place my wife has left. Therefore remain with me and be my own.'

He fares but ill who weds unwilling witch. When night came on they laid them down to sleep, and then the bride murmured a magic prayer, begging the awful Spirit of the Wind, the giant Eagle of the wilderness, to do his worst. A fearful tempest blew, and all night long the old black Indian was out-of-doors, working with all his power to keep the lodge from being blown away. As soon as he had pinned one sheet of bark into its place another blew away, and then a tent pole rattling in the rain bounded afar. It was weary work, but all night long the young bride slept in peace, until the morning came, and then he slept.

Then she arose, and, walking to the wood, sat down beside a stream and sang a song:

> There are many men in the world,
> But only one is dear to me.
> He is good and brave and strong.
> He swore to love none but me;
> He has forgotten me.
> It was a bad spirit that changed him,
> But I will love none but him.

And as she sat and sang, the sagamore her husband, paddling by in his canoe, heard the sweet song intoned in magic style, and all at once recalled what had been lost – the two strong giants, the cavern and the elf, the seven-headed monster and the fight, the sisters and the evil-minded men, and the black dog who leaped to lick his hand: it flashed upon him like some early dream brought out by sorcery. He saw her sit beside the stream, and still he heard her song, soft as a magic flute. He went to her, and in a minute he was won again.

And then she said, 'This world is ever false. I know another, let us go to it.' So then again she sang a magic spell, and as she sang they saw the great Culloo, the giant bird, broad as a thunder cloud, winging his way towards them. Then he came; they stepped upon him, and he soared away. But to this earth they never came again.

THE LAY NUN
WHO GAVE OF HERSELF

Jessica Amanda Salmonson

WHEN GUATAMA BUDDHA came to Benares, he stayed in a deer park called Isipatana. Near the park there was a devout lay nun, Suppiya, who devoted herself to the faith. She went to the Arama and, going from cell to cell, asked the mendicant monks, 'Who here is ill that I can nurse?'

There was a mendicant who had overreached himself in ascetic practices and lay as one dying in his cell. 'Sister,' he said, 'it is my belief that I can recover if I can obtain a bit of meat broth.'

Suppiya said, 'I will procure it for you at once, reverend sir.' She hurried to her house and gave orders to a servant, 'Quickly, go and see if there is any meat to be had.'

The servant sought throughout Benares for meat, but could find none. Suppiya was informed, 'The killing of animals is prohibited on this day, and there is presently no meat anywhere in the town that is ready.'

Suppiya said to herself, 'That monk will increase his sickness if he has no broth. He may well die. How can I fail in my promise to help him? There must be some manner by which I can procure meat for him.'

So saying, she drew forth a knife and cut a piece of flesh from her own thigh. She gave it to a maid and said, 'Hurry and prepare a broth from this meat, carefully so that all the strength will be got from it. Then take it to the Arama for the sick mendicant. If anyone should ask after me, tell them I have fallen ill.'

Then she bandaged her thigh, went into the inner chamber of the house, and took to her bed.

Suppiya's husband, who was also a lay devotee, returned that evening from a trip he had taken, only to find his wife abed. He asked, 'Are you ill, Suppiya?'

'I am ill.'

'But what is the matter?'

Then Suppiya told her husband what had transpired.

'How marvelous you are!' he said. 'How pious to give even of your flesh to an indigent! If you would give even this, surely you would deny nothing to your faith!'

Thus speaking elatedly of his wife's excellence, he left her, and hurried to the deer park Isipatana where all the lay devotees were gathering to hear Guatama speak.

Guatama turned to where Suppiya's husband was sitting and asked, 'Why is our splendid sister not among us?'

'She is sick.'

'Well, have her come to me in any case.'

'She is unable to walk, Lord.'

'Well then, go and bring her to me, carrying her in your arms.'

Thus Suppiya's husband hurried home, and, lifting her into his arms, carried her to the deer park and into the presence of the Buddha. In the very moment that the blessed one set eyes upon her, her terrible wound was healed. There was good skin there, with tiny hairs growing from it, soft and fine. Suppiya showed her gratitude with many words of praise and by prostrating herself before the blessed one whose gaze was miraculous.

Later that day, Guatama went into the Arama and asked, 'Who among the mendicants asked that meat be brought to him?'

He was led to the cell of the pale mendicant who was recovering from his illness.

Guatama asked, 'O Monk, has broth been brought to you?'

'It was brought, Lord.'

'Have you eaten it, O Monk?'

'It was very tasty, Lord.'

'Did you inquire, O Monk, how the meat was taken?'

'I did not inquire, Lord.'

'Oh foolish one, you have eaten human flesh. It will not do that mendicants take advantage of the faithful. Listen! Once a mendicant ate the flesh of an elephant, and it was his fate to be trampled by an elephant later in his life. Once some hunters killed a lion, and when a mendicant came begging alms, they gave him meat of the lion, which he devoured. The next day he was passing through the forest, when a lion leapt out and devoured him. During a famine, another mendicant was so hungry that he ate a serpent. He was soon after bitten by an adder, and so died. So as you can see, such meals are forbidden with good cause! But you have eaten human flesh. Do you not fear that men will descend upon the faith?'

'I fear it, Lord.'

'Then this once I will alleviate you of worry, for you have inadvertently upraised our sister Suppiya, whose act of goodness cleanses you of guilt. Her name will be sung in Heaven, and she will have rewards even in this life, not only in the next. Now up with you, and go into the world, rebuked and foolish one! Go about your mendicant business with repentance in you, and think never again to take advantage of the faithful.'

THE ONE-HANDED GIRL

Edward Steere

A N OLD COUPLE once lived in a hut under a grove of palm trees, and they had one son and one daughter. They were all very happy together for many years, and then the father became very ill, and felt he was going to die. He called his children to the place where he lay on the floor – for no one had any beds in that country – and said to his son, 'I have no herds of cattle to leave you – only the few things there are in the house – for I am a poor man, as you know. But choose: will you have my blessing or my property?'

'Your property, certainly,' answered the son, and his father nodded.

'And you?' asked the old man of the girl, who stood by her brother.

'I will have blessing,' she answered, and her father gave her much blessing.

That night he died, and his wife and son and daughter mourned for him seven days, and gave him a burial according to the custom of his people. But hardly was the time of mourning over, than the mother was attacked by a disease which was common in that country.

'I am going away from you,' she said to her children, in a faint voice; 'but first, my son, choose which you will have: blessing or property.'

'Property, certainly,' answered the son.

'And you, my daughter?'

'I will have blessing,' said the girl; and her mother gave her much blessing, and that night she died.

When the days of mourning were ended, the brother bade his sister put outside the hut all that belonged to his father and his mother. So the girl put them out, and he took them away, save only a small pot and a vessel in which she could clean her corn. But she had no corn to clean.

She sat at home, sad and hungry, when a neighbour knocked at the door.

'My pot has cracked in the fire, lend me yours to cook my supper in, and I will give you a handful of corn in return.'

And the girl was glad, and that night she was able to have supper herself, and next day another woman borrowed her pot, and then another and another, for never were known so many accidents as befell the village pots at that time. She soon grew quite fat with all the corn she earned with the help of her pot, and then one evening she picked up a pumpkin seed in a corner, and planted it near her well, and it sprang up, and gave her many pumpkins.

At last it happened that a youth from her village passed through the place where the girl's brother was, and the two met and talked.

'What news is there of my sister?' asked the young man, with whom things had gone badly, for he was idle.

'She is fat and well-liking,' replied the youth, 'for the women borrow her mortar to clean their corn, and borrow her pot to cook it in, and for all this they give her more food than she can eat.' And he went his way.

Now the brother was filled with envy at the words of the man, and he set out at once, and before dawn he had reached the hut, and saw the pot and the mortar were standing outside. He slung them over his shoulders and departed, pleased with his own cleverness; but when his sister awoke and sought for the pot to cook her corn for breakfast, she could find it nowhere. At length she said to herself,

'Well, some thief must have stolen them while I slept. I will go and see if any of my pumpkins are ripe.' And indeed they were, and so many that the tree was almost broken by the weight of them. So she ate what she wanted and took the others to the village, and gave them in exchange for corn, and the women said that no pumpkins were as sweet as these, and that she was to bring every day all that she had. In this way she earned more than she needed for herself, and soon was able to get another mortar and cooking pot in exchange for her corn. Then she thought she was quite rich.

Unluckily someone else thought so too, and this was her brother's wife, who had heard all about the pumpkin tree, and sent her slave with a handful of grain to buy her a pumpkin. At first the girl told him that so few were left that she could not spare any; but when she found that he belonged to her brother, she changed her mind, and went out to the tree and gathered the largest and the ripest that was there.

'Take this one,' she said to the slave, 'and carry it back to your mistress, but tell her to keep the corn, as the pumpkin is a gift.'

The brother's wife was overjoyed at the sight of the fruit, and when she tasted it, she declared it was the nicest she had ever eaten. Indeed, all night she thought of nothing else, and early in the morning she called another slave (for she was a rich woman) and bade him go and ask for another pumpkin. But the girl, who had just been out to look at her tree, told him that they were all eaten, so he went back empty-handed to his mistress.

In the evening her husband returned from hunting a long way off, and found his wife in tears.

'What is the matter?' asked he.

'I sent a slave with some grain to your sister to buy some pumpkins, but she would not sell me any, and told me there were none, though I know she lets other people buy them.'

'Well, never mind now – go to sleep,' said he, 'and tomorrow I will go and pull up the pumpkin tree, and that will punish her for treating you so badly.'

So before sunrise he got up and set out for his sister's house, and found her cleaning some corn.

'Why did you refuse to sell my wife a pumpkin yesterday when she wanted one?' he asked.

'The old ones are finished, and the new ones are not yet come,' answered the girl. 'When her slave arrived two days ago, there were only four left; but I gave him one, and would take no corn for it.'

'I do not believe you: you have sold them all to other people. I shall go and cut down the pumpkin,' cried her brother in a rage.

'If you cut down the pumpkin you shall cut off my hand with it,' exclaimed the girl, running up to her tree and catching hold of it. But her brother followed, and with one blow cut off the pumpkin and her hand too.

Then he went into the house and took away everything he could find, and sold the house to a friend of his who had long wished to have it, and his sister had no home to go to.

Meanwhile she had bathed her arm carefully, and bound on it some healing leaves that grew near by, and wrapped a cloth round the leaves, and went to hide in the forest, that her brother might not find her again.

For seven days she wandered about, eating only the fruit that hung from the trees above her, and every night she climbed up and tucked herself safely among the creepers which bound together the big branches, so that neither lions nor tigers nor panthers might get at her.

When she woke up on the seventh morning she saw from her perch smoke coming up from a little town on the edge of the forest. The sight of the huts made her feel more lonely and helpless than before. She longed desperately for a draught of milk from a gourd, for there were no streams in that part, and she was very thirsty, but how was she to earn anything with only one hand? And at this thought her courage failed, and she began to cry bitterly.

It happened that the king's son had come out from the town very early to shoot birds, and when the sun grew hot he felt tired.

'I will lie here and rest under this tree,' he said to his attendants. 'You can go and shoot instead, and I will just have this slave to stay with me!' Away they went, and the young man fell asleep, and slept long. Suddenly he was awakened by something wet and salty falling on his face.

'What is that? Is it raining?' he said to his slave. 'Go and look.'

'No, master, it is not raining,' answered the slave.

'Then climb up the tree and see what it is,' and the slave climbed up, and came back and told his master that a beautiful girl was sitting up there, and that it must have been her tears which had fallen on the face of the king's son.

'Why was she crying?' inquired the prince.

'I cannot tell – I did not dare to ask her; but perhaps she would tell you.' And the master, greatly wondering, climbed up the tree.

'What is the matter with you?' said he gently, and, as she only sobbed louder, he continued:

'Are you a woman, or a spirit of the woods?'

'I am a woman,' she answered slowly, wiping her eyes with a leaf of the creeper that hung about her.

'Then why do you cry?' he persisted.

'I have many things to cry for,' she replied, 'more than you could ever guess.'

'Come home with me,' said the prince; 'it is not very far. Come home to my father and mother. I am a king's son.'

'Then why are you here?' she said, opening her eyes and staring at him.

'Once every month I and my friends shoot birds in the forest,' he answered, 'but I was tired and bade them leave me to rest. And you – what are you doing up in this tree?'

At that she began to cry again, and told the king's son all that had befallen her since the death of her mother.

'I cannot come down with you, for I do not like anyone to see me,' she ended with a sob.

'Oh! I will manage all that,' said the king's son, and swinging himself to a lower branch, he bade his slave go quickly into the town, and bring back with him four strong men and a curtained litter. When the man was gone, the girl climbed down, and hid herself on the ground in some bushes. Very soon the slave returned with the litter, which was placed on the ground close to the bushes where the girl lay.

'Now go, all of you, and call my attendants, for I do not wish to stay here any longer,' he said to the men, and as soon as they were out of sight he bade the girl get into the litter, and fasten the curtains tightly. Then he got in on the other side, and waited till his attendants came up.

'What is the matter, O son of a king?' asked they, breathless with running.

'I think I am ill; I am cold,' he said, and signing to the bearers, he drew the curtains, and was carried through the forest right inside his own house.

'Tell my father and mother that I have a fever, and

want some gruel,' said he, 'and bid them send it quickly.'

So the slave hastened to the king's palace and gave his
message, which troubled both the king and the queen greatly.
A pot of hot gruel was instantly prepared, and carried over to
the sick man, and as soon as the council which was sitting was
over, the king and his ministers went to pay him a visit, bearing
a message from the queen that she would follow a little later.

Now the prince had pretended to be ill in order to soften his
parents' hearts, and the next day he declared he felt better,
and, getting into his litter, was carried to the palace in state,
drums being beaten all along the road.

He dismounted at the foot of the steps and walked up, a great
parasol being held over his head by a slave. Then he entered the
cool, dark room where his father and mother were sitting, and
said to them:

'I saw a girl yesterday in the forest whom I wish to marry, and,
unknown to my attendants, I brought her back to my house in a
litter. Give me your consent, I beg, for no other woman pleases
me as well, even though she has but one hand!'

Of course the king and queen would have preferred a
daughter-in-law with two hands, and one who could have
brought riches with her, but they could not bear to say 'No'
to their son, so they told him it should be as he chose, and that
the wedding feast should be prepared immediately.

The girl could scarcely believe her good fortune, and, in
gratitude for all the kindness shown her, was so useful and
pleasant to her husband's parents that they soon loved her.

By and by a baby was born to her, and soon after that the
prince was sent on a journey by his father to visit some of the
distant towns of the kingdom, and to set right things that had
gone wrong.

No sooner had he started than the girl's brother, who had
wasted all the riches his wife had brought him in recklessness
and folly, and was now very poor, chanced to come into the
town, and as he passed he heard a man say, 'Do you know
that the king's son has married a woman who has lost one of
her hands?' On hearing these words the brother stopped and
asked, 'Where did he find such a woman?'

'In the forest,' answered the man, and the cruel brother guessed at once it must be his sister.

A great rage took possession of his soul as he thought of the girl whom he had tried to ruin being after all so much better off than himself, and he vowed that he would work her ill. Therefore that very afternoon he made his way to the palace and asked to see the king.

When he was admitted to his presence, he knelt down and touched the ground with his forehead, and the king bade him stand up and tell wherefore he had come.

'By the kindness of your heart have you been deceived, O king,' said he. 'Your son has married a girl who has lost a hand. Do you know why she has lost it? She was a witch, and has wedded three husbands, and each husband she has put to death with her arts. Then the people of the town cut off her hand, and turned her into the forest. And what I say is true, for her town is my town also.'

The king listened, and his face grew dark. Unluckily he had a hasty temper, and did not stop to reason, and, instead of sending to the town, and discovering people who knew his daughter-in-law and could have told him how hard she had worked and how poor she had been, he believed all the brother's lying words, and made the queen believe them too. Together they took counsel what they should do, and in the end they decided that they also would put her out of the town. But this did not content the brother.

'Kill her,' he said. 'It is no more than she deserves for daring to marry the king's son. Then she can do no more hurt to anyone.'

'We cannot kill her,' answered they; 'if we did, our son would assuredly kill us. Let us do as the others did, and put her out of the town.' And with this the envious brother was forced to be content.

The poor girl loved her husband very much, but just then the baby was more to her than all else in the world, and as long as she had him with her, she did not very much mind anything. So, taking her son on her arm, and hanging a little earthen pot for cooking round her neck, she left her house with its great peacock fans and slaves and seats of ivory, and plunged into the forest.

*　　*　　*

For a while she walked, not knowing whither she went, then by and by she grew tired, and sat under a tree to rest and to hush her baby to sleep. Suddenly she raised her eyes, and saw a snake wriggling from under the bushes towards her.

'I am a dead woman,' she said to herself, and stayed quite still, for indeed she was too frightened to move. In another minute the snake had reached her side, and to her surprise he spoke.

'Open your earthen pot, and let me go in. Save me from sun, and I will save you from rain,' and she opened the pot, and when the snake had slipped in, she put on the cover. Soon she beheld another snake coming after the other one, and when it had reached her it stopped and said, 'Did you see a small grey snake pass this way just now?'

'Yes,' she answered, 'it was going very quickly.'

'Ah, I must hurry and catch it up,' replied the second snake, and it hastened on.

When it was out of sight, a voice from the pot said:

'Uncover me,' and she lifted the lid, and the little grey snake slid rapidly to the ground.

'I am safe now,' he said. 'But tell me, where are you going?'

'I cannot tell you, for I do not know,' she answered. 'I am just wandering in the wood.'

'Follow me, and let us go home together,' said the snake, and the girl followed him through the forest and along the green paths, till they came to a great lake, where they stopped to rest.

'The sun is hot,' said the snake, 'and you have walked far. Take your baby and bathe in that cool place where the boughs of the tree stretch far over the water.'

'Yes, I will,' answered she, and they went in. The baby splashed and crowed with delight, and then he gave a spring and fell right in, down, down, down, and his mother could not find him, though she searched all among the reeds.

Full of terror, she made her way back to the bank, and called to the snake, 'My baby is gone! – he is drowned, and never shall I see him again.'

'Go in once more,' said the snake, 'and feel everywhere, even among the trees that have their roots in the water, lest perhaps he may be held fast there.'

Swiftly she went back and felt everywhere with her whole hand, even putting her fingers into the tiniest crannies, where a crab could hardly have taken shelter.

'No, he is not here,' she cried. 'How am I to live without him?' But the snake took no notice, and only answered, 'Put in your other arm too.'

'What is the use of that?' she asked, 'when it has no hand to feel with?' but all the same she did as she was bid, and in an instant the wounded arm touched something round and soft, lying between two stones in a clump of reeds.

'My baby, my baby!' she shouted, and lifted him up, merry and laughing, and not a bit hurt or frightened.

'Have you found him this time?' asked the snake.

'Yes, oh, yes!' she answered, 'and, why – why – I have got my hand back again!' and from sheer joy she burst into tears.

The snake let her weep for a little while, and then he said –

'Now we will journey on to my family, and we will all repay you for the kindness you showed to me.'

'You have done more than enough in giving me back my hand,' replied the girl; but the snake only smiled.

'Be quick, lest the sun should set,' he answered, and began to wriggle along so fast that the girl could hardly follow him.

By and by they arrived at the house in a tree where the snake lived, when he was not travelling with his father and mother. And he told them all his adventures, and how he had escaped from his enemy. The father and mother snake could not do enough to show their gratitude. They made their guest lie down on a hammock woven of the strong creepers which hung from bough to bough, till she was quite rested after her wanderings, while they watched the baby and gave him milk to drink from the cocoa-nuts which they persuaded their friends the monkeys to crack for them. They even managed to carry small fruit tied up in their tails for the baby's mother, who felt at last that she was safe and at peace. Not that she forgot her husband, for she often thought of him and longed to show him her son, and in the night she would sometimes lie awake and wonder where he was.

*　　*　　*

In this manner many weeks passed by.

And what was the prince doing?

Well, he had fallen very ill when he was on the furthest border of the kingdom, and he was nursed by some kind people who did not know who he was, so that the king and queen heard nothing about him. When he was better he made his way slowly home again, and into his father's palace, where he found a strange man standing behind the throne with the peacock's feathers. This was his wife's brother, whom the king had taken into high favour, though, of course, the prince was quite ignorant of what had happened.

For a moment the king and queen stared at their son, as if he had been unknown to them; he had grown so thin and weak during his illness that his shoulders were bowed like those of an old man.

'Have you forgotten me so soon?' he asked.

At the sound of his voice they gave a cry and ran towards him, and poured out questions as to what had happened, and why he looked like that. But the prince did not answer any of them.

'How is my wife?' he said. There was a pause.

Then the queen replied:

'She is dead.'

'*Dead*!' he repeated, stepping a little backwards. 'And my child?'

'He is dead too.'

The young man stood silent. Then he said, 'Show me their graves.'

At these words the king, who had been feeling rather uncomfortable, took heart again, for had he not prepared two beautiful tombs for his son to see, so that he might never, never guess what had been done to his wife? All these months the king and queen had been telling each other how good and merciful they had been not to take her brother's advice and to put her to death. But now, this somehow did not seem so certain.

Then the king led the way to the courtyard just behind the palace, and through the gate into a beautiful garden where stood two splendid tombs in a green space under the trees. The prince advanced alone, and, resting his head against the stone, he burst into tears. His father and mother stood silently behind with a curious pang in their souls which they did not quite understand. Could it be that they were ashamed of themselves?

But after a while the prince turned round, and walking past them into the palace he bade the slaves bring him mourning. For seven days no one saw him, but at the end of them he went out hunting, and helped his father rule his people as before. Only no one dared to speak to him of his wife and son.

At last one morning, after the girl had been lying awake all night thinking of her husband, she said to her friend the snake:

'You have all shown me much kindness, but now I am well again, and want to go home and hear some news of my husband, and if he still mourns for me!' Now the heart of the snake was sad at her words, but he only said:

'Yes, thus it must be; go and bid farewell to my father and mother, but if they offer you a present, see that you take nothing but my father's ring and my mother's casket.'

So she went to the parent snakes, who wept bitterly at the thought of losing her, and offered her gold and jewels as much as she could carry in remembrance of them. But the girl shook her head and pushed the shining heap away from her.

'I shall never forget you, never,' she said in a broken voice, 'but the only tokens I will accept from you are that little ring and this old casket.'

The two snakes looked at each other in dismay. The ring and the casket were the only things they did not want her to have. Then after a short pause they spoke.

'Why do you want the ring and casket so much? Who has told you of them?'

'Oh, nobody; it is just my fancy,' answered she. But the old snakes shook their heads and replied:

'Not so; it is our son who told you, and, as he said, so it must be. If you need food, or clothes, or a house, tell the ring and it will find them for you. And if you are unhappy or in danger, tell the casket and it will set things right.' Then they both gave her their blessing, and she picked up her baby and went her way.

She walked for a long time, till at length she came near the town where her husband and his father dwelt. Here she stopped under a grove of palm trees, and told the ring that she wanted a house.

'It is ready, mistress,' whispered a queer little voice which made her jump, and, looking behind her, she saw a lovely palace made of the finest woods, and a row of slaves with tall fans bowing before the door. Glad indeed was she to enter, for she was very tired, and, after eating a good supper of fruit and milk which she found in one of the rooms, she flung herself down on a pile of cushions and went to sleep with her baby beside her.

Here she stayed quietly, and every day the baby grew taller and stronger, and very soon he could run about and even talk. Of course the neighbours had a great deal to say about the house which had been built so quickly – so very quickly – on the outskirts of the town, and invented all kinds of stories about the rich lady who lived in it. And by and by, when the king returned with his son from the wars, some of these tales reached his ears.

'It is really very odd about that house under the palms,' he said to the queen; 'I must find out something of the lady whom no one ever sees. I dare say it is not a lady at all, but a gang of conspirators who want to get possession of my throne. Tomorrow I shall take my son and my chief ministers and insist on getting inside.'

Soon after sunrise next day the prince's wife was standing on a little hill behind the house, when she saw a cloud of dust coming through the town. A moment afterwards she heard faintly the roll of the drums that announced the king's presence, and saw a crowd of people approaching the grove of palms. Her heart beat fast. Could her husband be among them? In any case they must not discover her there; so just bidding the ring prepare some food for them, she ran inside, and bound a veil of golden gauze round her head and face. Then, taking the child's hand, she went to the door and waited.

In a few minutes the whole procession came up, and she stepped forward and begged them to come in and rest.

'Willingly,' answered the king; 'go first, and we will follow you.'

They followed her into a long dark room, in which was a

table covered with gold cups and baskets filled with dates and cocoa-nuts and all kinds of ripe yellow fruits, and the king and the prince sat upon cushions and were served by slaves, while the ministers, among whom she recognised her own brother, stood behind.

'Ah, I owe all my misery to him,' she said to herself. 'From the first he has hated me,' but outwardly she showed nothing. And when the king asked her what news there was in the town she only answered:

'You have ridden far; eat first, and drink, for you must be hungry and thirsty, and then I will tell you my news.'

'You speak sense,' answered the king, and silence prevailed for some time longer. Then he said:

'Now, lady, I have finished, and am refreshed, therefore tell me, I pray you, who you are, and whence you come? But, first, be seated.'

She bowed her head and sat down on a big scarlet cushion, drawing her little boy, who was asleep in a corner, on to her knee, and began to tell the story of her life. As her brother listened, he would fain have left the house and hidden himself in the forest, but it was his duty to wave the fan of peacock's feathers over the king's head to keep off the flies, and he knew he would be seized by the royal guards if he tried to desert his post. He must stay where he was, there was no help for it, and luckily for him the king was too much interested in the tale to notice that the fan had ceased moving, and that flies were dancing right on the top of his thick curly hair.

The story went on, but the story-teller never once looked at the prince, even through her veil, though he on his side never moved his eyes from her. When she reached the part where she had sat weeping in the tree, the king's son could restrain himself no longer.

'It is my wife,' he cried, springing to where she sat with the sleeping child in her lap. 'They have lied to me, and you are not dead after all, nor the boy either! But what has happened? Why did they lie to me? and why did you leave my house where you were safe?' And he turned and looked fiercely at his father.

'Let me finish my tale first, and then you will know,' answered she, throwing back her veil, and she told how her brother had come to the palace and accused her of being a witch, and had tried to persuade the king to slay her. 'But he would not do that,' she continued softly, 'and after all, if I had stayed on in your house, I should never have met the snake, nor have got my hand back again. So let us forget all about it, and be happy once more, for see! our son is growing quite a big boy.'

'And what shall be done to your brother?' asked the king, who was glad to think that someone had acted in this matter worse than himself.

'Put him out of the town,' answered she.

RAYAMATI, THE SAVIORESS

Jessica Amanda Salmonson

A RISHTAMENI WAS THE son of Queen Siva and King Samudravigaya, who ruled one part of the twin-city of Sauryapura. Arishtameni was gifted with an excellent voice. His body was well proportioned and strong as a bull, and his skin was black.

Across the river were another king and queen. They had a daughter named Rayamati. Her beauty was greatly pronounced and she shone like the Lightning-goddess Rodasi. She was an aggressive girl, just like Rodasi. She could drive a chariot swiftly and was expert at throwing spears. In the game yards she rode horses along with the boys of the palace, holding the reigns in her teeth and wielding swords in both hands. However, on official occasions and in privacy, she loved to wear jewelry and silk and was exceedingly vain of her perfect, slender body.

Many said the prince and the princess were two parts of the same divinity, a blue lotus prince and white lotus princess. Almost from birth, their marriage was assumed, though there had never been an official betrothal. In the twin-city, on both sides of the river, romantic tales were invented about them, these becoming favorites in the dens of the storytellers and in small, pictorial booklets sold near the shrines of erotic deities.

They had been kept from one another, and had only seen each other's portraits. Even so, they believed in the truth of the tales woven about themselves. Each was in love with the portrait of the other. Neither had ever seen such unsurpassed beauty except in mirrors. They knew indeed their spirits were as one. For this and future lives, they would be together.

When both came of age, King Samudravigaya sent a messenger to King Ugrasena asking if Princess Rayamati would be willing to marry Prince Arishtameni.

King Ugrasena replied, 'Have the prince come to our palace, and I will present him to my daughter.'

Prince Arishtameni was so excited by the news, he could hardly speak to anyone. His smile was a beacon in his dark face and his eyes gleamed like precious stones, lit by the celestial happiness of his spirit. He bathed in herbal essences and performed other essential ceremonies. He wore a splendid blue robe and was greatly ornamented with sapphires. Carrying a vajra in his left hand and a mace sceptor in his right, he mounted a well-appointed elephant and looked like a splendid jewel on the elephant's head.

The prince rode under a raised umbrella. He was fanned with fans made from peacock feathers, held by two languid youths who sat behind him on the elephant's massive back. He passed through the shallow fording-place of the river and entered the city of the princess.

How his heart was beating! Everything was going so well. An army of footsoldiers went beside the elephant, their swords like polished golden moons, their spears ornate and jewel-encrusted, sweeping to and fro in a rhythmic sword-dance. Musicians followed in their wake, playing heavenly songs, and all these many fine attendants chanted sweet divine hymns of love and glory.

Along the way to the palace, the prince spied many things his sensitized heart had not been opened to before that day. There were animals kept in cages and tethered to trees, all of them miserable and frightened. Some were domestic beasts, others were wild and beautiful, and none of them were happy. All were destined to be sacrificed to sundry divinities, or slaughtered for celebratory meals; for the marriage of a prince and princess required huge feasts and numerous holy offerings.

'It is for the sake of my marriage all these beasts are suffering,' thought Prince Arishtemeni. Unexpectedly, his heart was burdened with unhappiness. As uplifted as he had felt the moment before, that was how low his emotions plunged. The low-caste people who crowded the sides of the street to catch a glimpse of him, how thin they were! How pitiful the rags that served as clothing! How could they gaze upon him with admiration when they themselves were always left to suffer?

Seeing these things, his heart felt constricted. He could barely breathe. He stopped the procession and climbed down from his elephant, embracing an old, decrepit kandala woman, to her great joy. She opened wide her toothless mouth and laughed, and the prince heard a musical echo of her lost youth that rent his heart further.

Then he removed his many jewels, passing them among the poor people by the road, whose misery had never previously affected him so much. How selfish he had always been in the palace of his father and mother! Now that his eyes were opened, he felt only shame and horror.

He tore off his silken garments and traded them to those who in their whole lives had worn only ragged pieces of cloth. Then he fled to Mount Raivataka.

When Rayamati heard that the beautiful prince had taken vows as a Jain ascetic, gaiety forsook her shimmering brow. She lamented, 'From the time I was small, everyone said it was preordained that he and I should marry. We were acclaimed in the temples as made for one another. Songs were written for us though we had never met, and storybooks were passed among the children who learned to recite fables of our former lives together. Now my life has come to a shameful impasse. He would rather live as a beggar than succumb to this marriage. Why should I do otherwise? I will be a nun!'

Having made her decision, she brought her maids to her, and had them pluck all the hairs from her head, until her pate was red and bald. The lovely tresses became a sheaf of sinister black hay, taken away to be enshrined.

Many of her maids lamented their mistress's decision, wailing in the palace as though Rayamati were dead. Others remained sombre, plucking out their hairs so as to join her.

The princess founded an order of mendicant nuns who travelled about the countryside struggling by means of their simplicity to achieve perfection and influence others to seek salvation by the ascetic path. The fame of the order spread throughout the country, and the place of Rayamati's enshrined hair was forever after a center for virgin pilgrimage.

In time, even the companionship of her fellow nuns came to

represent a luxury to Rayamati. 'Luxury is against my vow,' she told her beloved sisters, and, kissing the tears from their cheeks, said farewell. She started barefoot toward the sacred Himalayas, thinking of far places where her royalty would be unknown and she could live untethered by family, pride, prestige, or ambition.

On her way to Mount Raivataka, she thirsted, and begged at a wayside inn. The innkeeper was struck by her beautiful holiness, and gave her a sweet beverage in a golden cup, insisting she keep even the cup, which was an heirloom, telling her to sell it to finance her journey. After quenching her thirst, she put the golden cup inside her beggar's pouch, then strolled onward.

An unexpected storm burst from heaven. She knew at once that heaven was angry that she had kept the golden cup. However, she offered no apologies, for she meant to abandon it at a poor shrine where it might finance a roof, and gain nothing by it herself.

The rain fell on her in torrents. Her ragged garment became drenched. Her feet were covered with mud. She took refuge in a cavern. In the darkness, she removed her dripping garment.

Farther back in the cavern sat Rathanemi, the brother of the prince who had renounced the world and his marriage. Rathanemi had been travelling home from a farther place and, like Rayamati, found it expedient to take refuge from the rain. He realized the mendicant nun, undressing in the entry, could not see him in the depths of the cavern. He was laughing in his heart to see her naked. Because she gleamed like the Lightning-goddess, and was as beautiful as Sri Laksmi the Goddess of Fortune, the young prince could not help but fall in love with her at once.

Rayamati's peace of mind became disturbed. She gazed about, then detected Prince Rathanemi. She grew fretful upon realizing she was naked and alone with a young man. Folding one arm over her breasts, she squatted down and reached for her wet garment.

The prince put one foot on her garment so that she could not reclaim it. 'Dear, beautiful lady! I am Prince Rathanemi. Accept me for your lover and you will never have cause for regret. Come, let us enjoy pleasures together! After we have enjoyed one another, O slender one, you may reclaim the ascetic path at your leisure. Please, do not resist, for I love you greatly.'

Rayamati perceived that she must defend herself. As the Lightning-goddess was called the Spear of the Storm Clouds, so was Rayamati strong and able if violence was inescapable. She took a defensive posture, ready to maintain her honor and her vows. She said, 'If you were as beautiful as a god, I should have no desire for you. Remove your foot from my garment. Let us not be rude to one another while we await the passing of the storm.'

But Rathanemi gazed at her with doting eyes, and kept his foot upon her garment. As he moved neither to relieve her discomfort, nor to impose himself further, she relaxed somewhat. She took from her beggar's pouch the golden cup she had received as an offering from the wayside inn. Into the cup she vomited the sweet beverage. This she handed to the prince, saying, 'Drink! It was excellent this afternoon, sweet and refreshing.'

The prince drew away from her, disgusted. Rayamati said, 'Your elder brother vomited me out of his life to become an ascetic, as I have vomited the sweet brew into this golden cup. As for you, a strong and famous knight, fie! You wanted to quaff the vomited Rayamati, yet you reject Rayamati's vomited beverage! Rather than lower yourself so much, renounce your life at once!'

Having heard the beautiful and chastising words of the well-spoken and virtuous nun, Rathanemi was driven to repent his life, though until that moment he had imagined no flaw in his pursuits. He took vows and thereafter practiced austerities. When he achieved enlightenment late in life, he was welcomed into heaven by a company of divinities. He said, 'I am as you see me because of one who was wise and virtuous and turned me from the path of pleasure. Tell me, has she come to this place before me?'

'Alas,' said the company of divinities, 'it will be long before we have the pleasure of her presence. She has elected to remain upon the earth and save others. Rayamati is above us and below us. She is within us and without us.

She is in our past, our present, and our future. She is everywhere, and nowhere, and can neither be seen, nor forgotten.'

Thus said the divinities.

ECHO AND NARCISSUS

A. R. Hope-Moncrieff

T O THE RIVER-GOD Cephissus was born a son named
Narcissus, who seemed to his fond mother the most
beautiful of children, and anxiously she sought from the blind
prophet Tiresias to know his fate.

'Will he live to old age?' she asked; to which the dark-seeing
prophet made answer – 'If he shall not have known himself!'

What these mystic words meant, time only would show. The
boy grew up rarely beautiful, not only in his mother's eyes but
in all that were not blind. There was no maiden but cast loving
looks upon him; and less favoured youths must envy the charms
that, alas! made Narcissus vain above all sons of earth. Blushes,
sighs, and sparkling eyes were heeded by him but as tributes
to his loveliness; and when he had bloomed to the flower of
manhood, he was in love with himself alone.

Shunning all who would fain have been his companions,
it was his wont to walk apart in solitary places, lost in
admiration of the graceful form which he thought no eye
worthy to behold but his own. One day, as he wandered
through a wood, unawares he was spied by the wood-nymph
Echo, who loved him at first sight, but was dumb to open
her heart till he should ask its secret. For on her a strange
fate had been laid: Hera, displeased by her chattering tongue,
took away from her the power of speech unless in answer to
some other voice. So now, when Echo slunk lightly among the
thickets, shadowing the steps of that beautiful youth, eager as
she was to accost him, she must wait for him to speak first,
nor durst she show herself but at his desire. But he, given
up to his sweet thoughts of self, strolled on silently, and the
maiden followed him lovingly, unseen, till at last, as he halted

to drink from a cool spring, his ear was caught by a rustle in the branches.

'Who is there?' he exclaimed, raising his eyes to peer into the green shade.

'*There!*' came echoed back; but he saw not who spoke.

'What do you fear?' he asked; and the invisible voice answered –

'*Fear!*'

'Come forth here!' he cried in amazement, when thus his words were given mockingly back to him; and still the voice took no shape.

'*Here!*' was the reply; and now glided forth the blushing Echo, to make as if she would have thrown her arms round his neck.

But in the crystal pool the youth had caught another form that better pleased his eyes; and he roughly brushed away the enamoured nymph, with a harsh word.

'What brings you?'

'*You!*' she faltered, shrinking back from his frown.

'Begone!' he bid her angrily. 'There can be nothing between such as you and the fair Narcissus.'

'*Narcissus!*' sighed Echo, scarcely heard, and stole away on tiptoe to hide her shameful looks in the deep shade, breathing a silent prayer that this proud youth might learn for himself what it was to love in vain.

When left alone, Narcissus turned eagerly back to that spring in which he believed to have seen a fairer face. Like a silver mirror it lay, shining in sunlight, framed by a ring of flowery plants, as if to guard it from the plashing tread of cattle. On his knees at the edge, he stretched himself over the bright well, and there looked down upon a face and form so entrancingly beautiful, that he was ready to leap into the water beside it. A priceless statue it seemed, of one at his own blooming age, every limb chiselled like life, with features as of breathing marble, and curling locks that hung above ivory shoulders.

'Who art thou that hast been made so fair?' cried Narcissus; and the lips of the image moved, yet now came no answer.

He smiled, and was smiled back to. He flushed for delight, then the face in the water was overspread with rosy blood, its eyes sparkling like his own. He stretched out his hands towards it, and so the beautiful form beckoned to him; but as soon as his touch broke the clear surface, it vanished like a dream, to return in all its enchantment while he was content to gaze motionless, then again growing dim beneath the tears of vexation he shed into the water.

'I am not one to be despised,' he pleaded with his coy charmer, 'but such a one as mortal maidens and nymphs, too, have loved in vain.'

'*Vain!*' resounded the sad voice of Echo from the woods.

Again and again he leaned down to clasp that lovely shadow in his arms, but always it eluded him; and when he spoke entreating it to his embrace, it but simulated his gestures in unfeeling silence. Maddened by so strong allurement of his own likeness, he could not tear himself away from the mirror in which it ever mocked his yearning fancy. 'Alas!' was his constant cry, that always came sighing back from the retreats of the woeful nymph. Hour after hour, day after day, he hung over the pool's brink, nor cared to let food pass his lips, crying all in vain for that imaginary object of adoration, till at last his heart ceased to throb with despair, and he lay still among the water lilies that made his shroud. The gods themselves could not but be touched with pity for so fair a corse; and thus was Narcissus transformed into the flower that bears his name.

As for poor Echo, who had invoked such punishment on his cold heart, she gained nothing but grief that her prayer was heard. Out of sight, she pined away for despised love, till all left of her was an idle voice. And that still haunts the rocks where never since can she be seen by startled eyes; but always she must be allowed the last word.

VASAVADATTA
THE COURTESAN

Jessica Amanda Salmonson

T HERE WAS A courtesan of noble bearing and extraordinary
beauty. Her name was Vasavadatta. In the same city was a
youth named Upagupta who, though only a perfumer's son, was
perpetually rooting about in the regions of divine knowledge,
and excelled at occult learning. Everyone who saw him thought
that he was splendidly beautiful, therefore Vasavadatta became
curious to meet him. She sent her serving girl with a message for
Upagupta. When her maid returned, Vasavadatta said, 'Dear
child! Have you robbed that simple perfumer's son? You bring
back so many perfumes!'

'Dear mistress,' said the girl, 'Upagupta is surely the
handsomest man in the world! He is clever and charming.
He asked me to bring these perfumes to you as gifts, and to
apologize in his behalf, but he is certain the time is not yet
right for you to meet him.'

Vasavadatta's interest was piqued, and she developed a firm
longing for Upagupta. Indeed, she felt herself truly to be in love
with a youth as yet unmet. She sent her maid again, to announce
that Vasavadatta would be coming on such-and-such a night to
make love to Upagupta. Once more the maid returned with
starry eyes, and handed over to the courtesan twenty pieces
of gold, and Upagupta's message, 'It is not yet the time that
we should meet.'

'Dear child,' said Vasavadatta to her maid. 'Upagupta must
have heard somehow that I am the nation's most costly courtesan, and as an honest man, he lacks the five hundred pieces of
gold. Hurry, go tell him never to worry about this amount, for

I seek only to pursue pleasure with him.' But when the maid returned, Upagupta had reasserted his feeling that the time was not right for them to meet.

Some while later, a caravaneer came up from the north country to sell five hundred horses, all of them strong and swift. Having gained a trunk of gold from his sales, he then asked, 'Who is the best courtesan of your city?' He was told at once that Vasavadatta was the finest courtesan not only of the city, but of the nation. He gathered together five hundred pieces of gold, but more than that, he selected an array of excellent presents and set out for the house of Vasavadatta.

Messengers arrived to tell the courtesan of the caravaneer who would soon arrive with gifts and gold. Vasavadatta informed her client of the moment that he must leave immediately. He was a rowdy, unpleasant young man, but as the son of a guildmaster, he was spoiled, rich, full of himself, and accustomed to having his way. He refused to be dismissed. So Vasavadatta gave a shrill whistle which called into her house the seven armed maidens who people called 'the heavenly demonesses.' They beat the guildmaster's son black and blue and threw him in a cess pool. He lay in it a long time unable to climb out, all the while forming plans of vengeance.

When the relatives of the guildmaster's son learned of his mistreatment by a courtesan, they pressured the governor on the youth's behalf. In response, the governor sent soldiers to Vasavadatta's house. They cut off her hands, feet, nose, and ears, then threw her into the cremation grounds. She lay there in her blood, attended by her weeping serving maid. The news spread swiftly, and Upagupta heard of it. He said to himself, 'She sought me for sensual purposes, but now her hands, feet, nose and ears have been cut off. She has lost pride, passion, and joy. Now is the moment to discover her true nature.'

When Vasavadatta's maid saw the handsome youth coming toward the cremation grounds, she told her suffering mistress, 'Upagupta, to whom you sent me time and again, is drawing near.'

'Quickly,' said Vasavadatta, 'gather up my hands, feet, nose, and ears and place them where they belong about my body. Then cover me with a gown.'

Upagupta came and sat down beside her in the smoky

cemetery. Vasavadatta asked him, 'Have you come at last out of passion and desire? But here I am on the ground, laying in my blood, afflicted and suffering. Many times I sent for you, and you sent word back, telling me, "Sister, it is not yet time for us to meet." Today I am not so well disposed to sensual pleasures. Why have you waited until my lustre is gone?'

Upagupta said, 'How could I, seeking the road away from the cycle of rebirths, come to you for pleasure? Now sharp swords have cut from you all vanity and pleasure. I come not with desire, but with compassion. I wish to know your intrinsic nature.'

Vasavadatta said, 'I would like for you to have seen this body of mine when it was still a shining lotus, bedecked in silks and jewelry. How ashamed I am that you should see me, instead, plastered with blood and funereal ashes. Am I not a fearful thing, that once gave only joy and play and wonder?'

'I see nothing fearful in you,' said Upagupta. 'When you were covered in ornaments and excelled in all arts conducive to pleasure, none could see who you were. Now, free from trappings, your true form may be seen, and I think you are beautiful. I cannot understand that people love gross flesh, for it is but a living carcass. Why are people so attached to sinew, blood, and skin? When we observe those things that are beautiful on the outside, we know nothing of the inner being. They may well be corrupt and horrible. But a corpse that is obviously vile, what false sentiment need we suppress? Therefore we can see that part which was always good. Truly, in my father's trade, I have learned that a rich perfume can hide a foul odor. When tears of sorrow wash away falsity, what remains is the truth of our lives, a putrescent body that once we cherished to no end but death. Having given up desire, we lose also weariness, sadness, and suffering. We come to the tranquil center of the cosmic yoni, the pure light of nirvana.'

Hearing these words, and many others in their night-long discourse, Vasavadatta also came to be disgusted by the realm of desire. She gained a pure understanding of Truth, receiving the fruits of a non-returner's wisdom. An hour before dawn, she said, 'You have shown me the hidden road away from the heavily travelled path to the lower states of being. Until now, the light has been kept from me, yoked as I have been to pleasures and to sorrows. The meritorious realm is opening up to me! I can see the center of the cosmic yoni! Momentarily, blessed enlightened saint, I will leave your company. Glad I am to know that you will not weep for me, knowing as you do that my refuge is dazzling as a freshly opened lotus.'

Soon thereafter Vasavadatta arrived among the deities. The whole of the country saw the heavens open up to receive her splendid spirit. Upagupta came among them with the pieces of her body, to which the people paid homage. She was canonized as the Courtesan of the Noble Truth, whereas her persecutors were forgotten, and few knew even of the splendid deed of the Seven Heavenly Demonesses who had served Vasavadatta.

A few days after their mistress's escape to heaven, the seven demonesses broke into the house of the guildmaster by night, clubbing the whole family to death, sparing only the guildmaster's son, who lived many years without his ears, nose, feet, or hands, then was reborn to the lower realm, experiencing further torments.

PART VII:
WONDERS AND MYSTERIES

THE COURTESAN
WHO WORKED A MIRACLE

Jessica Amanda Salmonson

A SAGE STOOD BY the Ganges River. He had gathered about him a great crowd of admirers. All the citizens of the city of Pataliputta were there, as were many travellers from afar. Even the king of Pataliputta was in attendance.

'Only by good deeds and noble thoughts,' said the sage, 'are great things possible. By means of an Act of Truth, a king may ride in a chariot of fire drawn by lions. What is truth without action? A dam can be built to hold back a river, but can Truth do this without action?'

'Impossible!' the populace agreed. 'Truth requires action!'

But one voice was heard in the moment after the crowd had spoken together. That one voice came from Bindumati, a certain courtesan. She said, 'Truth requires nothing but itself to prove its power.'

All eyes fell upon her, as though she had blasphemed. She stepped forth from the crowd and stood at the river's edge. As even the sage challenged her with his eyes, she explained herself.

'Here I am, a lowly harlot in the city of Pataliputta. By the sale of my body do I make a livelihood. It keeps me from poverty, but it does not raise me to a noble status. Am I steeped in noble deeds? Could I, even aided by a million strong hands, turn back this river by means of a concerted action?'

They agreed she could not perform such a deed even with a million hands, but insisted also that it was because she lacked the purity required for action to be equated with truth.

'Observe, then,' said Bindumati, 'what faith in the Truth, rather than in truthful action, can achieve!'

Bindumati began to recite sacred hymns. At her back the mighty Ganges began to roil and rage. In a din of waves and whirlpools, it rolled itself backward, and flowed toward the Himalayas.

The king cried out, 'How is it possible the mighty Ganges is flowing backward?'

Filled with profound emotion, he hurried forth to the courtesan and asked her, 'Is it true that by faith you have used Truth to force back these waters?'

'It is true, sire.'

The king asked, 'How is it you have power of this magnitude, but live as a harlot? I have taken the Word to heart, and carried it forward by my actions. Yet beside you, my authority is insignificant, for never could I have turned back the mighty river.'

'It is not my power,' said Bindumati. 'It is the power of Truth.'

The king asked, 'How can that power be in a woman who lives without restraint, who plunders fools, who is full of transgressions?'

'That is just the kind of creature I am,' said Bindumati, as though she were proud of it. 'Therefore even my doubtful nature embodies Truth, which by itself can turn the worlds of divinity and humanity upside down. I live by Great Truth, so the waters turned back at my request.'

'What is this Great Truth that requires no further action?'

'O King, whosoever comes to me for pleasure, and carrying gold, whether he is a brahman, a tradesman, a prince, or a servant, I regard them as one. I make no distinctions. If I am told he is a slave, or an outcast, or an imbecile, I do not despise him. I neither fawn on him, nor dislike him; I do service to whoever buys me. This, O King, is the Truth by which I have turned back the Ganges.'

Then by raising her hands, she let the Ganges return to its normal path.

THE KING'S SON AND
THE WHITE-BEARDED SCOLOG

Jeremiah Curtin

NOT IN OUR time, nor the time of our fathers, but long ago, there lived an old king in Erin. This king had but the one son, and the son had risen up to be a fine strong hero; no man in the kingdom could stand before him in combat.

The queen was dead, and the king was gloomy and bitter in himself because old age was on him. The strength had gone from his limbs, and gladness from his heart. No matter what people said, they could not drive sorrow from him.

One day the king called up his son, and this is what he said to him, 'You are of age to marry. We cannot tell how long I'll be here, and it would cheer and delight me to see your wife; she might be a daughter to me in my last days.'

'I am willing to obey you,' said the son; 'but I know no woman that I care for. I have never seen any one that I would marry.'

With that, the old king sent for a druid, and said, 'You must tell where my son can find the right bride for himself. You must tell us what woman he should marry.'

'There is but one woman,' said the druid, 'who can be the right wife for your son, and she is the youngest daughter of the white-bearded scolog; she is the wisest young woman in the world, and has the most power.'

'Where does her father live, and how are we to settle it?' asked the king of the druid.

'I have no knowledge of the place where that scolog lives,' said the druid, 'and there is no one here who knows. Your son must go himself, and walk the world till he finds the young woman.

If he finds her and gets her, he'll have the best bride that ever
came to a king's son.'

'I am willing to go in search of the scolog's daughter,' said
the young man, 'and I'll never stop till I find her.'

With that, he left his father and the druid, and never stopped
till he went to his foster-mother and told her the whole story –
told her the wish of his father, and the advice the old druid had
given him.

'My three brothers live on the road you must travel,' said
the foster-mother; 'and the eldest one knows how to find that
scolog, but without the friendship of all of them, you'll not be
able to make the journey. I'll give you something that will gain
their good-will for you.'

With that, she went to an inner room, and made three cakes of
flour and baked them. When the three were ready, she brought
them out, and gave them to the young man.

'When you come to my youngest brother's castle,' said she,
'he will rush at you to kill you, but do you strike him on the
breast with one of the cakes; that minute he'll be friendly, and
give you good entertainment. The second brother and the eldest
will meet you like the youngest.'

On the following morning, the king's son left a blessing with
his foster-mother, took one for the road from her, and went
away carrying the three cakes with him. He travelled that day
with great swiftness over hills and through valleys, past great
towns and small villages, and never stopped nor stayed till he
came in the evening to a very large castle. In he went, and inside
was a woman before him.

'God save you!' said he to the woman.

'God save yourself!' said she; 'and will you tell me what
brought you the way, and where are you going?'

'I came here,' said the king's son, 'to see the giant of this
castle, and to speak with him.'

'Be said by me,' replied the woman, 'and go away out of this
without waiting for the giant.'

'I will not go without seeing him,' said the king's son. 'I have
never set eyes on a giant, and I'll see this one.'

'I pity you,' said the woman; 'your time is short in this life.
You'll not be long without seeing the giant, and it's not much
you'll see in this world after setting eyes on him; and it would

be better for you to take a drink of wine to give you strength before he comes.'

The king's son had barely swallowed the wine when he heard a great noise beyond the castle.

'Fee, faw, foh!' roared someone, in a thundering voice.

The king's son looked out; and what should he see but the giant with a shaggy goat going out in front of him and another coming on behind, a dead hag above on his shoulder, a great hog of a wild boar under his left arm, and a yellow flea on the club which he held in his right hand before him.

'I don't know will I blow you into the air or put my foot on you,' said the giant, when he set eyes on the king's son. With that, he threw his load to the ground, and was making at his visitor to kill him when the young man struck the giant on the breast with one of the three cakes which he had from the foster-mother.

That minute the giant knew who was before him, and called out, 'Isn't it the fine welcome I was giving my sister's son from Erin?'

With that, he changed entirely, and was so glad to see the king's son that he didn't know what to do for him or where to put him. He made a great feast that evening; the two ate and drank with contentment and delight. The giant was so pleased with the king's son that he took him to his own bed. He wasn't three minutes in the bed when he was sound asleep and snoring. With every breath that the giant took in, he drew the king's son into his mouth and as far as the butt of his tongue; with every breath that he sent out, he drove him to the rafters of the castle, and the king's son was that way going up and down between the bed and the roof until daybreak, when the giant let a breath out of him, and closed his mouth; next moment the king's son was down on his lips.

'What are you doing to me?' cried the giant.

'Nothing,' said the king's son; 'but you didn't let me close an eye all the night. With every breath you let out of you, you drove me up to the rafters; and with every breath you took in, you drew me into your mouth and as far as the butt of your tongue.'

'Why didn't you wake me?'

'How could I wake you when time failed me to do it?'

'Oh, then, sister's son from Erin,' said the giant, 'it's the poor night's rest I gave you; but if you had a bad bed, you must have a good breakfast.'

With that, the giant rose, and the two ate the best breakfast that could be had out of Erin.

After breakfast, the king's son took the giant's blessing with him, and left his own behind. He travelled all that day with great speed and without halt or rest, till he came in the evening to the castle of the second giant. In front of the door was a pavement of sharp razors, edges upward, a pavement which no man could walk on. Long, poisonous needles, set as thickly as bristles in a brush, were fixed, points downward, under the lintel of the door, and the door was low.

The king's son went in with one start over the razors and under the needles, without grazing his head or cutting his feet. When inside, he saw a woman before him.

'God save you!' said the king's son.

'God save yourself!' said the woman.

The same conversation passed between them then as passed between himself and the woman in the first castle.

'God help you!' said the woman, when she heard his story. ' 'Tis not long you'll be alive after the giant comes. Here's a drink of wine to strengthen you.'

Barely had he the wine swallowed when there was a great noise behind the castle, and the next moment the giant came in with a thundering and rattling.

'Who is this that I see?' asked he, and with that, he sprang at the stranger to put the life out of him; but the king's son struck him on the breast with the second cake which he got from his foster-mother. That moment the giant knew him, and called out, 'A strange welcome I had for you, sister's son from Erin, but you'll get good treatment from me now.'

The giant and the king's son made three parts of that night. One part they spent in telling tales, the second in eating and drinking, and the third in sound, sweet slumber.

Next morning the young man went away after breakfast, and never stopped till he came to the castle of the third giant; and a beautiful castle it was, thatched with the down of cotton grass, the roof was as white as milk, beautiful to look at from afar or near by. The third giant was as angry at meeting him as the other two; but when he was struck in the breast with the third cake, he was as kind as the best man could be.

When they had taken supper together, the giant said to his sister's son, 'Will you tell me what journey you are on?'

'I will, indeed,' said the king's son; and he told his whole story from beginning to end.

'It is well that you told me,' said the giant, 'for I can help you; and if you do what I tell, you'll finish your journey in safety. At midday tomorrow you'll come to a lake; hide in the rushes that are growing at one side of the water. You'll not be long there when twelve swans will alight near the rushes and take the crests from their heads; with that, the swan skins will fall from them, and they will rise up the most beautiful women that you have ever set eyes on. When they go in to bathe, take the crest of the youngest, put it in your bosom next the skin, take the eleven others and hold them in your hand. When the young women come out, give the eleven crests to their owners; but when the twelfth comes, you'll not give her the crest unless she carries you to her father's castle in Ardilawn Dreeachta (High Island of Enchantment). She will refuse, and say that strength fails her to carry you, and she will beg for the crest. Be firm, and keep it in your bosom; never give it up till she promises to take you. She will do that when she sees there is no help for it.'

Next morning the king's son set out after breakfast, and at midday he was hidden in the rushes. He was barely there when the swans came. Everything happened as the giant had said, and the king's son followed his counsels.

When the twelve swans came out of the lake, he gave the eleven crests to the older ones, but kept the twelfth, the crest of the youngest, and gave it only when she promised to carry him to her father's. The moment she put the crest on her head, she was in love with the king's son. When she came in sight of the island, however much she loved him when they started from the lakeside, she loved him twice as much now. She came to the ground at some distance from the castle, and said to the young man at parting –

'Thousands of kings' sons and champions have come to give greeting to my father at the door of his castle, but every man of them perished. You will be saved if you obey me. Stand with your right foot inside the threshold and your left foot outside;

put your head under the lintel. If your head is inside, my father will cut it from your shoulders; if it is outside, he will cut it off also. If it is under the lintel when you cry "God save you!" he'll let you go in safety.'

They parted there; she went to her own place and he went to the scolog's castle, put his right foot inside the threshold, his left foot outside, and his head under the lintel. 'God save you!' called he to the scolog.

'A blessing on you!' cried the scolog, 'but my curse on your teacher. I'll give you lodgings tonight, and I'll come to you myself in the morning'; and with that he sent a servant with the king's son to a building outside. The servant took a bundle of straw with some turf and potatoes, and, putting these down inside the door, said, 'Here are bed, supper, and fire for you.'

The king's son made no use of food or bed, and he had no need of them, for the scolog's daughter came soon after, spread a cloth, took a small bundle from her pocket, and opened it. That moment the finest food and drink were there before them.

The king's son ate and drank with relish, and good reason he had after the long journey. When supper was over, the young woman whittled a small shaving from a staff which she brought with her; and that moment the finest bed that any man could have was there in the room.

'I will leave you now,' said she; 'my father will come early in the morning to give you a task. Before he comes, turn the bed over; 'twill be a shaving again, and then you can throw it into the fire. I will make you a new bed tomorrow.'

With that, she went away, and the young man slept till daybreak. Up he sprang, then turned the bed over, made a shaving of it, and burned it. It was not long till the scolog came, and this is what he said to the king's son, 'I have a task for you today, and I hope you will be able to do it. There is a lake on my land not far from this, and a swamp at one side of it. You are to drain that lake and dry the swamp for me, and have the work finished this evening; if not, I will take the head from you at sunset. To drain the lake, you are to dig through a neck of land two miles in width; here is a good spade, and I'll show you the place where you're to use it.'

The king's son went with the scolog, who showed the ground, and then left him.

'What am I to do?' said the king's son. 'Sure, a thousand men couldn't dig that land out in ten years, and they working night and day; how am I to do it between this and sunset?'

However it was, he began to dig; but if he did, for every sod he threw out, seven sods came in, and soon he saw that, in place of mending his trouble, 'twas making it worse he was. He cast aside the spade then, sat down on the sod heap, and began to lament. He wasn't long there when the scolog's daughter came with a cloth in her hand and the small bundle in her pocket.

'Why are you lamenting there like a child?' asked she of the king's son.

'Why shouldn't I lament when the head will be taken from me at sunset?'

' 'Tis a long time from this to sunset. Eat your breakfast first of all; see what will happen then,' said she. Taking out the little bundle, she put down before him the best breakfast a man could have. While he was eating, she took the spade, cut out one sod, and threw it away. When she did that, every spadeful of earth in the neck of land followed the first spadeful; the whole neck of land was gone, and before midday there wasn't a spoonful of water in the lake or the swamp – the whole place was dry.

'You have your head saved today, whatever you'll do tomorrow,' said she, and she left him.

Toward evening the scolog came, and, meeting the king's son, cried out, 'You are the best man that ever came the way, or that ever I expected to look at.'

The king's son went to his lodging. In the evening the scolog's daughter came with supper, and made a bed for him as good as the first one. Next morning the king's son rose at daybreak, destroyed his bed, and waited to see what would happen.

The scolog came early, and said, 'I have a field outside, a mile long and a mile wide, with a very tall tree in the middle of it. Here are two wedges, a sharp axe, and a fine new drawing knife. You are to cut down the tree, and make from it barrels to cover the whole field. You are to make the barrels and fill them with water before sunset, or the head will be taken from you.'

The king's son went to the field, faced the tree, and gave it a blow with his axe; but if he did, the axe bounded back from the trunk, struck him on the forehead, stretched him on the flat of his back, and raised a lump on the place where it hit him. He gave three blows, was served each time in the same way, and had three lumps on his forehead. He was rising from the third blow, the life almost gone from him, and he crying bitterly, when the scolog's daughter came with his breakfast. While he was eating the breakfast, she struck one little chip from the tree; that chip became a barrel, and then the whole tree turned into barrels, which took their places in rows, and covered the field. Between the rows there was just room for a man to walk. Not a barrel but was filled with water. From a chip she had in her hand, the young woman made a wooden dipper, from another chip she made a pail, and said to the king's son –

'You'll have these in your two hands, and be walking up and down between the rows of barrels, putting a little water into this and a little into that barrel. When my father comes, he will see you at the work and invite you to the castle tonight, but you are not to go with him. You will say that you are content to lodge tonight where you lodged the other nights.' With that, she went away, and the king's son was going around among the barrels pouring a little water into one and another of them, when the scolog came.

'You have the work done,' said he, 'and you must come to the castle for the night.'

'I am well satisfied to lodge where I am, and to sleep as I slept since I came here,' said the young man, and the scolog left him.

The young woman brought the supper, and gave a fresh bed. Next morning the scolog came the third time, and said, 'Come with me now; I have a third task for you.' With that, the two went to a quarry.

'Here are tools,' said the scolog, pointing to a crowbar, a pickaxe, a trowel, and every implement used in quarrying and building. 'You are to quarry stones today, and build between this and sunset the finest and largest castle in the world, with outhouses and stables, with cellars and kitchens. There must be cooks, with men and women to serve; there must be dishes and utensils of every kind and furniture of every description; not a thing is to be lacking, or the head will go from you this evening at sunset.'

The scolog went home; and the king's son began to quarry with crowbar and pickaxe, and though he worked hard, the morning was far gone when he had three small pieces of stone quarried.

He sat down to lament.

'Why are you lamenting this morning?' asked the scolog's daughter, who came now with his breakfast.

'Why shouldn't I lament when the head will be gone from me this evening? I am to quarry stones, and build the finest castle in the world before sunset. Ten thousand men couldn't do the work in ten years.'

'Take your breakfast,' said the young woman; 'you'll see what to do after that.'

While he was eating, she quarried one stone; and the next moment every stone in the quarry that was needed took its place in the finest and largest castle ever built, with outhouses and cellars and kitchens. A moment later, all the people were there, men and women, with utensils of all kinds. Everything was finished but a small spot at the principal fireplace.

'The castle is ready,' said the scolog's daughter; 'your head will stay with you today, and there are no more tasks before you at present. Here is a trowel and mortar; you will be finishing this small spot at the fire when my father comes. He will invite you to his castle tonight, and you are to go with him this time. After dinner, he will seat you at a table, and throw red wheat on it from his pocket. I have two sisters older than I am; they and I will fly in and alight on the table in the form of three pigeons, and we'll be eating the wheat; my father will tell you to choose one of his three daughters to marry. You'll know me by this: there will be a black quill in one of my wings. I'll show it; choose me.'

All happened as the scolog's daughter said; and when the king's son was told to make his choice in the evening, he chose the pigeon that he wanted. The three sprang from the table, and when they touched the floor, they were three beautiful women. A dish priest and a wooden clerk were brought to the castle, and the two were married that evening.

A month passed in peace and enjoyment; but the king's son wished to go back now to Erin to his father. He told the wife what he wanted; and this is what she said to him, 'My father will refuse you nothing. He will tell you to go, though he doesn't wish to part with you. He will give you his blessing; but this is all pretence, for he will follow us to kill us. You must have a horse for the journey, and the right horse. He will send a man with you to three fields. In the first field are the finest horses that you have ever laid eyes on; take none of them. In the second field are splendid horses, but not so fine as in the first field; take none of these either. In the third field, in the farthest corner, near the river, is a long-haired, shaggy, poor little old mare; take that one. The old mare is my mother. She has great power, but not so much as my father, who made her what she is, because she opposed him. I will meet you beyond the hill, and we shall not be seen from the castle.'

The king's son brought the mare; and when they mounted her, wings came from her sides, and she was the grandest steed ever seen. Away she flew over mountains, hills, and valleys, till they came to the seashore, and then they flew over the sea.

When the servant man went home, and the scolog knew what horse they had chosen, he turned himself and his two daughters into red fire, and shot after the couple. No matter how swiftly the mare moved, the scolog travelled faster, and was coming up. When the three reached the opposite shore of the sea, the daughter saw her father coming, and turned the mare into a small boat, the king's son into a fisherman, and made a fishing-rod of herself. Soon the scolog came, and his two daughters with him.

'Have you seen a man and a woman passing the way riding on a mare?' asked he of the fisherman.

'I have,' said the fisherman. 'You'll soon overtake them.'

On went the scolog; and he never stopped till he raced around the whole world, and came back to his own castle.

'Oh, then, we were the fools,' said the scolog to his daughters. 'Sure, they were the fisherman, the boat, and the rod.'

Off they went a second time in three balls of red fire; and they were coming near again when the scolog's youngest daughter made a spinning-wheel of her mother, a bundle of flax of herself, and an old woman of her husband. Up rushed the scolog, and spoke to the spinner, 'Have you seen a mare pass the way and two on her back?' asked he.

'I have, indeed,' said the old woman; 'and she is not far ahead of you.'

Away rushed the scolog; and he never stopped till he raced around the whole world, and came back to his own castle a second time.

'Oh, but we were the fools!' said the scolog. 'Sure, they were the old woman with the spinning-wheel and the flax, and they are gone from us now; for they are in Erin, and we cannot take our power over the border, nor work against them unless they are outside of Erin. There is no use in our following them; we might as well stay where we are.'

The scolog and his daughters remained in the castle at Ardilawn of Enchantment; but the king's son rode home on the winged mare, with his wife on a pillion behind him.

When near the castle of the old king in Erin, the couple dismounted, and the mare took her own form of a woman. She could do that in Erin. The three never stopped till they went to the old king. Great was the welcome before them; and if ever there was joy in a castle, there was joy then in that one.

THE ADVENTURE OF
THE HOLY GRAIL

Alfred J. Church

I T FELL OUT on the Feast of Pentecost in a certain year when
the King and his knights were come back from worshipping
in the Minster they saw on the seats of the Round Table letters
newly written in letters of gold, 'Here ought to sit this one,' and
the name of a knight following, and on each seat a name. But on
the Perilous Seat was written, 'When four hundred winters and
fifty and four shall be accomplished then shall this seat be filled.'
Then Sir Lancelot, making count of the years, cried out, 'Then
ought this seat to be filled this same day, for this is the Feast of
Pentecost in the four hundred and fifty-fourth year. But I would
counsel that these letters be not seen, till the knight that is to fill
it be come.' So, by consent, was made a cloth of silk to cover
the seat. Then would the King have gone to his dinner. But Sir
Kaye the Seneschal said, 'If you go now to meat, you break the
old custom of the court, which is that you wait till you hear some
adventure.' While he spake there came in a squire, who said,
'Sir, I bring to you marvellous tidings.' 'What be they?' said
the King. 'There is floating on the river, as I have seen with
mine own eyes,' said he, 'a great stone, and in the stone is a
sword sticking.' Said the King, 'I will see this marvel.' So he
went to the river, and all his knights went with him. And when
they were come to the river, they saw the stone floating, and it
was like to red marble, and in it was stuck a fair and rich sword
on the handle of which was written in fine letters of gold, 'No
man shall draw me hence, but he only by whose side I ought to
hang, and he shall be the best knight in the world.' Said King
Arthur, 'Lancelot, this sword is surely yours; you are the best

knight in the world.' But Sir Lancelot answered soberly, 'Nay, sire, this sword is not mine, nor dare I put my hand to it, for it is not by my side that it ought to hang. And I know full well that whoso shall seek to take it and fail therein, it shall so wound him that he shall not easily be made whole.'

Then the King turned to Sir Gawaine, and said to him, 'Fair nephew, I bid you for the love of me, make trial of that sword.' Sir Gawaine said, 'I will obey your bidding,' and he took the sword by the handle, but could not move it. And the King thanked him for his endeavour, but Sir Lancelot said, 'Know that this sword shall so trouble you, that you will wish never to have set your hand thereto, no, not for the fairest castle in all the land.' 'Sir,' Sir Gawaine made answer, 'I could not disobey my uncle's commandment.' The King was troubled to hear this; nevertheless he bade Sir Percival try the sword. Then Sir Percival also set his hand to it, and drew at it strongly, but he could not move it at all. And when these three had failed, none others dared to put to their hands. 'Now, sir,' said Sir Kaye to the King, 'you may go to your meat, for you have seen a marvellous adventure.' So the King and his knights went to their meat, and all the seats were filled, save the Perilous Seat only.

While they thus sat at the meat, the squires serving them, there came to pass a marvellous thing. All the doors and windows of the palace shut themselves of their own accord, and yet the place was not darkened. Then spake the King, 'Fair knights, we have already seen many marvels this day; yet I doubt not that ere it be night we shall see yet greater.' And even as he spake there came into the hall an old man very venerable, clothed all in white, but no man knew whence he came. The old man brought with him a young knight, clad in red armour, without shield or sword, but with a scabbard only hanging by his side. The old man said to the King, 'Sir, I bring you this young knight who is of the lineage of Joseph of Arimathea; he shall accomplish marvellous things.' The King made answer, 'You are heartily welcome, sir, and this young knight also.' Then the old man bade the young knight doff his armour. And it was seen that he was clad in a coat of red satin, and a mantle furred with fine ermines on his shoulder. This done, the old man said to him, 'Follow me,' and so brought him to the Perilous Seat, whereby sat Sir Lancelot. Then the old man lifted up the cloth, and on the seat was written, 'This is the seat of Sir Galahad, the good knight.' The old man said, 'Be assured that this place is yours.' So the young knight sat him down in the seat with all boldness and said to the old man, 'Sir, you may now go your way, for you have done right well that which was commanded you. Commend me to my grandsire, King Pelleas, and say that I shall come to see him so soon as may be.' So the old man went his way, and there met him twenty noble squires who bare him company.

When the dinner was done, the King took Sir Galahad by the hand, and led him down to the place where the stone floated on the water, the Queen also, with many ladies, following. Said the King to Sir Galahad, 'Here is as great a marvel as ever I saw. Many knights have made trial of this sword to draw it from its place, but none have availed to do it.' 'Sir,' answered Sir Galahad, 'this is no marvel, for it is not their adventure but mine; so sure was I of this sword, that I brought none other with me, but only this scabbard that hangs by my side.' So saying, he laid his hand upon the sword, and drew it full easily out of the stone, and thrust it into the scabbard. Then he said to the King, 'This is the sword that belonged aforetime to Sir Balin, who was a passing good knight; therewith he slew his brother Sir Balan unawares, which thing was a grievous pity. This Balin also gave my grandfather, King Pelleas, a wound that has never been healed, no, nor shall be till I myself heal him.'

After this the King, willing to try Sir Galahad, of what mettle he was, bade all his knights joust together in a meadow that was by Camelot. So they jousted, and none bare himself more bravely than did Sir Galahad. Many knights of the Round Table he overthrew. But there were two whom he overthrew not, and these two were Sir Lancelot and Sir Percival. When the jousting was ended, then Sir Galahad unlaced his helmet before the King and the Queen and all the court, and they saw that he was so like unto Sir Lancelot, that never two knights in all the world were more alike than these two.

After this all the company repaired to the Minster, and from the Minster they repaired to the hall and sat down to meat. And as they sat they heard a great crack as of thunder, so loud that it seemed as if the hall were riven in twain. And in the midst of this thundering there entered a sunbeam, seven times brighter than was ever the light of the sun. And every knight, as he looked on his fellow, saw him fairer than he had ever seen him before. So they sat and gazed, none daring to speak a word, till there came into the hall the Holy Grail, a fair vessel of gold, covered all about with white samite, in which was the Holy Body. But how it was borne none saw, nor did any behold the Vessel itself, for it was closely covered about, but the hall was filled with a most heavenly odour. Then the Holy Grail departed out of the hall, and as none knew whence it came, so neither did any know whither it went.

When it was gone, the knights had breath to speak. First the King gave thanks to God who had suffered them to see the Holy Vessel at this Feast of Pentecost. After him Sir Gawaine spake out: 'We have been this day beguiled so that, though the Holy Grail came among us, yet we saw it not, so covered was it. Now, therefore, I make this vow that tomorrow I will set out seeking the Holy Grail, and that in this seeking I will continue for a twelvemonth and a day and will not return till I have seen it more plainly than it has been seen today.' And when the other knights of the Round Table heard Sir Gawaine so speak, they stood up, for the most part, and promised and vowed the same thing.

But the King was greatly troubled at this, and said to Sir Gawaine, knowing that it was he that stood up the first, and that the others took example by him, 'You have well-nigh slain me by this vow and promise, for you have bereft me of the fairest fellowship of knights that ever was in this world. For I am sure that they who shall depart on this quest shall never more meet together in this world.'

Now you shall hear how Sir Gawaine fared in the Quest. He rode many journeys forwards and backwards, seeking to join himself to Sir Galahad, and when he came to a certain abbey where Sir Galahad had been, he said to the monks, 'If I may meet Sir Galahad, I will not lightly depart from him, for all his strange adventures.' Then said one of the monks, 'He will not be of your fellowship.' 'Why so?' said Sir Gawaine. 'Because he is holy and you are sinful,' said he. The next day he rode to a certain hermitage where he asked a shelter of the hermit, which the good man willingly granted to him, asking him who he was and whence he came. 'I am of King Arthur's court,' said he, 'and my name is Gawaine, and I seek the Holy Grail.' 'I know you,' said the monk. Then Sir Gawaine told him how the monk at the abbey had called him a wicked knight. 'He might well say it,' said the hermit. 'You might have followed virtuous living when you were made a knight, but you would do otherwise. But Sir Galahad has chosen the better part. Therefore you shall fail and he shall prosper. Yet 'twere something should you do penance for your sins.' 'What penance shall I do?' 'said Sir Gawaine. 'What I shall set you,' answered the hermit. 'That may not be,' said Gawaine, 'we knights that seek adventure suffer pain enough.' Then the hermit said, 'God better you!' and held his peace.

Not many days after, Sir Gawaine met Sir Ector that was brother to Sir Lancelot. 'I am weary of this quest,' said he; and Sir Ector answered, 'I have met twenty knights, and they were all in the same case.' And riding on they came to a ruined chapel; and sitting down on the seats, fell asleep for weariness, and while they slept they dreamt, both of them, strange dreams. Afterwards they saw – for this was not a dream but a vision – a hand clothed in red samite, and in the hand was a candle burning very clear, and these two passed into the chapel, and so vanished out of their sight. And even as it vanished there came a voice to them saying, 'Ye knights that are evil of life and poor of faith, the adventure of the Holy Grail is not for you.'

When they had departed from the chapel, there met them a knight, who proffered to joust with them. 'Now,' said Sir Gawaine, 'since I left Camelot, there has no one proffered to joust with me.' 'Let me joust,' said Sir Ector. 'Nay,' answered Sir Gawaine, 'not so, but if I be beaten you shall come after me.' So the two jousted, and both fell to the ground. And when Sir Gawaine drew his sword, it was found that the other could not lift himself from the ground, for he was smitten through the body. 'Now you must yield you,' said Sir Gawaine. 'I am but a dead man,' answered the other, 'but take me to a house of religion where I may receive the Holy Sacrament.' 'I know of none such,' said Gawaine. But when the knight said that he would guide him, Gawaine set him on his horse, and sustained him till he came to the place. And when he had taken the Holy Sacrament, he prayed Sir Gawaine that he would draw the spear out of his body. 'I am a knight,' said he, 'of the Round Table, and we are sworn brethren, and I was in search of the Holy Grail, even as you, and now you have slain me. May God forgive you therefor.' And when the spear was drawn out from his body he died. Then Sir Gawaine and Sir Ector buried him, weeping the while, and so departed.

All this time they saw not Sir Galahad, but at the last they met with him and in this wise. At a certain castle they saw a party of knights that would enter by the gate, and another party that hindered them. They joined themselves to the knights without, and these got by far the better. Meanwhile Sir Galahad joined himself to the knights within and did great deeds of arms. And he came by chance to Sir Gawaine and smote him so hard that he brake through the helm and smote him to the ground and also carved in two the shoulder of his horse. This done he stole away secretly. Then said Gawaine, 'Now are the words of Lancelot come true that the sword in the stone would deal me such a buffet as I would not have for the best castle in the world. But now my quest is ended.'

Thus did Sir Gawaine fare in his Quest of the Holy Grail.

Now I will tell of Sir Lancelot.

After many adventures of which there is no need to tell, as he slept on a certain night there came a voice to him saying, 'Arise, Lancelot, and enter into the first ship that you shall find.' So he arose, and not long after came to a strand, and on the strand was a ship, into which he entered. In this he abode for a full month. And at the end of the month there came a knight riding. Him he saluted, saying, 'You are welcome.' And the knight saluted him again, saying, 'My heart is much inclined to you,' and asked his name. 'My name,' said he, 'is Lancelot du Lake.' 'No wonder,' said the other, 'that I love you, for you are my father,' 'Are you Sir Galahad?' said he; and when he knew that 'twas he, there was great joy between them, and they lived long time together in the ship.

After this there came one who said, 'Sir Galahad, you have been long time enough with your father; arise and go.' Said Sir Galahad to his father, 'I know that I shall not see you any more.' And Sir Lancelot said, 'Pray for me that God may keep me in His service.' While they talked, there came a voice, saying, 'Be careful to do well, for ye shall not see each other till the day of doom.' Then Sir Galahad mounted his horse and rode away.

Then a wind arose and drove the ship in which Sir Lancelot was for a whole month. At the end of the month he came to a castle, with two lions keeping the door, and heard a voice that said, 'Enter, Lancelot, and you shall have a part of your desire.' So he drew his sword for fear of the lions. But then came a dwarf that smote him on the arm so hard that the sword dropped out of his hand, and a voice said to him, 'Man of little faith, why trust you in your harness more than in your Maker?'

Then he made a cross on his forehead and passed by the lions, which harmed him not. So he went through many doors that opened before him, till he came to a door that was fast shut. And he knew that the Holy Grail was within. Then he prayed that God would show him something of that which he sought. But when the door opened, and he would have entered, there came a voice, saying, 'Enter not, Sir Lancelot; for it is not for you to do it.' Then he looked, and saw a table of silver and the Holy Grail on it, with red samite over it, and many angels round about, of whom one held a candle, and others divers other things. Then he entered the chamber and came near to the silver table. Whereupon there smote him on the face a fiery breath, and he fell to the ground, having lost all power over his body, and his hearing also and his speech. So he lay, well-nigh as one dead. But he was aware of many hands about him, which took him, and bare him out of the chamber, and cast him down without the door. And on the morrow, when it was day, the people of the place found him so lying, and wondered whether there was any life in him. And finding that there was life, they put him in a bed, where he lay without sense or speech for many days.

Thus did Sir Lancelot fare in the Quest.

* * *

After Sir Galahad left the King's court, he came to a castle where was King Bagdemagus. Said he to the King, 'What has brought you hither?' King Bagdemagus answered, 'In this castle there is a shield which if any man essay to wear about his neck, except he be worthy of it, he will either die within three days, or get some sore mischief. Now I am minded to essay it; and if I fail, then you shall essay it, for I know that you will not fail.' 'You please me well,' answered Sir Galahad, 'for I have as yet no shield.' On the morrow the King asked where this shield might be, and a monk showed it to him hanging behind the altar. It was white, with a red cross upon it. Then the King took it down from its place, and hung it about his neck, and so having put on his harness, went forth from the castle to seek adventures. But he took with him a squire, who should take news to Sir Galahad of how it fared with him. When they had ridden two miles, they came to a valley where there was a hermitage, and they saw a knight coming to meet them that was clad in white armour. And he had his spear in rest, and came on as fast as might be. The King also put his spear in rest and rode against the knight and brake his spear on him. But the knight smote the King on the shoulder, where the shield covered him not, and bore him from his horse. Then he lighted down from his horse, and took the shield from him, saying, 'This was great folly to bear a shield that may not be borne save by the best knight in the world.' And to the squire he said, 'Bear this shield to Sir Galahad, and greet him well from me.' The squire said, 'Tell me your name.' 'Take no heed of my name,' said the knight, 'for it is not for you to know. But be sure that this shield is for no man but Sir Galahad.' Then they carried the King to an abbey, where he was healed of his wound. But he scarce escaped with his life.

After this Sir Galahad rode away carrying the shield, and came to the hermitage. There the knight in white armour met him, and the two greeted each other right courteously, and when Sir Galahad would know the story of the shield, he told it to him, that it was borne in old time by a certain King Evelake against the Saracens, having been given to him by Joseph of Arimathea, and that when Joseph lay dying, he made a cross upon the shield with his blood, and that after this the shield was put away till the best knight in the world should come for it. After this the white knight vanished out of Sir Galahad's sight.

Then Sir Galahad, being now fully armed – for hitherto he had lacked a shield – rode on his way, and had many adventures. One while he met Sir Lancelot and Sir Percivale, that were the two strongest knights in the world, save, maybe, Sir Tristram of Lyonesse. And first he smote Sir Lancelot and his horse down to the ground, and afterward he served Sir Percivale in the same fashion, and this latter he had slain but that, by good chance, the sword swerved somewhat. But they knew not who he was till a recluse, that dwelt in a hermitage hard by, cried aloud, 'Hail, now, the best knight in the world.' This the two hearing, knew that it was Sir Galahad, and would fain have joined themselves to him, but he rode away as fast as he could.

Then he met with Sir Gawaine, and dealt him a very sore blow, and how he dwelt for a while with Sir Lancelot his father has been told already. Many other adventures he had, till there remained but one thing for him to do before the finding of the Grail, which thing was the healing of King Pelleas from the dolorous stroke which Sir Balin had dealt him, as has been told before.

When he came to the castle where King Pelleas dwelt, he and Sir Percivale and Sir Bors, for it was granted to them to be with him, they saw a man attired like to a bishop, with four angels about him. The angels set him in a chair before the table of silver whereon was the Holy Grail; then came in other angels, that bore candles of wax, and a towel, and a spear that dropped drops of blood in a marvellous fashion. And the man that was attired as a bishop said to the knights, 'This is the Holy Grail. Ye see it now, and shall see it yet more plainly in the place whither ye shall next go.' Then he gave them his blessing, and so vanished out of their sight.

Then went Sir Galahad to the spear, and touched the blood, and having touched it he anointed the King, who was straightway healed of his wound.

After this these three entered into a ship which carried them to a certain city of heathen folk, whose King put them in prison. But at the end of the year the king, having fallen sick, sent for them, and cried for mercy on what he had done. So they forgave him.

When he was dead the people of that city would not be content but they must have Sir Galahad to their king. And being King, he made for the table of silver a chest of gold to be a covering of the Holy Grail, and every day he and his companions said their prayers before it. At the year's end it was granted to Sir Galahad to see the Holy Grail full plainly, as no man ever saw it but he. When he had seen it, he went to Sir Percivale and kissed him, and also to Sir Bors and kissed him, and commended them both to God. This done, he bade them salute Sir Lancelot, and tell him, said he, 'that he remember how unstable is the world.' Having said this he died, and the angels carried his soul to heaven. And then came down a hand that took the Holy Grail and the spear, and carried them away.

Thus did Sir Galahad accomplish the adventure of the Holy Grail, because he was pure and without spot.

THE PRINCE WHO SOUGHT IMMORTALITY

Leonora Lang

O NCE IN THE very middle of the middle of a large kingdom, there was a town, and in the town a palace, and in the palace a king. This king had one son whom his father thought was wiser and cleverer than any son ever was before, and indeed his father had spared no pains to make him so. He had been very careful in choosing his tutors and governors when he was a boy, and when he became a youth he sent him to travel, so that he might see the ways of other people, and find that they were often as good as his own.

It was now a year since the prince had returned home, for his father felt that it was time that his son should learn how to rule the kingdom which would one day be his. But during his long absence the prince seemed to have changed his character altogether. From being a merry and light-hearted boy, he had grown into a gloomy and thoughtful man. The king knew of nothing that could have produced such an alteration. He vexed himself about it from morning till night, till at length an explanation occurred to him – the young man was in love!

Now the prince never talked about his feelings – for the matter of that he scarcely talked at all; and the father knew that if he was to come to the bottom of the prince's dismal face, he would have to begin. So one day, after dinner, he took his son by the arm and led him into another room, hung entirely with the pictures of beautiful maidens, each one more lovely than the other.

'My dear boy,' he said, 'you are very sad; perhaps after all your wanderings it is dull for you here all alone with me. It would be much better if you would marry, and I have collected here the portraits of the most beautiful women in the world of a rank equal to your own. Choose which among them you would like for a wife, and I will send an embassy to her father to ask for her hand.'

'Alas! your Majesty,' answered the prince, 'it is not love or marriage that makes me so gloomy; but the thought, which haunts me day and night, that all men, even kings, must die. Never shall I be happy again till I have found a kingdom where death is unknown. And I have determined to give myself no rest till I have discovered the Land of Immortality.'

The old king heard him with dismay; things were worse than he thought. He tried to reason with his son, and told him that during all these years he had been looking forward to his return, in order to resign his throne and its cares, which pressed so heavily upon him. But it was in vain that he talked; the prince would listen to nothing, and the following morning buckled on his sword and set forth on his journey.

He had been travelling for many days, and had left his fatherland behind him, when close to the road he came upon a huge tree, and on its topmost bough an eagle was sitting shaking the branches with all his might. This seemed so strange and so unlike an eagle, that the prince stood still with surprise, and the bird saw him and flew to the ground. The moment its feet touched the ground he changed into a king.

'Why do you look so astonished?' he asked.

'I was wondering why you shook the boughs so fiercely,' answered the prince.

'I am condemned to do this, for neither I nor any of my kindred can die till I have rooted up this great tree,' replied the king of the eagles. 'But it is now evening, and I need work no more today. Come to my house with me, and be my guest for the night.'

The prince accepted gratefully the eagle's invitation, for he was tired and hungry. They were received at the palace by the king's beautiful daughter, who gave orders that dinner should be laid for them at once. While they were eating, the eagle questioned his guest about his travels, and if he was wandering for pleasure's sake, or with any special aim. Then the prince told him everything, and how he could never turn back till he had discovered the Land of Immortality.

'Dear brother,' said the eagle, 'you have discovered it already, and it rejoices my heart to think that you will stay with us. Have you not just heard me say that death has no power either over myself or any of my kindred till that great tree is rooted up? It will take me six hundred years' hard work to do that; so marry my daughter and let us all live happily together here. After all, six hundred years is an eternity!'

'Ah, dear king,' replied the young man, 'your offer is very tempting! But at the end of six hundred years we should have to die, so we should be no better off! No, I must go on till I find the country where there is no death at all.'

Then the princess spoke, and tried to persuade the guest to change his mind, but he sorrowfully shook his head. At length, seeing that his resolution was firmly fixed, she took from a cabinet a little box which contained her picture, and gave it to him saying:

'As you will not stay with us, prince, accept this box, which will sometimes recall us to your memory. If you are tired of travelling before you come to the Land of Immortality, open this box and look at my picture, and you will be borne along either on earth or in the air, quick as thought, or swift as the whirlwind.'

The prince thanked her for her gift, which he placed in his tunic, and sorrowfully bade the eagle and his daughter farewell.

Never was any present in the world as useful as that little box, and many times did he bless the kind thought of the princess. One evening it had carried him to the top of a high mountain, where he saw a man with a bald head, busily engaged in digging up spadefuls of earth and throwing them in a basket. When the basket was full he took it away and returned with an empty one, which he likewise filled. The prince stood and watched him for a little, till the bald-headed man looked up and said to him: 'Dear brother, what surprises you so much?'

'I was wondering why you were filling the basket,' replied the prince.

'Oh!' replied the man, 'I am condemned to do this, for neither I nor any of my family can die till I have dug away the whole of this mountain and made it level with the plain. But, come, it is almost dark, and I shall work no longer.' And he plucked a leaf from a tree close by, and from a rough digger he was changed into a stately bald-headed king. 'Come home with me,' he added; 'you must be tired and hungry, and my daughter will have supper ready for us.' The prince accepted gladly, and they went back to the palace, where the bald-headed king's daughter, who was still more beautiful than the other princess, welcomed them at the door and led the way into a large hall and to a table covered with silver dishes. While they were eating, the bald-headed king asked the prince how he had happened to wander so far, and the young man told him all about it, and how he was seeking the Land of Immortality. 'You have found it already,' answered the king, 'for, as I said, neither I nor my family can die till I have levelled this great mountain; and that will take full eight hundred years longer. Stay here with us and marry my daughter. Eight hundred years is surely long enough to live.'

'Oh, certainly,' answered the prince; 'but, all the same, I would rather go and seek the land where there is no death at all.'

So next morning he bade them farewell, though the princess begged him to stay with all her might; and when she found that she could not persuade him she gave him as a remembrance a gold ring. This ring was still more useful than the box, because when one wished oneself at any place one was there directly, without even the trouble of flying to it through the air. The prince put it on his finger, and thanking her heartily, went his way.

He walked on for some distance, and then he recollected the ring and thought he would try if the princess had spoken truly as to its powers. 'I wish I was at the end of the world,' he said, shutting his eyes, and when he opened them he was standing in a street full of marble palaces. The men who passed him were tall and strong, and their clothes were magnificent. He stopped some of them and asked in all the twenty-seven languages he knew what was the name of the city, but no one answered him. Then his heart sank within him; what should he do in this strange place if nobody could understand anything? Suddenly his eyes fell upon a man dressed after the fashion of his native country, and he ran up to him and spoke to him in his own tongue. 'What city is this, my friend?' he inquired.

'It is the capital city of the Blue Kingdom,' replied the man, 'but the king himself is dead, and his daughter is now the ruler.'

With this news the prince was satisfied, and begged his countryman to show him the way to the young queen's palace. The man led him through several streets into a large square, one side of which was occupied by a splendid building that seemed borne up on slender pillars of soft green marble. In front was a flight of steps, and on these the queen was sitting wrapped in a veil of shining silver mist, listening to the complaints of her people and dealing out justice. When the prince came up she saw directly that he was no ordinary man, and telling her chamberlain to dismiss the rest of her petitioners for that day, she signed to the prince to follow her into the palace. Luckily she had been taught his language as a child, so they had no difficulty in talking together.

The prince told all his story and how he was journeying in search of the Land of Immortality. When he had finished, the princess, who had listened attentively, rose, and taking his arm, led him to the door of another room, the floor of which was made entirely of needles, stuck so close together that there was not room for a single needle more.

'Prince,' she said, turning to him, 'you see these needles? Well, know that neither I nor any of my family can die till I have worn out these needles in sewing. It will take at least a thousand years for that. Stay here, and share my throne; a thousand years is long enough to live!'

'Certainly,' answered he; 'still, at the end of the thousand years I should have to die! No, I must find the land where there is no death.'

The queen did all she could to persuade him to stay, but as her words proved useless, at length she gave it up. Then she said to him: 'As you will not stay, take this little golden rod as a remembrance of me. It has the power to become anything you wish it to be, when you are in need.'

So the prince thanked her, and putting the rod in his pocket, went his way.

Scarcely had he left the town behind him when he came to a broad river which no man might pass, for he was standing at the end of the world, and this was the river which flowed round it.

Not knowing what to do next, he walked a little distance up the bank, and there, over his head, a beautiful city was floating in the air. He longed to get to it, but how? neither road nor bridge was anywhere to be seen, yet the city drew him upwards, and he felt that here at last was the country which he sought. Suddenly he remembered the golden rod which the mist-veiled queen had given him. With a beating heart he flung it to the ground, wishing with all his might that it should turn into a bridge, and fearing that, after all, this might prove beyond its power. But no, instead of the rod, there stood a golden ladder, leading straight up to the city of the air. He was about to enter the golden gates, when there sprang at him a wondrous beast, whose like he had never seen. 'Out sword from the sheath,' cried the prince, springing back with a cry. And the sword leapt from the scabbard and cut off some of the monster's heads, but others grew again directly, so that the prince, pale with terror, stood where he was, calling for help, and put his sword back in the sheath again.

The queen of the city heard the noise and looked from her window to see what was happening. Summoning one of her servants, she bade him go and rescue the stranger, and bring him to her. The prince thankfully obeyed her orders, and entered her presence.

The moment she looked at him, the queen also felt that he was no ordinary man, and she welcomed him graciously, and asked him what had brought him to the city. In answer the prince told all his story, and how he had travelled long and far in search of the Land of Immortality.

'You have found it,' said she, 'for I am queen over life and over death. Here you can dwell among the immortals.'

A thousand years had passed since the prince first entered the city, but they had flown so fast that the time seemed no more than six months. There had not been one instant of the thousand years that the prince was not happy till one night when he dreamed of his father and mother. Then the longing for his home came upon him with a rush, and in the morning he told the Queen of the Immortals that he must go and see his father and mother once more. The queen stared at him with amazement, and cried: 'Why, prince, are you out of your senses? It is more than eight hundred years since your father and mother died! There will not even be their dust remaining.'

'I must go all the same,' said he.

'Well, do not be in a hurry,' continued the queen, understanding that he would not be prevented. 'Wait till I make some preparations for your journey.' So she unlocked her great treasure chest, and took out two beautiful flasks, one of gold and one of silver, which she hung round his neck. Then she showed him a little trap-door in one corner of the room, and said: 'Fill the silver flask with this water, which is below the trap-door. It is enchanted, and whoever you sprinkle with the water will become a dead man at once, even if he had lived a thousand years. The golden flask you must fill with the water here,' she added, pointing to a well in another corner. 'It springs from the rock of eternity; you have only to sprinkle a few drops on a body and it will come to life again, if it had been a thousand years dead.'

The prince thanked the queen for her gifts, and, bidding her farewell, went on his journey.

He soon arrived in the town where the mist-veiled queen reigned in her palace, but the whole city had changed, and he could scarcely find his way through the streets. In the palace itself all was still, and he wandered through the rooms without meeting anyone to stop him. At last he entered the queen's own chamber, and there she lay, with her embroidery still in her hands, fast asleep. He pulled at her dress, but she did not waken. Then a dreadful idea came over him, and he ran to the chamber where the needles had been kept, but it was quite empty. The queen had broken the last over the work she held in her hand, and with it the spell was broken too, and she lay dead.

Quick as thought the prince pulled out the golden flask, and sprinkled some drops of the water over the queen. In a moment she moved gently, and raising her head, opened her eyes.

'Oh, my dear friend, I am so glad you wakened me; I must have slept a long while!'

'You would have slept till eternity,' answered the prince, 'if I had not been here to waken you.'

At these words the queen remembered about the needles. She knew now that she had been dead, and that the prince had restored her to life. She gave him thanks from her heart for what he had done, and vowed she would repay him if she ever got a chance.

The prince took his leave, and set out for the country of the bald-headed king. As he drew near the place he saw that the whole mountain had been dug away, and that the king was lying dead on the ground, his spade and bucket beside him. But as soon as the water from the golden flask touched him he yawned and stretched himself, and slowly rose to his feet. 'Oh, my dear friend, I am so glad to see you,' cried he, 'I must have slept a long while!'

'You would have slept till eternity if I had not been here to waken you,' answered the prince. And the king remembered the mountain, and the spell, and vowed to repay the service if he ever had a chance.

Further along the road which led to his old home the prince found the great tree torn up by its roots, and the king of the eagles sitting dead on the ground, with his wings outspread as if for flight. A flutter ran through the feathers as the drops of water fell on them, and the eagle lifted his beak from the ground and said: 'Oh, how long I must have slept! How can I thank you for having awakened me, my dear, good friend!'

'You would have slept till eternity if I had not been here to waken you', answered the prince. Then the king remembered about the tree, and knew that he had been dead, and promised, if ever he had the chance, to repay what the prince had done for him.

At last he reached the capital of his father's kingdom, but on reaching the place where the royal palace had stood, instead of the marble galleries where he used to play, there lay a great sulphur lake, its blue flames darting into the air. How was he to find his father and mother, and bring them back to life, if they were lying at the bottom of that horrible water? He turned away sadly and wandered back into the streets, hardly knowing where he was going; when a voice behind him cried: 'Stop, prince, I have caught you at last! It is a thousand years since I first began to seek you.' And there beside him stood the old, white-bearded, figure of Death. Swiftly he drew the ring from his finger, and the king of the eagles, the bald-headed king, and the mist-veiled queen, hastened to his rescue. In an instant they had seized upon Death and held him tight, till the prince should have time to reach the Land of Immortality. But they did not know how quickly Death could fly, and the prince had only one foot across the border, when he felt the other grasped from behind, and the voice of Death calling: 'Halt! now you are mine.'

The Queen of the Immortals was watching from her window, and cried to Death that he had no power in her kingdom, and that he must seek his prey elsewhere.

'Quite true,' answered Death; 'but his foot is in *my* kingdom, and that belongs to me!'

'At any rate half of him is mine,' replied the Queen, 'and what good can the other half do you? Half a man is no use, either to you or to me! But this once I will allow you to cross into my kingdom, and we will decide by a wager whose he is.'

And so it was settled. Death stepped across the narrow line that surrounds the Land of Immortality, and the queen proposed the wager which was to decide the prince's fate. 'I will throw him up into the sky,' she said, 'right to the back of the morning star, and if he falls down into this city, then he is mine. But if he should fall outside the walls, he shall belong to you.'

In the middle of the city was a great open square, and here the queen wished the wager to take place. When all was ready, she put her foot under the foot of the prince and swung him into the air. Up, up, he went, high amongst the stars, and no man's eyes could follow him. Had she thrown him up straight? the queen wondered anxiously, for, if not, he would fall outside the walls, and she would lose him for ever. The moments seemed long while she and Death stood gazing up into the air, waiting to know whose prize the prince would be. Suddenly they both caught sight of a tiny speck no bigger than a wasp, right up in the blue. Was he coming straight? No! Yes! But as he was nearing the city, a light wind sprang up, and swayed him in the direction of the wall. Another second and he would have fallen half over it, when the queen sprang forward, seized him in her arms, and flung him into the castle. Then she commanded her servants to cast Death out of the city, which they did, with such hard blows that he never dared to show his face again in the Land of Immortality.

THE CHANGELINGS

Jessica Amanda Salmonson

A STRANGE CREATURE called the Huluk used to live in Lake Tualatin, now called Wapato Lake, a quiet shallow lake surrounded by gorgeous greenery. The Huluk is not there now, because it outgrew the lake, and went to live elsewhere. Today no one sees it; long ago, it was often seen. This story happened in bygone days when the Huluk still dwelt in that lake.

By nature sluggish, the Huluk waddled like a porcupine when it was out of the water. It dragged its big flat tail which was akin to that of a beaver, but spiked all about the rump with enormous quills. It had a long, slender, blunt-ended horn on the top of its head between its huge clamshell ears, above the eyes that were two protuberant half-globes, black and moist and never blinking.

The Huluk's horn was covered in red and white spots. The fur of the Huluk was slick and mottled.

Three children were out digging roots one day, a little girl, a little boy, and an older boy. The girl wore a sleeveless dress of seal fur interlaced with braids of mountain sheep wool. Upon her head she wore a bobcat-fur cap. The two boys wore striped coats of tanned deerskin decorated with red beads. When the creature came out of the water the little boy saw it first. At first he thought it was a beaver the size of a grizzly bear. He was a fearless boy, and the very idea of such a big beaver made him laugh.

'What are you laughing at?' asked his sister. 'What do you see?'

The little boy pointed and exclaimed, 'I like that creature's horn! I want it to belong to me!'

When his little sister saw it, she joined the laughter. The

horn was indeed very appealing. Together they ran toward the creature.

'Come back!' cried their older brother, understanding better the dangers of inexplicable beasts. He tried to run after his siblings, but his feet would not move, as though they were stuck in mud, or roots had grabbed him. The little ones did not listen to him, did not come back.

So the Huluk scooped up the little boy on its horn. Then it scooped up the little girl. They were taken into the water riding on the horn. From where the older child was standing knee-deep in muck, it looked as though they might have been impaled, but he wasn't sure, for they were obviously alive; he could still hear them laughing. As the creature slid into the lake, the older boy's legs were mysteriously freed from the muck, and he turned to flee.

He made it home and told his mother and father, 'Brother and sister have been carried away! The Tualatin lake-monster either drowned them or impaled them, I don't know which!'

Then the boy grew ill from his adventure. He lay down on a mat in the longhouse. He was sweating and moaning. His mother laid over him a cougar skin blanket, thoroughly tanned, and as she did so, she saw that he was covered with red and purple spots.

*   *   *

The father was called Wawinxpa, a chief. He took a carved box out from under a bench in the longhouse and opened it. He drew forth all his best clothes. He dressed himself in a shirt of tanned elkskin which his wife had decorated with beads and quills, tanned leggings and breechcloth, new moccasins of deerhide with the fur intact.

His marmot fur knife-belt was decorated with feathers from a white swan's back. His necklace consisted of bear claws, symbolic of warrior strength, plus the rare small shells of a shaman. He blacked his cheeks with pitch soot. Last of all he put on a headdress. It was made of white swan-feathers interspersed with red and black woodpecker-feathers. The circlet of feathers stuck straight up from his head.

Wawinxpa went to the place where his youngest children had

been taken away below the water. At the lake's edge he saw
a big hole and followed the Huluk's tracks into a cave. When
he came out the other side of the tunnel, the sky was made of
shimmering earth, and trees were growing downward from the
roof of the sky.

Off in the misty distance, he caught a glimpse of his children.
They were clinging to the speckled horn of the monster, which
trod slowly but steadily away. It moved awkwardly across
pitted earth, dragging its tail and gouging the ground with
its arrow-length quills, leaving a wide track that was easy to
follow.

The father pursued them through the dismal world up and
down deep gulleys. Time and again he caught sight of his
children, but the monster was never closer or farther. It was
always the same distance away. On the upper bank of the first
gulley Wawinxpa motioned with his hands and cried out for his
children to let go of the horn and come to him.

His children clung fast and called back, 'Father we are
different, different, different!'

The next day, from the top of the second gulley, he called to
them again. But they only replied, 'We are different, different!'
as they held fast to the Huluk's horn. The monster waddled on
and on, and though it never exerted itself, it managed somehow
always to keep the same distance. The father grew increasingly
despondent.

He made a camp each night in sheltered places low in one
or another gulley. Five days he stayed in the strange land. Five
times he ascended to a different gulley's ridge and called out,
'Come to me, my children, come!' He could never catch up to
them, and their reply was always the same.

After the fifth try, the father saw his children no more. He
looked everywhere, but the Huluk was no more to be seen.
Its wide trail vanished on a lava bed. Wawinxpa came out
of the cave, into the good world, but the world seemed less
good without his children. He went home and told his wife,
'The Tualatin monster has taken our children to live under the
mountain. All the trees in that place grow straight down out
of the sky. I saw our children on the horn of the monster, but
could not catch them.'

Then he sat down with his wife and together they cried.

The older son lay sick with fever, sleeping fitfully. His mother prepared strong medicinal teas of herbs, crab apple bark and spruce sap, but the boy could not keep liquids in him.

Through the night, Wawinxpa lay near his son and for a long time could not sleep for worrying that his last child would die.

Finally, Wawinxpa slept, and his night was filled with dreams. He drew dream-power into himself as he was sleeping. The next day his wife could not wake him. She waited patiently, watching her husband fretfully as she attended her sick son. Toward noon, Wawinxpa opened his eyes and said, 'I have seen them in my dream. I will try again to bring them home.'

Once more he made himself ready, wearing his many fine garments. He covered his forehead with black pitch. He made speckles on the rest of his face with red paint, white clay and coal. Then in the forest he twisted a long hazel rope and tied one end around his waist. The other end he tied to a tree beside Lake Tualatin. Then he swam out to the middle of the lake and peered down.

Deep in the clear, clear water he saw his children on the horn of the monster. He called down into the waters, 'Let go of the horn, my children, and swim up here to me!'

But they replied, 'Father, we are different, different, different.'

He swam about the middle of the lake until he was weary, with just the feathers of his headdress sticking up. The whole time he prayed and prayed for assistance from good spirits. He prayed to the clouds, to the lake, to the mountains, to the trees, to the birds and to the kindly spirit he had met in the forest when he came of age and which was always with him. Then he was so tired he couldn't even swim to shore. He sank from view, and would have drowned. His wife came wearing a cedar-bark dress and robe of interwoven seal, coon and bobcat furs. She pulled on the hazel rope, drawing her husband out of the water.

She raised him in her arms, wrapped him in a cougar hide blanket, and held him fast until he was warm.

The next morning, he went out into the lake again, with just his headdress of swan and woodpecker feathers showing in the distance. He called to his children, but their answer was the same as before. On the fifth day, he saw that his children had changed markedly. Their hair was gone. Their eyes were half-globes of darkness without lids. Their bodies had merged into one speckled body with two heads.

He called down to them, 'Children, swim up here to me!'

Both heads spoke at once, saying, 'Father, I am different, different, different.'

* * *

Wawinxpa's five days of prayers and ascetic acts had assisted in the recovery of his one remaining child. The boy had only white scars to show how the Huluk had seen him. On that last day of the father's prayer, fast, and swimming, the son came with his mother to the lakeshore. Together they pulled on the hazel cord.

For the last time Wawinxpa was drawn out of the water. He clung to his wife and son, and his feather headdress fell off to the ground. All he could say was, 'The children belong forever to the Huluk. Weep, my wife; weep, my only son; weep for they are different, different, different.'

THE STORY OF A GAZELLE

Edward Steere

T HERE ONCE LIVED a man who wasted all his money, and grew so poor that his only food was a few grains of corn, which he scratched like a fowl from out of a dust-heap.

One day he was scratching as usual among a dust-heap in the street, hoping to find something for breakfast, when his eye fell upon a small silver coin, called an eighth, which he greedily snatched up. 'Now I can have a proper meal,' he thought, and after drinking some water at a well he lay down and slept so long that it was sunrise before he woke again. Then he jumped up and returned to the dust-heap. 'For who knows,' he said to himself, 'whether I may not have some good luck again.'

As he was walking down the road, he saw a man coming towards him, carrying a cage made of twigs. 'Hi! you fellow!' called he, 'what have you got inside there?'

'Gazelles,' replied the man.

'Bring them here, for I should like to see them.'

As he spoke, some men who were standing by began to laugh, saying to the man with the cage: 'You had better take care how you bargain with him, for he has nothing at all except what he picks up from a dust-heap, and if he can't feed himself, will he be able to feed a gazelle?'

But the man with the cage made answer: 'Since I started from my home in the country, fifty people at the least have called me to show them my gazelles, and was there one among them who cared to buy? It is the custom for a trader in merchandise to be summoned hither and thither, and who knows where one may find a buyer?' And he took up his cage and went towards the scratcher of dust-heaps, and the men went with him.

'What do you ask for your gazelles?' said the beggar. 'Will you let me have one for an eighth?'

And the man with the cage took out a gazelle, and held it out, saying, 'Take this one, master!'

And the beggar took it and carried it to the dust-heap, where he scratched carefully till he found a few grains of corn, which he divided with his gazelle. This he did night and morning, till five days went by.

Then, as he slept, the gazelle woke him, saying, 'Master.'

And the man answered, 'How is it that I see a wonder?'

'What wonder?' asked the gazelle.

'Why, that you, a gazelle, should be able to speak, for, from the beginning, my father and mother and all the people that are in the world have never told me of a talking gazelle.'

'Never mind that,' said the gazelle, 'but listen to what I say! First, I took you for my master. Second, you gave for me all you had in the world. I cannot run away from you, but give me, I pray you, leave to go every morning and seek food for myself, and every evening I will come back to you. What you find in the dust-heaps is not enough for both of us.'

'Go, then,' answered the master; and the gazelle went.

When the sun had set, the gazelle came back, and the poor man was very glad, and they lay down and slept side by side.

In the morning it said to him, 'I am going away to feed.'

And the man replied, 'Go, my son,' but he felt very lonely without his gazelle, and set out sooner than usual for the dust-heap where he generally found most corn. And glad he was when the evening came, and he could return home. He lay on the grass chewing tobacco, when the gazelle trotted up.

'Good evening, my master; how have you fared all day? I have been resting in the shade in a place where there is sweet grass when I am hungry, and fresh water when I am thirsty, and a soft breeze to fan me in the heat. It is far away in the forest, and no one knows of it but me, and tomorrow I shall go again.'

So for five days the gazelle set off at daybreak for this cool spot, but on the fifth day it came to a place where the grass was bitter, and it did not like it, and scratched, hoping to tear away the bad blades. But, instead, it saw something lying in the earth, which turned out to be a diamond, very large and bright. 'Oh, ho!' said the gazelle to itself, 'perhaps now I can do something for my master who bought me with all the money he had; but I must be careful or they will say he has stolen it. I had better take it myself to some great rich man, and see what it will do for me.'

Directly the gazelle had come to this conclusion, it picked up the diamond in its mouth, and went on and on and on through the forest, but found no place where a rich man was likely to dwell. For two more days it ran, from dawn to dark, till at last early one morning it caught sight of a large town, which gave it fresh courage.

The people were standing about the streets doing their marketing, when the gazelle bounded past, the diamond flashing as it ran. They called after it, but it took no notice till it reached the palace, where the sultan was sitting, enjoying the cool air. And the gazelle galloped up to him, and laid the diamond at his feet.

The sultan looked first at the diamond and next at the gazelle; then he ordered his attendants to bring cushions and a carpet, that the gazelle might rest itself after its long journey. And he likewise ordered milk to be brought, and rice, that it might eat and drink and be refreshed.

And when the gazelle was rested, the sultan said to it: 'Give me the news you have come with.'

And the gazelle answered: 'I am come with this diamond, which is a pledge from my master the Sultan Darai. He has heard you have a daughter, and sends you this small token, and begs you will give her to him to wife.'

And the sultan said: 'I am content. The wife is his wife, the family is his family, the slave is his slave. Let him come to me empty-handed, I am content.'

When the sultan had ended, the gazelle rose, and said: 'Master, farewell; I go back to our town, and in eight days, or it may be in eleven days, we shall arrive as your guests.'

And the sultan answered: 'So let it be.'

All this time the poor man far away had been mourning and weeping for his gazelle, which he thought had run away from him for ever. And when it came in at the door he rushed to embrace it with such joy that he would not allow it a chance to speak.

'Be still, master, and don't cry,' said the gazelle at last; 'let us sleep now, and in the morning, when I go, follow me.'

With the first ray of dawn they got up and went into the forest, and on the fifth day, as they were resting near a stream, the gazelle gave its master a sound beating, and then bade him stay where he was till it returned. And the gazelle ran off, and about ten o'clock it came near the sultan's palace, where the road was all lined with soldiers who were there to do honour to Sultan Darai. And directly they caught sight of the gazelle in the distance one of the soldiers ran on and said, 'Sultan Darai is coming: I have seen the gazelle.'

Then the sultan rose up, and called his whole court to follow him, and went out to meet the gazelle, who, bounding up to him, gave him greeting. The sultan answered politely, and inquired where it had left its master, whom it had promised to bring back.

'Alas!' replied the gazelle,' he is lying in the forest, for on our way here we were met by robbers, who, after beating and robbing him, took away all his clothes. And he is now hiding under a bush, lest a passing stranger might see him.'

The sultan, on hearing what had happened to his future son-in-law, turned his horse and rode to the palace, and bade a groom to harness the best horse in the stable and ordered a woman slave to bring a bag of clothes, such as a man might want, out of the chest; and he chose out a tunic and a turban and a sash for the waist, and fetched himself a gold-hilted sword, and a dagger and a pair of sandals, and a stick of sweet-smelling wood.

'Now,' said he to the gazelle, 'take these things with the soldiers to the sultan, that he may be able to come.'

And the gazelle answered: 'Can I take those soldiers to go and put my master to shame as he lies there naked? I am enough by myself, my lord.'

'How will you be enough,' asked the sultan, 'to manage this horse and all these clothes?'

'Oh, that is easily done,' replied the gazelle. 'Fasten the horse to my neck and tie the clothes to the back of the horse, and be sure they are fixed firmly, as I shall go faster than he does.'

Everything was carried out as the gazelle had ordered, and

when all was ready it said to the sultan: 'Farewell, my lord, I am going.'

'Farewell, gazelle,' answered the sultan; 'when shall we see you again?'

'Tomorrow about five,' replied the gazelle, and, giving a tug to the horse's rein, they set off at a gallop.

The sultan watched them till they were out of sight: then he said to his attendants, 'That gazelle comes from gentle hands, from the house of a sultan, and that is what makes it so different from other gazelles.' And in the eyes of the sultan the gazelle became a person of consequence.

Meanwhile the gazelle ran on till it came to the place where its master was seated, and his heart laughed when he saw the gazelle.

And the gazelle said to him, 'Get up, my master, and bathe in the stream!' and when the man had bathed it said again, 'Now rub yourself well with earth, and rub your teeth well with sand to make them bright and shining.' And when this was done it said, 'The sun has gone down behind the hills; it is time for us to go': so it went and brought the clothes from the back of the horse, and the man put them on and was well pleased.

'Master!' said the gazelle when the man was ready, 'be sure that where we are going you keep silence, except for giving greetings and asking for news. Leave all the talking to me. I have provided you with a wife, and have made her presents of clothes and turbans and rare and precious things, so it is needless for you to speak.'

'Very good, I will be silent,' replied the man as he mounted the horse. 'You have given all this; it is you who are the master, and I who am the slave, and I will obey you in all things.'

So they went their way, and they went and went till the gazelle saw in the distance the palace of the sultan. Then it said, 'Master, that is the house we are going to, and you are not a poor man any longer: even your name is new.'

'What *is* my name, eh, my father?' asked the man.

'Sultan Darai,' said the gazelle.

Very soon some soldiers came to meet them, while others ran off to tell the sultan of their approach. And the sultan set off at once, and the viziers and the emirs, and the judges, and the rich men of the city, all followed him. Directly the gazelle saw them coming, it said to its master: 'Your father-in-law is coming to meet you; that is he in the middle, wearing a mantle of sky-blue. Get off your horse and go to greet him.'

And Sultan Darai leapt from his horse, and so did the other sultan, and they gave their hands to one another and kissed each other, and went together into the palace.

The next morning the gazelle went to the rooms of the sultan, and said to him: 'My lord, we want you to marry us our wife, for the soul of Sultan Darai is eager.'

'The wife is ready, so call the priest,' answered he, and when the ceremony was over a cannon was fired and music was played, and within the palace there was feasting.

'Master,' said the gazelle the following morning, 'I am setting out on a journey, and I shall not be back for seven days, and perhaps not then. But be careful not to leave the house till I come.'

And the master answered, 'I will not leave the house.'

And it went to the sultan of the country and said to him: 'My lord, Sultan Darai has sent me to his town to get the house in order. It will take me seven days, and if I am not back in seven days he will not leave the palace till I return.'

'Very good,' said the sultan.

And it went and it went through the forest and wilderness, till it arrived at a town full of fine houses. At the end of the chief road was a great house, beautiful exceedingly, built of sapphire and turquoise and marbles. 'That,' thought the gazelle, 'is the house for my master, and I will call up my courage and go and look at the people who are in it, if any people there are. For in this town have I as yet seen no people. If I die, I die, and if I live, I live. Here can I think of no plan, so if anything is to kill me, it will kill me.'

Then it knocked twice at the door, and cried 'Open,' but no one answered. And it cried again, and a voice replied:

'Who are you that are crying "Open"?'

And the gazelle said, 'It is I, great mistress, your grandchild.'

'If you are my grandchild,' returned the voice, 'go back whence you came. Don't come and die here, and bring me to my death as well.'

'Open, mistress, I entreat, I have something to say to you.'

'Grandchild,' replied she, 'I fear to put your life in danger, and my own too.'

'Oh, mistress, my life will not be lost, nor yours either; open, I pray you.' So she opened the door.

'What is the news where you come from, my grandson,' asked she.

'Great lady, where I come from it is well, and with you it is well.'

'Ah, my son, here it is not well at all. If you seek a way to die, or if you have not yet seen death, then is today the day for you to know what dying is.'

'If I am to know it, I shall know it,' replied the gazelle; 'but tell me, who is the lord of this house?'

And she said: 'Ah, father! in this house is much wealth, and much people, and much food, and many horses. And the lord of it all is an exceeding great and wonderful snake.'

'Oh!' cried the gazelle when he heard this; 'tell me how I can get at the snake to kill him?'

'My son,' returned the old woman, 'do not say words like those; you risk both our lives. He has put me here all by myself, and I have to cook his food. When the great snake is coming there springs up a wind, and blows the dust about, and this goes on till the great snake glides into the courtyard and calls for his dinner, which must always be ready for him in those big pots. He eats till he has had enough, and then drinks a whole tankful of water. After that he goes away. Every second day he comes, when the sun is over the house. And he has seven heads. How then can you be a match for him, my son?'

'Mind your own business, mother,' answered the gazelle, 'and don't mind other people's! Has this snake a sword?'

'He has a sword, and a sharp one too. It cuts like a flash of lightning.'

'Give it to me, mother!' said the gazelle, and she unhooked the sword from the wall, as she was bidden. 'You must be quick,' she said, 'for he may be here at any moment. Hark! is not that the wind rising? He has come!'

They were silent, but the old woman peeped from behind a curtain, and saw the snake busy at the pots which she had placed ready for him in the courtyard. And after he had done eating and drinking he came to the door:

'You old body!' he cried; 'what smell is that I smell inside that is not the smell of every day?'

'Oh, master!' answered she, 'I am alone, as I always am! but today, after many days, I have sprinkled fresh scent all over me, and it is that which you smell. What else could it be, master?'

All this time the gazelle had been standing close to the door, holding the sword in one of its front paws. And as the snake put one of his heads through the hole that he had made so as to get in and out comfortably, it cut it off so clean that the snake really did not feel it. The second blow was not quite so straight, for the snake said to himself, 'Who is that who is trying to scratch me?' and stretched out his third head to see; but no sooner was the neck through the hole than the head went rolling to join the rest.

When six of his heads were gone the snake lashed his tail with such fury that the gazelle and the old woman could not see each other for the dust he made. And the gazelle said to him, 'You have climbed all sorts of trees, but this you can't climb,' and as the seventh head came darting through it went rolling to join the rest.

Then the sword fell rattling on the ground, for the gazelle had fainted.

The old woman shrieked with delight when she saw her enemy was dead, and ran to bring water to the gazelle, and fanned it, and put it where the wind could blow on it, till it grew better and gave a sneeze. And the heart of the old woman was glad, and she gave it more water, till by and by the gazelle got up.

'Show me this house,' it said, 'from beginning to end, from top to bottom, from inside to out.'

, So she arose and showed the gazelle rooms full of gold and precious things, and other rooms full of slaves. 'They are all yours, goods and slaves,' said she.

But the gazelle answered, 'You must keep them safe till I call my master.'

For two days it lay and rested in the house, and fed on milk and rice, and on the third day it bade the old woman farewell and started back to its master.

And when he heard that the gazelle was at the door he felt like a man who has found the time when all prayers are granted, and he rose and kissed it, saying: 'My father, you have been a long time; you have left sorrow with me. I cannot eat, I cannot drink, I cannot laugh; my heart felt no smile at anything, because of thinking of you.'

And the gazelle answered: 'I am well, and where I come from it is well, and I wish that after four days you would take your wife and go home.'

And he said: 'It is for you to speak. Where you go, I will follow.'

'Then I shall go to your father-in-law and tell him this news.'

'Go, my son.'

So the gazelle went to the father-in-law and said: 'I am sent by my master to come and tell you that after four days he will go away with his wife to his own home.'

'Must he really go so quickly? We have not yet sat much together, I and Sultan Darai, nor have we yet talked much together, nor have we yet ridden out together, nor have we eaten together; yet it is fourteen days since he came.'

But the gazelle replied: 'My lord, you cannot help it, for he wishes to go home, and nothing will stop him.'

'Very good,' said the sultan, and he called all the people who were in the town, and commanded that the day his daughter left the palace ladies and guards were to attend her on her way.

And at the end of four days a great company of ladies and slaves and horses went forth to escort the wife of Sultan Darai to her new home. They rode all day, and when the sun sank behind the hills they rested, and ate of the food the gazelle gave them, and lay down to sleep. And they journeyed on for many days, and they all, nobles and slaves, loved the gazelle with a great love – more than they loved the Sultan Darai.

At last one day signs of houses appeared, far, far off. And those who saw cried out, 'Gazelle!'

And it answered, 'Ah, my mistresses, that is the house of Sultan Darai.'

At this news the women rejoiced much, and the slaves rejoiced much, and in the space of two hours they came to the gates, and the gazelle bade them all stay behind, and it went on to the house with Sultan Darai.

When the old woman saw them coming through the courtyard she jumped and shouted for joy, and as the gazelle drew near she seized it in her arms, and kissed it. The gazelle did not like this, and said to her: 'Old woman, leave me alone; the one to be carried is my master, and the one to be kissed is my master.'

And she answered, 'Forgive me, my son. I did not know this was our master,' and she threw open all the doors so that the master might see everything that the rooms and storehouses contained. Sultan Darai looked about him, and at length he said:

'Unfasten those horses that are tied up, and let loose those people that are bound. And let some sweep, and some spread the beds, and some cook, and some draw water, and some come out and receive the mistress.'

And when the sultana and her ladies and her slaves entered the house, and saw the rich stuffs it was hung with, and the beautiful rice that was prepared for them to eat, they cried: 'Ah, you gazelle, we have seen great houses, we have seen people, we have heard of things. But this house, and you, such as you are, we have never seen or heard of.'

After a few days, the ladies said they wished to go home again. The gazelle begged them hard to stay, but finding they would not, it brought many gifts, and gave some to the ladies and some to their slaves. And they all thought the gazelle greater a thousand times than its master, Sultan Darai.

The gazelle and its master remained in the house many weeks, and one day it said to the old woman, 'I came with my master to this place, and I have done many things for my master, good things, and till today he has never asked me: "Well, my gazelle, how did you get this house? Who is the owner of it? And this town, were there no people in it?" All good things I have done for the master, and he has not one day done me any good thing. But people say, "If you want to do anyone good, don't do him good only, do him evil also, and there will be peace between you." So, mother, I have done: I want to see the favours I have done to my master, that he may do me the like.'

'Good,' replied the old woman, and they went to bed.

In the morning, when light came, the gazelle was sick in its stomach and feverish, and its legs ached. And it said 'Mother!'

And she answered, 'Here, my son?'

And it said, 'Go and tell my master upstairs the gazelle is very ill.'

'Very good, my son; and if he should ask me what is the matter, what am I to say?'

'Tell him all my body aches badly; I have no single part without pain.'

The old woman went upstairs, and she found the mistress and master sitting on a couch of marble spread with soft cushions, and they asked her, 'Well, old woman, what do you want?'

'To tell the master the gazelle is ill,' said she.

'What is the matter?' asked the wife.

'All its body pains; there is no part without pain.'

'Well, what can I do? Make some gruel of red millet, and give to it.'

But his wife stared and said: 'Oh, master, do you tell her to make the gazelle gruel out of red millet, which a horse would not eat? Eh, master, that is not well.'

But he answered, 'Oh, you are mad! Rice is only kept for people.'

'Eh, master, this is not like a gazelle. It is the apple of your eye. If sand got into that, it would trouble you.'

'My wife, your tongue is long,' and he left the room.

The old woman saw she had spoken vainly, and went back weeping to the gazelle. And when the gazelle saw her it said, 'Mother, what is it, and why do you cry? If it be good, give me the answer; and if it be bad, give me the answer.'

But still the old woman would not speak, and the gazelle prayed her to let it know the words of the master. At last she said: 'I went upstairs and found the mistress and the master sitting on a couch, and he asked me what I wanted, and I told him that you, his slave, were ill. And his wife asked what was the matter, and I told her that there was not a part of your body without pain. And the master told me to take some red millet and make you gruel, but the mistress said, "Eh, master, the gazelle is the apple of your eye; you have no child, this gazelle is like your child; so this gazelle is not one to be done evil to. This is a gazelle in form, but not a gazelle in heart; he is in all things better than a gentleman, be he who he may."

'And he answered her, "Silly chatterer, your words are many. I know its price; I bought it for an eighth. What loss will it be to me?"'

The gazelle kept silence for a few moments. Then it said,

'The elders said, "One that does good like a mother," and I have done him good, and I have got this that the elders said. But go up again to the master, and tell him the gazelle is very ill, and it has not drunk the gruel of red millet.'

So the old woman returned, and found the master and the mistress drinking coffee. And when he heard what the gazelle had said, he cried: 'Hold your peace, old woman, and stay your feet and close your eyes, and stop your ears with wax; and if the gazelle bids you come to me, say your legs are bent, and you cannot walk; and if it begs you to listen, say your ears are stopped with wax; and if it wishes to talk, reply that your tongue has got a hook in it.'

The heart of the old woman wept as she heard such words, because she saw that when the gazelle first came to that town it was ready to sell its life to buy wealth for its master. Then it happened to get both life and wealth, but now it had no honour with its master.

And tears sprung likewise to the eyes of the sultan's wife, and she said, 'I am sorry for you, my husband, that you should deal so wickedly with that gazelle'; but he only answered, 'Old woman, pay no heed to the talk of the mistress: tell it to perish out of the way. I cannot sleep, I cannot eat, I cannot drink, for the worry of that gazelle. Shall a creature that I bought for an eighth trouble me from morning till night? Not so, old woman!'

The old woman went downstairs, and there lay the gazelle, blood flowing from its nostrils. And she took it in her arms and said, 'My son, the good you did is lost; there remains only patience.'

And it said, 'Mother, I shall die, for my soul is full of anger and bitterness. My face is ashamed, that I should have done good to my master, and that he should repay me with evil.' It paused for a moment, and then went on, 'Mother, of the goods that are in this house, what do I eat? I might have every day half a basinful, and would my master be any the poorer? But did not the elders say, "He that does good like a mother!"'

And it said, 'Go and tell my master that the gazelle is nearer death than life.'

So she went, and spoke as the gazelle had bidden her; but he answered, 'I have told you to trouble me no more.'

But his wife's heart was sore, and she said to him: 'Ah, master, what has the gazelle done to you? How has he failed you? The things you do to him are not good, and you will draw on yourself the hatred of the people. For this gazelle is loved by all, by small and great, by women and men. Ah, my husband! I thought you had great wisdom, and you have not even a little!'

But he answered, 'You are mad, my wife.'

The old woman stayed no longer, and went back to the gazelle, followed secretly by the mistress, who called a maid-servant and bade her take some milk and rice and cook it for the gazelle.

'Take also this cloth,' she said, 'to cover it with, and this pillow for its head. And if the gazelle wants more, let it ask me, and not its master. And if it will, I will send it in a litter to my father, and he will nurse it till it is well.'

And the maidservant did as her mistress bade her, and said what her mistress had told her to say, but the gazelle made no answer, but turned over on its side and died quietly.

When the news spread abroad, there was much weeping among the people, and Sultan Darai arose in wrath, and cried, 'You weep for that gazelle as if you wept for me! And, after all, what is it but a gazelle, that I bought for an eighth?'

But his wife answered, 'Master, we looked upon that gazelle as we looked upon you. It was the gazelle who came to ask me of my father, it was the gazelle who brought me from my father, and I was given in charge to the gazelle by my father.'

And when the people heard her they lifted up their voices and spoke:

'We never saw you, we saw the gazelle. It was the gazelle who met with trouble here, it was the gazelle who met with rest here. So, then, when such a one departs from this world we weep for ourselves, we do not weep for the gazelle.'

And they said furthermore:

'The gazelle did you much good, and if anyone says he could have done more for you he is a liar! Therefore, to us who have done you no good, what treatment will you give? The gazelle has died from bitterness of soul, and you ordered your slaves to throw it into the well. Ah! leave us alone that we may weep.'

But Sultan Darai would not heed their words, and the dead gazelle was thrown into the well.

When the mistress heard of it, she sent three slaves, mounted on donkeys, with a letter to her father the sultan, and when the sultan had read the letter he bowed his head and wept, like a man who had lost his mother. And he commanded horses to be saddled, and called the governor and the judges and all the rich men, and said:

'Come now with me; let us go and bury it.'

Night and day they travelled, till the sultan came to the well where the gazelle had been thrown. And it was a large well, built round a rock, with room for many people; and the sultan entered, and the judges and the rich men followed him. And when he saw the gazelle lying there he wept afresh, and took it in his arms and carried it away.

When the three slaves went and told their mistress what the sultan had done, and how all the people were weeping, she answered:

'I too have eaten no food, neither have I drunk water, since the day the gazelle died. I have not spoken, and I have not laughed.'

The sultan took the gazelle and buried it, and ordered the people to wear mourning for it, so there was great mourning throughout the city.

Now after the days of mourning were at an end, the wife was sleeping at her husband's side, and in her sleep she dreamed that she was once more in her father's house, and when she woke up it was no dream.

And the man dreamed that he was on the dust-heap, scratching. And when he woke, behold! that also was no dream, but the truth.

YUKI-ONNA

Lafcadio Hearn

IN A VILLAGE of Musashi Province, there lived two wood-cutters: Mosaku and Minokichi. At the time of which I am speaking, Mosaku was an old man; and Minokichi, his apprentice, was a lad of eighteen years. Every day they went together to a forest situated about five miles from their village. On the way to that forest there is a wide river to cross; and there is a ferryboat. Several times a bridge was built where the ferry is; but the bridge was each time carried away by a flood. No common bridge can resist the current there when the river rises.

Mosaku and Minokichi were on their way home, one very cold evening, when a great snowstorm overtook them. They reached the ferry; and they found that the boatman had gone away, leaving his boat on the other side of the river. It was no day for swimming; and the woodcutters took shelter in the ferryman's hut – thinking themselves lucky to find any shelter at all. There was no brazier in the hut, nor any place in which to make a fire: it was only a two-mat hut, with a single door, but no window. Mosaku and Minokichi fastened the door, and lay down to rest, with their straw raincoats over them. At first they did not feel very cold; and they thought that the storm would soon be over.

The old man almost immediately fell asleep; but the boy, Minokichi, lay awake a long time, listening to the awful wind, and the continual slashing of the snow against the door. The river was roaring; and the hut swayed and creaked like a junk at sea. It was a terrible storm; and the air was every moment becoming colder; and Minokichi shivered under his raincoat. But at last, in spite of the cold, he too fell asleep.

He was awakened by a showering of snow in his face. The door of the hut had been forced open; and, by the snow-light (*yuki-akari*), he saw a woman in the room – a woman all in white. She was bending above Mosaku, and blowing her breath upon him – and her breath was like a bright white smoke. Almost in the same moment she turned to Minokichi, and stooped over him. He tried to cry out, but found that he could not utter any sound. The white woman bent down over him, lower and lower, until her face almost touched him; and he saw that she was very beautiful, – though her eyes made him afraid. For a little time she continued to look at him; then she smiled, and she whispered: 'I intended to treat you like the other man. But I cannot help feeling some pity for you, because you are so young ... You are a pretty boy, Minokichi; and I will not hurt you now. But, if you ever tell anybody – even your own mother – about what you have seen this night, I shall know it; and then I will kill you ... Remember what I say!'

With these words, she turned from him and passed through the doorway. Then he found himself able to move; and he sprang up, and looked out. But the woman was nowhere to be seen; and the snow was driving furiously into the hut. Minokichi closed the door, and secured it by fixing several billets of wood against it. He wondered if the wind had blown it open; he thought that he might have been only dreaming, and might have mistaken the gleam of the snow-light in the doorway for the figure of a white woman: but he could not be sure. He called to Mosaku, and was frightened because the old man did not answer. He put out his hand in the dark, and touched Mosaku's face, and found that it was ice! Mosaku was stark and dead ...

By dawn the storm was over; and when the ferryman returned to his station, a little after sunrise, he found Minokichi lying senseless beside the frozen body of Mosaku. Minokichi was promptly cared for, and soon came to himself; but he remained a long time ill from the effects of the cold of that terrible night. He had been greatly frightened also by the old man's death; but he said nothing about the vision of the woman in white. As soon as he got well again, he returned to his calling – going alone every morning to the forest, and coming back at nightfall with his bundles of wood, which his mother helped him to sell.

One evening, in the winter of the following year, as he was on his way home, he overtook a girl who happened to be travelling by the same road. She was a tall, slim girl, very good-looking; and she answered Minokichi's greeting in a voice as pleasant to the ear as the voice of a song-bird. Then he walked beside her; and they began to talk. The girl said that her name was O-Yuki; that she had lately lost both of her parents; and that she was going to Yedo, where she happened to have some poor relations, who might help her to find a situation as servant. Minokichi soon felt charmed by this strange girl; and the more that he looked at her, the handsomer she appeared to be. He asked her whether she was yet betrothed; and she answered, laughingly, that she was free. Then, in her turn, she asked Minokichi whether he was married, or pledged to marry; and he told her that, although he had only a widowed mother to support, the question of an 'honorable daughter-in-law' had not yet been considered, as he was very young ... After these confidences, they walked on for a long while without speaking; but, as the proverb declares, *Ki ga aréba, mé mo kuchi hodo ni mono wo iu*: 'When the wish is there, the eyes can say as much as the mouth.' By the time they reached the village, they had become very much pleased with each other; and then Minokichi asked O-Yuki to rest awhile at his house. After some shy hesitation, she went there with him; and his mother made her welcome, and prepared a warm meal for her. O-Yuki behaved so nicely that Minokichi's mother took a sudden fancy to her, and persuaded her to delay her journey to Yedo. And the natural end of the matter was that Yuki never went to Yedo at all. She remained in the house, as an 'honorable daughter-in-law'.

O-Yuki proved a very good daughter-in-law. When Minokichi's mother came to die – some five years later – her last words were words of affection and praise for the wife of her son. And O-Yuki bore Minokichi ten children, boys and girls – handsome children all of them, and very fair of skin.

The country-folk thought O-Yuki a wonderful person, by nature different from themselves. Most of the peasant-women age early; but O-Yuki, even after having become the mother of ten children, looked as young and fresh as on the day when she had first come to the village.

One night, after the children had gone to sleep, O-Yuki was sewing by the light of a paper lamp; and Minokichi, watching her, said:

'To see you sewing there, with the light on your face, makes me think of a strange thing that happened when I was a lad of eighteen. I then saw somebody as beautiful and white as you are now – indeed, she was very like you.'

Without lifting her eyes from her work, O-Yuki responded:

'Tell me about her . . . Where did you see her?'

Then Minokichi told her about the terrible night in the ferryman's hut – and about the White Woman that had stooped above him, smiling and whispering – and about the silent death of old Mosaku. And he said:

'Asleep or awake, that was the only time that I saw a being as beautiful as you. Of course, she was not a human being; and I was afraid of her – very much afraid – but she was so white! . . . Indeed, I have never been sure whether it was a dream that I saw, or the Woman of the Snow.'

O-Yuki flung down her sewing, and arose, and bowed above Minokichi where he sat, and shrieked into his face:

'It was I – I – I! Yuki it was! And I told you then that I would kill you if you ever said one word about it! . . . But for those children asleep there, I would kill you this moment! And now you had better take very, very good care of them; for if ever they have reason to complain of you, I will treat you as you deserve!'

Even as she screamed, her voice came thin, like a crying of wind; then she melted into a bright white mist that spired to the roof-beams, and shuddered away through the smoke-hole . . . Never again was she seen.

PART VIII:
FULFILMENT AND FATE

BHADRA AND THE MENDICANT

Jessica Amanda Salmonson

M ANY PEOPLE HAVE heard the story of the demonic asuras who attacked a certain town and were carrying livestock and infants away through the air. They were rending warriors to pieces and causing much grief and bloodshed. At the height of the carnage, a fair princess ran forth, and, reciting an incantation, drew out of the forest a company of yaksas and yaksinis, who were like ghostly hunters and huntresses armed with bows and arrows and axes. These demi-gods and -goddesses fell upon the asuras mightily, and the town was saved.

Until this event, no one had known that Princess Bhadra had power over yaksas. Since that time, she has become famous for her abilities. But she was not born a great woman. It is hard to realize that previously she was hardly noticed by the divinities. And the first yaksini she ever met disliked her greatly. This is the story of how she angered a yaksini and learned by her fearful experience.

Bhadra had always lived an exemplary life for all outward appearances, performing such rituals and sacrifices as were expected of her, and causing no worry or concern to her father, King Kausalika, a widower. At no time had she known travail, or hunger, or suffering, and, while she meant no actual harm to anyone, she was selfish and vain without knowing she was these things, and caused grief to other people by her pride and careless indifference, scarcely knowing she was doing so.

She grew to be an exceedingly handsome young woman, taking for granted people's admiration. She was well versed in the Vedas, and was often reassured by the brahmans that as long as her family gave a percentage of their treasures to the priests, then King Kausalika's family, and especially his splendid daughter, would continue to prosper even into future lives.

It would have surprised her greatly to realize that in the Hall of the Offerings to Heaven, the divinities placed all her sacrifices in a room reserved to those called Stolid, Upright, and Insufferable. For all her earthly beauty, she was spiritually nondescript.

She was betrothed to Rudradeva, a good-looking brahman, and this was regarded by everyone, including Bhadra, as a superior match. She was quite pleased with the prospect of being Rudradeva's wife. She went about making her well-intended offerings at her family shrine in the deer park, and performing other rituals as were part of her preparations for the pending marriage. She burnt incense and presented rice cakes, flesh, prayers, and money to the Goddess of the shrine.

She liked to imagine the Heavenly Ones sitting in a neat row just like the brahmans, watching her pray, and smiling at her on account of her piety and her generally pleasing appearance. In actuality, the divinities were off somewhere else and, for that matter, didn't even know who she was.

A yaksini, or fairy-divinity, who was the guardian of the shrine, came as usual with a ho-hum and a who-cares, intending to gather up the smoke of Bhadra's incense, and the essence of the rice offering, and take these to the Room of the Upright and Insufferable. The meat and the money were of no concern to the yaksini, as such offerings were in actuality for the brahmans. As for Bhadra's prayers, the yaksini left those behind simply because there was no heavenly offering-room for banalities.

The yaksini was in a bad mood that day. For some while she had been bestowing good luck on visitors to the shrine, but yaksinis are somewhat unpredictable, and have to balance the good things they do with one or another offensive act. They tend to be just in their actions, however, even if human beings sometimes disagree with what a yaksa or yaksini considers justifiable.

The yaksini was invisible to mortals. Had she chosen to reveal herself, she might easily be mistaken for a beautiful young Goddess. She had firm round breasts and a flat stomach with a golden girdle. She had a lovely headdress and a third eye on her forehead. Although she usually had only two arms, she could sometimes reveal herself with four. She was a very elegant yaksini and delighted in punishing people who desecrated the shrine and rewarding those who were pious.

Unexpectedly, she felt something very pleasing in her vicinity. Despite her bad mood, an inexplicable feeling made her smile. She let loose of the essence of the rice and incense offered by Bhadra, and it dissipated into nothingness, not that it would be missed in heaven. She looked around for the source of the excellent emanations, and spied a Jain monk with filthy hands, praying in a gloomy corner of the shrine for the salvation of all the miserable and stupid people of the world.

This man, whose name was Bala, observed all rules in regard to walking, begging, speaking, vacuating, praying, restraining himself from idle pleasures, and being always attentive to duty. He protected his thoughts, speech, and body by subduing the senses. He was devoid of hatred and impurity. He never bathed, for Truth alone was his bathing pool, and his soul was among the cleanest of all mortals.

This mendicant was so humble in his heart, he did not even know he was a great sage, but thought himself nothing more than a small and undeserving monk whose simplicity and holiness might be noticed in heaven, but only if he was lucky, and his inarticulate prayers might sometimes be considered, but only because he was too pitiful to ignore.

'Ah, such a lovely monk,' said the yaksini. 'I shall take his prayers straightaway to the Room of the Saints of Truth!'

Princess Bhadra had had quite a different response to him. To be fair, it must be confessed that a yaksini cannot smell unbathed human skin, but is susceptible only to human spirit. Thus Bala made quite a different impression on Bhadra than on the yaksini. Even so, Bhadra was ungenerous. She was in the midst of a prayer she thought quite splendid. She had worked on it for a couple of days and was even thinking of having it published. Then an unexpected stench broke her concentration. She looked around and saw the mendicant, emaciated by austerities, with the most ragged clothing, and she shivered with disdain and dread of such a foul being.

Motioning to the row of brahman priests sitting by the altar, she indicated the presence of the vile beggar. The brahmans laughed at Bala, then went over to where he was sitting quietly.

They behaved like ruffians toward him. 'Look at this miserable swarthy monster with a boar hog's nose! What are you doing here, dirty little man with filthy clothes dangling from your soiled neck? Get out of here! Go away!'

The yaksini had often been annoyed by these brahmans, who were animal-killers and didn't know a good sacrifice from a bad one. They imagined themselves holy because of their high birth rather than their deeds, but they were, at best, insufferable prigs, and usually not even as good as that. She had given one of them a boil on the tip of his penis, and another, who was quite vain of his looks, was growing a wen on his cheek because the yaksini couldn't stand his pettiness and self-importance. She scowled at the brahmans, then looked to where Princess Bhadra sat quietly, wondering how to punish her. The princess was trying to look so innocent of the matter at hand, and was sitting in a very pretty lotus posture with her eyes averted. Yet she was all too eager to see the little monk gotten rid of.

The monk said to his persecutors, 'I am a chaste mendicant with no property. I eat neither meat nor cooked food. My mother was the chieftainess Gauri the Fair of a kandala tribe, the lowest caste, and my father was chief Harikesa the Yellow-haired. My tribe lives on the banks of the Ganges where it floods each spring. Life is difficult for them. I have become a Jain ascetic seeking always for the salvation of those who suffer. I have come here to pray and to beg for something to eat. Here at this shrine, much food is consumed, and much food is thrown away. Let a mendicant have what is thrown away.'

But the brahmans paid him no heed and dragged him out of the shrine and beat him at the edge of the grove. Then, to justify themselves and to feel magnanimous, they told him to go sit among the gardening rubble, where the leavings of each afternoon meal were composted. They promised to throw something edible to him later. He thanked them and went to sit atop the gardening rubble.

As Princess Bhadra was leaving the shrine grounds, the yaksini ran after her and leapt inside her body. By this means the yaksini came to the palace of King Kausalika. When a meal was served, Princess Bhadra was taken by the sudden impulse to throw food about. She snatched a fish from the plate of a young prince and threw it across the table, where it smote the king in the face, which considerably startled him. Bhadra laughed, then ran out of the room like a dart.

She went into the main greeting hall where stood her father's throne, and, climbing onto the dais, snatched his gold embroidered pillow and rent it all to pieces, laughing wildly the whole time. Servants and courtiers followed her about the palace as she caused damage here and there. When she began to break ancient vases and artifacts of incalculable value, she was finally restrained.

At her father's command, Bhadra was dragged kicking to her suite, where she was bound wrist and ankle to her bedposts. The whole while she was cursing her father and the memory of her mother and swearing all manner of vengeance on her maids who had helped tie her up. Everyone was weeping, as though she were dead and unreclaimable. Her betrothed, the brahman Rudradeva, was called to the palace for consultation. As he was versed in occult matters, he knew at once that she was possessed of a yaksini. He performed a severe exorcism, but the yaksini held fast to Bhadra's body, and caused her to say wicked things.

At last, Rudradeva thought to ask the yaksini what she wanted that caused her to hold onto the body of Bhadra. The yaksini spoke through Bhadra's mouth, saying, 'I am in love with Bala, the Jain monk who is staying in the holy grove, with no shelter and little to eat. If Bhadra will marry him, then I can experience his embrace for a full night. Only then will I leave the princess!'

Rudradeva was startled and unhappy, for Bhadra was to be his bride. Yet he went to the king and told him, 'Your daughter insulted an ascetic in the shrine today, and had the brahmans throw him out because of his odor. The yaksini of the shrine has possessed Bhadra in order to punish her rudeness. The fairy-spirit will not leave until Bhadra and the monk Bala have spent a wedding night together.'

As there was no other method, the king agreed to the marriage. The yaksini was informed she would soon have her wish. She then let Bhadra regain control of her senses. Repenting her aversion to the monk, Bhadra returned to the shrine and found the monk sitting on the compost heap. She said, 'Holy man! We must become married, for otherwise the yaksini of this shrine will not leave my body. You, in spite of your lowly kandala origins, can become a prince by wedding me! What greater reward can have come to you because of your austerities?'

Bala replied, 'I have vowed never to seek worldliness or pleasure. Think not ill of me if I reject your offer of marriage. As for the yaksini, I will speak to her in your behalf. Naughty yaksini! Do not trouble this young woman! You do me an injustice to punish anyone on my account. I suffer in this world so that others need not suffer!'

Thus chastised, the yaksini leapt out of Bhadra. She manifested herself as a pleasing young woman with three eyes and four arms. But feeling spurned and chastised, when she had sought only to act in his behalf, the mischievous part of her character rose again to the surface. She called forth ten yaksas from out of the trees, who looked like splendid young hunters. She told them, 'This ascetic wants to suffer! Beat him at once!' And the ten yaksas began to beat the monk at the yaksini's request.

Princess Bhadra threw herself upon the frail monk, pleading with an appeasing tone, 'Do not harm him! This chaste man, who would not accept me in marriage even when my father, King Kausalika, would have made him a prince, do you not know who he is? This is Saint Bala, a man of great piety and power, who could smite you easily if he were not so concerned even for your well-being! You might as well eat iron with your teeth as to treat this monk contemptuously! Come not against him with your willow sticks, lest he consume you in the fire of his virtue as moths are consumed when they dash toward an altar fire.'

When the yaksas heard these well-spoken words, they began to assist the sage, picking the thorns out of his ragged clothing, and bowing to him with admiration. The yaksini said, 'I have neglected my duties of late. I must take your excellent speech straightaway to the Hall of Offerings and the Room of Truth, where it will be enshrined as the first of your great offerings. From this day on, O Bhadra, you have power over yaksas and yaksinis. Because you are the protectress of a sage mighty in spirit, we bow to you.'

At that moment there fell a perfumed rain from heaven. The

yaksas produced drums and struck them, singing the praises of
Bala and Bhadra. The Jain monk said, 'The power of penance
has become visible. The Truth of the Law is that compassion
is great, anger is a small thing.'

Bhadra said, 'My life until now has been nothing. This shrine
that feeds brahmans, but which belongs to my father, I will
petition be turned over as a waystation for traveling ascetics.
Those priests who injure living things and slay pitiful animals
grow fat on the spoils of people's fear of dying. Let them find
another place! Birth and death are nothing, and compassion is
all. O blessed day that the yaksini possessed me! I will devote
my life to the care of wandering monks and nuns, and if my
betrothed Rudradeva wishes to pursue the brahman path, I will
never marry.'

THE REBORN DIVINITIES

Jessica Amanda Salmonson

EVEN DIVINITIES ARE subject to the cycle of birth and rebirth. Thus four of them came to the earth as mortals. They were born in a town called Ishukara, which was in the Kuru country long ago. In those days, the whole region was almost as beautiful as heaven.

They were born into noble families, two of the brahman caste, two within the royal house. They knew every pleasure.

One who was reborn was Yasa, whose beauty reflected her previous divinity. She married Bhrigu, a handsome youth who matched Yasa's sweet appearance.

The third to be reborn was Queen Kamalavati. Her husband was the famous King Ishukara. These two ruled in the country beautiful as heaven.

All four were born within days of one another. The children of the brahman grew up knowing the royal children, so all were fast friends, just as they had been in heaven. They retained a slight awareness of their heavenly origins, but rarely spoke of their suspicions. They hoped to escape the wheel of birth. They sampled all pleasures, abandoning them one after the other, no refinement being sufficient to fill the void within them. They grew fearful of birth, old age, and death.

Their aversion to both human and heavenly pleasures developed into a disgust for all the wickedness that was in the world. They desired liberation. They became filled with faith. One by one, they became Jain ascetics, first Bhrigu, then Yasa, then Kamalavati, and finally Ishukara.

Yasa's father was a famous brahman priest, well versed in the Vedas. He heard that his daughter and son-in-law were considering the ascetic path. He hurried to their house to dissuade them from rash decisions. He said, 'The Vedas tell us that there is no better world awaiting those who fail to procreate. My children, after you have studied the Vedas and have given offerings to priests; after you have had children to carry on the name of your house; and when you have lived a full life and grown old, that is the time to depart for the woods as praiseworthy ascetics.'

By his manner, they could see their father was consumed with grief. Yet he spoke importantly, as one who has grown used to giving sage advice, rarely hearing criticisms. They were sorry for him, seeing that he had been blown into terrible blazes of agony by the winds of delusion. He wept, cajoled, and bribed, but they were immovable, and more than a little surprised that he would demean himself so.

Yasa took her father's hands in hers. She said to him in a kindly way, 'The study of Vedas will not save us. The feeding of priests leads us from darkness to darkness. The birth of children binds others to the wheel of birth.'

Her husband added, 'Worldly pleasures bring momentary respite, but when we suffer, it goes on and on. Happiness is fleeting and anguish boundless, hence we cannot balance one with the other. The good things as well as the bad are obstacles holding us from our liberation. We must flee the pleasures if we are to flee the evils.'

Their father persisted. 'People who practice austerities do so in order to obtain wealth, position, and exquisite pleasures in another life. But you have these things for the asking. There is no reason for you to choose the austere path.'

Bhrigu replied, 'All who fail to abandon pleasure grieve day and night. Possessions cannot save us. We have this, but want that. We fret about robbers, so we hire guards, but the guards are themselves robbers. We have authority, but fear revolt. Wealth and power are no different from old age and death.'

Yasa said, 'What use are riches in the practice of religion? We shall live as mendicants, possessed of virtue rather than property, wandering from place to place.'

The sorrowful father lamented. 'Without you, I am bereft, as a bird without wings, as a merchant without goods, as a king standing amidst battle without followers. A snake sloughs its skin, just as you, my children, abandon grief and pleasure.

Perhaps you are admirable after all. Why should I live alone? Why should I not follow in the dusty prints of your naked feet? A fish breaks a weak net; a heron conquers gravity and flies away. So too will I escape all that I have lived to possess, and go with you!'

Therefore, without even closing up their houses, they set forth to seek perfection.

Now when Queen Kamalavati learned that Yasa and Bhrigu had taken vows of poverty, going so far as to convert their priestly father, she went quickly to speak with her husband, King Ishukara.

She was distraught with the world and with her own weakness in needing things. Thinking of her good friends striding barefoot from place to place, she was filled with admiration. For the first time she felt a strength well up inside her.

'Oh my husband,' said the queen. 'When in sickness someone vomits all that they have devoured, who would praise the man who hurried forth to feast upon that vomit? Yet you, my lord, have sent vassals to confiscate the property of the brahman family who has vomited everything to become ascetics. Remember this, my lord, that when we are dead, nothing in all we own can ever be salvation.'

'Why have you come to speak to me thus, O my Queen?' said the king, unused to such rebukes.

'My lord, as a bird hates its cage, so do I hate this world. I shall go forth to live as a nun, impoverished, without children or desire, without greed or hatred. Consider! When a forest is burning, the animals leap up and flee the forest. But what fools are we humans! The world is consumed with the fire of love and hate, yet we fail to escape what is blazing all about us. Those who have known pleasure, then renounce pleasure, are like the wind. They are birds unchecked in their flight.'

'Pray, O Queen, whose tongue is sweet and bitter to my ears, what would you have of me?'

'Consider the bird when it is held by its wings. It struggles, as we must struggle in our fetters. We must live as the wind, attached to no one place, affixed to no set objects. Pleasure is but a snare binding us to worldly existence, therefore we must put aside all that we have mistaken for treasure, then seek the greater destination. This, O great king Ishukara, is the wonderful truth that until this day has troubled me, but which now I am eager to embrace. O my husband, leave this kingdom and all the pleasures which have become dear to you! Abandon what pleases the senses! Give up idle amusements. Give up power. Become famed for severe penance and firm energy. By this means we shall both gradually obtain enlightenment.'

'O Queen, it is true that I have cluttered my existence with many things, fearful of birth and death, burying my fear in useless endeavors. You have won me over! In abandoning pleasure, we can at last seek an end to misery.'

All doubts were dispersed. The king descended from his throne, threw off his robes and crown, and together with his wife set out to seek perfection.

ISLAND OF THE OCEAN GOD

Peter Tremayne

M AC CUILL, which means 'son of the hazel', was, in fact, the son of the great god of eloquence and literacy, Ogma. He had so named his son for the hazel is a mystical tree and Ogma used it to signify the third letter of the alphabet which he had devised. And, indeed, Mac Cuill was the third son of Ogma for his brothers were Mac Gréine, 'son of the sun', and Mac Cécht, 'son of the plough'. The three brothers were married to three sisters: Mac Gréine was married to the goddess Éire, while Mac Cécht was married to her sister Fótla and Mac Cuill was married to the youngest sister named Banba.

There came a time when the gods themselves fell from grace, when the sons of Míl conquered them. And it was said that Mac Gréine was slain by the great Druid Amairgen; that Mac Cécht met his end from the sword of Eremon and that Mac Cuill was slain by the spear of Eber.

And when the gods were defeated by the sons of Míl, the wives of Mac Gréine, Mac Cécht and Mac Cuill – Éire, Fótla and Banba, went to greet the conquerors of the land of Inisfáil, the island of destiny.

'Welcome warriors,' cried Éire. 'To you who have come from afar this island shall henceforth belong, and from the setting to the rising sun there is no better land. And your race will be the most perfect the world has ever seen.'

Amairgen the Druid asked her what she wanted in reward for this blessing.

'That you name this country after me,' replied Éire. But her sisters chimed in that the country should be named after them. So Amairgen promised that Éire would be the principal name for the country while the poets of Míl would also hail the land by the names of Fótla and Banba. So it has been until this day.

Now as the sons of Ogma were gods, and therefore 'The Ever Living Ones', they could not die completely and so their souls were passed on through the aeons. And in the rebirths of Mac Cuill he began to lament the lost days of power, of the days he had been happy with Banba. He grew bitter and resentful with each rebirth until he was reborn as a petty thief in the kingdom of Ulaidh, which is one of the five provincial kingdoms of Éire. Each province was called *cúige* or a fifth and the five made up the whole and the whole, one and indivisible, governed by the Ard-Rígh, or High King.

There was no better thief in all Ulaidh than Mac Cuill and he became the terror of the land. His deeds came to the ears of the High King himself and he sent his personal Brehon, or judge, named Dubhtach, to the provincial king of Ulaidh, saying: 'Mac Cuill must be captured and punished.' Eventually, Mac Cuill the thief, was caught, and he was taken before the High King's Brehon. And there was a tall, white-haired man standing by the Brehon's side. They called him by the name of an ancient god of war, which is Sucat.

'Why should we not kill you for your evil life, Mac Cuill?' demanded Dubhtach the Brehon.

Now Mac Cuill was full of guile and he smiled.

'Kill me now, Brehon. I have reached my last rebirth on this earth. I cannot descend lower than a thief. I will have been wiped from the Brandubh board of this world.' Brandubh, which means 'black raven', was a wooden board game, which many compare to the eastern game of chess. 'Yet,' he added with evasive craft, 'Kill me now and there will be no hope of redemption, no hope of reparation for my sins. Spare me and perhaps there is still some goodness in my soul whereby I might change my life for the better.'

Now Mac Cuill spoke with irony, in mocking tones, but his words held some truth. The Brehon pondered and could reach no decision. Finally, it was Sucat who said: 'The decision is not for us to make, for man is often flawed in his perceptions of his fellows. What is justice for one is injustice for another. So let us leave it to the Creator to decide. You will have the judgment of the sea.'

Now the judgment of the sea can be a terrifying thing. But Mac Cuill, who had lived many lifetimes, was not afraid. And Sucat had the wrists of Mac Cuill bound in a chain of iron which he fastened by a padlock with his own hand. And he flung the key into the waves of the sea, saying to Mac Cuill: 'Loose not that chain until the key be found and brought to you.' The Brehon then had Mac Cuill taken to a boat which is called a curragh. The boat was without oars and without a sail and no food or drink was placed in it. This boat, containing Mac Cuill, was rowed several miles from the coast of Ulaidh and cast adrift. The fate of Mac Cuill was left to whichever way the winds and tides took him. Whoever found him could make a slave of him.

Now of all the ancient gods one of the last to live upon the Earth with their ancient powers was Manánnan Mac Lir, the tempestuous god of the oceans, who, with his angry breath, could raise large white-crested waves that could wreck entire fleets of ships. At the time of the fall of the gods, Manánnan Mac Lir had retired to his favourite island called Inis Falga which lay between Inisfáil and the Isle of the Mighty. Eventually that island became called after the great Manánnan and every Manxman is called, in his own tongue, Maninagh.

Now Manánnan, seeing the plight of Mac Cuill, reborn in a weak human body, was moved to compassion. He remembered the ancient times when he and Mac Cuill and the other Children of Danu had fought the evil Fomorii on the Plain of Towers to claim the Island of Destiny. So Manánnan breathed gently on the ship and sent a current which turned its bows towards his own mist-shrouded island of Inis Falga.

But even Manánnan's breath could not break the lock of the chain which bound Mac Cuill's wrists.

After several days the little boat, without oars or sails, and with Mac Cuill more dead than alive, bumped against a rocky shore.

Now on the island there were living two wise men named Conindri and Romuil. Both had heard the words of the Son of God and preached the new religion of love and forgiveness. They saw the half dead Mac Cuill and realised that his crimes must be great for him to have been cast into the sea in such a fashion. Yet they took him from the boat and laid him in their own beds and nursed him until he recovered his wit and strength.

As Mac Cuill was recovering, Conindri and Romuil spoke to him of the Creator and His Son and the new religion of love and brotherhood. And as they spoke, they did their best to unfasten the chain about Mac Cuill's wrists. But they could not do so, no matter how they tried.

Mac Cuill laughed. 'In a previous life I was a god. As I was once, so will your new God and His Son become – cast out and forgotten when they no longer serve the needs of the people.'

'You are proud, Mac Cuill. Our Lord taught: 'Blessed are the poor in spirit, for theirs is the kingdom of heaven.'

Mac Cuill laughed again. 'If poverty of spirit is a virtue than it does man little good. When men are poor in spirit, then the proud and haughty oppress them. When I was a god men were true and determined in spirit and resisted oppression.'

'But to him that smiteth thee on the one cheek offer also the other.'

Mac Cuill sneered.

'He who courts oppression shares the crime. If that is the teaching, then you are inviting further injury at the hand of the oppressor and thief.'

'Him that taketh away thy cloak, forbid not to take thy coat also. Give to every man that asketh of thee . . . Blessed be ye poor, for yours is the kingdom of heaven.'

Mac Cuill chuckled deeply, shaking his head.

'Now this new religion is ideal for a thief such as me. It tells people to accept with good grace when I rob them. The poor in spirit will not fight me. This is a good land and here I will prosper as a thief if all believe as you do. I will set forth to find a smithy to break my chains asunder.'

Mac Cuill set out and walked along the sea shore leaving the wise good men, Conindri and Romuil in sorrow behind him.

As he walked on the foreshore he heard a gentle singing and around a headland of rocks he came across a beautiful woman. The spot was called Langness in the parish of Kirk Malew. The girl sang sweetly.

> Come to our rich and starry caves
> Our home amid the ocean waves;

Our coral caves are walled around
With richest gems in ocean found.
And crystal mirrors, clear and bright.
Reflecting all in magic light.

Mac Cuill stopped and gazed upon the beautiful sad face. It reminded him of the one whom he had loved so long ago – the face of his wife in a former life – of Banba.

'Who are you, young maiden?' he demanded.

The young girl started and looked upon Mac Cuill and her eyes lit up in a smile of happiness.

'I am for you, son of the hazel,' she said.

'That cannot be. Nothing is for me unless I steal it. I am a thief and will take what I want.'

'I am Blaanid,' continued the girl, and reaching down beside the rock on which she sat, she drew forth a basket filled with coral and precious stones and other fabulous metals garnered from the ocean bed. 'You may have these, for we are all thieves now.'

'I will not accept that which is given when it is my place to take,' cried Mac Cuill in disgust. 'But if you can break the chains on my wrists, I will accept your gifts.'

Suddenly, Blaanid threw her arms around Mac Cuill and so surprised was he, and so great her strength, that she dragged him to the edge of the sea and plunged in. Though he struggled, she drew him downwards to the dwellings of the merfolk who lived beneath the waves. And Blaanid took Mac Cuill to a beautiful city under the sea. It was a place of many towers and gilded minarets and stood in all magnificence. It was deep down, beyond the region of the fishes where there was air which was strangely clear and the atmosphere serene. The streets were paved in coral and a shining kind of pebble which glittered like the sunbeams reflecting on glass. Streets and squares were on every side. Buildings were embossed with mother of pearl and shells of numerous colours and there were flashing crystals to decorate their walls.

But around the circle perimeter were countless wrecks of ships. Fearful wrecks, strewn on the slimy bottom, yet the city was protected from them. And among the wrecks, Mac Cuill saw the decomposing bodies of men, women and children.

There were countless eyeless skeletons, all scattered and on which the fishes gnawed. And from the dead peoples' skulls, which worms and fish inhabited, there arose a fearful wailing sound. The noise was so penetrating that Mac Cuill had to stop his ears.

'What manner of place is this?' he gasped.

Blaanid smiled and pointed. He could see people moving through the streets. He gasped, for he recognised his brothers and the other Children of Danu.

'This is our home now, and this could be your home. For you wish to exist by what you steal. The gods and goddesses are only left with theft in this new world. We have built our city from the ships that we entice to our mist-shrouded island and wreck upon the rocks above. Each ship comes tumbling through the seas to our city and we may take from them great heaps of pearls, wedges of gold, inestimable stones, unvalued jewels . . . thus our city prospers.'

Mac Cuill swallowed hard.

'And the souls of the dead sailors? Look at the bodies of the dead, of the drowned women and the children! Do you not hear their cries?'

'They are but poor in spirit,' Blaanid said. 'We grow accustomed to their wailing and take what we must.'

Mac Cuill grew sick in his soul. He stared into the face of Blaanid and he saw in it the face of Banba.

'Is this what we are reduced to?' he whispered.

Where once the Children of Danu had bestrode the earth in goodness and strength of spirit, Mac Cuill realised they had descended to thieves who preyed on the spiritual tragedy of others.

'This is but a shadow show of the choice you can make,' replied Blaanid.

'If there are choices still, then I shall choose to be released from my purgatory,' cried Mac Cuill. And he held out his chained wrists.

'Alas, wealth and prosperity can be yours but we cannot unchain your wrists,' replied Blaanid. 'You may remain in the realm of the Ocean God as you are or you may be reborn in the new religion and release your soul from its eternal bitterness. Here we have only illusions of the past.'

With that he found himself back on the headland of Langness in Kirk Malew.

He found himself staring at the grey seas and thought that he heard a whispering sound.

> Come to our rich and starry caves
> Our home amid the ocean waves . . .

Slowly he retraced his footsteps to where he had left Conindri and Romuil. They were standing as he had left them, for in earthly time he had not been long gone from their sight.

They smiled joyfully at his return.

'Tell me more about your God and his Son.'

And so they taught him. And he came to believe with a passion and they called him Maccaldus, for that was the form of his name in the language of the new religion. So Maccaldus, who had been the foremost thief of Ulaidh, felt repentance for his past lives and Conindri and Romuil took him to a stream and poured water over his head and confirmed him in the new religion.

That evening Conindri was cooking a fish that he had caught and he brought it to the table to divide between the three of them. As he cut open the fish they saw a key in its belly and Mac Cuill recognised it as the same one with which Sucat had locked the chains about his wrist. When he told Conindri and Romuil, they were astounded.

'Sucat Mac Calphurn is the foremost preacher of our faith which is why we call him Patricius – father of citizens.'

Conindri immediately unlocked the chains and they fell at Mac Cuill's feet.

The very next day Mac Cuill went out into the island of Inis Falga and began to preach the new religion. And he went up to the Lonan stone circle, near Baldrine, where he found the Druids, set in the ancient ways, about to sacrifice a human child. A stone altar had been heated by fire and it was proposed to throw the child upon it. As the child was being flung forward, Mac Cuill threw a phial of water that had been blessed by the saints and it landed on the stone before the child and split it asunder. And the child was not harmed.

Straightaway the Druids fled but Mac Cuill called them back

and he also called before him the King of Inis Falga and told
them henceforth to worship in the new religion.

One chieftain refused and this was GilColumb whose name
meant servant of the dove. But he was named with irony for he
was no follower of the peaceful path. And this GilColumb and
his three sons desired to kill Mac Cuill and one night they slunk
stealthily to the church which Mac Cuill had built. Mac Cuill
and his followers, hearing that his enemies were approaching,
guided his people into the subterraneous caverns beneath his
church.

With loud shrieks, GilColumb and his three sons, and his
followers, burst into the church.

'Where are you departed?' yelled GilColumb in anger, finding
no one there.

And Mac Cuill appeared before him with his pastoral staff.
GilColumb's followers stepped back in awe.

'What have you against me, GilColumb? Why have I offended
you that you should attack my sanctuary with slaughter in
mind?'

'Are you Mac Cuill, the former thief?' sneered GilColumb,
braver than his band of men.

'I am Maccaldus, the bishop of this land,' replied Mac Cuill
solemnly. 'I am the servant of the Christ.'

GilColumb laughed and raised his sword to smite him.

Mac Cuill, however, leaned forward and tapped GilColumb
over the heart with his pastoral staff. The impious chieftain
uttered an horrendous shriek and then his tongue clove to his
mouth. After six hours GilColumb died in agony and all those
who lived on Inis Falga realised that Mac Cuill was the one
chosen to bring them to the new religion.

Therefore, one evening, Manánnan Mac Lir himself appeared
before Mac Cuill on the foreshore.

'So it has come to this,' the old god said. 'We who were
young together on the Isle of Destiny are gods no longer.
Bitterness and rebirth have brought you to the human state
where now you preach a new philosophy. Our journeys through
life no longer converge nor even go in parallel direction. The
people no longer need the gods of their forefathers and
mothers.'

Mac Cuill was sad.

'There is no returning. This is the destiny of the world. No footsteps back.'

Manánnan shook his head.

'Perhaps I could have prevented this had I not blown you to this island which was my last refuge.'

'But that was written in the book of destiny, Manánnan son of Lir. Even before Danu, the divine waters, first moistened this earth.'

'People no longer believe in me and so I am reduced to a shadow and like a shadow I will be extinguished in the light of the new learning.'

'Your spirit shall abide among the grey seas and the misty mountains of this island for so long as one person remembers you,' replied Mac Cuill.

'One person?' mused the ocean god. 'Where would I find that one?'

'I shall remember you,' replied Mac Cuill softly.

Henceforth, Inis Falga was known as Ellan Vannin, the Island of Manánnan Mac Lir, which today is still known by the shortened version of the Isle of Man. Mac Cuill himself was known first as Maccaldus and then as Maughold and it is as St Maughold that he is still venerated in the Island of the Ocean God.

THE ROVER OF THE PLAIN

Henri Junod

A LONG WAY OFF, near the sea coast of the east of Africa, there dwelt a man and his wife. They had two children, a son and a daughter, whom they loved very much, and, like parents in other countries, they often talked of the fine marriages the young people would make some day. Out there both boys and girls marry early, and very soon, it seemed to the mother, a message was sent by a rich man on the other side of the great hills offering a fat herd of oxen in exchange for the girl. Everyone in the house and in the village rejoiced, and the maiden was despatched to her new home. When all was quiet again the father said to his son:

'Now that we own such a splendid troop of oxen you had better hasten and get yourself a wife, lest some illness should overtake them. Already we have seen in the villages round about one or two damsels whose parents would gladly part with them for less than half the herd. Therefore tell us which you like best, and we will buy her for you.'

But the son answered:

'Not so; the maidens I have seen do not please me. If, indeed, I must marry, let me travel and find a wife for myself.'

'It shall be as you wish,' said his parents; 'but if by and by trouble should come of it, it will be your fault and not ours.'

The youth, however, would not listen; and bidding his father and mother farewell, set out on his search. Far, far away he wandered, over mountains and across rivers, till he reached a village where the people were quite different from those of his own race. He glanced about him and noticed that the girls were fair to look upon, as they pounded maize or stewed something that smelt very nice in earthen pots – especially if you were hot and tired; and when one of the maidens turned round and offered the stranger some dinner, he made up his mind that he would wed her and nobody else.

So he sent a message to her parents asking their leave to take her for his wife, and they came next day to bring their answer.

'We will give you our daughter,' said they, 'if you can pay a good price for her. Never was there so hard-working a girl; and how we shall do without her we cannot tell! Still – no doubt your father and mother will come themselves and bring the price?'

'No; I have the price with me,' replied the young man, laying down a handful of gold pieces. 'Here it is – take it.'

The old couple's eyes glittered greedily; but custom forbade them to touch the price before all was arranged.

'At least,' said they, after a moment's pause, 'we may expect them to fetch your wife to her new home?'

'No; they are not used to travelling,' answered the bridegroom. 'Let the ceremony be performed without delay, and we will set forth at once. It is a long journey.'

Then the parents called in the girl, who was lying in the sun outside the hut, and, in the presence of all the village, a goat was killed, the sacred dance took place, and a blessing was said over the heads of the young people. After that the bride was led aside by her father, whose duty it was to bestow on her some parting advice as to her conduct in her married life.

'Be good to your husband's parents,' added he, 'and always do the will of your husband.' And the girl nodded her head obediently. Next it was the mother's turn; and, as was the custom of the tribe, she spoke to her daughter:

'Will you choose which of your sisters shall go with you to cut your wood and carry your water?'

'I do not want any of them,' answered she; 'they are no use. They will drop the wood and spill the water.'

'Then will you have any of the other children? There are enough and to spare,' asked the mother again. But the bride said quickly:

'I will have none of them! You must give me our buffalo, the Rover of the Plain; he alone shall serve me.'

'What folly you talk!' cried the parents. 'Give you our buffalo, the Rover of the Plain? Why, you know that our life depends on him. Here he is well fed and lies on soft grass; but how can you tell what will befall him in another country? The food may be bad, he will die of hunger; and, if he dies we die also.'

'No, no,' said the bride; 'I can look after him as well as you. Get him ready, for the sun is sinking and it is time we set forth.'

So she went away and put together a small pot filled with healing herbs, a horn that she used in tending sick people, a little knife, and a calabash containing deer fat; and, hiding these about her, she took leave of her father and mother and started across the mountains by the side of her husband.

But the young man did not see the buffalo that followed them, which had left his home to be the servant of his wife.

No one ever knew how the news spread to the kraal that the young man was coming back, bringing a wife with him; but, somehow or other, when the two entered the village, every man and woman was standing in the road uttering shouts of welcome.

'Ah, you are not dead after all,' cried they; 'and have found a wife to your liking, though you would have none of our girls. Well, well, you have chosen your own path; and if ill comes of it beware lest you grumble.'

Next day the husband took his wife to the fields and showed her which were his, and which belonged to his mother. The girl listened carefully to all he told her, and walked with him back to the hut; but close to the door she stopped, and said:

'I have dropped my necklace of beads in the field, and I must go and look for it.' But in truth she had done nothing of the sort, and it was only an excuse to go and seek the buffalo.

The beast was crouching under a tree when she came up, and snorted with pleasure at the sight of her.

'You can roam about this field, and this, and this,' she said, 'for they belong to my husband; and that is his wood, where you may hide yourself. But the other fields are his mother's, so beware lest you touch them.'

'I will beware,' answered the buffalo; and, patting his head, the girl left him.

Oh, how much better a servant he was than any of the little girls the bride had refused to bring with her! If she wanted water, she had only to cross the patch of maize behind the hut and seek out the place where the buffalo lay hidden, and put down her pail beside him. Then she would sit at her ease while he went to the lake and brought the bucket back brimming over. If she wanted wood, he would break the branches off the trees and lay them at her feet. And the villagers watched her return laden, and said to each other:

'Surely the girls of her country are stronger than our girls, for none of *them* could cut so quickly or carry so much!' But then, nobody knew that she had a buffalo for a servant.

Only, all this time she never gave the poor buffalo anything to eat, because she had just one dish, out of which she and her husband ate; while in her old home there was a dish put aside expressly for the Rover of the Plain. The buffalo bore it as long as he could; but, one day, when his mistress bade him go to the lake and fetch water, his knees almost gave way from hunger. He kept silence, however, till the evening, when he said to his mistress:

'I am nearly starved; I have not touched food since I came here. I can work no more.'

'Alas!' answered she, 'what can I do? I have only one dish in the house. You will have to steal some beans from the fields. Take a few here and a few there; but be sure not to take too many from one place, or the owner may notice it.'

Now the buffalo had always lived an honest life, but if his mistress did not feed him, he must get food for himself. So that night, when all the village was asleep, he came out from the wood and ate a few beans here and a few there, as his mistress had bidden him. And when at last his hunger was satisfied, he crept back to his lair. But a buffalo is not a fairy, and the next morning, when the women arrived to work in the fields, they stood still with astonishment, and said to each other:

'Just look at this; a savage beast has been destroying our crops, and we can see the traces of his feet!' And they hurried to their homes to tell their tale.

In the evening the girl crept out to the buffalo's hiding-place, and said to him:

'They perceived what happened, of course; so tonight you had better seek your supper further off.' And the buffalo nodded his head and followed her counsel; but in the morning, when these women also went out to work, the traces of hoofs were plainly to be seen, and they hastened to tell their husbands, and begged them to bring their guns, and to watch for the robber.

It happened that the stranger girl's husband was the best marksman in all the village, and he hid himself behind the trunk of a tree and waited.

The buffalo, thinking that they would probably make a search for him in the fields he had laid waste the evening before, returned to the bean patch belonging to his mistress.

The young man saw him coming with amazement.

'Why, it is a buffalo!' cried he; 'I never have beheld one in this country before!' And raising his gun, he aimed just behind the ear.

The buffalo gave a leap into the air, and then fell dead.

'It was a good shot,' said the young man. And he ran to the village to tell them that the thief was punished.

When he entered his hut he found his wife, who had somehow heard the news, twisting herself to and fro and shedding tears.

'Are you ill?' asked he. And she answered: 'Yes; I have pains all over my body.' But she was not ill at all, only very unhappy at the death of the buffalo which had served her so well. Her husband felt anxious, and sent for the medicine man; but though she pretended to listen to him, she threw all his medicine out of the door directly he had gone away.

With the first rays of light the whole village was awake, and the women set forth armed with baskets and the men with knives in order to cut up the buffalo. Only the girl remained in her hut; and after a while she too went to join them, groaning and weeping as she walked along.

'What are you doing here?' asked her husband when he saw her. 'If you are ill you are better at home.'

'Oh! I could not stay alone in the village,' said she. And her mother-in-law left off her work to come and scold her, and to tell her that she would kill herself if she did such foolish things. But the girl would not listen and sat down and looked on.

When they had divided the buffalo's flesh, and each woman had the family portion in her basket, the stranger wife got up and said:

'Let me have the head.'

'You could never carry anything so heavy,' answered the men, 'and now you are ill besides.'

'You do not know how strong I am,' answered she. And at last they gave it her.

She did not walk to the village with the others, but lingered behind, and, instead of entering her hut, she slipped into the little shed where the pots for cooking and storing maize were kept. Then she laid down the buffalo's head and sat beside it. Her husband came to seek her, and begged her to leave the shed and go to bed, as she must be tired out; but the girl would not stir, neither would she attend to the words of her mother-in-law.

'I wish you would leave me alone!' she answered crossly. 'It is impossible to sleep if somebody is always coming in.' And she turned her back on them, and would not even eat the food they had brought. So they went away, and the young man soon stretched himself out on his mat; but his wife's odd conduct made him anxious, and he lay awake all night, listening.

When all was still the girl made a fire and boiled some water in a pot. As soon as it was quite hot she shook in the medicine that she had brought from home, and then, taking the buffalo's head, she made incisions with her little knife behind the ear, and close to the temple where the shot had struck him. Next she applied the horn to the spot and blew with all her force till, at length, the blood began to move. After that she spread some of the deer fat out of the calabash over the wound, which she held in the steam of the hot water. Last of all, she sang in a low voice a dirge over the Rover of the Plain.

As she chanted the final words the head moved, and the limbs came back. The buffalo began to feel alive again and shook his horns, and stood up and stretched himself. Unluckily it was just at this moment that the husband said to himself:

'I wonder if she is crying still, and what is the matter with her! Perhaps I had better go and see.' And he got up and, calling her by name, went out to the shed.

'Go away! I don't want you!' she cried angrily. But it was too late. The buffalo had fallen to the ground, dead, and with the wound in his head as before.

The young man who, unlike most of his tribe, was afraid of his wife, returned to his bed without having seen anything, but wondering very much what she could be doing all this time. After waiting a few minutes, she began her task over again, and at the end the buffalo stood on his feet as before. But just as the girl was rejoicing that her work was completed, in came the husband once more to see what his wife was doing; and this time he sat himself down in the hut, and said that he wished to watch whatever was going on. Then the girl took up the pitcher and all her other things and left the shed, trying for the third time to bring the buffalo back to life.

She was too late; the dawn was already breaking, and the head fell to the ground, dead and corrupt as it was before.

The girl entered the hut, where her husband and his mother were getting ready to go out.

'I want to go down to the lake, and bathe,' said she.

'But you could never walk so far,' answered they. 'You are so tired, as it is, that you can hardly stand!'

However, in spite of their warnings, the girl left the hut in the direction of the lake. Very soon she came back weeping, and sobbed out:

'I met someone in the village who lives in my country, and he told me that my mother is very, very ill, and if I do not go to her at once she will be dead before I arrive. I will return as soon as I can, and now farewell.' And she set forth in the direction of the mountains. But this story was not true; she knew nothing about her mother, only she wanted an excuse to go home and tell her family that their prophecies had come true, and that the buffalo was dead.

Balancing her basket on her head, she walked along, and directly she had left the village behind her she broke out into the song of the Rover of the Plain, and at last, at the end of the day, she came to the group of huts where her parents lived. Her friends all ran to meet her, and, weeping, she told them that the buffalo was dead.

This sad news spread like lightning through the country, and the people flocked from far and near to bewail the loss of the beast who had been their pride.

'If you had only listened to *us*,' they cried, 'he would be alive now. But you refused all the little girls we offered you, and would have nothing but the buffalo. And remember what the medicine-man said: "If the buffalo dies you die also!"'

So they bewailed their fate, one to the other, and for a while they did not perceive that the girl's husband was sitting in their midst, leaning his gun against a tree. Then one man, turning, beheld him, and bowed mockingly.

'Hail, murderer! hail! you have slain us all!'

The young man stared, not knowing what he meant, and answered, wonderingly.

'I shot a buffalo; is that why you call me a murderer?'

'A buffalo – yes; but the servant of your wife! It was he who carried the wood and drew the water. Did you not know it?'

'No; I did not know it,' replied the husband in surprise. 'Why did no one tell me? Of course I should not have shot him!'

'Well, he is dead,' answered they, 'and we must die too.'

At this the girl took a cup in which some poisonous herbs had been crushed, and holding it in her hands, she wailed: 'O my father, Rover of the Plain!' Then drinking a deep draught from it, fell back dead. One by one her parents, her brothers and her sisters, drank also and died, singing a dirge to the memory of the buffalo.

The girl's husband looked on with horror; and returned sadly home across the mountains, and, entering his hut, threw himself on the ground. At first he was too tired to speak; but at length he raised his head and told all the story to his father and mother, who sat watching him. When he had finished they shook their heads and said:

'Now you see that we spoke no idle words when we told you that ill would come of your marriage! We offered you a good and hard-working wife, and you would have none of her. And it is not only your wife you have lost, but your fortune also. For who will give you back your money if they are all dead?'

'It is true, O my father,' answered the young man. But in his heart he thought more of the loss of his wife than of the money he had given for her.

URASCHIMATARO
AND THE TURTLE

David Brauns

T HERE WAS ONCE a worthy old couple who lived on the
coast, and supported themselves by fishing. They had only
one child, a son, who was their pride and joy, and for his sake
they were ready to work hard all day long, and never felt tired or
discontented with their lot. This son's name was Uraschimataro,
which means in Japanese, 'Son of the island', and he was a fine
well-grown youth and a good fisherman, minding neither wind
nor weather. Not the bravest sailor in the whole village dared
venture so far out to sea as Uraschimataro, and many a time
the neighbours used to shake their heads and say to his parents,
'If your son goes on being so rash, one day he will try his luck
once too often, and the waves will end by swallowing him up.'
But Uraschimataro paid no heed to these remarks, and as he
was really very clever in managing a boat, the old people were
very seldom anxious about him.

One beautiful bright morning, as he was hauling his well-filled
nets into the boat, he saw lying among the fishes a tiny little
turtle. He was delighted with his prize, and threw it into a
wooden vessel to keep till he got home, when suddenly the
turtle found its voice, and tremblingly begged for its life. 'After
all,' it said, 'what good can I do you? I am so young and small,
and I would so gladly live a little longer. Be merciful and set
me free, and I shall know how to prove my gratitude.'

Now Uraschimataro was very good-natured, and besides, he
could never bear to say no, so he picked up the turtle, and put
it back into the sea.

Years flew by, and every morning Uraschimataro sailed his

boat into the deep sea. But one day as he was making for a little bay between some rocks, there arose a fierce whirlwind, which shattered his boat to pieces, and she was sucked under by the waves. Uraschimataro himself very nearly shared the same fate. But he was a powerful swimmer, and struggled hard to reach the shore. Then he saw a large turtle coming towards him, and above the howling of the storm he heard what it said: 'I am the turtle whose life you once saved. I will now pay my debt and show my gratitude. The land is still far distant, and without my help you would never get there. Climb on my back, and I will take you where you will.' Uraschimataro did not wait to be asked twice, and thankfully accepted his friend's help. But scarcely was he seated firmly on the shell, when the turtle proposed that they should not return to the shore at once, but go under the sea, and look at some of the wonders that lay hidden there.

Uraschimataro agreed willingly, and in another moment they were deep, deep down, with fathoms of blue water above their heads. Oh, how quickly they darted through the still, warm sea! The young man held tight, and marvelled where they were going and how long they were to travel, but for three days they rushed on, till at last the turtle stopped before a splendid palace, shining with gold and silver, crystal and precious stones, and decked here and there with branches of pale pink coral and glittering pearls. But if Uraschimataro was astonished at the beauty of the outside, he was struck dumb at the sight of the hall within, which was lighted by the blaze of fish scales.

'Where have you brought me?' he asked his guide in a low voice.

'To the palace of Ringu, the house of the sea god, whose subjects we all are,' answered the turtle. 'I am the first waiting maid of his daughter, the lovely princess Otohimé, whom you will shortly see.'

Uraschimataro was still so puzzled with the adventures that had befallen him, that he waited in a dazed condition for what would happen next. But the turtle, who had talked so much of him to the princess that she had expressed a wish to see him, went at once to make known his arrival. And directly the princess beheld him her heart was set on him, and she begged him to stay with her, and in return promised that he should never grow old, neither should his beauty fade. 'Is not that reward enough?' she asked, smiling, looking all the while as fair as the sun itself. And Uraschimataro said 'Yes,' and so he stayed there. For how long? That he only knew later.

His life passed by, and each hour seemed happier than the last, when one day there rushed over him a terrible longing to see his parents. He fought against it hard, knowing how it would grieve the princess, but it grew on him stronger and stronger, till at length he became so sad that the princess inquired what was wrong. Then he told her of the longing he had to visit his old home, and that he must see his parents once more. The princess was almost frozen with horror, and implored him to stay with her, or something dreadful would be sure to happen. 'You will never come back, and we shall meet again no more,' she moaned bitterly. But Uraschimataro stood firm and repeated, 'Only this once will I leave you, and then will I return to your side for ever.' Sadly the princess shook her head, but she answered slowly, 'One way there is to bring you safely back, but I fear you will never agree to the conditions of the bargain.'

'I will do anything that will bring me back to you,' exclaimed Uraschimataro, looking at her tenderly, but the princess was silent: she knew too well that when he left her she would see his face no more. Then she took from a shelf a tiny golden box, and gave it to Uraschimataro, praying him to keep it carefully, and above all things never to open it. 'If you can do this,' she said as she bade him farewell, 'your friend the turtle will meet you at the shore, and will carry you back to me.'

Uraschimataro thanked her from his heart, and swore solemnly to do her bidding. He hid the box safely in his garments, seated himself on the back of the turtle, and vanished in the ocean path, waving his hand to the princess. Three days and three nights they swam through the sea, and at length Uraschimataro arrived at the beach which lay before his old home. The turtle bade him farewell, and was gone in a moment.

Uraschimataro drew near to the village with quick and joyful steps. He saw the smoke curling through the roof, and the thatch where green plants had thickly sprouted. He heard the children shouting and calling, and from a window that he passed came the twang of the koto, and everything seemed to cry a welcome for his return. Yet suddenly he felt a pang at his heart as he wandered down the street. After all, everything was changed. Neither men nor houses were those he once knew. Quickly he saw his old home; yes, it was still there, but it had a strange look. Anxiously he knocked at the door, and asked the woman who opened it after his parents. But she did not know their names, and could give him no news of them.

Still more disturbed, he rushed to the burying ground, the only place that could tell him what he wished to know. Here at any rate he would find out what it all meant. And he was right. In a moment he stood before the grave of his parents, and the date written on the stone was almost exactly the date when they had lost their son, and he had forsaken them for the Daughter of the Sea. And so he found that since he had left his home, three hundred years had passed by.

Shuddering with horror at his discovery he turned back into the village street, hoping to meet someone who could tell him of the days of old. But when the man spoke, he knew he was not dreaming, though he felt as if he had lost his senses.

In despair he bethought him of the box which was the gift of the princess. Perhaps after all this dreadful thing was not true. He might be the victim of some enchanter's spell, and in his hand lay the counter-charm. Almost unconsciously he opened it, and a purple vapour came pouring out. He held the empty box in his hand, and as he looked he saw that the fresh hand of youth had grown suddenly shrivelled, like the hand of an old, old man. He ran to the brook, which flowed in a clear stream down from the mountain, and saw himself reflected as in a mirror. It was the face of a mummy which looked back at him. Wounded to death, he crept back through the village, and no man knew the old, old man to be the strong handsome youth who had run down the street an hour before. So he toiled wearily back, till he reached the shore, and here he sat sadly on a rock, and called loudly on the turtle. But she never came back any more, but instead, death came soon, and set him free. But before that happened, the people who saw him sitting lonely on the shore had heard his story, and when their children were restless they used to tell them of the good son who from love to his parents had given up for their sakes the splendour and wonders of the palace in the sea, and the most beautiful woman in the world besides.

HOW THE SERPENT-GODS WERE PROPITIATED

Rachel Harriette Busk

L ONG AGES AGO there reigned over a flourishing province, a Khan named Kun-snang. He had a son named 'Sunshine' by his first wife who afterwards died. He also had a second son named 'Moonshine', by his second wife. Now the second wife thought within herself, 'If Sunshine is allowed to live, there is no chance of Moonshine ever coming to the throne. Some means must be found of putting Sunshine out of the way.'

With this object in view she threw herself down upon her couch and tossed to and fro as though in an agony of pain. All the night through also instead of sleeping, she tossed about and writhed with pain. Then the Khan spake to her, saying, 'My beautiful one! what is it that pains thee, and with what manner of ailment art thou stricken?' And she made answer –

'Even when I was at home I suffered oftwhiles after the same manner, but now is it much more violent; all remedies have I exhausted previous times, there remains only one when the pain is of this degree, and that means is not available.'

'Say not that it is not available,' answered the Khan, 'for all means are available to me. Speak but what it is that is required, and whatever it be shall be done, even to the renouncing of my kingdom. For there is nothing that I would not give in exchange for thy life.'

But for a long time she made as though she would not tell him, then finally yielding to his repeated inquiries, she said, 'If there were given me the heart of a Prince, stewed in sesame-oil, I should recover: it matters not whether the heart of Sunshine or of Moonshine, but that Moonshine being my own son, his heart would not pass through my throat. This means, O Khan, is manifestly not available, for how should it be done to take the life of Prince Sunshine? Therefore say no more, and let me die.'

But the Khan answered, 'Of a truth it would grieve me to take the life of Prince Sunshine. Nevertheless, if there be no other means of saving thy life, the thing must be done. I have not to consider "Shall the life of the Prince be spared or not?" but, "Which shall be spared, the life of the Prince, or the life of the Khanin?" And in this strait who could doubt, but that it is the life of the Khanin that must be spared by me? Therefore, be of good cheer, beautiful one, for that the heart of Prince Sunshine shall be given thee cooked in sesame-oil.'

This, he said, intending in his own mind to have the heart of a kid of the goats prepared for her in sesame-oil, saying, 'Behold, here is the heart of Prince Sunshine,' but to send away the Prince into a far country that she might not know he was not dead. Only when she was restored to health again, then he purposed to fetch back his son. But Moonshine being in his mother's apartments overheard this promise which the Khan had given, and he ran and told his brother all that the Khan, his father, had said, saying, 'When the Khan rises he will give the order to put thee to death; how shall this thing be averted?' and he wept sore, for he loved his brother Sunshine even as his own life.

Then Sunshine answered, saying, 'Seeing this is so, remain thou with our parents, loving and honouring them, and being loved by them. For me, it is clear the time is come that I must get me away to a far country. Farewell, my brother!'

But Moonshine answered, 'Nay, brother, for if thou goest, I also go with thee. How should I live alone here, without thee, my brother?' Therefore they rose quickly before the Khan could get up, and going privately to a priest in a temple hard by, that no one else might hear of their design and betray it to the Khan, they begged of him a good provision of baling-cakes, to support life by the way; and he gave them a good provision, even a bag-full, and they set out on their journey while it was yet night. It was the fifteenth of the month, while the moon shed abroad her light, and they journeyed towards the East, not knowing whither they went. But after they had journeyed many days over mountain and plain, and come to a land where was no water, but a muddy river the water whereof could not be drunk, and where was no habitation of man, Moonshine fell down fainting by the way. Sunshine therefore ran to the top of a high hill to see if he could discern any stream of water, but found none. When he came back Moonshine was dead! Then he fell down on the ground, and wept a long space upon his body, and at nightfall he buried it with solicitude under a heap of stones, crying, 'Ah! my brother, how shall I live without thee, my brother?' And he prayed that at Moonshine's next re-birth they might again live together.

Journeying farther on, he came to a pass between two steep rocks, and in one of them was a red door. Going up to the door, he found an ancient Hermit living in a cave within, who addressed him, saying, 'Whence art thou, O youth, who seemest oppressed with recent grief?' And Sunshine told him all that had befallen him. Without again speaking the Hermit put into the folds of his girdle a bottle containing a life-restoring cordial, and going to the spot where Moonshine lay buried, restored him to life. Then said he to the two princes, 'Live now with me, and be as my two sons.' So they lived with him, and were unto him as his two sons.

The desert where this Hermit lived belonged to the kingdom of a Khan dazzling in his glory and resistless in might. Now it was about the season when the Khan and his subjects went every year to direct the flowing of water over the country for fructifying the grain-seeds; but it was the custom every year at this season first, in order to make the Serpent-gods who lived at the water-head propitious, to sacrifice to them a youth of a certain age; and on this occasion it fell to the lot of a youth born in the Tiger-year. When the Khan had caused search to be made through all the people no youth was found among them all born in the Tiger-year. At last certain herdsmen came before him, saying, 'While we were out tending our cattle, behold we saw in a cave nigh to a pass between two steep rocks a Hermit who has with him two sons, and one of them born in the Tiger-year.'

When the Khan had listened to their words he immediately sent three envoys to fetch the Hermit's son for the sacrifice.

When the three envoys of the Khan had come and stood knocking before the red door of the Hermit's cave, the Hermit cried out to them, asking what they wanted of him. Then answered the chief of them, 'Because thou hast a son living with thee born in the Tiger-year, and the Khan hath need of him for the sacrifice; therefore are we come, even that we may bring him to the Khan.'

When the Hermit had heard their embassage, he answered them, 'How should a Hermit have a son with him out here in the desert?' But he took Sunshine, who was the youth born in the Tiger-year, and motioned him into a farther hole of the cave where was a great vessel of pottery; into this vessel he made him creep, then fastening the mouth of the vessel with earth, he made it to appear like to a jar of rice-brandy. Meantime, however, the Khan's envoys had broken down the door, and began searching through every recess of the cave. Finding nothing, they were filled with fury, and in their anger beat the Hermit on whose account they had come a bootless errand. But when Sunshine heard the men ill-treating the Hermit who had been to him as a father, he could not refrain himself, and called out from within the brandy-jar, 'Unhand my father!' Then the envoys immediately left off beating his father, but they turned and seized him and carried him off to the Khan, while the Hermit was left weeping with great grief at the loss of his adopted son, even as one like to die.

As the envoys dragged Sunshine along before the palace, the Khan's daughter was looking out of a window, and when she heard that the handsome youth was destined for the Serpent-sacrifice, she was filled with compassion. She went therefore to the men who had the charge to throw him into the water, saying, 'See how comely he is! He is worthy to be saved, throw him not into the water. Or else if you will throw him in, throw me in also with him.' Then the men went and showed the Khan her words; whereupon the king was wroth, and said, 'She is not worthy to be called the Khan's daughter; let them therefore be both sewn up into one bullock's skin, and so cast into the water.' The men therefore did according to the Khan's bidding, and sewing them both up in one bullock-hide together, cast them into the water to the Serpent-gods.

Then began Sunshine to say, 'That they should throw me to the Serpent-gods, because I was the only youth to be found who was born in the Tiger-year, was not so bad; but that this beautiful maiden, who hath deigned to lift her eyes on me, and to love me, should be so sacrificed also, this is unbearable!'

And the Khan's daughter in like manner cried, 'That I who am only a woman should be thrown to the Serpent-gods, is not so bad; but that this noble and beautiful youth should be so sacrificed also, this is unbearable!'

When the Serpent-gods heard these laments, and saw how the prince and the maiden vied with each other in generosity, they sent and fetched them both out of the water, and gave them freedom. Also as soon as they were set free, they let the water gently flow over the whole country, just as the people desired for their rice irrigation.

Meantime, Sunshine said to the Khan's daughter, 'Princess, let us each now return home. Go thou to thy father's palace, while I go back to the Hermitage, and visit my adopted father, who is like to die of grief for the loss of me. After I have fulfilled this filial duty, I will return to thee, and we will live for ever after for each other alone.'

The princess then praised his filial love, and bid him go console his father, only begging him to come to her right soon, for she should have no joy till he came back.

Sunshine went therefore to the Hermit, whom he found so worn with grief, that he was but just in time to save him from dying; so having first washed him with milk and water, he consoled him with many words of kindness.

The princess, too, went home to the palace, where all were so astonished at her deliverance that at first she could hardly obtain admission. When they had made sure it was herself in very truth, the people all came round her, and congratulated her with joy, for never had any one before been delivered from the sacrifice to the Serpent-gods.

Then said the Khan, 'That the Khan's daughter should be spared by the Serpent-gods was to be expected. They have the youth born in the Tiger-year for their sacrifice.'

But the princess answered, 'Neither has he fallen sacrifice. Him also they let free; and indeed was it in great part out of regard for his abnegation and distress over my suffering that we were both let free.'

Then answered the Khan, 'In that case is our debt great unto this youth. Let him be sought after, and besought that he come to visit us in our palace.'

So they went again to the cave in the rocky pass, and fetched Sunshine; and when he came near, the Khan went out to meet him, and caused costly seats to be brought, and made him sit down thereon beside him.

Then he said to him, 'That thou hast delivered this country from the fear of drought, is matter for which we owe thee our highest gratitude; but that thou and this my daughter also have escaped from death is a marvellous wonder. Tell me now, art thou in very truth the son of the Hermit?'

'No,' replied Sunshine, 'I am the son of a mighty Khan; but my step-mother, seeking to make a difference between me and this my brother standing beside me, who was her own born son, and to put me to death, we fled away both together; and thus fleeing we came to the Hermit, and were taken in by his hospitality.'

When the Khan had heard his words, he promised him his daughter in marriage, and her sister, to be wife to Moonshine. Moreover, he endowed them with immeasurable riches, and gave them an escort of four detachments of fighting-men to accompany them home. When they had arrived near the capital of the kingdom, they sent an embassage before them to the Khan saying, –

'We, thy two sons, Sunshine and Moonshine, are returned to thee.'

The Khan and the Khanin, who had for many years past quite lost their reason out of grief for the loss of their children, and held no more converse with men, were at once restored to sense and animation at this news, and sent out a large troop of horsemen to meet them, and conduct them to their palace. Thus the two princes returned in honour to their home.

When they came in, the Khan was full of joy and glory, sitting on his throne; but the Khanin, full of remorse and shame at the thought of the crime she had meditated, fell down dead before their face.

KOSHCHEI THE DEATHLESS

Alexander Afanasief

IN A CERTAIN country there once lived a king, and he had three sons, all of them grown up. All of a sudden Koshchei the Deathless carried off their mother. Then the eldest son craved his father's blessing, that he might go and look for his mother. His father gave him his blessing, and he went off and disappeared, leaving no trace behind. The second son waited and waited, then he too obtained his father's blessing – and he also disappeared. Then the youngest son, Prince Ivan, said to his father: 'Father, give me your blessing, and let me go and look for my mother.'

But his father would not let him go, saying, 'Your brothers are no more; if you likewise go away, I shall die of grief.'

'Not so, father. But if you bless me I shall go; and if you do not bless me I shall go.'

So his father gave him his blessing.

Prince Ivan went to choose a steed, but every one that he laid his hand upon gave way under it. He could not find a steed to suit him, so he wandered with drooping brow along the road and about the town. Suddenly there appeared an old woman, who asked:

'Why hangs your brow so low, Prince Ivan?'

'Be off, old crone,' he replied. 'If I put you on one of my hands, and give it a slap with the other, there'll be a little wet left, that's all.'

The old woman ran down a by-street, came to meet him a second time, and said:

'Good day, Prince Ivan! why hangs your brow so low?'

Then he thought:

'Why does this old woman ask me? Mightn't she be of use to me?' – and he replied:

'Well, mother! because I cannot get myself a good steed.'

'Silly fellow!' she cried, 'to suffer, and not to ask the old woman's help! Come along with me.'

She took him to a hill, showed him a certain spot, and said:

'Dig up that piece of ground.'

Prince Ivan dug it up and saw an iron plate with twelve padlocks on it. He immediately broke off the padlocks, tore open a door, and followed a path leading underground. There, fastened with twelve chains, stood a heroic steed which evidently heard the approaching steps of a rider worthy to mount it, and so began to neigh and to struggle, until it broke all twelve of its chains. Then Prince Ivan put on armour fit for a hero, and bridled the horse, and saddled it with a Circassian saddle. And he gave the old woman money, and said to her:

'Forgive me, mother, and bless me!' then he mounted his steed and rode away.

Long time did he ride; at last he came to a mountain – a tremendously high mountain, and so steep that it was utterly impossible to get up it. Presently his brothers came that way. They all greeted each other, and rode on together, till they came to an iron rock a hundred and fifty poods in weight, and on it was this inscription, 'Whosoever will fling this rock against the mountain, to him will a way be opened.' The two elder brothers were unable to lift the rock, but Prince Ivan at the first try flung it against the mountain – and immediately there appeared a ladder leading up the mountain side.

Prince Ivan dismounted, let some drops of blood run from his little finger into a glass, gave it to his brothers, and said:

'If the blood in this glass turns black, tarry here no longer: that will mean that I am about to die.' Then he took leave of them and went his way.

He mounted the hill. What did not he see there? All sorts of trees were there, all sorts of fruits, all sorts of birds! Long did Prince Ivan walk on; at last he came to a house, a huge house! In it lived a king's daughter who had been carried off by Koshchei the Deathless. Prince Ivan walked round the enclosure, but could not see any doors. The king's daughter saw there was someone there, came on to the balcony, and called out to him,

'See, there is a chink in the enclosure; touch it with your little finger, and it will become a door.'

What she said turned out to be true. Prince Ivan went into the house, and the maiden received him kindly, gave him to eat and to drink, and then began to question him. He told her how he had come to rescue his mother from Koshchei the Deathless. Then the maiden said:

'It will be difficult for you to get at your mother, Prince Ivan. You see, Koshchei is not mortal: he will kill you. He often comes here to see me. There is his sword, fifty poods in weight. Can you lift it? If so, you may venture to go.'

Not only did Prince Ivan lift the sword, but he tossed it high in the air. So he went on his way again.

By and by he came to a second house. He knew now where to look for the door, and he entered in. There was his mother. With tears did they embrace each other.

Here also did he try his strength, heaving aloft a ball which weighed some fifteen hundred poods. The time came for Koshchei the Deathless to arrive. The mother hid away her son. Suddenly Koshchei the Deathless entered the house and cried out, 'Phou, Phou! A Russian bone one usen't to hear with one's ears, or see with one's eyes, but now a Russian bone has come to the house! Who has been with you? Wasn't it your son?'

'What are you talking about, God bless you! You've been flying through Russia, and got the Russian air up your nostrils, that's why you fancy it's here,' answered Prince Ivan's mother, and then she drew nigh to Koshchei, addressed him in terms of affection, asked him about one thing and another, and at last said:

'Whereabouts is your death, O Koshchei?'

'My death,' he replied, 'is in such and such a place. There stands an oak, and under the oak is a casket, and in the casket is a hare, and in the hare is a duck, and in the duck is an egg, and in the egg is my death.'

Having thus spoken, Koshchei the Deathless tarried there a little longer, and then flew away.

The time came – Prince Ivan received his mother's blessing, and went to look for Koshchei's death. He went on his way a long time without eating or drinking; at last he felt mortally

hungry, and thought, 'If only something would come my way!'
Suddenly there appeared a young wolf; he determined to kill
it. But out from a hole sprang the she-wolf, and said, 'Don't
hurt my little one; I'll do you a good turn.' Very good! Prince
Ivan let the young wolf go. On he went and saw a crow. 'Stop
a bit,' he thought, 'here I shall get a mouthful.' He loaded his
gun and was going to shoot, but the crow exclaimed, 'Don't
hurt me; I'll do you a good turn.'

Prince Ivan thought the matter over and spared the crow.
Then he went farther, and came to a sea and stood still on the
shore. At that moment a young pike suddenly jumped out of the
water and fell on the strand. He caught hold of it, and thought –
for he was half dead with hunger – 'Now I shall have something
to eat.' All of a sudden appeared a pike and said, 'Don't hurt
my little one, Prince Ivan; I'll do you a good turn.' And so he
spared the little pike also.

But how was he to cross the sea? He sat down on the shore and
meditated. But the pike knew quite well what he was thinking
about, and laid herself right across the sea. Prince Ivan walked
along her back, as if he were going over a bridge, and came to
the oak where Koshchei's death was. There he found the casket
and opened it – out jumped the hare and ran away. How was
the hare to be stopped?

Prince Ivan was terribly frightened at having let the hare
escape, and gave himself up to gloomy thoughts; but a wolf,
the one he had refrained from killing, rushed after the hare,
caught it, and brought it to Prince Ivan. With great delight
he seized the hare, cut it open – and had such a fright! Out
popped the duck and flew away. He fired after it, but shot
all on one side, so again he gave himself up to his thoughts.
Suddenly there appeared the crow with her little crows, and set
off after the duck, and caught it, and brought it to Prince Ivan.
The Prince was greatly pleased and got hold of the egg. Then
he went on his way. But when he came to the sea, he began
washing the egg, and let it drop into the water. However was
he to get it out of the water? an immeasurable depth! Again
the Prince gave himself up to dejection.

Suddenly the sea became violently agitated, and the pike
brought him the egg. Moreover it stretched itself across the
sea. Prince Ivan walked along it to the other side, and then

he set out again for his mother's. When he got there, they greeted each other lovingly, and then she hid him again as before. Presently in flew Koshchei the Deathless and said:

'Phoo, Phoo! No Russian bone can the ear hear nor the eye see, but there's a smell of Russia here!'

'What are you talking about, Koshchei? There's no one with me,' replied Prince Ivan's mother.

A second time spake Koshchei and said, 'I feel rather unwell.'

Then Prince Ivan began squeezing the egg, and thereupon Koshchei the Deathless bent double. At last Prince Ivan came out from his hiding-place, held up the egg and said. 'There is your death, O Koshchei the Deathless!'

Then Koshchei fell on his knees before him, saying, 'Don't kill me, Prince Ivan! Let's be friends! All the world will lie at our feet.'

But these words had no weight with Prince Ivan. He smashed the egg, and Koshchei the Deathless died.

Ivan and his mother took all they wanted and started homewards. On their way they came to where the King's daughter was whom Ivan had seen on his way, and they took her with them too. They went further, and came to the hill where Ivan's brothers were still waiting for him. Then the maiden said, 'Prince Ivan! do go back to my house. I have forgotten a marriage robe, a diamond ring, and a pair of seamless shoes.'

He consented to do so, but in the meantime he let his mother go down the ladder, as well as the Princess – whom it had been settled he was to marry when they got home. They were received by his brothers, who then set to work and cut away the ladder, so that he himself would not be able to get down. And they used such threats to his mother and the Princess, that they made them promise not to tell about Prince Ivan when they got home. And after a time they reached their native country. Their father was delighted at seeing his wife and his two sons, but still he was grieved about the other one, Prince Ivan.

But Prince Ivan returned to the home of his betrothed, and got the wedding dress, and the ring, and the seamless shoes. Then he came back to the mountain and tossed the ring from one hand to the other. Immediately there appeared twelve strong youths, who said:

'What are your commands?'

'Carry me down from this hill.'

The youths immediately carried him down. Prince Ivan put the ring on his finger – they disappeared.

Then he went on to his own country, and arrived at the city in which his father and brothers lived.

There he took up his quarters in the house of an old woman, and asked her:

'What news is there, mother, in your country?'

'What news, lad? You see our queen was kept in prison by Koshchei the Deathless. Her three sons went to look for her, and two of them found her and came back, but the third, Prince Ivan, has disappeared, and no one knows where he is. The King is very unhappy about him. And those two Princes and their mother brought a certain Princess back with them; and the eldest son wants to marry her, but she declares he must fetch her her betrothal ring first, or get one made just as she wants it. But although they have made a public proclamation about it, no one has been found to do it yet.'

'Well, mother, go and tell the King that you will make one. I'll manage it for you,' said Prince Ivan.

So the old woman immediately dressed herself, and hastened to the King, and said:

'Please your Majesty, I will make the wedding ring.

'Make it, then, make it, mother! Such people as you are welcome,' said the king. 'But if you don't make it, off goes your head!'

The old woman was dreadfully frightened; she ran home, and told Prince Ivan to set to work at the ring. But Ivan lay down to sleep, troubling himself very little about it. The ring was there all the time. So he only laughed at the old woman, but she was trembling all over, and crying, and scolding him.

'As for you,' she said, 'you're out of the scrape; but you've done for me, fool that I was!'

The old woman cried and cried until she fell asleep. Early in the morning Prince Ivan got up and awakened her, saying:

'Get up, mother, and go out! take them the ring, and mind, don't accept more than one ducat for it. If anyone asks who made the ring, say you made it yourself; don't say a word about me.'

The old woman was overjoyed and carried off the ring. The bride was delighted with it.

'Just what I wanted,' she said. So they gave the old woman a dish full of gold, but she took only one ducat.

'Why do you take so little?' said the king.

'What good would a lot do me, your Majesty? if I want some more afterwards, you'll give it me.'

Having said this the old woman went away.

Time passed, and the news spread abroad that the bride had told her lover to fetch her her wedding-dress or else to get one made, just such a one as she wanted. Well, the old woman, thanks to Prince Ivan's aid, succeeded in this matter too, and took her the wedding-dress. And afterwards she took her the seamless shoes also, and would only accept one ducat each time. and always said that she had made the things herself.

Well, the people heard that there would be a wedding at the palace on such-and-such a day. And the day they all anxiously awaited came at last. Then Prince Ivan said to the old woman:

'Look here, mother! when the bride is just going to be married, let me know.'

The old woman didn't let the time go by unheeded.

Then Ivan immediately put on his princely raiment, and went out of the house.

'See, mother, this is what I'm really like!' says he.

The old woman fell at his feet.

'Pray forgive me for scolding you,' says she.

'God be with you,' says he.

So he went into the church and, finding his brothers had not yet arrived, he stood up alongside of the bride and got married to her. Then he and she were escorted back to the palace, and as they went along, the proper bridegroom, his eldest brother, met them. But when he saw that his bride and Prince Ivan were being escorted home together, he turned back again ignominiously.

As to the king, he was delighted to see Prince Ivan again, and when he had learnt all about the treachery of his brothers, after the wedding feast had been solemnised, he banished the two elder princes, but he made Ivan heir to the throne.

THE CIRCUMVENTION OF FATE

Jessica Amanda Salmonson

K ING LAKSHIMINDRA TOSSED and turned on his covers, his brow sweating, his eyes wildly staring but seeing none of the women who worriedly surrounded him.

Queen Behula placed her maids on all sides of King Lakshimindra and assigned them the tasks of cooling his arms and brow with moistened scarves and holding him still when he raved. 'Watch over him in my absence,' she commanded. She then hurried from the palace, wrapped in a dark cloak, leaping upon a pony. She rode swiftly and met secretly with the sorcerous Dakini.

The Dakini's breasts sagged into her lap. Her old face was chestnut brown. Although there had been no herald of the queen's coming, and none outside the palace knew of the king's illness, the Dakini naytheless was prepared in advance for the royal one's arrival.

The Dakini's hut was warm and dimly lit by red coals. Incense was fuming. Four yoginis in tiger skins sat in the shadows of the four corners of the room. The yoginis were the maiden pupils of the aged Dakini. They wove mystic signs with their fingers, murmured spells, and struck ringing bowls with tiny mallets.

Without exchanging greetings, the queen sat across the coal-pit opposite the Dakini. The wise one did not ask even one question as to why the queen had come, but said, 'O sorrowful queen, the Serpent-goddess Manasa has sent fire into the brain of the king. This very night, he will be taken by a fever-demoness, and never again will you see him. This is his punishment for having spurned the Goddess many times, calling her venomous and cruel.'

'I have propitiated Manasa with prayers and offerings,' said

Queen Behula, 'and warned my husband to avoid insults. But he listened only to brahmans, and ignored my counsel. Even so, I seek to preserve him. Have you no herb, poultice, or amulet that will aid me? I will pay you anything you desire.'

The Dakini said, 'Long ago have I given up desire. I seek no grand reward. I would help you freely, were it in my power, but the king's destiny was written on his forehead by the Goddess Bidahata-Purasha when he was six days old. Even his folly was written there, so he cannot be fully blamed. There is no poultice or amulet that will change the outcome of his life. Resign yourself, O Queen, and praise Manasa even in your saddest hour! The ways of Manasa are glorious. She seems cruel, but slays only that which keeps us from purity and happiness. Her beautiful cobra-naginis liberate all of us from this sphere of illusion.'

The queen said, 'Much as I have honored Manasa, even so, I am not prepared for this. I would fight even She that is loved in order to aid my beloved king Lakshimindra'

'Your prowess is well known,' said the Dakini. 'Only, speak not blasphemously of Manasa, for your sake and the sake of the world.'

'Come what may, I must strive to save my husband,' said Behula. 'Tell me in truth, if I sit up with him through this night, mopping his brow, praying for his recovery, cooling his body with fans when he is hot, warming him with my body when he is chilled, is there even then no chance of his survival?'

'If you swab his brow, and cool him when he is burning, and warm him when he is chilled, your devotion to him may well restore his health. Even so, two days hence, he will go riding on his elephant, and fall from it, and be accidentally trampled.'

The queen considered this, then asked, 'But if I keep him from riding his elephant, and insist he take only a horse, will he not be spared such a fate?'

'Just so. But when he rides his horse under the city gate, a stone will fall from the arch and kill him.'

'Oh! But suppose laborers are sent to tear down the arch this very night? How will a stone fall and kill him if the arch has been dismantled?'

'By such an act you can save him from this fate. But while he is hunting the royal deer, an arrow will be unleashed by his closest friend. That arrow will fall wild, and pierce your husband in the neck, from which wound he will not recover.'

'Suppose someone insists that he and his retinue hunt only with spears?'

'Then surely he will escape that danger. But upon his return home, he will seek his bath, and slip upon a tile. His head will crack open, and after many days of anguish, he will die raving.'

'But suppose his meal is ready even as he enters the palace, and a petulant queen will not let him dally from the table long enough to take a bath?'

'In that case, he will never break his skull. But there will be fish at the meal. A part of it will lodge in his throat. His face will become livid, and he will die gagging.'

'What if someone sitting near him snatches the fish from his plate and insists he eat only fruit the rest of the day?'

'Yes, that will save him, but fresh dangers await. When the king is in his bed that night, Manasa's cobra will slither through the curtains and bite him.'

'Suppose someone who loves him with her life stands guard with a sword! At risk to herself, she may behead the cobra, and save her king.'

'Yes, yes, but if Manasa is angered by the death of her serpent, the king will turn into a block of yellow stone. O Queen, give up your bold plans. Be courageous in your heart, and accept the will of Manasa.'

'Never!' said the queen, pounding the earthen floor with an open hand. 'I have honored her greatly, but in this one thing she finds a foe! I know what must be done! I know how I can save him!'

So saying, Behula stood and swept out of the hut. The four yoginis were singing a macabre dirge. The Dakini shook her wizened, hoary head and frowned as the queen departed.

She rode swiftly on her pony, returning to the palace. She hurried to the inner chambers. Shoving aside the maids who stood over the suffering king, Behula exclaimed, 'My husband! I know how to save you!' And drawing forth a dagger from her garments, she slit his throat.

THE DESTRUCTION OF KER-YS

Peter Tremayne

A T THE HOUR of the birth of Gwezenneg, prince of Bro Érech, a holy man foretold that he would be king. But the holy man also issued a warning; that on the day Gwezenneg ate pork, drank watered wine and renounced his God then he would surely die. And his death would come about by poison, by burning and by drowning. Such was the nature of this prophecy that everyone at the court of Bro Érech laughed and sent the holy man away to his hermitage with patronising smiles but with gifts lest he be a man of true prophecy.

The years went by and Gwezenneg grew to be a tall, handsome prince. It came about, as the holy man foretold, that he was acclaimed king of Bro Érech, a kingdom in the southernmost part of Armorica, the land by the sea, which we now called 'Little Britain'. Gwezenneg married a princess of Kernascleden named Gwyar and she bore him two sons. And Gwezenneg grew in fame and sought to extend the borders of his kingdom and fought several wars with neighbouring princes to expand his kingdom.

All the while, however, he was aware of the prophecy made at his birth.

One day he was hunting in the great forests of Pont Calleck by the edge of the great lake there when he came upon a beautiful young woman. Never had he beheld such beauty before. She sat on a log by the shore of the lake combing her hair with a silver comb ornamented with gold. The sun was shining on her so that her two golden yellow tresses, each one braided in four plaits, with a bead at the end of each, glistened like liquid fire.

She was dressed in a skirt of green silk, with a tunic of red, all embroidered with designs of animals in gold and silver. She bore a round golden brooch with filigree work decorated with silver. From her slender shoulders there hung a cloak of purple.

Her upper arms were white as the snow of a single night and they were soft and shapely. Her cheeks had the tinge of the foxglove of the moor upon them. Her eyebrows were coloured black and her eyes were as blue as the bugloss. Her lips were vermilion. The blush of the moon was on her fair countenance and there was a lifting pride in her noble face.

'Maiden, tell me your name,' demanded Gwezenneg, alighting from his horse and going on his knees before her as a tribute to her beauty.

She smiled softly, a dimple of sport in both her cheeks, and she answered with a gentle womanly dignity in her voice.

'I am called "whirlwind", "tempest" and "storm".'

'Lady, I would give the kingdom of Bro Érech to know you.' His children and queen, Gwyar, were all forgotten. 'Lady of the rough winds, come as my mistress to my royal palace at Vannes. I will grant you anything that is in my power.'

'Think well, on this, O king,' replied the girl. 'I have warned you of the storm to come. Do you still desire me?'

'I do.'

'Then I will come to your palace on the condition that no Christian cleric shall ever set foot there and that you must submit to my will in all things.'

Without even thinking, Gwezenneg, mesmerised by the deep blue of her eyes, agreed.

So the girl, who said her name was Aveldro, the whirlwind, came to the king's palace at Vannes.

Horrified, Gwyar, Gwezenneg's queen, took her children and went straightaway to Guénolé, the bishop, and, sobbing, asked him to intervene and cure her husband's infatuation. And when Guénolé came to Gwezenneg, the king would not listen to him. The bishop then turned to Aveldro, who was sitting unconcerned by the side of her lover. He demanded whether she felt guilt. Aveldro turned to him with a smile.

'Guilt is for the followers of your god, Gunwalloe,' she said, using the ancient form of his name so that he would know his pagan past. 'Guilt is not for those who follow the old ways.'

And Guénolé was enraged.

'Do you not follow the Christ?' he demanded.

'I cleave not to the cleric of your church,' she replied. 'They chant nothing save unreason and their tune is unmelodious in the universe.'

Then Guénolé cursed King Gwezenneg and reminded him that his doom had already been foretold.

Gwezenneg grew afraid at this but Aveldro caused a great wind to blow through the palace which swept the cursing cleric from its halls. Now Aveldro had done this feat of magic in order to put heart into Gwezenneg. But he was awed by her great power and realised that she was a *dryades*, that is to say, a female Druid. And he feared Guénolé's curse and the prophecy of his birth. So he waited until Aveldro had retired before he summoned a messenger and told him to go after Guénolé telling the bishop that Gwezenneg would come to him as soon as he could and confess all his sins, do penance, and with his blessing would eject Aveldro from his court.

The next evening Aveldro summoned him for the evening meal and a dish of meat was placed before the king.

'What meat is this?' he demanded of his cook, after he had chewed and swallowed a large piece. His cook looked uncomfortable.

'Why, we had no slaughtered beef nor mutton in the kitchen and so your lady,' he glanced awkwardly at Aveldro, 'told us to serve the pig we had slaughtered for the servants. She said that you would approve.'

And Gwezenneg went white for he knew the significance of eating pig. He reached for his wine glass to swallow the wine in order to wash out the unclean meat from his mouth. He took one swallow before spitting out the rest of the wine in disgust.

'What weak wine is this?' he demanded of the chamberlain, who had served the wine.

His chamberlain looked awkwardly at Aveldro.

'Why, sire, we had only one flagon of good wine left in the palace and so your lady told us to add a little water to it, so that it would go that much further. She said that you would approve.'

'God be damned!' swore Gwezenneg, rising up in anger from his place. Then, realising the nature of his unthinking curse, he sat down abruptly. Gwezenneg sat white-faced and stared at Aveldro who smiled a knowing smile.

Aveldro was a skilful Druidess for she could read the thoughts of the king of Bro Érech just as surely as if he had spoken them aloud. She knew that he planned to go to Guénolé and betray her. So that same night she evoked a vision which mesmerised him. And once more he pleaded for Aveldro to come to bed with him and make love and, in the vision, she consented.

Then Gwezenneg awoke from his love-making with a dry mouth and a great thirst which lay heavily on him.

'I thirst,' he moaned, 'but can find no water.'

Aveldro smiled beside him.

'I will go to the kitchen, my lover, and bring you some crystal, cold water to assuage your thirst.'

When she returned, she handed him a glass of water. He drained the glass and returned to sleep.

She watched his sleep and was satisfied for she had placed poison in the glass.

At dawn she was abruptly wakened by distant shouting. She smelt smoke and burning. It had happened that Gwyar, driven to distraction with her anger, had come upon the palace that night and set a fire under her husband's sleeping chamber.

Aveldro, taking a last look at her poisoned lover, decided to flee the palace. She had wanted to be there when Gwezenneg's body was discovered so that no blame would attach itself to her. But with the flames licking at the walls, she decided that her journey westward to her home must be precipitate. She escaped from the burning fortress and disappeared into the dawn light.

Now Gwezenneg, drugged with the poison, was not yet dead. For he was a strong and healthy man and it took a time for the poison to work through his system. The noise of shouting awoke him and he saw great flames engulfing his chamber. In discomfort from the poison, he staggered from his bed and, standing swaying, he gazed about him, finding himself amidst the smoke and crackling fires. He sought for a means of escape. The heat was intense but he managed to flee from the bedchamber as the blazing ridge poles of the roof came crashing down.

He made his way down the stone stairs, with the stones so hot that they burnt and blistered his bare feet, and found himself in the kitchens of the palace. There he was trapped by a great sheet of flame and in desperation he saw the tall water vats. In an effort to escape the flame, he clambered into the first vat which was filled with water. He plunged into its icy depth, intending to wait there until the flames had passed.

But the poison had so weakened him that he could not swim and after a minute or two he sank into the cold water of the vat and was drowned.

The next day, when Guénolé came to the smouldering ruins of the palace, the attendants of King Gwezenneg told him what had happened, for they had found the body of the king in the debris. Guénolé knew then that the prophecy had been fulfilled. But he knew also that the cause of it was the mysterious woman named Aveldro, the whirlwind. He vowed that Aveldro, who had denied the Living God, would have to pay reparation for this deed if ever she was found.

The time came when Guénolé left the sad kingdom of Bro Érech and set about a journey westward to the kingdom of Kernev, which is Cornouaille, which stretched south from the Monts d'Arrée and east to the River Ellé, beyond the great realm of Domnonia. Guénolé had heard that this kingdom of Kernev was still fiercely pagan. So he set out to convert it and he built a great monastery, which is called Landévennec, and slowly the people of Kernev turned to him and accepted his teachings.

However, Kernev was ruled by an eminent king called Gradlon. Gradlon ruled from a great city called Ker-Ys, which is 'the beloved place'. Ker-Ys was situated in what is now the Baie des Trépassés, that is the Bay of the Dead, just off the Pointe du Raz, for at the time the land of Kernev stretched over this area of the sea.

Ker-Ys was a mighty place and spoken of in awe by those merchants who had travelled to its massive walls.

Guénolé was put in a mind to see the city and to bring the word of the Living God to its king Gradlon.

One day, seated in his cell at Landévennec, he sent for his disciple, Gwion, who had been a fisherman from Kerazan and had often sailed the western coast around Kernev.

'Tell me of this Gradlon and Ker-Ys for tomorrow I mean to make a journey to see them.'

Gwion looked slightly worried.

'They hold steadfast to the old gods,' he warned his master.

'So did many of us until we heard the truth,' Guénolé replied complacently.

'Gradlon is certainly a fair king,' Gwion said. 'A sad king, though. Once, many years ago, Gwezenneg of Bro Érech tried to extend the borders of his kingdom to the west and into the territory of Kernev. He brought an army with him and crossed the River Scorv at Hennebont, which is the old bridge.

'It happened on that day Gradlon's wife and queen, Dieub, was visiting her kinfolk at Belon. And with her was her son Youlek the Determined. Gwezenneg and his warriors came down like a plague of locusts, slaughtering all before them and leaving behind the blackened earth stained red with blood. And the blood of Gradlon's wife, Dieub, was among that which had mingled with the sorry clay. And the blood of Gradlon's son, Youlek, also drenched the earth for Youlek had tried to protect his mother with his sword. And all the generations of Dieub's family were slaughtered.'

Guénolé was troubled when he heard this for Gwezenneg had been a Christian king and unworthy to have committed such a slaughter.

'Did Gradlon seek vengeance for the deed?'

Gwion shook his head.

'No; he sent his ambassadors to Gwezenneg asking for reparation and was refused. Each year, at the festival of Imbolc, he sent his ambassadors and they came back from Vannes empty handed. His daughter, Dahud-Ahes, whose beauty is renowned in the west, and who, it is said, is a mighty Druidess, demanded that her father take his army and seize that which Gwezenneg refused to give. Gradlon is a wise and worthy king and refused to lower himself to the actions of Gwezenneg.'

Guénolé was pleased then for he knew that Gradlon was such a king as he could convert to the true faith. But he was worried when he heard about Dahud-Ahes.

The next morning he set out for the west and Ker-Ys. The farther west he went the more forbidding the country became, with bare heathland and no trees but scrubland and little stone walls here and there as a means of enclosing the scanty crops which grew. There came a long, narrow spur of land, torn by waves on either side, overlooking the sea from a height of two hundred feet, and this was prolonged seaward into a chain of reefs. Then to the north was a low green plain, protected from the sea by a long, high dyke, which stretched between the Pointe du Raz and the Pointe du Van, for as we have said, this area was once land. The great dyke had built into it two massive gates which acted in the manner of a lock, and no one could open these gates, for they would flood the city. The gates were secured by a massive padlock to which there was but one golden key which Gradlon carried on a chain around his neck.

Guénolé rode up to the gates of Ker-Ys and demanded entrance and access to Gradlon. Gradlon readily admitted the man and listened to all he had to say.

'There is much that is true in what you say,' Gradlon conceded, after a while. 'I would learn more.'

'I would not!' rang out a voice.

A most beautiful woman entered the hall and from the way the attendants bowed low, Guénolé knew he was in the presence of Dahud-Ahes, daughter of Gradlon. As his disciple, Gwion, had said, she was a mighty Druidess.

Then Guénolé peered closer.

'Are you not known as Whirlwind?' he demanded.

Dahud-Ahes smiled condescendingly.

'What do you think?' she parried.

Guénolé gasped.

'Yes, by the Living God. You are Aveldro, who caused the death of Gwezenneg!'

Dahud-Ahes stood without shame.

'It was my right to take vengeance. Did not this Gwezenneg take the life of my mother, Dieub, and my brother Youlek? And did he not slaughter all my mother's family?'

'Yet you took his life by sorcery,' breathed Guénolé genuflecting.

'I took his life as he took the lives of my kin,' affirmed Dahud-Ahes.

Gradlon hung his head in shame.

'What you have done is not justice, daughter. Vengeance is not reparation.'

'Vengeance satisfies the soul,' replied Dahud-Ahes. 'My soul is at peace.'

'We are born bound to the great wheel of life, Dahud-Ahes,'

warned Guénolé. 'There is no action without a consequence. Just as Gwezenneg has paid for his action, so must you pay for your action.' He turned to Gradlon. 'King, I feel that you wish to reach out for the truth of the Living God. When the time comes you will find me at the city of Kemper.'

So he left the court of Gradlon.

That evening Dahud-Ahes was in her bed-chamber when, without warning, a young man of surpassing handsomeness entered. He was so handsome that Dahud-Ahes found herself trembling from her desire of him.

'You are no mortal man,' she murmured.

'I am Maponos, the god of love,' he replied with a smile. 'And of all the women on the earth, I have heard that you were the most beautiful. Now I have seen the truth of it with my own eyes. And I desire you. Come away with me and dwell with me in the palace of love, which is far to the west of this place.'

Dahud-Ahes lost all her rationality. Indeed, as Gwezenneg had fallen under her spell, she fell under the spell of this young man.

'I will,' she replied with vehemence.

Then the handsome Maponos hesitated.

'I have admitted my love for you. But before we go to my eternal palace, you must prove that you love me. The entrance to my palace is known only to myself and if you share this secret I need a token of your love.'

'I will do anything,' she replied simply.

'Then fetch the golden key of the gate in the dyke which hangs around your father's neck. Fetch it and unlock the gates.'

'But the whole city will drown,' protested Dahud-Ahes.

'Not so. If you believe in me I will not let it drown. Am I not a god and cannot I stop such floods? If you desire to live with me in all eternity then you must do this thing to prove your worthiness.'

For Dahud-Ahes there was never any doubt of her desire and she ran straightaway to her father's bedchamber and finding him asleep, she took the golden key and chain from around his neck. Then she hurried to the great gate where the handsome young god stood.

'Open the gate,' instructed Maponos, 'if you trust and desire me. Prove to me that you believe in me.'

She put the key in the lock, turned it and flung open the gate. The vast green frothy sea rushed in. Dahud-Ahes turned eagerly to the young man.

'Now save the city, for I have proved my love for you,' she cried.

The young man started to laugh. He laughed and as he did so his body was transformed into a twisted, ageing devil with the evil, sneering face of Gwezenneg. Then, with the laughter still echoing, the figure disappeared.

In terror and despair, Dahud-Ahes ran through the city of Ker-Ys raising the alarm. The sea rushed down, its waves like hungry mouths swallowing all in their path.

'Mount up, behind, my daughter!'

Gradlon rode up beside her on his fastest charger, and Dahud–Ahes was swung up behind. The king rode as hard as he could before the mighty, oncoming tide, the powerful sinews of his horse bursting with the effort. But the sea began to overtake them, to swallow them. Gradlon began to despair when he heard the voice of Guénolé.

'If you would save yourself and your people, Gradlon, throw your unworthy and shameful daughter off into the sea. She has betrayed you for her own desires.'

With aching heart, Gradlon did as he was bid. He pushed his pleading daughter back into the hungry waves. The seas began to recede although Ker-Ys remained submerged. But all the people of Ker-Ys managed to reach the safety of dry land except for Dahud-Ahes who was swept under the mighty waves. But because Dahud-Ahes was bound to the wheel of fate, because she was not the beginning nor the ending of its cycle, Guénolé took pity on her.

'You will live your time as one of the merfolk, living in the sunken palaces of Ker-Ys for all eternity!'

And so it is, throughout time, Dahud-Ahes, in the form of a mermaid, still lures unwary sailors, drawn on by her unsurpassed beauty, to the bottom of the sea. Thus, in the language of the Bretons, the place is called *Boé an Anaon* or the Bay of Suffering Souls.

Gradlon, meanwhile, went on in sorrow to Kemper, which is still called Quimper to this day. And he became a convert of Guénolé. When that venerable man returned to his monastery at Landévennec, Gradlon chose, as the bishop of his city, Corentin, and ended his days in the odour of sanctity, guided and sustained by Corentin who became patron of the town. And if you climb the cathedral that is in the Place St Corentin today you will find that a statue of Gradlon on horse-back stands between its two spires.

But beware of standing on the Pointe du Raz, listening to the whispering of the sea amongst the rocks; beware lest you hear the seductive calling of Dahud-Ahes.

STORY NOTES
AND ACKNOWLEDGEMENTS

The Ever-Living Ones

Peter Tremayne is the fiction-writing pseudonym of the Celtic scholar Peter Berresford Ellis (b. 1943) who has published many works on Celtic history and culture including *A Dictionary of Irish Mythology* (1987) and *A Dictionary of Celtic Mythology* (1992). The *Irish Democrat* said that he 'has done for Irish mythology what Robert Graves has done for Greek mythology.' As Peter Tremayne he has utilised his expert knowledge to write many fantasy novels and stories based on Celtic mythological themes.

The Celtic languages contain one of Europe's oldest and most vibrant mythologies. In fact the Irish language contains Europe's third oldest literature, for the oldest texts in Irish are predated only by Greek and Latin. Some 2,500 years ago the Celtic peoples spread through Europe from Ireland in the west to the central plain of Turkey in the east, and from Belgium in the north to as far south as Cadiz in southern Spain, and to Ancona, just north of the Apennines in Italy. They were the first non-Mediterranean civilisation to emerge into recorded history. Today, the Celts survive only on the north-west fringe of Europe and are divided into six modern cultures: the Irish, Manx and Scots, identified by their language as Goidelic Celts, and the Welsh, Cornish and Bretons, identified as Brythonic Celts. 'The Ever-Living Ones' contains not only Tremayne's reconstruction of the original Celtic Creation Myth but also the story of the fight between the Good and Evil gods and goddesses symbolised by the Battle of Magh Tuireadh (The Plain of Towers). This story is adapted mainly from the Irish *Leabhar Gabhála* (*Book of*

Invasions) whose earliest complete survival is in the *Leabhar na Nuachonghbhala* (popularly known as the *Book of Leinster*) compiled in AD 1150 by Fionn mac Gormain of Glendalough. The story is © 1995 by Peter Berresford Ellis. First printing original to this anthology. Used by permission of the author and the author's agent, A. M. Heath & Co.

The Star Maids and the Flea Man and The Star Maidens' Laughter

Although the author of over a hundred short stories, Jessica Salmonson (b. 1950) is probably best known for her heroic fantasy novels, such as the Tomoe Gozen trilogy, which recounts the adventures of a female Samurai in the world of Japanese myth. The sequence runs *Tomoe Gozen* (1981), *The Golden Naginata* (1982) and *Thousand Shrine Warrior* (1984). Another entrancing oriental fantasy is *Ou Lou Khen and the Beautiful Madwoman* (1985). Her short fiction often draws upon mystical legends. Relevant collections include *A Silver Thread of Madness* (1989), *Mystic Women* (1991), *The Mysterious Doom* (1993) and *Phantom Waters* (1995). These two stories are founded upon myths of the Tachi, Cahuilla and Maidu Indians of California as recorded by Edward W. Gifford and Gwendoline Harris Black in *California Indian Nights Entertainment* (1930). Both are © 1995 by Jessica Amanda Salmonson. First printing original to this anthology. Printed by permission of the author.

Bearskin Woman and Grizzly Woman

This is one of the creation myths of the Blackfoot Indians of North America. According to legend their tribe was founded by Napi, their folk hero, who saved the tribe from disaster at the time of the Great Catastrophe when they sought refuge in the great cave of Nina Stahu. The stars gave inspiration to the Blackfoot peoples as much as it did to many early cultures, and Jessica Salmonson has used one such myth here. The story is © 1994 by Jessica Amanda Salmonson. First published in *Daughters of Nyx 2* edited by Kim Antieau, 1994. Reprinted by permission of the author.

The Quest for Discovery

The legend of Theseus and the Minotaur is one of the best known of the Greek legends. For that reason I have avoided it here and instead selected a story about the youth of Theseus, the illegitimate son of Aegeus, King of Athens, who had to discover and prove his own identity. The story has been used by many writers, and I have selected here the interpretation by Andrew Lang. Lang (1844–1912) was a great Victorian folklorist and antiquarian. He is best remembered as the editor of twelve volumes of fairy stories which ran from *The Blue Fairy Book* (1889) to *The Lilac Fairy Book* (1910), but in his day he was a highly regarded authority on literature and the occult, contributing articles to many magazines as well as the *Encyclopedia Britannica*. Lang long held a fascination for the Greek myths. He collaborated with H. Rider Haggard on *The World's Desire* (1890), about the further adventures of Odysseus, and produced two volumes of his own retelling the key legends: *The Story of the Golden Fleece* (1903) and *Tales of Troy and Greece* (1907). It is from this last volume that 'The Quest for Discovery' is taken.

The Strange Tale of Caribou and Moose

Years ago I stumbled across a little book called *Canadian Wonder Tales* (1918) by Cyrus Macmillan. It was this book that first opened my eyes to the magical legends of the North American Indians. Macmillan (1882–1953) had followed in the footsteps of the Brothers Grimm and sought to capture the folk tales of North America. In his preface Macmillan passed his deepest thanks 'to the nameless Indians and habitants, the fishermen and sailors, the spinners and the knitters in the sun' from whose lips he heard these stories, adding that the stories were not of his own invention but were 'the common possession of the folk'. This research was the product of Macmillan's youth. It is interesting to note that the final proofs were corrected by him in the midst of the First World War while, as Major Macmillan, he was in the thick of the offensive at Vimy Ridge. One can easily imagine how the magic of North American myth would allow him to escape, if only for a moment, from the most horrendous carnage about him. Macmillan later became the head of the English Department at McGill University and a Member of the Canadian Parliament.

The Hero Makóma

This story comes from the Sena tribe in eastern Africa, from what is now the borders of Mozambique and Zimbabwe. It was drawn from oral tradition by the explorer and pioneer Kingsley Fairbridge (1885–1924). Fairbridge's family settled in Rhodesia in 1896. His father was a surveyor and explorer. Kingsley spent his teens exploring the wilds of Africa and learning the legends of the natives. He captured some of these memories in his Autobiography which became regarded as a classic of Rhodesian literature.

Prince Yamato Take

It was at the request of Andrew Lang that Yei Theodora Ozaki translated and edited a collection called *Japanese Fairy Tales* (1903), based upon a volume of Japanese myths and folktales compiled by Sadanami Sanjin. The insignia of the Empire consists of three treasures which have long been considered sacred. These are the Mirror of Yata, the Jewel of Yasakami and most precious of all, the Sword of Murakumo. The sword is the symbol of strength and talisman of invincibility of the Emperor. Nearly two thousand years ago this sword was kept at the shrines of Ite, the temples dedicated to the worship of Amaterasu, the powerful goddess of the Sun, from whom the Japanese emperors claim descent. 'The Story of Prince Yamato Take' reveals the background of the Sword and explains why its name was changed from Murakumo to Kasanagi, the grass-cleaver.

The Lad With One Sandal

My favourite of the Greek myths is the story of Jason and the Argonauts. It has everything. A fabulous quest, all the famous heroes, and travels into foreign lands facing many monsters and mysteries. It has fascinated many writers and is the subject of at least two excellent novels by Henry Treece and Robert Graves, as well as one of the better muscle-men dramas of the cinema, the 1963 film *Jason and the Argonauts* with excellent animation by Ray Harryhausen. It was also one of the favourite tales of the Greek poet Pindar, who lived in the sixth century BC and travelled throughout the Greek world reciting his famous narrative *Odes*. These *Odes* served as inspiration to Winifred Hutchinson who retold this story in her book, *The Golden Porch* (1907).

The Sons of Tuirenn

The adventures of the sons of Tuirenn have been likened to the tale of Jason and the Argonauts. It is a story about actions and consequences and represents Irish mythology at its best with warriors and gods facing an inescapable fate. This story is again based on an episode in the *Book of Invasions*. It is © 1995 by Peter Berresford Ellis. First printing original to this anthology. Used by permission of the author and the author's agent, A. M. Heath & Co.

My Lord Bag of Rice

Another story from *Japanese Fairy Tales* (1903) based on the stories by Sadanami Sanjin.

Prince Seyf el Mulouk

No book of legends would be complete without something from the Arabian Nights, which are amongst the best known legends in the world. I have, though, gone for something slightly different. The standard volumes of the Arabian Nights are based on the French translations by Antoine Galland under the familiar title of *The Thousand and One Nights*, but there was also a series called *The Thousand and One Days*, which, though well known in France, is almost unknown in the English-speaking world. *The Thousand and One Days* was the work of the French orientalist François Pétis de la Croix under the title *Persian Tales* (1710–12). He claimed his source as a Persian text called *Hazar Yek Ruz* which he acquired from a Dervish called Mocles whom he knew in Isfahan in 1675. These were tales that Mocles had collected from a variety of Arab, Indian and Turkish sources. Though English translations of de la Croix's work were made in 1714 and 1738, they then lay forgotten until the Victorian writer and scholar Justin Huntly McCarthy (1861–1936) made his own translation as *The Thousand and One Days* in 1892.

The Journey to Constantinople

Myths don't have to be from the dawn of time. Every generation and culture develops its own, and this was particularly true in the years after the reign of Charlemagne, or Charles the Great (AD 742–814), king of the Franks and Holy Roman Emperor. Such was the stature and power of Charles that he began to take on the legendary status of King Arthur. The number of legends are legion, many drawing not only upon his conquests but upon his deeply religious views and his penetrating wisdom, and two are presented here. The first, 'The Journey to Constantinople', whilst having its origins in France, travelled throughout Europe by way of balladeers and troubadours, eventually finding itself in Sweden. It is this Swedish version, collected by the Swedish ethnographer, Hans Shück, that is presented here. It was translated by William F. Harvey (not the same as the author of 'The Beast With Five Fingers') in a volume of Shück's works called *Mediaeval Stories* (1902).

Huon's Quest

The second of our Frankish legends deals with one of the most popular of the French *chanson de geste*, the story of 'Huon of Bordeaux'. It is believed this tale was first composed in the thirteenth century. Its popularity was such that it was amongst the earliest stories to be printed as a book. This was the English translation by Lord Berners which was printed by Wynkyn de Worde, Caxton's successor, in 1534. It was this version that was certainly known to Shakespeare who used the character of Oberon, the king of the fairies who helps Huon on his quest, in *A Midsummer Night's Dream* (1596).

Ascott Hope-Moncrieff (1846–1927) was a Scottish schoolmaster who found a more profitable career writing boys' adventure stories to which he turned full-time from 1865. In a career of over sixty years he produced more than a hundred books. Many drew upon old tales and legends, and increasingly these became of a scholarly nature. 'Huon's Quest' is taken from his volume *Romance and Legend of Chivalry* (1913).

Perseus and the Gorgon

Frequently in ancient myths we find kings fearful of their throne being usurped, usually by a son. The best known of these legends is that of Oedipus. His father was Laius, king of Thebes, who was told by an oracle that he would be killed by his son Oedipus. As a result Oedipus was exposed on a rock, but was found and reared and ultimately, fulfilling fate, killed his father and married his mother (both unwittingly). A similar fear haunted Acrisius, king of Argos, who was warned that his daughter, Danaë, would bear a son who would kill him. As a consequence he walled up his daughter in a stone tomb, but through the divine intervention of Zeus, she gave birth to Perseus. The story of Perseus, and his quest to fetch the head of the Gorgon Medusa fascinated the Victorian clergyman Charles Kingsley. Kingsley (1819–1875) is best known for his children's book *The Water Babies* (1863) but he had earlier written a volume of Greek legends, *The Heroes* (1856) which told not only of the adventures of Perseus, but also of Hercules, Theseus and Jason.

The Chimaera

Although Kingsley did not relate this version, one legend states that when Perseus beheaded Medusa, Pegasus, the winged horse, sprung from the blood. It was Pegasus who bore Perseus to the rescue of Andromeda. But Pegasus was a creature of the wild and not under the control of any mortal. Nevertheless Pegasus was tamed by another Greek hero, one who is less known than Perseus or Jason, but whose adventures are no less exciting. This was Bellerophon, one of the doomed Greek heroes, fated even more than Hercules. It was Bellerophon who tamed Pegasus and together they set off against the Chimaera, a fire-breathing dragon. This story is retold by Nathaniel Hawthorne (1804–1864) who included it in *A Wonder Book* (1852).

Hercules in Hell

Hercules, or more properly in Greek, Herakles, was the great-grandson of Perseus, and was dispossessed of his kingdom when the goddess Hera intervened and delayed his birth, thus making his cousin, Eurystheus, king of Tiryns. Nevertheless, Hercules was the favourite of Zeus, king of the gods, from whom he drew his great strength. This strength was present from his birth when Hera sent two snakes to kill him but the infant strangled them. Hercules however was to suffer bouts of madness and at one such time he killed not only his own children but those of his brother Iphicles. It was to atone for this that Hercules was bound to serve his cousin Eurystheus and that was how the twelve labours of Hercules began. The last and most difficult of these was his descent into the Underworld. In bringing together the story represented here I have blended elements from Charles Kingsley's version in *The Heroes* with those retold by Hope-Moncrieff in *Classical Mythology*, as well as drawing upon the extensive research of Robert Graves in *The Greek Myths*. This version is © 1995 by Mike Ashley.

Siegfried and the Dragon Fafnir

Siegfried is the archetypal hero of Teutonic and Scandinavian myth. His adventures are told in the *Nibelungenlied*, a series of connected narrative poems first laid down in German in the late twelfth century, but drawing on earlier tales in the Icelandic and Nordic eddas or sagas, most especially the *Volsunga Saga*. Siegfried can be alikened to the Greek Achilles, a hero made invulnerable as a child by bathing in the blood of a dragon, but having one vulnerable spot between his shoulder blades where a leaf had lain. The Nibelungs was the name given to those who guarded a vast treasure hoard which at length came into the possession of Siegfried. Siegfried's adventures have been immortalised over the last century thanks to the Ring Cycle of operas by Richard Wagner, but the legends had enthralled generations for centuries before. The extract used here comes from *The Story of Siegfried* (1882) by James Baldwin (1841–1925), an American historian and writer.

The Slaying of Grendel

When the Saxons and other Germanic tribes as well as the Vikings invaded the British Isles in the years from the fifth century on, they brought with them their own myths and sagas which rapidly passed into our native culture. The most famous of these legends is that of Beowulf, a Danish warrior of the fifth or sixth century. The adventures of Beowulf, particularly against the monster Grendel, would have been recounted endlessly to Danes settled in England, thinking of their homeland. The poem, which was written down around the year AD 1000, was probably extant for at least two centuries before that, and is the oldest surviving poem in Old English. The prose adaptation presented here is by Alfred Church (1829–1912), a classical scholar noted for his translation of Tacitus, and comes from his *Heroes of Chivalry and Romance* (1898).

The Lambton Worm

Many families have their own legends, especially amongst the nobility, and one of the most famous is that of the Lambton curse, which haunted the Earls of Durham for nine generations. Tradition came to link it with an earlier legend of the Lambton dragon which dates from at least the time of the Crusades in the twelfth century, and probably has links back to earlier legends like Beowulf and Grendel. The version presented here is from *The Grey Ghost Book* (1912) by Jessie Middleton who, at the turn of the century, wrote several books assembling stories of ghosts, superstition and family legends.

The Shadowy One

From Scotland comes a tale of the mysterious female warrior Scáthach, the Shadowy One. She ran a martial arts academy on the Isle of Skye, which takes its name from her – Sgitheanach, Isle of Shadows – where all the famous heroes of Éireann and Alba (Scotland) went for their military training. Scáthach appears infrequently in the 'Red Branch Cycle' of Irish myths, sometimes known as the 'Ulster Cycle'. More lengthy references appear in *Compert Scáthach Buanand (The Begetting of Scáthach the Victorious)* and *Tochmarc Emer (The Wooing of Emer)* whose fragmentary texts date to the tenth century. This is not only a story of warriors but of intense passion and jealousy. The story is © 1995 by Peter Berresford Ellis. First printing original to this anthology. Used by permission of the author and the author's agent, A. M. Heath & Co.

Bran and Branwen

This is one of the more famous stories from the *Mabinogi* (the Four Branches of the Mabinogion), the collective title for a group of tales which are the central surviving texts of Welsh mythology. The stories originate from different periods ranging from pre-Norman conquest through to the twelfth century. Elements of them appear in *The White Book of Rhydderch* (compiled *c.* 1300–1325) but the more complete text is in *The Red Book of Hergest* (compiled *c.* 1375–1425). The texts were not translated into English until Charlotte Guest began in 1838. Since then the tales have inspired many authors, especially Evangeline Walton and Alan Garner. The story included is © 1995 by Peter Berresford Ellis. First printing original to this anthology. Used by permission of the author and the author's agent, A. M. Heath & Co.

King Laurin's Rose-Garden

One of the principal characters in the German *Book of Heroes* is Dietrich von Bern. Dietrich is based on the historical character of Theodoric the Great, who established the great Eastern Gothic Empire in AD 493. Etzel, whom you also meet in this story, is Attila, the king of the Huns, although the lives of these two great conquerors did not historically overlap. Dietrich undergoes many fantastic adventures, not least when he encounters the dwarf-king Laurin (another name for Alberich) who has kidnapped his sister Künhild. That is where 'King Laurin's Rose-Garden' begins. The version here comes from *Epics and Romances of the Middle Ages* (1883) by Dr Wilhelm Wägner.

The Children of Loki

This is one of the many episodes from the heart of Nordic mythology. Loki, although classed as one of the Aesir – the chosen ones of Odin – was really something of a fallen angel. He was a mischief maker who fathers a family of evil creatures. The day comes when Odin sets out to face this evil once and for all. The story here has been extracted from *The Heroes of Asgard* (1857) by the Victorian novelist Annie Keary (1825–1879) and her sister Eliza. Annie Keary's best known work was *Castle Daly* (1875), set during the Irish famine.

When the Woman Chief was Young

This is based on a myth of the Klamath Indians in south central Oregon. The Klamath lived on the shores of Upper Klamath Lake and the Klamath Marsh and their culture is based heavily on the lakeside environment. This story is © 1995 by Jessica Amanda Salmonson. First published in *Phantom Waters* (Seattle: Sasquatch Press, 1995). Reprinted by permission of the author.

Tewdrig, Tyrant of Treheyl

This story derives from Cornish legend and is referred to in medieval hagiographies of Cornish saints, such as Gwinear, written in the twelfth century. Tewdrig also appears as a tyrant in *Bewnans Meryasek* (*Life of St Meryadoc*, a sixth-century bishop of Cornwall) which takes its place in literary importance as the only surviving full-length play about the life of a Cornish saint written in the Cornish language. The text of the surviving manuscript is dated AD 1504. This story is © 1995 by Peter Berresford Ellis. First printing original to this anthology. Used by permission of the author and the author's agent, A. M. Heath & Co.

Red Wolf's Daughter and Bloody Chief's Son

The Nez Perce Indians were so named by the French for their habit of having pierced noses. They live in Idaho and nearby Washington and Oregon. After the introduction of horses they became renowned horse breeders, but this legend goes back far earlier to the times of the battles with the Blackfoot tribe. This story is © 1995 by Jessica Amanda Salmonson. First published in *Phantom Waters* (Seattle: Sasquatch Press, 1995). Reprinted by permission of the author.

East of the Sun and West of the Moon

The title of this story has always been one of my favourites because it so evocatively captures the mystical enticement of other worlds. The story was originally collected by Peter Asbjörnsen (1813–1885) who with Jörgen Moe (1813–1882) had become encouraged to collect Norwegian folktales after discovering the works of the Brothers Grimm. The story was first collected in their *Norske Folkeeventyr* in the 1840s and translated into English in *Fairy Tales of All Nations* in 1849. The story became a favourite of William Morris (1834–1896) who included it in his long group of narrative poems *The Earthly Paradise*, a kind of Nordic Canterbury Tales, which Morris wrote between 1868 and 1870. These stories were later adapted into prose form by Madalen Edgar, in *Stories from the Earthly Paradise* (1919) and it is that version I have reprinted here.

The Barnacle Maid

Although this tale comes from the myths of the Salish Indians on the north-west coast of America, in Washington State and British Columbia it is reminiscent of so many legends of women who sacrifice themselves for their love. In most legends, as in Fouqué's retelling of *Undine* (1811), it is the sprite or nymph who falls in love with a human, but here the plot is twisted most effectively. The story is © 1992 by Jessica Amanda Salmonson and was first published in *The Mysterious Doom and Other Ghostly Tales of the Pacific Northwest* (Seattle: Sasquatch Press, 1992). Reprinted by permission of the author.

Battle on the Bridge of the Gods

The Columbia River has its birth in the Canadian Rockies. It meanders through the Northwest capturing other rivers such as the Snake and the Spokane, until it breaks mightily through the Cascade range between Mount Adams and Mount Hood, forming the Oregon–Washington border. After the river turns, there is a long, deep canyon, the Columbia River Gorge. The geographical, geological and meteorological oddities of this area have intrigued modern scientists, no less than they inspired aboriginal myths that still ring in our hearts with great authority.

Oregon's first historical novel was Frederic Homer Balch's *The Bridge of the Gods: a Romance of Indian Oregon* (1890), a national bestseller with many reprintings making the Bridge familiar to households in all quarters of America. A synopsis of a Klickitat telling of the myth is given as 'An Indian Legend' in Michael S. Spranger's compilation *The Columbia Gorge, A Unique American Treasure* (1984), and similar paraphrases in scores of popular books akin to Katharine B. Judson's *Myths and Legends of the Pacific Northwest* (1910) or Eleanor Marion Gridley's *Indian Legends of American Scenes* (1939). Clarence Orvel Bunnell's *Legends of the Klickitats* (1933) offers a series of interconnected tales associated with the Bridge, with a good deal of coloration derived as much from pioneer sentimentality as from the Klickitats. An overview of the myth can be found in Ella E. Clark's 'The Bridge of the Gods in Fact and Fancy' in *The Oregon Historical Quarterly*, March 1952.

Whether in enthographic or popular versions, there are contradictory variations of sequence and event. A variant supposes mounts Hood and St Helens were husband and wife; it was they who had the great fire-fight, with Hood getting the worst of it, since Loowit does seem to be a recollection of an all-powerful Earth-mother whose husband or husbands are her subordinates. In the majority of cases the antagonistic male mountains are Hood and Adams, who formed the pillars that upheld the sky-bridge. The St Helens Goddess who guards this bridge is sometimes a pure and noble virgin burdened by male possessiveness; elsetimes she is a coquette who intentionally arouses jealousy. The hag form lived either on the Bridge sharing fire with peoples who visited her from both sides, or she lived in her mountain attended by bats, seen by few.

Not every version identifies Loowit as fire-bringer, though many do. Her association with the region's most active volcano is invariable, indicating that she was indeed a Fire-goddess whether or not this was always recalled. Her name means 'Fire Top' and though no text suggests it, her hair may have been red, as was that of the nymphs or 'beaver women' who haunt rivers. There was among Salishan and Chinookan peoples a tradition that the oldest member of a family remained near the firepit at all times so the fire would never go out. This allowed the most enfeebled member of a family or tribe to continue to serve a necessary function. This appointment led to sundry legends of old women who hoard fire improperly without sharing it. In still other legends, it is the youngest of five brothers who guards the fire. A fifth of five brothers is roughly equivalent to the European idea of 'the seventh of seven sons' who possesses sorcery and wisdom. It may well be that in prehistory, the firepit guardian was a young priest or elderly priestess serving an Earth-mother not unlike the Hearth-goddesses of Europe served by Vestals. Loowit is, then, akin to the Greek Hestia or Roman Vesta, who was commonly identified with the Phrygian Mountain-goddess Cybele or Magna Mater, and whose youthful associate was Attis.

Loowit's wooers were Pahtoe the Fire Spirit of Mount Adams, grandfather of the Klickitat people who lived north over the semi-arid plains; and Wyeast the Wind Spirit of Mount Hood, grandfather of the Multnomahs who lived along the Willamette River. This supposes Loowit an ancestral divinity who had two husbands, even aside from their group role as geological personifications. Fire and Wind were certainly rational designations for the husband spirits, considering the actual weather patterns of the area. The Gorge, where dry and moist atmospheric conditions collide, is seasonally notoriously stormy. Winds from the west reach 100 miles per hour. The first time the American government put a weather station near the Gorge, the very next storm carried away all the instruments, as photographer Chuck Williams – himself a descendant of Cascade Indians – rather gleefully notes in his lovely volume *Bridge of the Gods, Mountains of Fire: A Return to the Columbia Gorge* (1980). So we can see how native mythmakers were actually teaching of natural phenomena, explaining how the hot breath of Pahtoe and the moist breath of Wyeast clash in the form of great battles at the Gorge.

Donald and Elizabeth Lawrence in 'Bridge of the Gods Legend: Its Origin, History and Dating,' in the mountaineer magazine *Mazama*, December 1958, speculate how the more expansive versions originated with Indian storytellers who were testing the limitations of white gullibility. Others suppose the legend was elaborated by whites themselves, with Indians re-adapting whatever parts they liked. Certainly the ethnographic texts, recorded directly from Indians, do not give such elaborate versions as found in the plethora of later popular books. It appears that prior to 1840, the Bridge was discussed in geologically feasible terms as a huge landslide-dam, and not as a supernatural epic. Early explorers were simply informed, 'We used to walk across without getting our moccasins wet.' Around seven hundred years ago, much of Greenleaf Peak and Table Mountain broke away in an earthquake, probably accompanied by nearby volcanic activity. A five square mile landslide was dumped into the river, and this was the actual Bridge of the Gods. Behind that bridge-dam, a great lake rose to five hundred feet and extended east to Umatilla. Many upstream villages were eradicated by inundation and loss of salmon runs. But the lake's overflow gradually weakened the landslide-dam, with attendant flooding catastrophes down river when the lake was finally unleashed. This story is © 1995 by Jessica Amanda Salmonson. Printed by permission of the author.

Story of The Three Strong Men

Charles Godfrey Leland (1824–1903) was a widely travelled authority on folklore throughout America and Europe. Although trained as a lawyer, which he practised between 1849 and 1853, he became a journalist and after the American Civil War travelled throughout Europe, settling for some years in London and Florence. He was the founder of the Hungarian Folklore Society and a President of the Gypsy-Lore Society. In his later years he travelled throughout New England collecting local stories which were published as *Algonquin Legends of New England* (1884).

The Lay Nun Who Gave of Herself

Some of the greatest tales come from Indian myth. This story is a Buddhist legend told in the *Milinda* (*Questions of Faith*) written in Sanskrit near the beginning of the Christian era. The story is © 1991 by Jessica Amanda Salmonson. First published in *Mystic Women: Their Ancient Tales and Legends* (Seattle: Street of Crocodiles, 1991). Reprinted by permission of the author.

The One-Handed Girl

This is one of the folk tales collected by Edward Steere in his travels around south-eastern Africa, especially the old colony of Zanzibar, and assembled in his book *Swahili Tales* (1870).

Rayamati, the Savioress

This legend of Jain asceticism is adapted from the *Uttarâdhyayana*. It is © 1991 by Jessica Amanda Salmonson. First published in *Mystic Women: Their Ancient Tales and Legends* (Seattle: Street of Crocodiles, 1991). Reprinted by permission of the author.

Echo and Narcissus

A simple tale from the later Greek myths captured by Ovid in his *Metamorphoses*, written at the very dawn of the Christian era. The version here is retold by Hope-Moncrieff from *Classical Mythology* (1913).

Vasavadatta the Courtesan

This is founded upon an episode from *Asokavadana (The Legend of King Asoka)* written in the second century AD but set several hundred years earlier. Asoka, who ruled in the third century BC, was the first to organise Buddhism as the state religion of India. This story is © 1991 by Jessica Amanda Salmonson. First published in *Mystic Women: Their Ancient Tales and Legends* (Seattle: Street of Crocodiles, 1991). Reprinted by permission of the author.

The Courtesan who Worked a Miracle

Another episode from the *Milinda*. © 1991 by Jessica Amanda Salmonson. First published in *Mystic Women: Their Ancient Tales and Legends* (Seattle: Street of Crocodiles, 1991). Reprinted by permission of the author.

The King's Son and the White-Bearded Scolog

One of the most refreshing volumes of legends I have read is *Hero-Tales of Ireland* by Jeremiah Curtin (1835–1906) which was first published in 1894, but is as lively today as ever.

The Adventure of the Holy Grail

It was impossible to compile a volume of legends without including at least one Arthurian story and there is none that has captivated the imagination of writers more than the quest for the Holy Grail. The Grail was the cup from which Christ drank the wine at the Last Supper and which later caught his drops of blood from the cross. It was brought by Joseph of Arimathea to Britain and supposedly hidden at Glastonbury, although research by Norma Lorre Goodrich suggests that the Grail Castle was on the Isle of Man. The significance of the Grail legend was first established in story form by the French romancist Chrétien de Troyes in *Le Conte del Graal* composed around 1190. It was further developed by the German poet Wolfram von Eschenbach in *Parzival* written a decade or two later, and was soon being embellished by the troubadours of the day. The version presented here recounts the legend in its simplest and purest form. It is from *Heroes of Chivalry and Romance* (1898).

The Prince Who Sought Immortality

I first encountered this story in a volume of Hungarian folktales selected by Gyula Ortutay (1910–1978), a noted Hungarian folklorist, but I was unable to secure the rights to the story. Fortunately I found an earlier and equally effective version by Leonora Alleyne, the wife of Andrew Lang. Mrs Lang has never received the full credit she deserves because it is she who translated, adapted and retold the bulk of the tales in Lang's long and popular series of *Fairy Books* for which he usually receives the credit.

The Changelings

This is a Wapato Lake legend from the Indians of Northwestern Oregon. It not only introduces us to the strange lake monster the Huluk, but like 'The Barnacle Maid' makes us aware of the transition from one state of existence to another, which is a common feature of the legends of the North American Indians. The story is © 1995 by Jessica Amanda Salmonson. First published in *Phantom Waters* (Seattle: Sasquatch Press, 1995). Reprinted by permission of the author.

The Story of a Gazelle

Another of the folk tales collected by Edward Steere in his travels around south-eastern Africa and assembled in his book *Swahili Tales* (1870). This one considers in particular the relationship between man and animals and their relative intelligence.

Yuki-Onna

I wanted to include at least one ghost story in this anthology, and the choice of one by Lafcadio Hearn was almost automatic. Hearn (1850–1904) was born in Greece, educated in France and England, emigrated to the United States in 1869 where he became a reporter, and then in 1891 settled in Japan as a writer and lecturer, becoming a Japanese citizen. His fascination with Japanese legends resulted in a number of books. This story comes from *Kwaidan* (1904).

Bhadra and the Mendicant

This is another Jaina tale based on characters and incidents from the *Uttarâdhyayana* along with alternative accounts of the legend. It is © 1991 by Jessica Amanda Salmonson. First published in *Mystic Women: Their Ancient Tales and Legends* (Seattle: Street of Crocodiles, 1991). Reprinted by permission of the author.

The Reborn Divinities

Another Jaina legend adapted from the *Uttarâdhyayana*. It is © 1991 by Jessica Amanda Salmonson. First published in *Mystic Women: Their Ancient Tales and Legends* (Seattle: Street of Crocodiles, 1991). Reprinted by permission of the author.

"Island of the Ocean God"

This story of Mac Cuill is based on a Manx legend from the Isle of Man. It is a curious one which seems to dwell on the death of the old gods, the naming of the Island and its conversion to Christianity. It also includes a description of an active watery-grave. The earliest source of the story is to be found in the *Liber Ardmachanus* (*Book of Armagh*), compiled by Feardomhnach in AD 807. This version is © 1995 by Peter Berresford Ellis. First printing original to this anthology. Used by permission of the author and the author's agent, A. M. Heath & Co.

The Rover of the Plain

This is a legend of the Thonga, or Tsonga, a Bantu-speaking people who live in southern Mozambique. The story was collected by the French ethnographer Henri Junod for his monograph *L'Etude Ethnographique sur les Baronga* and translated and adapted by Leonora Lang for *The Orange Fairy Book* (1906).

Uraschimataro and the Turtle

A Japanese folk legend collected by the German antiquarian David Brauns and published in *Japanische Märchen und Sagen* in 1885. This version was translated and adapted by Leonora Lang for *The Pink Fairy Book* (1897).

How the Serpent-Gods were Propitiated

This story is taken from the Saga of the Well-and-Wise-Walking Khan, a cycle of stories told by the Kalmouk nomads of eastern Tibet. The story-cycle is about two brothers, sons of a Khan, one of whom learns magic from seven magicians, and the other doesn't. The brother magician, seeking to impress the other, converts himself into a horse whom the other rides to the seven magicians. When they see a magic horse they try to kill it. A shape-changing battle ensues resulting in the brother killing the seven magicians. He knows he has done ill and his Master tells him to go to a distant grove where resides the Siddhî-kür (a dead body with magical powers) and bring it back. He must not talk to the Siddhî or it will return to its grove. Each time he tries he is tricked by a tale. This is the fifth tale. The stories were collected by the folklorist Rachel Busk (1818–1907) in *Sagas from the Far East* (1873).

Koshchei the Deathless

Koshchei is one of several evil spirits that haunt Russian legends and folktales. The cycle of stories in which he features comes to a climax in this tale where the hero confronts the spirit. The tale was collected by the Russian folklorist Alexander Afanasief (1826–1871) in *Russian Popular Legends* (1871). This version was translated by William S. Ralston in *Russian Folk-Tales* (1873).

The Circumvention of Fate

This story is founded upon a Bengali folk myth. It is © 1991 by Jessica Amanda Salmonson. First published in *Mystic Women: Their Ancient Tales and Legends* (Seattle: Street of Crocodiles, 1991). Reprinted by permission of the author.

The Destruction of Ker-Ys

We end where we started, with a Celtic legend, this one from Brittany. It features the popular motif of a city sinking beneath the sea, noted in Atlantis, Lyonesse and other legends, but this one introduces a Christian element. The earliest reference to it is in the eleventh-century *Cartulary of Redon*. This version is © 1995 by Peter Berresford Ellis. First printing original to this anthology. Used by permission of the author and the author's agent, A. M. Heath & Co.